YO-BUB-378

RENEWALS 691-4574

DATE DUE

WITHDRAWN
UTSA Libraries

The Age of Atonement

The Age of Atonement

The Influence of Evangelicalism on Social and Economic Thought, 1795–1865

BOYD HILTON

CLARENDON PRESS·OXFORD

1988

Oxford University Press, Walton Street, Oxford OX2 6DP

Oxford New York Toronto
Delhi Bombay Calcutta Madras Karachi
Petaling Jaya Singapore Hong Kong Tokyo
Nairobi Dar es Salaam Cape Town
Melbourne Auckland
and associated companies in
Beirut Berlin Ibadan Nicosia

Oxford is a trade mark of Oxford University Press

Published in the United States
by Oxford University Press, New York

©Boyd Hilton 1988

All rights reserved. No part of this publication may be reproduced,
stored in a retrieval system, or transmitted, in any form or by any means,
electronic, mechanical, photocopying, recording, or otherwise, without
the prior permission of Oxford University Press

British Library Cataloguing in Publication Data
Hilton, Boyd
The age of atonement : the influence of evangelicalism on
social and economic thought, 1795–1865
1. Great Britain—Economic Policy   2. Great Britain—Economic
conditions—1760–1860   3. Economics—Religious aspects—Christianity
I. Title.
261.1   HC255
ISBN 0-19-820107-9

Library of Congress Cataloging-in-Publication Data
Hilton, Boyd.
The age of atonement.
Bibliography: p.
Includes index.
1. Evangelicalism—England—History—19th century.
2. England—Social conditions—19th century.
3. England—Economic conditions—19th century.
4. Atonement.   5. Great Britain—Economic policy.
6. Economics—Religious aspects—Christianity.
I. Title.
BR1642.G7H55 1987   306'.3'0941   87-18579
ISBN 0-19-820107-9

Phototypeset by Dobbie Typesetting Service

Printed and bound in Great Britain by
Biddles Ltd, Guildford and King's Lynn

Library
University of Texas
at San Antonio

In memory of my father
KENNETH BOYD HILTON
and of
JACK GALLAGHER
former Vice-Master of Trinity College

PREFACE

> If every author were required to print a correct account of his cerebral development in his preface, a great saving of discussion might be effected.
>
> *The Phrenological Journal and Miscellany* 3 (1825–6), 51

Many years ago I started researching for a doctoral thesis on economic policies between 1815 and 1830. That period saw the cautious beginnings of policies which were to characterize the Victorian *Pax Britannica*— Free Trade, *laissez-faire*, sound money, and public retrenchment. I started out by asking several fairly mechanical questions about the process of policy formation. Were governments responding to pressure from extra-parliamentary lobbies? Did policy emerge through a process of political manœuvre, either at ministerial or parliamentary level? Was there a conscious application of economic doctrine, and how far did unconscious assumptions about the nature of the economy and society affect the outcome? My answers to these questions were largely negative, for most policies seemed to result from the pragmatic responses of officially minded ministers faced with practical problems like those of food supply, monetary instability, public indebtedness, a confusing and inefficient tariff.

And yet this conclusion was not entirely satisfactory, if only because years of academic cohabitation with those Tory ministers had left me with a strong impression of ideological differentiation. Liverpool, Canning, Huskisson, Wallace, Peel, Robinson, Dudley, Grant, and Goulburn, those so-called Liberal Tories who were mainly responsible for the new economic policies, seemed temperamentally different from their more paternalistic and protectionist colleagues—Castlereagh, Wellington, Eldon, Sidmouth, Bathurst, Ellenborough, and Vansittart. But is temperament the same thing as ideology? I returned to what I had written and discovered that at several points I had in fact attributed an implicit ideology to my Liberal Tories. This was at moments when they had acted with unnecessary fervour, as over the 1819 decision to resume cash payments, or else in irrational ways, as when in the summer of 1826 they had almost allowed the Government to break up over the question of issuing exchequer bills to firms in temporary trouble. In order to explain such things it was necessary to examine their often unspoken assumptions about economic roles and relationships. I came to think that I had not previously noticed the operation of ideological factors because I had been looking for the wrong ideology, for the ideology which nowadays we most often associate with *laissez-faire* individualism—that is, the 'classical' economic assumption that Free-Trade would lead to growth and increasing happiness. I remain convinced that such doctrines, even if they were held by many economists (which is questionable), had little impact on policy-making. Ministers sometimes appealed to the authority of Smith, Ricardo, and Senior when defending their actions in Parliament, and High Tories often accused them of having been contaminated by political economy, but their debt to this mode of thought was no more than superficial. Yet for all that, ministers were not working in an ideological vacuum. Looked at afresh, it became clear that there was another model of free-trade individualism, one *not* based on classical economics or the prospects of growth, or the superiority of the industrial sector, a model which I have tentatively labelled 'evangelical'.

There was only time to append a very brief statement of this alternative model to the published version of the thesis which appeared in 1979 under the title *Corn, Cash, Commerce*, and the present study is an elaboration of the same theme. I do not claim that evangelical ideology is a key to unlock all the secrets of policy formation in the first half of the nineteenth century—merely that it contributed more than 'classical economics' or utilitarianism to the formation of that public morality (or doctrine) in the context of which the new economic policy emerged and by which it was sanctioned.

Some historians will bridle at the mention of an ideology of *laissez-faire* individualism. Many have gone out of their way to remind us that hardly any writer took such views to extremes, or failed to allow significant exceptions in practice. Moreover, traces of an older paternalist tradition survived and periodically flourished, as in the first decade of Victoria's reign.[1] Nevertheless, it must surely be accepted that there was at this time a widespread presumption in favour of governments not interfering in social processes. As Oliver MacDonagh has perceptively pointed out, the period 1830–70 was an age of 'positive and aggressive individualism', and although some steps were taken towards collectivism and central-ization, they had to be taken 'surreptitiously and circuitously', being 'explained away as exceptions, as unusual necessities or even on occasions as subtle applications of the principle of individualism'.[2]

A recent book by E. F. Paul has suggested, as this book will do, that the shift to more government intervention in mid-century was brought

---

[1] David Roberts, *Paternalism in Early Victorian England* (1979), *passim*.
[2] Oliver MacDonagh, *Early Victorian Government 1830–1870* (1977), 9.

about by 'a change in moral perspective and not by alterations in pure economic theory'. In analysing this transformation, Paul considers that a 'Utilitarian moral imperative of general happiness supplanted the natural rights position', which had previously strengthened the case against state intervention.[3] The interpretation presented here overlaps to some extent with Paul's, but is based on an entirely different perspective, deriving mainly from theology and eschatology.

There is, of course, a long-standing theoretical debate on the relationship between religious or cosmological belief and social thought. This is not a theoretical work and it does not pretend to solve the problem posed by spiritual chickens and terrestrial eggs. Kitson Clark believed quite simply that 'what men think about their eternal destiny necessarily and profoundly affects their actions in temporal affairs'. Edward Norman, on the other hand, disparages the view that theology is basic to social thought, especially where the clergy are concerned. In his opinion the taste for political economy among early nineteenth-century clerics was merely modish, while the Church's involvement in society after about 1850 was not inspired by any normative beliefs but by its concern to win the respect and allegiance of the lower orders. Theological formulations, however hotly disputed, were simply metaphorical or self-justificatory, and such ideas as did affect the clergy's social perceptions 'derived from the surrounding intellectual and political culture and not, as churchmen themselves always seem to assume, from theological learning'.[4] The problem with this far from implausible thesis is that that 'surrounding culture' was in the nineteenth century itself saturated with 'traces of religion', as Dr Norman recognizes. Before 1850, especially, religious feeling and biblical terminology so permeated *all* aspects of thought (including atheism) that it is hard to dismiss them as epiphenomenal.

In relating social attitudes to theology, I have found it useful to relate both to developments in science or 'natural philosophy', one of the liveliest areas of early nineteenth-century thought. As with Dr Norman's clergymen, it is important to notice the social function which such knowledge performed. The devotional economists and assorted moralists who figure in this book belonged for the most part to an assertive upper middle class. This class, which looked to Robert Peel as an ideal of statesmanship, depended largely on *rentier* wealth and comprised not only capitalist-minded agrarians and City businessmen but also provincial élites

---

[3] Ellen Frankel Paul, *Moral Revolution and Economic Science: The Demise of Laissez-Faire in Nineteenth-Century British Political Economy* (Westport, Conn., 1979), 282–3 and *passim*.

[4] G. Kitson Clark, *The English Inheritance: An Historical Essay* (1950), p. 10; E. R. Norman, *Church and Society in England 1770–1970: A Historical Study* (Oxford, 1976), 10–12 and *passim*.

with metropolitan and Oxbridge aspirations. Scientific pursuits made a strong cultural appeal to such groups, anxious as they were to stress the importance of intelligence as against the *hauteur* of the aristocrat and the mutuality of the mob. For this reason, the swarm of writers who tried so hard to reconcile religion with political economy approached their endeavours as much from a scientific as a moralistic viewpoint, and in much the same way as they approached geology, astronomy, biology, and physics. Since C. C. Gillispie wrote his classic *Genesis and Geology* in 1951, many historians have emphasized the substantive influence of theological convictions on developments in science at this time. John Brooke on astronomy, David Gooding on magnetism, Crosbie Smith and P. M. Heimann on physics, Don Ospovat and L. Jacyna on biology, W. F. Bynum on natural history, Adrian Desmond on palaeontology, Pietro Corsi on all these areas, and many other scholars have contributed recently to this perspective.[5] In view of this, it seems reasonable to suppose that the course of political economy may also have been affected by theological—specifically by providentialist—assumptions.

Professor R. K. Webb wrote that Edward Norman's *Church and Society in England* 'has brought this line of inquiry close to an end. . . . The work surely does not need to be done again soon, in whole or in part.' Alas for historians, finality is almost never achieved—hence a further look at what is by now a very well raked-over problem. Whether there is any epistemological value attaching to quotations wrenched from context and scrunched together to furnish broad generalizations about the mentality of generations is, of course, open to question. This, nevertheless, is what has been attempted, and if the results are unavoidably impressionistic, they may at least provide a sense of how a society undergoing the 'great transformation' sought to understand and demystify its experiences.

---

[5] J. H. Brooke, 'Natural theology and the plurality of worlds: observations on the Brewster–Whewell debate', *Annals of Science*, 34 (1977), 221–86; P. M. Heimann, '*The unseen universe:* physics and the philosophy of nature in Victorian Britain', *The British Journal for the History of Science*, 6 (1972), 73–9; David Gooding, 'Empiricism in practice: teleology, economy, and observation in Faraday's physics', *Isis*, 73 (1982), 46–67. For references to the other authors mentioned see below, pp. 302–14.

ACKNOWLEDGEMENTS

I have incurred so many debts during the long preparation of this book that it is hard to know where my thanks should begin. Perhaps with the many hundreds of pupils who have had the argument in its successive versions foisted on them, and whose creative scepticism has helped me gradually to refine it. Very special thanks must go to Pietro Corsi, Colin Matthew, and Anthony Waterman. Among scores of other scholars from whose advice this book has benefited are Derek Beales, Richard Brent, David Carruthers, the late Sydney Checkland, Maurice Cowling, Bianco Fontana, Lawrence Goldman, Michael Hennell, Istvan Hont, Angus Macintyre, John Mason, Michael Murphy, Tim Morgan, Margaret Pelling, Robert Robson, Martin Rudwick, the late Eric Stokes, Norman Stone, Steven Swartzman, William Thomas, Stephen Taylor, David Thompson, and John Walsh. For permission to quote from manuscript materials in their possession I wish to thank: The Duke of Northumberland, The Earl of Harewood, Viscount Sidmouth, Sir Charles Graham, Bt., the Trustees of the British Library, the Trustees of the National Library of Scotland, the Trustees of the National Library of Wales, the Syndics of Cambridge University Library, the Edinburgh University Library and New College Library, Edinburgh, the Huntington Library, San Marino, California, His Grace the Archbishop of Canterbury and the Trustees of Lambeth Palace Library, the John Rylands University Library of Manchester, the Provost and Fellows of Oriel College, Oxford, the William R. Perkins Library, North Carolina, the Master and Fellows of Trinity College, Cambridge, and the Librarian of University College London. For instruction in and help with word processing, my thanks are due to Laura Cordy, and for help with day-to-day scholarship, to many scores of librarians but especially Rachel Clifford and Janice Fairholm of the Cambridge University Library. Most of all I thank my wife Mary and my children Thomas, Eliza, and Zoë, to whom the time which I have spent on 'the Atonement' (as they affectionately call it) has indeed seemed like 'an Age'.

Trinity College, Cambridge

CONTENTS

PART ONE   RELIGIOUS AND ECONOMIC THOUGHT   1

1. Evangelicalism in the Age of Atonement   3

2. The Rage of Christian Economics 1800–1840   36

PART TWO   THE CONTENT OF EVANGELICAL
SOCIAL THOUGHT   71

3. Poverty and Passionate Flesh   73

4. Profit and Prophecy: Evangelical Attitudes to Business   115

5. The Mind of Economic Man   163

6. The Politics of Atonement   203

PART THREE   AFTER THE AGE OF ATONEMENT   253

7. 'Incarnate and Incorporate': the Lord of Limit   255

8. Incarnational Social Thought in its Intellectual Context   298

9. Gladstonian Liberalism: the Last Days of Atonement   340

Epilogue   373

Bibliographical Appendix   379

PART ONE

Religious and Economic Thought

1

Evangelicalism in the Age of Atonement

Be fruitful, and multiply, and replenish the earth, and subdue it; and have dominion over the fish of the sea, and over the fowl of the air, and over every living thing that moveth upon the earth. Behold, I have given you every herb bearing seed, which is upon the face of all the earth, and every tree, in the which is the fruit of the tree yielding seed; to you it shall be for meat.

Genesis 1: 28–9

Cursed is the ground for thy sake; in sorrow shalt thou eat of it all the days of thy life; thorns also and thistles shall it bring forth to thee; and thou shalt eat the herb of the field; in the sweat of thy face shalt thou eat bread.

Genesis 3: 17–19

Introduction

The first half of the nineteenth century has been called 'The Age of Improvement'. But it was also an 'Age of Atonement', because improvement, like virtue, was not then thought of as its own reward, merely as terrestrial fumbling towards public and private salvation. This book examines the mind of the middle and upper classes during a period of social and economic upheaval. It is not an easy mind to characterize, for there was no consensus, but rather a 'war of ideas' which left most thinking men ambivalent, or torn between 'incompatible opposites'.[1] Yet there does seem to have been a dominant mode of thought, an amalgam of enlightenment rationalism and evangelical eschatology,[2] and its core or 'hinge' was the Christian doctrine of the Atonement.

The Age of Atonement began with an upper- and middle-class reaction against the French Revolution and English Jacobinism. G. M. Young cited Wilberforce's evangelical manifesto, *A Practical View of Christianity*

[1] Humphry House, *All in Due Time* (1955), 99; Marilyn Butler, *Jane Austen and the War of Ideas* (Oxford, 1975), *passim*.

[2] Trygve R. Tholfsen, *Working Class Radicalism in Mid-Victorian England* (1976), 34–72, suggests that both the dominant culture and the counter-culture of the day derived from the combined influences of evangelicalism, enlightenment rationality, and romanticism.

(1797), and Malthus's *Essay on the Principle of Population* (1798) as its classic texts.[3] Implicitly their common target was the Christian utilitarian philosopher William Paley, whose cosmic optimism seemed inappropriate to the times. Evangelicals thought that Paley was complacent about human nature, Malthusians that he was complacent about physical nature. He had, for example, welcomed population growth on the grounds that men are only likely to 'be fruitful and multiply' if they are also contented and thriving.[4] Yet here was Malthus apparently arguing that the pressure of population on food supplies blighted all earthly prospects of happiness. Pessimists were forced to conclude that man's impulse to copulate, and so to populate, was a sign of sin rather than a sign of obedience to God. 'Cursed is the ground for thy sake; . . . in the sweat of thy face shalt thou eat bread.' The years 1793–5 saw the onset of war and scarcity, which Malthus seemed to be depicting as permanent conditions of civilization. 'For they shall fall by the sword, by the famine, and by the pestilence' (Ezekiel 6: 11). Even more disturbing than the prophecy itself was the inference, which many drew, that the author of nature was either a butcher or a bungler. As the political economist Robert Torrens was to put it later, 'Paley, in his Natural Theology, . . . assumes . . . that the order of the universe shows intelligence and design; and this proves an intelligent cause-designing mind. But the Atheist denies that the order of the universe shows intelligence and design.'[5] And since, in the panicky, pessimistic 1790s, the atheist seemed to have a case, true believers like Wilberforce needed a more realistic or 'practical' viewpoint:

Christianity appears to me to consider the world as in a state of alienation from God, as lost in depravity and guilt; pointing out at the same time 'how we may escape from the wrath to come,' from the natural consequences of that guilt and depravity; and not only how we may be absolved from the guilt, but emancipated from the power of moral corruption. This must be effected by the power of the Holy Spirit. . . . It ought to be the grand object of every moral writer . . . to produce in us that true and just sense of the intensity of the malignity of sin . . . , and of the real magnitude of our danger, which would be likely to dispose us to exert ourselves to the utmost to obtain deliverance from the condemnation and emancipation from the power of sin. Now, here, Dr. Paley appears to me to fail.[6]

---

[3] G. M. Young, *Portrait of an Age: Victorian England* (1936; annotated edn G. Kitson Clark, 1977), 29.

[4] W. Paley, *The Principles of Moral and Political Philosophy* (1785), 587–636 (Bk. VI, ch. XI). 'The decay of population is the greatest evil that a state can suffer. . . . In the ordinary progress of human affairs, whatever, in any way, contributes to make a people happier, tends to render them more numerous.' Ibid., p. 589.

[5] W. Torrens to Macvey Napier, 28 Oct. 1830, Napier Papers, BL Add. MS 34614, fos. 426–7, printed in *Selection from the Correspondence of the late Macvey Napier*, ed. his son M. Napier (1879), 95.

[6] W. Wilberforce to Ralph Creyke, 8 Jan. 1803, *The Correspondence of William Wilberforce*, ed. R. I. and S. Wilberforce (1840), i. 247–53.

The disparagement was reluctant but fundamental. Whether one's faith was based on the individual conscience or on the harmonies of creation, Paley's eighteenth-century anodyne seemed inadequate to the needs of an age in which natural suffering and individual depravity were only too apparent.

The end of the Age of Atonement was less sudden but more self-conscious. By 1870 it was commonplace for Anglicans to assert that a theological transformation had recently taken place, whereby a worldly Christian compassion, inspired by the life of Jesus, had alleviated such stark evangelical doctrines as those of eternal and vicarious punishment. 'The Evangelical creed . . . foundered on the Impregnable Rock of Holy Scripture',[7] but it was also becalmed by an increasingly genteel sensibility. Unitarians naturally welcomed the derogation of original sin and divine punishment, and one of them, James Martineau, cited an erstwhile Unitarian, Frederick Denison Maurice, as 'the chief cause of a radical and permanent change in the "orthodox" theology, — viz., a shifting of its centre of gravity from the *Atonement* to the Incarnation'.[8] Wilberforce's eldest son Robert, a High Churchman, explicitly urged the Incarnation 'as the great objective fact of Christianity',[9] and even some evangelicals, who had always made a particular fetish of the Cross, began to stress the Christmas message more than that of Easter after about 1840. The *coup de grâce* came with the publication of *Lux Mundi: A Series of Studies in the Religion of the Incarnation* by a posse of High Churchmen in 1889. As Canon Vernon Storr commented a quarter of a century later, 'In all schools of theological thought, Christology rather than Soteriology, the Incarnation rather than the Atonement, now occupies the central position. In place of the *Christus Redemptor* stands the *Christus Consummator*.'[10]

The new emphasis on Jesus as man rather than as lamb, on religion as a guide to living as well as a passport to Paradise, is probably connected with the growth of Christian social action during the second half of the nineteenth century. 'It was the Incarnation . . . with which they desired

[7] Young, *Portrait of an Age*, 29. For a similar transformation among Nonconformists during the 1880s and 1890s, see Richard Helmstadter in *The Conscience of the Victorian State*, ed. Peter Marsh (Syracuse, NY, 1979), 135–72; R. W. Dale, *The Old Evangelicalism and the New* (1889), 5–63.

[8] James Martineau to Elizabeth Peabody, 9 Dec. 1876, *The Life and Letters of James Martineau*, by J. Drummond and C. B. Upton (1902), ii. 86–7.

[9] R. I. Wilberforce, *The Doctrine of the Incarnation of Our Lord Jesus Christ, in its Relation to Mankind and to the Church* (1848), 4, 218–19.

[10] V. F. Storr, *The Development of English Theology in the Nineteenth Century 1800–1860* (1913), 73; David Newsome, *Two Classes of Men: Platonism and English Romantic Thought* (1972), 80, suggests that this shift of emphasis is a 'pendulum swing' which theology undergoes from time to time.

to see the laws of political economy brought into contact', wrote Henry Scott Holland in 1890.[11] Incarnationalist economists such as Wilfrid Richmond and Llewellyn Davies have been depicted as forming a link between idealist or Social Darwinist philosophies on the one hand, and the practical work of the Christian Socialists and their satellites on the other.[12] What might be called soteriological economics, however, the earlier political economy of original sin and redemption, has either been ignored or else dismissed as vapid self-justification on the part of a selfish and brutal capitalist class. Against this, it will be suggested here that religious belief was important in shaping *as well as* rationalizing the economic philosophy of the period. It was commonplace then to refer to 'the sacred laws of political economy' and 'the Gospel of Free Trade', and while such slogans may be trite, they are not necessarily meaningless.

Admittedly, the metaphysical content of what might be called *high* political economy, evident enough in its eighteenth-century Scottish phase,[13] becomes less apparent from the 1820s onwards, as 'professionals' such as Ricardo, Senior, and the Mills began to develop a technical expertise which was quite different from the normative approach of most clerics.[14] The professionals' determination to treat economics as a branch of secular knowledge won them a reputation for satanity. However, this book is not concerned with the dialectics of the Political Economy Club or with formal statements of doctrine, but with the underlying attitudes and assumptions of the period, which are seen best in the writings of amateur practitioners, many of whom wrote from an avowedly moralistic, and often specifically Christian, standpoint. It is they who provide the most vivid insight into the 'official mind' of the period, and it is they—more than the 'classical' economists—who throw light on the ideological elements (which must not of course be exaggerated) behind the policies of Free Trade and the Gold Standard.

Many of these Christian, and especially evangelical, writers developed their views in conscious opposition to utilitarian or classical economics. With hindsight, however, it can be seen how similar the two philosophies

[11] H. Scott Holland's preface to Wilfrid Richmond, *Economic Morals: Four Lectures* (1890), p. xi.
[12] Melvin Richter, *The Politics of Conscience: T. H. Green and his Age* (1964), 47–50, 97–135, 316–17; Peter d'A. Jones, *The Christian Socialist Revival, 1877–1914: Religion, Class, and Social Conscience in Late-Victorian England* (Princeton, NJ, 1968), 3–30; Stefan Collini, *Liberalism and Sociology: L. T. Hobhouse and Political Argument in England 1880–1914* (Cambridge, 1979), 13–50. See other references at p. 299 below.
[13] *Wealth and Virtue: The Shaping of Political Economy in the Scottish Enlightenment*, ed. Istvan Hont and Michael Ignatieff (Cambridge, 1983), *passim*; Stefan Collini, Donald Winch, John Burrow, *That Noble Science of Politics: A Study in Nineteenth-Century Intellectual History* (Cambridge, 1983), 25–61; Biancamaria Fontana, 'Political Economy in the *Edinburgh Review*, 1802–1832', Cambridge University Ph.D. (1983), 65–160.
[14] D. P. O'Brien, *The Classical Economists* (Oxford, 1975), 1–20.

were, besides leading to identical policy recommendations. This book seeks to determine which aspects of the ideology of *laissez-faire* individualism can be attributed to the evangelical ethos, and which are more appropriately regarded as utilitarian in inspiration. It also seeks to explain why some evangelicals subscribed to that ideology and others did not. The main thrust of the book, therefore, is to explore the tensions that arose from the conflict between the two types of evangelicalism, and from the relationship between one type of evangelicalism and parallel modes of thought.

Evangelicalism in the Early Nineteenth Century

The word 'evangelical' is seriously inadequate, being in some ways too vague and in others too precise. ('Puritan' might be a less misleading term, but one which has less contextual resonance.) While almost every historian acknowledges the role of evangelicalism in shaping the mentality of the period, none has yet defined its impact at all precisely, and the task may well be impossible, for it was not a precise phenomenon. Unfortunately, most of the questions asked by Canon Smyth as long ago as 1943 remain to be investigated,[15] and many of the best studies are as yet unpublished. In this book 'evangelical' refers to the third and fourth generations of the revival begun by Wesley, and the main emphasis is on the established clergy, Anglicans and Scottish Presbyterians. This is the world of the Clapham Sect—of William Wilberforce, Henry Thornton, Zachary Macaulay, and John Venn—as well as of Henry Elliott, Isaac Milner, Charles Simeon, Edward Bickersteth, Thomas Chalmers, Henry Ryder, Hannah More, Daniel Wilson, John and Charles Sumner. Evangelicalism, national and provincial, was undoubtedly an important element in the mentality of the *haute bourgeoisie* that dominated British politics from 1784 to the 1840s, a combination of *rentier* economic interests, office-holding, and social notability. But it is not merely that Wilberforce and Thornton, for example, gave powerful support to Pitt and Liverpool, or that permanent officials like James Stephen and Charles Trevelyan influenced policy formation in the 1830s and 1840s. More important is the extent to which evangelicalism's distinctive middle-class piety fostered new concepts of public probity and national honour, based on ideals of oeconomy, frugality, professionalism, and financial rectitude. In other words, 'evangelical' in this book refers less to persons—to the 'Saints' at Westminster and the 'Slopes' in their parishes—than to a gamut of attitudes and beliefs, the evangelical *Weltanschauung* as it affected the established clergy in the first half of the nineteenth century.

---

[15] Charles Smyth, 'The evangelical movement in perspective', *The Cambridge Historical Journal*, 7 (1941–3), 160–74.

As Roger Anstey has pointed out in a brief but perceptive summary,[16] 'the world-view of Evangelicals was primarily theological and it was distinctive'. Not that its theology was original, for its doctrines were all culled from the Judaeo-Christian scheme, being 'part of the heritage of the Church through the ages' as well as being held by many contemporaries who were not evangelicals. What distinguished evangelicals was the emphasis they gave to particular doctrines, and the fervour with which they practised 'vital religion'. Indeed, the fervent aspects of this 'religion of the heart', its stress on conversion and grace as against the dry rationalism of the eighteenth century, are most frequently stressed, but, for all that, most evangelicals stood inside and partly depended on the rationalistic and mechanistic tradition of eighteenth-century natural theology. Essentially theirs was a simple and wholly *un*mysterious form of worship, which may be summarized as follows. A sharp discontinuity exists between this world and the next. God transcends this world, and his providence is responsible for everything that happens in it. His creatures are all in a state of natural depravity, weighed down by original sin, and life is effectively an 'arena of moral trial', an ethical obstacle course on which men are tempted, tested, and ultimately sorted into saints and sinners in readiness for the Day of Judgment. Then, souls will be despatched either to Heaven or to Hell, literally conceived as states of eternal felicity and everlasting torment. The all-important contractual relationship is directly between each soul and its maker, and such intermediaries as priests and sacraments are of relatively little significance. The organ of redemption is the individual conscience, and the means are provided by Christ's Atonement on the Cross, which purchased ransom for the sins of all mankind. Justification comes through faith in that Atonement, and through faith alone, for though good works, sanctification, and holiness are important, they cannot precede faith. Rather, faith in the Atonement sanctifies the sinner as well as justifying him, and so prepares his heart for the Heaven which will be his home. This, in essence, was the evangelical 'scheme of salvation', as it can be found in Henry Venn's *Complete Duty of Man* (1763), Thomas Scott's *Commentaries* (1788–92), and Wilberforce's *Practical View*. Its centrepiece was an 'economy of redemption' in which souls were bought in the cheapest market and sold in the dearest.

Of course the above sketch obscures some important differences of opinion. One issue that was no longer regarded as fundamental (except in Scotland) was predestination, on which Wesley and Whitefield had famously disagreed. There is some evidence that in the early nineteenth century the nominal, or so-called 'moderate', Calvinism of the *Christian*

---

[16] Roger Anstey, *The Atlantic Slave Trade and British Abolition 1760–1810* (1975), 157–99.

Guardian (1809–49) was losing ground to the increasingly Arminian bias of the *Christian Observer* (1802–74). Like Simeon, Wilberforce emphatically believed that 'an effective offer of salvation was made to every man born into the world',[17] and he was always anxious to point out that even those evangelical clergy who *did* admit to Calvinist beliefs 'not only never bring the mysterious subject into their public ministrations, but hold it speculatively in a far more relaxed and even doubtful way, than their predecessors of a former generation'.[18] This was probably true, for though 'moderate Calvinists' like Venn, the Milners, Newton, and Scott clung to the doctrine of particular election, Walsh shows that they did not emphasize it, or let it lead them into a deterministic view of reprobation. Drawing more on Augustine than on the Institutes of Geneva, they held that Christ died for *all* men's sins, ensuring a universal redemption though not of course universal salvation.[19] There were here the remnants of a serious theological dispute. Most 'moderate Calvinists' believed that God was the author of salvation but not of sin, which was man's own doing, whereas Arminians tended to believe that 'the *worm* was from God as well as the *gourd*',[20] and that God used both good and evil powers in the administration of his providence. In the former case the contest for each man's soul lay between God and Satan, in the latter case 'merely' between Christ and Satan. But it is clear that by 1815 the differences had come to seem artificial,[21] since both camps were at one on the ever-present danger of backsliding, and on a man's need to exercise constant moral vigilance and choice, whether God had pre-ordained his actions or not.

---

[17] *Memoirs of Joseph John Gurney: With Selections from His Journal and Correspondence*, ed. Joseph Bevan Braithwaite (Norwich, 1854), i. 408.

[18] W. Wilberforce to Lord Liverpool, 30 Sept. 1820, Liverpool Papers, BL Add. MS 38191, fos. 280–3.

[19] J. D. Walsh, 'The Yorkshire Evangelicals in the eighteenth century: with especial reference to Methodism', Cambridge University Ph.D. (1956), 27–36.

[20] Josiah Pratt in *The Thought of the Evangelical Leaders: Notes of the Discussions in the Eclectic Society, London during the years 1798–1814*, ed. John H. Pratt (1856; reprinted Edinburgh, 1978), 468–9. 'All *good* is from the ordinary and concurring will of God; and all *evil* from His permissive will; and everything, whether good or evil, is from His overruling will, guiding it to His own ends.' Ibid.

[21] S. C. Orchard, 'English evangelical eschatology 1790–1850', Cambridge University Ph.D. (1969), 23; Walsh, 'Yorkshire Evangelicals', pp. 42–3; G. F. A. Best, 'The Evangelicals and the Established Church in the early nineteenth century', *The Journal of Theological Studies*, NS, 10 (1959), 73–5; Elizabeth Jay, *The Religion of the Heart: Anglican Evangelicalism and the Nineteenth-Century Novel* (Oxford, 1979), 51–3, 84–6; R. H. Martin, *Evangelicals United: Ecumenical Stirrings in Pre-Victorian Britain, 1795–1830* (Metuchen, NJ and London, 1983), 15–18. For contemporary views of the irrelevance of the distinction between Calvinism and Arminianism, see Hannah More to Bishop Beadon, 1801, *The Life of Hannah More with Selections from Her Correspondence* (1856), pp. 220–1, and *Memoirs of the Life and Correspondence of Mrs. Hannah More*, by William Roberts (2nd edn, 1834), iii. 128–30.

Much more important was the growing split within Anglican evangelicalism between the respectable Clapham Sect and its followers on the one hand, and the pentecostal, pre-millenarian, adventist, and revivalist elements on the other. These can for convenience be termed 'the moderate' and 'extreme' factions within evangelicalism. As Edward Thompson has shown so memorably with respect to evangelical Methodism,[22] the emotion and enthusiasm of the extremists could easily slip into a masochistic chiliasm, a revelling in pain as though it were a mark of grace. Their cult of leadership, and increasingly apostolic and ecclesiological attitudes, marked them off still further from the moderate individualists of Clapham. Where moderates 'preached Christ and Him crucified', extremists celebrated 'not Christ crucified merely, but Christ risen . . . , and Christ to be again present in person' very soon.[23] Pre-millenarianism, or the view that the Second Coming must precede the thousand-year reign of felicity on earth, can be found in the pages of the dissenting *Evangelical Magazine* (1793–1904), the *Morning Watch* (1829–33), and less extreme but strongly Calvinist—Alexander Haldane's *Record* (1828–1923), which took over from the moderate *Christian Observer* as the best-selling evangelical journal during the 1830s. Within middle-class Anglican circles, extreme evangelicalism spread rapidly from the mid-1820s onwards, thanks to economic alarms, Catholic Emancipation, constitutional crisis, cholera, and other 'signs' of an impending divine initiative. The antinomianism of these extremists, and their often apocalyptic other-worldliness, undoubtedly alienated many serious-minded evangelicals of the younger generation, and helped to push potential leaders such as Gladstone, Stanley, Acland, Newman, Manning, and Robert Wilberforce away towards the High Church.[24]

A striking example of the difference between moderates and extremists is the way that each reacted to suffering and trial. Both accepted that 'whom the Lord loveth He chasteneth', and that there was therefore 'a discipline of affliction' and 'mercy in the curse'.[25] Nevertheless, moderate evangelicals like those of the Clapham Sect were generally able to take

[22] E. P. Thompson, *The Making of the English Working Class* (1965), 350–400. On Joanna Southcott and other popular pre-millenarians, see J. F. C. Harrison, *The Second Coming: Popular Millenarianism 1780–1850* (1979), *passim*.

[23] H. C. Whitley, *Blinded Eagle: An Introduction to the Life and Teaching of Edward Irving* (1955), 60.

[24] On this split see Orchard, 'Evangelical eschatology', pp. 75–104; Jay, *Religion of the Heart*, pp. 88–105; David Newsome, *The Parting of Friends: A Study of the Wilberforces and Henry Manning* (1966), 10–12; D. N. Hempton, 'Evangelicalism and eschatology', *The Journal of Ecclesiastical History*, 31 (1980), 179–94; Ernest R. Sandeen, *The Roots of Fundamentalism: British and American Millenarianism 1800–1930* (Chicago and London, 1970), 3–41.

[25] Revd Henry Melvill, 'Mercy in the Curse: A Sermon', *The Pulpit*, 48 (1846), 124–32.

a more cheerful view of private and even national misfortunes. Their conviction of personal 'guilt and depravity', and their recognition of the need for 'emancipation from the power of sin', was none the less vivid for being cool and sober, but they were joyously optimistic about the availability of grace, and tended to regard temporal setbacks in the light of divine encouragement to reformation and redemption before it was too late. God smites terrestrially those whom he most loves, in the hope that he will then not need to inflict condign punishment on them eternally. 'Affliction was good for him, and it was sent: the bright and dazzling prospect of a sunny day was obscured. He needed consolation, and it was vouchsafed: for he that hath torn will heal; he that hath smitten will bind up.'[26] The sequence of sin, suffering, contrition, despair, comfort, and grace — so common in moderate evangelical homiletic — shows that pain was regarded as an essential part of God's order, and as bound up with the machinery of judgment and conversion. 'Every thing is exactly proportioned: the degree of suffering corresponds with the measure of offence.'[27] Pre-millenarian extremists, on the other hand, such as Irving and the Recordites, regarded pain as a sign of 'dislocation' in God's order.[28] They accepted it as a mark of God's sadistic regard for a nation or a life, and even welcomed it as a sign that the last days were nigh at hand. But they were less confident than the moderates about the world's capacity for inculcating virtue, and they tended to preach resignation rather than the need for discipline.

Though there be enough of trial inwardly and outwardly in all ages to keep the soul in active life, and holy discipline, and progressive sanctification, yet when the Almighty thereto adds sore trials of His providence — bereavements, losses, crosses, persecution, perils, and sword — we are to regard them as so many fostering and nutritious measures to hasten ourselves into premature perfection, and raise us to a preternatural purity; and those who endure such afflictions patiently are to account themselves highly favoured of the Lord, and to reckon that His grace and His providence are working together for their good.[29]

In Irving's view, only martyrdom, leading to 'assurance' — that is, conscious-ness of the power of the Holy Spirit operating within oneself, independently of sanctification or good works — and so to 'final perseverance', could suffice to vanquish the Devil. 'We are but promised to live by the altar,

[26] William Howels, *Sermons, &c. &c.*, with a memoir by Charles Bowdler (1833–4), i, p. xxiii.

[27] Charles Jerram, *A Treatise on the Doctrine of the Atonement* (1828), 316.

[28] Haddon Willmer, 'Evangelicalism 1785 to 1835', Cambridge University Hulsean Prize Essay (1962), 125.

[29] Edward Irving, 'The perversion and use of suffering', *Miscellanies from the Collected Writings of Edward Irving* (1865), 306.

and the rest is so much burdensome stewardry. . . . Though the worst come to the worst, what mattereth it?'[30]

The danger was that such evangelicals could become obsessed by sin, damnation, and suffering. Charles Simeon, the 'maker' of so many moderate evangelicals during his ministry at Cambridge (1783–1836), contended against the extremists that religion was 'calculated to make us happy', and 'loved to see religion in a cheerful dress'. Service to God did not in his eyes require a retreat into other-worldliness, but proper everyday conduct *in* the world.[31] Not surprisingly, he denounced the Irvingites as doing great harm to the church, and as lacking in Christian sobriety. 'Their mode of promoting humility and devotion originated in vanity, pride, and carnality.'[32] Even before 1826, when Irving began to 'speak in tongues' and prophesy the millennium, his ministry had been attacked by the moderates for its lack of pathos.

The grand and the sublime are his elements. To strike terror is his delight. . . . His aim is almost always to come at the hearts of men through their apprehensions, and by depicting the awful attributes of the Deity, and the fallen condition of his creatures, with more or less success, to force repentance, by a sort of moral torture, into the bosom of despair.[33]

Such a strategy implied crushing and voiding men of individual personality, making them 'self-emptied', as Irving's colleague Drummond put it.[34] Now this was never the Clapham Sect's way, for all its concern to remind mankind of the wrath to come. One of the most popular of all moderate evangelical sermons was on 'the expulsive power of a new affection' by a Scotsman, Thomas Chalmers, who will play a central part in this study. One should not try to 'displace from the human heart its love of the world' merely by bullying it with tales of the world's worthlessness, since this will merely leave the heart 'emptied' of all affection. The 'true' way is to make the heart 'exchange an old affection for a new one' by giving it something else, 'even God, as more worthy of its attachment'.[35] Enthusiasm for the Cross, rather than mere repression of one's own depravity, was the secret of moderate evangelical religion.

[30] Irving to Revd John Martin, 21 Jan. 1826, A. L. Drummond, *Edward Irving and His Circle* (1937), 101. Martin had lost his savings in the 1825–6 banking crash.

[31] Simeon to Duchess of Beaufort, 13 May 1823, and to a father, 17 July 1823, *Memoirs of the Life of the Rev. Charles Simeon: With a Selection from his Writings and Correspondence*, ed. William Carus (1847), 578–9, 586.

[32] Simeon to J. J. Gurney, 26 Jan. 1832, ibid., pp. 688–90.

[33] James Fleming, *The Life and Writings of the Rev. Edward Irving* (1823), 20.

[34] Henry Drummond to Revd Henry Blunt, March 1832, in the author's private possession.

[35] Thomas Chalmers, *The Expulsive Power of a New Affection* (1861), 3–10 [first published in *The Works of Thomas Chalmers* (Glasgow, 1836–42), vi. 209–18].

We can see why moderate evangelicals, anxious to redeem mankind, often fretted more over sinful insouciance than over outright wickedness. The latter is so obvious that its perpetrators are likely to become conscience-stricken 'ere it is too late', but outwardly good men are often unaware of their peril. Since it is not sinful activity but lack of faith for which men are condemned to Hell, an apparently innocent life is often more dangerous spiritually than a career of heinous crime. And if, as 'Our Lord says, "Every idle word that men shall speak, they shall give account thereof in the day of judgment"', then 'talkative people are to be pitied, if old. It is quite an infirmity of old age.'[36] In some ways, smaller sins could be considered more reprehensible than greater ones, as a moderate or 'rational' evangelical of the following generation explained.

Profane men have dared to sneer at the fact, that man lost paradise, and incurred eternal death, by partaking of the forbidden fruit; and they have presumed to arraign the punishment as utterly disproportionate to the crime. Yet, in very deed, the smallness of the temptation may be regarded as the gauge of the depth of the faithlessness and rebellion of the creature in disobeying his Creator . . . [and] enhances instead of alleviating the turpitude of the violation.[37]

The point is important for what follows, since it explains how moderate evangelicals could regard the economy—a sphere of activity in which so many of God's creatures engaged unthinkingly—as an arena of great spiritual trial and suspense. Self-righteous men guilty of economic peccadilloes might stand in even greater danger than murderers and revolutionaries. The latters' plight was only too evident to themselves as well as to others, but 'how shall we convince *amiable* characters of their natural depravity?' This was a recurring anxiety of the members of the Eclectic Society of London, an assembly of moderate Anglican evangelicals.[38]

Another important point of issue between moderate and extreme evangelicals was the question of whether providence operates 'generally' and predictably through natural and immutable laws of cause and effect, or 'specially' by *ad hoc* and *ad hominem* interventions in terrestrial affairs.[39] Of course the distinction was not a rigid one, and many of those who thought of providence as working neutrally through physical or secondary laws also reserved a place for 'special' interventions from

---

[36] Revd Richard Cecil in Pratt, *Thought of the Evangelical Leaders*, p. 304.

[37] Hugh Stowell, *A Model for Men of Business: Or, Lectures on the Character of Nehemiah* (1854), 141–2.

[38] Revd Basil Woodd in Pratt, *Thought of the Evangelical Leaders*, p. 507.

[39] See Jacob Viner, *The Role of Providence in the Social Order: An Essay in Intellectual History* (Philadelphia, 1972), pp. 1–26, on providentialist thought in the eighteenth century. On the doctrine of special providence see Jay, *Religion of the Heart*, pp. 97–102.

time to time, especially in judgments on whole nations,[40] and in the vital matter of securing individual conversions.[41] But by and large, the Clapham Sect believed that 'the judicial and penal visitations of Providence occur . . . in the way of natural consequence'.[42] God had instituted a permanent moral law on earth, a 'natural' and predictable in-built system of rewards and punishments appropriate to good and bad behaviour. Almost always in the case of individuals, and sometimes in the case of communities, suffering was the logical consequence of specifically bad behaviour. It could therefore incite as well as guide men to virtuous conduct in the future, but they must of course take the opportunity to examine their own actions in the light of their sufferings. As Chalmers put it,

It is the constancy of nature that gives such confidence to the experimental philosopher in the manipulations of chemistry. And it is just the same constancy in the world of mind, or because of the doctrine of necessity realized there also, that we enter with any comfort or confidence on the management of human nature. It is because of this, that in our treatment of the human spirit, we ply all those various elements of hope, and fear, and conscience, and a sense of interest, and everything else that we have found to be of efficacy in leading our fellows on to the determinations of prudence and of virtue.[43]

Pre-millennialists, however, regarded this sort of attitude as blindness to the workings of providence. 'The irreligious world mocks at, and the religious world'—meaning the Clapham Sect—'cannot see, God's hand in any thing, either in pestilence, state, or Church', lamented the Irvingite, Henry Drummond.[44] For pre-millennialists, temporal misfortunes were always 'special' or 'particular' judgments on men and nations, inflicted for unspecifiable spiritual offences, and requiring miraculous suspensions of natural law. One should react to suffering with resignation, even with

[40] For example, *The Christian Observer*, 31 (1831), 383–4, considered that cholera came from 'Him by whom nations and empires rise and fall'. See Best, 'Evangelicals and the Established Church', op. cit., pp. 64–6; Owen Chadwick, *The Victorian Church* (1966–70), i. 451–2.

[41] And individual conversions were thought to be of even more importance than national judgments. See Henry A. Boardman, *The Great Question: Will You Consider the Subject of Personal Religion?* (1855), 41: 'Marathon and Thermopylae, Trafalgar and Waterloo, the proudest of earth's battle-fields, . . . dwindle into insignificance when compared with the mighty conflict involved in the *salvation* of a single individual.'

[42] William Wilberforce to Earl Bathurst, 4 July 1816, *Report on the Manuscripts of Earl Bathurst, preserved at Cirencester Park*, Historical Manuscripts Commission, 76th Report (1923), 418.

[43] Thomas Chalmers, *Institutes of Theology* [*Posthumous Works of Thomas Chalmers*, ed. William Hanna (Edinburgh, 1847–9), viii. 337]. For Chalmers's qualifications on this point see below, pp. 361–2. See also Revd Josiah Pratt in Pratt, *Thought of the Evangelical Leaders*, pp. 468–9.

[44] Drummond to Blunt, March 1832, loc. cit.

masochistic gratitude, and also of course with redoubled devotions and spiritual self-abasement; but one was not to suppose that the pain was a consequence of our own mistakes (as distinct from our general sinfulness), or that one could prevent sufferings in future by acting in accordance with natural laws. Providence always acted miraculously, and it was presumptuous to expect to comprehend its dispensations, or to seek, by rational and prudential calculations of one's behaviour, to avoid its blows in future.

We can see this distinction at work in a way that is particularly relevant to the theme of this book in the debate which was conducted in the *Christian Observer* on the food shortages of 1800. For an age obsessed by Malthusian predictions of mass starvation, the most potent weapon of a wrathful providence was obviously famine. Most contributors to the debate followed Adam Smith in blaming the shortages on the economic selfishness of forestallers, regraters, and monopolists, in whom was manifest the original depravity of mankind, but one correspondent (styled 'B. T.') objected that to blame men in this way was to deny 'the hand of God so awfully displayed in the dispensation'.[45] 'B. T.' argued that famine should be regarded as a special retribution for national sins, such as participation in the Slave Trade, whereas moderate evangelicals claimed that it was the 'probable' and predictable consequence of specific wrong behaviour on the part of individuals.

Chapters 3 and 6 below will argue that this difference of opinion about the way in which providence operates helps to explain why evangelicals were divided on matters of social and economic policy. Because Shaftesbury, Drummond, Sadler, and many more were prominent philanthropists, bitterly opposed to the prevailing *laissez-faire* ethos of their day, many commentators have used the term 'evangelicalism' as though it were synonymous with 'benevolence' and 'philanthropy'.[46] Yet in this study evangelicals are described as helping to create and to buttress the very capitalist philosophy that was under attack. In explaining this paradox it is necessary to generalize, a dangerous occupation in an area so imprecise as the history of attitudes, but it is suggested[47] that those who held an interventionist view of providence, who saw God as constantly directing earthly affairs by special warnings and judgments, also believed that governments on earth should take an interventionist approach to social and economic problems. So Shaftesbury and Drummond were paternalists; Irving and the *Morning Watch* frequently denounced the Clapham evangelicals for their indifference to wage-slavery at home; and the 'B.T.'

---

[45] *Christian Observer*, 1 (1802), 226–30.
[46] Even at the time, as Owen has pointed out, 'in the public mind the word "philanthropist" became all but synonymous with "evangelical"'. David Owen, *English Philanthropy 1660–1960* (Cambridge, Mass., 1964), 93.
[47] See below, pp. 91–8, 211–15.

referred to above was one of the few contributors to the *Christian Observer* to defend England's 'humane' Poor Laws.[48] On the other hand, moderate evangelicals seemed to match their *laissez-faire* or neutral conception of providence with a similar approach to the 'Condition of England'. They wished to make society operate as closely to 'nature' as possible by repealing interventionist laws. Then men could be left to work out their own salvation, to find their own peace, and joy, and spiritual life in the course of their worldly duties.

In other words, moderates believed that ninety-nine out of a hundred events are predictable consequences of human behaviour. Governments should interfere with men's lives as little as possible, so that men can exercise 'self-help'—the only means to salvation, both spiritually and economically—in a world beset with temptation, and meant for trial and judgment. Extremists saw no such predictability, but a perpetual—and to mortal eyes arbitrary—governance, and thought that those whom it had pleased God to place in positions of worldly influence should exercise a similar measure of control over society. In this study the word 'evangelical', when it occurs without qualification, refers to the former and—so far as the upper classes are concerned—more widespread body of thought, conveniently enshrining doctrines of self-help, *laissez-faire*, and Free Trade.

Disputation between pre- and post-millennialists is, of course, a long-standing feature of theological controversy and in no sense confined to the nineteenth century. Normally, however, it is post-millennialists who have a paternalist or activist approach to the affairs of this world, and their opponents who are fatalistic and uncaring. Thus Professor Oliver points out that much depends on the way in which a millennialist envisages the transition from the world as it is to the world as it shall be. 'If continuity is stressed, the millennium becomes simply a progressively achieved improvement upon the present. If discontinuity is stressed, then it becomes its complete reversal. In the former case the transition is smooth, gradual and peaceable; in the latter, it is abrupt, revolutionary and violent.'[49] Since pre-millennialists hold that improvement can only take place *after* the Second Coming, which itself must be preceded by chaos and deterioration, there is no incentive (and some disincentive) to set about repairs. Post-millennialists, on the other hand, see the need as well as the possibility of building towards the new Jerusalem by human agency, and therefore take a more interventionist approach towards social problems. Yet in the

---

[48] See below, pp. 98–100, 205–8. See also Edward Irving, 'Signs of the Times in the Church', *The Morning Watch: or, Quarterly Journal on Prophecy, and Theological Review*, 1 (1829), 664.

[49] W. H. Oliver, *Prophets and Millennialists: The Uses of Biblical Prophecy in England from the 1790s to the 1840s* (Auckland, 1978), 21.

early nineteenth century these roles seem to have been reversed, for it was the post-millenarian moderates who wished to leave economic relationships alone, and the pre-millenarians—Irving, Drummond, and Shaftesbury—who called for paternalistic intervention. The explanation of this apparent paradox is that 'improvement' then was generally envisaged in moral rather than material terms, and that the post-millenarian moderates, however callous their economic attitudes may appear to modern eyes, were actually the more paternalist in this other sense of wishing to control the morals of the nation. Indeed, they supported *laissez-faire* economic and social policies precisely because these would best nurture individual morality. God runs the material world on *laissez-faire* lines, in the sense that he does not often meddle with his own mechanism, and so man should not meddle either. On the other hand, the moral world does require man's intervention—hence the numerous Bible and Missionary Societies which the moderates sponsored. For their own part, the pre-millennialists agreed that it was their rivals who were the paternalists—and they despised them for it. Bible Societies and the like were devices of impotent but presumptuous men, attempting to do the Almighty's work for him, and to no avail, since God would 'not let the desire of promoting salvation—much less the desire of promoting civilization and the amelioration of moral and political society—be joined with his glory'. In pre-millenarian eyes, a successful ministry did not consist in 'this man or that man saved, much less is it nations saved by wholesale', but in providing a faithful witness to the truth of an imminent millennium.[50] Nowadays we are accustomed to think of economic conditions and relationships as primary, and so it is the extremists or pre-millenarians who seem to us to have been the paternalists. At the time, however, it was the Clapham Sect and suchlike moderate evangelicals who seemed presumptuously bent on amelioration.

At all events, moderates regarded pain as part of God's joyous plan for the moral redemption of mankind, while pre-millenarian extremists saw it as a sign that the thousand-year reign of felicity could not be long delayed. In a sense, what both were trying to do was to reconcile the evil and suffering, which after 1789 were felt to dominate the world, with the continuing existence of a powerful and loving God.

If extremists thought that moderate evangelicals were presumptuous in trying to assist God, the latter in turn condemned the extremists for underestimating the importance of right behaviour. 'He does not sufficiently unite the preceptive or cautionary parts of Holy Writ with what are considered the consolatory and elevating', wrote Daniel Wilson

---

[50] E. T. Vaughan, *A Letter to Edward Bickersteth on the Lawfulness, Expediency, Conduct and Expectation of Missions* (Leicester, 1825), 11–12. See below, p. 287.

of the Genevan pietist, Malan. Another moderate, Basil Woodd of the Eclectic Society, complained that Malan 'maintains positions, which in their tendency, relax the necessity of repentance and practical faith. . . . It is unscriptural and dangerous to speak of *salvation* as already granted and obtained.'[51] Extreme pre-millennialists were, as David Newsome has pointed out, 'assured'—that is, they were at ease in their faith, whereas most moderates would have agreed that to be at ease is to be unsafe.[52] It follows paradoxically that in order to feel potentially safe, the latter had also to feel *un*easy, just as they also liked to pretend that they had led licentious lives in youth, so that they might feel the more regenerate in maturity. It is therefore misleading of Noel Annan to write that the consolatory aspects of justification by faith fortified the Clapham evangelicals from all '*ultimate doubt*', thereby fitting them for public service.

Unlike a man who believes in justification partly by works and never therefore quite knows what the score is—who never knows how many of his bad actions have atoned for his good actions [*sic*]—the Evangelical's mind is at rest on the ultimate question. He knows that he is saved. The knowledge that God does not forget his saints gives him strength to labour in the vineyards of the world.[53]

Now this is highly debatable. The pre-millennialist Lord Shaftesbury may indeed have gained confidence in this way, but do-gooders from Clapham usually lacked precisely this sort of assurance. For most believers, faith is at least as elusive a commodity as good works, and perhaps more so since unlike them it cannot be catalogued on some sort of spiritual balance sheet. Evangelicals *professed* to believe, but could never quite be sure that they did so. Were they not Pharisees and hypocrites, pretending to a faith which they had not? Hannah More, for example, feared that she did not profit as much as she should from pious company—'it evaporates in self-satisfied feelings, and serious talk, without reaching the heart'. Craving spontaneity and frequently doubting their own sincerity, moderate

[51] Timothy Stunt, 'Geneva and British Evangelicals in the early nineteenth century', *Journal of Ecclesiastical History*, 32 (1981), 39, 44; *Christian Observer*, 19 (1820), 402.

[52] Wilberforce told his son Samuel that, unlike Methodists, 'we know that religion does not consist in the assurance of our salvation; so have written all our *sound* divines—Baxter, Doddridge and all'. Newsome, *Parting of Friends*, p. 47; J. H. Newman, *Parochial and Plain Sermons* (new edn., 1868), i. 13. See Josiah Pratt's in Pratt, *Thought of the Evangelical Leaders*, p. 500: 'We should distinguish between an assurance of *feeling* and an assurance of *inference*. The Holy Spirit enables the Christian to *infer* from what God has wrought. . . . We must not preach the duty of assurance as a duty *per se*. But the duty of living in that state with which assurance is connected.'

[53] Noel G. Annan, *Leslie Stephen: His Thought and Character in Relation to his Time* (1951), 116; N. G. Annan, *Leslie Stephen: The Godless Victorian* (1984), 151–2. However, Joseph Milner, *Sermons on St Paul's Epistle to the Colossians*, ed. James Fawcett (1841), 115, supports Annan's view that evangelicals thought it difficult to know 'what the score is' with respect to good works.

evangelicals condemned all behaviour which threatened the autonomy of self, like acting, or impersonation, or speaking in tongues. If anything, public service was less the outcome of spiritual assurance than a means by which convinced sinners, ever conscious of Satan at their elbows, sought release from guilt and a buttress for precarious faith.[54] To quote Chalmers again,

Under the economy of 'Do this and live,' the great point of anxiety with him who is labouring for the good of his soul, is, 'O that I had obedience!' Under the economy of 'Believe, and ye shall be saved,' the great point of anxiety with him who is labouring for the good of his soul, is, 'O that I had faith!' . . . Men may make a work of faith . . . [but] in the doing of this work, there may be felt all the darkness, and all the anxiety, and all the spirit of bondage, which attached to the work of the old covenant.[55]

Certainly evangelicalism contributed to, rather than detracted from, the sense of anxiety, precariousness, and doubt which prevailed among the 'upper ten thousand' during the first half of the nineteenth century.

'Feeling' was felt to be important because religion was assumed to be natural or inductive. 'Natural religion is . . . written in the feelings of the human heart.'[56] On the debit side, this led to an indifference towards the intellectual and artistic aspects of belief. A theology which has to be understood *and* felt must necessarily be simple, for one cannot *feel* a complex schema. There was a popular view, which some of their leaders criticized,[57] that 'a certain poverty of understanding' was 'inseparable from religious zeal'. Their sense of 'the indispensable importance of a child-like spirit' followed from their belief that passions and feelings, occasionally even tantrums, were surer guides than understanding and intellect. Christianity required, in Wilson's opinion, 'child-like simplicity of mind', a 'docile and humble temper, in which alone there is a recipiency,

[54] See Hannah More's journal, 29 Apr. 1798, in Roberts, *Life of Hannah More*, iii. 59. See also T. Chalmers, *The Duty of Giving an Immediate Diligence to the Business of the Christian Life* (Edinburgh, 1815), 9–17 [*Works*, xii. 77–86]. Ian Bradley, 'The Politics of Godliness: Evangelicals in Parliament 1784–1832', Oxford University D.Phil. (1974), 12–14, quotes Hannah More's *Christian Morals* (1813), i. 126, on how the most talented feel most accountable, and go into the world to escape from guilt. Evangelicals who did *not* share this sense of anxiety were felt to be noteworthy. See *Memoirs of Samuel Hoare by his Daughter Sarah and his Widow Hannah: Also Some Letters from London during the Gordon Riots*, ed. F. R. Pryor (1911), 35.

[55] T. Chalmers, 'Introductory essay', *Tracts by the Rev. Thomas Scott* (Glasgow, 1826), pp. xxii–xxiii [*Works*, xiii. 184–5; *Select Works of Thomas Chalmers*, ed. W. Hanna (Edinburgh, 1854–63), xii. 366–7]. See the discussion on anxiety and 'the strain of Puritanism' in Walter E. Houghton, *The Victorian Frame of Mind, 1830–1870* (New Haven, 1957), 61–4.

[56] Thomas Bernard, *Report of the Society for Bettering the Condition of the Poor*, iii (1802), 36.

[57] T. Chalmers, *The Christian and Civic Economy of Large Towns* (1821–6), i. 17–18 [*Works*, xiv. 39].

a capacity for admitting truth'.[58] Grace would not enter a vessel that was too smart by half. Chalmers was smart, but the quality stressed by most of those who heard him for the first time was his 'child-like simplicity of mind' (J. J. Gurney), his 'fresh and child-like simplicity' (McLeod Campbell), his 'almost infantile simplicity of manner' (Archibald Alison), his 'energy of a giant and . . . simplicity of a child' (Gladstone). A head stuffed with thought cannot *feel*, and it is necessary to *feel* the Atonement, to get *under the blood* in the words of the hymn. What is required is a character 'as clear, translucent, and homogeneous as the object glass of a great telescope', having been 'fused', like it, 'again and again in the white-heat of affliction'.[59]

Now there was obviously a danger that all this 'longing to be under the blood', with its emphasis on feeling, grace, and conversion, could degenerate into the promiscuous, romantic craving for spiritual experience which moderate evangelicals so despised in their extremer brethren. It is therefore important to stress that, while on the one hand they found eighteenth-century natural religion too cold and impersonal, moderate evangelicals were thoroughly 'dry' as well as 'low'. The members of the Eclectic Society were always anxious to distinguish evangelical devotion from enthusiasm, the latter being little more than an attack of nerves, a sort of mental inflammation to be expected of 'a bacchanalian, an actor, a fop'.[60] In the same way, feeling was distinguished from mere sensation. Thus theatre was condemned because, like Roman Catholicism, it took hold of the senses, whereas true religion 'appeals to the reason and conscience'.[61] 'They who are [evangelicals] from Reason *and* Feeling must be happiest and safest', mused a perceptive commentator, the author of *Sense and Sensibility* (1811),[62] while Wilberforce considered that 'the reasoning part of the public . . . is also the feeling part'.[63] There is obviously an ambiguity here which was never quite resolved, but it is important to stress the rational aspects of moderate evangelicalism, if only because many accounts (including a recent and very interesting study of liberal pacifism during the Napoleonic Wars) exaggerate its irrational aspects. J. E. Cookson believes that because they started from the facts

[58] Daniel Wilson, *The Evidences of Christianity* (1828–30), i. 45–9.
[59] *The Thorough Business Man: Memoirs of Walter Powell, Merchant Melbourne and London*, by Benjamin Gregory (1871), 185.
[60] R. Cecil in Pratt, *Thought of the Evangelical Leaders*, pp. 294–5.
[61] J. Pratt, ibid., p. 160. Plays were thought to 'have a tendency to give a romantic turn of mind', while oratorios were worse since they were also profane. R. Cecil, ibid., p. 161. For a sensitive discussion of this theme see Doreen M. Rosman, *Evangelicals and Culture* (1984), 70–9.
[62] Jane Austen to Fanny Knight, 18 Nov. 1814, *Jane Austen's Letters to her Sister Cassandra and Others*, ed. R. W. Chapman (2nd edn, Oxford, 1952), 410 (italics added).
[63] Wilberforce to Bathurst, 4 July 1816, loc. cit.

of man's depravity and need for redemption, evangelicals possessed a faith which was essentially mysterious and emotional, and that—despite some points in common—this distinguishes them from the Unitarians and other 'rational Christians' who led the opposition to the war against France.

Evangelicals . . . were not 'rational' in their apprehension of religious truth. They found and sustained their faith in marvelling at the mystical processes of the Holy Spirit, in intense devotion to Jesus Christ and in acceptance of the bible as an authority which needed piety rather than intellect to be understood. The rational Christian found it impossible to agree that the God-given intellectual capacity of man could be of so little account in the contemplation of the divine. He could not accept, if an all-wise, all-powerful deity was to be known by his works, that the feeling of an individual that he had been redeemed from sin provided the same certainty as the realisation that the Creation was a universe of harmony and perfection. Moreover, the rational Christian, in possession of this teleology, was able to hold fast to the potential of human nature, where the evangelical, beginning with his own depravity, was impressed by its corruption.[64]

Such a view of evangelicalism may fit a Joanna Southcott or an Edward Irving; it may also fit many Nonconformists, who probably dominated Cookson's vision since unlike Anglicans they were often opposed to the war against France. But moderate evangelicals were in their own way extremely rational, and believed just as much in the potential as in the depravity of humankind. Their faith also was teleological, though the purpose (or 'perfection') that they divined in the universe was different from that of the 'Friends of Peace'. The latter looked for beauty and happiness, of which some saw in the French Revolution a glorious harbinger. Anglican evangelicals, meanwhile, shared in polite society's abhorrence of the Revolution, and did not suppose that either beauty or happiness—or peace, for that matter—was to be found in the temporal world. Extremists may have moved from here to a mystical nihilism, but the moderates clung to a view of nature as both constant and perfectly constructed. The *telos* was not, however, happiness but justice, that is, punishment—justice being regarded in an individualistic rather than a distributive light—and this priority in turn led to an emphasis on sin which may strike the modern mind as irrational, but was not in fact.

In other words, the moderate evangelicalism which developed after 1789 represented a shift in natural religion from *evidences* to *paradoxes*, that is, from examples of benign contrivance in the natural world to demonstrations of how superficial misery may work inner improvement. Those who found it impossible to point to the obvious harmonies of nature as evidence of the goodness and good sense of the deity had to argue instead

[64] J. E. Cookson, *The Friends of Peace: Anti-War Liberalism in England 1793–1815* (Cambridge, 1982), 8–9.

that *apparent* nastiness, like war and famine, was—to those who understood the divine economy—a blessing in disguise. This point can be illustrated with reference to the fashionable study of the earth's surface. There were still many Scriptural Geologists prepared to argue that the world was a model of harmonious forces. John Rooke, for example, political economist and free trader, attacked Ricardian pessimism over rent on geological grounds, arguing against it that the 'economy of Providence' was evident in all the layers of the earth. On the other hand, an evangelical geologist like Thomas Gisborne the elder, who saw only chaos and disruption among the rocks, did not so much abandon natural theology as stand it on its head:

The earth, as to its exterior strata, is not at present in the same condition in which it was when it came forth from the hand of its Creator; but has manifestly undergone universal and violent and overwhelming convulsions of such a nature as to spread general destruction among the animated inhabitants of its surface at the time of the catastrophe. . . . A convulsion thus effected by the hand of the Creator, and reducing, at the time of its occurrence, the inhabited surface of the earth into a state of desolation and ruin, does not appear to admit of any other explanation than the following: that a moral change calling for such an event had taken place in that portion of the inhabitants of the earth, which was endued with moral agency and responsibility; in other words, that mankind had offended their Creator, by transgression of his laws, and had brought upon themselves penal consequences of disobedience.[65]

Such penalties were welcome, moreover, since suffering conduces to remorse and regeneration, thus affirming God's concern for his creatures. It is impossible to say whether a pessimistic view of things after 1789 led men to search for a lapsarian theology, or whether the latter was an autonomous development which coloured men's views of reality. The paradigmatic nature of moderate evangelicalism as an adaptation of natural theology to a fallen world is, however, obvious.

In consequence, perhaps, of the common tendency to regard evangelicalism as irrational, it has often been assumed that it was bitterly antipathetic to the scientific developments of the first half of the nineteenth century.[66] But this is only true of those extremists like Shaftesbury, Irving, Frederick Nolan, and supporters of the *Record*, who did indeed oppose any

[65] T. Gisborne, *The Testimony of Natural Theology to Christianity* (1818), 64–5; John Rooke, *Geology as a Science, applied to the Reclamation of Land from the Sea, &c* (1838), esp. 3–10, 328–56. On Gisborne see John H. Overton, *The English Church in the Nineteenth Century (1800–1833)* (1894), 74–6.

[66] Young, *Portrait of an Age*, pp. 24–5; Jack Morrell and Arnold Thackray, *Gentlemen of Science: Early Years of the British Association for the Advancement of Science* (Oxford, 1981), 224–45.

accommodation with science and scholarship.[67] Those who, on the contrary, supposed that there was a permanent natural law operating in the universe looked to science with confident expectation. Thus Chalmers and Sumner, for example, were anxious to show the hand of God at work in the formation of rocks and in the movement of the heavens, as well as in the economic operations of society. William Buckland, a professional geologist who was able at one stage to present his findings in an explicitly biblical light, was much patronized by evangelicals such as Bishop Barrington of Durham, G. S. Faber, Samuel Wilks, and J. B. Sumner.[68] J. D. Yule makes an important point here in his study of the Genesis/ geology debate between 1800 and 1840. Those writers who attempted to twist the findings of the geologists to fit the Genesis story he calls 'scriptural geologists'. Those who reinterpreted Genesis to fit geology are 'geological hermeneutists'.[69] Generally speaking, the evangelicals fell into the former category, while more 'moderate and intellectual' divines are found among the latter. However,

If religious periodicals are to be trusted, the dividing line between these groups fell within the ranks of the Evangelicals, with the *Christian Guardian* consistently supporting the work of the 'Scriptural Geologists', while the *Christian Observer* and the majority of the rest preferred to accept what was agreed upon by most professional geologists and sought to find an interpretation of the Scriptures which did not involve their contradicting any acknowledged geological 'fact'.[70]

A relevant case here might be that of Charles Girdlestone, described by the *Dictionary of National Biography* as a biblical commentator of 'the moderate evangelical school'. In discoursing on the cholera epidemic of 1832, he praised the 'goodness and severity of God' and was convinced that the only remedy lay 'in Jesus Christ, in the atonement of his blood'.

---

[67] Frederick Nolan, *The Analogy of Revelation and Science*, 1833 Bampton Lectures (Oxford, 1833), 9–10: 'The rejection of miraculous agency in any scheme of Science, which entrenches on the province of Revelation, must be consequently not merely contrary to the first principles of theology, but to every sound deduction of reason.'

[68] Nicolaas A. Rupke, *The Great Chain of History: William Buckland and the English School of Geology 1814–1849* (Oxford, 1983), 14–15, 64. See below, pp. 235–6. Bishop Barrington was also, with Thomas Bernard, a patron of Sir Humphry Davy, and tried to persuade him to take Holy Orders. Davy declined, but promised that he would 'lose no opportunity of making those [scientific] deductions which awaken devotional feelings, and connect the natural with the moral sense'. Davy to Bernard, ?1805, *Memoirs of the Life of Sir Humphry Davy*, by John Davy (1836), i. 272–3.

[69] The 'geological hermeneutists' fell into two main categories: the first attempted to overcome the discrepancy between geological and biblical 'time' by adopting Chalmers's formula, that a large interval must have elapsed at some point in the Genesis story; the second followed G. S. Faber in redefining the biblical word 'day' so as to signify a period longer than twenty-four hours, even so long as six thousand years.

[70] John David Yule, 'The impact of science on British religious thought in the second quarter of the nineteenth century', Cambridge University Ph.D. (1976), 328.

Yet he was every bit a natural theologian and far from unscientific in his outlook. The numerical laws of gravitation, of planetary motion, and—thanks to John Dalton's recent advances—of chemical combination, proved for Girdlestone the existence of God, while mathematics provided a means whereby the mind might divine that existence.[71]

Girdlestone professed to have been greatly influenced by John Leslie's *Philosophy of Arithmetic* (1817). In Scotland the turning-point in evangelical attitudes to science had come with the celebrated Leslie affair of 1805. This was the abortive attempt of the so-called Moderate Party in the Presbyterian Church of Scotland[72] to prevent the election of John Leslie to the Chair of Mathematics at Edinburgh University. His fault was to have endorsed, in a footnote to *An Experimental Inquiry into the Nature and Propagation of Heat* (1804), Hume's notorious doctrine of causation. Hume's theory, that 'the relation of cause and effect is nothing more, at bottom, than a constant and invariable sequence', and its elaboration by Thomas Brown, Professor of Moral Philosophy at Edinburgh (1810–20), was regarded as an enormous challenge to natural theologians and their 'proofs', and became as great a bogey in its sphere as Malthusianism was among social theorists.[73] To many it betokened

the accursed system of individualisation fathered by Locke, and brought to its full monstrous growth by Brown in his essay on cause and effect, and most dextrously chemicalised and naturalised by Sir John Leslie. What a dismal dream we and the world, and *what* we must then put in the place of God, would be, if cause and effect, cause and effect, marched on like spectre kings in Macbeth, with as little connection, and in no more vital method and order.[74]

A striking fact about the Leslie affair is that the Evangelicals were to be found in support of Leslie, that is of free speculation and scientific progress, while the Moderate Party came across as religious bigots and narrow adherents to the Westminster Confession. This was of course a startling reversal of roles. The Moderate Party contended that to regard causation

---

[71] Charles Girdlestone, *Number: a Link between Divine Intelligence and Human: An Argument* (1875), 1–34; C. Girdlestone, *On the Goodness and Severity of God, during the Prevalence of Cholera: A Sermon* (Birmingham, 1832), 6.

[72] 'Moderate' here refers to the dominant party in the Church of Scotland during the late eighteenth and early nineteenth centuries, and must not be confused with those evangelicals in England whom we have deemed to be 'moderates' as distinct from 'extremists'.

[73] See Pietro Corsi, 'Natural theology, the methodology of science and the question of species in the works of the Reverend Baden Powell', Oxford University D.Phil. (1980), 224. Thomas Brown, *Observations on the Nature and Tendency of the Doctrine of Mr. Hume, Concerning the Relation of Cause and Effect* (1804; 2nd enlarged edn 1806), *passim*. Brown argues against Hume's doctrine of the power of 'custom', and for man's intuitive conception that the same antecedents will produce the same consequences.

[74] Samuel Clark to Edward Strachey, Easter Day 1840, *Memorials from Journals and Letters of Samuel Clark*, ed. his wife (1878), 142.

as no more than observed 'conjunctions' and 'sequences' of events was to deny that the harmonies of the natural world *proved* the existence of a wise and designing First Cause a posteriori. But, as Ian Clark has written, 'while the Moderates were still tenaciously defending their old positions the Evangelicals were slowly becoming aware that even the so-called "scepticism" of Hume might be woven into the fabric of Christian apologetics'. For the bedrock of evangelical belief was an a priori argument based on every man's conscience and common sense, something which Hume did not impugn, and which Leslie and Brown explicitly defended.[75]

Ian Clark believes that the Leslie affair marks a powerful shift in the Scottish theological consensus from natural theology to revelation, from George Hill's 'evidences' to Chalmers's view that natural theology can only give us 'inklings' of the truth, and that it was 'quite overrated by those who would represent it [rather than conscience] as the foundation of the edifice'.[76] Equally important, it marks the point where Scottish evangelicals accommodated themselves to a scientific notion of causation, and there is more to this than Clark's suggestion that the Humean theory left inductive religion unscathed. In a positive way, this idea of law as 'constant conjunction' buttressed the evangelical 'scheme' of salvation. The point is that the Moderate Party had never really needed a theory of temporal sequence. God was the cause, and his effects were conceived as operating spatially, as it were, in mechanical harmony. As we have seen, the moderate evangelicals of Clapham, like Chalmers, did not abandon natural theology, but inserted a temporal sequence—sin followed by punishment—which required a notion of causality to supplement that of the First Cause. Leslie endorsed that notion, as well as consolidating the evangelical view that, in the final analysis, faith is a product of innate conscience.

Anyway, early nineteenth-century evangelicalism cannot be dismissed as anti-intellectual or irrational. In Scotland again, Rice has identified a 'new' group of 'often learned, often even fashionable' Presbyterian evangelicals, who 'followed their own group of philosophers, the common sense school founded by Thomas Reid and later led by Dugald Stewart'.

[75] J. Veitch, 'A memoir of Dugald Stewart', *The Collected Works of Dugald Stewart*, ed. Sir William Hamilton (Edinburgh, 1854–60), x, p. lxxviii.

[76] T. Chalmers, *On the Power Wisdom and Goodness of God as Manifested in the Adaptation of External Nature to the Moral and Intellectual Constitution of Man*, Bridgewater Treatise No. 1 (1833), ii. 283–90 (reprinted as *On Natural Theology* in *Works*, ii. 395–9); Ian D. L. Clark, 'The Leslie controversy, 1805', *Records of the Scottish Church History Society*, 14 (1960–2), 179–97. J. B. Morrell, 'The Leslie affair: careers, kirk, and politics in Edinburgh in 1805', *The Scottish Historical Review*, 54 (1975), 63–82, is a salutary but less than wholly persuasive warning not to read too much theological and philosophical significance into the affair.

These men mainly desired abolition of the Slave Trade as 'an act of atonement for national sins', but such a sentiment by no means signified a surrender of reason to emotion. For, as Rice comments,

By an extraordinary religious alchemy, these years saw the whole weight of the Scottish intellectual elite shift from the moderate party of the Old Kirk to the evangelical one. . . . This was a change from a situation wherein high learning and vital religion were antithetical, to one wherein they were compatible if not inseparable.[77]

This assessment is important, given the part which Scottish political economists generally and Thomas Chalmers especially played in the national debate on the economy. And though one could not go so far in discussing the situation in England, it is the case that moderate evangelicals in this period achieved an intellectual respectability, and an acknowledged role in rational debate, without which they could hardly have exercised so much official influence.

'Permeation by Filtration': the Spread of the Evangelical Influence

Clearly the term 'evangelical' covers a range of theological positions, but still more problematic is the fact that it is seriously frayed at the edges. By 1850 about one-third of Anglican clergymen, including many of the brightest and best, may have been designated 'Evangelical' with a capital letter, and so could the vast majority of Nonconformists. Ian Bradley calculates that there were then between two and three million Anglican Evangelicals out of a population in England and Wales of eighteen million.[78] Even so, evangelicalism could hardly have had the impact ascribed to it if it had been confined to those who formally acknowledged the label. G. M. Young pointed out that *morally* it imposed itself on many who were indifferent or even hostile to its religious basis.[79] This begs the question of whether evangelicalism affected the thought of non-evangelicals, or whether it was merely one vocabulary among many for expressing ideas deriving from some other source. Either way its ramifications were widespread and pervasive.

[77] C. Duncan Rice, *The Scots Abolitionists 1833–1861* (Baton Rouge and London, 1981), 25–6.

[78] Ian Bradley, *The Call to Seriousness: The Evangelical Impact on the Victorians* (1976), 52. The estimate of one-third originated with [W. J. Conybeare], 'Church parties', *Edinburgh Review* 98 (1853), 338, but it is considered too high by W. R. Ward in *A History of the Methodist Church in Great Britain*, ed. R. Davies, G. Rupp, and A. R. George (1965–83), ii. 86, and by Owen Chadwick, *Victorian Church*, i. 446.

[79] G. M. Young, *Portrait of an Age*, p. 24. Elsewhere Young spoke of 'the imponderable pressure of the Evangelical discipline'. Ibid., p. 21.

The affinity between evangelicals and Tractarians has long been something of an historical commonplace.[80] Gladstone, for example, despised the individualism implicit in evangelical teaching, its derogation of sacraments and of apostolical authority, but his fundamentalist belief 'in a degeneracy of man, in the Fall—in *sin*—in the intensity and virulence of sin', as well as his absorption in the Atonement, was a clear legacy of an evangelical upbringing.[81] William Sewell's ascetic doctrine that virtue consists of doing what is unpleasant strongly resembles that of the fictional evangelical, paterfamilias Pontifex.[82] J. H. Newman admitted in the *Apologia Pro Vita Sua* that the evangelical creed had imbued his youthful intellect with 'impressions of dogma, which, through God's mercy, have never been effaced or obscured'.[83] George Landow has suggested that when evangelicals were not stressing the need for personal conversion, nor Tractarians the Apostolical Succession and corporate holiness, then the two groups sounded much the same.[84] Perhaps the *real* difference lies in the respective doctrines of conversion and reserve. Evangelicals stressed the eternal conflict between good and evil, and man's hope of sudden conversion as grace flooded into the empty vessel of his soul. For Tractarians such a doctrine resembled too closely the despised tenets of liberalism, the view that man could choose his own way amid a clash of conflicting opinions. John Keble and Isaac Williams therefore promulgated the principle of 'Reserve in communicating Christian Knowledge' (*Tract LXXX*), the idea that truth has to be 'wrung from nature's close reserve', and that members of a church are only educated into the mysteries of faith gradually and in response to their holy lives. This led to an emphasis on the apostolic tradition and on the sacraments, on purity and sanctity, which was not in keeping with evangelical priorities, but Horton Davis considers that the Oxford Movement's evangelical roots, and especially the doctrine that personal religion was a response to divine favour, helped to check its tendency towards a quasi-materialist conception of grace, where the validity of the sacraments is regarded as independent of the faith of the recipient.[85]

[80] Yngve Brilioth, *Evangelicalism and the Oxford Movement* (1934), 1–53; Yngve Brilioth, *The Anglican Revival: Studies in the Oxford Movement* (1933), 29–44; Newsome, *Parting of Friends*, pp. 12–16; Herbert Clegg, 'Evangelicals and Tractarians', *Historical Magazine of the Protestant Episcopal Church*, 35 (1966), 111–53, 237–94, and 36 (1967), 127–8.

[81] Gladstone speaking to Mrs Humphry Ward, 8 Apr. 1888, as reported in *The Life of Mrs. Humphry Ward*, by Janet Penrose Trevelyan (1923), 59. See below, pp. 344–5.

[82] Sewell, *Christian Morals* (1840), 179–209, 404–7, reviewed in *The British Critic and Quarterly Theological Review* 29 (1841), 1–44.

[83] J. H. Newman, *Apologia Pro Vita Sua: being a Reply to a Pamphlet entitled 'What, then, does Dr. Newman mean?'* (1864), 58.

[84] George P. Landow, *Victorian Types Victorian Shadows: Biblical Typology in Victorian Literature, Art, and Thought* (Boston and London, 1980), 16–20.

[85] Horton Davis, *Worship and Theology in England* (Princeton, NJ, 1961–75), iii. 210–82.

Conversely, one must not underestimate the evangelicals' attachment to a visible church or their awareness of the need for establishments. The publication of Froude's *Remains* (1838–9) and the secessions from Oxford to Rome were to embitter relations between the two movements in the 1840s, and an attempt to turn the *Church of England Quarterly Review* into an organ of 'Evangelical High Churchmanship' in 1840 met with little success.[86] But until then, Oxford and Clapham should be regarded as complementary rather than antagonistic spheres of influence.

More surprising, perhaps, are evangelical's links with Broad or Liberal churchmen. It is well known that the latitudinarian Thomas Arnold despised 'the party', as he called the Clapham Sect, because of their 'infinitely little minds' and the 'seeming wish to keep the world and the Church ever distinct, instead of labouring to destroy the one by increasing the influence of the other, and making the kingdoms of the world indeed the kingdoms of Christ'. Yet even his attitude was ambivalent, for he clearly saw that only 'the party' came at all close to sharing his own moral seriousness and enthusiasm. Stanley remarked that Arnold 'felt most keenly his differences with the so-called Evangelical party, to which, on the one hand, he naturally looked for co-operation, as the body which at that time was placed at the head of the religious convictions of the country, but from which, on the other hand, he was constantly repelled'.[87] Walter Houghton has pointed out that 'underlying the sectarian differences between Arnold, Newman, and the Evangelicals, there is a fundamental continuity of aim which springs from their common indebtedness to John Wesley and the religious movement he initiated in the eighteenth century'.[88] Certainly Arnold's view that life is a series of trials, and that these should turn out to be 'our greatest advantages' spiritually,[89] is typical, and his famous last words to his son would be less understandable if divorced from the evangelical temper of the times: 'Thank God, Tom, for giving me this pain: I have suffered so little pain in my life, that I feel it is very good for me: now God has given it to me, and I do so thank Him for it.'[90] Duncan Forbes has referred to the 'latent evangelicalism' of such Liberal Anglicans as Arnold, Whately, J. C. Hare, Thirlwall, and Milman, with their overriding concern for the salvation of the individual soul amid the ruins of the empires which they studied as historians.[91]

[86] Peter Toon, *Evangelical Theology 1833–1856: A Response to Tractarianism* (1979), 41–2.

[87] *The Life and Correspondence of Thomas Arnold*, by Arthur Penrhyn Stanley (1844), i. 255 [5th edn (1845), i. 286]; Arnold to Revd F. C. Blackstone, 14 Mar. 1828, ibid., i. 76 [i. 90].

[88] Houghton, *Victorian Frame of Mind*, p. 228.

[89] Stanley, *Life of Arnold*, i. 45 [i. 50].   [90] Ibid., ii. 328 [ii. 337].

[91] Duncan Forbes, *The Liberal Anglican Idea of History* (Cambridge, 1952), 131.

If such links between Broad and Low Church seem surprising, even someone like Byron, who scoffed at orthodox doctrines of sin, retribution, and damnation, can be said to have been 'touched by the sweep of the Evangelical wave'.[92] As Kingsley observed, Byron had 'the most intense and awful sense of moral law—of law external to himself',[93] and though he angrily denounced the Calvinist dogmas of his own upbringing, he could never quite believe his own rebuttals. Then there was Lady Bessborough, Byron's 'Lady Blarney', whom one would not readily associate with moral propriety, but who could innocently interrupt a gossipy love letter to make earnest observations about sabbath observance.[94] Even if this was merely 'sermons and soda water the day after', it does illustrate the way in which puritanical piety was able to infiltrate many unexpected areas of early nineteenth-century society. No one quite coined the phrase 'We are all evangelicals now', but Jane Austen came close: 'I am by no means convinced that we ought not all to be Evangelicals, and am at least persuaded that they who are so from Reason *and* Feeling, must be happiest and safest.'[95]

It is important to be clear about this, since in this book evangelical attitudes will be attributed to many who would not have been regarded as 'Evangelicals' with a capital 'E'. A case in point is Edward Copleston, Provost of Oriel College, Oxford (1814–28), and Bishop of Llandaff (1828–49), whose social and economic ideas were in many respects typical of those described here as 'evangelical', and who is of particular interest since he actually exercised a direct, if brief, influence on official policy-making.[96] He was conventionally regarded as a High Churchman, and has also been seen as a 'rationalistic' pioneer of Liberal Anglicanism, but no one has ever suggested that he was an Evangelical. And quite rightly, for Copleston's abhorrence of predestinarianism[97] made it impossible for

---

[92] H. J. C. Grierson, 'Byron and English society', *Byron, the Poet*, ed. W. A. Briscoe (1924), 67.

[93] Charles Kingsley, *Miscellanies* (1859), i. 311–13. Young, *Portrait of An Age*, p. 25 n., glossed this by calling Byron 'an Evangelical gone wrong'.

[94] Lady Bessborough to Granville Leveson Gower, 14 Aug. 1810, *Lord Granville Leveson Gower: Private Correspondence 1781 to 1821*, ed. Castilia Countess Granville (1916), ii. 358–9, and quoted in *The Context of English Literature: The Romantics*, ed. Stephen Prickett (1981), 141.

[95] Jane Austen to Fanny Knight, 18 Nov. 1814, loc. cit. On feminine susceptibility to evangelicalism, see F. K. Prochaska, *Women and Philanthropy in Nineteenth-Century England* (Oxford, 1980), 8–17.

[96] See below, pp. 126–7, 223, 234–5.

[97] 'Surely there may be a power reserved [to God] of influencing the *will*, whether by presenting motives, or immediately by secret impulse, without impairing its freedom; as there may be a power reserved of modifying upon particular occasions, of abating, augmenting, or suspending the laws of the material world, without destroying that system, or even changing it, which to our reason appears to be the established order.' Copleston to Ward, ?1825, *Memoirs of the Political and Literary Life of Robert Plumer Ward*, by Edmund Phipps (1850), ii. 124–5.

him to associate with a type of churchmanship tainted, however misleadingly, with Calvinism. But when Edward Irving first came to London's
Caledonian Chapel in 1822—this was before his adventist phase when
he was still regarded as a devotee of Chalmers—Copleston was delighted
with what he heard and anxious to 'go again'.[98] It seems, moreover, that
Copleston always spoke kindly of evangelical clergy,[99] and Simeon—
surely a touchstone of moderate evangelical orthodoxy—claimed on
making Copleston's acquaintance in 1822 that he 'accords more with my
views of Scripture than almost any other person I am acquainted with'.[1]
Three chance comments such as these do not indicate that Copleston
was a covert Evangelical with a capital 'E', but may remind us that
we are dealing with an amorphous set of ideas and attitudes, capable
of seeping into minds that were sometimes formally hostile to the type
of churchmanship they represented.

Another example is provided by William Vernon Harcourt (1789–
1871), son of an Archbishop of York and a founder member of the
British Association for the Advancement of Science. It is fashionable to
suppose that, since Broad Churchmen would accommodate most easily
to Darwinism in the 1860s, earlier attempts by clerics to advance scientific
knowledge must have been conducted by prototypes of the Broad Church,
that is by so-called Liberal Anglicans. The late Faye Cannon pioneered
the idea of a mainly Cambridge network of 'scientific Broad Churchmen',
an intellectual coterie based around Whewell, Peacock, Herschel, Babbage,
Maurice, the Hares, and the Wordsworths,[2] and in their recent author-
itative work Morrell and Thackray contrive to imply that while nearly
all evangelicals were hostile to science, nearly all scientists (including
Harcourt) must, in so far as they had any religious beliefs, be Liberal
Anglicans.[3] Yet if Harcourt was a friend of the High Churchman Walter
Hook, he was also a friend of Wilberforce and a former pupil of Isaac
Milner, while his approach to religion was quite unscientific. The *'theory
of religion'* was, he admitted, entirely contained in those Gospel truths
which he had learned at his mother's knee, though 'advancing years
[had] brought with them experimental proof of the sinfulness of human

[98] Copleston to John Murray, 22 Dec. 1822, Murray MSS.
[99] *Memoirs of Sir George Sinclair, Bart., of Ulbster,* by James Grant (1870), 177.
[1] Simeon to Revd T. Thomason, 26 Apr. 1822, in Carus, *Memoirs of Simeon,*
pp. 567–8.
[2] Walter F. Cannon, 'Scientists and Broad Churchmen: an early Victorian intellectual
network', *The Journal of British Studies,* 4 (1964), 65–88; Susan Faye Cannon, *Science
in Culture: The Early Victorian Period* (New York, 1978), esp. 29–71; for some cogent
doubts as to the religious and intellectual coherence of this network, see Pietro Corsi in
Isis, 70 (1979), 593–5.
[3] Jack Morrell and Arnold Thackray, *Gentlemen of Science: Early Years of the
British Association for the Advancement of Science* (Oxford, 1981), 224–45.

nature'.[4] He believed in the possibility of miracles, but also in clockwork laws of nature, especially in 'the law of pain to amend the moral condition of mankind'.[5] His sermon *The Present Time a Probation* is indeed as comprehensive a statement of moderate evangelical eschatology as one could hope to find.

This [Gospel] system is a Divine provision of corrective discipline for reclaiming free agents from an exceptional condition of moral defilement; there our material world is shown to be a temporary land of exile from the presence of God out of which the redeemed spirit escapes through the gate of suffering and death; there the apparent flaw in the system of Divine government proves to be a merciful plan for bringing the greatest good out of that evil, which by the abuse of his liberty man has heaped upon himself.

It is ours, brethren, standing amidst the revolutions of a fearful *machinery*, to regard the changes and chances of our mortal life with an eye to this their true intent; it is ours to appreciate rightly the conditions of a probationary state. If pain and suffering are our path to the noblest excellences of our nature, and consequently to its greatest blessedness, if the temptations of every kind which assail us, once conquered, lead the victor on the road to glory, . . . there we see clearly how this preliminary order of things . . . may well consist with the wisdom and benevolence of God.[6]

This is undoubtedly the authentic voice of Wilberforce, Simeon, and Chalmers, and reminds us that even such a 'progressive' churchman as Harcourt inhabited what may be called an evangelical frame of reference.

The relationship of evangelicalism to utilitarianism is of particular importance to the historian of economic thought, since 'official' political economy in the nineteenth century is generally located within the body of Benthamite ideas. Lord Shelburne once described Bentham's system of jurisprudence as a type of 'legal Protestantism', and recently Peter Mathias has applied the same conceit to the pre-evangelical 'economic Protestantism' of Adam Smith.

Each individual, in a society composed of discrete individuals anxious to maximise their own interests, was equidistant from the market, and equal before the market. The truth about the relations between the individual and the market was certain and could be codified and in the hands of every individual—in the form of simplified gospels if not the complete, sophisticated testament. There was to be no priesthood with special sacramental authority, with access to the market on preferred terms, no intervening bodies between the individual and the market enjoying special status and particular favours, seeking to interpret the rules of

---

[4] W. V. Harcourt to Sir Thomas Blomefield, 12 Dec. 1832, *The Harcourt Papers*, ed. Edward Harcourt (privately printed, Oxford, 1880–1905), xiii. 307–9.

[5] W. V. Harcourt to the Duke of Argyll, 22 July 1867, ibid., xiv. 256–7.

[6] *Sermons by the Rev. William Vernon Harcourt*, ed. W. F. Hook (1873), 54–5.

the market in their favour by monopoly, tariffs or discretionary advantage. Only special cases, each needing separate justification, could deny the operation of this rule.[7]

Now in some respects this description applies equally well to the evangelical scheme of economics discussed below, but with the important difference— already noted—that in the post-Malthusian gloom of the Age of Atonement it was no longer possible to assume with Smith that the market would serve to maximize material happiness. In evangelical hands enlightened self-interest meant not that private vices would conduce to public good but that public and private calamities might, in a state of probation, conduce to future virtue. The market would yield not material but moral and spiritual benefits, would engender remorse, which in turn would foster self-denial, the latter being the hinge on which evangelical economics turned, the counterpart of altruism in the philosophy of Smith and of chivalry in that of Alfred Marshall.

Now at first sight this emphasis on self-denial distinguishes evangelicalism from utilitarianism, against whose hedonistic egoism it was in part a reaction. Yet Benthamism also contained a puritanical emphasis on self-denial, at least in the short term. 'To abstain from the enjoyment which is in our power' and 'to seek distant rather than immediate results'— Houghton has pointed out that this sounds like an evangelical discoursing on the here and the hereafter, but in fact it was the most *un*evangelical Nassau Senior explaining the secret of commercial success.[8] Halévy has explained how an instinct 'to sacrifice present pleasure in the hope of future, and purchase happiness at the cost of labour and suffering' gave classical economics, and utilitarianism generally, an 'element of asceticism' which was almost religious. 'British individualism is a moderate individualism, a mixture whose ingredients are often mingled beyond the possibility of analysis, a compound of Evangelicalism and Utilitarianism.'[9] And of course the two movements joined forces to 'reform' the treatment of paupers, lunatics, criminals, alcoholics, Indians, and other unfortunates.[10] Even so, the differences are obvious and important. Evangelicals were adamant that virtuous action must be spontaneous, that there was no ethical value in doing good by command. Even theological utilitarians like Paley, on the other hand, concerned with the consequences of actions rather than with men's motives, considered that a man who obeys the law because

---

[7] Peter Mathias, 'Malthus and the transition from optimism to pessimism in classical economic thought' (unpublished seminar paper, 1981), p. 2.

[8] Houghton, *Victorian Frame of Mind*, pp. 249–50; Nassau William Senior, *Political Economy* (1836; 2nd edn for *Encyclopaedia Metropolitana*, 1850), 60.

[9] E. Halévy, *A History of the English People in the Nineteenth Century*, trans. E. I. Watkin and D. A. Barker (1924–47), i. 586–7.

[10] See below, pp. 215–18.

he is law-abiding or fearful of punishment is ethically as laudable as one who obeys out of conviction. In Bentham's deontology, it is the state which metes out reward and punishment, the object of which is the 'conversion' of the citizen from his naturally anti-social disposition. With evangelicals it is of course God who dispenses justice, and it is the sacrifice of earthly pleasure, rather than the pursuit of long-term pleasures, which can best guarantee a final and lasting reward.[11] In other words, all life is to be regarded as short-term, since all long-term ends and aims lie in eternity.

In assessing the intellectual influences which operated on any individual reformer, it is difficult to disentangle the contributions of these two parallel and complementary movements. Perhaps, as Halévy warned, they are 'mingled beyond the possibility of analysis'. Nevertheless, this book will make the attempt, and will suggest for a start that if, in the early nineteenth century, many men shared a predominantly *mechanistic* and *individualistic* cast of thought—if, as was sometimes said, 'love of system' prevailed over 'love of truth'—this probably owed more to the vague but diffusive sway of evangelicalism than to Bentham (whom few can have read) or the Philosophic Radicals. There can be no doubt that the evangelicalism of the period *was* individualistic in its concern for the spiritual struggle facing each mortal soul. There is also no doubt that it was a *mechanistic* religion, whose votaries conceived of souls as though they were suspended between opposing forces of sin and grace, their only hope of safety lying in that '*hinge* of Christian truth', the Atonement. Mechanical also was its conception of the world as an equilibrium state and of man as 'standing amidst the revolutions of its fearful machinery'. No less mechanical was the exaggerated extent to which Anglican evangelicals rigidly structured their lives. In Hugh McLeod's words, 'Nation, monarch, established church, social hierarchy, sabbath, bible, marriage, family, work: round these sacred symbols, each heavily laden with emotional significance, life revolved' with a regular 'moral dynamic'.[12]

A static-cum-cyclical conception of time accompanied the evangelicals' view of the world as a probationary state, but it was also a hallmark of early nineteenth-century attitudes generally, and may be a clue to the sway which evangelicalism exercised. Forbes, for example, has demonstrated brilliantly how Liberal Anglicans thought of history in essentially cyclical terms. The 'domination of the clock' and the monotony of factory life no doubt impressed a heightened sense of recurrent time

---

[11] The analogy was recognized in [J. Bentham and T. P. Thompson], *The 'greatest happiness' principle in morals and government* (1829–30), iii. 37–8: both evangelicalism and utilitarianism were, they argued, based on the precept 'Do as you would be done by', but the latter applied only earthly sanctions to enforce it.

[12] Hugh McLeod, 'Recent studies in Victorian religious history', *Victorian Studies*, 21 (1977–8), 255.

on thousands of people to whom life was a curse;[13] while the guiltily comfortable middle classes, to whom it was a blessing, characteristically felt the urge to 'redeem' the precious gift by accounting for every spent moment in minutely detailed diaries. It may well be that it was those who possessed a different sense of the passage of time, a Whig perception of history perhaps, or a Utopian confidence in future progress, who were best able to shelter from the dominant evangelical ideology. Chapter 8 will suggest that a more dynamic sense of time past and future, as encouraged by historical inquiry and by geological and biological advances, helped to defeat that ideology in the 1850s and 1860s, and to replace a social theory based on what Spencer called 'statics' with a form of 'social dynamics'.

But if earlier nineteenth-century thinkers took an essentially static view of society, they did not do so with the confidence of medieval Schoolmen. Much of the intellectual tension of the period derives from the ambivalence of men who felt the seductions of future growth but who feared the consequences horribly. 'We have . . . the fact before us, that England is largely in advance of the rest of the world; that few nations are following up her footsteps, and of these, none rapidly.' This was not the triumphalist statement it might appear to be. The writer was a political economist of Tory views, who naturally regarded England as not a 'safe specimen of the career of a people so developing their productive forces', and who longed for 'the air of purer, though poorer communities'.[14] Nevertheless, the dilemma was one which exercised so-called Liberals as well as Tories. James Currie (1756–1805), for example, was a Liverpool physician of Whiggish sympathies, who had studied medicine and metaphysics at Edinburgh University. In 1804 his son Wallace was an undergraduate at the same university, and attending lectures by Dugald Stewart, Professor of Moral Philosophy and soon to be an outspoken defender of John Leslie in his struggle for the Chair of Mathematics. In a fatherly letter James Currie commended Stewart's lectures—there was 'nothing like them, certainly, to be found any where'—but he wished that Wallace would also go to hear Professor Thomas Hope: 'Chemistry is, not merely in point of fashion but of real utility, the branch of natural philosophy most important to be known. It is the combination of chemistry with mechanics that has made so very large an addition to human powers in latter times: e.g. in the steam engine.' Currie proceeds at once to ask what Stewart has to say about Malthus's doctrines. Currie himself has read them

---

[13] E. P. Thompson, 'Time, work-discipline, and industrial capitalism', *Past and Present*, 38 (1967), 56–97, reprinted in *Essays in Social History*, ed. M. W. Flinn and T. C. Smout (Oxford, 1974), 39–77.
[14] Richard Jones, *Lectures on the Political Economy of Nations* (n.p.d.), 34, 47–9.

carefully, feels that they are exaggerated, yet 'cannot wholly resist the evidence of their truth'. Political economy has 'dwelt too little on this serious and melancholy truth, that there may be, and that there often is, a morbid excess of population, contributing to the vice and misery of a people'.[15]

It is easy to see how Currie's thoughts were running as he wrote this letter. Chemistry, mechanics, Watt's invention of the steam engine, Smith's discovery of the 'division of labour', all contributed to the Utopian atmosphere created—for some—by the American and French Revolutions, to hopes of growth, civilization, and the improvement of mankind. But Currie was also a realist, and the indulgence of such hopes merely led him on to Malthus and the principle of population, whose truth could not be wholly resisted.

The following examination of social theories will reveal a persistent oscillation between optimism and pessimism, a constant uncertainty as to whether happiness or misery best testified to God's efficient governance of the mortal world. With its dual stress on depravity and salvation, evangelicalism was particularly well suited to convey this ambiguity. Before we consider how it did so, however, it is necessary to examine how Christian moralists generally, and not just evangelicals, responded to the challenge of the new political economy. And since we are mainly concerned with metropolitan culture, with the confessions of a social and ecclesiastical establishment[16] and the apologetics of an economic élite, the best places to seek out that response are the universities of Oxford, Cambridge, and Edinburgh.

---

[15] James to Wallace Currie, 29 Jan. 1804, *Memoir of the Life, Writings, and Correspondence of James Currie of Liverpool*, ed. William Wallace Currie (1831), ii. 241–4.

[16] Nonconformist grievances were concentrated on questions of civil and political discrimination, and they only became involved in questions of economic policy with the campaign against the Corn Laws, which like Tithes were regarded as a plank in the Anglican establishment's monopoly of power and privilege. Anyway, many of them, Methodists especially, tended to regard Christianity as a means to happiness on earth as well as afterwards. There are indications that some dissenters took up a more retributive theology in mid-century, just as Anglicans were abandoning it, and this may reflect a greater sense of social achievement on their part, leading them to embrace conservative apologetics as well.

2
The Rage of Christian Economics
1800–1840

We hear nothing on all sides, at dinners, parties, in church and at the theatre, but discussions on political economy and the distresses of the times.

H. U. Addington to Charles Vaughan, 2 Mar. 1826,
C. R. Vaughan MSS, C.2

So great and absorbing is the interest which the present discussions excite that all men are become political economists and financiers, and everybody is obliged to have an opinion.

The Greville Memoirs, ed. H. Reeve (1875), i. 81 (20 Feb. 1826)

Christian Economics in the Universities

Evangelical economics was part of something wider and more vague which may be called 'Christian economics', and Christian economics was a reaction against—but also part of—the great vogue for political economy during the first half of the nineteenth century. It should therefore not be confused with the tradition of thought which repudiated political economy as a mode of inquiry improper in itself. The latter often borrowed from Christian precept but was really romantic, high Tory, and anti-utilitarian. Its exponents included nostalgic agrarians like Robert Southey and David Robinson of *Blackwood's Magazine*, populists like William Cobbett, and prophets like S. T. Coleridge and Thomas Carlyle.[1] Coleridge thought the 'democratical oligarchy of glib economists' and their 'narcotic' fancies quite contemptible,[2] while Carlyle saw the rage of political economy as one more sign that men were 'grown mechanical in head and in heart,

---

[1] William D. Grampp, 'Classical economics and its moral critics', *History of Political Economy*, 5 (1973), 359–74. For Robinson see H. Perkin, *The Origins of Modern English Society 1780–1880* (1969), 245–52; S. Rashid, 'David Robinson and the Tory macroeconomics of *Blackwood's Edinburgh Magazine*', *History of Political Economy*, 10 (1978), 258–70.
[2] *Letters, Conversations and Recollections of S. T. Coleridge* (1836), i. 137 [ed. T. Allsop (1864), 73].

as well as in hand'.[3] Then there were Tractarians, such as Pusey and J. H. Newman, for whom scriptural revelation was the only guide to truth, in the economic as in any other sphere. Christian economists, on the other hand, accepted the new science of political economy, and merely assailed what they took to be its dominant, anti-landlord, anti-clerical, and viciously secular formulation by Ricardo and the *Westminster Review* radicals.

Needless to say, this so-called Ricardian or classical school was the most corny of straw men. Few 'Christian economists' displayed much analytical rigour or really understood what political economy was about. This is particularly the case as the latter became rapidly more technical after the founding of the Political Economy Club in 1821. Until then the distinction between 'professional' and 'Christian' economics is more easily blurred. For in the eighteenth century, and in Scotland especially, political economy had signified the whole science of government and society, and had therefore blended moral and to some extent theological considerations with purely technical investigations into the creation and distribution of wealth.[4]

There are many reasons why political economy became so popular after 1800. In the first place, there was the need for governments to take economic policy initiatives in a period of revolutionary discontent and total war. Speenhamland (1795), the Property Tax (1798), Combination Laws (1799 and 1800), suspension of cash payments (1797), Sinking Fund (1786), Corn Law (1804), Orders in Council (1806/7), and suchlike were bound to stir controversy. Then there was the debate (to some extent aroused by these acts of government) as to whether agriculture or commerce was the true basis of national wealth. The agrarians (sometimes dubbed 'physiocrats')—Malthus (1803), Lauderdale (1804), Spence (1807), and Chalmers (1808)—and the *économistes*—Mill and Torrens (1808)—thus added a dash of socio-economic spice to what most people thought was a 'dry and repulsive' subject.[5] In Meek's opinion, 'it was

---

[3] Thomas Carlyle, 'Signs of the times' (1829), *Critical and Miscellaneous Essays: Collected and Republished* (2nd edn, 1840), ii. 270 [*Centenary Edition of the Works of Thomas Carlyle* (1896–9), xxvii. 63].

[4] See below, pp. 163–70.

[5] T. R. Malthus, *Essay on the Principle of Population: or, a View of its Past and Present Effects on Human Happiness, with an Inquiry into our Prospects respecting the Future Removal or Mitigation of the Evils which it occasions* (2nd edn, 1803), 430–51; Lord Lauderdale, *An Inquiry into the Nature and Origin of Public Wealth and into the Means and Causes of its Increase* (1804); W. Spence, *Britain Independent of Commerce, or, Proofs, deduced from an Investigation into the True Causes of the Wealth of Nations, &c* (1807); T. Chalmers, *An Inquiry into the Extent and Stability of National Resources* (Edinburgh, 1808); [?Henry Brougham], 'Spence On Commerce', *The Edinburgh Review, or Critical Journal*, 11 (1808), 429–48; J. Mill, *Commerce Defended: An Answer to the Arguments by which Mr. Spence, Mr. Cobbett, and Others, have Attempted to Prove*

largely in the course of these debates that British political economy was finally purged of the Physiocratic elements . . . and moulded into something like the form it was eventually to assume in the hands of Ricardo'.[6] Political economy also constituted a central element in the manufacturing middle-class provincial culture of the period after 1770, a culture which tended to combine *either* Tory politics and evangelicalism *or* Whig/Radical politics and Unitarianism.[7] Meanwhile, the chief intellectual source of political economy was to be found in Edinburgh, where Dugald Stewart, biographer and interpreter of Adam Smith, was inspiring an army of mainly Whig disciples. By their writings in the *Edinburgh Review* and their salon *conversaziones* at Bowood, Lansdowne House, and Holland House, Horner, Jeffrey, Brougham, Macvey Napier, Mackintosh, Lauderdale, Erskine, and Lansdowne were to incorporate 'economics' into political and public discussion, and to give it a Whiggish reputation that disgusted many of the party's leaders, such as Grey and Russell.[8]

According to Cockburn, the 'liberal young' of Edinburgh had been 'immersed in chemistry and political economy', deriving their 'mental food' from Smith and Hume (among others) even before Stewart began his series of political economy lectures (c.1800–8). Even so, there is abundant testimony to Stewart's impact on impressionable young minds in those heady, emotional years during and immediately after the repressive regime of Judge Braxfield. To Cockburn 'his lectures were like the opening of the heavens. I felt that I had a soul.'[9] Stewart attempted gently and respectfully to deflect opinion away from Smith in favour of Turgot and the physiocrats. His lectures were not technically

that Commerce is Not a Source of National Wealth (1808); R. Torrens, *The Economists Refuted: or, an Inquiry into the Nature and Extent of the Advantages derived from Free Trade* (1808). See Bernard Semmel, *The Rise of Free Trade Imperialism: Classical Political Economy, the Empire of Free Trade, and Imperialism 1750–1850* (Cambridge, 1970), 48–64.

[6] Ronald L. Meek, *The Economics of Physiocracy: Essays and Translations* (1962), 345.

[7] John Seed, 'Unitarianism, political economy and the antimonies of liberal culture in Manchester, 1830–50', *Social History*, 7 (1982), 1–25; S. G. Checkland, 'Economic attitudes in Liverpool, 1793–1807', *The Economic History Review*, 2nd series, 5 (1952–3), 58–75.

[8] Russell had been a pupil of Stewart 1809–12, but probably did not hear the political economy lectures. A firm believer in the moral superiority of agriculture to manufacturing, he was to vilify fashionable political economy before becoming a convert to it during the 1830s. See Hilton, *Corn, Cash, Commerce*, p. 143.

[9] Henry Cockburn, *Memorials of His Time* (Edinburgh, 1856), 24–7, 45–6 [ed. Karl F. C. Miller (Chicago and London, 1974), 22–5, 41]. Collini, Winch, Burrow, *That Noble Science of Politics*, pp. 25–61; Biancamaria Fontana, 'Political economy in the *Edinburgh Review*, 1802–1832', Cambridge University Ph.D. (1983), 120–69; Pietro Corsi, 'The heritage of Dugald Stewart: Oxford philosophy and the method of political economy, 1809–1832', forthcoming in *After Adam Smith: Crossroads in Early Nineteenth-Century Political Economy*, ed. Istvan Hont (Cambridge, 1987).

sophisticated,[10] but they placed the subject firmly within the 'common sense' intuitionist tradition of Reid and Hutcheson, and against the Benthamite philosophy which was fashionable in England. Thomas Brown, following Stewart in the Chair of Moral Philosophy and Political Economy, ignored the latter part of his duties, while John Wilson, who was elected by a Tory coup in 1820, had never given economics a thought. He was eventually provoked into delivering perfunctory lectures every second year by an abortive attempt of the Whigs to set up a separate chair of political economy for J. R. McCulloch in 1825.[11] The latter lacked friends at court, however, being an Edinburgh reviewer and (in his own words) 'the only Edinburgh economist who has embraced the doctrines of Ricardo'.[12] He considered that Huskisson was 'almost my only friend' in the matter, and indeed there is evidence that Huskisson and Robinson would have moved against Wilson had the project not been thwarted by Liverpool, Melville, Peel, and Canning.[13] McCullough had been lecturing privately since 1820, but he moved south in 1828, so that Stewart's mantle eventually fell on the celebrated Glasgow preacher and pastor Thomas Chalmers, Professor of Moral Philosophy at St Andrews since 1823. Chalmers had sat at Stewart's feet in Edinburgh in 1800, probably at the first course of political economy lectures, for his strongly physiocratic *Enquiry into the Extent and Stability of Natural Resources* (1808) contains much that seems to derive from Stewart. It was written before the religious crisis and conversion of 1810, which was to condition all Chalmers's subsequent attitudes. The regenerate Chalmers will be presented later as the main exemplar of evangelical economics.

In effect, what Chalmers did after his conversion was to *evangelicalize* the Scottish economics of Stewart and Horner. An evangelical germ was already present, of course, as John Clive noticed in his study of the *Edinburgh Review* in its early days.

---

[10] See Alison's opinion in *Some Account of My Life and Writings: An Autobiography by Sir Archibald Alison*, ed. Lady Alison (Edinburgh and London, 1883), i. 50–1. Alison was also disturbed by Stewart's endorsement of Malthusian population theory. See below, p. 62.

[11] Elsie Swann, *Christopher North [John Wilson]* (Edinburgh and London, 1934), 173–83; J. B. Morrell, 'Science and Scottish university reform: Edinburgh in 1826', *British Journal for the History of Science*, 6 (1972–3), 47–8; D. P. O'Brien, *J. R. McCulloch: A Study in Classical Economics* (1970), 57–60.

[12] McCulloch's words as reported in Torrens to Place, 30 Sept. 1818, Place Papers, BL Add. MS 37949, fos. 70–1.

[13] 'Christopher North': *A Memoir of John Wilson*, ed. his daughter Mrs Gordon (Edinburgh, 1862), ii. 85–7. See McCulloch to Napier, 23 Apr. 1825, Napier Papers, BL Add. MS 34613, fos. 295–7; McCulloch to Huskisson, 27 May 1825, Huskisson Papers, BL Add. MS 38746, fos. 215–16; Canning to Huskisson, 11 June 1825, ibid., fo. 236.

Their native country supplied the reviewers with a two-fold heritage: Puritanism and Enlightenment. They retained the ethical postulates of the former along with the intellectual presuppositions of the latter. Scottish Whigs disseminating this heritage to a public impelled to bid it welcome by the combined impact of French and industrial revolutions must take a place, however humble, beside the Evangelicals as progenitors of the nineteenth-century English middle-class ethic.[14]

Scottish political economy was based almost entirely on Adam Smith and Quesnay, and did not become involved in the technical disquisitions which were to characterize the subject in England after 1810. It is not at all surprising, therefore, to find a pupil of Stewart and the foremost Whig spokesman on political economy (after Horner's death in 1817) writing: 'I have always been inclined to suspect myself that some of the differences so much insisted upon between Malthus and Ricardo and Say are of much less consequence particularly in a practical view than many of their readers and it appears those writers themselves appear to consider them.'[15] The *Edinburgh* believed passionately in Free Trade as a means of unfolding the operations of nature, and condemned as 'artificial' all wealth spawned by monopoly and protection, but its approach to such matters was more moralistic than scientific.

In England political economy came later. Horner complained in 1803 that while there were ten lecture courses to be heard on chemistry, there was no one in London to speak on political science.[16] When it came it was, as suggested, more technical and less overtly philosophical than in Scotland, though the dominance of Bentham, James Mill, and Ricardo meant that it was based on a utilitarian or materialist conception of economic man, who balanced in his mind the pains of labour against the pleasures of profit. It was the bullion and corn law debates of 1810–11 and 1814–15 respectively, followed by Ricardo's *Principles of Political Economy* in 1817, which brought the subject to the forefront of public attention. Mrs Marcet's *Conversations on Political Economy* (1816), a sequel to *Conversations on Chemistry* (1806), at once sold enormously and passed through several editions. Then came the series of annual Ricardo Memorial Lectures, delivered in London by McCulloch from 1824

[14] John Clive, *Scotch Reviewers: The* Edinburgh Review, *1802–1815* (1957), 150. Clive points out the irony in all this, since the *Review* frequently lambasted evangelicals, along with Methodists, 'as fanatical children of darkness'.

[15] Lansdowne to Drummond, 9 Nov. 1820, Alnwick Castle, Northumberland MSS, Drummond Papers, C/1/355. Portsch makes a good case for supposing that, despite McCulloch's agreement with Ricardo on such questions as gluts, the *Review* remained essentially Malthusian, thanks to its editor Francis Jeffrey. S. R. Portsch, 'The odd man out', *Victorian Periodicals Newsletter*, 11 (1978), 133–4.

[16] F. Horner to L. Horner, 1803, *Memoir of Leonard Horner*, ed. Katharine M. Lyell (1890), i. 5–6.

to 1827.[17] The first was attended by many distinguished politicians and businessmen, the biggest 'catch' being William Huskisson, President of the Board of Trade. His coming was 'chiefly important', according to the Whig McCulloch, on the grounds that it would 'remove any obstacle, on account of political opinions, to young Tories coming to my private prelections'.[18] Seven or eight hundred attended the 1825 session, and McCulloch was exultant. 'At present the rage is for Political Economy, and if not a lion, I am at all events a lion's whelp.'[19] Attendances were well down in 1826, however, which may have reflected the public's disillusion with the latest fashions in political economy following the financial crash of December 1825. Even his 'best friends, the merchants and bankers', stayed away.[20] Despite this setback, McCulloch became the first (if not very successful) holder of the Chair of Political Economy at London University (1828-37). Sadly, he had to report that 'the study of Political Economy is decidedly less popular now than it was four years ago'.[21] Even so, McCulloch was to have an important if indirect effect on official policy through his private pupil, S. J. Loyd, the future Lord Overstone. 'On this subject [political economy] I cannot forget that you have stood to me *in loco parentis*', wrote a grateful Loyd while at the height of his influence.[22]

Meanwhile the first Chair of Political Economy at an English university had been established in Oxford in 1825. There had been what Checkland calls some 'donnish dabbling' before then, by Edward Tatham, Edward West, Edward Copleston, and the Regius Professor of Modern History, Henry Beeke.[23] As early as 1801, Prime Minister Addington had insisted

---

[17] O'Brien, *J. R. McCulloch*, pp. 45-57.

[18] McCulloch to Napier, 2 May 1824, *Correspondence of Macvey Napier*, pp. 38-40. It seems that Huskisson was furtive about supporting a Whig and a 'professional' economist. Apparently James Mackintosh extracted a promise that he would attend the second and third lectures but not the first. McCulloch to Napier, 5 Apr. 1824, Napier Papers, BL Add. MS 34613, fo. 230. Huskisson was of the opinion that 'a course of reading' could do more good than desultory attendance at lectures in attempting to master a 'branch of abstract science, the knowledge of which cannot be assisted or promoted by experimental illustrations'. Huskisson to McCulloch, 1 June 1825, copy Peel Papers, BL Add. MS 40378, fos. 310-11.

[19] McCulloch to Napier, 2 and 23 Apr. 1825, Napier Papers, BL Add. MS 34613, fos. 291-5. Dudley, Calthorpe, Lascelles, and Leveson Gower were among the audience.

[20] McCulloch to Napier, 2 Apr. 1827, ibid., fos. 385-6; O'Brien, *J. R. McCulloch*, pp. 61-8.

[21] J. R. McCulloch, 'To the Council of the University of London', 22 Dec. 1828, University College London MSS.

[22] Loyd to McCulloch, 4 Jan. 1843, *The Correspondence of Lord Overstone*, ed. D. P. O'Brien (Cambridge, 1971), i. 333.

[23] S. Rashid, 'The Beeke good: a note on the origins of the 'Giffen good'', *History of Political Economy*, 11 (1979), 606-7; S. G. Checkland, 'The advent of academic economics in England', *The Manchester School of Economic and Social Studies*, 19 (1951), 43-70, esp. 44-7; W. R. Ward, *Victorian Oxford* (1965), 50-1. On Copleston see below, pp. 126-7, 223, 234-5.

that Beeke should promote the study of political economy, and from then until 1813 the Professor lectured on it once a term. From 1812 to 1823 he privately lectured the Chancellor of the Exchequer, Nicholas Vansittart, offering him a great deal of advice on fiscal and financial affairs. In 1814 Addington (now Lord Sidmouth, Home Secretary) demanded that Beeke's successor, Edward Nares, should work the subject up from scratch — perhaps the first example of manpower planning applied by government to an English university. There is even a story that the Prime Minister, Lord Liverpool, whose eloquent espousals of Free Trade in the Lords debates of 1812 and 1820 took many by surprise, advised Nares on what to say in the economics lectures, which were delivered for the first time in 1817.[24]

Whether ministers had anything to do with Henry Drummond's decision to endow the Oxford Chair in 1825 is not known. Drummond was a man of 'wonderful individuality'[25] and an extreme evangelical, though otherwise quite impossible to stereotype. Banker, protégé of Pitt, and Tory MP (1810–13), he suddenly became 'satiated with the follies of the fashionable world' in 1817, sold up his huge estates, and entered on a lifelong mission to convert Jews and other heathen to Christianity. His Oxford initiative was taken before February 1825 at the latest, and may have owed something to his connections (though they were not particularly close) with Copleston and Peel.[26] Soon after this, in 1825–6, alarmed by the insane speculation that was taking place in Latin American mining shares, he began, in his own words, 'to direct attention to the events connected with the close of the Christian dispensation'.[27] He was a founder member of, and chief host to, Edward Irving's Catholic Apostolic Church, of which he became in turn an Apostle, Evangelist, Prophet, and finally Angel. He supported the new *Morning Watch* and bitterly attacked his former friends, the moderate evangelicals of Clapham, 'lovers of their own institutions, and of wealth; boasters of their charitable, and missionary exploits',[28] complacent, pharisaic prigs who thought they could co-operate with God to bring about the millennium, instead of

---

[24] *A Versatile Professor: Reminiscences of the Rev. Edward Nares*, ed. G. C. White (1903), 208, 239–42; Lord Sidmouth, 'Rules and regulations respecting the Professors of Modern History and Languages', Sidmouth Papers, Devon County Record Office MS 152M/C1814/OA, copy in Peel Papers, BL Add. MS 40459, fos. 151–2.

[25] *The Life of Edward Irving illustrated by His Journals and Correspondence*, by Mrs Oliphant (1862), i. 389.

[26] Both Drummond and Copleston believed that monetary fluctuations, rather than human depravity, were the cause of poverty, and Drummond had sent his 1819 tract on the currency to Copleston for comment. Copleston to Drummond, 17 Oct. 1820, Northumberland MS C/1/102.

[27] H. Drummond, *Abstract Principles of Revealed Religion* (1845), p. iii.

[28] H. Drummond, *A Defence of the Students of Prophecy* (1828), 116; Oliver, *Prophets and Millennialists*, pp. 107–10.

leaving all to the divine initiative. In other words, Drummond became a pre-millennialist, believing that the Second Coming must precede the reign of felicity on earth, and also that the event was likely to be heralded by earthly troubles and disruption, such as were taking place before his eyes. Catholic Emancipation, Parliamentary Reform, and cholera (1829-31) confirmed his hopeful alarms, and it was joked that in the latter year he gave up insuring his life.[29] But as we saw above,[30] belief in leaving things to divine initiative did not conduce to a *laissez-faire* social philosophy. Drummond preached and practised the virtues of landed paternalism within what he saw as an organic and hierarchical society, setting up allotments for labourers as early as 1818. He vilified 'orthodox' political economy with its *laissez-faire* individualism, and was scornful of *économistes* like James Mill, who considered merchants, mere men of the world, to be more significant in the scale of national wealth than landlords.[31]

It is not particularly surprising that this pre-millennial High Tory should have struck up an alliance with the Radical Francis Place; nor that the issue on which High Tory and Radical came together should have been the currency. In much of their correspondence Drummond adopted a rather too self-consciously Cobbettian demotic, describing himself as a beer-swilling 'chew bacon', and he liked to twit Place for being a wine connoisseur and 'march-of-mind' sophisticate from 'Lunnon'.[32] It *is* surprising to discover that he lobbied on behalf of the Whig McCulloch in the matter of the London Chair of Economics in 1827.[33] Perhaps the explanation is that the two men agreed on several doctrinal points. They both opposed the monetary system as it had been set up in 1819, and both believed after 1825 that it would lead to a mass 'explosion'. They both thought Ricardo wrong in supposing that convertibility alone would prevent periodic over-issues, and espoused what later came to be known as the 'Currency Principle', which held that a paper circulation should fluctuate exactly as though it had been metallic.[34] Moreover, McCulloch frequently quoted Drummond's tract of 1826 to counter the popularly

[29] Charles Merivale to W. H. Thompson, Oct. 1831, *Autobiography and Letters of Charles Merivale, Dean of Ely*, ed. J. A. Merivale (Oxford, 1898), 168.

[30] See above, pp. 14–17.

[31] [H. Drummond], *Cheap Corn Best for Farmers, proved in a Letter to George Holme Sumner* (1825), 4–9.

[32] Drummond to Place, 4 Apr. 1827 and 8 Feb. 1835, Place Papers, BL Add. MS 37949, fos. 200, 332.

[33] McCulloch to Drummond, 13 June 1827, Drummond Papers, C/1/285.

[34] H. Drummond, *Elementary Propositions on the Currency* (4th edn, 1826), 3–69; [J. R. McCulloch], 'Fluctuations in the supply and value of money — banking system of England', *Edinburgh Review*, 43 (1826), 263–98; [J. R. McCulloch], 'Commercial revulsions', ibid., 44 (1826), 84–93.

held view that the Corn Laws were of benefit to farmers. Drummond thought that only the landlords benefited, and they but slightly, and that farmers suffered along with all other capitalists from the general depression of profits which resulted from those laws. Agricultural labourers suffered too because, like other labourers, they depended on the profits of capital for employment. 'Nobody can deny', he concluded, 'that it is better to have all commodities cheap than dear; and the sure way to have them the cheapest, is to let the public buy them wherever they please.'[35] As late as 1839–42 Drummond was still arguing that the ports ought to be opened to foreign corn, in order to relieve a starving population, though he had shifted ground on the question of profits from capital. Now he thought that agriculturalists should be compensated by a reduction in mortgages and settlement charges, and that active steps should be taken to limit the spread of manufacture, so that they would not be beneficiaries of Free Trade, or make of the whole country 'one Birmingham or Manchester'.[36] In view of this clear if qualified support for a free trade in corn, it is somewhat surprising that, when repeal finally came in 1846, Drummond should have prophesied as a consequence,

the destruction of all those things which God has instituted in a Christian monarchy as certainly as those things have been overthrown in France: such as, the annihilation of entails, that is, of family and hereditary interests as distinguished from merely personal interests; the destruction of primogeniture; the ruin of many widows and orphans; the minute subdivision of lands as in France; an universal attack on tithes, and on the compulsory support of cathedrals and parish churches. It is now to be shown how by all these ways Britain becomes the head of that system which God has denounced by His prophets under the name of Tyre.[37]

But then, of course, it is possible that the pre-millenarian Drummond might actually have relished the prospect of these catastrophes. For him, as for Stewart, Free Trade was a means of revealing the order of nature, and Drummond's vision of nature included a belief in providential catastrophes. So though he saw 1846 as the final hammer blow to society, he blamed Peel much less than he blamed the Whig Reform Act of 1832, which had made the eventual overthrow of the aristocracy inevitable, and he had even *less* sympathy for the protectionists of 1846, whose opposition to the 'inevitable' repeal of the Corn Laws was misconceived. Yet he never compromised his agrarian paternalism, and was fond of remarking that Seth's ancestors had been yeomen while Cain's had

---

[35] [Drummond], *Cheap Corn Best for Farmers*, pp. 22–32 and *passim*; O'Brien, *J. R. McCulloch*, pp. 379–85.

[36] H. Drummond, 'Justice to corn-growers and to corn-eaters' (1839), in *Speeches in Parliament and some Miscellaneous Pamphlets of the late Henry Drummond*, ed. Lord Lovaine (1860), ii. 143–56.

[37] H. Drummond, *Letter to the Bishop of Winchester on Free Trade* (1846), 17–18.

been manufacturers. Probably he half welcomed 1846 as herald of the 'last things'.[38]

Maybe Drummond thought that Oxford University was the place 'to take hold of all the science of the secular world, [and] wrest it from the hands of the agents of the devil'.[39] More likely his decision to endow a Chair of Economics was one which he would not have taken after his conversion to 'Irvingism'. As early as 1826 he was admonishing a friend from Clapham that

like other branches of Politics, [political economy] is a ticklish one for a Christian to meddle with: they cannot be conducted upon Christian principles, nor ever will be, till *The* King reigns in righteousness, Sin and its concomitant curse is removed from the earth, the Lion and the lamb lay down beside each other, this world has received its baptism of fire, as well as its baptism of water, for it, like a Christian, receives no good from one, untill it has received the other, and then only is it a fit dwelling for God.[40]

Certainly, it is not evident that Drummond took any further interest in the Oxford Chair after his conversion to pre-millennialism, and he can hardly have approved of its first incumbent. Nassau Senior (Professor 1825–30 and 1847–52) was a Whig and a far less evangelically minded one than McCulloch—indeed, he stood at the farthest end of the theological spectrum from Drummond, rejecting the doctrines of inspiration, free will, providence, Atonement, and divine retribution.[41] He came to exemplify the *laissez-faire* tradition of political economy, but was thoroughly 'secular' in his approach: 'I am no metaphysician, and a very ill-read moralist. I never read Locke or Stewart, or Brown or Reid, or indeed anything on these subjects, except Aristotle, Paley, and Adam Smith.'[42] His inaugural lecture revealed a mechanical view of society which must have offended Drummond's organicist sensibilities: 'the machinery of civilized society is worked by so many antagonist springs; the dislike of labour, the desire for immediate enjoyment, and the love

[38] Ibid., pp. 23–4. Drummond claimed that signs of the ending of an existing 'dispensation' were almost always political, and that the sudden implementation of Free Trade in such a way as not merely to redistribute wealth within a class but to overthrow the wealth of a class whom God had instituted was one such sign. Ibid., p. 12.

[39] Ibid., pp. 9–10.

[40] Drummond to Zachary Macaulay, 15 Nov. 1826, California, Huntington Library MS, MY 218.

[41] See extracts from Senior's 'Essay on materialism and immortality', in S. Leon Levy, *Nassau W. Senior 1790–1864: Critical Essayist, Classical Economist and Adviser of Governments* (1943; new edn, Newton Abbot, 1970), 214–17, in which he dissents from the doctrines of retribution and a future state of rewards and punishments. Senior to Whately, 14 July 1827, ibid., pp. 57–8.

[42] Senior to Napier, 17 May 1845, *Correspondence of Macvey Napier*, pp. 497–8.

of accumulation are . . . perpetually counteracting one another'.[43] Senior's main aim was to assert the scientific nature of the subject in opposition to those who pressed the claims of everyday 'practical sense'. He defended political economy against the charge that it was amoral by appealing to utility—it would promote the maximization of wealth, which in turn would banish economic insecurity and enable citizens to develop feelings of benevolent sympathy with each other, and a desire for each other's happiness. Accumulation for future use, or saving, was in Senior's eyes the only source of moral improvement, sobriety, frugality, and law-abidingness.[44]

Senior's former tutor, intimate friend, and successor in the Drummond Chair (1830–1), Richard Whately, also disclaimed concern with the relationship between political economy and virtue. His views were much the same as Senior's, though presented in a more morally didactic form. He had been reluctant to take on the professorship, but

some of my friends have persuaded me that this is a sort of crisis for the science in this place, such, that the occupying of the office by one of my profession and station may rescue it permanently from disrepute. Religious truth . . . appears to me intimately connected, at this time especially, with the subject in question. *For it seems to me that before long, political economists, of some sort or other, must govern the world.* . . . Now the anti-Christians are striving hard to have this science to themselves.[45]

Whately believed that morality was not to be derived entirely from the Bible, and that political economy could help Christians to discover it. Since religion could not disprove science, its practitioners should fight for the establishment of truth in scientific terms.

Whately was less confident than Senior about the possibility of producing *extra* wealth through competition, and more concerned with the social and moral effects of different systems of distribution. His less-eligibilist cynicism comes out in a comment to a friend that 'if good boys have a larger slice of cake than the rest, this does not indeed increase the amount of cake, but it may increase good conduct'.[46] He did not have much time to develop his earlier work on logical definitions in political economy before being elevated to the See of Dublin by the new Whig government. There he was instrumental in founding the Political Economy Chair at Trinity College, and in disseminating his version of economic

---

[43] N. W. Senior, *An Introductory Lecture on Political Economy* (1827), 8–9.
[44] Ibid., pp. 11–17. Senior cited James Mill's *History of British India* on this point.
[45] *Life and Correspondence of Richard Whately*, by E. Jane Whately (1866), i. 66–7. This was a common complaint—for example [G. Poulett Scrope], 'The Archbishop of Dublin on Political Economy', *The Quarterly Review*, 46 (1831–2), 49, complained that economists were beginning to 'trespass on the domain of the moralist and the statesman'.
[46] Whately, *Life of Whately*, i. 77.

truth through the medium of school textbooks.[47] Meanwhile, back in Oxford, Forster Lloyd held the Drummond Chair during 1832–7, and made a distinguished technical contribution to analysis, but his tenure was followed by another strenuous attempt to combat such 'anti-Christian economics'. Frederick Denison Maurice was even less professionally qualified for the post than Whately had been, but was urged to stand for it by William Sewell and other Tractarians who admired his *Subscription No Bondage* (1835); and so,

finding there was no one else ready to come forward on this ground, that political economy is not the foundation of morals and politics, but must have them for its foundation or be worth nothing, I have consented to be proposed. . . . I shall of course endeavour to master the details of the subject. . . . If the university can do anything to save us from being a nation of money-getters, it should surely try, and I should feel it no dishonourable office to be a hewer of wood to it while it was so engaged.[48]

In the opinion of H. J. Rose, a high church theologian, Maurice would propound 'far more wholesome' views of political economy 'and *its limits*' than the starry-eyed Liberals who had monopolized the subject hitherto.[49] For these reasons, Maurice was clearly the favourite candidate, until his Tractarian backers suddenly turned against him. For if the account given by his rival for the post, Herman Merivale, is correct, the Drummond Chair seems to have fallen into the hands of the High Church. Merivale wrote to the editor of the *Edinburgh Review* in January 1837 that he did not expect to be elected, partly because he was a Whig, 'and partly from some peculiar views respecting the subject prevalent among the higher flyers at Oxford. They imagine the science as at present studied to be altogether delusive and dangerous, and that it ought to be rendered subordinate to their own High Church scheme of Christian Ethics.' Six months later he reported that he had most unexpectedly won the contest.

Great objection had been taken to my politics, and [Maurice] . . . was carrying all before him and was pretty sure of success, when in an unfortunate hour for himself he chose to promulgate some unsound opinions on the matter of infant

---

[47] S. Rashid, 'Richard Whately and Christian political economy at Oxford and Dublin', *Journal of the History of Ideas*, 38 (1977), 147–55; J. M. Goldstrom, 'Richard Whately and political economy in school books 1833–80', *Irish Historical Studies*, 15 (1966–7), 131–46; Ray E. McKerrow, 'Archbishop Whately, human nature, and Christian assistance', *Church History*, 50 (1981), 166–81; S. Rashid, 'Richard Whately and the struggle for rational Christianity in the mid-nineteenth century', *Historical Magazine of the Protestant Episcopal Church*, 47 (1978), 293–311.
[48] Maurice to Julius Hare, 29 Nov. 1836, *The Life of Frederick Denison Maurice chiefly told in His own Letters*, ed. F. Maurice (1884), i. 210.
[49] H. J. Rose to Dr Bliss, 3 Dec. 1836, copy Bliss Papers, BL Add. MS 34572, fo. 120.

baptism.[50] This of course sealed his fate as a Political Economist, and I being protected by the obscurity of my tenets on those subjects, which have never been exposed to the public, got to the windward of him.[51]

Maurice did eventually concoct a synthesis between God and Mammon which many found acceptable, a political economy based on the principle of co-operation rather than competition,[52] but times were against him in the Oxford of 1837. Meanwhile, Merivale, once appointed, declared himself a thoroughgoing Seniorite in his belief that political economy was a 'distinct and sovereign' science and not a branch of ethics.[53]

In Cambridge political economy was left to the initiative of a few individuals. The Regius Professor of Modern History from 1807, William Smyth, was a friend of Ricardo and did his best to imbue students with the 'somewhat repulsive' study of the subject.[54] Then there was George Pryme, an evangelical friend of Simeon, who, reading Adam Smith as a boy, had thrilled to the possibilities of infinite wealth opened up by the division of labour principle.[55] He wintered in Edinburgh one year, along with several other Cambridge dons, in order to hear Stewart lecture,[56] but he afterwards claimed to 'adhere to the school of Locke, not that of Reid and Dugald Stewart'.[57] He began rather reluctantly to lecture on political economy in 1816, and became the first professor of that subject (1828–63), though undergraduate attendances were thin. More important, or at any rate more interesting, was a nucleus of dons centred on Trinity, adherents of Reid rather than of Locke, who were attempting during the 1820s and 1830s to develop a science of society suitable for the nineteenth century, as Stewart's had been for the eighteenth. The central figures here were William Whewell, Adam Sedgwick, John

---

[50] F. D. Maurice, *Letters to a Member of the Society of Friends* (1837), 65–160 [reissued as vol. i of *The Kingdom of Christ* (1837–8)].

[51] H. Merivale to Napier, 16 Jan. 1837 and June 1838, Napier Papers, BL Add. MS 34618, fos. 8–10, 146–7. See Ward, *Victorian Oxford*, p. 115. For confirmation of Merivale's analysis, see Pusey to Acland, ?Jan. 1837, *Memoir and Letters of Sir Thomas Dyke Acland*, by A. H. D. Acland (1902), 81.

[52] See below, pp. 322–32.

[53] H. Merivale, *An Introductory Lecture on the Study of Political Economy* (1837), 12. Senior himself was defeated by Travers Twiss in December 1841, but returned to the Chair in 1847, by which time the High Church party had lost ground following Newman's secession to Rome.

[54] K. T. B. Butler, 'A "Petty" Professor of Modern History: William Smyth (1765–1849)', *Cambridge Historical Journal*, 9 (1947–9), 220.

[55] *Autobiographic Recollections of George Pryme*, ed. his daughter (Cambridge, 1870), 23.

[56] G. Pryme, *A Syllabus of a Course of Lectures on the Principles of Political Economy* (Cambridge, 1816), p. vii n.

[57] Pryme to Whewell, 27 Oct. 1841, Whewell Papers, Trinity College Cambridge Add. MS a.58[17].

Cazenove, John Herschel, and Richard Jones.[58] Whewell and Jones were keen to involve scientists like Humphry Davy, and government advisors like William Jacob, in the crusade to overturn a Ricardian orthodoxy which they found 'palpably mischievous and immoral', 'dogmatical', and 'pernicious'.[59] Jones became Professor of Political Economy at King's College, London (1833–54), and from 1835 he also held the Chair at the East India College, Haileybury, in succession to Malthus. It was not Jones, however, but the charismatic geologist Sedgwick who caught attention, with his celebrated *Discourse on the Studies of the University*, delivered in Trinity College chapel in December 1832 and published the following year. It included a plea for a better political economy, one which would dispel the notion that wealth was the only means to security and happiness. He dared to hope

that it may, in the end, assist in enabling men to see more deeply into the sources of social happiness or national greatness—that it may allay the bitterness of national animosity; teaching kingdoms, as well as individuals, how much they gain from mutual support and mutual good-will—and more than all, that it may (when combined with Christian knowledge), help to enlighten the pressure of such evils as belong to our fallen nature, and are among the unavoidable conditions of our probation.[60]

Sedgwick's sermon made a considerable impact in intellectual circles, as great as or greater perhaps than Keble's sermon on National Apostasy delivered in St Mary's, Oxford, the following July.

Political Economy as Natural Theology

Clerical economists had to overcome a widespread conviction that political economy was not only dry and repulsive but wicked and dangerous. If the sound of words like *corn* and *drawback* 'seemed a profanation of Stewart's voice',[61] this was because the mere discussion of such materialistic subjects threatened to open up Jacobinical inquiries into the utility of thrones and altars. Popular enthusiasm for political economy after 1815 did nothing to reassure the propertied classes. As late as 1830 Whately encountered strong moral prejudices against the subject, and Chalmers was not being entirely fanciful in fearing 'secular contamination' and

---

[58] Cannon, *Science in Culture*, pp. 29–71; Lawrence Goldman, 'The origins of British "social science": political economy, natural science and statistics, 1830–1835', *Historical Journal*, 26 (1983), 587–616.

[59] Jones to Whewell, 27 Sept. 1827, Whewell Papers, c.52[15].

[60] Adam Sedgwick, *A Discourse on the Studies of the University* (Cambridge, 1833), 75.

[61] Cockburn, *Memorials*, p. 175 [1974 edn, p. 169].

'encroachments of earthliness' as a result of his studies.[62] This prejudice resulted partly from a conventional antipathy to utilitarian ethics, and to what Coleridge called 'the general contagion of its mechanic philosophy'. Ethically, it seemed to many that political economy 'recognized no duties which it could not reduce into debtor and creditor accounts on the ledgers of self-love, where no coin was sterling which could not be rendered into *agreeable sensations*'.[63] Even Copleston, despite his enthusiasm for the subject and support for its inclusion in the university syllabus, thought that it would be better taught to older persons, rather than

when the affections are young and growing, and liable to be cramped and stunted by the views of human nature which it continually presents. There is perhaps something in all theoretical views of society, which tends to harden the feelings, and to represent man as a blind part of a blind machine.[64]

Copleston, like many intellectuals, was anxious to systematize moral philosophy 'scientifically', but not in front of the children.

Christians found the psychology of the profit motive distasteful because it made virtue 'a question of calculation—a matter of profit or loss'.[65] Worse still, it contravened Christian notions of grace, self-sacrifice, and worldlessness. Early nineteenth-century clerics did not have the Puritan doctrine of *calling* as a refuge for bad conscience.[66] Moreover, political economy's competitive ideal of society, and especially the ecological competition at the heart of its population theory, offended against the influential natural theology tradition, with its view of the world as sublimely harmonious. Natural theologians had argued from the design of the universe for the existence of a beneficent and omnipotently purposeful Creator, but the dismal science's picture of the world seemed to suggest that, on the contrary, God was mad, bad, and dangerous. When Whately observed that the only difficulty in theology was the existence of evil in the universe, he was thinking—most *un*evangelically—of natural rather than moral evil, of such 'apparent frustrations of . . . benevolent design' as wars, famines, and tornadoes.[67]

It was characteristic of Oxford that Whately and some of his successors in the Drummond Chair, such as Lloyd (1832–7), Merivale (1837–42),

[62] See Chalmers's Journal, 31 July and 4 Aug. 1825, *Memoirs of the Life and Writings of Thomas Chalmers*, by William Hanna (Edinburgh, 1852), iii. 93–4.

[63] S. T. Coleridge, *The Statesman's Manual: or the Bible the Best Guide to Political Skill and Foresight: a Lay Sermon, addressed to the Higher Classes of Society* (1816), pp. xvii, 34 [ed. R. J. White for *The Collected Works of Samuel Taylor Coleridge*, general ed. Kathleen Coburn (1971–) No. 6, pp. 28, 76].

[64] E. J. Copleston, *A Reply to the Calumnies of the* Edinburgh Review *against Oxford* (Oxford, 1810), 173–4.

[65] Sedgwick, *Discourse*, p. 57.　　　　　　　　[66] See below pp. 116, 375–6.

[67] R. Whately, *Introductory Lectures on Political Economy* (1831), 114–15.

and George Rickards (1852-7), assumed that if the Ricardians had made political economy seem dismal, then they must have founded it on logical or semantic error; whereas in Cambridge, where the natural sciences were better established, the assumption was rather that Ricardianism must be mistaken as to the true facts. So while Whately tried to make 'a sort of continuation of Paley's "Natural Theology," extending to the body-politic some such views as his respecting the natural',[68] Whewell, Jones, and other Cambridge luminaries led what they called an inductivist attack on Ricardo. The facts of life, *once properly ascertained*, would assuredly illuminate the wit and wisdom of the deity; *apparent* evils would show up in their true if paradoxical light as *real* benefits, further evidences of divine contrivance. 'If inductive science be true it must harmonize with all the great truths of religion.'[69] This was the faith in which early nineteenth-century scientists pushed forward their inquiries, in economics just as in biology and geology. Whewell believed that, to deal 'inductively' with moral sciences, it was first necessary to build up hundreds of examples of human conduct, and Sedgwick described the proper role of the political economist as 'observing and classifying phenomena, from which he deduces consequences that are to him *in the place of* moral laws'.[70] In this way Christianity promoted rather than impeded scientific investigation, though of course it often distorted scientific interpretation. It was not the case that, for Whewell, 'political economy could *become* apologetics', as Sydney Checkland suggested in his brilliant pioneering survey, but rather that Whewell developed an inductivist approach as a consequence of his desire to 'make science fall in with a contemplative devotion'.[71] A letter from Whewell to Jones in 1826 makes it clear that the apologetics preceded the economics. Whewell wished to include some references to population theory in a course of sermons on natural evidences for 'the activity and

---

[68] Whately, *Life of Whately*, i. 67.

[69] Whewell to H. J. Rose, 12 Dec. 1826, *William Whewell: An Account of his Writings with Selections from his Literary and Scientific Correspondence*, by I. Todhunter (1876), ii. 78. Whewell uses 'inductive' to mean 'based on objective evidence', which is not the same as the Scottish 'common sense' meaning of 'innate'. See below, pp. 163-5. Whewell was to write one of the 'Bridgewater Treatises' on natural theology, of which Malthus observed: 'The proofs of design are indeed every where so apparent that it is hardly possible to add much to the force of the argument as stated and illustrated by Paley; but still it is gratifying to contemplate the new illustrations which the almost infinite variety of nature furnishes.' Malthus to Whewell, 1 Apr. 1833, Whewell Papers, a.209[12].

[70] Whewell to Jones, 25 Feb. 1831, Whewell Papers, c.51[99]; Sedgwick, *Discourse*, p. 74 (italics added); William L. Miller, 'Richard Jones: a case study in methodology', *History of Political Economy*, 3 (1971), 198-207; N. B. de Marchi and R. P. Sturges, 'Malthus and Ricardo's inductivist critics: four letters to William Whewell', *Economica*, NS, 40 (1973), 379-93; S. Rashid, 'Richard Jones and Baconian historicism at Cambridge', *Journal of Economic Issues* 13 (1979), 159-73.

[71] S. G. Checkland, 'The propagation of Ricardian economics in England', *Economica*, NS, 16 (1949), 49; Whewell to Jones, 26 Feb. 1827, Todhunter, *Whewell*, ii. 82-3.

omnipresence of the Deity', mainly with reference to physical science, but he had to concede that 'when I come to the indications of benevolent design in the moral frame of society, I have not such an habitual familiarity with the view of the subject in its details as to write with the confidence and vehemence which would be becoming'.[72] Jones was looked on by his friends as the chosen instrument of natural theology in this sphere, and a 'knight errant' to spread the inductivist faith,[73] which is why they became so irritated by his notoriously dilatory methods. He in his turn was frustrated by

the hold that systems palpably mischievous and immoral have gained upon the public mind, [and] the difficulty of gaining a *hearing* for principles of a different complexion and got at in a different and less dashing manner and in the spirit of a less presumptuous philosophy.[74]

Whewell and Jones were Tories, believing Ricardo's principles to be 'entirely false',[75] and denouncing 'fallacies so very palpable as those of "Free Trade"'.[76] Like Malthus, they rejected Say's Law and anticipated crises of underconsumption or gluts,[77] and they were firm in the belief that 'rank and inequality of ranks and progress of agriculture and such matters are good things'.[78] Their explicit targets were the *Millites*, and they dismissed Whately's and Senior's 'nonesense' as 'puerile' deductions from false Ricardian principles.[79] In return Whately considered that if only Jones 'had studied Logic to learn the value and proper nature of definitions', he would have spared his readers much 'tedious logomachy'.[80] Never was Oxford logic and Cambridge natural science so starkly differentiated, but the differences were also political. Whately's argument for the 'connexion of political economy with natural theology', based on the notion of 'divine wisdom' providing for 'the *progress* of society', was the sort of Whiggish proposition that Whewell spurned; while, as Pietro Corsi has suggested, the latter's methodological attack on the subject was probably a way of undermining its distasteful policy recommendations.[81]

[72] Whewell to Jones, 10 Dec. 1826, Todhunter, *Whewell*, ii. 79–80.
[73] Jones to Whewell, 25 Feb. 1831, Whewell Papers, c.52²¹.
[74] Jones to Whewell, 27 Sept. 1827, ibid., c.52¹⁵; see Jones to Babbage, 21 Feb. 1833, Babbage papers, BL Add. MS 37187, fos. 428–9.
[75] Whewell to Forbes, 14 July 1831, Todhunter, *Whewell*, ii. 122.
[76] Whewell to Jones, 29 Oct. 1851, ibid., ii. 370.
[77] Whewell to Jones, 12 Aug. 1847, ibid., ii. 341.
[78] Whewell to Jones, Dec. 1826, ibid., ii. 81–2; R. Jones, *An Essay on the Distribution of Wealth, and on the Sources of Taxation* (1831), 286–329.
[79] Jones to Whewell, 24 Feb. 1831, Whewell Papers, c.52²⁰.
[80] Whately to Hawkins, 18 Dec. 1831, Oriel College Oxford MS, Ca.184.
[81] Pietro Corsi in private conversation.

Whately's favourite example of the way in which providence works through 'human faults and follies' for beneficial ends was taken, unadventurously enough, from *Wealth of Nations*, and concerned the victualling of a large city like London by myriads of middlemen in the grain trade. 'Men, who think each of nothing beyond his own immediate interest, . . . combine unconsciously to employ the wisest means for effecting an object, the vastness of which it would bewilder them even to contemplate.' The task is not done by human wisdom, and yet '*wisdom* there surely is, in this adaptation of the means to the result actually produced'.

The heavens do indeed 'declare the glory of God;' and the human body is 'fearfully and wonderfully made'; but Man, considered not merely as an organized Being, but as a rational agent, and as a member of society, is perhaps the most wonderfully contrived, and to us the most interesting, specimen of divine Wisdom that we have any knowledge of.

Economic competition, in other words, included within itself a wealth of 'unconscious co-operation'.[82]

As Checkland has observed, there was a fundamental philosophical difference between Whewell and Whately with respect to the status of the individual conscience.[83] The former held that man possesses an independent moral faculty, an intuitive sense of what is right and wrong, and that any account of how men do or should make economic choices ought to be predicated on that fact. Whately agreed *in theory* that men possess intuitive moral faculties, but thought that this had little, if any, relevance to the way in which they make economic decisions. In his economic psychology, therefore, he was a 'dependent moralist' like Paley, holding that men's concepts of right and wrong depend on the pleasure and pain which attend certain acts. As Whewell put it, Whately assumed that 'principles of action are known by consciousness and do not require detailed observation', such as Whewell himself recommended.[84] The basis of all economic life, for Whately, was *exchange*, and if in practice men showed consciousness of the long-term benefits of co-operation if, that is, their private vices proved to be public virtues, as in the case of the victuallers—this was 'natural' proof that God had endowed man with a social instinct.[85] Whately also rejected the complaint that

[82] Whately, *Lectures on Political Economy*, pp. 103–10. The word 'adaptation' was a staple of early nineteenth-century natural theology.

[83] Checkland, 'Advent of academic economics', op. cit., pp. 57–8. My debt to Professor Checkland's early writings on this subject will be evident. See also Richard Yeo, 'William Whewell, natural theology and the philosophy of science in mid-nineteenth-century Britain', *Annals of Science*, 36 (1979), 493–516.

[84] Whewell to Jones, 15 July 1831, Todhunter, *Whewell*, ii. 123.

[85] For interesting comments by an economist who followed Whately in this respect, see Stanley Jevons's journal, 5 Apr. 1857, *Papers and Correspondence of William Stanley Jevons*, ed. R. D. Collison Black and R. Könekamp (1972–81), i. 157–9.

utilitarian economists were indifferent to motive, and willing to let ends justify the most selfish means. Like Senior, he argued that wealth was the high road to civilization, leisure, dissemination of knowledge, and abolition of mechanical toil, and that these in turn would transform men's motives and actions. In other words, though only selfish enterprise can improve the human environment, its improvement will in turn discourage selfish instincts. Even 'inferior motives', therefore, like the propensity for profit, 'constitute, as it were, a kind of scaffolding, which should be taken down by little and little, as the perfect building advances, but which is of indispensable use till that is completed'.[86]

Whately was an optimist—far more optimistic than Ricardo, for example, on the question of what was likely to happen to wage rates under capitalism—and he agreed with Senior that increased foreign commerce would promote international peace. He believed that man could no more have 'civilized' himself without 'the agency of a divine *Instructor*' than he could have 'made himself' without 'the agency of a divine *Creator*', and he accepted that much essential instruction derived from Revelation. Thus the 'division of labour' principle derived from Genesis, where one of Eve's sons tilled the ground and the other kept cattle.[87] Pursuit of that principle would in time create sufficient wealth to solve all problems in respect of distributive justice. Such Paleyan complacency was to influence the 'orthodox' economics of J. S. Mill, Richard Cobden, and *The Economist*, and was epitomized in the 1859 inaugural lecture of the Oxford Professor of Modern History, Goldwin Smith:

To buy in the cheapest and sell in the dearest market, the supposed concentration of economical selfishness, is simply to fulfil the command of the Creator, who provides for all the wants of His creatures through each other's help; to take from those who have abundance, and to carry to those who have need. It would be an exaggeration to erect trade into a moral agency; but it does unwittingly serve agencies higher than itself, and make one heart as well as one harvest for the world.[88]

Optimism was all very well—and indeed was commonplace by the time Goldwin Smith spoke these words—but in the first half of the nineteenth century, amid darkening gloom and with change and decay all around, such optimism as Whately's seemed to many to be incompatible with what Sedgwick called 'our fallen nature' and 'our probation'. In fact, the

---

[86] Whately, *Lectures on Political Economy*, pp. 176–7.

[87] R. Whately, *On the Origin of Civilization: A Lecture to the Young Men's Christian Association* (1854), 19. See Whately to Sedgwick, 19 Feb. 1860, BL Egerton MS 3020, fos. 5–14, where Whately opines that the hardest part to swallow of the doctrine of evolution is 'the *last* step of all,—the advance of the Savage-*man* into the civilized, without external help'.

[88] Goldwin Smith, *An Inaugural Lecture* (Oxford and London, 1859), 33.

economic apologetics of Oxbridge made little public or popular impact, because they did not chime with the dominant evangelical ethos of the day. Whately's belief in man's social instinct went right against evangelical assumptions as to natural and original depravity. Abhorring those aspects of faith which appeared irrational, mysterious, emotional, he denied the doctrine of special providence, and thought it 'a mistake . . . to assume that the usual and natural effect of affliction was improving to the moral character',[89] as evangelicals tended to do. Far from ennobling, distress invariably depraved its victims. Whately was scornful of the stock evangelical explanation of suffering, based on man's probationary state. Such a rationalization, he objected, 'amounts to something more than a state of trial: it is a distinct provision made by the Deity for the moral degradation of his rational creatures'.[90] Meanwhile Richard Jones railed against 'the hypocrisy and fanaticism exhibited while living and while dying' by the converts of 'silly' Claphamites.[91] Unfortunately, perhaps, fanaticism was part of the spirit of the age. It was all very well for someone like Whewell to assert that political economy need not seem dismal. More influential were those writers who were only too happy to acknowledge the dismal nature of a world in alienation from God, as providing an arena for the exercise of man's best, redemptive faculties. Of these writers the most important was the 'second most influential Scotsman of his generation'—after Sir Walter Scott—the evangelical divine, Thomas Chalmers.

The English Face of Thomas Chalmers

'I got on the top of a coach for Clapham, whither I had been invited by Mr. Dealtry, the minister thereof. He had a large party of parishioners to dinner, whom he wanted to impregnate with my views.'[92] Whether Chalmers was the original man on the Clapham omnibus, merely articulating the conventional wisdom of his day, or whether he helped to impregnate his generation with that wisdom, is difficult to determine. Either way his influence was enormous—and not just in Scotland. Hugh Miller, the geologist, thought that Chalmers 'may be said rather to have created than to have belonged to an era'; Gladstone remembered him as 'a man greatly lifted out of the region of mere flesh and blood'; Sterling regarded him as a potential 'prophet' to 'lament over' and 'teach' a

---

[89] *Memoirs of Richard Whately, Archbishop of Dublin, with a Glance at his Contemporaries and Times*, by W. J. Fitzpatrick (1864), ii. 62.

[90] Whately, *Lectures on Political Economy*, p. 189.

[91] Jones to Whewell, 23 Nov. 1822, Whewell Papers, c.52⁹.

[92] Chalmers to his wife, 24 Sept. 1822, Hanna, *Life of Chalmers*, ii. 349–50. William Dealtry (1775–1847), FRS, succeeded John Venn in the evangelical living of Clapham in 1813. He was a strong supporter of the British and Foreign Bible Society, and became Professor of Mathematics at East India College, Haileybury.

'pampered' and 'degraded' people; 'not one man [but] a thousand men', opined Sydney Smith. 'His was a voice that filled the world, the English-speaking world at any rate, from end to end', wrote F. H. Doyle, while Patrick Dove called him a second Luther, whose influence rolled 'like a mighty wave of good over the whole surface of the land', and Simeon thought him 'raised up by God for a great and peculiar work'.[93] Much has been written about him too, but it has been somewhat fragmentary, reflecting the disparate nature of his achievement. His disquisitions on astronomy and geology are being taken increasingly seriously by historians of science. Historians of economic policy remember him with some asperity as the arch-opponent of all systems of compulsory poor relief. Social historians salute the pioneer of urban missionary activity, especially his experiments in the St John's Parish of Glasgow, 1819–23, where he sought to create a sort of urban feudalism. Theologians respect his epistemological contributions to natural religion, while church historians puzzle over his slightly uncomfortable leadership of the Scottish Free Church in the Disruption of the 1840s. He was also widely celebrated as 'the man who began that baptism, so to speak, of political economy with Christianity, which was the main thing needful to bring about its regeneration'.[94]

But above all he was a magnificent preacher—the man who 'adjusted the pulpit to the exigencies of the age'[95]—and it was his sermons which brought him popular veneration in Scotland and fashionable éclat in England. He came to fame suddenly in 1817. In January he published his *Discourses on the Christian Revelation, viewed in connection with the Modern Astronomy*, previously delivered from the pulpit of the Tron Church in Glasgow. The volume went through nine editions and nearly twenty thousand copies inside the year, and, as Hazlitt testified, 'ran like

---

[93] For Hugh Miller see John Anderson, *Reminiscences of Dr Chalmers* (1851), 401; for Smith see Ian Henderson, 'Thomas Chalmers', Ronald Selby Wright, *Fathers of the Kirk: Some Leaders of the Church in Scotland from the Reformation to the Reunion* (1960), 130; [W. E. Gladstone], 'Memoir of Norman Macleod', *The Church Quarterly Review*, 2 (1876), 494; [John Sterling], 'The state of society in England', *The Athenaeum*, 1 (1828), 487; *Reminiscences and Opinions of Sir Francis Hastings Doyle 1813–1885* (1887), 101–2; Patrick E. Dove, *Account of Andrew Yarranton, the Founder of English Political Economy* (Edinburgh, 1854), 100–1; Simeon to J. W. Cunningham, 22 Oct. 1821, Carus, *Memoirs of Simeon*, pp. 552–4. But Simeon also thought Chalmers 'too sanguine. He does not sufficiently see, that a Chalmers is necessary to carry into effect the plans of Chalmers. But . . . if we cannot all follow him closely, we may yet tread in his steps.'

[94] John Lalor, *Money and Morals: a Book for the Times* (1852), p. vii. There has recently appeared a long-overdue modern biography of Chalmers, Stewart J. Brown, *Thomas Chalmers and the Godly Commonwealth in Scotland* (Oxford, 1982). This is an accomplished and in many respects superb biography, but it is relatively weak on Chalmers's theology and on his social and economic thought. See below, pp. 87–8.

[95] Blaikie in *Dictionary of National Biography*. There is a reference to Chalmers's *deep mouth* in Hugh Miller, *My Schools and Schoolmasters: Or, The Story of My Education* (Edinburgh, 1854), 530.

"wild-fire" through the country'.[96] The heavens were of course the last refuge of the natural theologian, being still beautiful and undefiled by wars, famines, or pestilences, and George Canning was not alone in finding the book's 'most magnificent passages' consolatory.[97] Then in May Chalmers made his first conquest of London. He began by declaiming at the London Missionary Society in a crowded Surrey Chapel on 1 Corinthians 14: 22–5. His friend Thomas Smith described the scene:

Dr. Chalmers has just finished the discourse before the Missionary Society. All my expectations were overwhelmed in the triumph of it. Nothing from the Tron pulpit ever exceeded it, nor did he ever more arrest and wonderwork his auditors. I had a full view of the whole place. The carrying forward of minds was never so visible to me: a constant assent of the head from the whole people accompanied all his paragraphs, and the breathlessness of expectation permitted not the beating of a heart to agitate the stillness.[98]

A less favourably disposed witness confirms the impact of this and several other sermons during the following fortnight:

Canning was in raptures—Sir James Mackintosh full of them. Bobus Smith . . . permitted himself to be carried away with the stream. Besides these, Wilberforce, Romilly, Huskisson, Lord Binning, Lord Elgin, Lord Harrowby, and many more of rank and influence, forthwith sought him out. They formed part of his congregation wherever he preached, and vied with one another in their anxiety to do him honour in society.[99]

'All the world wild about Dr. Chalmers', echoed Wilberforce, 'Canning . . . quite melted into tears'.[1] On his way back to Scotland, Chalmers reflected that Wilberforce was his 'most valuable acquisition', though he counted Grenville and Canning to be 'very splendid acquaintances' also.[2]

'Acquisition' to what, exactly? Probably to his great crusade of the next fifteen years—abolition of compulsory assessments for the relief of the poor. In the course of his London sermons Chalmers denounced all forms of legalized charity, and he first won prominence in public controversy with articles on pauperism in the March 1817 and February 1818 numbers

---

[96] William Hazlitt, 'Rev. Mr. Irving', *The Spirit of the Age: Or Contemporary Portraits (1825)*, 97–8 [*The Complete Works of William Hazlitt*, Centenary Edn, ed. P. P. Howe (1930–34), xi. 44–5]. See Hannah More to Mr Harford, 21 Apr. 1817, Roberts, *Memoirs of Hannah More*, iv. 18.

[97] *Memoirs of the Life of Sir James Mackintosh*, ed. R. J. Mackintosh (1835), ii. 343.

[98] Hanna, *Life of Chalmers*, ii. 99.

[99] [G. R. Gleig], 'Memoir of Dr. Chalmers', *Quarterly Review*, 91 (1852), 428.

[1] Wilberforce's journal, 25 May 1817, *Life of William Wilberforce*, iv. 324–5.

[2] Hanna, *Life of Chalmers*, ii. 106. Elgin, who was acting as Chalmers's manager in England, told Grenville that Chalmers was delighted with his conversation. Elgin to Grenville, 27 May 1817, Additional Dropmore Papers, BL Add. MS 59008, fos. 92–3. For Wilberforce's 'esteem and love' for Chalmers, see Wilberforce to Sinclair, 3 Feb. 1829, Grant, *Memoirs of Sir George Sinclair*, pp. 356–7.

of the *Edinburgh Review*. He became obsessed with the evil effects of poor laws, and his parochial experiments, first in Kilmany, then at St John's, were expressly designed to demonstrate that even the poorest of communities could, if sufficiently 'godly', be self-supporting without resorting to institutionalized philanthropy. Industrial suburbs could be assimilated into rural parishes, each with its team of voluntary helpers, deacons, and curates, under strict clerical control. Rigorous attention to the homes, families, individual personalities, and immortal souls of the poor would induce a frugal self-reliance on their part, and encourage a sufficiency of spontaneous concern on the part of their relatives and betters. Compulsory assessment would therefore be unnecessary. But above all, it was essential to remove the prevailing 'character of earthliness' from the subject of pauperism, to demonstrate its 'powerful and most intimate alliance with the spiritual interests of our population'.[3]

Chalmers adumbrated these views in the first volume of his *Christian and Civic Economy of Large Towns* in 1821, but before he could convince Parliament he had to investigate conditions in England. On his next southern tour, in 1822, he tried to avoid publicity, having 'no room for anything . . . but pauperism'. Instead he managed to conquer the affections of a large section of the evangelical establishment. In Liverpool he stayed with the evangelical merchant John Gladstone, MP. Gladstone had 'greatly delighted' Chalmers in 1817, while his own 'delight was beyond expression', but now Chalmers found that Gladstone, though still 'most sensible and judicious', was too preoccupied with politics in general 'to have turned the powers of his gifted and vigorous mind' to a right view of pauperism.[4] His fellow philanthropists, Samuel Hope and James Cropper, were more responsive. Indeed, the latter must have been particularly susceptible to Chalmers's message, having been imbued by his mother 'with a sense of the corrupting power of business and wealth'.[5] In Manchester Chalmers fraternized with Daniel Grant, James Brierley, Thomas Potter, and 'the most philosophical chemist in the land', John Dalton. In Birmingham he stayed with Wilberforce's brother-in-law,

---

[3] Chalmers to Thomas Babington, 1 Nov. 1822, Trinity College Cambridge MSS, Babington Papers, 20⁴. For the St John's experiment see R. A. Cage and E. O. A. Checkland, 'Thomas Chalmers and urban poverty: the St. John's Parish experiment in Glasgow, 1819–1837', *The Philosophical Journal*, 13 (1976), 37–56; R. A. Cage, *The Scottish Poor Law 1745–1845* (Edinburgh, 1981), 90–110; Brown, *Thomas Chalmers*, pp. 122–51. For Chalmers's influence on later activity see Olive Checkland, *Philanthropy in Victorian Scotland: Social Welfare and the Voluntary Principle* (Edinburgh, 1980), 32–7, 299–337.

[4] Hanna, *Chalmers*, ii. 106, 332–3; Mrs Gladstone to Tom Gladstone, 12 June 1817, S. G. Checkland, *The Gladstones: A Family Biography 1764–1851* (Cambridge, 1971), 87.

[5] Checkland, *The Gladstones*, p. 127. Cropper suffered, much more than Gladstone, from the Puritan dilemma that enjoined thrift yet abhorred accumulation. See below, pp. 101, 116

Richard Spooner, and also with Lord Calthorpe, who was 'most particularly attentive' and became his frequent companion and chaperon. In Gloucester he met the Revd. Hunter, in Bristol Rowland Hill, in Southampton Sturges Bourne ('discomposed a little' at the thought of annihilating poor rates altogether), in Portsmouth Sir George Grey. And then at last to London and to Clapham, where Elgin, Grenville, Calthorpe, Babington, Zachary Macaulay, Robert Grant, Buxton, Vansittart, Teignmouth, William Smith, Clarkson, Wilberforce, Bickersteth, and many others of the evangelical establishment fêted the great celebrity. He fell in also with the Gurneys and with many other Quakers, 'the most serviceable philanthropists we meet with', but his real desire was to make 'auxiliaries in the cause' among Anglican clergymen.[6] He also enjoyed 'much of kindred and substantial discourse with Mr. Malthus'. On the way home he stayed with Babington in Leicestershire, where he met William Wolryche Whitmore, 'a very great Parliamentary acquisition to the good cause', before returning to Glasgow in October. Announcing his findings in Chadbandese, he roundly declared the English system of compulsory legal assessment for poor relief to be 'a moral nuisance, a bane, a burden, an excrescence on the body politic, a sore leprosy, which has spread itself over ten thousand parishes of England'.[7]

The battle for abolition was on, but Chalmers was anxious not to anticipate public opinion. In 1823 Brougham spent many hours in Glasgow trying to persuade him that the House of Commons might be taken by storm on the Poor Laws, and recommending Whitmore as the man to take the lead. Chalmers, however, was sensible of the 'extreme touchiness of public opinion' on the subject,

and while most impregnably confident in the result of a fair trial in the English parishes, it is a matter of uncertainty whether the trial will yet be allowed by the English Parliament, and the point for deliberation is whether the cause might not suffer by prematurely exposing it to the hazard of such a rejection as would discourage a renewal of the attempt.[8]

If they moved too quickly, public men might be panicked into making a premature declaration *against* reform, which they would then have to abide by.[9] So for all his propaganda he was a cautious political realist. He even seconded a motion in the General Assembly of the Church of Scotland *against* Kennedy's bill, which he had helped to draft and which was then pending in Parliament, for the compulsory abolition of all poor

---

[6] Chalmers to Elgin, 14 Sept. 1822, copies Peel Papers, BL Add. MS 40351, fos. 127–8; Additional Dropmore Papers, ibid., 59008 fos. 154–5.
[7] For an account of the tour see Hanna, *Life of Chalmers*, ii. 330–63.
[8] Chalmers to Babington, 6 Jan. 1824, Babington Papers 20[6].
[9] Chalmers to Babington, 1 Nov. 1822, ibid. 20[4].

rates in Scotland forthwith.[10] He preferred to build up his official acquaintance until the time was right. The Home Secretary, Robert Peel, who had unsuccessfully sought a meeting with Chalmers in 1822, and had since asked to be sent instalments of the *Christian and Civic Economy*, finally made contact in 1827. Chalmers had come south again to consecrate his former curate Edward Irving's new church in Regent Square, and also to discuss an offer made by Brougham and Zachary Macaulay of the Moral Philosophy Chair at London University. After the sermon Peel snatched 'a deal of kind conversation' on Scottish university politics, pauperism, and 'my sermons, all of which he had read'.[11] Then Robert Wilmot Horton came up to lobby for a scheme of assisted emigration, which was *his* pet solution to the problem of poverty, but it is likely that the two *fanaticks* talked past each other. Another new acquaintance in the congregation, who probably did not listen much either, despite his 'curiosity', was Coleridge.

Chalmers did not move to London University in 1827, but took up the Chair of Theology at Edinburgh in the following year instead. He had a second, more formal, meeting with Peel on pauperism in 1830, having been invited south by Thomas Spring Rice to give evidence before a Select Committee on the State of the Poor in Ireland. His entourage this time included Wilberforce, Mackintosh, J. C. Colquhoun, Lansdowne, Buxton, Teignmouth, Leonard Horner, Robert Inglis, Calthorpe, Joseph Gurney, Dr Lushington, Bishop J. B. Sumner, Samuel Hoare, Baptist Noel, and Elizabeth Fry.[12] Young William Gladstone, still an undergraduate, risked being rusticated from Christ Church when he broke bounds to hear the Scotsman preach at a dissenting chapel.[13] Chalmers toured again in 1833, and at the meeting of the British Association in Cambridge met up with many leading scientists—Sedgwick, Whewell, Lubbock, Babbage, Herschel, Airy, Forbes, Brewster, Rowan Hamilton, and Buckland—as well as with Simeon, Malthus, and Richard Jones.[14] Then he went to London to see Whitmore, Senior, Commissioner Chadwick, and Under-Secretary Stephen, and also Le Bas of the East India College, a friend of Malthus and Jones.

---

[10] For the various misunderstandings connected with Kennedy's bill see Brown, *Thomas Chalmers*, pp. 154–62.

[11] Hanna, *Life of Chalmers*, iii. 161–2; Chalmers to Peel, 27 Sept. 1822, Peel papers, BL Add. MS 40351, fo. 177.

[12] Hanna, *Life of Chalmers*, iii. 249–89; Chalmers to Peel, May 1830, Peel Papers, BL Add. MS 40400, fo. 189.

[13] *Reminiscences of Francis Hastings Doyle*, pp. 101–2; John Morley, *The Life of William Ewart Gladstone* (1903), i. 59.

[14] For Chalmers at Cambridge see Morrell and Thackray, *Gentlemen of Science*, p. 173; *Life of Sir William Rowan Hamilton, including Selections from his Poems, Correspondence, and Miscellaneous Writings*, by Robert Perceval Graves (Dublin and London, 1882–9), ii. 50–3.

The climax of Chalmers's social success came in 1838 when he delivered a series of highly topical *Lectures in Defence of Religious Establishments* in Hanover Square Rooms.

Dukes, marquises, earls, viscounts, barons, baronets, bishops, and members of Parliament, were to be seen in every direction. After some considerable delay and impatient waiting, the great charmer made his entrance and was welcomed with clappings and shouts of applause, that grew more and more intense till the noise became almost deafening.[15]

So wrote a member of the audience, and Chalmers's biographer and son-in-law, William Hanna, adds:

The concluding lecture was graced by nine prelates of the Church of England. The tide that had been rising and swelling each succeeding day now burst all bounds. Carried away by the impassioned utterance of the speaker, long ere the close of some of his finest passages was reached, the voice of the lecturer was drowned in the applause, the audience rising from their seats, waving their hats above their heads, and breaking out into tumultuous approbation. Nor was the interest confined to the lecture-room. 'Nothing', says Dr. Begg [of the Church Extension Committee], 'could exceed the enthusiasm which prevailed in London. The great city seemed stirred to its very depths.'[16]

It was further recounted that both Phillpotts and Blomfield listened on this occasion to 'the most popular divine in Christendom, . . . with the most profound attention, and, if any faith is to be placed in Lavater's theory of physiognomy, with the greatest delight'.[17]

When Dr John Brown described Chalmers as 'a *solar* man', who 'drew after him his own firmament of planets', all 'bound to the great massive luminary in the midst',[18] he was writing in a Scottish context. Nevertheless, it is obvious from the above that Chalmers also exercised an important gravitational influence in the national galaxy as well. Moreover, though he was for the most part non-political, his contacts and sympathies were largely with the so-called Liberal Tories. He opposed Parliamentary Reform but supported Catholic Emancipation, repeal of the Corn and Combination Laws, reduction of tariffs, and an income tax, while his closest political associates—Wilberforce, Calthorpe, and Whitmore—all supported the Liberal Tories.[19] Chalmers shared a 'mutual reverence' with both Canning and Peel, and 'hailed with delight the career upon which Mr. Huskisson had so auspiciously entered' in

[15] Rev. J. A. Clark, *Glimpses of the Old World* (1847), ii. 96-7.
[16] Hanna, *Life of Chalmers*, iv. 38-9.
[17] Grant, *Memoirs of Sir George Sinclair*, p. 174. For Gladstone's response to the lectures see below, pp. 340-1.
[18] John Brown, *Horae Subsecivae*, 2nd series (Edinburgh, 1861), 62.
[19] On Liberal Toryism see below, pp. 218-36.

1823.[20] Sir James Graham, Huskisson's adherent in economic matters after 1828, also became a close friend and warm admirer, while Chalmers's support for Peel during the latter's moral and political crusade of 1837–9 was a factor in the revival of Conservative fortunes north of the border. He had intense conversations during Peel's emotional visit to Glasgow in 1837 to be inaugurated as Rector of the University of Glasgow, and was overjoyed to hear the Tory leader pledge support for the Church Extension movement in Scotland. If he would not have gone as far as his evangelical accomplice Colquhoun in declaring Peel 'to be the very prophet of the Lord',[21] he undoubtedly did see in him the instrument of 'a kind Providence'.[22]

Chalmers's standing in the Liberal–Conservative establishment has been forgotten, for the simple reason that it collapsed very suddenly. Gladstone's extreme disappointment with the 1838 lectures was not in itself important, but was a straw in the wind.[23] In 1839 an Edinburgh physician W. P. Alison, brother of the Archibald Alison who had found Stewart's lectures unsatisfactory, launched a full-scale attack on Chalmers's parochial and voluntarist approaches to the problem of poverty. In a specially arranged and widely attended debate between the two men at the Statistical Section of the 1840 British Association in Glasgow, Alison contended for a much more interventionist, environmentally oriented approach to pauperism. Most of the audience considered that Alison carried the argument, even though a histrionic Chalmers scored debating-points.[24] Meanwhile Archibald Alison was intriguing to squash Chalmers's candidature for the vacant Chair of Divinity at Glasgow University. Conceding that Chalmers was by far the best-qualified candidate, and also a man of 'great powers and fervent genius', Alison complained to Graham that he was impractical, too accustomed to regard mankind as an extended congregation, and blind to the native selfishness of most men once they have left the church doors.

---

[20] Hanna, *Life of Chalmers*, iii. 298–9. Brown, *Thomas Chalmers*, p. 195, is mistaken in supposing that Chalmers opposed the economic policies of the Liverpool government after 1823.

[21] *Disraeli's Reminiscences*, ed. Helen M. Swartz and Marvin Swartz (1975), 31–2. Graham described Colquhoun sympathetically as 'warm almost to enthusiasm in his religious feelings', and as having a wide following in Scotland. Graham to Peel, 14 Nov. 1837, Graham Papers in the possession of Sir Charles Graham Bt., available on microfilm in Cambridge University Library, General series, Bundle 34 (draft); Graham to Stanley, 9 Nov. 1837, ibid.

[22] Chalmers to Peel, 1 Dec. 1837, Hanna, *Life of Chalmers*, iv. 29–30.

[23] See below, pp. 340–1.

[24] Olive Checkland, 'Chalmers and William Pulteney Alison; a conflict of views on Scottish social policy', A. C. Cheyne (ed.), *The Practical and the Pious: Essays on Thomas Chalmers (1780–1847)* (Edinburgh, 1985), 130–40; Morrell and Thackray, *Gentlemen of Science*, pp. 294–5.

Thus while sincerely anxious to promote the welfare of the poor, he has all his life supported a visionary and Utopian system in regard to them, which has gone far to lead the public astray, on the subject of parochial institutions, and perpetuate that frightful misery in our great towns to the reality of which pestilence and famine have at length awakened the nation.[25]

Alison need not have worried, for Chalmers's role in the controversy over lay patronage in the Scottish Church had already alienated Peel irrevocably, and also Graham, who had succeeded Peel as Lord Rector of the University. All Graham's 'prepossessions and feelings' were 'favourable' to the Evangelicals, and as recently as November 1837 he had regarded them as the Tories' 'tower of strength in Scotland', but now he was outraged by their inconsistency in demanding public money to build new churches while denying the state any rights over livings, and saw that what they were doing would lead to disruption.[26] When Lord Sandon wrote to him in support of Chalmers's claims to the Glasgow chair, arguing that rejection of 'the most distinguished theologian of Scotland' would shatter the Conservative forces north of the border, Graham replied dustily. He seems to have taken more notice of Lord Aberdeen, who expressed himself with great bitterness about Chalmers, 'the author of all the mischief which has taken place', a 'really unprincipled' and 'wretched . . . subversive'.[27] Peel let it be known that 'Were I Lord Rector, I would *not* vote for Dr. Chalmers (highly as I value and respect him for some qualities)',[28] and so in October Graham went up to Glasgow to vote against Chalmers in the professorial competition. The alliance was over. 'It is like taking leave', wrote a lachrymose but unchastened Chalmers to Graham, 'of a much-loved acquaintance, from whom perhaps for life we are to be separated.'[29] Five years later the Peel Government, instigated partly by Graham, offended Chalmers further when it accepted the Alisons' suggestion for a commission of inquiry (1843-4) into the Scottish Poor Laws. But by this time the Disruption, which brutally undermined the cohesion of parish life in Scotland, had rendered Chalmers's schemes for voluntary parochial contributions quite impracticable.

[25] Alison to Graham, 17 Sept. 1840, Graham Papers, General series, Bundle 40.
[26] Graham to George Sinclair, 13 Oct. 1841, ibid., Bundle 139A; Graham to Colquhoun, 6 Sept. 1840, ibid., Bundle 40 (copy); Graham to Stanley, 21 Oct. 1838, ibid., Bundle 36 (copy).
[27] Sandon to Graham, 23 Sept. 1840, Graham to Sandon, 25 Sept. 1840, ibid., Bundle 139A; Aberdeen to Graham, 11 and 17 Sept. 1840, 19 Oct. 1840, ibid.
[28] Peel to Graham, 30 Sept. 1840, ibid., Bundle 40.
[29] Chalmers to Graham, 4 Jan. 1840, ibid., Bundle 139A.

Two Models of Free Trade: the 'Natural' and the 'Dynamic'

For Chalmers, clearly, political economy was secondary to, and grew out of, his lifelong crusade to correct the problem of poverty in industrial cities. He might not have taken it up at all had he not moved from his Glasgow parish in 1823 to the Chair of Moral Philosophy at St Andrews University. The third volume of *Christian and Civic Economy* in 1826 was noticeably more academic than its predecessors. He had begun to lecture on economics to a class of graduate students in 1824–5, and by 1827 he could write in his journal that his 'chief earthly ambition' was 'to finish a treatise on Political Economy, as the commencement of a series of future publications on Moral Philosophy and Theology'.[30] In November 1830, while at Edinburgh, he began a course of weekly lectures, and then began writing up his notes in the second half of 1831, 'by way of bidding a last adieu to the subject, and by way of acquitting myself of all further attention to it'.[31] This 'longing and lingering look behind' emerged in 1832 as *On Political Economy, in connexion with the Moral State and Moral Prospects of Society*, a highly Malthusian treatise which Hanna regarded as 'the favourite child of his intellect'.[32] It was followed in 1833 by the first of the Bridgewater Treatises, *On the Adaptation of External Nature to the Moral and Intellectual Constitution of Man*, which put his economic ideas even more fully into the context of evangelical natural theology.

'Your Political Economy is creating a great sensation here', wrote Senior in 1832.[33] However, apart from John Cazenove in the *British Critic*, the reviewers were unfriendly. Poulett Scrope was dismissive, Perronet Thompson sarcastic, and McCulloch, though respectful, did not wholly conceal what he privately thought of the work, which was: 'a tissue of abominable absurdities . . . a more thorough piece of quackery never came into my hands'.[34] Even so, Chalmers has retained a modest place in the 'history of economic thought' as a Malthusian. Marx wrote contemptuously about 'Parson Malthus and his pupil, the arch-Parson Thomas Chalmers', and Joseph Schumpeter, in his magisterial survey, designated Chalmers the 'McCulloch' of the Malthusian school, meaning

---

[30] Chalmers's journal, 1 Jan. 1827, Hanna, *Life of Chalmers*, iii. 298.

[31] Chalmers to Babington, 8 Feb. 1832, Babington Papers 20¹².

[32] Hanna, *Life of Chalmers*, iii. 299.

[33] Senior to Chalmers, 28 July 1832, New College Edinburgh MSS, Chalmers Papers, CHA 4.189.57–8.

[34] [G. P. Scrope], 'Dr. Chalmers *On Political Economy*', *Quarterly Review*, 48 (1832), 39–64; [T. Perronet Thompson], 'Dr. Chalmers *On Political Economy*', *Westminster Review*, 17 (1832), 1–33; J. Cazenove, 'Chalmers — *On Political Economy*', *British Critic, Quarterly Theological Review, and Ecclesiastical Record*, 12 (1832), 306–47; McCulloch to Napier, 3 Aug. 1832, Napier Papers, BL Add. MS 34615, fo. 382.

that he presented the master's ideas to a wider audience and in a more acceptable form, as McCulloch reputedly did for Ricardo.[35] Malthus called Chalmers 'my ablest and best ally'.[36]

It is not possible to elaborate here on the academic controversy that surrounds the Ricardian and Malthusian schools. The former is often taken to epitomize orthodox classical economics, but if the core of Ricardianism lay in its theories of value, rent, wage, and trade, then it had largely been discredited by the time of Torrens's famous *num* question to the Political Economy Club in 1831: 'Are any of the principles first advanced [by Ricardo] now acknowledged to be correct?' O'Brien considers that by then De Quincey and James Mill were the only true Ricardians left, in that they alone still thought in terms of a 'corn model' economy.[37] To non-professionals, however, the important ideological questions dividing Malthus and Ricardo were not these, but the former's physiocracy and the latter's confidence that, in favourable conditions, Say's law of markets would operate to ensure that supply created its own demand. On these points Ricardo, who died in 1823, is seen to have triumphed posthumously over Malthus, and to have dominated formal economic thought until the Keynesian revolution of the 1930s discredited Say's Law. It seems likely, however, that whatever professional economists thought, the Malthusian perspective retained a hold over 'Christian economists' and over the 'official mind' until the 1850s.

The point to bear in mind is that during the first half of the nineteenth century the British were extremely ambivalent in their attitude to the unprecedented economic growth around them. In this sense the Spence–Mill debate of 1807–8 was merely an academic offshoot of a general uncertainty in which a mood of 'change and decay' vied with exhilaration and patriotic optimism. The fact that Britain was perceived to be the only industrializing country, the fact that the take-off first became noticeable

[35] Karl Marx, *Capital: A Critical Analysis of Capitalist Production*, translated from the 3rd German edn by Samuel Moore and Edward Aveling and ed. Frederick Engels (1887), ii. 630 n. Joseph A. Schumpeter, *History of Economic Analysis*, ed. E. B. Schumpeter (New York, 1954), p. 487.

[36] Malthus to Chalmers, 21 July 1822, Chalmers Papers, CHA 4.21.51-2.

[37] O'Brien, *The Classical Economists*, p. 43. See Ronald L. Meek, 'The decline of Ricardian economics in England', *Economica*, NS, 17 (1950), 43–62, revised and reprinted in R. L. Meek, *Economics and Ideology and Other Essays: Studies in the Development of Economic Thought* (1967), pp. 51–74; B. J. Gordon, 'Say's Law, effective demand, and the contemporary British periodicals, 1820–1850', *Economica*, NS, 32 (1965), 438–46; Malthus to Whewell, 31 May 1831, Whewell Papers a.209[11]: 'I confess I felt that when I almost stood alone in my differences with Mr. Ricardo, and was compared to Dr. Priestley amidst the new discoveries in chemistry, it would not finally be so. But I was hardly prepared to expect that in so short a time as has since elapsed, one of the questions in the Political Economy Club should be [this one]. . . . My apprehension at present is that the tide is setting too strong against him.'

during a highly artificial state of 'total' war and therefore might not be natural, the fact that 'time' was conceived as following a cyclical course which might just as easily lead back as well as forward: all this meant that the supreme question, not always susceptible to a clear-cut answer, was whether to applaud and encourage, or to lament and stifle, this process of economic and industrial growth. Now historians have tended to assume that the political battle between Free Trade and Protection, which played such a dominant part in the public life of the day, mirrored the debate between forward-looking *économistes* and backward-looking agrarian 'physiocrats' and mercantilists. However, the matter was not quite so simple.

Certainly Chalmers and Malthus were both Tories and agrarian 'physiocrats', anxious to stress that unproductive spending by the idle rich made an important contribution to the economy as a whole. Chalmers accepted uncritically the Malthusian theory of population and the Malthusian theory of gluts. Loyal to 'the Empire of demand and supply', both men believed that profit margins would be eroded by accumulation and by competition among capitalists, whereas Ricardo and McCulloch thought that the threat would come from increasing labour costs, themselves affected by diminishing returns to agriculture.[38] On these matters Malthus and Chalmers were in almost total agreement, *but*—and the point is crucial—Chalmers was an *out-and-out* free trader whereas Malthus, a free trader in principle, allowed many exceptions in practice, even advocating controls in the important corn and capital markets.[39] Chalmers had broken with Tory tradition in preferring direct to indirect taxation as early as 1808, in a physiocratic pamphlet which borrowed heavily from Spence, and from at least 1819 he was calling for the repeal of the Corn Laws.[40] Now since agrarian physiocracy is usually supposed to have pointed to Protection in the nineteenth century, the way in which Chalmers combined it with Free Trade is of considerable importance for an understanding of evangelical economics.

Whether they stressed the evidences of design in the universe, or the fact that life was a time of probation, most early nineteenth-century Christians saw the world as a stationary state, and lacked any dynamic conception of the economy such as that adumbrated (though perhaps not

---

[38] Malthus to Napier, 19 May 1823, Napier Papers, BL Add. MS 34613, fo. 160; J. R. McCulloch, *A Discourse on the Rise, Progress, Peculiar Objects, and Importance of Political Economy* (Edinburgh, 1824), 10.

[39] In practice Malthus was also more pragmatic than Chalmers on the question of the Poor Laws, realizing that in the current state of public opinion the most that could be expected was an 'improved administration' and not abolition. See Malthus to Chalmers, 21 July 1822, loc. cit.

[40] Chalmers to Wilberforce, 15 Dec. 1819, Hanna, *Life of Chalmers*, ii. 250–1.

anticipated) by Adam Smith. Whereas Ricardo would have been dissatisfied with securing '*some* prosperity' for his country if he could have achieved more, and equated stagnation with national misery, most clerical economists shared what Keynes called Malthus's 'vaguer intuitions' that there was a *natural* (and therefore limited) rate of economic growth, based on a *natural* or effective level of consumer demand.[41] Activity and exertion were desirable, since men should make proper use of the divine gifts of mind and muscle, but *progress*, in the sense of growth, was not the object of their economics. Movements of the economy, like those of history, were seen as cyclical rather than as linear-progressive. Thus, despite their underconsumptionist analysis, neither Chalmers nor Malthus favoured public works, for fear that they would increase excess capacity in the long run. A static outlook on the economy gave them no desire to stimulate production, since they believed that only checks to population and production could make the nation happier.[42]

Thus Chalmers emphasized over and over again in his political economy lectures at St Andrews that, after reading Malthus, he was unable to agree with the author of *The Wealth of Nations* (still his favourite text) that economic progress was possible. Neither governments nor individuals could create employment, since manufacturers could supply *only* their own products, while the equivalent of those products must come from elsewhere. All branches of the economy, except agriculture, were liable to oversupply, but this was not to be lamented since, notwithstanding Smith and Ricardo, a stationary state of population and wealth is likely to be happier than a progressive one.[43] A mercantilist obsession with the growth of exports was therefore delusive and harmful, in Chalmers's opinion—indeed, even Malthus thought that he 'pushed too far the doctrine of the non-importance of foreign commerce'.[44]

[41] Ricardo to McCulloch, 23 Mar. 1821, *The Works and Correspondence of David Ricardo*, ed. Piero Sraffa and Maurice H. Dobb (Cambridge, 1951–5), viii. 359; Malthus to Ricardo, 16 July 1821, ibid., ix. 20; J. M. Keynes, *Essays in Biography* (1933), 122–3 [Royal Economic Society, *The Collected Writings of John Maynard Keynes* (1971–   ), x. 88]. Ricardo used the term 'natural rates', but as a counterfactual model only. See Maxine Berg, *The Machinery Question and the Making of Political Economy 1815–1848* (Cambridge, 1980), 45–7.

[42] B. A. Corry, *Money, Saving and Investment in English Economics 1800–1850* (1962), 66, 125–32; J. R. Poynter, *Society and Pauperism: English Ideas on Poor Relief, 1795–1834* (1969), 226–7, shows that when Malthus did suggest public works, he intended that they should be directed towards *un*productive employment (e.g. the decoration of estates), so as to divert capital *from* productive labour. See also O'Brien, *The Classical Economists*, pp. 231–2. The Prime Minister, Lord Liverpool, also thought that public works would slow down the economy while tiding labourers over until times improved. Hilton, *Corn, Cash, Commerce*, pp. 86–7.

[43] Chalmers, *On Political Economy*, pp. 443–4 [*Works*, xx. 28].

[44] Malthus to Chalmers, 19 Feb. 1833, Chalmers MSS, New College Edinburgh, CHA.

Now it is obvious that Radicals often took up Free Trade as an agent of growth, while Tories often clung to Protection as a means of preventing it. For Coleridge, Whewell, and some other Christian writers, attachment to the Corn Laws was a despairing attempt to stem the tide of industrialization. Less well appreciated is the fact that many agrarians of a Liberal–Tory persuasion assumed that the best way to save agriculture was to go along with Free Trade. Since they regarded industrial towns as profoundly *un*natural, man-made blots on God's landscape, the unforeseen consequences of government monopolies and other fiscal anomalies, it followed that anything which reduced such temporal interference with nature must be good for agriculture. During the 1820s Chalmers believed that a free trade in religion would benefit Protestants, even in Ireland, since persecution was working to protect the Roman Catholic faith;[45] in the same way he believed that Protection was undermining agriculture by making it less efficient, and that Free Trade would benefit it. In this respect Chalmers was closer to Dugald Stewart than to Horner. When Stewart lauded Free Trade as a means of moving 'nearer and nearer to the order of nature', he looked at 'nature' through mainly physiocratic eyes. His pupil Horner also celebrated Free Trade as one of those discoveries which had 'unfolded the operations of nature', though *he* took 'nature' to favour 'progress' from an agrarian to a commercial society.[46] Chalmers, like Stewart, desired that his country should attain to 'nature and justice and liberty in her commercial relations',[47] but this in no way contradicted his belief in an expanded agricultural sector.[48] Protection merely expanded commerce artificially—and temporarily—beyond its natural limits, and should give way to 'the philosophy of Free-trade, the essence of which consists in leaving this mechanism to its own spontaneous evolutions', so as to reveal 'a striking testimony to the superior intelligence of Him who is the author both of human nature and of human society'.[49]

---

[45] But later Chalmers expressly opposed Free Trade in religion on the grounds that there was no 'natural demand' for faith as there was for bread and profits. T. Chalmers, *Lectures on the Establishment and Extension of National Churches* (Glasgow and London, 1838), 44–5: 'It is not with man's intellectual, or his moral, as it is with his animal nature. . . . There is no natural hungering or thirsting after righteousness; and before man will seek that the want should be supplied, the appetite must first be created.' I am grateful to Dr Colin Matthew for this reference.

[46] D. Stewart, *Lectures on Political Economy* [*Collected Works of Dugald Stewart*, ix. 210]; F. Horner, 'M. Canard, *Principes d'Économie Politique*', *Edinburgh Review*, 1 (1802–3), 446.

[47] Chalmers to Wilberforce, 15 Dec. 1819, Hanna, *Life of Chalmers*, ii. 250.

[48] Berg, *The Machinery Question*, p. 86. Chalmers repudiated the doctrine of diminishing returns to agriculture, and saw the prospect of modest growth for the agricultural sector under Free Trade.

[49] [T. Chalmers], 'The political economy of the Bible', *The North British Review*, 2 (1844–5), 29.

We are not, therefore, of the number of those who rate very high the economic advantages of the system of free trade. . . . [Yet] there are certain attendant moral benefits . . . which render the adoption of the system one of the best and wisest achievements of an enlightened national policy.[50]

To understand what these moral benefits are, it is important to remember that God was presumed to rule by tempting and testing, judging and punishing his children. Evangelicals therefore found the mechanistic aspects of political economy perfectly acceptable. Barriers to Free Trade, like monopolies, protective duties, and preferences, not only offended the unprivileged, but were elements of friction obscuring God's clockwork providence.

There were then two discrete, if sometimes overlapping, models of Free Trade in the first half of the nineteenth century. The more familiar is that of the professional economists like Ricardo; the more widespread and probably more influential was that of evangelicals like Chalmers. The former was expansionist, industrialist, competitive, and cosmopolitan. Its objective was economic growth through capital accumulation and the international division of labour, which, as James Wilson of the Anti-Corn Law League asserted, would mean more money and more happiness for all people and all classes.[51] The psychological premiss on which it was based was that individuals balance the desire of profit against the disutility of labour: 'the master principle of individual interest [is] the power which connects and maintains the whole system, as gravitation regulates the movements of the heavenly bodies'.[52] Thanks to Brougham and the *Edinburgh Review*, to Senior, Cobden, J. S. Mill, and Robert Lowe, this version of Free Trade became increasingly popular from the 1840s on. Essentially optimistic, it took no part in the 'rejection' of Paley,[53] and indeed Wilson's *Economist* openly affirmed its devotion to that philosopher.[54] The alternative, evangelical, version of Free Trade may be characterized as static (or cyclical), nationalist, retributive, and purgative, employing competition as a means to education rather than to growth. Its psychological premiss was not self-interest but the supremacy of economic conscience, the latter innate in man yet needing to be nurtured

[50] Chalmers, *On Political Economy*, pp. 519-20 [*Works*, xx. 99-100]. [T. Chalmers], 'Stirling's *Philosophy of Trade*', *The North British Review*, 6 (1846-7), 100-1; predicted 'mortifying disappointment' for all who supposed that Free Trade would lead to prosperity, but still thought that Free Trade was essential 'for the moral good of a harmonious and happy understanding between all the orders of British society'.

[51] James Wilson, *Influences of the Corn Laws, as Affecting All Classes of the Community, and Particularly the Landed Interests* (1839), 49-99 and *passim*.

[52] [H. Brougham], 'Plans of national improvement, &c', *Edinburgh Review*, 5 (1804-5), 16.

[53] On the 'rejection of Paley' see above, pp. 4-5, and below, p. 171.

[54] See below, pp. 246-7.

into a habitude through the mechanism of the free market, with its constant operation of temptation, trial, and exemplary suffering.

Malthus recognized the problem of underconsumption in a capitalist economy, which Ricardo more or less denied as a theoretical possibility, yet he did not prescribe measures to stimulate demand for productive labour. Trapped in a world of finite resources, economically as well as ecologically, the Malthusian's instinct was rather to restore equilibrium by diminishing production, both of people and of things. Malthus did not soften this vision with allusions to 'the hidden hand of providence' in the manner of a Mrs Marcet,[55] which may be why his commitment to *laissez-faire* policies remained shaky. Evangelical economics, on the other hand, rested firmly on providentialism, and was the result of injecting 'conscience', leading to 'abstinence' on the part of producers, into a basically Malthusian model. J. S. Mill, whose *Principles of Political Economy* (1848) came to epitomize the economics of neo-Ricardian optimism, sneered at Chalmers's endeavours 'to inculcate on capitalists the practice of a moral restraint in reference to the pursuit of gain',[56] yet, however impracticable, this was what early nineteenth-century social morality was all about. But before we examine this doctrine of 'abstinence' as it was meant to apply to capitalists, we must first look at the ways in which evangelicals tackled the still more pressing problem of the poor.

[55] Patricia James, *Population Malthus: His Life and Times* (1979), 313–14, 403.
[56] J. S. Mill, *Principles of Political Economy with Some of their Applications to Social Philosophy* (1848), ii. 90 [ed. V. W. Bladen for *The Collected Works of John Stuart Mill*, general ed. J. M. Robson (1963–   ), iii. 571].

PART TWO

The Content of Evangelical Social Thought

3

Poverty and Passionate Flesh

He that will not work, neither shall he eat.

St Paul in 2 Thessalonians 3: 10

If any man choose to marry, without a prospect of being able to support a family, he should have the most perfect liberty so to do. . . . [But] he should be taught to know, that the laws of nature, which are the laws of God, had doomed him and his family to starve for disobeying their repeated admonitions; that he had no claim of *right* on society for the smallest portion of food, beyond that which his labour would fairly purchase.

T. R. Malthus, *An Essay on the Principle of Population* (2nd edn, 1803), 539–40.

The Spectre of Malthus

We have seen how Malthus's *Essay on Population* impressed Dr James Currie of Liverpool.[1] A bizarre anecdote in one of Currie's letters to his son shows just how horribly Malthus could impact on sensitive minds, nurtured during the rationalist optimism of the Enlightenment. It concerns a man of liberal education, whose mind had been deranged by Utopian beliefs in 'the improvement of the human race, and the perfectibility of man', and who was referred to Currie for treatment. The patient was deluded into thinking that he could make men happy, and so in order to sober him Currie innocently 'urged . . . the objection, that when men became so happy as he proposed to make them, they would increase too fast for the limits of the earth'. Undaunted, the man promptly devised a scheme for enlarging the surface of the globe, which he sent to the Prime Minister. In desperation at what seemed a hopeless case of Utopianitis, Currie prescribed Malthus's *Essay* as the ultimate antidote. The consequences are described in the following terms.

He read it with the utmost avidity and seeming attention. In my visits I did not mention the subject to him, but desired the keeper to watch him narrowly.

---

[1] See above, pp. 34–5.

After finishing the perusal, he got pen, ink, and paper, and sat down, seemingly with an intention to answer it, or to write notes upon it. But he did not finish a single sentence, though he began many. He then sat down to read the book again, aloud, and finished this second perusal in a few days, not omitting a single word, but stopping at times, and apparently bewildered. I now spoke to him, and introduced the subject, but he was sullen and impatient. He became very thoughtful, walked at a great pace in his airing-ground, and stopped occasionally to write, if I may so speak, words, but more frequently numbers, with a switch in the sand. These he obliterated, as I approached him. This continued some days, and he appeared to grow less thoughtful; but his mind had taken a melancholy turn.

One afternoon he retired into his room, on the pretence of drowsiness. The keeper called him in a few hours, but he did not answer. He entered, and found the sleep he had fallen into was the sleep of death. He had 'shuffled off this mortal coil.'

At the moment I write this, his copy of Malthus is in my sight; and I cannot look at it but with extreme emotion.[2]

This was an extreme case, but undoubtedly population theory posed by far the biggest challenge to belief in a divinely ordered and harmonious world. One of Malthus's aims, in fact, had been to refute the complacent Utopianism of writers like Godwin, who argued that the abolition of rank and riches would promote the happiness, welfare, and 'perfectibility' of mankind. According to Malthus, social inequalities were useful in creating those aspirations and insecurities which alone could 'goad' men to be good, by persuading them to restrain their propensities for pleasure and to overcome their disappetite for labour. For man is born 'inert, sluggish, and averse from labour, unless compelled by necessity'.[3] 'It is the hope of bettering our condition, and the fear of want, rather than want itself, that is the best stimulus to industry.'[4] Mere appeals to asceticism and self-denial, however, were hardly less convincing and much less appealing than Benthamite hedonism, and so to clinch his theories Malthus had to show that an unbridled pursuit of pleasure would have socially disastrous consequences. Writing in the wake of the 'great hunger' that had preceded the French Revolution, and amid anxieties caused by the scarcity of 1795 in his own country, it is not surprising that he should have singled out sexual indulgence, leading to procreation, as the greatest threat to society. Whereas Godwin believed that the animal passions would

---

[2] James to Wallace Currie, 19 Feb. 1804, *Memoir of James Currie*, ii. 249–51.

[3] [T. R. Malthus], *An Essay on the Principle of Population, as it affects the Future Improvement of Society: With Remarks on the Speculations of Mr. Godwin, M. Condorcet, and Other Writers* (1798), 363. The following account will be brief as the subject has already been covered by many writers, most notably by R. A. Soloway, *Prelates and People: Ecclesiastical Social Thought in England 1783–1852* (1969), and by A. M. C. Waterman, 'The ideological alliance of political economy and Christian theology, 1798–1833', *Journal of Ecclesiastical History*, 34 (1983), 231–44.

[4] Malthus, *Essay on the Principle of Population* (2nd edn, 1803), 475 [(7th edn, 1872), 382].

wither away in irrelevance as civilization advanced, much as Whately was to postulate the decline of middle-class avarice, Malthus was sure that civilization ('equality of conditions') must not be allowed to advance *until* human morality ('activity and energy of mind') had been attained.[5] Some highly theoretical postulates about geometrical and arithmetical ratios were added to give teeth to the argument that growth of population must periodically outstrip the supply of food, causing wars, famines, and pestilences. Whereas population growth had once been welcomed by many writers (including Malthus)[6] as making nations strong at war, Malthus now seemed to be saying that wars were to be tolerated as eliminating unnecessary and insupportable parts of the population. In the famous gaunt phrase, God had invited too many mortals to nature's feast.

It became a major aim of Christian demographers after Malthus to reassert the hospitality of nature, so as to repair the damage done to Paley's model of universal harmony. Paley himself attempted to do this by suggesting that it was 'part of the scheme of Providence, that the earth should be inhabited by a shifting, or perhaps a circulating population. . . . When old countries are become exceedingly corrupt, simpler modes of life, purer morals, and better institutions, may rise up in new ones, whilst fresh soils reward the cultivator with more plentiful returns.'[7] Eventually this argument would be used by spokesmen of the various evangelical missionary societies, as a way of illustrating the perfect contrivance with which God had caused the spread of the gospel to distant parts of his globe.

He is sending scarcity on these [Scottish highlands], that, by the rod of famine, the Celtic races may be driven out to other lands. . . . They are a religious, reverential people—a people of deep piety. Is it not for the regeneration of the coming time such men go forth, that the Providence of God selects such for the heads to the future nations?[8]

And yet, though many missionary societies flourished during the first forty years of the century, this particular argument was not in vogue at that time. Chalmers for one was emphatic in his opinion that the emigration

[5] Ibid. (5th edn, 1817), ii. 278 [(7th edn, 1872), 284].

[6] This was in an unpublished essay written before Malthus had read Godwin. See Gertrude Himmelfarb, *The Idea of Poverty: England in the Early Industrial Age* (1984), 102 n.

[7] W. Paley, *Natural Theology: or, Evidences of the Existence and Attributes of the Deity, collected from the Appearances of Nature* (1802), 513 [(15th edn, 1815), 478–9]. For Paley's appreciation of Malthus's *Essay*, see *Memoirs of William Paley*, by G. W. Meadley (Sunderland, 1809), 152–3.

[8] Alexander Ewing, 'Lochaber No More: Sermon on Highland Emigration' (1852), quoted in *Memoir of Alexander Ewing, Bishop of Argyll and the Isles*, by A. J. Ross (1877), 212. By 1831 even Malthus was prepared to acknowledge that, 'in this age of emigration', the population problem had shifted to the New World. Malthus to Whewell, 28 Feb. 1831, Whewell Papers, c.53².

of the excrescent part of the population could merely delay the Malthusian dilemma temporarily, and that the fundamental problem of imbalance between earth's population and food supplies would remain.

So Christian apologists had either to protest that the principle of population was empirically wrong,[9] or else to show that it contained the seeds of its own solution by elaborating Malthus's own two, somewhat unobtrusive, qualifications. The first of these was contained in Chapter Eighteen of the first (1798) edition of the *Essay*, and omitted from later versions. Since 'suffering was necessary to create exertion, and exertion seems evidently necessary to create mind', and 'mind' was an indispensable ingredient of 'foresight', Malthus was able to suggest that population pressure might have been expressly designed to promote agricultural 'activity' and ingenuity in the form of capitalization. This was, after all, the classic age of the Agricultural Revolution, when high prices were chasing what Chalmers called the 'margin of cultivation' up the hillsides, and when livestock was multiplying as rapidly as mankind.

Two writers in particular developed this 'activity' argument. Thomas Southwood Smith (1788–1861) is best known as a 'sanitarian',[10] and so it is tempting to see him as a precursor of mid-century attitudes, but this is misleading insofar as his social philosophy was individualistic rather than environmental. Religion mastered him from the age of nineteen, when he threw off his parents' Calvinism and became a Unitarian. From then on he challenged the 'spirit of the age' by protesting ceaselessly that God's *love* was a more powerful ingredient than his *justice*, and that a loving God would not inflict eternal punishment on his earthly creatures. With this optimistic eschatology went a refusal to be fatalistic about worldly troubles. 'What *can* be improved *must* be improved and *will* be improved until man in society reflects the benevolent purposes of the Almighty.'[11] The ordinary state of mankind was one of ease and positive enjoyment, from which it followed that pain is infrequent, extraordinary, and 'corrective'— a word he used in a worldly, not a spiritual sense.[12] Thus natural problems like scarcity set in train a process of adaptation and evolution which led on to felicitous solutions. Like Malthus in the first edition, he believed social inequality to be useful in 'goading' men to greater effort:

In a state of society in which every man's share of the conveniences and comforts of life depends upon himself; in which he must look wholly to his own conduct

---

[9] See, for example, John Weyland, jun., *The Principles of Population and Production, as they are affected by the Progress of Society: with a View to Moral and Political Consequences* (1816), 1–162. James Bonar, *Malthus and His Work* (1885), 355–98, discusses Malthus's critics.

[10] See below, pp. 270, 307–8.

[11] Southwood Smith, *Illustrations of the Divine Government* (Glasgow, 1816), 95.

[12] Smith, *The Divine Government* (5th edn, 1866), 105.

and character for the acquisition and preservation of wealth, and honour, and power, and fame; . . . in a state of society so constituted, the great incentives to human action, hope, and fear, must be afforded with unfailing strength and increasing constancy.[13]

This optimistic, neo-Paleyan response—the law of population as an incentive to social and economic improvement—was given much wider currency by the evangelical John Bird Sumner, whom Peel was to appoint Bishop of Chester in 1828, and Russell Archbishop of Canterbury twenty years later. *A Treatise on the Records of the Creation, and on the Moral Attributes of the Creator; with particular reference to the Jewish History, and to the consistency of the Principle of Population with the Wisdom and Goodness of the Deity* (1816) was, as Richard Soloway has pointed out in his masterly summary, the channel through which most early nineteenth-century Churchmen learned their Malthus.[14] Like Southwood Smith, Sumner regarded over-population as the main incentive to 'exertion', though he refined the argument by celebrating private property, itself the product of population pressure on scarce resources, as a crucial link between the 'economy of nature' and human virtue. In his scenario, men are forced by want to labour, and then to exchange with each other the fruits of their labour, so that 'universal welfare (such welfare at least as is consistent with an imperfect state) is the consequence'.[15] According to Copleston, Sumner's exegesis 'beautifully developed the high moral and religious blessings which . . . hang over [Malthus's] discovery'.[16]

This benign solution to the population problem, through increased exertion and capitalization in agriculture, probably influenced the thinking behind the notorious Corn Law of 1815, but in that same year Ricardo, Edward West, and Malthus himself effectively countered it with their law of diminishing returns to agriculture.[17] Human exertion in the form of

---

[13] Ibid., pp. 75–108, especially p. 96. Dugald Stewart took a similarly optimistic line, accepting the truth of the law of population, but emphasizing the counter-influence of 'habits and ideas' in determining demographic responses to the pressure of scarcity. He did not presuppose a 'miraculous reformation in the moral character of a people', and thought that such reformation could only *follow* changes in the law. See Collini, Winch, and Burrow, *That Noble Science of Politics*, p. 35.

[14] Soloway, *Prelates and People*, pp. 96–101; on Sumner's later pessimism, ibid., pp. 153–4. See R. S. Dell, 'Social and economic theories and pastoral concerns of a Victorian archbishop', *Journal of Ecclesiastical History*, 16 (1965), 196–208.

[15] J. B. Sumner, *A Treatise on the Records of the Creation* (1816), ii. 113–14, 149. See also George Miller, *Lectures on the Philosophy of Modern History* (Dublin, 1816–28), i. 69–70.

[16] [E. Copleston], *A Second Letter to Robert Peel, on the Causes of the Increase of Pauperism, and on the Poor Laws* (Oxford, 1819), 23. Patricia James points out that Sumner made Malthusianism 'theologically respectable' and helped to change the views of the *Quarterly Review* on the subject. James, *Population Malthus*, p. 348.

[17] Hilton, *Corn, Cash, Commerce*, pp. 117–25.

marginal inputs of capital, or of labour, or of land could not after all yield limitless additional supplies of food. Even though Chalmers continued to insist unfashionably on the productive capacities of a thoroughly mechanized and capitalized agriculture,[18] God's apologists—including Chalmers—were forced to look to the other side of the food/population equation, to turn from 'the enlargement of resources in the outer world of matter, . . . to the establishment of habit and principle in the inner world of mind'.[19] This is what Malthus himself had done (but again unobtrusively) in the second (1803) and subsequent editions of the *Essay*. Here he had dropped the argument from exertion, but had also softened the rigours of the positive checks to population—the wars, famines, and pestilences—by supposing 'another check to population possible, which does not strictly come under the head either of vice or misery'—that is, the 'preventive' check of sexual restraint.[20] Now he was extolling moral rather than physical exertion, and attempting to escape the grip of the ecological pincer by shrinkage rather than growth.

The doctrine of moral restraint helped to repair the damage done to natural theology by the first edition of the *Essay*; wars and famines were not written into the universe after all. On the other hand, it contradicted Revelation, since God had clearly required Noah to increase and multiply.[21] None the less, Sumner endorsed the 'preventive check' every bit as emphatically as he lauded 'exertion',[22] and in the following year the evangelical James Bicheno placed it in the context of a jungle. 'It is an universal law of the wise and supreme Governor of the earth, that *the constant tendency of all animated beings is to increase beyond the subsistence prepared for them.*' Wise, because it was in the struggle for subsistence that the lion had developed his innate strength, the fox his native cunning, and the dog his latent power of smell. The very same '*wise*, as well as *merciful* and *just*' dispensation would eventually winkle out the potential of mankind, which consisted of moral faculties— 'honesty, temperance, fidelity, and persevering industry'.[23] Predictably,

[18] Berg, *The Machinery Question*, p. 86.

[19] Chalmers, *On Political Economy*, p. 71 [*Works*, xix. 83].

[20] Malthus, *Essay on the Principle of Population*, 2nd edn (1803), p. vii [(7th edn, 1872), p. vii]. Malthus believed that all methods of birth control were evil, except abstinence.

[21] For an attack on Malthusianism from this viewpoint, see [R. B. Seeley], *Remedies Suggested, for some of the Evils which constitute 'The Perils of the Nation'* (1844), 116–17.

[22] Sumner, *Treatise on the Records of Creation*, ii. 166–9.

[23] James E. Bicheno, *An Inquiry into the Nature of Benevolence, chiefly with a View to elucidate the Principles of the Poor Laws, and to show their Immoral Tendency* (1817), 76–90. Others were consoled by the nutritional aspect of Malthus's case for depopulation, because it gave relief from 'an uneasy feeling' on the subject of carnivores. Buckland to Drummond, 16 Jan. 1837, Northumberland MSS, Drummond Papers, C/1/72; William Buckland, *Geology and Mineralogy Considered with Reference to Natural Theology*,

Whately's way of making the same point was more anodyne, but he too drew a distinction between the savage and the civilized. Defending Malthus from professed friends who had 'made him a tool for noxious purposes', Whately pointed out that it was not a case of God having 'made Man too prolific, or the earth too barren'. It was rather that having made man rational, God had placed him in just the sort of ecological trap to stimulate rational thought, and to direct him towards the long-term advantages of sexual abstention. Then, as the nation grew richer under the influence of a wise political economy, men would cultivate higher pleasures, which would more than compensate them for the absence of sex. For though Malthus had shown that man has a *tendency* to overpeople the world, in order to do so he would have to behave like the savage he is not.[24]

Interestingly, Whately thought that Malthus would have been less disastrously misunderstood if, instead of saying that wars, famines, and pestilences were the 'necessary' consequences of sexual abandon, he had merely said that they were 'unavoidable' ones.[25] This distinction between 'necessary' and 'contingent' truth may seem trivial, but Whately had a point. Like Southwood Smith and Sumner, he was a thoroughgoing Arminian in his emphasis on individual free will, and so saw little moral opportunity for those living in the realms of necessity. In this he differed from Chalmers, who, for all his faith in individual responsibility, could never entirely suppress a native Calvinism,[26] and was apparently prepared to lend spiritual countenance to virtuous acts performed under duress. It was Chalmers who erected the 'preventive check' into a system of moral theology, in which prudence and chastity were not merely rational responses to crisis, but spiritual imperatives in their own right. As Robert Young puts it, 'where Malthus had stressed a dismal law of nature alleviated by moral restraint, Chalmers focused on moral restraint itself'.[27]

There is then a symbiosis between the optimistic, *adaptational* approach of neo-Paleyans like Southwood Smith and Whately, and the more fundamentalist, *conversionist* approach of the evangelicals, Sumner, Bicheno, and Chalmers. The two approaches had much in common, and both pointed towards freer trade and a *laissez-faire* social policy. The

---

Bridgewater Treatise No. 6 (1836), 129–34. Drummond objected that animals (including carnivores) had pre-existed Adam, by whom death was supposed to have come into the world (Romans 5: 12).

[24] Whately, *Lectures on Political Economy*, pp. 164–6.

[25] Whately to Senior, 1835, Whately, *Life of Whately*, i. 301.

[26] *Life Letters and Journals of Sir Charles Lyell*, ed. his sister-in-law (1881), i. 331.

[27] R. M. Young, 'Malthus and the evolutionists: the common context of biological and social theory', *Past and Present*, 43 (1969), 120.

difference—detectable for the most part in emphasis, nuance, and imagery—lies in their respective spiritual contexts. Thus, when Southwood Smith writes of Malthusianism as a 'moral discipline' for improving character, and of life as 'a state of discipline in which . . . the human being should be prepared for a higher and happier state', his phraseology is typical of the Age of Atonement, but the sentiments are not in his case evangelical. More like Whately, he saw the march of civilization, education, and generosity as a gradual process of tuition, fitting men for a future existence in Heaven. Having no concept of natural depravity or of the urgent need for conversion, Southwood Smith was not only a post- rather than a pre-millennialist but a very relaxed millennialist altogether. Again, when Bicheno observes that 'the human mind cannot be stationary', he seems to share the evolutionary cosmic optimism of Southwood Smith, but the jungle metaphor points the difference, as does his emphasis on fear more than on hope, on punishment and suffering more than on rewards and satisfaction. Chalmers thought that 'repentance, sorrow, humiliation, contrition at the thought of his past misconduct' were man's 'only means' for appeasing God's wrath,[28] whereas Southwood Smith believed that men might discover godliness in their quest for 'wealth, and honour and power, and fame'. Chalmers thought that salvation was more important than physical comfort, whereas Southwood Smith regarded poverty as incompatible with spiritual health. The crucial difference is, of course, that for Chalmers and Sumner the world was merely an 'arena of moral trial', an 'imperfect state' capable of but a limited amount of 'welfare', whereas for Southwood Smith the world was cherished by God and designed for ultimate perfection. The distinction was drawn most neatly and explicitly by Paley in his *Natural Theology*, where life was described as a state of 'moral probation' but 'not a state of retribution: it is not a state of punishment'.[29]

However, the distinction must not be drawn *too* rigidly. Not all writers were conscious of it themselves, and some occasionally slipped from one mode to the other. Even the tone of voice can be misleading— Chalmers, for all his emphasis on sorrow and humiliation, could be quite cheerful. The fact remains that evangelical social theory was separate from (as well as dependent on) the natural law/natural harmony tradition. Historians have been more aware of the latter, with its optimistic, Utopian prediction that Free Trade could solve all social problems, but the evangelical mode was probably more widespread and probably more influential.

[28] Chalmers, *On the Power Wisdom and Goodness of God*, ii. 295-6 [*Works*, ii. 405].
[29] Paley, *Natural Theology*, pp. 561-2 [(15th edn, 1815), 525-6].

Chalmers and the Problem of Poverty

Southwood Smith regarded sexual restraint as the apotheosis of Christian awareness; Chalmers seems to have seen it as a necessary prelude to conversion. He regarded his own generation as peculiarly blessed, God having magnanimously instituted the Malthusian trap as a formula for carrying out the evangelicalization of the nation. Faced with the immediate threat of wars, famines, and pestilences, men were being *forced* 'to elevate their minds above their passionate flesh', and such enforced self-denial put them in a proper mental condition for the receipt of divine grace. While a xenophobic youth in 1808, Chalmers had actually welcomed population increase as a means of combating the armies of Napoleon, but that was before his own religious crisis and conversion at Kilmany in 1810–11. By the time he came to write the influential *Christian and Civic Economy of Large Towns* in 1821, he had embraced and exaggerated the Malthusian message.[30] Official poor relief in England, like the parochial assessments that existed in parts of Scotland, were 'amiable' in intent but 'cruel' in their consequences, for they encouraged men to marry improvidently and live in idleness. Not that at this stage Chalmers saw an antidote to pauperism in political economy, or in the cold and cautious maxims of Mrs Marcet and Miss Martineau. Improvidence was unavoidable 'so long as the sensual predominates over the reflective part of the human constitution, . . . so long as there is generally a low and grovelling taste among the people, instead of an aspiring tendency towards something more in the way of comfort, and cleanliness, and elegance'.[31] And, like Robert Southey, he believed that the only way to inculcate such sagacity, foresight, and self-esteem was by Christian missionaries undertaking intensive house-to-house visitation and religious exhortation, such as he himself was attempting in Glasgow. Evangelists did not themselves need to know any political economy, for merely by rescuing labourers from 'the dominion of sensuality', they would encourage modes of behaviour in 'practical conformity' with the lessons of political economy and so unwittingly promote the temporal good of society. The transformation would not be rapid, and one would have to 'weather for a season the annoyance of . . . mendicity', but such Christian evangelism was the only sure way to effect a moral regeneration of society.[32]

[30] Chalmers does not seem to have read Sumner's *Treatise* until November 1827. Hanna, *Life of Chalmers*, iii. 209.

[31] Chalmers, *Christian and Civic Economy*, i. 7–10 [*Works*, xiv. 29–32]. See L. J. Saunders, *Scottish Democracy 1815–1840: The Social and Intellectual Background* (1950), 209–21.

[32] Chalmers's evidence to a Select Committee in *Collected Works*, xvi. 285–421; Brown, *Thomas Chalmers*, pp. 190–2.

Chalmers never relaxed his moral paternalism. The 'Christian education of the people' forms the climax of his *Political Economy* of 1832. But the emphasis changed after he had abandoned his heroic personal role among Glasgow's slums in 1823, and became involved in the academic study of political economy from 1824. Now he came to emphasize the wisdom of providence in having created the wages fund as a mechanism for inducing good behaviour. Since the size of that fund is fixed at any one time, there must be an inverse relationship between wage levels and the supply of labour. Accordingly, only the poor could help the poor by subduing their 'passionate flesh' and limiting their own numbers. It was thus that, as he put it so memorably in his *Bridgewater Treatise*:

Political economy is but one grand exemplification of the alliance, which a God of righteousness hath established, between prudence and moral principle on the one hand, and physical comfort on the other. However obnoxious the modern doctrine of population, as expounded by Mr. Malthus, may have been, and still is, to weak and limited sentimentalists, it is the truth which of all others sheds the greatest brightness over the earthly prospects of humanity — and this in spite of the hideous, the yet sustained outcry which has risen against it. This is a pure case of adaptation, between the external nature of the world in which we live, and the moral nature of man, its chief occupier. There is a demonstrable inadequacy in all the material resources which the globe can furnish, for the increasing wants of a recklessly increasing species. But over and against this, man is gifted with a moral and a mental power by which the inadequacy might be fully countervailed; and the species in virtue of their restrained and regulated numbers, be upholden on the face of our world, in circumstances of large and stable sufficiency, even to the most distant ages. The first origin of this blissful consummation is the virtue of the people; but carried into sure and lasting effect by the laws of political economy, through the indissoluble connection which obtains between the wages and the supply of labour.[33]

Here Chalmers was employing Malthus's market theory of wages against Ricardo's subsistence theory. The latter stipulated that competition among the bosses would always force down wage levels towards the price of staple food. But Ricardo also thought that the price of food, in existing monopolistic conditions, was determined by the cost of growing it on the very worst land in cultivation. Rent was then defined as the difference between the price of food, which was common to all soils, and the actual cost of producing it on different soils. In Chalmers's hands, this theory of rent was harnessed, like that of wages, to the prevailing natural theology. Geologists at that time were accustomed to deduce a presiding design in nature from the way that wastage of soil was nicely balanced

---

[33] Chalmers, *On the Power Wisdom and Goodness of God*, ii. 49–51 [*Works*, ii. 142–3.]

by the supply from the disintegration of the upland rocks, which were worn and pulverized at the precise rate necessary to keep up a good vegetable mould on the surface of the earth. Chalmers weighed in with the suggestion that the 'provision' of a fund called rent out of the surplus fertility of the soil was, since rent effectively paid for all the amenities of civilization, a most 'wondrous and beautiful adaptation between the state of external nature and the mechanism of human society'.[34] This was tantamount to saying that working-men should limit their own numbers, not in order that each of them might command a greater share of the wages fund, but—and in this Chalmers was making a concession to the subsistence theory of wages—in order that the aggregate size of that fund might be kept down, and the resources allotted to rent, source of all permanent happiness, might be increased.

A Scottish evangelical Congregationalist, James Haldane, once complained that Chalmers ignored the natural depravity of mankind.[35] He could not have been more wrong, since original sin was Chalmers's starting-point. But it *is* true that, like most moderate evangelicals, Chalmers was optimistic about man's capacity, under duress, to turn away from sin. In this way he combined a Judaic vision of the stern and vengeful Jehovah with the 'warm, and affectionate, and evangelical spirit of the New Testament'.[36] Political economy merely assisted by demonstrating that virtue and material happiness rise and fall together. If men live immorally they will sink into destitution; if they live like Christians they will 'augment indefinitely, not the produce of the earth, nor the produce of human industry, but that proportion of both which falls to their share'.[37] In labouring for eternity, they will unconsciously ensure their own material improvement—a quite different proposition from Whately's, that men improve their own temporal position thanks to their unconscious social instincts. The priest who teaches that licentious behaviour is a mortal sin, and the political economist who demonstrates that wages vary inversely with the supply of labour, are complementary witnesses to God's benevolence.

So it was not merely self-defeating, as Whately and Senior thought, to dole out alms to the poor, on the grounds that the latter would quickly procreate themselves back into all their old misery. Chalmers further

---

[34] Chalmers, *On Political Economy*, pp. 46–7 [*Works*, xix. 60]. On connections between geology and political economy see below, pp. 149–54.

[35] [J. Haldane], *A Letter on the Causes and Cure of Pauperism* (Glasgow, 1818), 3–13, cited in Brown, *Thomas Chalmers*, p. 122.

[36] Chalmers, *Christian and Civic Economy*, i. 23 [*Works*, xiv. 43].

[37] Chalmers, *On Political Economy*, p. 28 [*Works*, xix. 42]: 'In labouring for the good of their eternity, they have reaped, by the way, those blessings which religion so abundantly sheds over the pilgrimage that leads to it.'

believed that it would be spiritually vicious to let men off God's carefully contrived ecological hook, and undo by misplaced sentiment and humanity the 'moral ordination' which was built into the natural world. Chalmers, no less than Wilberforce, rebelled against Paley's picture of the deity as a fond and affectionate parent, and urged instead ' a fuller view of God's moral nature', based on his 'righteousness' as well as his 'benevolence'. 'We are then on firmer vantage-ground for the establishment of a Natural Theology, in harmony, both with the lessons of conscience, and with the phenomena of the natural world.'[38] Indeed, Chalmers claimed to have taken up lecturing on political economy in the first place because his moral philosophy students had been excited by the distinction which he had drawn, with respect to questions of poverty and poor relief, 'between the two virtues of Humanity and Justice'.[39] With his characteristic tenacity of thought and phraseology, he wrote twenty years later that 'Utilitarians and Socinians would overbear this distinction [between justice and benevolence] by resolving all the moralities into benevolence alone . . . nay carrying this principle upward to the divine character. . . . It is thus that they would set aside the doctrine of the Atonement.'[40] Nothing could define more sharply Chalmers's divergence from the philosophy of Southwood Smith.

It was then a cardinal tenet of Chalmers, and the clutched straw of his natural theology, that *the world is so constituted that if we were morally right we should be physically happy*. Men suffer physically because they disobey God's laws of nature, but such suffering may operate to render them more obedient in future. 'Prudence and virtue will verily have their rewards', while sin will 'always' lead to suffering, here as well as hereafter.[41]

Natural theology was one thing, but what about Revelation and Christ's injunctions to the rich to care for the poor? Chalmers would not accept that the New Testament contradicted his attitude to the Poor Laws. The Apostles had apparently refrained from dispensing charity on the ground that it took up time which should be given to teaching the Word. Even Christ had relieved from want and hunger only twice, while in

[38] Chalmers, *On the Power Wisdom and Goodness of God*, ii. 100–3 [*Works*, ii. 206–10]. Young, 'Malthus and the evolutionists', op. cit., pp. 124–5, is mistaken in thinking that Chalmers's conception of an 'Old Testament, judicial and vengeful God' contradicted the ethical and psychological assumptions of the period. See below, pp. 270–4.

[39] *Evidence taken by the Commissioners for Visiting the Universities of Scotland: Volume III, University of St. Andrews*, 2 Aug. 1827, p. 61 [PP 1837, xxxvii. 87].

[40] [Chalmers], 'Political economy of the Bible', *North British Review*, 2 (1844–5), 49. See below, pp. 178–9.

[41] Ibid., p. 30. See Chalmers's chapter 'On the capacities of the world for making a virtuous species happy', *On the Power Wisdom and Goodness of God*, ii. 97–130 [*Works*, ii. 206–47].

John 6: 26-7, he had refused to do so. (This was a rather twisted interpretation of the text, 'Labour not for the meat that perisheth, but for the meat which endureth unto everlasting life.'). Chalmers even found it significant that Christ had refused to perform the Miracle of the Loaves and the Fishes for a third time. On the other hand, Christ frequently relieved men from disease, so that there was a

distinction which ought to be observed between a charity for mere indigence, and a charity for disease. A public charity for the one tends to multiply its objects — because it enlists the human will on the side, if not of poverty, at least of the dissipation and indolence which lead to poverty. A public charity for the other will scarcely, if ever, enlist the human will on the side of disease.[42]

Clearly, Chalmers was not one of those extreme evangelical fatalists who, seeing cholera and other epidemics as a special intervention of God, regarded any mortal attempts to cure the disease, other than by prayers and fasting, as impious.[43] Chalmers preferred to think of such retributions as the consequences of (as yet) 'undivined' — but none the less divinely designed — 'secondary causes' operating in the universe. Anyway, working-class poverty did not come suddenly like an epidemic, nor did it come 'undivined'. It was the necessary and inescapable consequence of licentious habits, which could only be cured by 'sustained evangelical tuition', emphasizing the eternal retribution that awaits all reprobates.[44]

Chalmers's Place in Nineteenth-century Social Thought

It would not be difficult to compile a long list of social reformers who were inspired by Chalmers and tried to follow his example. According to R. K. Webb, one man who took Chalmers to America (and thence back into English Unitarianism) was Joseph Tuckerman, a Unitarian philanthropist who started a city mission for the poor at Boston in 1826.[45] There was also the Baptist Francis Wayland, President of Brown University from 1827, and the Rev. George Boardman of New York, though the latter was perhaps more Whatelyan than Chalmerian in the optimism of his natural theology.[46] At home one could cite Edward

---

[42] [Chalmers], 'Political economy of the Bible', op. cit., p. 47. The same point is made in Chalmers, *The Example of Our Saviour a Guide and an Authority, in the Establishment of Charitable Institutions* (1819), *passim* [*Works*, xii. 11–46].

[43] See R. J. Morris, *Cholera 1832: The Social Response to an Epidemic* (1976), 131–2 and chapter 7 *passim*.

[44] [Chalmers], 'Political economy of the Bible', op. cit., pp. 8–17.

[45] R. K. Webb in *Times Literary Supplement*, No. 3,891 (1976), 1266.

[46] Joseph Dorfman, *The Economic Mind in American Civilization 1606–1933* (New York, 1946–59), ii. 758–71; George N. Boardman, 'Political economy and the Christian ministry', *The Bibliotheca Sacra*, 23 (1866), 73–107.

Bickersteth, John Lalor, and Robert Whytehead. But it is not being claimed that Chalmers created so much as that he articulated, and to a greater extent than most acted on, those attitudes. The Surrey evangelical Charles Jerram was preaching and applying similar principles long before Chalmers, while Ralph Wardlaw, a fellow member of the Glasgow Literary and Commercial Society, was on the way towards similar opinions by 1817.[47] There is no evidence either of direct influence on James Stevens, whose *The Poor Laws an Interference with the Divine Laws by which the Interests and Welfare of Society are Maintained* (1831) took Chalmers's message to extremes. Stevens believed that the gradual but total abolition of poor relief was essential for the sake of society and of the moral character of its members:

To prevent the possibility of death from famine, to prevent the possibility of actual want, may appear a desirable object. But we forget that it is in this very possibility, that the efficiency of those laws of God by which society is governed, consists. From observations on the state and order of the world, we are fully authorized to infer, that it is the will of God, as expressed in the laws of nature, that the life of man should depend upon various contingencies; as upon his own exertions and character, the good will of others, advantages of situation, and so forth. . . . We find that upon this very contingency and uncertainty of subsistence, upon this very possibility of utter destitution (and if there is a possibility, — there are likely to be instances) the integrity of the social compact, the prevention of actual vice, the industry and happiness of man, the peace and security of the political body, are made to depend. Physical evil, it is a well-known fact, is necessary for the promotion of moral good.[48]

In short, poor laws were the work of 'unskilful man, intermeddling with an intricate and delicate piece of machinery'.[49] It was to reduce the degree of muddling and intermeddling that the free trade movement was mainly directed, and of course it welcomed the 'less eligibility' principles of the New Poor Law in 1834 as at least a step in that direction. For, as Chalmers put it, *laissez-faire* in poor relief would 'restore the natural balance [of society], as in the case of trade' the free movement of commodities would restore 'earth's natural balance'.

It should be said at this point that Chalmers has not always been regarded as a spokesman for the *Zeitgeist*, or as an apostle of *laissez-faire*

[47] Charles Jerram, *The Impolicy of the General Administration of the Poor-Laws* (1802); C. Jerram, *Considerations on the Impolicy and Pernicious Tendency of the Poor-Laws* (1818); *The Memoirs and A Selection from the Letters of the late Rev. Charles Jerram*, by James Jerram (1855), 275–8; *Memoirs of the Life and Writings of Ralph Wardlaw*, by William Lindsay Alexander (Edinburgh, 1856), 179–81.

[48] James Stevens, *The Poor Laws an Interference with the Divine Laws by which the Interests and Welfare of Society are Maintained* (1831), 64–5.

[49] Ibid., p. 79.

social theory. Sydney Checkland suggested that he ploughed a 'lonely furrow', while David Roberts depicts him as a 'stern Calvinist' paternalist and as such 'somewhat untypical'. Stewart Brown prefers to see him either as a 'backward-looking' mercantilist or else as a 'prophet' of something like collectivism. Trygve Tholfsen, more plausibly, regards him as the precursor of those Smilesian ideals of working-class improvement and respectability which were to characterize the mid-nineteenth-century consensus.[50] In view of these informed opinions, it is necessary to elaborate on the justification for depicting Chalmers in strictly *laissez-faire* terms.

In part the problem arises through failure to distinguish clearly between moral and material paternalism. Chalmers's economic individualism, though rigorous and unequivocal, can easily be obscured in selective quotation by the force with which he peddled a strictly *moral* paternalism. The combination was typical of the period. By and large, economic paternalists tended to be relatively indifferent to the need for moral reform, while individualists enthused about it. Thus Alison, Sadler, and Robert Owen, all real paternalists assuming the best about human nature, thought that characters would improve *automatically* as social conditions improved, and that intense moral suasion was unnecessary. It was the individualists, those who saw that characters must be reformed *before* it would be safe to improve material conditions, who also saw the need for moral didacticism to complete the process. It is therefore misleading to write, as Brown does many times over, of Chalmers's 'rejection of the radical individualism of *laissez-faire* capitalism', and of his alternative 'vision of the nation as a Godly Commonwealth', inspired by paternalist, covenanting traditions,[51] for in fact Chalmers would have seen no contradiction between the two visions. Repeatedly, Brown presents Chalmers as fundamentally opposed to 'economic individualism', as 'an oracle — a social prophet, who had early recognised the dangerous tendencies of Classical Liberal economic theory and had been willing to struggle in isolation for the Godly Commonwealth ideal which alone could save the nation'.[52] This verdict is supported by a quotation from the *Christian Guardian*, citing Chalmers's view that labourers must help themselves

---

[50] Tholfsen, *Working Class Radicalism*, pp. 133–4; David Roberts, *Paternalism in Early Victorian England* (1979), 26, 42; Checkland, 'Propagation of Ricardian economics', *Economica*, 16 (1949), 44.

[51] S. J. Brown, 'Thomas Chalmers and the Godly Commonwealth: 1780–1847', University of Chicago Ph.D. (1981), abstract.

[52] Brown, *Thomas Chalmers*, pp. 189, 194–9, 225, and *passim*. Elsewhere Brown suggests that in Chalmers's eyes the 'greatest benefit' to be derived from Free Trade was that it would demonstrate to working-men that Protection was *not* the cause of their sufferings! Ibid., p. 196. Other authorities have also supposed that, because of his other views, Chalmers must have been a protectionist. See Berg, *The Machinery Question*, p. 87.

through foresight and self-denial, and that the function of governments is to educate people for this work. The last point may sound paternalist, but in fact such a philosophy was very close in practice to that of the secular writers whose 'Classical Liberal economic theory' Chalmers was supposed to be attacking—to Ricardo, for example, who made the same points that poor relief would encourage over-population and that the upper classes had no obligation 'to feed as well as to take care of and educate the children of . . . the poor'.[53] Neighbourhood, parish, and family were all important for Chalmers, it is true, but because they were conducive to the development of individual awareness, not because they contradicted them. A moral paternalism like his, which had to operate within a context of economic individualism, was no paternalism at all in the conditions of early nineteenth-century industrialization. The poor wanted 'bread before bibles', but Chalmers believed that bread was impossible without bibles, and if he had seen any conflict between the two, there is no doubt where his priority would have lain: 'I should count the salvation of a single soul of more value than the deliverance of a whole empire from pauperism.'[54] The spiritual priority seems very different from Ricardo's, yet it powerfully reinforced classical economic liberalism. As Brian Stanley has put it, Chalmers's writings were 'probably the most important single channel whereby the tenets of utilitarianism and political economy were mediated to the evangelical world'.[55] To see him as the spokesman of a paternalist counter-culture is quite mistaken.

What then of the view which sees Chalmers as anticipating mid-Victorian liberal reformism? Certainly, he often employed a language of *embourgeoisement* very similar to that of later nineteenth-century middle-class reformers. When he argues that delayed marriages entail a 'season of anticipation', which serve to 'recall the sexual feelings, and to fix and concentrate them upon one object', and that this gives working-men 'a farther reach of anticipation than before', making them capable of 'looking onward with forecast and preparation, not only for the distant futurity on the other side of death, but for the nearer futurities of our earthly existence',[56] he sounds not wholly unlike J. S. Mill, for example. Moreover, this view that Chalmers anticipated later modes of social thought gains plausibility from the fact that C. S. Loch, secretary of the Charity

[53] Ricardo to James Mill, 12 Dec. 1818, *Works and Correspondence of Ricardo*, vii. 359–60.

[54] Chalmers to James Brown, 30 Jan. 1819, Edinburgh University Library MS, DC.2.57, fo. 62.

[55] Brian Stanley, ' "Commerce and Christianity": providence theory, the missionary movement, and the imperialism of free trade, 1842–1860', *Historical Journal*, 26 (1983), 74 n. 18.

[56] [Chalmers], 'Political economy of the Bible', *North British Review*, 2 (1844–5), 21–7.

Organisation Society founded in 1869, was inspired by the St John's experiment in formulating his ideal of scientific philanthropy.[57] On the other hand, Loch's religious beliefs, and consequently his conception of working-class 'reformation', differed profoundly from Chalmers's, while it will shortly be seen that the very notion of charity *organization* entirely contradicted Chalmers's emphasis on individualism and spontaneity. Loch even sanctioned the involvement of the state and the use of legal assessments in securing social welfare for the poor. Then again, Chalmers's emphasis on 'comfort, and cleanliness, and elegance' resembles mid-nineteenth-century ideals of *embourgeoisement*, while his desire that the poor should invest in savings banks seems to presage the ideas of the Christian Socialists with their Provident Societies, and of Gladstone with the Post Office Savings Bank. In fact his attitude, like that of Wilberforce, another proponent of savings banks, was subtly different, as is clear from an article he wrote in 1820. Here he showed great sensitivity to the dilemmas of working-class existence—how in glutted markets labourers have to work doubly hard merely to provide subsistence for their families, and how they thereby glut the market for their produce still further, and stave off the day of their deliverance. Chalmers thought that the poor had enough to do battling against their own sexuality, and he did not want them to have to cope with cyclical depressions as well. Besides, such fluctuations introduced an arbitrary element into working-class existence, distorted the ecological mechanism, and gave the poor a plausible excuse for their misfortunes. Chalmers wished them to invest their meagre savings—not in order that they could become petty capitalists, contributing to fluctuations, themselves, but so that such fluctuations might make less impact on their lives. When the market became overstocked, instead of working harder, workers would be able to go off on holiday, read, walk, or even play, until the glut had dispersed.[58] This was hardly the same as the mid-Victorian ethos of hard work, thrift, ambition, and upward mobility.

The 'Evangelicalization' of Parson Malthus?

It was undoubtedly in this moralistic and even evangelical form that Malthusian population theory was most widely disseminated. An intriguing if peripheral question, and one which has stimulated much recent research,

---

[57] On Loch see C. S. Mowat, *The Charity Organisation Society 1869-1913: Its Ideas and Work* (1961), 63–78 and *passim*.

[58] [T. Chalmers], 'State and prospects of manufacturers', *Edinburgh Review*, 33 (1820), 386–7, 394–5 [*Works*, xx. 378–80, 392–3]. See also [Chalmers], 'Stirling's *Philosophy of Trade*', *North British Review*, 6 (1846–7), 92–3; Chalmers, *On the Power Wisdom and Goodness of God*, ii. 47 [*Works*, ii. 141].

is the extent to which Malthus himself may have been influenced by what Sumner and Chalmers did to his theory. If the most obvious distinguishing feature of evangelicalism is its emphasis on life as a moral trial, there is some evidence that Malthus was indeed affected. As Le Mahieu has pointed out, the first edition contains an explicit theodicy—a belief, attuned to natural theology, that scarcity is ordained by providence in order to stimulate hard work and social mobility. Malthus seems to have been influenced here by his Unitarian teachers, Wakefield and Frend, and the first edition certainly gave great offence to the orthodox in so far as it 'equivocated on Original Sin, neglected Jesus, and denied Hell'.[59] The *New Annual Register* for 1799 was disturbed by his supposition that 'the moral situation of man in this world is not a state of trial'.[60] When the second and third editions of the *Essay* made no references (approving or otherwise) to moral trial, the *Christian Observer* sarcastically congratulated the author on not having repudiated the doctrine of eternal punishment, nor having 'entertained' his readers with a 'theory of the grand operation of nature for exciting mind out of matter'.[61] No doubt such changes were more instrumental than theological. Whereas the first edition had envisaged population pressure as encouraging the 'growth of mind', the second more or less took growth of mind as its premiss, in the sense that men were assumed to be capable of exercising the 'preventive check'. But then the fourth (1807) and fifth (1817) editions contained explicit if not wholly committed references to 'probation', and to 'the necessity of practising the virtue of moral restraint in a state *allowed to be* a state of discipline and trial'.[62] Such grudging admissions nicely illustrate the process of evangelical creep, affecting even some of those who were unsympathetic. Malthus admitted that he had been persuaded to revise his theology by unknown but 'competent' friends in the Church of England,[63] and he was thought by his friend William Otter, the Bishop

---

[59] D. Le Mahieu, 'Malthus and the theology of scarcity', *Journal of the History of Ideas*, 40 (1979), 470. This article caps a recent move away from an older view, expressed in 1969 by Robert Young, 'Malthus and the evolutionists', op. cit., p. 118, that 'Paley stresses perfect adaptation; Malthus stresses conflict, . . . Darwin synthesises them. Struggle both explains and produces adaptation'. For a middle view, see P. J. Bowler, 'Malthus, Darwin, and the concept of struggle', *Journal of the History of Ideas* 37 (1976), 631–50: 'Malthus . . . *did* break away from the belief that the relationship of each species to its environment, or to nature as a whole, is harmonious', but 'he did not abandon the idea of natural harmony as far as the internal workings of society are concerned'. See also S. M. Levin, 'Malthus and the idea of progress', ibid., 27 (1966), 92–108.

[60] Quoted in James, *Population Malthus*, pp. 66–7.

[61] *Christian Observer*, 4 (1805), 539.

[62] Malthus, *Essay on the Principle of Population* (4th edn, 1807), ii. 478 [(5th edn, 1817), iii. 423–4] (italics added).

[63] J. M. Pullen, 'Malthus's theological ideas and their influence on his principle of population', *History of Political Economy*, 13 (1981), 39–54; S. Rashid, 'Malthus's *Principles* and British economic thought, 1820–1835', ibid., pp. 55–79; Edmund N. Santurri,

of Chichester, to have altered several expressions for the fifth edition after reading Sumner, for whom he felt 'profound respect'.[64]

On the practical implications of population theory for poor relief, Malthus, it will be remembered, dubbed Chalmers his 'ablest and best ally'. Until the success of the St John's experiment, Malthus had 'almost despaired . . . and almost begun to think that in a highly manufacturing state where so large a portion of the population must be subject to the fluctuations of trade, and the consequent sudden variations of wages, it might not be possible entirely to give up a compulsory provision without the sacrifice of too many individuals to the good of the whole'.[65] Chalmers's work in Glasgow was apparently able to reassure Malthus that a 'fundamental change in the habits and manners of the great mass of our people' was a practical possibility after all, so that when the latter told Whewell in 1831 that he had been 'unfortunate' in his followers, and that his theories did not bear 'the gloomy aspect given to them by many of my readers', it seems unlikely that he had his evangelical interpreters, Sumner and Chalmers, in mind.[66]

Evangelicals as Paternalists: Sinclair, Sadler, and Oastler

But how representative were Sumner and Chalmers of evangelicals generally, and of the early nineteenth-century frame of mind? We have seen that some famous evangelicals were noted for their paternalism, in the conventional sense of the word, meaning that they advocated material and not just moral support for the poor. In the early years of Victoria's reign, especially, many evangelicals participated in the paternalist backlash

---

'Theodicy and social policy in Malthus' thought', *Journal of the History of Ideas*, 43 (1982), 315–30; A. M. C. Waterman, 'Malthus as a theologian: the *First Essay* and the relation between political economy and Christian theology', *Malthus Past and Present*, ed. J. Dupâquier, A. Fauve-Chamoux, and E. Grebenik (1983), 195–209; J. A. Banks, *Victorian Values: Secularism and the Size of Families* (1981), 12–21.

[64] W. Otter, 'Memoirs of Robert Malthus', in T. R. Malthus, *Principles of Political Economy Considered with a View to their Practical Application* (1820; 2nd edn, 1836), lii–liii. Otter implies that Malthus grew more pious with age. James, *Population Malthus*, pp. 119–20, shows how the third (1806) edn of the *Essay* countered a charge contained in a letter to the *Christian Observer*, 4 (1805), 539–41, as to Malthus's 'morality of expediency'. And it may be significant that the word 'starve' in the motto to this chapter is replaced by the word 'suffer' in the fourth (1807) edition of the *Essay*, ii. 321–2. For Malthus's public tribute to Sumner's *Treatise* see *Essay*, 5th edn (1817), ii. 277.

[65] Malthus to Chalmers, 29 Aug. 1821, Chalmers Papers, CHA 4.18.21–2. Admittedly, Malthus still considered that the higher and middle classes were not yet mentally prepared for abolition of the Poor Laws. Malthus to Chalmers, 21 July 1822, ibid., 4.21.51–2. There is no evidence to support the claim in James, *Population Malthus*, pp. 428–34, that Malthus persistently slighted Chalmers's 'pathetic' efforts to ingratiate himself, and anyway Chalmers was hardly an ingratiating type of person.

[66] Malthus to Whewell, 28 Feb. 1831, Whewell Papers, c.53².

against the 'march of mind',[67] insisting that the lamentable 'Condition of England' was a consequence of *laissez-faire* social theory. So evangelicals were divided, and nothing illustrates the chasm among them better than the following report of a conversation which Chalmers had in 1847, the final year of his life, with Richard Oastler. The subject was a bill then before Parliament to limit the maximum amount of labour for women and children in the textile industry to ten hours each day.

CHALMERS: I see this Bill is contrary to the Principles of Free Trade.
OASTLER: Decidedly. If Free Trade be right, the Ten Hours' Bill is wrong.
CHALMERS: I am a Free Trader, and cannot support any measure that is opposed to it.
OASTLER: That is very strange. I thought you were a Christian.
CHALMERS: And so I am.
OASTLER: What! a Christian and a Free Trader? You surprise me.
CHALMERS: How so?
OASTLER: Why, Dr. Chalmers, it was from you I learned that Free Trade was anti-Christian. When a youth I read your *Astronomical Lectures*, and in one of them you treated on the responsibility of the rich . . .
CHALMERS: What has that to do with Free Trade?
OASTLER: Everything.[68]

Oastler was, of course, being thoroughly disingenuous, since he must have known perfectly well what Chalmers's views were on Free Trade. The clash of views is nevertheless fundamental, and needs to be explained if the term 'evangelicalism' is to carry any weight as an interpretative concept.

A complicating factor, which we encountered in Chapter 1, is that while not all nominal Evangelicals subscribed to the theories described here as evangelical, many people who were not nominal Evangelicals did so. Thus at first sight there is — according to the theory — something topsy-turvy about a correspondence that took place between Sir George Sinclair and the *Quarterly*'s leading reviewer John Wilson Croker in 1840. Sinclair was a Scottish evangelical MP, and Croker was a High Tory, a High Churchman, a lifelong champion of prescription as the only way to keep 'everything in its place', and a scourge of utilitarianism, which he thought

---

[67] On this backlash see Roberts, *Paternalism in Early Victorian England*, *passim*; Himmelfarb, *The Idea of Poverty*, pp. 177–206. For specifically evangelical moves towards paternalism after 1830, seen from a different aspect than the one presented here, see J. Douglas Holladay, '19th century evangelical activism: from private charity to State intervention, 1830-50', *Historical Magazine of the Protestant Episcopal Church*, 51 (1982), 53–79.

[68] Cecil Driver, *Tory Radical: The Life of Richard Oastler* (New York, 1946), 468–9. This section is based on Boyd Hilton, 'The role of Providence in evangelical social thought', *History, Society and the Churches: Essays in Honour of Owen Chadwick*, ed. Derek Beales and Geoffrey Best (Cambridge, 1985), 215–33.

would reduce society to 'a fortuitous concourse of atoms'.[69] Yet it was Sinclair who wrote a 'sentimental'—that is to say, paternalist—pamphlet on poor relief, and Croker who took the more robust view. The latter's tone is grimmer than Chalmers's but the perspective is similar. Unlike Sinclair, he defended the utilitarian New Poor Law of 1834:

It is the first Law of nature, the primal curse of an angry, but all-wise Creator, that we [i.e. 'the great mass of mankind'] should earn our bread in toil and pain, and by the sweat of our brow. . . . It is meet and right, and our bounden duty, to help the weak, and to alleviate distress, as far as our means allow; but to tell the working classes that *any* power can relieve them from their state of *want and dependence* is to impugn, as it seems to me, the dispensations of Providence, and to disorder the frame of society. . . . How can the rich give them bread? *Only* by giving work.[70]

It would be foolish to suggest that Croker was a closet or unconscious evangelical, just because he appealed to providence, befriended Drummond and Sinclair, admired Wilberforce's *Practical View*, and achieved what one pious commentator acknowledged to be a 'beautiful' death-bed realization that 'the entire depravity of man and the eternal justice of God could never have been reconciled without a Mediator'.[71] The point is simply to show how even a conventionally pious but 'high-and-dry' Anglican of the old school, and an habitual opponent of *laissez-faire* liberalism, could succumb to an evangelical view of man's condition, and slip from there into support for liberal economic policies.

More importantly, why did a devout evangelical like Sinclair *not* subscribe to 'evangelical' doctrine on poor relief, and does the fact that so many of the evangelicals dissented from it invalidate the view that there was such a doctrine? We saw in Chapter 1 that the explanation might have something to do with theology, and with whether one's evangelicalism was of the extreme type, or moderate and rational.[72] Working on these lines, we can find a clue to Sinclair's paternalism in the comments of a friend and biographer as to his occasional religious doubts and dilemmas:

At times his faith was clouded, and the prosperity of the wicked, and the preponderating mass of evil and suffering in the world, perplexed him sorely and disquieted his spirit, for he took to heart the sins and sufferings of others, and their lack of advantages and good moral influences, and his heart was full of pity even for the outcasts of society, whom he always regarded as objects of compassion.[73]

---

[69] Croker to Sinclair, 8 Jan. 1834, Grant, *Memoirs of Sir George Sinclair*, p. 219.
[70] Croker to Sinclair, Aug. 1840, ibid., pp. 223–4. Eleven years later, Croker deprecated the way in which Christian Socialists blamed the government of the day for evils which were 'natural', 'irremediable', 'providential'. [J. W. Croker], 'Revolutionary literature', *Quarterly Review*, 89 (1851), 491–543.
[71] Grant, *Memoirs of Sir George Sinclair*, p. 228.
[72] See above, pp. 15–17.   [73] Grant, *Memoirs of Sir George Sinclair*, p. 468.

In other words, Sinclair's soft-hearted attitude to pauperism, his compassion for those who suffer, was linked to his indignation that wicked men often succeed. He thought that life was unjust, or, as his biographer James Grant put it, 'at times he was not free from perplexities and painful feelings in regard to the moral government of God'. Croker had no such doubts, and neither did most moderate, 'natural law' evangelicals. They were confident that *laissez-faire* policies would reveal a providential order, and that that order would be a *just* one. Sinclair took a more paternalist approach because he doubted the efficacy and fairness of God's judicial machinery. It is no surprise to find, therefore, that he was a supporter of the Recordite campaigns in Parliament, and a close friend of such prophetic writers as the Irvingite George Mandeville, 3rd Duke of Manchester, and Robert Jocelyn, 6th Earl of Roden. It has already been suggested that Recordite evangelicalism is distinguishable from the moderate and respectable version by its rejection of a Newtonian or 'natural law' conception of providence. Its view was rather that God exercised a perpetual superintendence by means of special providences. The task of temporal governments was to imitate the divine, to exercise their own paternal superintendence in the light of these providences—to interpret them, and legislate accordingly. Croker meanwhile had no patience with the doctrine of special providence, even though it once seemed that his health might have been miraculously affected:[74] 'To look for *special providences* in such trivial matters, seems to us to mistake wholly any individual man's share in the general distribution of God's infinite but equal dispensations.'[75]

'Infinite but *equal*': this was what Sinclair could not be certain about. However, James Grant suggests that his prayers were finally answered, and that he too came at last to believe in permanent laws of natural justice, and in the 'equality' of God's dispensations. This may explain why he switched during the 1840s to a more robust, *laissez-faire* approach to poverty. In his *Observations on the New Scottish Poor Law* (1849), Sinclair regretted having supported the extension of the Poor Law to Scotland, 'unmindful of the solemn warnings, inculcated . . . by . . . Dr. Chalmers, who clearly foresaw and emphatically predicted the ruinous consequences which the Poor Law would necessarily produce'.[76] Now he accepted that compulsory assessments were destroying all industry, all prudence, temperance, contentment, gratitude, veracity, and natural affection in the workers, as well as all benevolence in the rich.

[74] Myron F. Brightfield, *John Wilson Croker* (1940), 116.

[75] [J. W. Croker], 'Life of Wilberforce', *Quarterly Review*, 62 (1838), 247.

[76] George Sinclair, *Observations on the New Scottish Poor Law* (Edinburgh, 1849), 17–26, 42–9, 79.

Sinclair's paternalism, however short-lived, is important because it reminds us that there was this alternative aspect of evangelicalism. Indeed, the reputations of Lord Shaftesbury, Henry Drummond, Richard Oastler, Thomas Sadler, William Marsh, and Parson Bull of Byerly are such that some historians have equated the term 'evangelicalism' with humanitarian paternalism. Theirs was certainly a thoroughgoing rejection of political economy and liberal individualism. In 1824 Drummond called for an extension of England's relatively generous poor relief policies to Ireland, as '*the* cure' for her problems, and he hated the harsh New Poor Law of 1834.[77] Sadler denounced in turn the law of population, the New Poor Law, usury, Free Trade, and competition. The 'passion for cheapness' only benefited men with fixed incomes, and Bullionism merely enabled rich capitalists to keep down aspiring members of the lower middle classes by restricting paper credit. Sadler's biographer and *alter ego*, the paternalist Robert Benton Seeley, was if anything even more outspoken. The 'preventive check' was 'a direct inspiration of the Father of lies—of him whose grand occupation and delight it is, to render earth a foretaste of Hell'.[78] Seeley preferred the political economy of the Chinese, based as it was on the desirability of human multiplication. Seeley and Sadler did not think it was necessary to encourage working-class abstinence, but even if it was, it could only be 'supplied by hope, and inculcated by kindness'. If labourers were forced into despair, on the other hand, they would become ever more reckless. 'In short, deal paternally with your people, and they will repay your care. Feel for them; supply those wants which they cannot supply for themselves; guard them from the oppression of those who would "make haste to be rich".'[79]

Shaftesbury, Marsh, Sadler, and Seeley were, like Sinclair, all associated with the pentecostal wing of evangelicalism, which may help to explain their social attitudes. Shaftesbury was a fervent pre-millenarian, obsessed with prophecy and with the imminence of the Second Advent, even though he sometimes found the language of the *Record* too extreme.[80] Marsh

---

[77] Drummond to Peel, 17 Dec. 1824, Peel Papers, BL Add. MS 40371, fo. 159; Drummond to Place, 30 Dec. 1836, Supplementary Place Papers, BL Add. MS 37949, fo. 307.

[78] *Memoirs of the Life and Writings of Michael Thomas Sadler* [by Robert Benton Seeley] (1842), 610 n. See also J. C. Gill, *The Ten Hours Parson: Christian Social Action in the Eighteen-Thirties* (1959), 131–2, 178–93; J. C. Gill, *Parson Bull of Byerly* (1963), 62–77.

[79] [Seeley], *Memoirs of Michael Thomas Sadler*, p. 621.

[80] Geoffrey B. A. M. Finlayson, *The Seventh Earl of Shaftesbury 1801–1885* (1981), 102–5, 160–1. Soloway, *Prelates and People*, pp. 34, 137, confuses James Bicheno with his pre-millenarian father. This is important, for the son's *An Inquiry into the Nature of Benevolence chiefly with a View to elucidate the Principles of the Poor Laws, and to show their Immoral Tendency* (1817) is a robustly *laissez-faire* tract, and not the type of social theory to be expected of a pre-millennialist.

was a pre-millennialist and supporter of Shaftesbury, anxious that the weary and heavy-laden should be refreshed with material charity.[81] Sadler collaborated with Recordite MPs during his years in Parliament (1829–32), while Seeley wrote regularly for the *Record* and was a prominent pre-millenarian prophet, obsessed with the imminence of divine vengeance. Pauperism was God's 'scourge that our own hands are twisting, for the purposes of severe chastisement'. 'The season of sunshine and of calm is too palpably past: the rain is about to descend; the floods to come, and the winds to blow.'[82] He held the greatest contempt for Chalmers, while Chalmers in turn attacked Seeley with uncharacteristic bitterness: 'They who would divorce Theology from Science'—whether political economy, geology, or whatever—'are, in effect, . . . the enemies of both.'[83] Chalmers's Christian economics was scientific, based on a theory of constant law in the universe, and therefore excluded the interventionist God of the paternalists.

The career of Edward Bickersteth also illustrates the links between pre-millennialism and paternalism. Zealous secretary of the Church Missionary Society (1815–31), he was brought up as a moderate, and greatly distrusted all species of prophesying and speaking in tongues. A turning-point came, however, in 1833 when he suddenly realized the need for 'the personal coming of Christ *before* the Millennium',[84] while at the same time he became a keen supporter of Shaftesbury's political campaigns. There was also the lawyer Samuel Richard Bosanquet (1800–82), who, despite his support for Chalmers's St John's scheme and hostility to official Poor Laws, peddled a paternalism of the most extreme, even *Blanquist* kind. In his view the poor were not poor through any fault of their own,[85] but were victims of the ruling liberal philosophy. Epistemologically he attacked the Aristotelianism prevalent among Christians, and like Irving tried to show that assurance of faith could be real. 'By study and experience in heavenly things, we can possibly attain to a kind of acute and quickened moral sense, by which we shall be enabled to feel and verify this compatibility [of free will and grace], after it has been revealed to us, though not entirely to reason upon it and explain it.'[86] Characteristically,

---

[81] *The Life of the Rev. William Marsh*, by his daughter (1867), 259, 285.

[82] [R. B. Seeley], *The Perils of the Nation: An Appeal to the Legislature, the Clergy, and the Higher and Middle Classes* (1843), 21, 144–8, 399.

[83] [Chalmers], 'Political economy of the Bible', *North British Review*, 2 (1844–5), 3.

[84] *Memoir of Edward Bickersteth*, by T. R. Birks (3rd edn, 1852), ii. 42–68.

[85] S. R. Bosanquet, *The Rights of the Poor and Christian Almsgiving Vindicated: Or the State and Character of the Poor, and the Conduct and Duties of the Rich, Exhibited and Illustrated* (1841), 205–90 and *passim*; S. R. Bosanquet, *A Letter to Lord John Russell on the Safety of the Nation* (1848), 3–33.

[86] S. R. Bosanquet, *A New System of Logic, and Developement* [sic] *of the Principles of Truth and Reasoning: Applicable to Moral Subjects and the Conduct of Human Life* (1839), 196 and *passim*.

Bosanquet was convinced that he was living amid the 'last times' of national degeneracy and apostasy. His *Principia* of 1843 is full of highly charged admonitions about 'spiritual incest', 'the image of the beast','the noisome and grievous sore'. All Britain's current ills—romanticism, political economy, commercial epicureanism, mechanicism, fictitious capitalism, infidelity, pauperism, and revolution—had their origin in the passion for 'liberty', for 'liberty is sin'.[87] Instead he placed his hope in *The Successive Visions of the Cherubim Distinguished and Newly Interpreted, showing the Progressive Revelation through Them of the Incarnation and of the Gospel of Redemption and Sanctification* (1871).

Yet another exemplar of this tradition was the novelist Charlotte Elizabeth Tonna. Her stories of urban despair and degradation in the 1830s and 1840s were, as she intended, powerful propaganda for the Ten Hours Movement. Her pre-millenarian views, meanwhile, are paraded in a tract of 1842 on *Principalities and Powers*, published by Seeley and Burnside and with a foreword by Bickersteth. The volume is devoted to the activities of Satan, with 'his daring, cunning, and cruelty', and of the angels whose task it is to minister to earth during these last days. It concludes with the promise that the Second Coming is imminent: 'The period that remains is but as an hour', and then after a brief reign of terror 'shall the night-watch of the Church give place to the glories of a day that knows no going down of the sun'.[88]

Richard Oastler does not fit the present argument so well, since there is no evidence of pre-millennialism in his religious attitudes. There is not much evidence of religiosity at all, in fact, and it may be that the evangelical appellation has stuck to him—illogically—as a consequence of his paternalist activities. 'The Bible is put out, and Miss Martineau is come in', was how he welcomed the New Poor Law. A 'Demon called *Liberalism*' was abroad in the land—the 'March of Intellect, Political Economy, Free Trade, Liberal Principles', all were 'destroying the peace of the cottage and the happiness of the palace'. More vividly than anyone else he denounced the mechanistic, self-acting, atomistic philosophy of his day, which was divorcing the profit motive from the spiritual parts of human nature, and destroying the older view that men are all members of one another in an organic social harmony.[89]

---

[87] S. R. Bosanquet, *Principia: A Series of Essays on the Principles of Evil Manifesting Themselves in these Last Times in Religion, Philosophy, and Politics* (1843), 166–75 and *passim*.

[88] Charlotte Elizabeth [Tonna], *Principalities and Powers in Heavenly Places* (1842), 320–1.

[89] Driver, *Tory Radical*, pp. 293–7, 430–4. For Recordite objections to Free Trade long after the policy had become heavily entrenched in the public mind, see *The Record*, 23 July 1855, p. 2, cited in Norris Pope, *Dickens and Charity* (1978), 55–6.

There is, then, to recap, a distinction to be made between moderate or 'Clapham' evangelicalism on the one hand, and the more extreme or Recordite variety on the other. In the 1830s the latter made much the more noise and may even have dominated the movement, though they had little sway in the highest circles of government. Until then, however, it was the moderates who held the initiative, as well as exercising considerable influence in society at large. Spiritually individualistic, and lacking the Recordites' cult of personality and leadership, they preferred to leave a wise and predictable ('legible') providence to its own devices, rather than trying to intercede with God and influence his operations. Evangelical politics are discussed more fully below,[90] but it can be said here that the moderates, unlike Sadler and Oastler, favoured Free Trade and *laissez-faire* in the conduct of temporal affairs. They supported slave emancipation because slavery was obviously incompatible with free will individualism, but were notoriously much less concerned about wage slavery and the other social evils of their own land. The one thing needful was, they thought, the redemption of individual sinners, whether paupers, criminals, alcoholics, or money-crazed capitalists. The way to achieve it was by moral suasion and the offer of a hopeful Gospel, within a context of spiritual terror; the way to lose it was by tender-hearted relief of the consequences of sin, such as Oastler and Sadler were advocating. As Sumner put it, Christ's benevolence had been directed towards 'the soul rather than the body; the concerns of another world, and not the present'.[91]

Evangelicals as Individualists: the SBCP

The many reports of the Society for Bettering the Condition of the Poor, founded by Thomas Bernard, William Wilberforce, and Bishop Barrington of Durham in 1798, are probably the best source for the study of moderate evangelical attitudes in this matter. It is evident that the passionate moral paternalism is not matched by a material paternalism, that there was little desire for the *practical* relief of poverty. From the beginning, the SBCP emphasized the need to suppress vice and encourage industry, œconomy, frugality, and self-discipline.[92] It was anxious to set the poor up in cottages, but chary of bestowing cash. Moral and religious education was 'the true *medicine of the soul*',[93] and material charity should be confined

---

[90] See below, pp. 205–15.

[91] J. B. Sumner, *The Evidence of Christianity, derived from its Nature and Reception* (1824), 234–5.

[92] For an account of its work see Poynter, *Society and Pauperism*, pp. 91–8.

[93] T. Bernard, *19th Report of the Society for Bettering the Condition and Increasing the Comforts of the Poor* (1803), 31–2, quoted in *Christian Observer*, 2 (1803), 178–80.

to providing symbolic marks of self-respect, such as—since fustian maketh man—decent clothes. Bernard's open letter to the Bishop of Durham, the Society's President, emphatically disapproved of the practice, recently adopted in 'Speenhamland' parishes, of making up family earnings to a certain sum in proportion to the number of mouths to be fed. The ill consequences of charity mattered far more than the good motives which inspired it.

The Poor Laws of England have held out a false and deceitful encouragement to population. They promise that unqualified support, that unrestricted maintenance, to the cottager's family, which it is not *possible* for them to supply; thereby inducing the young labourer to marry, before he has made any provision for the married state; and, in consequence, extinguishing all prospective prudence, and all consideration for the future. . . . *Whatever encourages and promotes habits of* INDUSTRY, PRUDENCE, FORESIGHT, VIRTUE, *and* CLEANLINESS *among the poor, is beneficial to them and to the country; whatever removes, or diminishes, the incitement to any of these qualities, is detrimental to the* STATE, *and pernicious to the* INDIVIDUAL. This is the POLAR STAR of our benevolent affections; directing them to their true end.[94]

Long before Sumner and Chalmers, Bernard pointed out that although Christ had freely instructed and healed, 'we read of no extraordinary, or gratuitous, supply of food; except in the wilderness, where there were no ordinary means by human industry'. And like them he believed that, though spiritual succour should be offered to everyone, financial relief ought to be conditional on the recipient having already shown signs of moral regeneration.[95]

Such free will individualism, which was entirely opposed to Sadler's environmentalism, was the hallmark of public evangelicalism. It is therefore misleading to claim, as Cowherd does in his valuable study, that there was ever a basic conflict between 'the sentimental benevolence of the Evangelical humanitarians' and the callous brutality of 'natural law reformers'. The passage in Bernard's *Letter to the Bishop of Durham*, which Cowherd cites on three occasions, simply does not substantiate the view that Bernard was anti-Malthusian. Nor were any of the 'humanitarian' reformers identified by Cowherd—Pitt, Gilbert, and George Rose— remotely evangelical; the latter even opposed the Anti-Slavery campaign.[96]

[94] Bernard, Introductory letter to *The Reports of the S.B.C.P.*, 3 (1802), 10–11, 20–1.

[95] Ibid., p. 11 n. See also John Venn's report for the SBCP at Clapham, cited in Michael Hennell, *John Venn and the Clapham Sect* (1958), 144–5; Soloway, *Prelates and People*, p. 79.

[96] Raymond G. Cowherd, *Political Economists and the English Poor Laws: A Historical Study of the Influence of Classical Economics on the Formation of Social Welfare Policy* (Athens, Ohio, 1977), 15–16, 22, 31, 45, and *passim*. T. Bernard, *A Letter to the Bishop of Durham on the Measures now under the consideration of Parliament for Promoting and Encouraging Industry, and for the Relief and Regulation of the Poor* (1807), 60–2.

Nor is it the case that the *Christian Observer* at first opposed Malthus's law of population, then accepted it in 1807 (while holding out against its implications for the Poor Laws), and finally embraced it zealously around 1812.[97] Far from succumbing gradually to natural law theory in this way, most evangelicals had been immersed in it all along.

'The Greatest of these is Charity': Evangelical Philanthropy

'The poor ye will have with ye always.' It was of course a commonplace among educated people that the labouring classes 'must be kept poor, or they will never be industrious'.[98] Some moralists added tautology to fatalism: 'The poor must always undergo a certain degree of privation, or they would not be poor.'[99] It seemed clear from Job that high Heaven itself was ranged into a hierarchy of ranks, orders, and dignitaries. It also seemed to many that, even if poverty was deemed to be an evil, 'the wide prevalence of evil in the world' was 'proof that God cannot expect us to harass ourselves incessantly in resisting it. He doubtless permits it, as affording an arena for our energies. . . . But it could never be meant that our own enjoyment is to be nullified by it. . . . Our Saviour himself was not always teaching or relieving distress.'[1] Anyway, it was mistaken to suppose that the poor were any less happy than the rich, since 'that elastic adaptation of the mind to its permanent situation, which we call the power of habit, equalizes the apparent inequalities of fortune; and blunts the edge of imagined hardships'. Men in different stations have different 'dispositions and tastes', and those who bemoan the fate of the

---

[97] Cowherd, *Political Economists and Poor Laws*, p. 38. The first three volumes of the *Christian Observer* (1802–4) make no mention of Malthus, population, or Poor Laws. The fourth (1805), pp. 539–41, includes a letter to the editor attacking the utilitarian or 'expediency' morals of Malthus and Paley (which Malthus answered in his third edition of 1806 — James, *Population Malthus*, pp. 119–20), but praising the substantive message of the *Essay on Population*. A review article in the sixth vol. (1807), pp. 450–66, opposed the Poor Laws in principle, though it was cautious about immediate abolition, as was Malthus himself. This article also asserted that the law of population had been sent by 'our Maker to try us'. The article may have been written by the editor, Zachary Macaulay; Wilberforce supposed that it was Bowdler's, and that it was an 'excellent critique'. *Life of Wilberforce*, iii. 350. The language of later volumes of the *Christian Observer* does not significantly differ from this, though it is true, as Cowherd points out, that evangelical opposition to the Poor Laws, like secular opposition, increased considerably after 1816.

[98] [A. Young], *The Farmer's Tour through the East of England* (1771), iv. 361.

[99] John Weyland, jun., *Observations on Mr. Whitbread's Poor Bill and on the Population of England* (1807), 62.

[1] Copleston to Whately, 24 Oct. 1824, *Memoir of Edward Copleston, Bishop of Llandaff: With Selections from his Diary and Correspondence*, by W. J. Copleston (1851), 99–100.

poor are mostly persons who are not poor and imagine that it must be awful to be so.[2]

And yet such moralists also thought that the rich had a duty to give money, as well as other things, to the poor. 'Save all you can, but lest frugality become avarice, give all you can', was potent advice derived from Wesley. The society which deprecated official poor relief on anything more than the scale of a safety net was also a society which indulged in an enormous amount of private charity. Moreover, as David Owen observed, 'philanthropy, like Victorian society as a whole, became tinctured with the evangelical spirit'.[3] Bernard, Sumner, and Chalmers certainly believed in the obligation of the rich to give to the poor privately, even though they inveighed against official relief. Whately gave away about £8,000 during 1846-9, even while he was denouncing outdoor relief and the extension of the Poor Laws to famine-smitten Ireland.[4] Wilberforce regularly alienated one-quarter of his income as a bachelor, while Thornton continued even after marriage to give away one-third. Sumner, Blomfield, and Ricardo were all 'generous' individuals in this sense, and Sumner (it should be said) was an effective and caring bishop. What evangelicals insisted on was that each act of charity, besides discriminating between deserving and undeserving recipients—which Poor Law bureaucracies might not do properly—must be heartfelt, 'spontaneous and individual' on the part of the giver,[5] must be in short a genuinely 'free-will offering'.[6] State systems of relief, or any form of charitable organization, merely transformed benevolence from a thing of loving 'gratulation' into a complex tissue of legal rights between rich and poor. 'All the tenderness of charity on the one hand, and all its delicacy on the other, have been put to flight, by this metamorphosis of a matter of love, into a matter of angry litigation.'[7] Poor Laws made recipients resentful and dependent,

---

[2] Sumner, *Treatise on the Records of Creation*, ii. 267, quoted approvingly by William Otter, *A Sermon upon the Influence of the Clergy in Improving the Condition of the Poor* (Shrewsbury, 1818), 42-3 n.

[3] Owen, *English Philanthropy*, p. 95. On some shortcomings in this excellent account see Brian Harrison, 'Philanthropy and the Victorians', *Victorian Studies*, 9 (1965-6), 353-74; reprinted in B. Harrison, *Peaceable Kingdom: Stability and Change in Modern Britain* (Oxford, 1982), 217-59. For an early but influential discussion of these themes see Reinhard Bendix, *Work and Authority in Industry: Ideologies of Management in the Course of Industrialization* (New York and London, 1956), 60-116. On the institutional interstices of evangelical philanthropy see Ford K. Brown, *Fathers of the Victorians: The Age of Wilberforce* (Cambridge, 1961), esp. 317-60; Martin, *Evangelicals United*, *passim*.

[4] Soloway, *Prelates and People*, p. 163.

[5] Chalmers to Malthus, 12 Dec. 1821, National Library of Scotland MS 3112, fos. 228-9.

[6] Chalmers, *On the Power Wisdom and Goodness of God*, ii. 25 [*Works*, ii. 129]. In the first half of the nineteenth century, that is before about 1856, 'spontaneous' meant 'internalized' rather than 'effortless'. I am grateful to Mr Geoffrey Hill for this point.

[7] Chalmers, *On Political Economy*, pp. 403-4 [*Works*, xix. 405].

discouraged self-help and 'mutuality' among them, and rendered the act of charity itself morally neutral. Compulsion was the last thing God had ordained in the matter. Sinclair pointed out that, in recommending charity to the Corinthians, Paul had added, ' "I speak not by *commandment*" (2 Corinthians 8), thus explicitly *disclaiming* compulsion'.[8] Employment and bounty must be provided for the poor but *voluntarily*, 'since it is upon the single circumstance of their being voluntary, that God has made to depend the exercise of kindness and benevolence by the one class, and of dependence and gratitude by the other; by which feelings, and by which feelings alone, the necessary union between the two grand divisions of the community is formed and cemented'.[9] According to Bernard, God had deliberately clouded his instructions in the matter of charity, so that man's faculties might be morally exercised in elucidating them. 'If, indeed, this science were *easily* to be acquired, and the bearings, the limits, and the boundaries *precisely and correctly* ascertained, one of the most potent incentives to benevolent researches would cease; the kind and amiable affections of the heart might lose their influence; and every sentiment congenial with charity, might stagnate in torpid inactivity.'[10] 'Our own souls would famish under this vicarious sort of piety', echoed another who despised the mid-century passion for '*organized* benevolence, for "Institutions" '.[11]

It seems obvious that, in discussing charity in these terms, such writers were thinking at least as much about the spiritual needs of the giver as about the material needs of the poor. This is where evangelical attitudes can be distinguished from the secular approach of, say, F. M. Eden and Whately, and also from the more generous concern of Archdeacon Paley. The trouble was that charity might bless the giver but damn the recipient. God had given rich people the power to give or to withhold, and the obligation was to God, not to the potential beneficiaries.[12] 'Our object is not to annihilate charity', wrote Sumner, 'but to render it profitable both to the giver and receiver.' Chalmers frequently stressed the 'superior blessedness of the giver to that of the receiver'.[13] It was commonly assumed that the rich were in greater spiritual danger than the poor, more

---

[8] Sinclair, *Observations on the New Scottish Poor Law*, p. 39. Bentham depicted Paul as Anti-Christ in *Not Paul, but Jesus*, by 'Gemaliel Smith' (1823), 371–3.

[9] Stevens, *Poor Laws an Interference with Divine Laws*, p. 24.

[10] T. Bernard, *Report of S.B.C.P.*, 3 (1802), 9.

[11] Revd H. A. Boardman, *The Bible in the Counting-House: a Course of Lectures to Merchants* (1854), 268–9.

[12] Bicheno, *Inquiry into the Nature of Benevolence*, p. 70; on Bicheno see Poynter, *Society and Pauperism*, pp. 231–2.

[13] [J. B. Sumner], 'Poor-Laws', *Supplement to the Fourth, Fifth, and Sixth Editions of the Encyclopaedia Britannica* (Edinburgh, 1824), vi. 306; see Chalmers's sermon of 1815 in *Works*, xi. 399–435; Jerram, *Memoirs of Charles Jerram*, p. 180.

subject to temptations and so more liable to damnation. Responsible use of one's wealth through philanthropic disbursements might just appease God's wrath, but only if done *personally* and in a *spontaneous* frame of mind. It was not enough to contribute a proportion of one's income unthinkingly, or to make subscriptions to charitable societies. Routine good works could never guarantee salvation, since they did not betoken a right state of heart and mind. It was thought to be too common for men to give money to Christ but no longer 'their *personal* exertion'.[14] 'God wants not money alone — the silver and the gold are His; but He wants your heart, your feelings, your time, your anxiety. . . . A Christian may as well give over his faith into the hands of a public body . . . as cast his charity over to a public body.'[15] The devout Robert Hamilton took disorganized spontaneity to extremes, being 'in his charities, . . . solicitous that his left hand should not know what his right hand did'.[16] Bernard was adamant that his hope of mercy depended on his assisting the poor to the utmost of his power. 'If we provide for the sick and needy', wrote an evangelical-turned-Tractarian, Francis Paget, 'we shall ourselves be delivered in the day of trouble'. 'Without the poor', echoed another evangelical, Henry Melvill, the wealthy would find it 'hard to make progress in genuine piety'. James Sweet thought that the only *real*, which was to say *spiritual*, advantage possessed by the rich was that they had the wherewithal to be charitable.[17] Their dependence, commented another evangelical, the poetaster Robert Montgomery, was the greatest of the 'benefits conferred by the poor upon the rich': 'the sublime cause of Philanthropy is greatly strengthened by the poor'.[18] Indeed, one argument *against* giving permanent endowments to the poor was that it was better to 'let the benevolence of the present age relieve the distress of the present age'.[19] Generations must make sacrifices as well as individuals.

Note how different all this was from the usual eighteenth-century view of charity, as expounded by Paley. In his view, the duty of the rich was

---

[14] [Anon.], 'The gold and the silver are the Lord's', *The Evangelical Magazine and Missionary Chronicle*, NS, 33 (1855), 580–1.

[15] E. Irving, 'True charity', *Miscellanies from the Collected Writings of Edward Irving*, p. 372.

[16] Robert Hamilton, *The Progress of Society* (1830), p. xviii.

[17] Francis E. Paget, *The Warden of Berkingholt: or, Rich and Poor* (1843), 64; Revd Henry Melvill, 'The least of service to the greatest', *Sermons, Preached on Public Occasions* (1846), 47–8; Revd J. B. Sweet, 'The worth and proper use of wealth', *Sermons for Sundays, Festivals, and Fasts, and other Liturgical Occasions*, ed. Revd Alexander Watson (1845–7), second series, iii. 356–8, quoted in Roberts, *Paternalism in Early Victorian England*, pp. 152–3.

[18] Revd Robert Montgomery, *Outlines of Discourses, expanded in Short Expositions of Religious and Moral Truths* (1850), 199–210.

[19] [J. W. Gilbart], *The Moral and Religious Duties of Public Companies* (1846), 44 n.

primarily to the poor and not to God. He agreed that riches and poverty
were 'alike trials; have both their duties and temptations', but he did not
consider the former to be a more dangerous spiritual state. Dwelling
characteristically on rewards rather than punishments, he considered that
the right use of greater talents (or trust) would be more highly rewarded
than the right use of lesser ones.[20] Paley also considered that the poor
had a *claim* to charity, 'founded in the law of nature' and deriving from
the original holding of property. The rich should be 'charitable upon a
plan' rather than spontaneously, and therefore he preferred efficient public
charities to private activity. He acknowledged the dangers of boastful
ostentation inherent in organized philanthropy, and admitted that Christ
had once enjoined secrecy in alms-giving, but he also countered this central
plank of evangelical benevolence with the text, 'Let your light so shine
before men, that they may see your good works', and follow your
example.[21] At all events, charity meant giving money and other material
things, not merely love, advice, or goodness of heart.

Paley's views were of course unfashionable during the Age of Atonement,
but later in the century, as works came to be emphasized above piety,
Christians turned back to the regulation of benevolence. Thus the Charity
Organisation Society, while it followed Chalmers on the need to be discrim-
inate in the matter of who should receive relief, altogether abandoned
his injunction to leave *giving* to the individual. It was in this mid-Victorian
climate that philanthropy came to be regarded as a badge of social esteem,
and petty notables clamoured to be 'on the notepaper' of as many
charitable institutions as possible. With ostentation went a spurious
attempt at scientific precision. A collection of prize essays sponsored by
the Evangelical Alliance in 1853 toyed with the question of precisely *how
much* a man was required to give by divine law: 'The Scripture Rule of
Religious Contribution; or in what proportion should a believer in
Revelation dedicate his property to the Cause of God'; 'An essay on the
right appropriation of the profits of business, salaries, wages, and income
in general'.[22] Precise rules should be laid down and matters no longer
'left to the decision of the selfish'. Such views would have scandalized
moralists in the earlier nineteenth century, when the application of any
precise 'measure of Christian liberality' was thought to undermine the
spontaneity — and anxiety — with which the performance of good works

[20] Paley, *Natural Theology*, pp. 567–8 [(15th edn, 1815), pp. 531–2].
[21] Paley, *Principles of Moral and Political Philosophy*, pp. 202–14 [Bk. III, Pt. II,
ch. 5]. Paley considererd that charitable bequests beyond the 'normal' amount should be
given secretly in order to avoid boasting, but that up to that amount monies should
be given openly.
[22] *Gold and the Gospel: The Ulster Prize Essays on the Scriptural Duty of Giving in
Proportion to Means and Income* (1853), p. ix and *passim*.

needed to be accompanied if it was to go down as a mark of spiritual grace. In mid-century, James William Gilbart averred that one was more likely to give cheerfully if one gave a predetermined amount, rather than when each act of charity presented 'a conflict between the suggestions of liberality and those of selfishness'.[23] He did not see that it was precisely this conflict, and the victory to which it could lead, that made evangelicals most truly cheerful. This was why they thought that the rich should give money away during their own lifetimes, under the sole dictate of conscience, and not vicariously in wills.[24]

So giving by command, because one had to or thought that one had to, reduced philanthropy to an unthinking, conventional routine. Thus Sumner took his 'argument for Christian charity . . . from the disinterested and self-denying example of Christ himself, and not from the positive commands of his religion'.[25] According to an evangelical Fellow of All Souls, the poor toiled with their limbs, but the rich toiled 'by the still more painful exercise of the mind, and straining of the spirit',[26] and the greatest strain of all lay in deciding how unselfish to be with one's wealth. The 'quality' of Walter Powell's beneficence 'was *not strained*', and yet there was no question of letting charity drop like gentle rain from heaven. True benevolence was '*eminent*, and conspicuous, not oozing in drops, but falling in showers, or flowing in streams'.[27] Unstrenuous or frivolous giving, on the other hand, ate 'out the very bowels of true charity'.[28] As Irving said, 'He wants your heart, your feelings, your time, your anxiety.' Men must half not wish to give, but then must do so joyously, for charity must be '*cheerfully* dispensed' as well as 'prompt, *spontaneous*, and free'. It must hurt, and the hurt must be enjoyable. It must be prompt and unplanned, but also '*steady* and uniform, not arbitrary, capricious, and eccentric'. It must be done as a matter of '*principle*, and not merely of feeling, an obligation of conscience, and not only an excitement of the passions'. It must be '*self-denying* and laborious . . . not an effeminate compassion', but 'clothed in *humility*' and modelled 'in the love of God'.[29] In short, like evangelical faith itself it must be both 'spontaneous' *and* 'systematic', as the merchant Walter Powell's allegedly was: 'With

[23] [Gilbart], *Moral and Religious Duties of Public Companies*, p. 43.

[24] For Gladstone's agreement on this point, see Philip Magnus, *Gladstone: A Biography* (1954), 258.

[25] Sumner, *Evidence of Christianity*, p. 234.

[26] Thoms Garnier, *Plain Remarks upon the New Poor Law Amendment Act, more particularly addressed to the Labouring Classes* (Winchester, 1835), 25–6.

[27] John Angell James, *Christian Philanthropy: as exemplified in the Life and Character of the Late Joseph Sturge* (1859), 14.

[28] E. B. Pusey, *Chastisements Neglected Forerunners of Greater: A Sermon, preached on the Day appointed for a General Fast and Humiliation* (1847), 24.

[29] James, *Christian Philanthropy*, p. 15.

him, giving was not only a principle, but also a pleasure and a passion. He gave to indulge the godlike propensity and *penchant* of his renewed nature. . . . It was, in fact, the only luxury in which he indulged. He was "given to" giving.' Generosity so mastered Powell, apparently, that he had to fight to exercise self-control.[30]

Evidently, charity was less a social act than a vehicle for a frame of mind. The evangelical banker John Thornton 'devoted his time and thoughts' to it. 'To form, and execute plans of usefulness; to superintend, arrange, and improve upon those plans; . . . to form acquaintance, and collect intelligence for this purpose; to select proper agents, and to carry on correspondence . . . were the hourly occupations of his life.'[31] According to his panegyrist Edwin Hodder, Samuel Morley gave '*himself* with his money'.[32] You should not only give to, but also 'humble yourself to those of poor estate', admonished Irving.[33] It was essential to have personal contact with them, and not merely for the purpose of picking out which ones were deserving of help. Business was commonly regarded as a 'hardening influence', since the selfishness and worldliness which were inseparable from it formed a protective shell of indifference, 'through which the whispers of light celestial voices and the touches of light celestial fingers can find no way'. 'Tell me, busy men, is the ear as keen as it once was to the appeals of misery?'[34] Owen notes that nineteenth-century philanthropists were frequently single, or widowed, or childless, and suggests that sometimes 'charitable interests took the place of a family'.[35] A remark of Thomas Arnold's is relevant here. He supposed that evangelicals underrated the importance of charity because they read St Paul more than any other part of the Bible, and because St Paul had been writing for a society which had not suffered from the problems of population and poverty.[36] Nevertheless, Arnold mediated evangelical attitudes into that ethos of public school manliness which he did so much to disseminate. Here he is congratulating his nephew on the latter's forthcoming marriage, and remarking on the hardening tendencies of bachelor life in the city:

The most certain softeners of a man's moral skin, and sweeteners of his blood, are, I am sure, domestic intercourse in a happy marriage, and intercourse with

---

[30] Gregory, *The Thorough Business Man: Memoirs of Walter Powell*, pp. 311–21.

[31] [Thomas Scott], *The Love of Christ the Source of Genuine Philanthropy: A Discourse on the Death of John Thornton* (1791), 7–8.

[32] *The Life of Samuel Morley*, by Edwin Hodder (1887), 291–2. On Morley's charitable activities see Owen, *English Philanthropy*, pp. 401–8.

[33] E. Irving, 'True charity', *Miscellanies*, p. 370.

[34] Revd J. Baldwin Brown, quoted in Hodder, *Life of Samuel Morley*, pp. 286–7.

[35] Owen, *English Philanthropy*, p. 424.

[36] Arnold to Augustus Hare, 24 Dec. 1830, Stanley, *Life of Arnold*, i. 262 [(5th edn, 1845), i. 293–5].

the poor. It is very hard, I imagine, in our present state of society, to keep up intercourse with God without one or both of these aids to foster it.[37]

Soft skin and sweet blood: Arnold's metaphors are less corpuscular than the standard evangelical argot, but the sentiments are similar. Merely to be present in the cottages of the poor, to be in attendance at death-beds, to be kind to and popular among them, was to achieve a kind of grace.[38] Chalmers made the impact he did because he had actually done these things, and, as he never tired of saying, it was not enough to help the poor, one had to love them too.

And one cannot love on compulsion. Moralists deprecated official poor relief for the same reason that they thought it would be wrong to subject working-class marriages to a legal means test.[39] The point was made lucidly by Copleston, whose relations with evangelicalism have already been discussed.[40] At first sight, Copleston's views seem untypical. His *Letter to Peel on the pernicious effects of a variable standard of value* (1819) emphatically blamed post-war distress on fluctuations in the currency, not on the depravity of the poor themselves. It even defied political economy by calling on employers to raise wages artificially as a way of meeting this situation. Such paternalism was only superficial, however. His real message was that once monetary fluctuations had been prevented by the return to the Gold Standard—and it was the main burden of his pamphlet to recommend this—then moralists would once more be able to round on paupers and accuse them of depravity, and the iron law of wages could once more be allowed to operate. There was nothing soft-hearted in this: he preferred 'the wholesome terrors of a workhouse' to the 'false humanity' of legal assessments for relief.[41] Charity was a divine imperative, so it could not be a governmental one as well.

That what all individuals *ought to do*, it is the business of the laws to *make* them do, is a plausible position, and has actually been adopted by some of the ablest and most virtuous men. But nothing in reality is more fallacious—nothing less congruous with the nature of man, and with that state of discipline and trial

---

[37] Arnold to John Ward, 7 July 1832, ibid., i. 287–8 [i. 326–7].

[38] Chalmers, *Christian and Civic Economy*, i. 29–30 [*Works*, xiv. 49–50]. The General Society for Promoting District Visiting was founded in 1828, and by 1831 it employed 573 visitors making 165,000 calls.

[39] Bicheno, *Inquiry into the Nature of Benevolence*, p. 99: 'To produce any good, it must be a voluntary restraint enforced by self-government, and not a compulsory one by the law.'

[40] See above, pp. 29–30.

[41] [E. Copleston], *A Letter to Robert Peel, on the Pernicious Effects of a Variable Standard of Value, especially as it regards the Condition of the Lower Orders and the Poor Laws* (Oxford, 1819), 34.

which his present existence is clearly designed to be. . . . An action to be virtuous must be voluntary.[42]

'Clearly designed to be'; two years earlier Malthus had 'allowed' that the world was 'a state of discipline and trial'. This was the admission which enabled evangelicalism to encroach on the general thought of the day, and which marks Copleston's approach from that of the utilitarians. Though the latter accepted many of the evangelicals' policy prescriptions, and agreed on the best treatment for lunatics, criminals, and paupers (broadly, 'less eligibility'), they were more concerned with consequences than with motives, with behaviour than with belief, and so regarded a willingness to obey a law of charity as being as valuable ethically as an original disposition to be charitable. Such a view was anathema to Chalmers, however: 'the force of law and the freeness of love cannot amalgamate the one with the other. Like water and oil they are immiscible.'[43]

Of course, there were voices raised against this philosophy. A. C. Cheyne has presented the Scotsman Patrick Brewster as an evangelical antithesis of Chalmers. Convinced that the national calamities were caused by inequality of wealth and by corporate rather than individual sin, Brewster supported 'moral force' Chartism and compulsory poor relief. He joined with William Alison in attacking Malthus's 'infidel philosophy' and Chalmers's injunctions to 'give as little as possible' or 'nothing at all'. 'So devotedly self-denying are they, for the good of others,—so superhumanly kind to their neighbour,—that rather than hazard the increase of human suffering by feeding the hungry, they will peril their own immortality, by a wilful act of disobedience to God.'[44] Brewster's sarcasm would not have been lost on Harold Skimpole, who 'almost' felt that his benefactors should be grateful to him, for giving them 'the opportunity of enjoying the luxury of generosity' (*Bleak House*, ch. 6).

Charity in the Irish Famine

If anything, Chalmers's self-help philosophy hardened with age. In his last community experiment, the West Port scheme of 1844, he allowed even less *material* relief to be given to the poor than he had done at St John's.[45] However, he lived just long enough to witness the Irish potato failure, which struck in the autumn of 1845, and his response, elaborated in an

---

[42] [E. Copleston], *Second Letter to Peel on Pauperism and the Poor Laws*, pp. 17–18; Norman, *Church and Society in England*, pp. 62–4.

[43] Chalmers, *On the Power Wisdom and Goodness of God*, ii. 24 [*Works*, ii. 128].

[44] Patrick Brewster, *The Seven Chartist and Military Discourses* (Paisley, 1853), 97–101; A. C. Cheyne, *The Transforming of the Kirk: Victorian Scotland's Religious Revolution* (Edinburgh, 1982), 19–28.

[45] Brown, *Thomas Chalmers*, pp. 354–63.

article of 1847, is extremely interesting. He emphatically did not blame political economy for the mass starvation, nor did he relinquish the ideal of Free Trade. The Whig government guided by Sir Charles Trevelyan, the Assistant Secretary at the Treasury who was responsible for administering relief, had, he thought, responded with humanity and intelligence. Chalmers did, however, make two important concessions to the critics of political economy. In the first place, he admitted that Free Trade could only operate beneficially, so as to 'reveal the order of nature', where there was abundant competition and no possibility of monopoly or combination. Free Trade was therefore inapplicable in pre-capitalist Ireland, since there was simply not sufficient competition to ensure a providential rationing of food along the lines described by Adam Smith. In such circumstances it might be necessary to resort to relief committees, food depots, and requisitioning. The second concession was crucial. Chalmers drew a distinction between scarcities which were spread lightly over the entire nation, as in 1800–1, and famines which attacked just one part of a nation virulently, as in 1845–7. In the former case, the principles of Free Trade should not be violated, but in the latter 'a due liberality' was requisite from those parts of the country which were not suffering. In 1800–1 corn dealers and other middle-men had rightly been *left alone* as agents of 'a higher hand, of Him . . . who can make even the selfishness of individuals work out a country's salvation'.[46] But the 1845–7 famine was localized, since the majority of Englishmen were enjoying 'wonted jollity and abundance' and 'all sorts of luxurious and even riotous indulgence':

Providence equalized the visitation of about fifty years back; and the consequent equality of distribution which laid the necessity of spare living upon all, might be regarded as the effect at once of *a direct ordering from God*. Providence had laid upon us now, not a heavier visitation than then, but has laid the full weight of it on the distant extremities of our United Kingdom; and left the task of equalization—if there be enough of wisdom and mercy below for the accomplishment of the task—to the ordering of man.[47]

So although such things should normally be left to private charity, the present abnormal situation required that the state should supplement it by donations of money to enable those who were starving to buy meal. Chalmers had always supported direct taxation, if only as a gesture of conciliation by the upper classes, and he now hoped that the government would utilize taxation, rather than a public loan, for the purpose of transferring resources from one part of the nation to another.

[46] [T. Chalmers], 'Political economy of a famine', *North British Review*, 7 (1847), 252.
[47] Ibid., pp. 259–60 (italics added).

Stewart Brown regards this article as an eleventh-hour repudiation of all that Chalmers had said before. 'Chalmers's godly commonwealth ideal succumbed to the grim realities of the great famine of 1846–7, which both devastated the Celtic population and destroyed his confidence in the sufficiency of purely voluntary benevolence. . . . His social thought had finally run full circle. . . . He returned to many of his 1808 views' in favour of paternalism and Protection.[48] This diagnosis is misleading. Chalmers's only deviation from the principle of Free Trade, and his only criticism of Trevelyan, derived from a wish that the government would suspend distillation from grain—and this not so much because it used up potential foodstuff as because it was morally abominable 'that the Scotch might luxuriate in spirits, and the English in their potations of beer as usual', while Irishmen starved.[49] The article closes with a repetition of all Chalmers had ever said on the degrading effects of compulsory state relief, and a further attack on the recent decision to extend such relief to Ireland. Nevertheless, Stewart Brown might argue that Chalmers's call for state action in this crisis practically contradicted his usual *laissez-faire* approach, even if he clung to it in theory. But a careful examination of his phraseology will show that his response to the Famine was less of a departure from evangelical economics than might be supposed.

The important point was that the Famine was not 'a *direct* ordering from God', as those of 1795 and 1800–1 had been. Now in modern parlance the word 'direct', as applied to providence, seems to designate a 'special' or 'immediate' intervention by the Almighty in the affairs of his world. In the nineteenth century, however, 'direct' meant not 'immediate' but 'straight', 'undeviating', or 'without intervening agency', and was applied to the motions of planets. 'Direct actions' were those 'which took effect without intermediate instrumentality', and the term 'direct-acting' was applied to the new steam-engines and pumps of the 1840s. The popular evangelical preacher Hugh McNeile could define a 'direct tendency' as one which operated 'according to the known and ordinary course of events'.[50] So the term 'direct providence' implied a natural law, clockwork view of God's worldly government, and was the opposite of 'special providence'.

Clearly, Chalmers considered that the 1795 and 1800–1 scarcities were examples of natural law providence, and that the appropriate governmental response was *laissez-faire* so as to let that providence operate

---

[48] Brown, *Thomas Chalmers*, pp. 367–9.

[49] [Chalmers], 'Political economy of a famine', op. cit., p. 277.

[50] H. McNeile, 'The famine a rod of God; its provoking cause—its merciful design' (1847), *British Eloquence: Sacred Oratory*. First Series. Sermons by Eminent Living Divines of the Church of England (London and Glasgow, 1856), 87; *Oxford English Dictionary*.

without hitch. 1845–7 was different: the fact that famine was restricted to Ireland and parts of western Scotland was evidence that it fell outside the ordinary, mechanical, natural law course of providence. It must be a message, a warning, a 'special providence' which, as we saw when discussing Sinclair, called for an interventionist response from the government. Thus, in attacking the new Irish Poor Law, Chalmers asked,

Is such a season of perplexity and pressure, when extraordinary visitations should be met by means alike extraordinary—is this the time for building up another system for the ordinary relief of the poor? Better, we do think, that emergencies like the present were met by the operation of some such expedients as did not leave one trace of themselves upon the statute-book. . . . The method of relief for the present should have been made as peculiar as the emergency itself is peculiar.[51]

W. P. Alison, as we have seen, opposed Chalmers in almost every particular by this time. It is no surprise, therefore, to find him writing that the Irish Famine 'ought not to be regarded *merely* as a visitation of Providence, calling for temporary aid from the rest of the nation, but as an indication of a previously unsound condition of the population, . . . which demands permanent remedies'.[52]

Most Englishmen would have agreed that the Famine was not a case of peculiar providence but a mechanical application of cause and effect. Unlike Alison, they would have located the cause in the Irish themselves, in their sloth and fecklessness. Many saw it also as a punishment for Catholicism, and here a 'special' element might be acknowledged in respect of the Maynooth Grant of the year before. Others were not censorious of the Irish, but accepted that there was little anyone could do besides pray. Chalmers took a somewhat different line. He had always argued that visible nature was 'rigidly undeviating' and constant, but that God does respond to man's prayers at a higher, invisible level. Every now and again he also performs a miracle—that is to say, he alters the course of the lower, visible realm, that which is not responsive to prayer.[53] The Famine was clearly such an event, and so excessive prayerfulness seemed inappropriate. Accordingly, he derogated from his usual rule of

---

[51] [Chalmers], 'Political economy of a famine', op. cit., pp. 280, 284. An admirer of Chalmers believed that those who argued for non-interference in the present crisis, 'lest we should only aggravate the disease', must be persons who looked 'no higher than to human agencies and to second causes'. Revd T. Garnier, *A Sermon, in behalf of the Suffering Irish and Scotch* (Winchester, 1847), 18.

[52] William Pulteney Alison, *Observations on the Famine of 1846–7, in the Highlands of Scotland and in Ireland, as illustrating the Connection of the Principle of Population with the Management of the Poor* (Edinburgh and London, 1847), 9 (italics added).

[53] 'On the consistency between the efficacy of prayer—and the uniformity of nature', in Chalmers, *Works*, vii. 234–62.

laissez-faire by recommending measures of mitigation. And yet despite his compassion for the sufferings of the Irish, and refusal to regard them as self-inflicted, it is obvious that his main concern was with the *spiritual* significance of the event for the English ruling class with which, despite being a Scotsman, he identified. As with the case of charitable giving by the wealthy, it was those who were *not* suffering who were being put to the real trial. Several times in the article he implied that it was the stigma on England which most alarmed him about the Famine. Unless the British government acted swiftly, 'we shall have again and again to incur the misery and disgrace of those hideous starvations which have scandalized the world'.[54] Acts of national charity, of England towards Ireland, might have all the atoning, redemptive effects that private benevolence confers upon its practitioners.

Now is the time for Britain to step forward . . . to acquit herself generously, openly, freely, towards Ireland—and by her acts of princely but well-directed munificence to repair the accumulated wrongs of many generations. The chastisements of this dreary period have not been joyous but grievous; but thus might they be made to yield the peaceable fruits of righteousness to those who have been exercised thereby—

—meaning, of course, the rulers in England, not the starving in Ireland.[55] This is not an abandonment of the principle of voluntary benevolence in favour of state aid, as Brown avers, but a call for the British state to exercise, in an hour of special providence, a voluntary benevolence towards Ireland. Chalmers ended on a note of affirmation, one which reminds us again that it is better to give than to receive:

But with all the blunders of England's legislation, the heart of England is in its right place—bent with full desirousness on Ireland's large and lasting good. . . . With the guidance and guardianship of the Holy Providence above, a harvest of good will ensue from this great temporary evil; and Ireland, let us trust and pray, will emerge from her sore trial, on a bright and peaceful career to future generations.[56]

'What has [the responsibility of the rich] got to do with Free Trade?', asked Chalmers, and Oastler answered, 'Everything'. Oastler thought that the responsibility of the rich could not be exercised without help from the state, by means of social welfare reforms, whereas Chalmers believed that in normal circumstances state aid would undermine responsibility by coming between providence and the individual sinner.

In retrospect, however, it seems clear that the Irish Famine, like the return of cholera in 1848, played a part in the rejection of evangelical

---

54 [Chalmers], 'Political economy of a famine', op. cit., p. 275.
55 Ibid., p. 282.   56 Ibid., p. 289.

attitudes. Not surprisingly, it gave rise to a huge number of tracts and sermons, many of which expressed bewilderment at the recent dispensations of providence, as well as dissatisfaction with the accepted canons of *laissez-faire* social theory. 'O! tell me not of the demoralising effects of charity at a time when whole masses of my fellow-countrymen are melting away like snow before the breath of the advancing scourge! Insult not my understanding, my compassion, my Christianity, by attempting to argue me out of my benevolent intentions.'[57] As the day appointed for a General Fast (24 March 1847) approached, hundreds heralded the Famine '*as a visitation* — a chastisement for our national sins and crimes — for the grasping, gambling, monopolising, covetous spirit, which of late has engrossed the minds of all ranks and classes of men'.[58] But was it retribution on the Irish themselves? Few could be so sure of this as Sir Charles Trevelyan, a moderate evangelical with a Clapham background who regarded 'dependence on others' as 'a moral disease', and the Famine as 'the judgment of God on an indolent and unself-reliant people'. As God had 'sent the calamity to teach the Irish a lesson, that calamity must not be too much mitigated'.[59] However, the Tractarian Henry Phillpotts admitted that the sufferers were unlikely to have been more wicked than he himself had been, and suggested that 'one of the most important and most improving trials of our faith, is the *imperfect* state of retributive justice'.[60] Unfortunately, 'natural law' evangelicals needed to believe that retributions were perfectly just, but of course the justice might be hidden from men's eyes. Thus Gladstone saw Ireland, not as the *object*, but as the *minister* of God's retribution.[61] England must atone by relieving Ireland, or else expect 'a fearful retribution' on herself.[62] Unfortunately, the more money England disbursed, the less she seemed capable of the necessary self-abasement. Much of the money raised for relief came in ways associated with public amusements — charity-balls, parish dances, and fêtes. Instead of self-denial and humiliation, there was 'the bribe of a public ball! . . . this mockery of the name of charity . . . *charity* the handmaiden of dissipation. . . . To every thing there is a season . . . a time to mourn and a time to *dance*'.[63] 'HEAR the rod' cried a thousand

---

[57] Garnier, *Sermon on the Suffering Irish and Scotch*, p. 20.

[58] Revd Charles Vansittart, *A Sermon on Famine: the Expediency of a Public Fast, and the Duty of Personal Abstinence in the Present Time of Dearth* (1847), 9.

[59] Jenifer Hart, 'Sir Charles Trevelyan at the Treasury', *English Historical Review*, 75 (1960), 99.

[60] Henry Phillpotts, *A Sermon preached on the Day appointed for a General Fast, and Humiliation before God* (Exeter, 1847), 12.

[61] W. E. Gladstone to his wife, 12 Oct. 1845, *Correspondence on Church and Religion of William Ewart Gladstone*, ed. D. C. Lathbury (1910), ii. 266. See below, pp. 351–2.

[62] *The Witness*, 6 Mar. 1847.

[63] Phillpotts, *Sermon on the General Fast*, pp. 17–18.

preachers, words which express as well as any the principle of vicariousness which was so powerful during the Age of Atonement. 'Hear', not 'feel', for the purpose of suffering was often to disturb the consciences of those in comfortable earshot. But this doctrine itself began to be questioned after the Famine. Would a loving God scourge his people in quite so horrible a manner, or butcher Irishmen to atone for English guilt?

Evangelicals, like economists, believed in a 'hidden hand'; unlike economists, they believed that the 'hidden hand' held a rod. Moderate evangelicals were further assured that the rod was wielded justly, in response to human behaviour. The Irish Famine, among other things, forced them to rethink their views about the Almighty. In admitting that the Famine must be an example of special providence, Chalmers managed to sustain his social theories, but the admission itself helped to undermine confidence in providence theory generally. All this led to a mid-century re-evaluation of social policy, which is discussed in Chapters 7 and 8. But first we must consider how evangelicals tackled the problems posed by the political economists' theory of commerce.

4

Profit and Prophecy
Evangelical Attitudes to Business

Babylon the Great—the *commercial world* of selfish competition, *drunken with the blood* of God's people, *whose merchandise is the bodies and souls of men*—her doom is gone forth.

> Charles Kingsley, *Alton Locke* (1862), ii. 295

Gold undoubtedly approximates to the nature of a criterion; but to consider it, in a commercial country, as possessing any more sacred character than that of a commodity, is one of those inconceivable absurdities which may be classed with faith in rotten bones and transubstantiation.

> John Galt, *Diary Illustrative of the Times of George IV* (1838–9), iv. 294–6

On the Tendency of Capital to Procreate

It might be supposed that the well-to-do stressed the 'rigours of mercy' and the 'need to be cruel to be kind' simply in order to keep the poor in their place, but it can be said in extenuation that they often adopted a similar approach to their own position in the economy. In an age of enormous money-making and intense religiosity, the rich were sorely troubled by Christ's injunctions as to the 'spiritual superiority of the poor', his frequent allusion to 'the perils of wealth, and the difficulties it interposes in the way of salvation'.[1] Working-men might be animals, 'upon a level with the beasts that perish',[2] their mortal souls and temporal prospects alike threatened by the sin of copulation, but the upper classes felt themselves to be standing in far graver spiritual danger from a sin every bit as mortal—speculation. They would not end up on the parish, but there was a fiery workhouse in the sky, 'Hell's hot jurisdiction', awaiting the ungodly:

---

[1] J. H. Newman, 'The danger of riches', *Parochial Sermons* (1834–42), ii. 383–99; W. E. Gladstone, *Gleanings of Past Years, 1843–78* (1879), v. 119. See E. B. Pusey, *The Danger of Riches* (Oxford, 1850), 8–9: 'riches . . . are, in themselves contrary to the Cross of Christ'.

[2] Peter Gaskell, *The Manufacturing Population of England: Its Moral, Social, and Physical Conditions* (1833), 282.

The poor are not pious, and the rich are not pious, and God is lashing one with the other. The poor deserve to be scourged, and they are so—they are limited, stinted, pressed upon. The rich deserve to be scourged, and they are so—they are alarmed, uneasy, dissatisfied, tormented by ennui, and languor and mala conscientia.[3]

It was possible to argue along the lines of the old Puritan ethic, that successful labour in the sphere to which God had called one was pleasing in his sight, and the Parables of the Talents and of the Wise Steward were frequently appealed to.[4] However, a society so immersed in evangelical values derived little consolation from such pleadings. Success, pleasure, profit were all *felt* to be immoral and spiritually dangerous. 'Lay not your treasure on earth, where moth and rust doth corrupt, but lay up for yourself treasures in Heaven' (Matthew 6: 20–1).

So what about the profit motive, fundamental to the pleasure/pain calculus of political economy? '*Profit* is in mercantile dealings, what *gravitation* is in the system of the universe: and no problem is worth listening to, which supposes the absence of that universal principle.'[5] As we have seen, hedonistic views of human behaviour, whether sex- or profit-oriented, presented great difficulties for those attempting to reconcile political economy with the Christian ideal of self-denial and other-worldliness.

When Chalmers wrote the first volume of his *Christian and Civic Economy* in 1821, he was not unduly bothered about this. He stated there that political economy had only posed a moral dilemma for Christians since 1798. Until then it had been dominated by the theory of commerce, and Adam Smith had proved beyond doubt that free trade and *laissez-faire* policies would elevate commerce 'to the pitch of its uttermost possible elevation'. Governments should leave the field 'to the love of gain, and the spirit of enterprise, and the sharp-sighted sagacity, that guides almost all the pursuits of interest, and the natural securities for justice, between man and man in society'. It was only with the theory of population that Christian morality had entered political economy, for though *laissez-faire* policies should also obtain with respect to poor relief, much more was

---

[3] [M. S. G.], *Letters to J. E. Gordon, Esq. M.P.* (1832), 25. The evangelical Quaker businessman J. J. Gurney claimed that the most 'salutary chastisements' he had received from God had 'arisen out of being . . . a "monied man" ', Gurney's journal, 10 July 1825, Braithwaite, *Memoirs of Gurney*, i. 299.

[4] See, for example, Joseph Milner, 'Parable of the Rich Man and Lazarus, considered', *Practical Sermons*, ed. Isaac Milner (1801; 4th edn, 1821), ii. 246–50; Edmund Butcher, *Sermons, for the Use of Families* (1798; 3rd edn, 1819), i. 21–47: 'Be not slothful in business . . . for diligence fits man for Heaven.' Butcher was a Unitarian; in the nineteenth century this argument was kept up by the more traditional, non-evangelical wing of the Quaker movement.

[5] [Copleston], *Letter to Peel on a Variable Standard of Value*, pp. 61–2.

needed in the way of the spiritual elevation of the people before the Malthusian dilemma could be overcome.[6]

Despite his almost Whatelyan optimism about commerce, however, Chalmers was an evangelical and could not simply shrug aside the question of economic motives in rapt contemplation of economic consequences. He was well aware that the profit motive was potentially dangerous, and to the end of his life he regarded the *Commercial Sermons* (1820) as his most important work. These sermons, which sought to inculcate 'commercial morality' and 'spiritual discipline in money matters', contain the seeds of much subsequent homilizing by Chalmers and others, though the tone is much less urgent than it was to become later.

An affection for riches, beyond what Christianity prescribes, is not essential to any extension of commerce that is at all valuable or legitimate; and, in opposition to the maxim, that the spirit of enterprise is the soul of commercial prosperity, do we hold, that it is the excess of this spirit beyond the moderation of the New Testament, which, pressing on the natural boundaries of trade, is sure, at length, to visit every country, where it operates with the recoil of those calamities, which, in the shape of beggared capitalists, and unemployed operatives, and dreary intervals of bankruptcy and alarm, are observed to follow a season of overdone speculation.[7]

He aimed, therefore, to lift businessmen to 'the standard of the Gospel', just as he also preached abstinence to the poor. 'Let your moderation shine before men' became his slogan. 'Men respect the moderate man, while they distrust the showy extravagance which is meant to dazzle, but seldom deceives, and never increases social respect', declared one avowed Chalmerian.[8]

Chalmers never abandoned such biblical injunctions, any more than he abandoned the need for Christian instruction of the poor. But as he gave up pastoral duties for pedagoguery and political economy, his emphasis changed. In the first place he read Malthus's *Principles of Political Economy* (1820), a work which for him at any rate contained a message every bit as dramatic as the 1798 *Essay*. In the latter Malthus had prophesied a recurrence of wars, famines, and pestilences as passion between the sexes caused the working population to outpace the world's natural resources. Less stridently, the *Principles* predicted a recurrence

---

[6] Chalmers, *Christian and Civic Economy*, i. 4–10 [*Works*, xiv. 26–32].

[7] T. Chalmers, *The Application of Christianity to the Commercial and Ordinary Affairs of Life, in a Series of Discourses* (Glasgow, 1820), pp. v–vi [*Works*, vi, pp. vi–vii]. For a long and flattering review of these 'Commercial Sermons' see *Christian Observer*, 20 (1821), 372–83, 441–53.

[8] Revd Joseph B. Owen, *Business without Christianity, with some Statistics and Illustrative Incidents: A Lecture delivered before the Young Men's Christian Institute of Manchester* (1855), 29–34.

of capital and commodity gluts as middle-class avarice outpaced the natural limits of consumer demand. In other words, Malthus rejected Say's law of markets, the basis of Ricardo's political economy, and its assumption that in favourable conditions supply would always create its own demand. Chalmers seized on this and also on Malthus's market theory of wages, even though they contradicted the benign view which he had formerly held of commerce under free trade conditions. Thanks to the *Principles* he came to see that there were economic as well as ecological limits to the progress of society.

The dispute between Malthus and Ricardo was conducted amicably and at a technical level, but the events of the middle twenties were to make Chalmers's adoption of underconsumptionism more than merely academic. He began the third volume of *Christian and Civic Economy* on 9 November 1825 and completed it on 19 January 1826. These were terrifying and panicky weeks for the capitalist establishment. Hundreds of firms were bankrupted, and the Bank of England itself very nearly stopped payments. It is clear from the preface that Chalmers was moved to make late alterations to the work,[9] and that it marked a shift in his concern, at least temporarily, from pauperism to the analogous problems of capitalism. For the drama of December 1825, together with Malthus's conviction that such events were inevitable and recurrent, gave a new urgency to the views he had put forward in the *Commercial Sermons*.

A major theme of the third volume of *Christian and Civic Economy* was that capital is 'a follower in the train of national prosperity' and not a cause of it as the Ricardians thought, and further that it had the power to recover from cyclical depressions as swiftly as population could make good the ravages of war or disease:

A prevalent physical distemper might seize upon households, and carry off many families. The consequent abundance of provisions will speedily bring forward other families in their room. A prevalent moral distemper, even that of ruinous extravagance, might seize upon merchants, and sweep away many of our capitals. The consequent abundance of profits will construct other capitals, and raise up other capitalists, with a rapidity like that of magic.[10]

In both cases, individuals would suffer during the spontaneous process of adjustment, but the nation as a whole would not. Moreover, in both cases God had provided men with a choice between positive and preventive 'checks':

Neither in population, nor yet in capital, are the preventive checks carried so far as to supersede the positive. It is because of the too frequent and too early

---

[9] Chalmers, *Christian and Civic Economy*, iii, pp. v, viii.
[10] Ibid., iii. 324 [*Works*, xvi. 54–5].

marriages, that the field of competition for labour, and for wages, is overcrowded; that families jostle out each other; that so many are outcasts from well-paid employment; that disease is engendered among them by spare living, and thins the over-peopled land of its numbers, by the premature deaths of infancy and childhood. To the mere student of political science, it may wear the air and boldness of a paradox, when we affirm of capital, that too little goes into the stock for immediate consumption, and too much is adventured upon the field of commerce—that the competition for business, and for its profits, is greatly overcrowded—that traders jostle out each other, and so many become outcasts from safe or gainful merchandise—that what disease does with the redundant population, bankruptcy does with the redundant capital of our land; relieving the overdone trade of its excess, and so reducing capital within those limits beyond which it cannot find any safe or profitable occupancy.[11]

Sumner had hinted at this analogy ten years earlier when he had pointed out that 'if prudential restraint, i.e. the *preventive check*, is disregarded, . . . famine, war, or epidemics will arise, just as bankruptcy will come upon a man who takes no care of his fortune'.[12] However, it was Chalmers who made the analogy central to his argument, and was congratulated for doing so by Malthus himself in a private letter of January 1827.[13] It then became the leading idea of Chalmers's *Political Economy* of 1832. This, like all his economic treatises, suffers from a preacher's repetitiousness, and chapter four may be said to labour 'the parallel between population and capital, both in respect of their limits and their powers of expansion', *ad nauseam. Political Economy* made many obvious class points—for example, the claim that unproductive consumption by the idle rich is of public benefit, and that national debts usefully slow the economy down by preventing the productive employment of capital. Its main theme, however, was that just as overpopulation causes low wages and starvation, so a 'supersaturation of capital' lowers profits and leads to bankruptcies. In effect, what Chalmers was doing was to transform Malthus's long-run stagnation thesis into an explanation of business cycles. Because of man's innate avarice, 'splendid extravagance is followed by splendid bankruptcy, out of the wrecks and ashes of which there suddenly arises a phoenix as splendid as before'—a 'rotation' which in turn was severely detrimental to sober business habits and to 'private virtue and happiness'.[14] Man was

---

[11] Ibid., iii. 325 [*Works*, xvi 56].

[12] Sumner, *Treatise on the Records of Creation*, ii. 166.

[13] Malthus to Chalmers, 18 Jan. 1827, Chalmers Papers, CHA 4.80.19–20. Malthus basically agreed with Chalmers, but thought him too dismissive of manufacturers, and did not agree that teachers and legislators should be placed among the class of wealth creators. He accepted Chalmers's 'slowly receding limits', but insisted that variations in profits could occur within these limits due to supply and demand. See also Malthus to Chalmers, 6 Mar. 1832 and 16 Feb. 1833, ibid., CHA 4.185.32 and 4.210.5–6.

[14] Chalmers, *On Political Economy*, pp. 123–4 [*Works*, xix. 134].

thus locked in a situation where his sins caused fluctuations and fluctuations encouraged sin, and his only hope of release was through the power of Christ.

Chalmers had to be more sensitive about the feelings of the middle classes than he had about those of the poor, which may explain why he was more sparing of spiritual intimidation when berating them. But it is obvious from the analogy he drew with population theory that he regarded bankruptcy as a positive check, like pestilence, to elevate capitalists' minds above what he might have called their passionate fleshpots. 'There is a moral preventive check, which, if put in steady operation throughout the labouring classes, would keep wages high', and 'there is an analogous check, which, operating among capitalists, would keep profits high'.[15] 'Either expenditure or bankruptcy is just as requisite, whether to prevent or correct the redundancy of capital, as disease or the providential check is requisite, whether to correct or to prevent the redundancy of population.'[16] What was needed in both cases was an improved 'collective will', and in predicting the coming of this Utopia he sometimes indulged in sacrificial imagery.

The accumulating policy of Dr. Adam Smith will at length give way, before the doctrine that capital has its limits as well as population, and that the Christian liberality of merchants would not only secure them from the woes denounced in the Bible against those who, hasting to be rich, pierce themselves through with many sorrows, but would induce a far more healthful state of commerce than it is possible to maintain with the distempered over-trading of the present day.[17]

Vision and Reality: Notions of Wealth in an Age of Speculation

Many writers besides Chalmers inveighed against the abandoned Mammonism of the age. The central text here might be Coleridge's *Lay Sermon* of 1817, which attributed almost all contemporary evils to an 'overbalance of the commercial spirit' and its invasion even of the agricultural domain.[18]

---

[15] Chalmers, *On Political Economy*, p. 515 [*Works*, xx. 95]. Chalmers acknowledged T. Perronet Thompson as having drawn the same analogy.

[16] [Chalmers], 'Stirling's *Philosophy of Trade*', *North British Review*, 6 (1846–7), 92. Note the use of 'providential' to mean 'prudential'. This conflation perhaps reflects the mid-century emphasis on self-help as distinct from divine will.

[17] [Chalmers], 'Political economy of the Bible', *North British Review*, 2 (1844–5), 52.

[18] S. T. Coleridge, 'Blessed are Ye that Sow beside all Waters': A Lay Sermon, addressed to the Higher and Middle Classes, on the existing Distresses and Discontents (1817), 45–6, 95–6 [ed. R. J. White for *Collected Works of Coleridge*, No. 6, pp. 169–70, 202]. This can be contrasted with Chalmers's view that the very great contribution made by commerce to civilization was that it had led agriculture out of the 'feudal' or 'lazaroni system' and into capitalism. Chalmers, *On Political Economy*, pp. 56–9 [*Works*, xix. 69–72].

Many moralists shared Chalmers's desire for a type of political economy consonant with 'revealed truth'—with the Scriptures, the Fathers, Canon Law—and capable of implanting asceticism in place of avarice as man's basic economic instinct.[19] The Tractarians, Pusey, Newman, and Keble, as well as their young political ally Gladstone, all sought such a concoction during the thirties and early forties. What distinguishes Chalmers from them is his individualism and complete rejection of economic paternalism. In 1820 he might still have thought that it was possible to instil Christian behaviour among his merchant congregation by simple exhortation. By 1826 he had come to see that an 'elevated collective will' could only be achieved by businessmen through active participation in a divinely ordered world. Whereas Coleridge the protectionist was confident that 'the Spirit of Commerce is itself capable of being at once counteracted and enlightened by the Spirit of the State, to the advantage of both',[20] Chalmers was a free trader who considered that the state had no role to play in regulating either poor relief or commerce. For the same reasons he profoundly disagreed with monetary paternalists like David Robinson of *Blackwood's* and Thomas Attwood, who wished to see the Bank of England damping down fluctuations by counter-cyclical currency controls, or lending money to firms caught up in commercial difficulties.[21] Chalmers thought all such policies undesirable because they would obscure the providence of God apparent in the business cycle.

It will now be clear how Chalmers could desire Free Trade but *not* economic growth.[22] Quite simply, he no longer thought that Free Trade would boost commerce to the pitch of 'uttermost elevation', since God had clearly devised practical limits, not merely ultimate restrictions on the supply of land, but much more immediate ones in the form of trade depressions. Trade was already pressing close to its natural limits, despite many existing 'artificial barriers' such as monopolies and protective tariffs. It followed that such barriers could be at once removed, with many attendant moral and social advantages, and without producing an economic explosion.[23]

Living in the lowlands of Scotland, Chalmers could hardly denounce *all* economic activity as satanic, like some of the more rabid contributors to *Blackwood's Magazine*. His belief in 'natural demand' and in 'the natural boundaries of trade' encouraged him to distinguish, however vaguely,

---

[19] Checkland, 'Advent of academic economics', *Manchester School*, 19 (1951), 66–70.
[20] Coleridge, '*Blessed are Ye that Sow beside all Waters*', pp. 125, 132 [Collected Works, No. 6, pp. 223, 228].
[21] Perkin, *The Origins of Modern English Society*, pp. 244–52; Hilton, *Corn, Cash, Commerce*, pp. 224–6.
[22] See above, pp. 64–70.
[23] Chalmers, *On Political Economy*, pp. 518–21 [*Works*, xx. 98–101].

between 'legitimate' and 'illegitimate' business; between 'solid commerce', which was God's instrument for the development of his world, and 'excrescent trade', which was fictitious, vicious, and selfish, 'the blotch and distemper of our nation'.[24] It was the same sort of distinction which Colquhoun in 1806, Sumner in 1816, Chalmers himself in 1826, and the vast majority of the political nation thereafter, drew between 'pauperism' and 'poverty', imputing misfortune to the one state and depravity to the other.[25] And it was just as absurd. Risk being inseparable from profit, the line between fair trade and foul is impossible to draw. No doubt it was used as a cover for some socially conservative attitudes. Bad traders were not so much those who defrauded their customers, or borrowed money in order to invest it, or engaged in 'under-selling' (a word Chalmers preferred to competition), but anyone who tried to become rich too quickly, at an unnatural rate. Inevitably such a doctrine condemns the little man 'struggling to raise his head above the waters',[26] while it is hard to see how plutocrats like Thornton and Gurney could ever be thought to have succumbed to such a vice. Though Chalmers did not want to keep small businessmen down by paternalist action—by monopolies or discretionary banking (i.e. 'real bills')— he clearly thought that a *laissez-faire* economy would automatically perform the task of snuffing out the impatient and ungodly.

Whatever the ulterior motives, this distinction between wealth that was 'visionary' and that which was 'real' was fundamental to Chalmers and to a great many of his contemporaries. Such moralists could speak complacently of 'a line beyond which firms have no moral *right* to extend their business', since they were confident that 'every one who is capable of moral distinctions must perceive . . . the difference between the usual workings of a speculating mania and the sober methods of legitimate commerce'.[27] The 'ambitious and restless spirit in man' was held to be 'apart, and *altogether distinct from* that honourable spirit of enterprise which is content with its moderate share of advancement'.[28] Aspirations for self-improvement in themselves were held to be laudable, 'the vital force that makes the machinery go round', but once they overstepped the law of righteousness, the machinery would spin giddily out of control, creating what was commonly called a 'vortex'. To prevent this it was

[24] Chalmers, *On Political Economy*, pp. 229–32 [*Works*, xix 235–8].
[25] P. Colquhoun, *A Treatise on Indigence* (1806), 8–9, 48–9; Sumner, *Treatise on the Records of Creation*, ii. 92; Poynter, *Society and Pauperism*, p. 202.
[26] T. Attwood to E. Davenport, 22 June 1826, John Rylands Library Manchester MSS, Bromley Davenport Monuments (Attwood), fos. 43–52.
[27] H. A. Boardman, *The Bible in the Counting-House*, pp. 96, 127.
[28] Revd George Fisk, 'The moral influence of the commercial spirit of the day', *Lectures to Young Men, delivered before the Y.M.C.A. in Exeter Hall, 1847–8* (1848), 285 (italics added).

necessary to 'destroy the vermin, but cherish the noble plant on which they feed'.[29] 'The old school—slow and sure'[30] was frequently held up in virtuous contrast to the madness of present times, when men thought nothing of spending capital faster than they could recoup it. 'Over-trading is *fast* trading; is, in fact, the criminal folly against which the Word of God so clearly warns us—the *making haste to be rich*, which is never innocent, but always culpable and baneful.' Many people believed that '*over*-trading far more than otherwise unsound trading is chargeable with all the ruin of those vast commercial earthquakes, all the wrong of those ruthless mercantile massacres. It is excessive much more than deliberately fraudulent adventure which brings on commercial convulsion.'[31] This explains how fraudulent rogues like George Hudson and John Sadleir could be regarded in a romantic and almost an heroic light, while those who tried to jump above their proper economic stations were invariably castigated as sinful.

Over-trading was always referred to as 'speculation', in some circles the most pejorative of all commonly used words in the first half of the nineteenth century, in that it implied not merely economic irresponsibility but even philosophic doubt and atheism. Jane Austen used the term to characterize the irreverent, capricious, and spiritually restless Crawfords in *Mansfield Park*,[32] while the hero of a mid-century evangelical novel could be described as having 'a speculative turn of mind', which fortified itself 'against superstition by a course of infidel literature'.[33] Indeed, the reason why nineteenth-century moralists did not by and large cite the creation of personal wealth as a sign of divine favour may have been their sense that wealth was by definition more shadowy, fictitious, and precarious than of old. Formerly, it would be said, a man's fortune depended on the amount of gold he possessed, but now it depended mainly on the solidity of his credit. 'If man were not a fallen creature, if sin were not enthroned in his heart, we should say that there could be no more danger in this than in the existence of self-interest and its mutuality.'[34]

---

[29] [Anon.], 'The morals of business', *Meliora: a Quarterly Review of Social Science in its Ethical, Economical, Political, and Ameliorative Aspects*, 1 (1859), 46–56.

[30] Edmund Yates, *Kissing the Rod: A Novel* (1866), iii. 88.

[31] Gregory, *The Thorough Business Man: Memoirs of Walter Powell*, p. 293.

[32] See Tony Tanner's introduction to Jane Austen, *Mansfield Park* (1814; Penguin English Library edn, Harmondsworth, Middlesex, 1966), 7–36, which sees the novel in terms of an allegorical battle between 'the quiet thing!' and 'evil', the latter taking the guise of speculation and economic improvement. For *Mansfield Park* as an evangelical novel see Warren Roberts, *Jane Austen and the French Revolution* (1979), 136–54.

[33] [W. J. Conybeare], *Perversion: Or, the Causes and Consequences of Infidelity: A Tale for the Times* (1856), i. 197. This novel is discussed in Robert Lee Wolff, *Gains and Losses: Novels of Faith and Doubt in Victorian England* (New York and London, 1977), 282–98.

[34] Fisk, 'Moral influence of the commercial spirit', op. cit., p. 276.

But 'speculativeness' seemed to be inherent in modern commerce and reflected, not mutuality of need, but modern man's 'ingenious, solitary, subtle, overreaching, and distant-looking mind'.[35]

The concern shown by clerics and other moralists for the souls of speculators was by no means vicarious, for they were all to a greater or lesser extent participants in the share-trafficking and scrip-mongering of the times. It is obvious that they wanted to pluck as much legitimate fruit from a *rentier* economy as possible, without descending into iniquity. So they insisted that at its best commerce was a supremely moral activity, 'sacred', 'noble', and 'divine'. Chalmers, as we have seen, appreciated keenly how manufacturing industry could degrade and demean, but commerce— 'beauteous intercourse'—was capable of effecting a beneficial 'moral transition' in its practitioners. In order to succeed a merchant needs to have a good name, and he will behave well in order to get one. Thus does God employ human selfishness to promote human virtue. Moreover, 'the very soul and life of commercial activity' is confidence and the trust which merchants repose in one another. Trusting and being trustworthy in turn breed habits and thoughts which leave their mark on the soul.[36] In the same vein, Gladstone reflected privately that belief was really a form of 'spiritual exchange'—the trading of time, thought, money, health, and influence for the inward gifts of God and the likeness of Christ— which was probably why the Bible resorted so frequently to business metaphors. At its best commerce provided a framework of Christian discipline in ordinary life, which could prepare men in time for spiritual trading:

Where there is a real interest and desire, as there certainly is in the pursuit of money, men proceed with activity, with earnestness, with precision: they apply all their powers, what-ever they may be: they do not make much of small difficulties but little of great ones: *they venture the present for the sake of the future*: they thrust aside out of their path every thing that is frivolous and trivial with reference to the main object: their whole life falls into order and discipline, all the movements of it have a purpose, and the consciousness of that purpose shapes and governs all those movements either sensibly or if insensibly yet not less truly.[37]

Unfortunately, the mechanical nature of much commercial routine was likely to dull a man's sensibility and to make him less morally dis- criminating. Worse still, the merchantman, however honest and moderate

---

[35] Fisk, 'Moral influence of the commercial spirit', op. cit., p. 286.

[36] Chalmers, *Application of Christianity to Commerce*, pp. 73–7 [*Works*, vi. 60–4]. See also William Romaine Callender, jun., *The Commercial Crisis of 1857: its Causes and Results* (1858), 9–10.

[37] W. E. Gladstone, 'Memorandum on theology', 1 Jan. 1855', *The Gladstone Diaries*, ed. M. R. D. Foot and H. C. G. Matthew (Oxford, 1968–   ), v. 1 (italics added).

in his ambitions, could hardly help thinking of the world in terms of 'secondary causes irrespective of God'. As an evangelical preacher put it,

He lives in an atmosphere and amidst a mechanism of secondary causes. He hears the motions of its wheels around him continually; and the sounds of the mechanism too often exclude the sounds of God's voice of tenderness and love speaking to him from the mercy-seat, and from the cross of the Redeemer. . . . The secondary causes by which he acts . . . shut out God as the moral governor of the world.[38]

It was in this mechanical context that commercial crises could come to seem beneficial, timely reminders of the existence of providential government. If nothing else they brought home to businessmen their ambivalent moral status. Because the love of money was compatible with outward respectability and with the forms of Christian observance, merchants and financiers were liable to a false sense of security, lacking that certainty of their own danger which often led voluptuaries and criminals to 'repent ere it was too late'. So God in his mercy sent recurring reminders that they were *not*, in either an earthly or a spiritual sense, secure.[39] These reminders were those business catastrophes which played such an important part in forming the mental imagination of the period.

There had been monetary and commercial disorders in the eighteenth century, of course (1788, 1793, 1797), but nothing to compare with the crises of 1825–6, 1837–9, 1847–8, 1857, and 1866 not to mention several lesser hiccups. The causes of such phenomena are complex.[40] Accelerator theory suggests that an increase in fixed capital formation caused successive shocks to the economy which forced it into a cyclical mode. It may also be that Britain's position as the world's only 'developed' economy, reliant on trade with primary producing countries, forced her growth into such a pattern, as cyclical upturns led inevitably to worsening terms of trade. Contemporary analysis concentrated on two quite different types of explanation, however: monetary mismanagement by government or Bank of England, and human avarice and ambition.

Monetary Policy and Theories of Value

Nearly all clerical economists were staunch Bullionists—that is, they supported Britain's return to the Gold Standard, which Pitt had been forced

---

[38] Fisk, 'Moral influence of the commercial spirit', op. cit., pp. 287–8.

[39] T. Nolan, 'The fever of monetary speculation', *Twelve Lent Lectures on 'The Signs of the Times', for the Year 1858* (1858), 92–3.

[40] A. D. Gayer, W. W. Rostow, and A. J. Schwartz, *The Growth and Fluctuation of the British Economy 1790–1850* (Oxford, 1953), esp. ii. 531–616; *British Economic Fluctuations 1790–1839*, ed. D. H. Aldcroft and P. Fearon (1972), 74–130, 188–219.

to abandon in 1797. This is not the place to discuss the bullionist controversy, but one aspect of it relates to the problem discussed in this chapter—the early nineteenth century's ambivalent attitude to wealth, the feeling that some of it was legitimate and some of it was not.

The period off the Gold Standard (1797–1821) coincided with the most hectic and most visible stages of economic growth, a period in which it seemed to commentators that mushroom fortunes and satanic towns and cities were developing almost overnight. It was inevitably a matter of debate whether all this wealth was speculative and insubstantial— 'shadowy and ideal', to use Copleston's terms, or whether it was real and 'of sterling worth'.[41] Anti-Bullionists generally urged the second position, arguing that the economy had outgrown the Gold Standard, and that to force prices back down to a correspondence with the 1797 par value of gold would merely kill off much sound and useful enterprise.[42] It would be to sacrifice the 'real world' to an abstract theory. Bullionists, on the other hand, were often unable to conceal a certain *schadenfreude* at the thought of stifling some of the bubble fortunes of the *nouveaux riches*, though few were as candid or as artless as Harriet Martineau in admitting that as a child she had relished the prospect of a national bankruptcy, so that 'all, *except landowners*, [would have] to begin the world again, and start fair'.[43] 'The *real* and the *false* people' is how one Tory back-bencher referred to society, and by 'real' he meant 'rural', by 'false' he meant the 'unfortunate portion of the population which inhabited great manufacturing towns'.[44] Many still thought in court/country terms, regarding the rural economy as more natural and 'real' than trade and manufactures. This, of course, is why Chalmers was able to think that Free Trade would ultimately benefit agriculture more than industry; the former was 'natural', and Free Trade would bring the economy nearer to the 'order of nature'. The controversy surfaced in Copleston's *Letter to Peel* (1819), which objected to the way in which the Chancellor of the Exchequer (Vansittart) had cited new canals and three new London bridges as evidence that wartime wealth was not fictitious. 'Till the bubble bursts all goes well', chided Copleston, but Vansittart should remember what had happened to the South Sea Company of old, and 'wait till the experiment is fairly over, before he

[41] [Copleston], *Letter to Peel on a Variable Standard of Value*, pp. 83–4.

[42] T. Attwood to Edward Tatham, 11 Apr. 1820, Additional Dropmore Papers, BL Add. MS 59418, fos. 22–3: 'The whole mass of society is oppressed beyond endurance by these *protected values*, and therefore it is quite certain that society will ultimately shake them off.'

[43] H. Martineau, *Introduction to the History of the Peace: From 1800 to 1815* (1851), p. cclxiv (italics added).

[44] Sir Thomas Lethbridge in House of Commons, 28 Feb. 1822, *Parliamentary Debates*, 2nd series, vi. 856.

pronounces on its success'.[45] Less obviously, the controversy also colours the parliamentary debates of 1822 on the currency question.[46]

Generally speaking, those who thought that the wartime prosperity might be only apparent rather than real tended to want some 'real' criterion by which to assess it, and the obvious one was money. Bullionist theory was largely based on the work of three writers: the evangelical banker Henry Thornton, the Jewish stockbroker David Ricardo; and the Scotch reviewer and pupil of Stewart, Francis Horner. Although their work was technical and betrayed little moral fervour, it seems clear that Bullionism appealed to the religious because it implied a fundamentalist approach to the question, 'What is value?'. To have taken a relativist approach would have seemed to them as dangerous as taking a relativist approach to the question, 'What is truth?' (Ricardo's sin being not relativism but the fact that his labour theory was unduly anthropocentric). Of course, there had long been Christian overtones in the way that money and debt were described, as is clear from such words as 'redeem', 'convert', keeping 'faith' with creditors, and 'credit' itself, but it was in the nineteenth century that such phrases became staples of political debate. Grenville talked quite seriously about the 'sacred standard of metallic value' and the 'sacrilege' of the Bank Restriction, while Tierney described Bullionism as his 'creed'.[47] Conversely, clerics began to talk for the first time in the nineteenth century about the 'standard of the Cross' and the 'standard of our faith';[48] just as evangelical literary critics talked of 'the *necessity of returning to the* OLD LEGITIMATE AND ESTABLISHED STANDARD', an 'UNVARYING STANDARD OF CRITICAL TASTE AND LAW', free from the political prejudices which in their eyes disfigured contemporary journals.[49] And the best standard was the Gold Standard, for gold appeared to be an impartial measure of value, common to all goods, as felicity was taken by Benthamites to be the common coin of all human sensations. Of course, to go for gold (rather than felicity) was to take a conservative view of economic relationships (and a jaundiced attitude towards much of the wealth that had been generated in wartime). But

[45] [Copleston], *Letter to Peel on a Variable Standard of Value*, pp. 80–2.

[46] Hilton, *Corn, Cash, Commerce*, pp. 96–7.

[47] Grenville in House of Lords, 21 May 1819, *Parliamentary Debates*, 1st series, xl. 651, 654–5; Tierney in House of Commons, 2 Feb. 1819, ibid., xxxix. 215.

[48] Daniel Wilson, *Evidences of Christianity* (1828–30), i. 20–1. On the word 'standard' see *OED; The Penny Cyclopaedia of the Society for the Diffusion of Useful Knowledge*, 21 (1841), 175; Revd Gavin Struthers, *The History of the Rise of the Relief Church* (Edinburgh and London, 1848), p. 293; Revd John Macpherson, *The Westminster Confession of Faith* (Edinburgh, 1881), 1.

[49] Edward Clarkson, *Robert Montgomery and His Reviewers: With Some Remarks on the Present State of English Poetry, and on the Laws of Criticism* (1830), 5, 149. Montgomery, described by the *Dictionary of National Biography* as having 'an unfortunate facility in florid versification', was much taken up by evangelicals for his devotional poetry.

perhaps it is not surprising that in a money-owning or *rentier* economy debate should have focused on the question of whether money possesses intrinsic value.

There was a substantial minority which thought that it did not. It included the combative and controversial Rector of Lincoln College, Oxford, Edward Tatham. He was a maverick in all economic and philosophical matters. Thus he spoke out against the common assumption, deriving from Adam Smith and endorsed by most evangelical moralists, that the enormous rise of the National Debt was an unfavourable development. Private debt was bad for the debtor but good for the creditor, and since in the case of the public debt the nation played both roles, that debt could not be publicly detrimental. The funds were in fact 'the great wheel of national circulation', directing money to the sources of enterprise and preventing it from being locked up in mortgages and marriage portions. The way to reduce the Debt's burden was, not to try to pay it off, but to chip away at its value by a gentle, perpetual increase of the amount of money in circulation.[50] Unsurprisingly, Tatham later became an advocate in high places of Attwood's anti-bullionist proposals.[51] He argued that paper money, 'however fictitious or artificial it may be called', had 'wrought itself so deeply in the very vitals of this mercantile and agricultural country, that without it, and without a full supply of it too, all its business will be confounded, and all its economy overturned'. 'Money is the blood of the body politic. Stop the current of this blood, and disorder or death must be the consequence.'[52] His main thrust was that there was 'no such thing in nature . . . as a *fixed* and invariable standard as a measure of value'.[53] Such relativism perhaps reflects Tatham's philosophical position, his inductivist attack on Aristotelian logic and on the syllogistic reasoning dominant in Oxford. Truth was of course constant and uniform in the divine mind, but it was modified and varied as it passed through the human faculties of intellect, will, and imagination.[54]

Another relativist was Coleridge, who as early as 1817 presented a sophisticated analysis of the 'periodical revolutions of credit' occurring every twelve to thirteen years.[55] Like Tatham he was scornful of Bullionists:

[50] Edward Tatham, *A Letter to William Pitt on the National Debt* (1795), *passim*. On Tatham see Vivian Green, *The Commonwealth of Lincoln College 1427-1977* (Oxford, 1979), 360-86.

[51] Tatham to Grenville, 13 Apr. 1820, Additional Dropmore Papers, BL Add. MS 59418, fo. 21.

[52] Edward Tatham, *A Letter to Lord Grenville on the Metallic Standard* (Oxford, 1820), 4-5.

[53] Ibid., pp. 19-24.

[54] Edward Tatham, *The Chart and Scale of Truth, by which to find the Cause of Error*, 1790 Bampton Lectures (Oxford, 1790), esp. i. 1-74, 306-74.

[55] Coleridge, 'Blessed are Ye that Sow beside all Waters', p. 97 [*Collected Works of Coleridge*, No. 6, p. 203].

The necessity of a *Standard*—or rather the want of insight into the important truth that in a given degree of trade and commerce, already more than attained in this country, the standard must be *ideal*, not a real commodity, itself to be measured—this is the πρωτον ψευδος, the fundamental error.[56]

Money, according to Coleridge, was '*whatever* has a value among men according to what it *represents*, rather than to what it *is*'.[57] He had merely contempt for 'narcotic Bullionists'[58] like Ricardo, whose desire for an invariable standard was the corollary of their belief in absolute value, and he partly anticipated Samuel Bailey's argument that value consists in the relations between objects as exchangeable commodities, rather than in anything positive and intrinsic.[59]

It must not be supposed that such questions were disputed only by philosophers. They dominated the 1811 debates in Parliament on the Bullion Report, which Horner, Huskisson, and Thornton had concocted the previous year. Thus, in rejecting the relativist view that precious metals 'acquired their value entirely from any convention of agreement', Huskisson insisted on their 'intrinsic value. They were money before they were coined.'[60] When Castlereagh countered by talking of 'a sense of value in reference to currency as compared with commodities', Canning was bitingly scornful. He would not take advice from proponents of '"abstract currency"—from those who, after exhausting in vain every attempt to find an earthly substitute for the legal and ancient standard of our money, have divested the pound sterling of all the properties of matter, and pursued it under the name of the "ideal unit", into the regions of non-entity and nonsense'. Dr Johnson had refuted Berkeley's theory of the non-existence of matter by simply kicking a stone; in the same spirit Canning asserted that the one pound note was more than 'a creature of the imagination'.[61]

So the moral Bullionists believed that with an absolute measure of value, like the Gold Standard, it would be possible to measure the *real* worth of economic enterprise. It followed that governments should adopt a 'neutral'

[56] Coleridge to William Mudford, 9 Feb. 1819, *Collected Letters of Samuel Taylor Coleridge*, ed. E. L. Griggs (Oxford, 1956–71), iv. 920.

[57] S. T. Coleridge, 'Bullion commerce' (1811), *Essays on His own Times, forming a Second Series of The Friend*, ed. his daughter (1850), iii. 862–3 [ed. David V. Erdman for *Collected Works of Coleridge*, No. 3, ii. 238–42].

[58] Ibid., iii. 858 (*Collected Works of Coleridge*, No. 3, ii. 228–30).

[59] M. Dobb., *Theories of Value and Distribution since Adam Smith* (1973), 98–9; B. Gordon, 'Criticism of Ricardian views on value and distribution in the British periodicals, 1820–1850', *History of Political Economy*, 1 (1969), 370–87. On Bailey see below, pp. 166–7.

[60] Huskisson in House of Commons, 7 May 1811, *Parliamentary Debates*, xix. 971.

[61] Canning in House of Commons, 8 May 1811, ibid., xix. 1087–90. See below, p. 223.

monetary policy, in order to keep that standard as inviolate as possible. We have seen how Copleston condemned successive changes in the money supply as causing fluctuations, and therefore furnishing citizens with an excuse if they fell into poverty; how he advocated cash payments in order to force men to be responsible for their own destinies.[62] In exactly the same way, he complained that government intervention in the money market would give bankrupts an alibi for financial failure. An 'unnatural state' of monetary insecurity frustrated all men's attempts to plan ahead, raised the unworthy to 'sudden opulence', smashed the unlucky, and in both cases impaired the 'mercantile character'. Adherence to a Gold Standard, on the other hand, would restore a 'natural' economy, and would establish in economic affairs 'that principle of self-correction which the analogy of nature teaches us is the universal law of her constitution'.[63] There is clearly some affinity here with Burke, who had attacked the *assignats* because their fluctuating values had tempted men to spend and speculate rather than acquire savings and property.[64]

'Self-correction' of course was what the politicians meant by 'things finding their own level', that stock response of the committed *laissez-faire* do-nothing liberal. It provoked Coleridge's famous jibe — 'But Persons are not *Things* — but Man does not find his level. Neither in body nor in soul does the Man find his level!' *Laissez-faire* was appropriate, in Coleridge's eyes, only to the Mosaic chaos, before the world's 'brute tendencies had been enlightened by the Word . . . and before the Spirit of Wisdom moved on the *level-finding* Waters'.[65]

Henry Drummond also opposed the fashionable emphasis on self-help and individual responsibility. He blamed cyclical problems on a fluctuating money supply, and was scornful of the official doctrine that human wickedness, in the form of 'over-trading', was to blame. He insisted that speculation could only hurt the speculator himself and not the community as a whole, since money over-invested in one commodity would lead to a withdrawal of money from other commodities or from the funds. It followed that, since many of the people who were suffering from the collapse of the markets in 1826 were clearly innocents, any over-trading must have been the consequence of an inundation of depreciated paper.[66]

---

[62] See above, p. 107.

[63] [Copleston], *Letter to Peel on a Variable Standard of Value*, pp. 37, 88; Copleston to Whately, 3 July 1841, *Memoir of Copleston*, pp. 85–6.

[64] J. G. A. Pocock, 'The political economy of Burke's analysis of the French Revolution', *Historical Journal*, 25 (1982), 335–9.

[65] Coleridge, *'Blessed are Ye that Sow beside all Waters'*, p. 101 [*Works of Coleridge*, vi. 206].

[66] H. Drummond, *Elementary Propositions on the Currency: With Additions, showing their Application to the Present Times* (1819; 4th edn, 1826), 49–51; Lovaine, *Speeches and Miscellaneous Pamphlets of Drummond*, ii. 27–8. In the 1848 edition of *Elementary*

Elsewhere Drummond, while agreeing that 'speculation produces ruin', reversed the usual order of argument by insisting that 'fluctuation produces speculation'.[67] The point is that unlike moderate evangelicals he was obsessed, not by individual sinfulness, but by the derangement of whole communities, fluctuation being a sure sign of national malady.

The Trade Cycle and the Millennium

It is impossible to make precise delineations in tracing the history of attitudes, but it is noticeable that 'events'—in this case, mainly publications and comments on events—tend to cluster, as they did in 1825–6. The financial collapse of December 1825 was comparable both in substance and in dramatic effect to the Wall Street crash of 1929. The 'storm' came, moreover, at a time when there seemed not a cloud in the sky, and ravished equally the 'innocent and the guilty'.[68] Not surprisingly, it was greeted as a sublime example of special providence, an awful pointer to national wickedness, much as the equally undiscriminating cholera was to be greeted in 1831–2.[69] According to Macaulay's later reflections, Cobbett claimed that the crash was a culmination of all his prophecies, and ejaculated: 'Will the Quakers and Unitarians now venture to deny that there is a God?'—by which he meant of course a retributive, evangelical kind of God.[70] Thomas Arnold seems to have awoken to his 'lively sense of social evils' in 1826, to a feeling of 'deep disease' in the nation, and Anthony Ashley Cooper, the future Lord Shaftesbury, was turned from a life of frivolity to one of remorse-ridden philanthropy.[71] It was in the same year that Drummond and Irving gave their new twist to the evangelical revival by founding the Catholic Apostolic Church at Albury, confident in the belief that 'events were visibly marching forward' to a 'great visible era of doom and triumph'. As Irving's biographer put it,

---

Propositions on Currency, pp. 13–14, Drummond argued that over-issue had forced interest rates down to the level of the public funds, which had in turn caused over-trading and the 1847 crash. He desired to see a fixed amount of money in circulation, but was informed by one Chancellor of the Exchequer that it was necessary for the circulation to vary with circumstances. Goulburn to Drummond, 2 Dec. 1841, Northumberland MS, C/1/1881—ii.

[67] Drummond, *Cheap Corn Best for Farmers*, p. 31.

[68] George G. Babington to Thomas Babington, 23 Dec. 1825, Babington Papers, 2[74].

[69] Morris, *Cholera 1832*, pp. 129–58.

[70] Lord Granville to Lord Canning, 14 Feb. 1856, *The Life of Granville George Leveson Gower, Second Earl Granville*, by Lord Edmond Fitzmaurice (1905), i. 164–5. It seems that at this time Cobbett regarded Unitarians as a peculiar sect of usurious Jews. *Cobbett's Weekly Political Register*, 63 (1827), 261; George Spater, *William Cobbett: The Poor Man's Friend* (Cambridge, 1982), ii. 591 n. 78.

[71] Stanley, *Life of Arnold*, i. 45 [5th edn (1845), i. 50]; Finlayson, *Shaftesbury*, pp. 21–3.

That time was clearly a time of expectation. An age of great events was just over, and the public mind had not yet accustomed itself to the domestic calm. At home the internal economy of the country was swelling with great throes—agonies in which many people saw prognostics most final and fatal. Out of all the visible chaos, what a joyful, magnificent deliverance, to believe—through whatsoever anguish the troubled but short interval might pass—that the Lord was coming visibly to confound his enemies and vindicate his people![72]

Irving's father-in-law was ruined by rash investments in a joint-stock banking company in 1826. Whether this had anything to do with his mood or not, his sermons of that time keep coming back to the way in which, in one day, Britain had been shaken by the Almighty and toppled from the peaks of boastful success, leaving a trail of 'boundless ruin and desolation, spreading on all sides, to the day of judgment'. God had destroyed our credit because he wished to 'wound us in the part we deem most invulnerable'.[73] Another prominent London evangelical, the Revd Henry Budd, made similar points. As recently as July 1825 he had lamented the corrupting effects of national wealth, the gaming, speculation, and covetousness. Six months later he was almost pleased to feel the hand of God on the nation's back. 'Fleets and armies, and art and science, and political power, have been the gods of our idolatry; but the chief idol has been our national credit . . . But God has . . . shewn us, that in one moment, almost without warning, He can tumble it to the ground.' Budd was convinced that Parliament should make a special effort to abolish colonial slavery as an atonement and propitiation.[74]

It is unnecessary to quote at length, but such views were common coin, especially in evangelical circles. The *Christian Observer*, for example, referred interminably to 'our commercial sins, and the retributive distresses which have accompanied them'.[75] A quarter-century later, it was still insisting that only God, not do-gooders, could arrest the downward course of speculators, as only God could save alcoholics or gamblers of race-course and table.[76] Thomas Nolan pointed out that, according to James, Luke, Peter, and Timothy, it was prophesied that covetousness would characterize *the last days* before the Second Advent of Jesus, a time (as pre-millenarians supposed) of evil and suffering.[77]

[72] Oliphant, *Life of Edward Irving*, i. 388–97. The popular pre-millenarian Zion Ward also 'took off' in 1826.

[73] Edward Irving, 'Remarks on commercial distress', *The Pulpit*, 6 (1826), 27–8.

[74] Henry Budd to Revd C. J. Bird, 30 July 1825, 16 Jan 1826, and 10 Feb. 1826, *A Memoir of the Rev. Henry Budd: comprising an Autobiography, Letters, Papers, and Remains* (1855), 435–8. Conventionally, Budd thought that the Gold Standard would enable Britain 'to return to a natural state' and cure the fever of speculation.

[75] *Christian Observer*, 32 (1832), 127–8.

[76] Ibid., NS, 242 (1858), 81.

[77] Nolan, 'The fever of monetary speculation', op. cit., pp. 87–94.

1825–6 was sudden and unexpected. By 1847–8 the regularity, pre-dictability even, of the business cycle encouraged a belief that crashes were a result of regular rather than special providence. Gladstone considered the Irish Famine to be a calamity 'most legibly Divine' because there was 'a total absence of such second causes as might tempt us to explain it away',[78] but the all-too-inevitable collapse of the railway investment mania in 1847 had no such 'special' connotations. It was no longer so readily assumed that, where the business cycle was concerned, God was intervening to punish the nation for its sins—nor was it feasible to go on blaming the troubles on government interference with the money supply. Instead it was argued that the victims of business failure must themselves have evinced economic guilt, perhaps by attempting too much too soon, however honourable their behaviour might seem to be on the surface. They had been placed on a moral obstacle course devised by providence, and had been up-ended. For bankruptcies were not 'mysterious visitations, inscrutable as potatoe-rot or rinder pest', but the logical outcome of sin. 'The laws of business are laid down by the Governor of the world with as much firmness and precision as the laws which make the universe the "Kosmos,"—the perfection of order and beauty.'[79]

An influential exponent of this sort of thinking was Samuel Jones Loyd, Lord Overstone, a banker and parliamentarian who exercised some considerable influence over the monetary policies of Peel and his successors. He was a deeply religious man who had almost decided to take orders, and though there is no evidence that he ever called himself an evangelical, it is likely that if he had been a generation older he would have associated with the moderate evangelicalism of Wilberforce's Clapham and Simeon's Cambridge. According to his *Times* obituarist, he was concerned with the 'sound' truths of religion rather than with 'theological speculation'.[80] He held a literal and vivid belief in hell-fire, and felt that there could be no 'meaning and purpose of life, . . . of all our virtuous feelings, of self-sacrifice, of moral struggle, of *Conscience*, unless we can look upon life as a state of trial and preparation, and upon death as a great change no doubt, but as the starting point of real life'.[81] He took a suitably robust attitude to social problems, having supported the New Poor Law,[82] and like most moderate evangelicals he opposed paternalist intervention (such

[78] Gladstone to Henry Manning, 9 Mar. 1847, Lathbury, *Correspondence on Church and Religion*, ii. 275–6. See below, pp. 351–2.

[79] Gregory, *The Thorough Business Man: Memoirs of Walter Powell*, pp. 205, 294.

[80] *The Times*, 19 Nov. 1883, p. 8a–c.

[81] Overstone to G. W. Norman, 15 Nov. 1868, *The Correspondence of Lord Overstone*, ed. D. P. O'Brien (Cambridge, 1971), iii. 1161.

[82] Overstone in House of Lords, 4 Aug. 1862, *Parliamentary Debates*, 3rd series, clxviii. 1171–3.

as licensing bills) on the grounds that it was impossible 'to make people moral by Act of Parliament', without reference to 'reason and conscience'.[83]

Overstone's support for free trade policies did not betoken a desire for economic growth, but rather deflected his anxiety as to the consequences of past expansion. He was alarmed at 'the increase, which proceeds in geometrical rate, of our manufacturing capital, and therefore of our manufacturing population and our machinery'.[84] Free Trade might create outlets, and so prevent a convulsion of all this productive capacity and subsequent stagnation. Overstone was a leading member of the so-called Currency School of monetary theorists, advocates *par excellence* of the belief in money (coin and paper) as something tangible and intrinsic, altogether different from frothy, insubstantial credit. Peel's 1844 Bank Charter Act, which adhered faithfully to his views, went further than ever in securing a neutral monetary policy on the part of government and Bank, and in ignoring the money-potential of cheques, deposits, and credits. In theory this neutral policy was meant to discourage speculation, but some at least of the policy-makers never really believed this. 'Storms and tempests are not more certain and inevitable in the material world, than are the periodical convulsions of commercial affairs; and they both answer similarly useful purposes.'[85]

Overstone's analysis of the trade cycle, though technical and relatively unpolemical, rested characteristically on psychological factors. In this he followed Thornton, the first writer to emphasize how much such factors could affect public credit. For Overstone the 'established cycle' started 'in a state of quiescence,—next improvement,—growing confidence,—prosperity,—excitement,—overtrading,—convulsion,—pressure,—stagnation,—distress,—ending again in quiescence'.[86] Such periodic convulsions were clearly specimens of regular and not special providence, from which it followed that the sufferers must all be guilty ones, that 'monetary pressure' did not 'convert *real* prosperity into embarrassment and ruin—Such pressure detects real unsoundness and brings it to a crisis.'[87]

---

[83] Ibid., 3 June 1862, clxvii. 282.

[84] Loyd to Norman, 28 Sept. 1841, O'Brien, *Correspondence of Overstone*, i. 328–9.

[85] S. J. Loyd, *Remarks on the Management of the Circulation: and on the Condition and Conduct of the Bank of England and of the Country Issuers, during the Year 1839* (1840), 104, in Lord Overstone, *Tracts and Other Publications on Metallic and Paper Currency* (1858), 132; S. J. Loyd, *Thoughts on the Separation of the Departments of the Bank of England* (1844), 4–5: 'To guard against commercial convulsions is not the direct or real purpose of the Bill', since such things will recur so long as the 'hope of gain influences human minds'.

[86] Loyd, *Reflections suggested by a Perusal of Mr. J. Horsley Palmer's Pamphlet on the Causes and Consequences of the Pressure on the Money Market* (1837), 44; he was to repeat this diagnosis frequently, O'Brien, *Correspondence of Overstone*, i. 63.

[87] Overstone to Norman, 4 Nov. 1856, O'Brien, *Correspondence of Overstone*, ii. 679.

It is *false* prosperity—*undue* Credit, and *over*-trading which alone are pinched and embarrassed by Monetary pressure—and in producing this result does not Monetary pressure really render good service to the community—by exterminating noxious weeds and destroying the seeds of spreading mischief.[88]

Like the New Poor Law, belief in the efficacy of monetary pressure was also a feature of Ricardian economics, but there the aim was to promote growth, not business morality. A short shower of bankruptcy would eliminate inefficient rather than morally 'noxious' businesses, thus enabling the efficient ones to expand more confidently. Evangelical economists, however, did not wish to promote growth so much as the fear of God among capitalists, and they thought that this could only occur where there was an unregulated market operating freely in a context of Christian exhortation, the two combining to create what Chalmers liked to call an 'elevated collective will'. George Combe, the nearest thing to an early nineteenth-century psychologist,[89] was deeply impressed by Overstone's contribution. Like him he thought that the 'ruin and desolation' of 1847–8 had had 'a brighter side', since 'the great sufferers on that occasion were the improvident persons who had bought or manufactured goods, or purchased shares or other property beyond their means of paying for them, and the creditors who had imprudently trusted them'.[90]

Those who stretched beyond their means might be 'improvident', but their punishment was undoubtedly providential. The following quotation from an evangelical magazine shows how literally some moralists believed that the business cycle sought out 'real unsoundness':

In this speculating world, amid all these risks and ventures which perhaps must be entered into to make business prosperous and to keep pace with the age, it is only a very strong religious spirit, a practical exercise of religion, that can make anyone judge accurately between legitimate and reckless commercial speculation. . . . It is here, as Butler so well points out, that the great moral trial lies. . . . From the danger we are all in of taking our moral standard from the tone of the common morality of society, we are apt to forget the higher standard of the law of CHRIST. We are every now and then recalled to a sense of the difference of these two standards by some tremendous commercial failure; in which we see that speculation has been carried so far into the region of uncertainty and risk, that trust and confidence has been abused, and the ruin of one man has involved in it that of hundreds, who trusted him. *Now we only see this by reason of the failure of the speculation*, not from the speculation itself: had that proved

---

[88] Overstone to G. C. Lewis, 6 Nov. 1856, ibid., ii. 682.
[89] See below, pp. 189–202.
[90] George Combe, *The Currency Question, considered in relation to the Act of the 7th and 8th Victoria, Chap. 32, commonly called the Bank Restriction Act* (1855–6; 10th edn, 1858), 16.

successful instead of disastrous, many would not have seen the immorality at all.[91]

By the time that this was written, providentialism was becoming unfashionable among Anglicans. Christ's law was coming to be identified with his teaching as recorded in the New Testament, rather than having to be inferred from what happens in the natural world. But though it is a late quotation, it encapsulates very well the attitudes current in the first age of capitalism, when speculation had appeared to be the sin of sins.

Debt as a Release from Doubt: the Atoning Bankrupt

If speculation was the supreme sin, charity was conventionally regarded as the supreme virtue. Yet Burke was only one of many writers who pointed out that, while charity was a Christian's 'obligatory duty', it came 'next in order after the payment of debts'.[92] As we have seen, business crashes were widely supposed to search out the guiltiest debtors and punish them, but not everyone could accept that they really did this. Such scepticism undoubtedly contributed to the mid-century shift in attitudes,[93] but before about 1850 it was usual to defend the providentialist position by pointing out that in the land of Mammon vastly more people were guilty than the prosperous producers, distributors, and financiers. During the 'excitement' phase of a business cycle whole communities became 'crazed', and even in ordinary times a widespread 'passion for cheapness' betokened degradation on the part of consumers as well as producers. Manufacturers were merely obliging the public when they produced what George Fisk condemned as 'practical lies', shoddy ostentatious goods, produced at less than cost price. Fisk insisted that there was 'a mutuality of guilt' between buyer and seller, producer and consumer in such matters.[94]

Then there was the problem of joint-stock associations and public companies, increasingly plentiful from the 1830s onwards. Should innocent partners be punished alongside the guilty, and, if they were,

[91] [Anon.], 'Life's problems', *The Ecclesiastic and Theologian*, 22 (1860), 261–4 (original italics).

[92] Edmund Burke, *Thoughts and Details on Scarcity, originally presented to the Right Hon. William Pitt in 1795* (1800), 18 [*The Works and Correspondence of Edmund Burke* (new edn, 1852), v. 197].

[93] See below, p. 265.

[94] Fisk, 'Moral influence of the commercial spirit', op. cit., pp. 283–4. Another lecturer to the YMCA a decade later, a Baptist whose mission to the poor at St Giles, Bloomsbury, was in conscious imitation of Chalmers, made exactly the same point. Revd William Brock, 'Mercantile morality: A lecture', *Lectures delivered before the Young Man's Christian Association, in Exeter Hall, from November 1855, to February 1856* (1856), 450–1.

then what became of the notion that failure invariably denoted guilt? Did companies have consciences? An elaborate explanation was provided by James William Gilbart of the London and Westminster Bank. As a leading member of the Banking School, that is, someone who argued in opposition to Overstone and the Currency School that banks should be allowed a discretion over their issues, he was much exercised by the problem of companies' economic responsibility or 'conscience'. In his view joint-stock companies *were* 'moral agents, . . . capable of virtuous and vicious actions', just like individuals, and similarly 'responsible to a superior power, who will reward or punish them, according to their works'.[95] If whole nations were capable of sin, and made liable to the 'moral discipline' of collective punishment, why not companies? Moreover, as children of the third and fourth generations could often testify (Exodus 20: 5–6), 'it is not inconsistent with the principles of the Divine government for persons to suffer for the wickedness, or to be rewarded for the righteousness of those with whom they are socially connected'. 'Every individual member of a public body, whether a nation, a family, or a company, should induce that body to walk in the path of uprightness', or else 'bear a portion of the collective punishment'.[96] Moreover, when companies *did* fail, Gilbart felt even more certain that the punishment was justified than he did in the case of individuals. His reasoning here is slightly bizarre. Individuals do not always meet with their just deserts in life, as Job discovered, because 'the present state is not a state of final retribution', and earthly afflictions are intended 'chiefly as instruments of moral discipline'. Companies, on the other hand, though they are indeed moral agents, are not in Gilbart's view capable of going to Heaven—he thought such a notion 'too wild to need refutation'—and so it must be supposed that their just deserts are met in the here and now.

The righteous Governor of the world must reward the good and punish the wicked.

But this is not done in the present world.

Therefore there must be a future world, in which this retribution will take place . . .

The righteous Governor of the world must reward the good and punish the wicked whether those actions are performed by public bodies, or private individuals.

But the public companies who now perform good or evil actions will not exist in a future world.

---

[95] [J. W. Gilbart], *Moral and Religious Duties of Public Companies*, p. 4. Gilbart thought that banks should not vary the rate of dividend, since this merely encouraged gambling in shares; instead they should keep to a steady rate, so that the profits of one year could be used to meet the deficiencies of another. Ibid., p. 20. Compare Chalmers on the poor's rates, see above, p. 89.

[96] Ibid., pp. 10, 13.

Therefore public companies must be rewarded or punished in the present world . . .

It is only in the present world that such collective bodies [as nations, cities, joint-stock companies] can, in their corporate capacity, be either punished or· rewarded.[97]

There was the further point that since companies existed to obtain wealth, the only way in which they could be rewarded or punished was by adding to or taking from that wealth. One cannot suppose of a board of share-holders, as one can of individuals, that financial success conceals remorse and sorrow, or that business failure masks inward satisfaction and content-ment. The only criterion of happiness and distress is monetary loss and gain. It followed, according to Gilbart, that in the case of companies 'righteousness will bring wealth, and wickedness will bring poverty'.[98]

In the case of individuals it was nowhere near so clear that the victims of a financial crash would be those who deserved to suffer. Even so, this did not necessarily undermine confidence in the retributive justice of the trade cycle, because in that evangelically conditioned climate there was a tendency to regard innocent bankrupts as sacrificial offerings, beloved of God, and atoning vicariously for the sins of a commercially fallen world. This is a theme of *Perversion: or, the Causes and Consequences of Infidelity. A Tale for the Times* (1856) by William J. Conybeare. It is a typical homily on the theme of every man's need for a personal God, a novel whose hero, the consumptive Charles Bampton, moves from vice and weakness to a dysenteric redemption (a 'falling asleep in Christ') at Scutari. The turning-point comes when he suddenly perceives that the soul of commercial man 'is a mere gland for the secretion of lucre', and that only Christianity can rescue it [ii. 175].

The sense of personal guilt made this belief [in God] a necessity to him; he felt that he needed pardon from the Author of all law, reconciliation with the Source of all good. . . . 'How can I make atonement for my transgression? How can I be brought into harmony with the moral order of His universe? How can I gain pardon, and holiness, and peace?' [iii. 229–31.]

How? It requires the sacrifice of a brilliant Oxford don. A young academic, Hawkins, has the world at his feet when his wealthy merchant father undertakes a ruinous speculation and becomes a bankrupt in circumstances which dishonour the family name. Reduced to beggary and shame, and deserted by his fiancée, Hawkins nearly succumbs to brain fever before turning to Christ, but in his regenerate condition it is he who ministers to and converts Bampton, currently a prey to pantheistic and necessarian

---

[97] [J. W. Gilbart], *Moral and Religious Duties of Public Companies*, pp. 50–1. See also McNeile, *Famine A Rod of God*, pp. 68–9, 87.
[98] [Gilbart], *Moral and Religious Duties of Public Companies*, p. 57.

influences. 'Conscience', argues Hawkins, 'cries out indignantly that good is different from evil, that sin is sinful, and that guilt demands atonement, and . . . a heavenly deliverer' [iii. 270–1]. Hawkins finally dies in spasms, but not before he has accomplished his redemptive operation on Bampton's soul. The latter's final days are spent in practical Christianity and at Scutari helping Florence Nightingale. As a mark of grace, perhaps, he is spared 'the struggling death of consumption', and allowed instead to die from 'the painless exhaustion which follows dysentery' [iii. 322].

It is clear from the popular fiction of the period as well as from tracts and sermons that the prospect of bankruptcy and financial collapse pervaded men's minds. Fiction's best-known evangelical financier is probably Bulstrode, the banker of *Middlemarch* (1871–2) who inspired George Eliot's acute description of the role of 'fear' in the workings of the puritan conscience:

Night and day, while the resurgent threatening past was making a conscience within him, he was thinking by what means he could recover peace and trust — by what sacrifice he could stay the rod. His belief in these moments of dread was, that if he spontaneously did something right, God would save him from the consequences of wrong-doing. For religion can only change when the emotions which fill it are changed; and the relation of personal fear remains nearly at the level of a savage. [bk VI, ch. 61.]

Bulstrode's case points the Malthusian analogy particularly well. The collapse of his deceitfully spun financial web is said to have 'blighted' his many clients 'like a damaged ear of corn'. Dickens liked to describe the bubble speculations inspired by Merdle in *Little Dorrit* (1857) as a 'contagion' and an 'epidemic'. That novel contains a graphic account of life in the most notorious debtors' prison, the Marshalsea. Smallweed in *Bleak House* (1853) illustrates another favourite point of Victorian homily—that usurers often try to force men into their debt, not for the sake of the interest payments, but in order to exercise power over them. 'They were his game—his bagged foxes—the sport of his new gentility.'[99] Perhaps the most relevant of all Dickens's novels is *Nicholas Nickleby* (1838). Its villain is Nicholas's uncle Ralph, a company promoter whose activities during 1825–6 had ruined poor but honest speculators like his own brother, Nicholas's father. As one critic puts it, Ralph could only atone for this behaviour by repentance and the performance of charity, a course of action he scornfully rejects. On the contrary, his heartless conduct towards his victims in the course of the novel prepares

[99] Catherine Frances Gore, 'An account of a creditor', *Temptation and Atonement, and Other Tales* (1847), ii. 171.

the reader 'for Ralph's ultimate ruin, and for his terrible end'.[1] There are variations of the theme in Thackeray's *Vanity Fair* (1847–8) and Mrs Craik's *John Halifax Gentleman* (1857), and later (less evangelical) manifestations in Trollope's *The Way We Live Now* (1875) and Meredith's *Beauchamp's Career* (1876), but the most revealing tale of all for a study of early Victorian attitudes is probably *Hard Cash. A Matter-of-Fact Romance* (1863) by Charles Reade.

This novel expresses in an unusually blatant way the unconsciously held idea that credit is virtuous, speculation corrupting, and debt sinful. Chapter Eight describes how the upright and honourable banker Richard Hardie turns into a depraved monster. The background is a railway mania, graphically depicted, in which bishops, princes, peers, and charwomen jostle each other for scrip in the 'bubbling iron, . . . all to get rich in a day'. For a long time Richard holds out manfully against this 'Arithmetic of Bedlam', but eventually succumbs as he sees paupers becoming million-aires overnight. Before long he is buying shares merely to sell them again at a premium. 'But it is dangerous to be a convert, real or false, to Bubble', warns Reade; 'the game is to be rash at once, and turn prudent at the full tide.' When things begin to falter, Richard battles against the threat of insolvency with fortitude, dignity, and honour, so that for months no one could 'guess the doubts and fears, the hopes and despondencies, which agitated and tore the heart and brain that schemed, and throbbed, and glowed, and sickened by turns, beneath that steadily modulated exterior'. But then comes a final blow, the collapse of some good securities in Turkish stock, and in order to surmount it Hardie is driven to raiding his children's trust funds. The ploy keeps him afloat, 'but the peril, and the escape on such terms, left him gasping inwardly'. While in this precarious state Hardie enters on a career of cheating, which includes robbing his son's friend David Dodds of fourteen thousand pounds. Most heinous of all, he bribes the Commissioners in Lunacy to certify his son, in order to have him incarcerated in an asylum and cheated of his inheritance. The denouement is oddly machinated: a few chapters from the end, Turkish stock rise back to par and Richard becomes wealthy again. 'With this revived the habits of his youth; no more cheating: nothing could excuse that but the dread of poverty.'[2] Regenerate, Hardie

---

[1] N. Russell, '*Nicholas Nickleby* and the commercial crisis of 1825', *The Dickensian*, 77 (1981), 144–50. See also John R. Reed, 'A friend to Mammon: speculation in Victorian literature', *Victorian Studies*, 27 (1983–4), 179–202.

[2] This may seem an odd philosophy on Reade's part, but note how Hugh Stowell, *A Model for Men of Business: or, Lectures on the Character of Nehemiah* (1854), 12–13, comments that one should not be surprised when apparently upright merchants are depraved by the experience of failure, since 'In truth, the man is not greatly altered; his altered condition has called out what was latent in his breast.' On the doctrine of final perseverance in this con-text see Miss E. J. Whately, *Evangelical Teaching: its Meaning and Application* (1871), 32–3.

restores to Dodds all the 'hard, hard Cash' that he had extorted from him, love and certainty triumph, and the novel ends with a famous if fatuous apostrophe to cosy domestic bliss.

Reade's own philosophical views are obscure, but it is known that he grew up in an atmosphere of militant evangelicalism, and was greatly influenced by his pietistic and Calvinist mother, a close friend of the evangelical disputant G. S. Faber.[3] The most obviously didactic point made in *Hard Cash* is the barbaric treatment of lunatics, which was also a prime evangelical concern at that time. In the present context, the novel's investigation of the moral contrasts between cash and floating capital, between 'real' and 'false' value and values, touches the centre of the Victorian preoccupation with success. 'O immortal cash! You, like your great inventor have a kind of spirit as well as a body; and on this, not on your grosser part, depends your personal identity. So long as that survives, your body may be recalled to its lawful owner from Heaven knows where.' [i. 227–37, iii. 342–3: Chs. 8 and 55.]

Typically, Victorian moralists envisaged successive phases of business life. The manly honest trader is tempted, falls, is terrorized, and then smashed, and in the process he may or may not achieve a state of grace. Ideal merchants and financiers, who never succumbed to temptation, were a staple of contemporary biography and widely advertised, especially perhaps in nonconformist circles. There was Joseph Sturge, for example, a devout Quaker of the evangelical variety, a corn trader during the period of fluctuating markets which set in after 1815, and later the founder of the Compleat Suffrage Movement and friend of Cobden. His journals of the 1820s record his periodic losses, with pained reflections that his 'trials' had not had 'that purifying effect upon me for which they are no doubt intended'. Nevertheless, his biographer assures us that he consciously adjusted the time spent in prayer to the size of his profits, and, 'as if conscious of the peril he incurred', he redoubled his devotions 'at those seasons when he was drawn most deeply into the dizzying vortex of commercial competition and activity'.[4] Samuel Morley, the hosiery manufacturer, furnishes another example of the breed, but the fullest account of a mercantile angel is probably Benjamin Gregory's hagiography of a little-known evangelical Methodist from Tasmania, Walter Powell. The latter subscribed fully to the Old Testament, 'Arnoldian', retributive values of the period—Gregory calls it 'the "Tom Brown" school of theology'—'If a boy smite thee on the one cheek, hit him on the other

---

[3] For a perceptive account of the evangelical influences apparent in Reade's work see Wayne Burns, *Charles Reade: A Study in Victorian Authorship* (New York, 1961), 26 ff., 60 ff. Burns comments that Reade sometimes envisaged God as a humanitarian with sadistic propensities, in support of his cruelty-hating Christ. Ibid., p. 167.

[4] *Memoirs of Joseph Sturge*, by Henry Richard (1864), 37–45.

also . . . [Powell] bore throughout his life the stigmata of this bluff saintship.'[5] He was, it seems, aggressive and combative, combining self-confidence and daring with frugality, consideration, punctuality, industry, and methodical habits. 'Business-life was not a something apart, or even distinct, from his spiritual life. Business was part of his religion, whilst religion was the whole of his business.'[6] Needless to say, Powell gave enormous amounts to charity, reserving only a modest competence for himself. His 'mercantile salvation' was of course his 'moderation' and refusal to speculate, and this was made possible by the application of conscience and 'a heroic and martyr-like trust in God'.[7] Not only conscience, but confidence that if God loathed bad merchants, he adored good ones, that 'every mercantile activity throbs, and its pulsation is immortality'.[8]

Although evangelical religion was the only *sure* antidote to Mammon, certain earthly balms, like domestic felicity and kindness to inferiors, could certainly help. Country rambles, contemplation of the stars or of the ocean, could give a busy merchant smatterings of taste and imagination, enabling him to return to the counting-house with broadened mental culture.[9] Rural life reminds us constantly of God's handiwork, whereas mortals 'seem to move and govern all, and to be the providence of cities'.[10] The Romantic poets may have looked to the countryside for intimations of the sublime, and for the opportunity to discover their own souls through communion with nature, but for more and more moralists the countryside was coming to seem a mere retreat from, and an antidote to, the 'real' life of the cities. 'It is in no small measure through metropolitan capital, energy, intelligence, and piety, that the mighty conflict with sin is carried forward, which is, by the blessing of God, to result in the general diffusion of Christianity.'[11] The reason is that, by some spiritual dialectic, 'great wickedness causes a reaction to great holiness'. A dead level of worldliness destroys faith, but the presence of 'an actual moving enemy' like Mammon calls dormant energies into play, and creates a spiritual 'progression by antagonism'.[12]

The last point brings us to the mysteries of temptation, a condition which was regarded by evangelicals as 'a token that we are God's'.[13] Thus William Henry Hutchings attacked eighteenth-century writers

---

[5] Gregory, *The Thorough Business Man: Memoirs of Walter Powell*, pp. 16–17. See below, p. 274.

[6] Ibid., pp. 183–4.   [7] Ibid., pp. 201, 291–2, and *passim*.

[8] Brock, 'Mercantile morality', op. cit., pp. 457.

[9] H. A. Boardman, *The Bible in the Counting-House*, pp. 251–2.

[10] Ibid., p. 294.   [11] Ibid., p. 295.

[12] [Anon.], 'Life's problems', op. cit., p. 261. See below, p. 349.

[13] W. W. Champneys, 'Temptation: A sermon', *The Pulpit*, 69 (1856), 397–400.

for having discounted literal interpretations of the Temptation in the
Wilderness, on the grounds that the story did no good to man and reflected
ill on God. On the contrary, 'the trial is from God, Who permits it, and
has arranged it, in order to keep the soul low, when, from the very presence
of the gift of Divine favour, there may be a risk of self-exultation'.[14] Here
is the common moderate evangelical assumption that God, far from being
locked in equal combat with Satan, actually controls the latter's operations.
In the present context it justified a belief that, since the corollary of debt
was credit, and since one could only get into debt if one had previously
been worthy of credit, a 'real' person must flirt with debt, however
'perilous' it was to do so, must overcome his own personal devil. 'Thrice
happy the man who sleeps solvent upon his pillow. But scarcely less pitiful
the wretch who lays his head there absolutely debtless;—untrusted either
because untrustworthy, or because unwilling to accord credit in return!'[15]
Bicheno, who anticipated so many of Chalmers's thoughts, regarded
resistance to the profit motive as a means of developing a 'nobler moral
structure', through a 'competition of physical and moral qualities . . .
striving for the ascendancy'.[16] Horace Bushnell considered that no one
was 'more genuinely Christ-like' than the honest merchant.[17] The most
explicit statement comes from another American, H. A. Boardman, who
openly aspired to be 'another Chalmers' of commercial homiletic.[18] A
biblical fundamentalist, convinced that 'in the economy of redemption,
. . . without shedding of blood there is no remission',[19] Boardman's
writings are a repetitious vade-mecum of evangelical attitudes to business.
Like Chalmers, whose *Commercial Sermons* were a direct inspiration,
Boardman sometimes paid lip-service to an optimistic, Cobdenite, natural
theology of commerce, that 'system of interchanges founded on the organic
structure of the globe, and mercifully designed by the Author of our being
to subserve the most salutary ends in our physical and moral training'.
But far more prominent in his analysis is the refining effect of personal
trial and retribution.

Luther specified *temptation* as one of the three things requisite to make a minister.
It is equally indispensable to make a merchant; and a business-life involves a
perpetual trial of one's principles. It furnishes incessant openings for the suggestions of avarice, falsehood, extortion, and jealousy. It daily invites to indolence

---

[14] William Henry Hutchings, *The Mystery of the Temptation: A Course of Lectures*
(1875), 3–10.
[15] Gore, *Temptation and Atonement*, ii. 159.
[16] Bicheno, *Inquiry into the Nature of Benevolence*, p. 94.
[17] Horace Bushnell, 'How to be a Christian in trade', *Sermons on Living Subjects*
(1872), 266–7.
[18] H. A. Boardman, *The Bible in the Counting-House*, p. 3.
[19] H. A. Boardman, *The Great Question*, pp. 116–20.

or to rashness. And no man can, year after year, repel the Protean-like enticements to wrong-doing which lurk along the avenues of trade, and make their way into every counting-house, and insinuate themselves into every business-transaction, without becoming both a wiser and a better man.

Finally, failure in business impresses better than anything else 'a becoming sense of God's universal Providence'.[20]

Understandably, such writers, including Chalmers, wished to remove one of the central planks of scriptural economics, the Usury Laws, which lingered on the statute book until 1854, though in desuetude. Bentham, Paley, and Ricardo also wanted this, because they thought that repeal would encourage capitalists to lend and mechanics to invent. Evangelicals had no such desire for economic expansion, but they did believe that if capitalists were to achieve commercial (and spiritual) salvation through resisting temptation, then they must first be tempted to the utmost. Their detractors, such as Richard Jones, feared that repeal of the Usury Laws would be 'a fearful and intricate experiment upon the moral habits of the great body of the people',[21] not realizing perhaps that this was exactly what it was intended to be. William Sewell, a Tractarian whose moral philosophy is difficult to distinguish from that of moderate evangelicals, countered that the money-market ought never to be 'suppressed', because it constituted 'a field and discipline for some of men's greatest virtues', including self-control.[22]

The aetiology of business immorality is easy to reconstruct from countless sermons and novelettes. Once 'fallen', commercial man becomes a prey to materialism. His business absorbs too much of his life, and colours all his thoughts and actions, leaving no time for 'legitimate' and 'enlightened moral' amusement. 'Hence these jaundiced, dyspeptic, jaded, emaciated, rheumatic, neuralgic, paralytic pill-boxes and boluses, ruins of men, who crowd the streets of mercantile and manufacturing cities, occupy counting-houses, and stand at Change.'[23] Master and man are equally ground down by 'this sad intensity of modern life': the former is liable to lunacy and sudden death, the latter is subjected to political economy's 'division of labour' and to a consequent alienation from the

---

[20] Boardman, *The Bible in the Counting-House*, pp. 50–2.

[21] [R. Jones], *Reasons against the Repeal of the Usury Laws* (1825), p. 3. Characteristically, Jones favoured government controls, on the grounds that natural demand for profit may, as in the case of the opium trade, be illegitimate.

[22] W. Sewell, *Christian Politics* (1844), 226. On Sewell's relationship to evangelicalism see above, p. 27. The first known defence of the usurer Shylock by a literary critic was [Richard Hole], 'An apology for the character and conduct of Shylock', *Essays, by a Society of Gentlemen, at Exeter* (Exeter, 1796), 552–73. Hole thought that Shylock's cruel conduct towards Antonio 'accorded with [Jewish] ideas of retributive justice', and was much less reprehensible than the prodigality of Lorenzo and the undutifulness of Jessica.

[23] [Anon.], 'The philosophy of amusement', *Meliora*, 6 (1864), 199.

work process. Gradually intensity turns into terror and creates deep psychological scars. Even honourable traders become 'tremulous and giddy' when contemplating the magnitude of their transactions, and the anxiety shows in their faces. 'The fear, not the fact—the fear of overtrading may so excite the mind of the man of vast enterprise, that he may, by finesse and contrivance, seek to veil the vastness of his transactions from other eyes, lest they should suspect, what by-and-bye may be the fact, that he has gone beyond his balance, and that a crash may follow the indiscretion, by which millions may suffer.'[24] When such a business starts to falter, the unfortunate partners dare not mention the fact, even to wives and children, for fear of shaking their own credit, 'and this suppression of misery, is worse than the misery itself'.[25] Inevitably the crash occurs, and, as if to emphasize the transitory nature of all temporal wealth, business failure brings immediate oblivion. 'The erasure of the name from the doors and of the memory of the firm from their friends were almost simultaneous.'[26]

'Did he fling himself down? who knows? for a vast speculation had fail'd?' [Tennyson, Maud, Part I, section i, §3]. For as many as flung themselves down, there were others who achieved through trial their modicum of grace. Perhaps not many emulated Henry Austin, a fiery evangelical banker who became ordained after going bankrupt in 1815, but many took seriously Irving's view that 'scanty poverty' was to be embraced as a trial of faith.[27] It is often recorded that victims of business crashes showed relief and even elation when the long-expected blow struck. 'We shall be the better for passing through the ordeal', confided Gladstone's father in 1826, a comment which gives point to Disraeli's description of Archibald Constable as indulging in an 'ecstasy of pompous passion' while on the point of his 'fatal and shattering bankruptcy' the year before.[28] The hero of Edmund Yates's Kissing the Rod. A Novel (1866) is one who learns unselfishness only after going bust—deserted by his wife, 'whom he had won with money', all he feels is worry and pity for her in her privations. They are reconciled at last, and parted only by death. 'It is indeed a kind Providence which superintends our concerns, and brings us into difficulties, that we may know who can extricate us out of them.' If this is tantamount to saying that God runs a 'protection racket', it is also a logical inference from the doctrine of the Trinity.

[24] Fisk, 'Moral influence of the commercial spirit', op. cit., pp. 278–9.
[25] E. Irving, 'Remarks on commercial distress', op. cit., p. 28.
[26] Yates, Kissing the Rod, iii. 90.
[27] Irving, 'Covetousness produced by natural affection', The Collected Writings of Edward Irving, ed. G. Carlyle (1864–5), iv. 455.
[28] John Gladstone to Robertson, 12 Jan. 1826, Checkland, The Gladstones, p. 155; Swartz, Disraeli's Reminiscences, p. 10.

We saw earlier that 'nature' could sometimes help to keep a merchant sound. It could also play its part in redeeming the fallen. In *The Moneyed Man, or, the Lesson of a Life* (1841) by the free trade novelist Horace Smith, who was a friend of Cobden, a weak and depraved protagonist eventually turns from his 'blind idolatry of wealth' towards 'self-purification' and 'moral redemption'. The turning-point comes shortly after he discovers that the family bank has broken. Just as he is on the verge of throwing himself into the Thames, he decides on an impulse to flee instead to the countryside, where, coming upon a secluded valley, the throbbings of his heart subside in ecstasy:

Never, no never, shall I forget the sensations that suddenly overwhelmed me at the sight of that beautiful, that majestic, that sublime spectacle. . . .

All was brightness and rapture, as if heaven and earth were celebrating their hymeneals amid universal smiles and love. . . .

'So then', I ejaculated, 'there are natural and simple pleasures, of whose existence I had no previous knowledge; pleasures which a pauper may command, and which are far more exquisite than all the sensual indulgences of the wealthiest voluptuary.'[29]

In evangelical argot a state of debt was always sinful, but an honourable bankruptcy—one in which the bankrupt strove to ensure that no one but himself ultimately suffered—was, of course, more than compatible with Christian virtue.[30] Evangelical families showed signs of pleasure at gaining an opportunity to be so noble. The Gurneys kept calm in the crisis of 1825, 'feeling the Lord to be near to us'.[31] Henry Thornton fils was judged to have 'gained so largely in character' during his period of near failure, 'and in the esteem, confidence and attachment of all the great bankers, that he will I am persuaded be ultimately a gainer even in a worldly point of view by his sharp trial'.[32] It was essential to keep a 'wax-like countenance' of calm during the crisis; the thing to fear was 'fear itself', which spread irrational panic and caused unnecessary failures. The Thornton case is vividly described in letters from Marianne Thornton to Hannah More.[33] In Marianne's account, the heroism of young Henry is characteristically contrasted with that of the 'villain', his partner Peter Free. The latter had apparently monopolized control of the company's affairs for some time past, and had displayed 'a spirit of speculation, a love of concealing what he did, *making the best* of a story', and other

---

[29] Horace Smith, *The Moneyed Man, or, the Lesson of a Life* (1841), ii. 102–37.
[30] Hugh Stowell, *The Christian Man in the Business of Life: A Lecture* (1856), 29–32.
[31] Gurney's journal, 23 Nov. 1825, Braithwaite, *Memoirs of Gurney*, i. 300.
[32] Zachary Macaulay to Thomas Babington, 15 Dec. 1825, Babington Papers, 27[150].
[33] E. M. Forster, *Marianne Thornton, 1797–1887: A Domestic Biography* (1956), 106–24.

conduct which was not 'strictly honourable and *therefore* not prudent'. When the crisis came suddenly, Free panicked, raved, and repined, could not act sensibly, and wanted to declare himself bankrupt on the spot, while another partner blubbed like a five-year-old. Henry manfully took the helm (Marianne slips into a Pittite simile here: 'there was something in the sight of so youthful a pilot weathering such a storm') several of his father's old friends rallied round, and the firm was eventually kept afloat. To Marianne, 'a special Providence seems to watch over those walls. Those same qualities of high honour, strict principle, and fearless integrity which once built it up, have now saved it from falling.' Henry himself considered that 'breaking' had made him great in the eyes of the world, while the Governor of the Bank of England reassured him, 'Since none of it is your doing, I can only tell you this is just the scene to make a man of you.' Richard Oastler was another evangelical whose bankruptcy allegedly revealed his 'mental and moral grandeur'. He paid his creditors and then, unlike Thornton, quitted business altogether.[34]

The 'Common Context' or 'Science in Culture'

So Malthus's was a double-headed spectre: wars, famines, and pestilence stalked the hovels of the poor as business crashes bedevilled the imagination of the bourgeoisie. But then it has often been pointed out that catastrophic and apocalyptic visions were common currency in the earlier nineteenth century, as exemplified in John Martin's painting *The Destruction of Pompeii and Herculaneum* (c.1821), and Bulwer-Lytton's novel *The Last Days of Pompeii* (1834). George Landow has suggested that the image of shipwreck is a popular element in the literary iconology of the day, and that 'the bourgeois version of this experience of the world is bankruptcy'.[35] The metaphor was undoubtedly popular. Burke warned against creating 'oceans of boundless debt', Chalmers bemoaned the 'ocean of contingency' on which businessmen 'floated' precariously, and a thousand other writers denounced the 'sea of speculation'.[36] Maybe thoughts of the biblical deluge encouraged such figures of speech. Bankrupts were often depicted as shipwrecks, floundering and splashing in their struggles to stay afloat, their very efforts to save themselves leading to the capsize

---

[34] Driver, *Tory Radical*, pp. 23–4.

[35] George P. Landow, *Images of Crisis: Literary Iconology, 1750 to the Present* (Boston and London, 1982), 110–11.

[36] Chalmers, *Application of Christianity to Commerce*, p. 275 [*Works*, vi. 206]. Elsewhere Chalmers, in a celebrated image, depicted the entire earth as floating 'on the ocean of vacancy, . . . the theatre of such a competition, as may have all the desires and all the energies of a divided universe embarked upon it'. Chalmers, *A Series of Discourses on the Christian Revelation, viewed in connection with the Modern Astronomy* (1817), 200 [*Works*, vii. 140–1].

of others. On the other hand, righteous men laid down their buoys, 'so that the waters of life may be navigated as nearly as possible secure from the danger of shipwreck'. People who did not maintain themselves from the savings of their former labours were shutting their eyes to 'breakers ahead'.[37] Peel drew an analogy between the fluctuations of the waves, caused by physical forces, and the fluctuations of society, caused by moral ones.[38] Storms were dangerous but beneficial. 'Storms are necessary in every department of Nature, physical, political, moral, religious—to clear the atmosphere', reflected Overstone stoically.[39] Violent quarrels were thought to have a similar purgative effect. It has been 'a salutary, albeit sharp medicine to your moral system', was how one evangelical curate admonished his contrite younger brother after trouncing him in a family dispute.[40]

Even more pervasive perhaps were geological metaphors. Business crashes were conventionally referred to as 'commercial earthquakes' and 'mercantile seizures'. 'He who, advanced in life, is living from hand to mouth, cultivates his vineyard on the slope of a volcano.'[41] Explosions of all sorts were thought to be caused by the build-up of internal pressures, an idea borrowed from contemporary wisdom in chemistry and mechanics. Coleridge was as usual scornful when such images were used to justify *laissez-faire* economics. 'We shall perhaps be told too, that the very Evils of this System, even the periodical *crash* itself, are to be regarded but as so much superfluous steam ejected by the Escape Pipes and Safety Valves of a self-regulating Machine.'[42]

Certainly the notion of 'release' was a powerful one. Boardman, for example, described business cycles as alternating 'periods of inflation and redundancy'. 'Without shedding of blood there can be no remission of sins', and since money was always thought of as the 'life-blood of the nation', it is no wonder that the regular and ritualistic spilling of blood every ten years or so was thought to be purifying. 'We have been crammed with circulating medium', wrote one pious banker, 'and we ought to have less of it amongst us.' Attwood more than once alluded to business crashes in the language of sexual release, while there was also a scatological variant, the 1825 crisis being 'the explosion of a noxious vapour which had been long gradually accumulating'.[43] Such themes appealed particularly

[37] William Ellis, *A Layman's Contribution to the Knowledge and Practice of Religion in Common Life* (1857), 298, 318.

[38] See below, p. 231.

[39] Overstone to Norman, 5 Sept. 1874, O'Brien, *Correspondence of Overstone*, iii. 1266-7.

[40] Mary Blamire Young, *Richard Wilton: A Forgotten Victorian* (1967), 70-6.

[41] Ellis, *Religion in Common Life*, p. 318.

[42] Coleridge, '*Blessed are Ye that Sow beside all Waters*', p. 100 [*Collected Works of Coleridge*, No. 6, p. 205].

[43] *Diary illustrative of the Times of George the Fourth*, ed. John Galt (1838-9), iv. 346.

to the indigestive Carlyle, whose imagery, as John Burrow has pointed out, 'is igneous, saturated, like the paintings of John Martin, with the Vulcanist geology; . . . its calculated aesthetic effects are those of the terror-sublime. Historical change, in *The French Revolution*, is a fearful apocalypse of convulsive heavings, belchings, terrifying crackings of the surface of assumed normality, seas of fire, driven through the vents, overspreading the earth.'[44] Thus was society obsessed by seizures, by spasms (remember Edward Hawkins's death throes, by earthquakes and volcanoes, by 'the *expulsive* power of a new affection'.

This brings us, briefly and superficially, to a consideration of what Robert Young has called the 'common context' of scientific debate in the first half of the nineteenth century.[45] Christians who wrote and read about economics wrote and read also about the natural and physical sciences. It is clear that the idea of analogies between the sciences was a widespread assumption at that time,[46] and resemblances between work in different branches of knowledge are not hard to find. If, as is widely accepted by historians, natural philosophy and theology impinged on the development of scientific thought, there is every reason to suppose that it affected the science of society as well.

The science most closely connected with political economy was geology. Both disciplines were greatly in vogue during the late eighteenth and early nineteenth centuries, and both had to beat off the challenge of those who thought them potentially irreligious. Moderate evangelicals took a lively and on the whole constructive attitude to geology, though the extremists who came into prominence during the 1830s were less tolerant, and after about 1835 evangelical attention turned to other matters, such as the growing Tractarian threat from Oxford. Moreover, both economics and geology had become locked into a tension between conflicting views as to time scale. The 'division of labour' principle as promulgated in *The Wealth of Nations* (1776) and the fashionable cry of Free Trade, together with the observed facts of economic expansion, were opening men's eyes to the possibility of endless growth, but on the other hand the *Essay on Population* (1798), and the scarcities and famines which affected England and Ireland, reminded them of the inescapable limits within which society revolved. In the same way, Smith's near contemporary James Hutton hinted at the infinite vastness of time and space in his *Theory of the Earth* (1785–8), and the empirical work of paleontologists and cartographers

[44] John Burrow, *A Liberal Descent: Victorian Historians and the English Past* (Cambridge, 1981), 255.

[45] Robert M. Young, 'Natural theology, Victorian periodicals and the fragmentation, of a common context', *Darwin to Einstein: Historical Studies on Science and Belief*, ed. Colin Chant and John Fauvel (1980), 69–107.

[46] See below, p. 175.

was uncovering a vast amount of earth history as layers on layers of rock and fossil remains were catalogued; but, on the other hand, it was difficult to throw off the scriptural message that the earth was but a few thousand years old. Given their biblical preconceptions, geologists had to cram more and more geological 'events' into the limited amount of time prescribed by Genesis, and this not unnaturally led to an emphasis on cyclical development, punctuated by sudden and large-scale catastrophes like floods and earthquakes.[47] Cuvier's *Essay on the Theory of the Earth* (1811; translated 1813) also popularized the view that successful species in the past must have needed revolutionary catastrophes to displace them, since he felt that they could surely have adapted to merely gradual changes in the universe. Volcanoes, especially, fitted the prevailing ideas of 'catastrophe' and 'release mechanism', and explanations of the sort put forward by the Oxford geologist Charles Daubeny—that they resulted from water reacting with the uncombined bases of alkalis and earths underground—were extremely popular.[48] For so long as the limit of time assigned to the earth's past remained so circumscribed, it was hard for men to accept the notion of uniformitarian progress put forward in Charles Lyell's *Principles of Geology* (1833).

J. B. Sumner and Chalmers were prominent among the small army of 'scriptural geologists' and followed Cuvier in arguing that, though Noah's Flood had been the only 'general destruction or revolution' to have taken place *since* the creation (as described by Moses), there had obviously been worlds existing before the 'genesis' of the present one, earlier worlds of which fossil evidence was now accumulating, and 'from the wreck of which our globe was organized'.[49] The most prominent of such apologists was William Buckland, whose celebrated inaugural lecture as Reader in Geology at Oxford in 1819 followed Sumner fairly closely. Buckland insisted that he had not 'read a word of the Huttonian or Wernerian doctrines' until after he had gathered the geological 'facts' necessary to form his devout conclusions.[50] At all events, his claim to have unearthed

[47] Martin J. S. Rudwick, *The Meaning of Fossils: Episodes in the History of Palaeontology* (1972), 101–63; R. Hooykaas, *Natural Law and Divine Miracle: The Principle of Uniformity in Geology, Biology and Theology* (Leiden, 1963).

[48] C. Daubeny, *A Description of Active and Extinct Volcanos* (1826), 357–60, 390–3.

[49] Sumner, *Treatise on the Records of Creation*, i. 284–5; Chalmers, 'Remarks on Cuvier's *Theory of the Earth*', *The Christian Instructor* (1814) [*Works*, xii 349–72]; Leroy E. Page, 'Diluvialism and its critics in Great Britian in the early nineteenth century', in *Towards a History of Geology*, ed. Cecil J. Schneer (Cambridge, Mass., and London, 1969), 262–4; Charles Coulton Gillispie, *Genesis and Geology: A Study in the Relations of Scientific Thought, Natural Theology, and Social Opinion in Great Britain, 1790–1850* (Cambridge, Mass., 1951), 210–16. On Chalmers as a catastrophist see Walter Cannon, 'The problem of miracles in the 1830s', *Victorian Studies*, 4 (1960–1), 15–18.

[50] Buckland to Drummond, 16 Jan. 1837, Northumberland MSS, Drummond Papers, C/1/72.

scientific evidence in confirmation of the Mosaic account of the Deluge, in *Vindiciae Geologicae* (1820) and *Reliquiae Diluvianae* (1823), won him much popular favour as well as public preferment.[51] The former work was reviewed for the *Quarterly* by John Barrow, but in a wholly technical or scientific manner which displeased the author, who had been anxious for 'something higher, and . . . more philosophical'.[52] The task of noticing *Reliquiae Diluvianae* therefore fell to Copleston, whose lavish praise centred on Buckland's having 'introduced new and convincing proofs of providential design—of that system of final causes, which is deeply impressed on the whole mechanism of nature'. Moreover, Buckland's catastrophist theory of the Flood, and his view that despite the universal destruction a few human beings had been allowed to survive, suggested to Copleston that an 'immediate', 'positive', or 'special' providence had been at work; though he was careful to add that even if the Flood had been due to natural causes, as geologists like Greenough were suggesting, this would in no way impugn the doctrines of Christianity, since 'even miraculous agency is often, nay generally, combined with natural means'.[53]

An interesting and important, but slightly misleading, judgment on this geological controversy was made in 1951 by C. C. Gillispie. He pointed out that before Darwin progressive or 'uniformitarian' geologists like Greenough and then Lyell maintained

that their hypotheses contributed more powerfully to an exalted understanding of the omnipotence and omniscience of a Creator whose initial design was sufficient for all His purposes than did the Neptunist and catastrophist effort to cast the world into the bosom of an uncertain and ubiquitous Providence. The doctrine of final cause was attacked by no one. The trouble was not that progressives themselves rejected the idea of purposeful design, but that their opponents instinctively felt that eliminating providential direction would lead in that direction. If material phenomena are sufficiently explained by natural causation, the argument for design might be strengthened, but the evidence of control would be weakened. And in the nineteenth century, unlike the eighteenth century, orthodox natural theology was more interested in control than design. It was chiefly on this account that Huttonian and uniformitarian theories were suspect.[54]

---

[51] See below, pp. 235–6.

[52] William Gifford to John Murray, July and Sept. 1823, H. and H. C. Shine, *The Quarterly Review under Gifford: Identification of Contributors 1809–1824* (Chapel Hill, 1949), 84.

[53] [E. Copleston], 'Buckland—*Reliquiae Diluvianae*', *Quarterly Review*, 29 (1823), 158–9, 165; Copleston to Grenville, 1 Sept. 1823, Additional Dropmore Papers, BL Add. MS 59416, fos. 92–3.

[54] Gillispie, *Genesis and Geology*, p. 226.

Gillispie may well be correct in saying that nineteenth-century natural theologians stressed control more than design, but it is an over-simplification to identify catastrophism with belief in an interventionist as distinct from general providence. The financial collapse of 1825 did strike many observers as 'special' because of its unexpectedness, but by 1857 the regularity of business crashes made them seem perfectly compatible with divine design and forethought. The point is rather that to a generation under the evangelical spell, sudden catastrophe could seem to be an outcome, all too mechanically predictable, of mankind's wickedness and contrary behaviour, as Thomas Gisborne assured the readers of his geological jottings in 1818.[55]

Publication of Lyell's *Principles* in 1833 made the scriptural literalness of *Reliquiae Diluvianae* hard to accept, as Buckland himself recognized.[56] In the *Edinburgh Review* for 1837, the most overtly evangelical scientist of his day, David Brewster, upbraided those scriptural geologists who tried to argue from Genesis that the earth was young and that the stories of the six-day creation and the Flood explained all known phenomena, since the facts were clearly against such a belief. For Brewster the real answer was to be found in Hutton's cyclical view that, though man was a recent creation, various animal species went back much further, proving that there had been 'another distinct period of the living world', and that as planets revolve, so worlds succeed each other cyclically in time, with 'no vestige of a beginning—no prospect of an end'.[57] In this way geologists had

outstripped the theologian, by discovering the true interpretation of the first page of sacred writ—and have proved, by infallible evidence, that, previous to the creation of man, the earth was inhabited by races of animals that were successively overwhelmed by great and destructive convulsions; and that new races, different from those which preceded them, and from those which now occupy our globe, were created by the immediate interposition of divine power.[58]

Forewarned by the Bible, Brewster had no doubt that when the present cycle was done, the earth would be 'burnt up', and 'new heavens and

---

[55] See above, p. 22.
[56] William Buckland, *Geology and Mineralogy Considered with Reference to Natural Theology*, Bridgewater Treatise No. 6 (1836), 8–33. See Michael Bartholemew, 'Lyell and evolution: an account of Lyell's response to the prospect of an evolutionary ancestry for man', *British Journal for the History of Science*, 6 (1972–3), 261–303.
[57] [D. Brewster], 'Geology and mineralogy', *Edinburgh Review*, 65 (1837), 5–6. Brewster told the Edinburgh Philosophical Institution in 1851 that man could not have survived the storms, earthquakes, and irruptions that marked the world's period of preparation, and that even if he could have done so, his presence was not required 'for his intellectual powers could have had no suitable employment'. *The Home Life of Sir David Brewster*, by his daughter Mrs Gordon (Edinburgh, 1869), 226–8.
[58] [Brewster], 'Geology and mineralogy', op. cit., p. 2.

and a new earth shall replace the ruins of a world'. Thus did God make 'even the convulsions of the material world subservient to the civilisation and happiness of his creatures'.[59] Like his lifelong friend Chalmers, Brewster was a moderate evangelical, believing in the grand truths—original sin, the Atonement, the Trinity, election, and the eternity of punishment—and he opposed the 'assurance of faith' claimed by more extreme evangelicals as the 'height of presumption and self-righteousness'.[60] His emphasis on earthquakes and volcanoes did not imply belief in a hyperactive, interventionist God, but fitted in with his conception of a mechanical order of things.

The link between evangelical social thought and evangelical science can be pointed up by reference to those who strongly opposed both. Charles Poulett Scrope, for example, was someone whose thought ran counter to the philosophy of 'Atonement' in every way. He wrote prolifically on geology and political economy and was extremely scornful of Chalmers's ideas on both subjects. He was an Anti-Bullionist, and regarded the resumption of cash payments as having defrauded productive industry of £1,500,000,000. He recommended the setting up of a National Bank, the par value of whose notes would be fixed, not with reference to gold, but according to the average price of various commodities, and then guaranteed by law.[61] Like Drummond he denied the possibility of gluts, except as a result of monetary mismanagement by the Bank; believed in the unlimited capacity of the globe for food production; utterly opposed the attempts of Malthus and Chalmers to restrict the enjoyment of marital conjugality;[62] and hailed the extension of the Poor Law to Ireland in 1838 as 'most just and righteous', albeit not without some unfortunate side-effects.[63] A uniformitarian in geology, he utterly rejected Daubeny's dramatic version of volcanic activity: eruptions would be 'comparatively constant, tranquil, and invariable' if it were not for the accidental obstruction of vents in the earth's surface.[64] In the *Quarterly Review* for 1835 he praised Lyell for having created an epoch in geological science, for having dispelled a hitherto universal belief in 'revolutions and convulsions, deluges or cataclysms', and shown 'by what succession of

---

[59] Ibid., pp. 3, 15.   [60] Gordon, *Home Life of Brewster*, pp. 312–14.
[61] G. Poulett Scrope, *An Examination of the Bank Charter Question, with an Inquiry into the Nature of a Just Standard of Value, and Suggestions for the Improvement of our Monetary System* (1833), 20–9, 60–6; G. P. Scrope, *On Credit Currency and its Superiority to Coin* (1830), 32–5. See Scrope to Charles Babbage, n.d., Babbage Papers, BL Add. MS 37201, fos. 423–5.
[62] G. P. Scrope, *Principles of Political Economy, deduced from the Natural Laws of Social Welfare, and applied to the Present State of Britain* (1833), 211–16, 269–89.
[63] G. P. Scrope, *The Irish Poor Law: How Far it has Failed? and Why?* (1849), 5.
[64] G. P. Scrope, *Considerations on Volcanos, leading to the Establishment of a New Theory of the Earth* (1825), 61–2.

secondary causes' the globe's 'Great Author and Designer gradually moulded and fashioned it to his use'.

TIME is, in truth, the master-key to the problems of geology. And the concession of an unlimited period for the working of the existing powers of nature has permitted us to dispense with comets, deluges, and other prodigies which were once brought forward, *ad libitum*, to solve every difficulty in the path of the speculating geologist.[65]

As we shall see,[66] the abandonment of Malthusian restraints with respect to growth in the 1850s was to have much the same effect on political economy as Scrope's realization that there were 'unlimited drafts' to be 'made upon antiquity' had had upon geology: both helped to dispel the notion of an inevitable sequence of cycles and revolutions.[67] Scrope was sorry that, despite the great boost his researches had given to the 'progressivists', Lyell himself clung to a cyclical view of the passage of time, albeit one in which cycles were held to be gradually 'diminishing in violence'.[68]

Medicine in this period was a more technically advanced subject than geology and less liable to scriptural distortion. Not that it did not furnish material for the natural theologians. Paley had dilated on the human anatomy in introducing his argument from design, and the introduction to Thomas Watson's influential textbook of 1843, *Lectures on the Principles and Practice of Physic*, rehearses most of the conventional pieties. Thus the body is an 'exquisite contrivance', a perfect adaptation of means to ends, and the way in which one kidney will enlarge to take over if its twin becomes inefficient is comparable to the law of political economy which states 'that the supply of a marketable commodity is regulated by the demand for it'. The profession of medicine was still only on its way towards respectability, and Watson's appeals on its behalf were alive to the prevailing moral tone. A career in medicine is 'a salutary school of mental and of moral discipline', its numerous trials having great power to 'chastise the feelings' of practitioners. 'The sad varieties of human pain and weakness . . . should rebuke our pride, while they quicken our charity. Still more important, the study of disease justifies God's moral government, for

---

[65] [G. P. Scrope], 'Lyell's *Principles of Geology*', *Quarterly Review*, 53 (1835), 407–10.

[66] See below, pp. 262–3, 300–1.

[67] Martin J. S. Rudwick, 'Poulett Scrope on the volcanoes of Auvergne: Lyellian time and political economy', *British Journal for the History of Science*, 7 (1974), 205–42, has used linguistic evidence to suggest that Scrope's geology may have been influenced by his views on population theory. The literature on the connections between geology and political economy is surveyed by Salim Rashid, 'Political economy and geology in the early nineteenth century: similarities and contrasts', *History of Political Economy*, 13 (1981), 726–44.

[68] [Scrope], 'Lyell's *Principles of Geology*', op. cit., pp. 447–8.

It is ours to know in how many instances, forming indeed a vast majority of the whole, bodily suffering and sickness are the natural fruits of evil courses; of the sins of our fathers, of our own unbridled passions, of the malevolent spirit of others. We see, too, the uses of these judgments, which are mercifully designed to recall men from the strong allurements of vice, and the slumber of temporal prosperity; teaching that it is good for us to be sometimes afflicted.

And if nothing else, the constant presence of death reminds doctors that their time is short, and that only God can redeem, as only he can heal.[69]

Moral and theological considerations were not always as explicit as this, however. The historian Karl Figlio sees academic medicine in the early nineteenth century 'as a bearer of bourgeois ideology', 'redefining' health problems so as to emphasize 'personal responsibility for illness' and to absolve the industrial work process from blame. He points out that this function corresponds to what Marx had to say on the cash nexus.

For Marx, the commodity exchange characteristic of liberal capitalist society replaced all qualitative differences by the single abstract measure of exchange value. People were reduced to abstract labour power, which was sold as a commodity. From a social point of view everyone was the same, so that the actual social differences between people had to come from natural ones. Thus *social inequality* was naturalized by an ideology based on *social equality*.

For Figlio, medicine did likewise by identifying health with self-discipline, with a sound constitution and a wholesomeness of person, and while one may be sceptical of that part of his argument which emphasizes bourgeois conspiracy and intention, it is certainly the case that spiritual and mental health was thought to precede physical well-being. *Mens sana ergo corpus sanum.*[70]

The commonest cause of death, and the subject of most medical investigation, was fever. The spasmodic nature of cholera, with visitations in 1831–2, 1847–8, 1853–4, and 1866, caught public attention far more than greater, more constant, but less dramatic killers such as enteric typhus, and inevitably it was a fruitful subject for those who liked to reflect on the dispensations of providence.[71] It was said that 'excitement

---

[69] Thomas Watson, *Lectures on the Principles and Practice of Physic* (1843), i. 2, 13–17.

[70] Karl Figlio, 'Chlorosis and chronic disease in nineteenth-century Britain: the social constitution of somatic illness in a capitalist society', *Social History*, 3 (1978), 167–97. See below, pp. 307–8, on the way in which mid-century medical attitudes reversed this order of priorities.

[71] On the question of cholera and providence, Morris points out that in 1832 Anglicans tended to be vague about the sins for which society was being punished, whereas Nonconformists, and especially Methodists, were often very specific. He suggests that this is because Anglicans, exercising power in society, liked to think of God's power as being mediated through themselves, whereas Dissenters preferred a God who was in detailed charge of events, picking his victims with infinite care. R. J. Morris, *Cholera 1832: The Social Response to an Epidemic* (1976), 129–58.

performs in the moral world an office analogous to the attraction of gravitation in the physical world'.[72] Excitement, implying stimulation, was a common scientific term of the day, in chemistry as well as in medicine, where a distinction was made between diseases of excitement and diseases of debility. Pulmonary tuberculosis was among the latter, and it is perhaps significant that its popular name derived from economics. Adam Smith may have regarded consumption as the proper end of production, but in the popular mind the word retained some of its pejorative seventeenth-century meaning, as the destructive or wasteful employment of productive matter. In that sense the term 'underconsumption' was meaningless, and it is unsurprising that economic crises should have been regarded rather as cases of overproduction, requiring evacuation.

In the same way, the commonest treatment for fever was the evacuation of the circulating system, and there was considerable debate between those who favoured 'heroic bloodlettings' periodically and those who advocated smaller and more frequent bleedings.[73] Blood-letting seemed indicated because of the way in which fevers were diagnosed in the first half of the nineteenth century. Significantly its heyday coincided with that of 'anticontagionism'. In the eighteenth century most English doctors, unlike their French counterparts, had seen fevers as both contagious and debilitating. They had therefore been opposed to bleeding, as this would merely make the debility worse. But from about 1805 a growing number of doctors, including many who had been discharged from military service, came round to the view that fevers were inflammatory, and that they should be met by bleeding. 'Immediate' and 'copious' blood-letters in the first half of the nineteenth century, such as John Armstrong, Benjamin Welsh, and Henry Clutterbuck, all argued that fever was in some way 'congestive' and 'inflammatory', an 'over-loading' of the body, possibly caused by dietary excess or other forms of intemperance. For without a Pasteur to show how diseases could come from bacteria *outside* the body, it was easily assumed that the body must have generated its own infirmities. 'There is nothing outside a man which by going into him can defile him; but the things which come out of a man are what defile him' (Mark 7: 15). This assumption, that disease was internal and intrinsic, led doctors to think that shedding of the body's main internal constituent, blood, might bring relief. It was a view that was strengthened, as Margaret Pelling has shown, by the fact that 'fever appeared as the fundamental phenomenon in a large number of diseased conditions where the whole

---

[72] Thomas Doubleday, *On Mundane Moral Government demonstrating its Analogy with the System of Material Government* (Edinburgh and London, 1852), 27.

[73] For a summing up on this debate see Watson, *Lectures on Physic*, i. 214–23; Lester S. King, 'The blood-letting controversy: a study in the scientific method', *Bulletin of the History of Medicine*, 35 (1961), 1–13.

body was affected', and that 'its explanation had, therefore, to be in terms of those fluids or organic systems (the circulatory, the nervous) which were capable of determining the state of the whole constitution'. Whereas French doctors, abandoning their habits of the previous century, looked more and more for *local* explanations of inflammation, doctors in Britain clung to the idea of systemic, 'essential or idiopathic fever, that is, a generalised febrile state', probably caused by an abnormal pathology of the fluids.[74] Bleeding was thought to act, not directly on the disease, 'but rather by a kind of counter-impression on the system, by which the disease is influenced in a secondary way'; that is, it aroused the body to what was often referred to as a 'panic', in the same way that a cold bath, extreme pain, alcohol, or violent emotion might do.[75] Such heroic medicine, though fashionable, continued to be opposed by contagionists, who still insisted that fevers were debilitating and should not be bled. And by 1840 there were increasing doubts about the practice of bleeding. Blood, it was noticed, was spurting neither so far nor so fast as it had in the 1820s. 'Just as improved economic conditions had been cited to explain the lack of direct debility and excess of inflammatory activity' earlier in the century, 'now massive unemployment in the woollen manufactories was cited to explain a debilitating destitution among the poor due to dietary insufficiency and predisposing to contagion.'[76]

The question here is whether changing medical fashions can be linked to changing social and economic theories. On this it may be useful to consider what one scholar has described as 'the American prologue of the anticontagionist revolution':[77] that is, the work of two 'liberal' physicians, Benjamin Rush and Noah Webster, who in the immediate post-revolutionary period abandoned the tradition of their former colonial masters (which was still against vigorous bleeding) in favour of eighteenth-century French practices.[78] Rush was of a Quaker background but had 'gotten' vital religion by reading the work of the 'New Light' Presbyterians of the 1740s Great Awakening—disciples of Jonathan Edwards and fervent believers in sin, redemption, and national retributions. Since then he had become acquainted with many famous *philosophes* and had studied

[74] Margaret Pelling, *Cholera, Fever and English Medicine 1825–1865* (Oxford, 1978), 1–7, 14–24.

[75] Henry Clutterbuck, *Lectures on Blood-letting* (Philadelphia 1839), 12, quoted in King, 'Blood-letting controversy', loc. cit., p. 5. H. Clutterbuck, *On the Proper Administration of Blood-Letting, for the Prevention and Cure of Disease* (1840), 125.

[76] Peter H. Niebyl, 'The English bloodletting revolution, or modern medicine before 1850', *Bulletin of the History of Medicine*, 51 (1977), 479–80.

[77] Erwin H. Ackerknecht, 'Anticontagionism between 1821 and 1867', ibid., 22 (1948), 569.

[78] Benjamin Rush, *Medical Inquiries and Observations* (4th edn, Philadelphia, 1815) iv. 223.

medicine at Edinburgh, where he befriended the liberal Dr Currie, later
of Liverpool, but though he complemented his redemptionist instincts
with a dash of enlightenment, he never abandoned them. Pilloried by
Cobbett as the 'murderous Dr Sangrado',[79] Rush even bled maniacs,
considering them too to be suffering from a form of fever.[80] Believing
as he did in 'an indissoluble union between physiology, metaphysics, and
Christianity . . . so . . . that they mutually afford not only support but
beauty and splendor to each other',[81] it is not surprising that he also drew
a connection between medicine and economics, between too much money
in the body politic and too much blood in the body natural, between
'overtrading' and 'overloading'. Nothing distressed him more after the
Declaration of Independence than the introduction of paper money. 'Every
dollar . . . is replete with poison to the liberties and virtue of our country.'
Paper money and the funding system fostered speculation and forestalling,
ruined widows and orphans, erected a monied aristocracy, 'created our
canine appetite for wealth, . . . reduced regular industry and virtuous
economy to the rank of sniveling virtues, and rendered "enterprise and
successful speculation" the only mark of civic worth'.[82] A copious
bleeding of poisonous bankrupts was, in Rush's view, the only road back
to Republican virtue, and would conduce to the gradual improvement
of mankind. 'Civilization, human knowledge, and liberty . . . the heralds
of religion', would eventually ensure that evil was 'ultimately annihilated'
and secure the 'Atonement of all'.[83]

Like Webster, Rush was convinced that the yellow fevers of 1793–1803
had been *local* in origin, due to the 'epidemic constitution of the atmosphere', that they had not been imported. This was an essential premiss for
those who believed in the poison *within*. He even subscribed to Webster's
view, which gained a certain currency in England, that earthquakes
were also associated with this 'epidemic constitution of the atmosphere':
'derangements in the whole animal and vegetable creation, *in* the *sky*,
on the earth, and *under* the earth, all combine to prove the domestic origin
of epidemic diseases'.[84] Like other anticontagionists, Rush objected to
the Quarantine Laws, imposed against foreigners at the instigation of a
majority of doctors, who thought that the fevers had been imported.

[79] For the dispute with Cobbett see *Letters of Benjamin Rush*, ed. L. H. Butterfield
(Princeton, NJ, 1951), ii. 1213–18.
[80] Rush to John Seward, 28 Dec. 1796, ibid., ii. 784.
[81] Rush to Thomas Jefferson, 2 Jan. 1811, ibid., ii. 1075.
[82] Rush to John Dunlap, 3 July 1779, ibid., i. 232–3; to John Adams, 21 Jan. 1781
and 21 Dec. 1810, ibid., i. 261 and ii. 1073; to James Madison, 27 Feb. 1820, ibid., i. 539.
[83] Rush to John Seward, 28 Dec. 1796, ibid., ii. 783; to John Montgomery, 6 June
1801, ibid., ii. 834.
[84] Rush to N. Webster, 9 Dec. 1800, ibid., ii. 828; to T. Pickering, 30 Sept. 1799,
ibid., ii. 816. *British Critic* 16 (1800), 160–8.

Quarantine was a despotic weapon, offensive to Rush's Republican sensibilities; it was also leading to retaliation against American merchants.[85]

So did a preference for blood-letting indicate a capitalist mentality? A famous suggestion to this effect occurs in Erwin Ackerknecht's seminal article of 1948.[86] Commenting on the widespread acceptance of anticontagionist views in Europe during the first half of the nineteenth century — that is, a refusal by most doctors to believe that plague merely 'spread' from town to town and nation to nation — Ackerknecht suggests that wilful liberal progressivism was largely responsible for this misunderstanding. Contagionism seemed to be an irrational medieval heresy that needed to be extirpated; a handy tool of despots, an excuse for quarantine and suchlike assaults on personal liberty; a tool of mercantilism also, in that it militated against contacts with other nations. Anticontagionists 'wrote long and detailed dissertations of exactly how many millions of pounds, francs or dollars were yearly lost through the contagionist error'.

Quarantines meant, to the rapidly growing class of merchants and industrialists, a source of losses, a limitation to expansion, a weapon of bureaucratic control that it was no longer willing to tolerate, and this class was quite naturally with its press and deputies, its material, moral, and political resources behind those who showed that the scientific foundations of quarantine were naught, and who anyhow were usually sons of this class.[87]

Leading anticontagionists like Maclean, Chervin, Magendie, Aubert-Roche, and Virchow were 'known radicals and liberals', while most contagionists were apparently high-ranking military officers and bureaucrats, so it is not surprising that in Continental Europe 'the ascendancy of anticontagionism coincides with the rise of liberalism, its decline with the victory of the reaction' after 1848.[88] Of course, as Ackerknecht acknowledges, there were respectable scientific reasons for opposing contagionism in the generation *before* germ theory, when it was assumed that any contagion must be carried in the air, while Pelling has warned us that any simple dichotomy between contagionists and their opponents is hard to maintain after about 1835, and impossible where *formal* medical science

---

[85] Rush to James Madison, 23 June 1801, Butterfield, *Letters of Rush*, ii. 835–6.

[86] Ackerknecht, 'Anticontagionism between 1821 and 1867', op. cit., pp. 589–92.

[87] Ibid., p. 567. Ackerknecht points out, pp. 568–9, that though many experts were non-committal in theory, they tended towards anticontagionism in the great *practical* test, which was opposition to quarantine.

[88] Ibid., pp. 589–91. See [Anon.], 'Contagion of plague, and policy of the Quarantine Laws', *The British Review, and London Critical Journal*, 13 (1819), 439–59, for the view that governments should legislate against the plague, as the Jewish lawgiver stayed the plague by placing himself between the dead and the living.

is concerned. Even so it seems a reasonable hypothesis, since most English doctors were liberal and bourgeois, that political and intellectual factors worked powerfully in favour of anticontagionism.[89]

Nevertheless, the connection probably needs to be explained more subtly than this. Recently Peter Niebyl has refined Ackerknecht's argument by suggesting that medical liberalism in its blood-letting phase was less concerned to attack government bureaucracy than to uphold the autonomy of individual bodies. He finds a clue as to what liberal medicine was about in the criticism which a French liberal physician, L. J. Begin, made on the concept of 'the autocratism of nature'. This implied that

there was 'a conflict between the morbific causes and the organic powers'—the latter being the autocrat who needs supportive therapy. Begin considered this an absurd 'medicine of symptoms,' symptoms which were supported and stimulated—the very opposite of bloodletting, which was used to remove the oppressive cause. Thus, the modern practice of thought that the body needs support in its fight against the contagious agent was apparently alien to liberal thought at that time. This would explain why therapy in general, and bloodletting in particular, and not simply contagionism, were so crucial . . . The medical liberal was not so much concerned with the real bureaucracy as he was with making the human body the symbolic autocracy attacking foreign invaders.[90]

In other words, the essence of medical liberalism was dualism. The body was conceived as an autonomous vessel invaded by morbific powers which needed to be repelled, in the same way that the soul had to be purged of sin. The idea of contagion, on the other hand, like those of uniformitarianism, evolution, conservation, and organic recycling, threatened this essential separation of man from the material world. The triumph of these concepts in the middle of the nineteenth century was to shift medical thinking away from the autonomous but mind-dominated body and towards the 'autocratism of nature'.

Margaret Pelling considers that this mid-century change of attitude was a logical outcome of the scientific debates: anticontagionism led certain doctors to consider the environmental factors in disease, which in turn led to improvements in sanitary provision in the 1850s and 1860s. Ackerknecht and Niebyl are more willing to consider ideological reasons for the shift of opinion. In 1856 an early historian of medicine from

---

[89] Morris, *Cholera 1832*, pp. 183-4; see A. A. MacLaren's review of the same in *Social History*, 3 (1978), 108-10; and also A. A. MacLaren, 'Bourgeois ideology and Victorian philanthropy: the contradictions of cholera', *Social Class in Scotland: Past and Present*, ed. A. Allan MacLaren (Edinburgh, n.d.), 36-54. Thomas Watson, a contagionist, claimed that anticontagionist blood-letters tended to 'liberal opinions in politics and religion'.
[90] Niebyl, 'English bloodletting revolution', op. cit., pp. 481-2; L. J. Begin, *Treatise on Therapeutics* (New York, 1829), i. 26.

Germany, August Hirsch, observed that 'the more the belief in the contagious nature of cholera became widespread in the medical world, the smaller became the number of facts in which contagious genesis could not be proven', on which Ackerknecht comments: 'this suggests that to a certain extent emotional conversion, based on the accumulated despair of repeated cholera epidemics and the normal "swing of the pendulum," preceded intellectual insight and discovery, rather provoking than being provoked by the latter'.[91] Niebyl meanwhile argues that the move away from bleeding in the treatment of fevers during the forties *preceded* the scientific observations and academic controversies of the fifties. 'The rise and fall of bloodletting' was less the result of medical advances than of a 'revolution . . . in men's minds'.

It is of course men's minds that are the subject of this study, and the point of this superficial digression into medical history is simply to suggest how strongly men were conditioned to interpret all aspects of life in terms of revolutionary cycles. As we saw, Rush regarded famines, volcanoes, and epidemics as interrelated, a consequence of 'derangement *in* the *sky*, *on* the earth, and *under* the earth'. F. D. Maurice demanded, 'do you think there may be no gout, palsy, and *delirium tremens*, brought on in [the body politic], as well as in the natural body, by gluttony and by intoxication? Do we never hear of speculations and panics which at once suggest the thoughts of fever and of ague?'[92] In this context it is not surprising that business crashes should have been regarded by many as a similar sort of sudden disaster to cholera, but one which affected the lives of the bourgeoisie, one that was far worse indeed than the mere epidemics and starvations which befell the poor. No doubt when life is impoverished death can be assumed to be a merciful release, agonizing death a 'moral discipline' in the nick of spiritual time; the well-to-do, on the other hand, are susceptible to terrible losses and shame. William Ellis, philanthropist and founder of the Birkbeck Schools, agreed with Chalmers that the only way to prevent bankruptcies was by proper Christian instruction in the obligations of business. But he could not understand why this need was not being tackled more urgently than it was.

What are the measures adopted, on the occurrence of calamities of *far less magnitude* than those in which bankruptcy involves its victims? When any particular district is visited by epidemic, is not inquiry instituted into the causes, with a view to their removal if possible? When death takes place out of the ordinary course, is not an inquest held?[93]

---

[91] Ackerknecht, 'Anticontagionism between 1821 and 1867', op. cit., p. 590.
[92] F. D. Maurice, *On the Reformation of Society, and How All Classes may Contribute to it: A Lecture* (Southampton and London, 1851), 12.
[93] Ellis, *Religion in Common Life*, p. 319 (italics added).

Clearly death was thought to be a lesser calamity than debt, and not only by unworldly clerics. Thus in setting his face against relief to famine-ridden Ireland, Trevelyan could aver that death by starvation was 'a discipline', and a smaller evil than bankruptcy.[94]

Not surprisingly, Chalmers's medical antagonist, W. P. Alison, the proponent of official or legal charity, opposed the miasmatic theory of fever in favour of environmentalist explanations. In arguing that only security — not suffering — could induce moral restraint in working-men, Alison revised Malthus's famous dictum: 'It *is not the fear of lowering but the hope of maintaining or bettering their condition*, which really constitutes [the] preventive check.'[95] Alison was to medicine what Scrope was to geology; both of them point towards the ideas of the mid-century, in social as well as in scientific thought. We shall see in Chapter 8 how the ideology of Atonement succumbed to a gentler interpretation of nature and a more benign approach to social problems, but first we must consider how that ideology had permeated the more formal philosophy of the earlier nineteenth century, and also how it had operated in public life.

---

[94] Jenifer Hart, 'Sir Charles Trevelyan at the Treasury', *English Historical Review*, 75 (1960), 99.

[95] W. P. Alison, *Observations on the Management of the Poor in Scotland, and its Effects on the Health of the Great Towns* (Edinburgh, 1840), 98. See Flinn's introduction to Edwin Chadwick, *Report on the Sanitary Condition of the Labouring Population of Great Britain* (1842; ed. M. W. Flinn, Edinburgh, 1965), 63–5.

5

The Mind of Economic Man

In the present state, all which we enjoy, and a great part of what we suffer, *is put in our own power*. For pleasure and pain are the consequences of our actions; and we are endued by the Author of our nature with capacities of foreseeing these consequences.

> Joseph Butler, *The Analogy of Religion, Natural and Revealed, to the Constitution and Course of Nature* (1736), Part 1, Ch. 2.

Is not man's early prudence often the cause of his prosperity in *later* life, and his folly, though for a moment it may produce gratification, *finally* the cause of his ruin? . . . In moral causation, time is not to be measured by the flow of mechanical or physiological events;— not by the clock, or by the pulse. Moral causation has its own clock, its own pulse, in the progress of man's moral being; and by this measure of time is the relation of moral cause and effect to be defined.

> W. Whewell, *Are Cause and Effect Successive or Simultaneous?* (Cambridge, 1842), 7, 14.

Epistemology and Economics

Its critics were generally agreed that technical political economy was too abstract and theoretical, but, in demanding that it become more 'inductive' or empirical, different critics meant different things. As we have seen,[1] there was a Cambridge school which bewailed the shortage of information as to how economic man actually behaves. 'To obtain consequences from principles is Deduction; to obtain general truths from particular facts is Induction', pronounced Whewell,[2] as he encouraged Jones to accumulate particular facts that would refute the Ricardian theory of rent. Oxford critics, on the other hand, and indeed most Christian economists, were less concerned with factual observation than with the psychological premises of human behaviour. This involved them more in problems of moral philosophy and epistemology than in the sort of technical questions debated at the Political Economy Club, such as the nature of

---

[1] Above, pp. 50–2.
[2] W. Whewell, *Of a Liberal Education in general: and with Particular Reference to the Leading Studies of the University of Cambridge* (1845), 18.

profits and rent or the effects of machinery. They regarded economics as a branch of natural science, and 'mind' as the medium through which all science — that is, all knowledge of the natural world — was mediated. It was Stewart's message, especially, that a science of economics could only be formed by men with 'habits of metaphysical thinking'.[3]

To some this orientation was profoundly irritating. In particular, plain men's Tories suspected that it was a process of mystification through which Christian economics could follow secular political economy along the road to Free Trade. 'What the devil can the *pure metaphysics* of *political economy* mean?' expostulated Jones, after reading the phrase in the *Edinburgh Review*.[4] Whewell sympathized: the phrase was inappropriate, since metaphysics signified 'your way of getting your principles', and in political economy 'there are no peculiar principles of observation or deduction employed'. 'Never mind', he reassured Jones, 'you and Malthus belong not to the *metaphysical* but to the *ethical* school of Political Economy.'[5]

However, this was a distinction contemporary moralists were rarely prepared to make. To them the word 'moral' had epistemological as well as ethical connotations, the two categories being intimately connected. When Currie congratulated Stewart on the dissemination of Reidian philosophy in England; when Allen surmised that Horner was probably 'much more inclined to Hume's metaphysics than to Reid's', despite his veneration for Stewart; and when Pryme declared that he was for Locke rather than for Reid or Stewart; these were not trivial slogans but declarations of considerable moment to the intelligentsia of the day.[6]

The reference is of course to those rival schools of philosophy, the utilitarian tradition of Locke and Hume and the Scottish 'common sense' school of Reid and Stewart. To some extent the latter had developed in

[3] D. Stewart, *Dissertation: exhibiting the Progress of Metaphysical, Ethical, and Political Philosophy, since the Revival of Letters in Europe*, (1815–21), *Collected Works of Dugald Stewart*, i. 477 and n. See Elie Halévy, *The Growth of Philosophic Radicalism*, trans. Mary Morris (1928), 433–78; Karl M. Figlio, 'The metaphor of organization: an historiographical perspective on the bio-medical sciences of the early nineteenth century', *History of Science*, 14 (1976), 42–5.

[4] Jones to Whewell, 14 Aug. 1822, Whewell Papers, Trinity College Cambridge Add. MS c.52⁶. See [H. Brougham], 'Lord Lauderdale, *On Public Wealth*', *Edinburgh Review*, 4 (1804), 344, on 'the abstract doctrines of national riches; the distinctions between the kinds of wealth; the pecularities in the modes of its distribution; the variations in its quantity, and in the sources of its production; in a word, what we may denominate the pure metaphysics of political economy'.

[5] Whewell to Jones, 16 Aug. 1822, Todhunter, *Whewell*, ii. 48–50.

[6] Currie to Stewart, 14 July 1794, *Memoir of James Currie*, ii. 320; J. Allen to M. Napier, 25 Mar. 1843, *Correspondence of Napier*, pp. 424–5; Pryme to Whewell, 27 Oct. 1841, Whewell Papers, c.58¹⁷. See Richard Yeo, 'William Whewell, natural theology and the philosophy of science in mid nineteenth century Britain', *Annals of Science*, 36 (1979), 495–8.

response to the implicit atheism of the former. Thus Chalmers argued that a science of metaphysics was only necessary because an 'acute' but dangerous 'metaphysician'—presumably Hume—had succeeded in impugning the infallibility of common sense as a guide of life. Chalmers thought that Hume (if that was whom he had in mind) 'must be fought with his own weapon, and another metaphysician must arise to meet and over-match him . . . just to restore to common sense all its prerogatives'.[7] Briefly, utilitarians believed that the mind was a passive agent, acquiring knowlege through sensations—ultimately pleasure and pain—and organizing it through the association of ideas; whereas the Scottish 'common sense' school held the mind to be an active agent, endowed with various faculties and with certain intuitive knowledge. Since faculty psychology was a means of extending natural theology from the physical to the human world, it was especially pertinent to the human science of political economy. We have seen how Whately and others liked to depict the market as proof of God's wise and wonderful fabrication of society, but even more wondrous was the way in which he had implanted perfectly harmonious drives (or market responses) in our own breasts. This line of argument can be found to some extent in Hutcheson and Mandeville, but really begins with the 'common sense' theories of Adam Smith.

Smith's *Theory of Moral Sentiments* (1759) was based on the idea that human behaviour is mainly governed by intuited, sub-rational instincts. Man also has a capacity for 'sympathy', an area of mind somewhere between instincts and human reason, but reason itself is relegated to a very inferior position. Sentiments are innate and normally infallible, but reason is frequently wayward, and never more so than when it is exercised by governments on man's behalf in the form of mandatory or prohibitory laws. As Jacob Viner has pointed out,

Smith's analysis of the sentiments is in form and in fact partly naturalistic and inductive. It is also, however, partly providentialist and teleological, and it is so expressly, deliberately, and repetitively. It is in fact an extension, the only systematic and elaborate one I know of, to the subrational behaviour patterns of mankind of a type of providentialist explanation which . . . a long line of predecessors had already applied systematically to the physical universe, to the organic world of plants and animals, to animal and human anatomy and physiology, and to the instincts which man shares with the animals.[8]

The Wealth of Nations (1776) was not explicitly based on the same hypothesis, but in it Smith connected man's *original* commercial instinct

---

[7] [T. Chalmers], 'Causes and cure of pauperism', *Edinburgh Review*, 29 (1818), 278-9 [*Works*, xx. 328-9].

[8] Viner, *The Role of Providence in the Social Order*, pp. 77-82.

with a psychological drive to truck and barter rather than with a rational pursuit of economic gain.[9] The point was developed in a little-known work by an evangelically minded clergyman, Richard Raikes's *Considerations on the Alliance between Christianity and Commerce* (1806),[10] and more famously by Samuel Bailey (1791–1870), the writer who came closest to answering Chalmers's call for a new metaphysics of political economy.[11]

Bailey was a Sheffield merchant, an isolated and original thinker, a utilitarian in philosophy, and a sort of Philosophic Radical in politics. One of his strongest beliefs, which earned the commendation of James Mill, was that since man's opinions are independent of his will, he is not responsible for them and should not be punished or reproved on their account.[12] He objected to the conventional definition of political economy as the study of laws governing the production and distribution of wealth, on the grounds that it was much too wide. Economics was not concerned, for example, with comparative systems of husbandry or with the best method of making roads, but merely with 'moral or mental laws, or, in other words, those laws of human nature on which the economical condition of nations depends'.[13] Adam Smith's discussion of the pin factory was in this view as much a consideration of motives — why people divide their labour — as of the effects of such division on the community. Why do vendors take advantage of an increase in the paper circulation to demand more money for their commodities? All economic laws concern 'the voluntary actions of men', and the confidence with which political economists can predict that the exchanges will fall in response to an over-issue of paper money, or that in a competitive economy the profits of different branches of trade will tend to be the same, proves that 'the volitions of mankind are under the influence of precise and ascertainable causes'. Bailey's point is that, though the wills of thousands of men are free and their actions voluntary, we can nevertheless predict how they will react to different events, just as we can predict the effects of mechanical operations, such as the tendency of water to find its own level. There was 'uniformity of causation' in mental and moral as well as in physical phenomena, in the operations of the understanding as well as in the process of geological formations. Bailey was a determinist

---

[9] Ibid., pp. 47, 79–80.

[10] [Richard Raikes], *Considerations on the Alliance between Christianity and Commerce* (1806) esp. 20–3.

[11] Checkland, 'Propagation of Ricardian economics', *Economica*, 16 (1949), 52.

[12] [S. Bailey], *Essays on the Formation and Publication of Opinions, and on Other Subjects* (1821), 1–94. See Ursula Henriques, *Religious Toleration in England 1787–1833* (1961), 241, 250–4.

[13] Samuel Bailey, *Discourses on Various Subjects: Read before Literary and Philosophical Societies* (1852), 108–12.

and a warm admirer of the American theologian Jonathan Edwards.[14] In attacking the economists' notion of *intrinsic value* he struck at the roots, not of orthodox political economy only, but at the common moral assumptions of his day. Value was not, according to Bailey, *real* or *absolute*, but only relative, 'an effect produced on the mind'. It derived from men's perceptions of utility, and so 'an inquiry into the cause of value is, in reality, an inquiry into those external circumstances, which operate so steadily upon the minds of men, in the interchange of the necessaries, comforts, and conveniences of life, as to be subjects of inference and calculation'.[15]

Bailey's theories of value and profits presupposed that mankind possesses a common set of constant social instincts. In this he was at one with Chalmers, whose opposition to 'meddlesome' Poor Laws was based on the assumption that they interfered with such common instincts. God had implanted in our breasts the two impulses most necessary for social harmony — the prescriptive right of property (or possessory principle) and benevolence (or the compassion felt by possessors for non-possessors) — but the Poor Law undermined both principles by giving the poor a *lien*, however tiny, in the land, and by making benevolence compulsory and controversial. Abolition of the Poor Law would not only improve society by reducing numbers, but would also re-harmonize men's social instincts. Whately and Senior, meanwhile, took the intuitional approach to political economy further still, arguing that the science was founded 'on a very few general propositions, which are the result of observation, or consciousness, and which almost every man, as soon as he hears them, admits as familiar to his thoughts, or at least, as included in his previous knowledge'.[16] Thus Senior employed introspective observation or 'consciousness' to extend the Ricardian theory of rent: all economic gains made as a consequence of 'extraordinary powers of body and mind', all 'processes in manufacture which are protected by secrecy or by law', and all 'peculiar advantages from situation or connexion', should be regarded as analogous to 'rent', in the sense of extra profit made because of some advantage over one's competitors.[17]

[14] Ibid. [S. Bailey], *Essays on the Pursuit of Truth, on the Progress of Knowledge, and on the Fundamental Principle of All Evidence and Expectation* (1829), esp. 239–48; [S. Bailey], *Questions in Political Economy, Politics, Morals, Metaphysics, Polite Literature, and Other Branches of Knowledge* (1823), 257–62.

[15] [S. Bailey], *A Critical Dissertation on the Nature, Measures, and Causes of Value: Chiefly in reference to the Writings of Mr. Ricardo and his Followers* (1825), 1, 180; Robert M. Rauner, *Samuel Bailey and the Classical Theory of Value* (1961), 4–5, 67, and *passim*.

[16] Senior, *Introductory Lecture on Political Economy*, p. 7.

[17] Senior's Appendix to R. Whately, *Elements of Logic* (1826; 2nd edn, 1827), 319. For Jones's contempt for this Appendix see Jones to Whewell, 24 Feb. 1831, Whewell papers, c.52[20].

George Grote provides an example of the way in which such psycho-epistemological concerns could affect economic thought. In 1818 Grote was a young City banker, a friend of Ricardo and of the future Lord Overstone. He had imbibed a good deal of conventional piety from a strict evangelical mother, and was himself intensely religious, given to praying compulsively out loud at frequent intervals.[18] Two years earlier he had set out on a course of self-education, beginning with Lessing, Berkeley, Kant, and Hume, and then in 1818 he began on political economy (Say, Smith, Turgot, Ricardo), interspersing it with Butler's *Dissertation on Virtue*, Lessing's theology, Aristotle's *Politics*, and Kant's *Anthropology*. The fruit of all this was a paper on 'The Metaphysics of Political Economy', written during January 1819,[19] and noteworthy for its strikingly strong statement of the introspective or 'common sense' method in economic science. Concerning the process of wealth creation, Grote conceded that it was important to make inductions from the *facts* concerning production,

but it is manifest, that if there are any fundamental rules, immediately and inseparably connected with the existence and action of individual interest in the human mind, an appeal to our own bosoms will be at once the shortest and most infallible mode of discerning those rules. By this quick but certain process, we shall obtain general principles applying to an immense class of particular cases, without the trouble which the investigation of those cases must necessarily require.

Grote cites, as an example of innate knowledge, the *fact* that men will only give something away in exchange for something else which both gratifies and is scarce. Hence *utility* and *scarcity* constitute the foundations of exchangeable value. Another example is the *fact* that quantities of labour will always be equally rewarded—hence the quantity of labour involved determines the price of a commodity. In *discovering* these things, Ricardo had, according to Grote, 'wonderfully simplified, indeed almost remodelled, the department of Political Economy, by linking it more closely to its source in the human mind and by placing its basis in the invariable and universal laws of individual interest'. With respect to the sexual instinct, and to the important role of capital in food production, Malthus had proved 'beyond dispute' but *laboriously* what he might have demonstrated much more quickly. 'We ascertain this general Law of Population by an immediate appeal to the fundamental conditions of human existence, without the necessity of recurring to an examination of particular countries and states of society.'[20]

---

[18] O'Brien, *Correspondence of Overstone*, i. 189 n.
[19] *The Personal Life of George Grote*, by Mrs Harriet Grote (1873), 29–37.
[20] Grote, 'The metaphysics of political economy', Grote Papers, BL Add. MS 29530, fos. 84–90.

In 1819, shortly after writing this, Grote met James Mill and through him Bentham. As his biographer puts it, 'the meeting with Mill was momentous for Grote's further development', or as J. S. Mill put it, Grote 'rapidly seized on my father's best ideas'.[21] An obvious parallel is with James Mill's own meeting with Bentham in 1808, an event which had led him to discard the 'common sense' beliefs he had sipped from Stewart, and to take up utilitarianism instead.[22] In the same way Grote succumbed at once, not only to utilitarianism, but to political reform and—more painfully—to unbelief. By 1822 he was able to write up some notes by Bentham into a pseudonymous attack on natural religion, pointing out that to depict God as 'an almighty Being by whom pains and pleasures will be dispensed to mankind during an infinite and future state of existence', was to depict him as no less than a monstrous and capricious tyrant. Such a religion terrorizes and restrains without conducing to beneficent actions (the punishment being too remote to have much of a tutelary effect), confuses the intellectual faculties by dissociating belief from experience, and creates a 'standing army' of priests whose concern is to help the aristocracy thwart the interests of the community.[23] By 1822 Grote had also turned against Reid's doctrine of 'common sense', and against the notion that moral feelings are innate and primary, since if they were there could not be any general standard of reference or correction.[24] Now he argued 'that the proper evidence of metaphysical science is *human action*—not *our own consciousness*, as Dugald Stewart maintains'. Consciousness can reveal 'the metaphysics of one individual mind alone', is liable to self-deceit and self-importance, and is further flawed by the fact that it really comprises only the memories of consciousness. It followed that metaphysical science had to be based on the *actions* of men: 'human pains and pleasures therefore and the circumstances most essentially promotive and preventive of each, will be the first to strike our eyes'. Nothing could be further from the views expressed in his political economy paper of four years previously.[25]

[21] M. L. Clarke, *George Grote: A Biography* (1962), 19–21; J. S. Mill, *Autobiography* (1873), 72 [ed. John M. Robson and Jack Stillinger for *Collected Works of John Stuart Mill*, general editor J. M. Robson (Toronto and Buffalo, 1981–   ) i. 75].

[22] Halévy, *Growth of Philosophic Radicalism*, pp. 249–51, 444–55.

[23] ['Philip Beauchamp'], *An Analysis of the Influence of Natural Religion on the Temporal Happiness of Mankind* (1822). I have followed the analysis in Clarke, *George Grote*, pp. 30–2, closely.

[24] Grote, 'Morals', June 1822, Grote Papers, BL Add. MS 29528, fos. 23–37.

[25] Grote, 'MSS essays: on metaphysical science', ibid., fos. 1–8. The volume is marked on the binding in another hand 'Logical and metaphysical essays, 1818', but this seems unlikely since the watermark on the paper is 1822. It is equally unlikely that Grote could have written such a piece in the same year as his 'Political economy'.

Grote's metamorphosis clearly illustrates the divergence between Stewart's Scottish school and London's philosophic radicalism. The differences are to some extent obscured by a common concern for Free Trade (in its widest sense) and reform, but they are important. The former was probably more influential in the world of politics and among the intelligentsia, if only because it was more compatible with the evangelical ethos of the times. In theology, the conflict between 'common sense' and 'utility' was frequently personalized in terms of those two giants of Anglican apologetics, Butler and Paley. There have been just two references to Butler so far in this book,[26] yet his impact on intellectual debate during the early and middle years of the nineteenth century was sufficiently prodigious as to require further investigation.

Bishop Butler and the Zeitgeist

Joseph Butler (1692–1752) was a Dissenter turned Churchman who attended Oriel College, Oxford, in 1714–17 and thereafter lived a life of relative clerical obscurity punctuated by promotion, ending up as Bishop of Durham. His Rolls Sermons (1726), The Analogy of Religion, Natural and Revealed, to the Constitution and Course of Nature (1736), and the Dissertations on Personal Identity and Virtue (1736) were addressed to the religious and philosophical disputes of his own day, yet they made only a modest impression outside intellectual circles before the nineteenth century. When Wilberforce pressed Butler on the younger Pitt, the latter remarked sardonically that the writer seemed to raise more doubts than he resolved, while Fox apparently thought Butler a bad teacher of reasoning, since anything could be proved by analogy.[27] He was mainly appreciated by members of the Scottish 'common sense' school, and his philosophy was carried into the nineteenth century by Dugald Stewart.

Some idea of how Butler's reputation fluctuated can be gained from his publishing history. There seem to have been ten editions of the Analogy between 1736 and 1800, then four in the 1800s (including Halifax's edition of the Complete Works), four again in the 1810s, three in the 1820s, five in the 1830s, five again in the 1840s, and eight in the 1850s. Yule calculates that there were eleven editions of the various sermons before 1810, but then suddenly five in the 1830s, four in the 1840s, and nine in the 1850s. There was also a medley of epitomes, abridgements, and commentaries. A comparative lull during the 1860s and 1870s was followed by a revival in the last two decades of the century, though Yule

[26] See above, pp. 135, 163.
[27] Recollections of the Table-Talk of Samuel Rogers, ed. Alexander Dyce (1887), 14; R. I. and S. Wilberforce, Life of Wilberforce, i. 95.

detects a different approach by this time, one which regarded Butler as a Christian 'classic' rather than as a philosopher of contemporary significance, which he had certainly been during the first half of the century.[28]

To a large extent the surge in Butler's popularity was at the expense of Paley, dissatisfaction with whom we noted in the first paragraph of this book. There were twenty-nine editions of Paley's *Evidences of Christianity* between 1794 and 1816, and another five before 1830, but only six more by 1860 and a further two by 1900. There were twenty-five editions of the *Natural Theology* between 1802 and 1830, but only seven more during the remainder of the century.[29] Rivalry between Paley and Butler was most noticeable at Cambridge, where the former had played a dominant part in the curriculum since 1787. The *Evidences*, *Natural Theology*, and *Principles of Moral Philosophy* were incorporated, with Butler's *Analogy* and *Sermons*, into the revised examinations of 1821–2 in such a way that, as Garland writes, 'Paley touched everybody', so that even those alumni who later rejected his ideas 'often spelled out their early debt to his works'. It was the Trinity sages—Whewell, Sedgwick, J. C. Hare, and Connop Thirlwall, followed by the 'Apostle', F. D. Maurice— who set out systematically to denigrate Paley as a mere utilitarian egoist. Whewell's *Elements of Morality* (1845) was pure Butler with touches of Kant, though his boast that Butler was now accepted as the official moral philosophy of Cambridge (as well as of Trinity) was mere bravado. Paley survived the sniping, and retained a considerable hold in that home of the natural sciences for the remainder of the century. His *Evidences* continued to be compulsory reading for the Tripos until 1909, and only disappeared as an optional subject for all students in 1920.[30]

Though Butler's Cambridge champions were mainly concentrated in Trinity, that was the college most closely attuned to the public and political life of the time. However, it was mainly in Oxford, where Paley's works— though well known—had never been so popular,[31] that generations of future statesmen bit deep on Bishop Butler. In this case the dominant

---

[28] Yule, 'Impact of science on British religious thought', Cambridge University Ph.D. 165–7.

[29] Hamish F. G. Swanston, *Ideas of Order: Anglicans and the Renewal of Theological Method in the Middle Years of the Nineteenth Century* (Asser, The Netherlands, 1974), 5.

[30] For the campaign against Paley see Martha McMackin Garland, *Cambridge before Darwin: The Ideal of a Liberal Education, 1800–1860* (Cambridge, 1980), 52–69). Possibly Garland slightly exaggerates the success of this campaign, outside Trinity. For Francis Wayland's substitution of Butler for Paley in the Moral Philosophy course at Brown University in about 1830, see Joseph L. Blau's introduction to F. Wayland, *The Elements of Moral Science* (New York, 1835; new printing of 2nd 1837 edn, Cambridge Mass., 1963), p. xli. For Wayland see above, p. 85.

[31] Corsi, 'Natural theology, the methodology of science, and the question of species', Oxford D.Phil. (1980), 254.

society was Oriel, where Copleston had tilted at Paley as early as 1810. It was his Noetic colleagues, Whately and Hampden, who were mainly responsible in 1832 for installing the *Analogy* as one of only two set-books in 'Greats' alongside Aristotle's *Ethics*, the latter having been compulsory reading for all BA students since 1809.[32] Butler's influence must have been felt before 1832, however. The young evangelical J. H. Newman was deeply appreciative of him, and Hampden's *An Essay on the Philosophical Evidences of Christianity* (1827) is seeped in his thought. Indeed, if T. T. Carter, a life-long devotee, is to be believed, the *Analogy* had already become 'the authorized standard of Philosophy' by the time he was up at Christ Church in 1827–30. A year behind Carter, Gladstone certainly read Butler, though it was not until later, around 1835, that he became besotted.[33] By 1840, at any rate, the *Analogy* had become a staple ingredient of an Oxford diet consisting otherwise of classical literature and history, and smatterings of Aristotle (especially the *Ethics*) and the Scotsmen Stewart, Reid, and Hamilton. Newman, no longer an evangelical but a Tractarian, announced in 1840 that 'the real influence of [Butler's] work is only just now beginning!', while the latitudinarian Thomas Arnold, Regius Professor of Modern History, averred that Butler was the only English divine worth bothering about.[34] There was support also from a High Churchman, William Sewell, Professor of Moral Philosophy, who lectured enthusiastically on Butler's *Sermons* during the 1840s, placing them in a context of Platonic philosophy.

Probably Sewell was less enthusiastic about the *Analogy*, since he disliked the rationalist or Aristotelian bias of Oxford studies.[35] Yet in fact it was the *Analogy*, rather than the *Sermons*, which attracted most attention and assent. Gladstone was revolted by the latter's ethical postulates when he encountered them in 1830, and ten years later another

---

[32] [Copleston], *Reply to the Calumnies of the* Edinburgh Review, p. 180; R. D. Hampden, *Introduction to the Second Edition of the Bampton Lectures, of the Year 1832* (2nd edn, 1837), 37 n. *Some Memorials of Renn Dickson Hampden*, ed. Henrietta Hampden (1871), 16 n., 21; William S. Knickerbocker, *Creative Oxford: Its Influence in Victorian Literature* (Syracuse, NY, 1925), 52–76; Ward, *Victorian Oxford*, p. 214. For the use made of Butler by Oxford Aristotelians see Frank M. Turner, *The Greek Heritage in Victorian Britain* (New Haven and London, 1981), 326–40.

[33] *Life and Letters of Thomas Thellusson Carter*, by W. H. Hutchings (1903), 9. On Gladstone see below, pp. 340–9.

[34] J. H. Newman, 'The Catholicity of the Anglican Church' (1840), *Essays Critical and Historical* (1872), ii. 57; Stanley, *Life of Arnold*, ii. 64 n [5th edn (1845), ii. 66 n.].

[35] Sewell was cited above, p. 27, as an example of someone who combined High Churchmanship with evangelical attitudes. It should be added that his attitudes were closer to Irving's than to Chalmers's. See, for example, his sermon on the cholera as a 'special' punishment of the nation because of its class warfare. Man's only resource in the crisis was to 'pray, pray, pray', and not to suppose that the laws of nature could be 'stronger than the will of God'. William Sewell, *An Address to a Christian Congregation on the Approach of the Cholera Morbus* (Oxford, ?1831), 4–8, 56.

undergraduate was thankful that Oxford attempted 'nothing quite so foolish or contradictory' as at Cambridge, where Paley's *Moral Philosophy* and Butler's *Sermons* were uneasily combined.[36] The *Analogy*, however, seemed unassailable. To Butler's detractors there was something obsessional about the way in which it became a dark blue 'fetish'—'the Oxford Koran, . . . a universal solvent of the theological difficulties'.[37] Matthew Arnold was wrily contemptuous of the way in which Butler and Aristotle came to be regarded, not as commentators, but as inspired witnesses to revealed truth:

Your text-book was right; there were no mistakes *there*. If there was anything obscure, anything hard to be comprehended, it was your ignorance which was in fault, your failure of comprehension. . . . Whatever was hard, whatever was obscure, the text-book was all right, and our understandings were to conform themselves to it.[38]

This situation continued until the later 1850s when reformers, led by Pattison and Jowett, assaulted Butler just as Whewell and Sedgwick had once assaulted Paley.[39]

Butler's conquest of Tractarian Oxford and its satellite parishes is well known.[40] Less familiar, and in the present context more significant, was the way in which moderate evangelicals adopted him. Wilberforce frequently appealed to his authority; Chalmers is rumoured to have been first converted to Christianity by perusal of the *Analogy*, and he certainly made Butler's ideas the basis of his natural theology;[41] Sumner's *Records of Creation* acknowledge a specific debt, as did Bishop Bathurst of Norwich and a great many Nonconformist evangelicals.[42] Lord Overstone was wont to refer starkly to 'the great Bishop Butler'. In 1825 a future Bishop of Calcutta, the evangelical Daniel Wilson, produced an edition of the

---

[36] Samuel Clark to Edward Strachey, 24 Feb. 1840, *Memorials of Samuel Clark*, pp. 131–6. See Clark to Strachey, Easter Day 1840, ibid., pp. 140–4: 'I . . . am more than ever in wonder at Paley's keeping his standing at Cambridge. Butler, of all our old established ethical writers, is the great witness for *man*.' But for subsequent doubts lest Butler be too negative, see Clark to Strachey, 25 May 1840, ibid., pp. 148–51.

[37] *Reminiscences by Goldwin Smith*, ed. Arnold Haultain (New York, 1910), 65; Goldwin Smith, *Rational Religion, and the Rationalistic Objections of the Bampton Lectures for 1858* (Oxford, 1861), 76–7.

[38] M. Arnold, 'Bishop Butler and the *Zeit-geist*', *Last Essays on Church and Religion* (1877), 62–3.

[39] See below, pp. 337–9.

[40] See Swanston, *Ideas of Order*, *passim*, for an exhaustive account of Butler's influence on Hampden, Maurice, Mansel, and Newman. For a sketchier but useful general account of Butler's reception in the nineteenth century see E. C. Mossner, *Bishop Butler and the Age of Reason: A Study in the History of Thought* (New York, 1936), esp. 198–229.

[41] Hanna, *Life of Chalmers*, i. 146.

[42] Such as the Congregationalists Henry Rogers (1806–77) and Richard Winter Hamilton (1794–1848). Hanna, *Life of Chalmers*, iii. 403.

Analogy with a 161-page introduction, which was warmly admired by Sumner, Charles Bird, and also Copleston.[43] It was to serve as the main evangelical rival to Halifax's edition until Joseph Angus's version with commentary of 1855. Indeed, the evangelical scheme of redemption was essentially Butlerian, though it is not clear whether this accounts for Butler's posthumous popularity, or whether vestiges of eighteenth-century good sense survived into the nineteenth so as to enable a soteriological scheme to permeate the minds of many who distrusted the more emotional, sanctimonious, and pentecostal elements of evangelicalism.

The nineteenth century was not really interested in Butler's dispute with the deism of his own day. Why then did he have such a posthumous appeal? No doubt there are some trivial explanations. His influence at Oxford may have had something to do with the fact that he was in many respects an ideal teaching aid. Leslie Stephen quipped that it was Paley's 'utter inability to be obscure' which won him the contempt of subsequent generations.[44] If so, Butler probably hit just about the right degree of obscurity. Bagehot thought that the jejune analytical approach rendered his works 'apt exercises for the critical intellect', and made 'truth when found seem more valuable from the difficulty of finding it'. Clark thought that the 'clumsiness and faults of style' indicated a cardinal Victorian virtue, lack of 'humbug'.[45]

Then, and perhaps strangely, many nineteenth-century readers seemed to find comfort in the *Analogy*'s famous dictum that 'probability is the guide of life'. This tame premiss, which it is said *almost* saved James Mill from infidelity,[46] aroused considerable excitement. Is it too trite to suggest that, in a period of social and ideological upheaval, Butler's probabilism gave an uncanny sense of relief? After all, it was distress at their lack of certainty, as much as the reasons for it, which bothered troubled minds. Butler's doctrine that certainty is unimportant, that *probable* evidence is good enough, may have provided an antidote to insecurity. We have seen that evangelicals had a longing for assurance of salvation, and that the wilder elements found it in prophecy and in calculations of the millennium. The more responsible resisted this, but were relieved to be told that certainty is unattainable, that God-fearing law-abiding citizens will *probably* enter Paradise. Probability could be

[43] C. S. Bird to his brother, 9 Sept. 1828, *Sketches from the Life of Charles Smith Bird*, by Claude S. Bird (1864), p. 121; Overstone to Norman, 18 Jan. 1879, O'Brien, *Correspondence of Overstone*, iii. 1318–19.

[44] Leslie Stephen, *Essays on Freethinking and Plainspeaking* (1873), 37.

[45] [W. Bagehot], 'Rogers's Life of Bishop Butler', *The Prospective Review: A Quarterly Journal of Theology and Literature*, 10 (1854), 543 [*The Collected Works of Walter Bagehot*, ed. Norman St John-Stevas (1965–86), i. 235]; Clark to Strachey, Easter Day, 1840, loc. cit.

[46] J. S. Mill, *Autobiography*, pp. 38–9 [*Collected Works of Mill*, i. 41].

hitched to the Reidian catalogue of contingent truths, like Williams's *Reserve in the Communication of Christian Knowledge* or Newman's on the *Development of Christian Doctrine*. If it seemed to contradict the evangelical emphasis on conversion—on the sudden infiltration of the human vessel by divine grace—those who could not be sure that they had ever experienced such a thing were likely to feel comforted.

Connected with probabilism was a fashion for analogical reasoning, another form of contingent truth. It was a central feature of scientific thinking at this time, one that struck a contemporary mind as especially 'pleasing' and 'consolatory'.[47] Prickett has demonstrated the importance of analogical reasoning in Keble's response to Butler,[48] and the same is true of many other moralists. Reading Butler carefully for the first time in 1852, the Duke of Argyll was convinced by its 'fundamental conception of an analogy', which complemented his own adolescent studies of animal mechanics. In a subsequent reflection he complained that Butler's late nineteenth-century detractors seemed 'blind to the power of analogy in all the operations of the mind, to the place it takes and the part it plays in everything that we can understand, as an explanation of anything in the world'.[49] An explanation of *anything!* Analogy was a spatial way, and probabilism a temporal way, of conceiving some order in a world which no longer believed in Paleyan canons of order. Analogy and probabilism were ways of fumbling towards Wordsworth's 'eternal fitness of things' in a world where fitness was not superficially obvious.

An obvious attraction of the *Sermons* was their emphasis on the supremacy of conscience as an intuitive moral sense and the source of all ethical judgments. This was the aspect of Butler which Hutcheson, Reid, Kames, and Stewart had valued, and it naturally appealed to those who detested the utilitarian, consequentialist ethics of Paley and

---

[47] D. Stewart, *Elements of the Philosophy of the Human Mind* (London and Edinburgh, 1792-1827), ii. 235-9, 382-401, 432-4 [*Works of Stewart*, iii. 176-9, 284-98, 320-2]. For analogical reasoning in medicine see Pelling, *Cholera, Fever and English Medicine*, pp. 109-20, 189-206, 229-86; for physics see Richard Olson, *Scottish Philosophy and British Physics 1750-1880: A Study in the Foundations of the Victorian Scientific Style* (Princeton, 1975), 48-52, 95-121, 219-51, 289-330; for chemistry see J. H. Brooke, 'Organic synthesis and the unification of chemistry—a reappraisal', *British Journal for the History of Science*, 5 (1970-1), 363-92. See also Hooykaas, *Natural Law and Divine Miracle: The Principle of Uniformity*, pp. 154-62.

[48] Stephen Prickett, *Romanticism and Religion: The Tradition of Coleridge and Wordsworth in the Victorian Church* (Cambridge, 1976), 107-8.

[49] *Autobiography and Memoirs of the Eighth Duke of Argyll*, ed. the dowager Duchess of Argyll (1906), i. 354-5. For Argyll as a late nineteenth-century individualist see below, pp. 363-5. See F. Wayland, *A Discourse on the Philosophy of Analogy* (Boston, 1831), quoted in *American Philosophical Addresses 1700-1900*, ed. Joseph L. Blau (New York, 1946), 355.

Bentham.[50] Bentham himself attacked the notion of conscience as one of 'many contrivances for avoiding the obligation of appealing to any external standard, and for prevailing upon the reader to accept of the author's sentiment or opinion as a reason and that a sufficient one for itself'.[51] But Arnold, Whewell, and Coleridge—who not surprisingly much preferred the *Sermons* to the *Analogy*—all applauded Butler's rooting of morality 'upon ideas, altogether distinct from consequences',[52] and evangelicals also appreciated his emphasis on conscience.[53] As early as 1789 Thomas Gisborne had led an evangelical charge against Paley in favour of Butler's intuitionism, while Chalmers repeatedly hailed Butler as the 'first discoverer' of the 'natural supremacy of conscience'.

The success of the *Analogy*, meanwhile, is related to the way in which the nineteenth century redefined natural theology. Butler's intention had been to refute the deists of his own day, who accepted that there was a divine creator of the universe but who could not stomach the harsh, cruel God of Christian revelation. His method was to show that the natural world contained anomalies not to be resolved this side of Paradise, and that these anomalies were analogous to the cruelties and harshness found in scriptural Christianity (just as one would expect if God were the author of *both* the natural world *and* revelation). As has often been pointed out, this was a double-edged argument, ensuring that the later nineteenth-century retreat from deism would for many people carry with it a corresponding rejection of Christianity. It was also an inadequate one, in that for revelation to have any point it should surely explain the anomalies of nature, and not merely reflect them analogically. But this did not signify for early nineteenth-century apologists, whose enemy was still deism, not atheism.[54] It is clear that the Butlerian view, more than any other, suited the cosmic unease of the first half of the nineteenth century—the feeling that the natural world was full of anomalies: though now, of course, the analogy was being reversed, in that the Bible was

[50] J. B. Schneewind, *Sidgwick's Ethics and Victorian Moral Philosophy* (Oxford, 1977), 64: Reid 'carried the Butlerian combination of religion, epistemology, and ethics into an extended argument against Hume's scepticism, empiricism, and utilitarianism'.

[51] J. Bentham, *An Introduction to the Principles of Morals and Legislation* (1780; 2nd edn, 1823), ed. J. H. Burns and H. L. A. Hart for *The Collected Works of Jeremy Bentham*, general editor J. H. Burns (1968–   ), 25–6.

[52] Hazlitt, *Complete Works*, xvii. 113, xx. 216; W. Whewell, *Lectures on the History of Moral Philosophy in England* (1852), 110.

[53] T. Gisborne, *The Principles of Moral Philosophy Investigated, and briefly applied to the Constitution of Civil Society: together with Remarks on the Principle assumed by Mr. Paley as the Basis of all Moral Conclusions, and on other Positions of the same Author* (1789), 141; T. Chalmers, *On the Power Wisdom and Goodness of God*, i. 68–9 [*Works*, i. 319]. For an excellent discussion of Butler's impact in this respect see Schneewind, *Sidgwick and Victorian Moral Philosophy*, esp. pp. 7–8, 418–20.

[54] D. Wilson, *Evidences of Christianity*, i. 26–32.

being used to justify post-Malthusian doubts about natural theology, not the other way round. No wonder then that historical and textual criticism of the Bible was to prove so devastating for this line of argument in the mid-century.

Both Butler and Paley recognized the twin incentives of pleasure and pain,[55] but Paley laid all his emphasis on the former. In his benevolent picture of the world, occasional suffering is, to quote Garland, 'an accidental, unintended by-product in a complex and essentially joyful creation'. God much prefers to work his purposes by means of pleasures, so he allows healthy young animals to devour old and weak ones in order to prevent the latter from dying miserable slow deaths.[56] When Butler talks of 'godly government by a system of rewards and punishments', however, it is easy to see that his emphasis is on the latter, and this suited the nineteenth-century mood. The cosmic optimism of Paley, Whately, and Southwood Smith played an opposition role not unlike that of deism in Butler's day, and represented the mechanistic equivalent of the romantic pantheism of Wordsworth, Shelley, and Keats, for whom beauty *was* truth. Butler's power derived from the way in which he combated such optimism, a contribution which Bagehot analysed with his usual robust common sense. 'Now of the poetic religion there is nothing in Butler. No one could tell from his writings that the universe was beautiful' — and, of course, most early nineteenth-century pessimists had thought that it was not—

But in return and by way of compensation for this, there is a religion of another sort, a religion . . . of *superstition*. The source of this . . . is in the conscience, . . . to most men a principle of fear. . . . A sensation of shame, of reproach, remorse, of sin, . . . is what the moral principle really and practically thrusts on most men. Conscience is the condemnation of ourselves. We expect a penalty.[57]

In other words, having set up *conscience* as the animating principle of all actions, Butler implies that in at least nine cases out of ten this will be a bad conscience, inviting or wanting punishment. Since men live in a 'deep and intimate anxiety of guilt, . . . and the painful anticipation

---

[55] [Anon.], 'Whewell on Butler and Paley', *The Theologian and Ecclesiastic*, 6 (1848), 193: 'According to Paley, the Will of GOD is the absolute standard, general happiness is the *index* of right and wrong. Butler makes general happiness, probably, the absolute standard, conscience the index.'

[56] Garland, *Cambridge before Darwin*, p. 55; Paley, *Natural Theology*, pp. 507–16 [15th edn (1815), 473–81]. Buckland used the same argument in his Bridgewater Treatise, *Geology and Mineralogy*, i. 129–34, much to the disapproval of the anti-Paleyan Sedgwick. Sedgwick to W. D. Conybeare, 5 Dec. 1836, *The Life and Letters of Adam Sedgwick*, by J. W. Clark and T. McK. Hughes (Cambridge, 1890), i. 469–71.

[57] [Bagehot], 'Rogers's Life of Bishop Butler', *Prospective Review*, 10 (1854), 534 (*Works*, i. 226–7).

of its punishment', justice can be understood as the link between virtue and reward, sin and suffering. The earthly state is one of probation, implying perpetual trial, difficulty, and danger, a condition expressly designed by God for the moral discipline and development of his creatures.[58]

So Butler's natural theology fitted far better into the evangelical view of a flawed world than Paley's. The point was made as succinctly as possible by a writer (almost certainly Wilberforce) in the *Christian Observer* for 1803:

The goodness of God is the only moral attribute which is apprehended by Dr. Paley to be manifest, from the appearances of the natural world. No observation occurs . . . concerning the holiness or justice of the deity; nothing of those tendencies of virtue to produce happiness, and of vice to produce misery, which are so judiciously collected and so unanswerably enforced by Bishop Butler, and analogically applied as proofs that the world is not now in the state in which it originally proceeded from the hands of the Creator, but that it is evidently in a state of degradation and ruin—that the Creator is a moral governor.[59]

The Christian's task was not merely to acknowledge God's benevolence but, more importantly, to 'inquire concerning the means of avoiding the effects of his punitive justice in a future world, from the manifest indications of it in this'. In a Butlerian tract of 1818, Gisborne objected that Paley had ignored 'Holiness as an Attribute of God',[60] and as we have seen, Chalmers's *Bridgewater Treatise* also praised God's *righteousness* rather than his *benevolence*: 'We are then on firmer vantage-ground for the establishment of a Natural Theology.'[61]

This personification of the conflict in terms of Paley and Butler is not merely a caprice of hindsight. In *Chalmeriana* (1853) J. J. Gurney, leader of the evangelical Quakers, recorded a conversation with his friend Thomas Chalmers in 1830. It began with Chalmers on Butler—his

---

[58] J. H. Newman, *An Essay on the Development of Christian Doctrine* (1845), 51: 'Conscience, the existence of which we cannot deny, is a proof of the doctrine of a Moral Governor, which alone gives it a meaning and a scope; that is, the doctrine of a Judgment to come is a development of the phenomenon of conscience.' W. E. Channing, *Discourses, Reviews, and Miscellanies* (1834), i. 462: 'It is the lawgiver in our own breasts, which gives us the idea of divine authority.'

[59] *Christian Observer*, 2 (1803), 373; compare Wilberforce to Creyke, 8 Jan. 1803, see above, p. 4. See Joseph Butler, *The Analogy of Religion, Natural and Revealed,– to the Constitution and Course of Nature* (1736), 68 [*The Works of Joseph Butler*, ed. Samuel Halifax (Oxford, 1820), i. 96; ed. W. E. Gladstone (Oxford, 1896), i. 92]: 'There is a kind of moral government implied in God's natural government: virtue and vice are naturally rewarded and punished as beneficial and mischievous to society.' Smith had also said that prosperity and adversity were ordinarily distributed in such a way as to reward virtue and punish vice. Adam Smith, *The Theory of Moral Sentiments* (1759; 6th edn, 1790), i. 412–27 [ed. D. D. Raphael and A. L. Macfie for *The Glasgow Edition of the Works and Correspondence of Adam Smith* (Oxford, 1976), i. 165–70].

[60] Gisborne, *Testimony of Natural Theology to Christianity*, pp. 7–8.

[61] See above, p. 84.

original, powerful, and 'unsophisticated mind'—and turned via Leibniz and Southwood Smith to Paley. Gurney alluded to Smith's Paleyan volume, *Illustrations of the Divine Government*, which was so popular with the Unitarians and which

> solves all the attributes of God into pure *benevolence*—denominates sin 'moral evil'—ascribes it to the direct appointment of God, and presumes to infer that it not only promotes the general good, but, taken in connexion with its corrective consequences, in the end enhances the happiness of the sinner. . . .
>
> CHALMERS: It is a dangerous error to reduce the divine attributes to the single quality of goodness. Our best metaphysicians (especially Brown) teach us that the *ethical virtues* are in their nature unalterably independent. Justice is an ethical virtue, distinct in its origin, character, and end, and must not be confounded with any other. Those principles apply to the moral attributes of God. . . . The harmony, yet distinctness, of the divine moral attributes is most instructively inscribed on the atonement of Christ.
>
> GURNEY: Surely, *that* is a point where justice and benevolence meet; where God has displayed at once his abhorrence of sin and his mercy to the sinner.
>
> CHALMERS: Brown had very low and inadequate views of the character of God. The same may be said of Paley. Witness his founding his system of morals on expediency.

The two men agreed, however, that Paley's 'best' book, *Horae Paulinae*, written during the early stages of the French Revolution and published in 1790, marked a considerable spiritual improvement on what had gone before. (It is probably not a coincidence that this was to be the most popular of Paley's books in Oxford.) A rumour was current that when he was dying in 1805, Paley had expressed remorse for having written the *Moral Philosophy*, and Gurney concluded that Paley's various sermons, if arranged chronologically, would display 'a gradually progressive change from a sort of semi-Pelagianism to a sound evangelical view of Christianity. It is delightful to be able to ascribe such a man as Paley to the company of true believers in a crucified Redeemer.'[62] There are indeed grounds for thinking that Paley was affected by the rapid *evangelicalization* of attitudes around the turn of the century, just as Malthus may have been.[63] Certainly his posthumously published sermons have much to say about sin, repentance, and the atoning work of Christ. 'The utilitarian Paley is still there', comments Yule, but has been 'subordinated to evangelical doctrine'.[64]

At all events, Bishop Butler's 'scheme of salvation', based on pains and penalties, sin and redemption, and Atonement through the vicarious and

[62] John Joseph Gurney, *Chalmeriana; or, Colloquies with Dr. Chalmers* (1853), 26–30; Braithwaite, *Memoirs of Gurney*, i. 419–20.
[63] See above, pp. 89–91.
[64] Yule, 'Impact of science on religious thought', p. 186.

propitiatory sacrifice of Christ, contained all the theological ingredients of nineteenth-century evangelicalism.[65] Nevertheless, it lacked some of the essential spirit. A detractor, Pattison, considered that 'in order to make the proof of revelation universal', Butler had been 'obliged to resolve religion into the moral government of God by rewards and punishments, and especially the latter. It is this anthropomorphic conception of God as the "Governor of the Universe" . . . which excludes on principle not only all that is poetical in life, but all that is sublime in religious speculation.'[66] Interestingly, this worry had also been entertained by devoted evangelical adherents of Butler like Wilson, Wardlaw, and Chalmers, and underlay their attempts to recast him in the mould of 'vital religion'.[67] It was because they found Butler deficient in the purely emotional aspects of Christianity, in its 'particular grace' and in those elements which are 'most effectual in subduing the heart of man and training him for heaven',[68] that they set out to leaven him with some evangelical yeast. Wilson's introductory essay tags on to Butler's scheme those things he finds wanting in it: a quest for holiness, and not merely for what the world .calls *virtue*; a concern for motives, piety, regular devotions, and self-examination; a sense of 'the stupendous recovery of man provided in the Gospel'; a more *forensic* interpretation of the mechanism of the Atonement; a view of the Holy Ghost; and generally, a more scriptural, less philosophic approach to the language of religion. This may seem to us to be a large set of omissions in Butler, but Wilson was able to attribute them all to Butler's 'inadequate view of the fallen state of man'—a failing venial enough in one who had died forty years before the French Revolution. So while the *Analogy* contained a good deal about man's state of 'degradation', thanks to Adam and Eve, there was also too much for Wilson's taste about man's capacity for 'favouring virtue' and about his 'principle of amendment'. If God was to receive due credit for redeeming men, then those men must be shown to be far less capable of self-help than this.[69] It was the aim of Wilson's 1825 edition to place Butler in the proper context at last. An admiring colleague of Wilson, Charles Jerram, wrote to agree about 'the argument of Butler retaining all its force, or even augmented force, on the

[65] D. Wilson, 'Introductory essay' to J. Butler, *Analogy of Religion*, ed. D. Wilson (1825; 7th edn, Glasgow 1841), p. cv.

[66] Mark Pattison, 'Tendencies of religious thought in England, 1688–1750', *Essays and Reviews* (1860), 293.

[67] Wilson, 'Introductory essay', op. cit., pp. cv–cvi. For Butler's underestimation of man's depravity see Ralph Wardlaw, *Christian Ethics: or, Moral Philosophy on the Principles of Divine Revelation* (1823; 2nd edn, 1834), 113–56.

[68] Copleston to Wilson, April 1825, *The Life of Daniel Wilson, with Extracts from his Journals and Correspondence* (1860), i. 161.

[69] Wilson, 'Introductory essay', op. cit., pp. cxix–cxlv.

supposition of your statement of evangelical truth being the basis of the system'.[70]

Wilson's evangelical 'placing' of Butler was not uncontroversial, however. J. J. Blunt in the *Quarterly* objected that ' "the *entire* corruption," or "the *total* moral ruin" of man, or the "alienation of his *whole* moral nature from God," which Mr. Wilson would have had introduced by Butler, is a doctrine which that profound inquirer did not hold; and, moreover, is a doctrine, which, if established, would, in our opinion, shake his argument to its foundations. . . . To allow [that man has] a *"moral sense,"* and yet to insist on a *"total moral* ruin," appears to us as incongruous as to allow some sense of hearing, and yet to insist on a total deafness.' If men were totally depraved, the redemption of some of them would be a case of 'arbitrary', not 'moral' government, continued the future Lady Margaret Professor of Divinity (1839–55), but as it is, he has given all men the wherewithal to discover faith in Christ.

No man can vindicate more nobly or more thankfully [than Butler] the merciful scheme of the atonement, (if there be any one part of his book more satisfactory than another, it is where he handles this vital question;) but that does not entail upon him the necessity of *effacing* the image of its Creator altogether from the soul of the unregenerate man, as a preliminary step.[71]

To do that would be to confound 'the charity of a Titus with the cruelty of a Nero'. This was a good debating-point but probably little more, since evangelicals saw no incompatibility between the doctrines of conscience and of total depravity. Certainly, Gladstone only ceased to be revolted by Butler's ethics when around 1835 he placed them in the context of Augustinian theology,[72] and then he became convinced that beneath its sober language the *Analogy* contained all the soteriological passion that Wilson could want. Still, the *Christian Observer* continued to object to Butler's treating of the *conscience* 'as though it were no partaker of common fall and deterioration of our nature', and for many evangelicals it was not until Joseph Angus's 1855 edition and *Notes* that the *Analogy* at last had 'a hue of Evangelical truth shed over some of the arguments'.[73]

Perhaps Butler appealed so widely in the Age of Atonement because he managed to combine the Scottish and evangelical doctrine of conscience with the utilitarian doctrine of consequentialism—put *conscience* into

---

[70] Jerram to Wilson, 1825, *Life of Wilson*, i. 162.
[71] [J. J. Blunt], 'The writings of Bishop Butler', *Quarterly Review*, 43 (1830), 211–13. Blunt was Lady Margaret Professor of Divinity at Cambridge 1839–55.
[72] See below, p. 342.
[73] *Christian Observer*, NS, 217–28 (1856), 571–2. See *The Evangelical Magazine*, NS, 33 (1855), 771–2, for a similar comment.

the machine, as it were. In this way he combined the attractive qualities of Bentham and Coleridge, whom J. S. Mill called the two seminal influences of the day. The core of utilitarian moral theory, especially as elaborated by Bentham, was consequentialist, in that the ethical value of an action was estimated by considering what effect it had on the actor and on others, not by making judgments as to the actor's motives and intentions. The appeal of such an approach is that we can be tolerably certain what the consequences of an act are, but must always remain ignorant as to the actor's state of mind. Paley's ethics were utilitarian because they expressed the same consequentialist truth the other way round and in a religious context. God gives man innate desires and God rules the world. Since the *natural* world is a good place, so men's desires—whose fulfilment largely makes the world what it is—must also be good. Paley's critics frequently complained that he was unable to believe in the existence of a 'natural conscience' because he 'seems to suppose, that conscience must be taken to be independent of the consequences of acts', whereas Butler—making intention the 'pivot' of conscience—realized that this could not be so.[74] Thus it is not surprising that, in the first half of the nineteenth century, Butler's ethics should have appealed to those who craved an intuitive or non-consequentialist basis of morality.

So far Butler was an intuitionist, but unlike Coleridge his writings included a consequentialist message as well. This involved him in philosophical contradictions as to whether men should obey the dictates of self-love or conscience, and whether acts of self-love have good consequences or coincide with acts inspired by benevolence. But this was not something which unduly worried his nineteenth-century admirers, sharing as they did his view of a cosmic moral order.[75] Like Paley, Butler believed that the world was divinely ordered in such a way that it was a *consequence* of men's gratified appetites. Unlike Paley, Butler's admirers believed that those appetites must be bad ones, since in the post-Malthusian, post-1789 gloom, the world—which was the consequence of those appetites—seemed itself to be so bad. Butler's consoling message was simply that suffering, even—perhaps especially—vicarious suffering, is beneficent because it can pay the debt of sin. Since the drunkard harms his own children, then, by a process of substitutionary punishment, his sins are partly paid for. Thus the section of the *Analogy* which seemed most prominent to contemporaries was that which compared the divine act of atonement with the natural processes of mediation in the ordinary course of life. In Butler the Fall accounts for the anomalies of nature—such

[74] Richard Wildman, *The Anatomy of Scepticism, and Metaphysics of Science* (1853), 94–103.
[75] Schneewind, *Sidgwick and Victorian Moral Philosophy*, pp. 7–8, 418–20.

as the many ways in which good can come out of evil—while in Paley they are shrugged off as unintentional by-products of the Creation. Butler based his faith on evidences, but kept those evidences sufficiently flimsy to be in themselves a moral probation and discipline for would-be believers. Such 'probable' evidences were more rewarding than 'irresistible' truth, since the latter required no moral effort on the part of the believer.

It is not difficult to see Butler's relevance for political economists. Having anticipated all those nineteenth-century moralists who railed against the idea of 'compulsory virtue', he was frequently appealed to by writers opposed to poor relief for undeserving vagrants.[76] More generally, Smith, Stewart, and Whately all approved his argument that self-love could be a virtuous emotion quite distinct from selfishness, and that the world would be a better place if more self-love, properly controlled and moderated, were practised. Indeed, it seems likely that, during the first half of the nineteenth century, the doctrine of 'enlightened self-interest' was envisaged more often in a Butlerian than in a Benthamite context, more with an eye to individual probity than to public benefit.

Chalmers and a Natural Theology of Conscience

More than anyone it was Chalmers who adapted Butler's ethics and theology to nineteenth-century evangelicalism. Not that his spiritual and philosophical history was a straightforward one. As a youth he had entertained religious doubts induced by reading Holbach's *System of Nature* (1770). He was led out of scepticism by James Beattie's *An Essay on the Nature and Immutability of Truth* (1770), as well as by Robison's lectures on natural philosophy at Edinburgh University. Then had come a period of attachment to the Moderate Party in the Kirk, during which he strongly opposed such doctrines as those of atonement and justification by faith. It was only with his evangelical conversion in 1809–11 that he imbibed Wilberforce, Thomas Scott, Baxter, and above all Butler, but from then on he seems to have needed little else by way of spiritual refreshment.[77] He followed Butler in moving a posteriori 'from the felt experience of a judge within the breast to the inference of a Judge above and over us, who planted it there'.[78] Man possesses an 'original and independent

---

[76] See, for example, J. E. Bicheno, *An Inquiry into the Poor Laws, chiefly with a View to examine them as a Scheme of National Benevolence, and to elucidate their Political Economy* (1824), 138–41. Butler is not mentioned in the 1817 pamphlet of which this is a revised version.

[77] Daniel F. Rice, 'Natural theology and the Scottish philosophy in the thought of Thomas Chalmers', *Scottish Journal of Theology*, 24 (1971), 23–46.

[78] [T. Chalmers], 'Morrell's *Modern Philosophy*', *North British Review*, 6 (1846–7), 311. Having become acquainted with German philosophy towards the end of his life, Chalmers decided that the 'supremacy of conscience' was identical with Kant's 'Categorical Imperative'.

intellectual constitution', to which 'external nature' is adapted.[79] 'Blind and unconscious matter cannot . . . evolve the phenomena of mind', and the authority of natural theology depends on man's knowing intuitive truths.[80] One of the reasons that Chalmers found Malthus's 'preventive check' compelling was its implication that *all* men, including the lowest, possess a moral sense. In rebutting the argument that a benevolent God would surely not rule by eternal rewards and punishments, or render the prospect of salvation so precarious, Chalmers (following Butler's *Analogy*) pointed to the 'economy' of the earth, to the 'daily course of natural providence', where rewards and punishments were equally in evidence— 'foreseen pleasures and pains . . . fitted to induce one line of conduct and deter from another'. Eternal damnation merely mirrors sublunary misfortunes, all of which are petty punishments designed to dissuade men from actions

committed for the sake of a present tempting gratification, as when intemperance is followed up by disease; and these eventual pains or chastisements are often far greater than the immediate enjoyment, as when the disgrace of a whole lifetime results from the indulgence, which lasts but for a moment, of some ungovernable passion; and frequently a long delay intervenes between the commission and its penalty, as when the secret fraud or profligacy, it may be of many years back, at length breaks out, to the consequent ruin of the perpetrator either in character or circumstances; and when these natural punishments do come, it is often with an astounding suddenness, and when they are altogether unlooked for.

Chalmers's point is that, since the 'heedlessness of one stage of life' *always* leads to 'wretchedness' in the later stages, why cavil at the Christian doctrine of hell-fire? Why cry 'Peace, when there is no peace, and cherish a delusive security, as if in the hands of an indulgent God who will not bear too hard . . . but make allowance for the frailty of [human] nature, and the force of external temptations?'[81] In other words, we should not criticize God's spiritual cruelty, since it is perfectly consistent with his terrestrial government. Incidentally, Chalmers went even further round the circular argument than Butler in claiming that, since *in practice* vice is not always punished on earth and virtue is not always rewarded, there logically *must* be an afterlife where appropriate dispensations can be made. Either 'unavenged sins against God', and 'unredressed injustice between man and man', meet with an 'equitable adjustment in a future state',[82]

[79] Chalmers to Whewell, 4 Mar. 1834, Whewell MS a.202[25].

[80] Chalmers, *On the Power Wisdom and Goodness of God*, i. 37 [*Works*, i. 286].

[81] T. Chalmers, *A Course of Lectures on Butler's 'Analogy of Religion'* (1839), [*Posthumous Works*, ix. 15–18].

[82] The term 'equitable adjustment' was frequently used at that time by those such as Cobbett who wished for a revision of debts and contracts to take account of the changed value of money consequent upon the return to specie payments in 1821.

or else we must admit that our world is 'a deep moral enigma', a 'perfect moral anarchy'.[83] Here again Chalmers stands Paley on his head: it is not the perfection but the very imperfection of the universe which proves the existence of God and of God's Heaven.

Butler had identified three constituents of mind: self-love, benevolence or disinterestedness, and conscience, which is lord of all. When the dictates of self-love and conscience differed man should, it seems, obey the latter, but fortunately God had so wonderfully contrived the world that in most instances there was no conflict. In Chalmers's hands, however, natural theology celebrated, not Butler's well-ordered world—Robespierre and Malthus had put paid to that notion—but man's well-ordered mind. That man is good—that his faculties, emotions, and intellect are ruled over by conscience—is the repetitious argument of Chalmers's Bridgewater Treatise *On the Moral and Intellectual Constitution of Man*. The material universe may reveal God's *cleverness*, but only man's conscience—'a mechanism of obvious contrivance'—suggests that the Creator is benevolent as well.[84]

We derive pleasure from acting virtuously and misery from being vicious. Rectitude is thus its own reward, and sin its own punishment, from which it was possible to infer 'that we lived under the administration of a God who loved righteousness and who hated iniquity'.[85] Here Chalmers was celebrating the Butlerian idea of conscience which Bagehot was to deride, but which excited many nineteenth-century moralists, and not only evangelicals.[86] 'But besides the pleasures and pains of conscience', Chalmers continued, 'there is, in the very taste and feeling of moral qualities, a pleasure or a pain.' It was yet another mark of God's forethought,

more especially as exemplified in the reciprocal influences which take place between mind and mind in society; for the effect of this adaptation is to multiply both the pleasures of virtue and the sufferings of vice. The first, the original pleasure, is that which is felt by the virtuous man himself; as, for example, by the benevolent, in the very sense and feeling of that kindness whereby his heart is activated. The second is felt by him who is the object of this kindness—for

[83] Chalmers, *Lectures on Butler's 'Analogy'* [*Posthumous Works*, ix. 12].

[84] Chalmers, *On the Power Wisdom and Goodness of God*, i. 38, 62 [*Works*, i. 288, 310].

[85] Chalmers, 'Institutes of theology', [*Collected Works*, vii. 122–3; *Posthumous Works*, vii. 104–5].

[86] [J. G. Lockhart], 'Chalmers's sermons', *Blackwood's Edinburgh Magazine* 5 (1819), 462–8: 'Alas! the perfectibility of human nature is but an idle dream. . . . But admit the doctrine of depravity and the fall of man, and while thus his nature is rendered more awful and mysterious, yet does his history on earth become less unintelligible. His griefs, his agonies, his melancholy, and his despair, are then reasonable things—while, otherwise, they would be but foolishness and mockery. . . . This is Chalmers's great message.'

merely in the conscious possession of another's good will, there is a great and distinct enjoyment. And then the manifested kindness of the former awakens gratitude in the bosom of the latter; and this, too, is a highly pleasurable emotion. And lastly, gratitude sends back a delicious incense to the benefactor who awakened it. By the purely mental interchange of these affections there is generated a prodigious amount of happiness; and that, altogether independent of the gratifications which are yielded by the material gifts of liberality on the one hand, or by the material services of gratitude on the other.

Natural theology was thus transferred from the physical to the mental world and applied to the relations between men. 'Honest and universal good-will' in every wealthy bosom, 'gratitude back again' from the beneficiaries, true kindness oscillating 'from one heart and countenance to another', 'universal courteousness in our streets', commercial integrity and confidence, of such things was a Paradise upon earth made possible.[87]

Clearly Chalmers's intention in the Bridgewater Treatise was to attack utilitarianism (which, after Stewart, he called 'the selfish system of morals') along intuitionist or 'common sense' lines.[88] 'What is the first departure of every argument but an intuition, and what but a series of intuitions are its successive stepping-stones?' We must 'assume' things rather than try to 'prove' them by logic, syllogism, or deduction.[89] Butler and Brown had demonstrated that the final object of a desire (e.g. food) is quite separate from the pleasure attendant on its gratification (eating). Yet although he followed Reid, Beattie, and Stewart here, Chalmers was an evangelical and so opposed to the theological 'Moderatism', based on Enlightenment rationality, which was the usual complement of 'common sense' in Scotland. As Daniel Rice has shown,[90] the reconciliation of 'common sense' with evangelicalism, that is, with an anthropology of sin, grace, and redemption, informs all Chalmers's natural theology. Nature is constant, and faith in its constancy proves *both* God's existence *and* man's capacity for faith anterior to experience.[91] 'Common sense' assures us of the universality of human nature—by which Chalmers means that

---

[87] Chalmers, *On the Power Wisdom and Goodness of God*, i. 171–3 [*Works*, ii. 19–20].

[88] For this division in nineteenth-century moral philosophy see J. B. Schneewind, 'Moral problems and moral philosophy in the Victorian period', *Victorian Studies*, 9 (1965–6), supplement, pp. 29–46.

[89] Chalmers, *On the Power Wisdom and Goodness of God*, i. 36–7 [*Works*, i. 285]. Not that utilitarians were abashed. See, for example, [T. Perronet Thompson], 'Dr. Chalmers's *Bridgewater Treatise*', *Westminster Review*, 39 (1834), 12: 'O for five minutes of Jeremy Bentham after meat, to hang up such useless verbiage upon the pot-hook of his nose!'

[90] Rice, 'Natural theology and Scottish philosophy in Thomas Chalmers', *Scottish Journal of Theology*, 24 (1971), 23–46.

[91] Chalmers, *On the Power Wisdom and Goodness of God*, i. 169 [*Works*, ii. 16–17].

all men possess a moral sense, though not all men are moral. On the contrary, men are totally depraved, 'rebels' to God's moral government.[92] 'Christianity in its very essence is the religion of sinners; and the sinfulness of all men is the very basis on which the remedial system of the gospel is proposed for the acceptance of the world.'[93] As Rice puts it, Chalmers's natural theology goes no further than to pose a religious question which can only be resolved outside natural theology, by the Bible doctrine of the atonement. It was a way of marrying Scottish 'common sense' to its evangelical antithesis, something which Copleston also attempted, though unlike Chalmers he started from the former and worked toward the latter. Thus in a letter to the novelist-politician Robert Plumer Ward Copleston criticized the common practice 'of making *natural religion* the introduction to the revealed', yet at the same time he admitted that the goodness of God, which was 'indisputable', found 'a perfect accordance . . . in the scheme of Christian redemption by a suffering Messiah', and acknowledged that deism had helped to prepare him for Christianity. Contemplation of the moral law within his own breast filled Copleston, like Chalmers, with an even greater sense of awe than contemplation of the starry heavens.[94]

So Chalmers's version of natural theology, what he called 'moral dynamics', was distinctly man-centred and also subservient to the gospel message of redemption. In this lies his affinity with such scientists as Whewell and Herschel who, as Roger Smith has explained, argued for

an anthropomorphic philosophy in which the experience of force was believed to be the meaningful reference for all kinds of causal events. They argued that the mind, rather than physical science, applied intelligible experiences of causation. This argument placed the idea of free will at the centre of nature and interpreted free will as a source of natural events.

This 'volitional' or 'dynamic' theory of causality went with a phenomenalist psychology, in which 'force' was held to link the active mind with passive matter surrounding it.[95] It was an assumption very widely shared during

[92] Chalmers, 'Discourses illustrative of the connection between theology and general science', *Works*, vii. 345.

[93] Chalmers, 'Institutes of theology', [*Collected Works*, vii. 409; *Posthumous Works*, vii. 384]. See Edmund Phipps's comment in Phipps, *Memoirs of Plumer Ward*, ii. 126 n: 'Without physical evil, where would be the virtues of fortitude, patience, resignation, charity, long suffering, . . . and without . . . moral evil, our gratitude to the First Person of the Trinity for his gracious promise, to the Second for his inestimable sacrifice, and to the Third for that assistance by which alone we can ever resist moral evil, would fail.'

[94] Copleston to R. P. Ward, ?1825, Phipps, *Memoir of Plumer Ward*, ii. 120-27. For further discussion of Chalmers's natural theology see below, pp. 361-2.

[95] Roger Smith, 'Physiological psychology and the philosphy of nature in mid-nineteenth century Britain', Cambridge University Ph.D. (1970), 216, 224-70.

the Age of Atonement by evangelicals as well as by those who abhorred them. The realization after 1850 that mind and matter, mind and body, might be subject to the *same* laws was to have dramatic effects on all aspects of thought, as Chapter 8 will show.

Butler, Paley, and the Economics of Free Trade

It has been a recurrent theme of this book that commitment to fashionable social and economic policies could derive from opposing philosophical and theological positions. As we saw in Chapter 2,[96] there was an optimistic model whereby it was thought that Free Trade would wondrously unfold the harmonies of physical nature, which man had merely to contemplate passively. There was also a retributive model, which described Free Trade as revealing both physical *dis*harmony (competition) and human adaptability (or willingness to obey the rules of the market). The distinction clearly has some relevance to the conflict between Butlerian and Paleyan modes of thought.

Paley, said Fitzjames Stephen, 'was obviously a cheerful sanguine man, naturally disposed to enjoy himself and take a bright view of things'; Butler, as obviously, had a 'contrary disposition'.[97] Unlike his contemporaries Shaftesbury, Bolingbroke, and Pope, Butler believed that rational animals do not always prevail over irrational ones, and that good men cannot unite because they do not recognize each other.[98] He would have been bewildered by Cobden's 'certain' assurance 'that in this world the virtues and the forces go together, and the vices and the weaknesses are inseparable'.[99] Yet many of Cobden's contemporaries held an equally sanguine or Paleyan view of nature, even of the principle of population, a point which may be obscured by the emphasis we have been placing on evangelical gloom and social pessimism. Where Malthus deduced that man could achieve one kind of happiness (security) if he forwent more immediate gratifications, Paley inferred a more benign law of nature from the fact 'that the Deity has added *pleasure* to animal sensations, beyond what was necessary for any other purpose, or when the purpose, so far as it was necessary, might have been effected by the operation of pain'. Brougham — an eccentric, admittedly, but not a bad guide to the mentality of *Edinburgh Review*

---

[96] Above, pp. 64–70.
[97] James Fitzjames Stephen, *Horae Sabbaticae: Reprints of Articles Contributed to The Saturday Review* (3rd series, 1892), 77.
[98] Butler, *Analogy*, I, iii, pp. 59–61 [*Works*, ed. Halifax (1820), i. 84–7; ed. Gladstone (1896), i. 82–4]. See James Bonar, *Moral Sense* (1930), 60.
[99] 'Speech on the American war at Rochdale', 24 Nov. 1863, *Speeches on Questions of Public Policy by Richard Cobden*, ed. John Bright and James E. Thorold Rogers (1870), ii. 106.

Whiggism—concluded from this that sex (the 'superfecund propensity') proves how the universe is governed more by inducement than by denouncement, by reward more than punishment. As Paley had pointed out, God might well have forced us to procreate on pain of death—instead he has added a sensational 'bounty'.[1] Brougham's final word—contrasted as it was in economic terminology with 'duty'—points the moral.

With a few exceptions (most notably McCulloch) professional economists were thoroughly *un*Butlerian and opposed to the Scottish metaphysics of retribution. James Mill and, less consciously, Ricardo held to the 'natural harmony' theories of the French physiocrats—Turgot, Quesnay, and their successor, Say. Senior, as we saw, could not 'attribute wrath to the Deity or . . . justice', and his conception of liberty was as negative as that of Hobbes: 'most men think that free will consists in the power of controlling oneself. I understand by it only the absence of physical restraint.' Torrens declared his allegiance to the philosophy of the Rev. Alexander Crombie, who seems to have persuaded him to become a political economist in the first place. And Crombie, although he was an exponent of 'faculty' natural theology like Chalmers, held a much rosier view of nature, being fulsome in his laudation of God's 'adorable attributes', 'transcendent perfections', 'purely benevolent' and 'stupendous works', which assured us that man's undoubted suffering would shortly issue in a glorious resolution.[2] Yet important though these political economists were in developing doctrine, it is not clear that any of them exercised particular sway over what might be called public opinion. In order to understand the optimistic version of Free Trade, it might be better to concentrate on a publicist whose concern with social policy was secondary to his philosophy of mind. George Combe is an appropriate choice, if only because he was a Scotsman whose influence in national life was comparable to that of Thomas Chalmers, though it was exercised less among members of the social establishment than among those who aspired to be members.

Phrenology and Political Economy

George Combe (1788–1858) was an indefatigable champion of phrenology, a scientific false start which was condemned and derided by

---

[1] Henry Brougham and Charles Bell, *Paley's Natural Theology, with Illustrative Notes* (1836), ii. 138. See T. Southwood Smith, *The Divine Government* (5th edn, 1866), 95: 'Pleasure is annexed to the performance of the animal and vital functions, . . . [for] no other reason . . . but the pure benevolence of Him in whom we live.'

[2] Senior to Whately, 14 July 1827, Levy, *Nassau Senior*, pp. 57–8; Alex Crombie, *Natural Theology: or Essays on the Existence of Deity and of Providence, on the Immateriality of the Soul, and a Future State* (1829), ii. 608–9; Robert Torrens, *An Essay on Money and Paper Currency* (1812), p. v; Torrens to Napier, 20 Oct. 1830, *Correspondence of Macvey Napier*, p. 95.

many—but not all—of the respectable thinkers of the day. Despite constant rebuffs, Combe found himself on the borderline where all sorts of intellectual networks met, and therefore figures prominently in any discussion of social and moral science during the second quarter of the nineteenth century. A frail and sensitive boy, brought up in Edinburgh's gloomy Calvinist atmosphere, he was terrified of teasing adults and greatly distressed at the sight of cruelty to animals. The harsh discipline meted out at one of his schools quite demoralized him, and he much preferred a later academy where, in place of beatings, there were girls who created 'a kindly and gentle tone of feeling'.[3] Not surprisingly, he rebelled against the God of the evangelicals, though he would never be entirely able to shake off his fears of eternal hell-fire. What mainly worried him, however, was his inability to control his own passions. Realizing that he had a hyperactive brain, he determined to conquer his impulsiveness, irritability, and excitement 'by doing everything with deliberate slowness. He took a walk, and measured his steps to the time of a dead march, in spite of much eagerness to quicken his pace'. He spoke very slowly also, and never committed himself to anything without long deliberation, which may explain why he remained a bachelor until he was nearly forty-five, despite being 'decidedly partial to the married state'.[4] Whereas evangelicals craved spontaneity, it seems that Combe did his best to avoid it. By such means he managed, in his biographer's opinion, to keep wonderfully calm through a lifetime's disputation, while reducing antagonists to paroxysms of exasperation. Despite this successful mastery of his own passions, however, Combe's efforts to understand the workings of the human mind were for a long time unrewarded. He could eke no comprehension from Locke, Hutcheson, Smith, Hume, or Stewart, and for many years gave up moral philosophy and epistemology as the obscurantist tools of a worthless intellectual élite.

It was in this state of social and philosophical frustration that he chanced to attend one of Spurzheim's Edinburgh lectures in 1815. Gall and Spurzheim were the Continental exponents of phrenological 'science', and, after a characteristic period of hesitation, Combe seems to have been swept up by its doctrines in the manner of an evangelical experiencing conversion. From then on, in Leslie Stephen's words, he 'propagated the doctrine with the zeal of a religious missionary'.[5] Like his brother Andrew, a doctor, Combe had often been 'repelled and puzzled by the representations from

<hr>

[3] *The Life of George Combe*, by Charles Gibbon (1878), i. 1–24. On Combe see David de Giustino, *Conquest of Mind: Phrenology and Victorian Social Thought* (1975), 3–9, 25–34, 117–66.

[4] Gibbon, *Life of George Combe*, i. 80–1, 85. Needless to say, he examined the lady's head before marrying her. Ibid., i. 285.

[5] Stephen in *Dictionary of National Biography*, iv. 885.

the pulpit and in the Catechism, of the corrupt condition and dreadful prospects of man', and neither knew any peace of mind on religious questions until they came across phrenology.[6] They came to see it as a panacea for all social and philosophical difficulties, for, as George wrote to Chalmers in 1823, 'Phrenology appears to be precisely what Reid and Stewart and Brown, and many other eminent philosophers sought for but did not find, a true system of human nature.'[7]

By this Combe meant that the 'metaphysicians' had vainly tried to deduce a philosophy of mind from their own consciousness. Locke and Hume had regarded the mind as a sheet of white paper, on which ideas of evil and virtue could be impressed from without. Reid and Stewart had more plausibly postulated a form of faculty psychology, with categories similar to those used later by Gall and Spurzheim, but their subsequent deductions had been highly speculative. Phrenologists, on the other hand, confidently identified mind as a function of the brain, and defined the latter as an aggregate of about thirty-five parts or organs, each one subserving a distinct mental faculty, like *amativeness, combativeness, firmness, veneration, conscientiousness, adhesiveness* (the desire to love and be loved), and *ideality*. Other things being equal, the size of an organ was taken to be an index of its power.[8] Phrenology was therefore half-way between anatomy and a primitive form of psychology.[9] Whereas Butler, Reid, Stewart, and Brown had *assumed* that man has a moral sense, and Hume had *asserted* that men are attracted to 'justice', and Smith had *postulated* a faculty of 'sympathy' as the source of moral approbation, Combe felt able to demonstrate scientifically that some persons did, while others did not, possess each of these attributes.[10] He could thus assure his friend Whately, who took the 'science' seriously and claimed to 'like its metaphysics', that his moral region was enormously large in relation to the base of the brain. 'It is the large size of the organs of the moral sentiments which communicates that vivid love of mankind, that reliance on the power of right, and that weight of character which distinguish your Grace.'[11]

___

[6] Andrew Combe to George Combe, 8–14 Dec. 1841, *The Life and Correspondence of Andrew Combe*, by George Combe (Edinburgh, 1850), 406–7.

[7] Combe to Chalmers, 19 Feb. 1823, Chalmers MS, CHA 4.24.82.

[8] Gibbon, *Life of George Combe*, i. 95, 204.

[9] But see Roger James Cooter, 'The cultural meaning of popular science: phrenology and the organization of consent in nineteenth-century Britain', Cambridge University Ph.D. (1978), 101–2, 360 n. 75.

[10] G. Combe, *Lectures on Moral Philosophy, delivered before the Philosophical Association, at Edinburgh, 1835–6* (Boston and London, 1840), 9–35.

[11] George Combe to Whately, ?1831, Gibbon, *Life of George Combe*, i. 259–60, 264–6. Combe praised Sedgwick's famous *Discourse on the Studies of the University* for proclaiming the inadequacies of Locke and Paley, but lamented its neglect of phrenology as the missing link in moral philosophy. [G. Combe], 'Sedgwick on the studies at Cambridge', *The Phrenological Journal and Miscellany*, 9 (1834–6), 1–6. Combe regarded

Combe thought that he himself proved the point that love of justice (beyond mere selfish gain) went with a large organ of conscientiousness.

Phrenologically, Combe contrasted three types of person: first, those in whom the moral and intellectual propensities are large and the animal propensities only moderate in size. Such men can clearly tell right from wrong, and should therefore be punished if they allow their animal bumps so far to preponderate as to lead them into crime. Then there are those like Whately in whom both higher and lower propensities are large; 'the full influence of the animal feelings has been felt; but they never had the ascendancy. There was at all times a vigorous monitor within who never slept.'[12] Finally there are those whose animal organs far outmeasure their higher ones. Such men should not be punished for giving way to temptation, but merely restrained.[13]

In all this Combe was working toward a materialist explanation of mind, in much the same way as Hartley had used association psychology, Erasmus Darwin neurology, and Horne Tooke philology, and if he had stopped at this point he would have deserved the charges of 'materialism' and 'determinism' which were so often thrown at him. In fact, his theory of mind had yet to be wedded to a conception of natural theology, one that was largely Butlerian though he would not have admitted it. As with so many of the people who figure in this study, the year 1825 was decisive, a time when 'he was tending towards his most hazardous speculations'. These appeared in a paper on 'Human responsibility as affected by phrenology', produced in a 'spirit of infuriation' during January 1826, and were later developed in his most famous and notorious book, *The Constitution of Man, considered in relation to External Objects* (1828). He recorded to a friend,

Now all fear and doubt and hesitation are removed. I have got a hold of the principle of the Divine administration, and most holy, perfect and admirable it appears. Now I can say for the first time in my life that I love God with my whole heart and soul and mind; because now I see Him as an object altogether gratifying to Benevolence, Veneration, Hope, Ideality, Conscientiousness, Comparison, and Causality.[14]

In other words, Combe had come to a realization that there is a direct— that is, mechanically consistent[15]—and benevolent moral government of the world, God's laws being plainly written in nature for the benefit of

---

Brown as the philosopher who came closest to a phrenological exposition of man's mental constitution. See Combe to Chalmers, 5 Dec. 1826, Chalmers MS, CHA 4.54.42.

[12] G. Combe to Whately, ?1831, Gibbon, *Life of George Combe*, i. 264–6.

[13] Ibid., ii. 41, i. 130.

[14] G. Combe to Revd David Welsh, 11 Feb. 1826, Gibbon, *Life of George Combe*, i. 180, 183–4.

[15] See above, pp. 13–14.

man. As he put it in 'Human responsibility',

God intended the moral sentiments and intellect to rule the actions of man, and constructed the human mind and physical nature with a determinate relation to these faculties, so that conduct in conformity to their dictates should be followed by happiness, and conduct in opposition to them should produce misery; just because, in the first instance, man would act in harmony with the scheme of creation; and in the second, in opposition to it.[16]

Man's task was therefore to observe which actions do practically produce happiness and beneficence, so that they might in future comply with each separate law of nature. Children must be shown how the moral constitution of things is adapted, 'as a means of wholesome discipline and enjoyment, to their own bodies and minds'. They must then be made 'to train their veneration and conscientiousness to respect that constitution and these adaptations, and to act in harmony with them'.[17] Phrenology would help by providing a clear account of an individual's 'innate capacities . . . and of the effects of external circumstances in modifying them'. Man's nature is progressive, and phrenology helps to educate him. Reveal a criminal's propensities to him, explain to him the laws of nature as they affect hygiene, dietetics, or political economy, and you will be able to persuade him that he is the arbiter of his own fate, and that right conduct will maximize his happiness.[18]

So in God's harmonious world all suffering is the consequence of one's own (or one's parents') wrongdoings. Combe had the grace to bear in good part the loss of some investments in American railways, certain as he was that losers on these occasions always reaped their just deserts. Lying on what he thought was his death-bed, he accepted the agonizing bouts of pain as 'the result of some error committed in ignorance of God's law, and believed that it was only because of ignorance that they could not be alleviated. He was patient in his agony, and anxious to learn its cause that he might warn others.'[19] In casual moments he seems to suggest that achievement of perfect phrenological awareness would lead to immortality: 'disease, death, disappointment . . . these misfortunes, *should they come*, will be the consequences of past departures from His laws' on the part 'of ourselves or of our forefathers'.[20] For the trouble with men is that 'they do not *reflect*. We live in an age of practical infidelity to any divine government of the affairs of men on the principle of cause and effect.'[21]

---

[16] Gibbon, *Life of George Combe*, i. xii, 183.
[17] G. Combe to Whately, 24 Feb. 1847, Lambeth Palace Library, Whately MS 2164, fos. 45–8.
[18] Gibbon, *Life of George Combe*, i. xiv, 147–8, 163–5.
[19] Ibid., ii. 345.
[20] Ibid., ii. 187 (italics added).
[21] Combe to Cobden, 16 Nov. 1847, Cobden Papers, BL Add. MS 43660, fos. 80–1.

All this, of course, bypassed the question of original sin. Not surprisingly, the most virulent opposition to Combe came from the Evangelical Party in Scotland, with their strong attachment to the Westminster Confession. At first Calvinists had found phrenology not unattractive, since its stress on organs of amativeness, acquisitiveness, and so on seemed to confirm their notions of human depravity. They quickly turned hostile when Combe suggested that such organs were in themselves beneficent, that evil occurred only when the organs of the lower animal propensities were larger than those of the moral and intellectual faculties, and that physiological and hereditary factors mainly determined these relative sizes.[22] 1831–2 saw an exodus of evangelicals from the Phrenological Society, including the departure of Combe's close friend David Welsh. Combe himself was unrepentant. Phrenology was for him 'the philosophy of the New Testament', able to show how the precepts of Jesus, such as the Sermon on the Mount, 'can be rendered really practical'.[23] The notion that men should be good Christians merely to avoid future punishment was selfish and base. 'It is impossible to love a Being whom we fear', he wrote in 1828, 'and habitual consciousness of liability to eternal misery enslaves the mind, and renders it unfit to entertain generous emotions.' Far better a religion which excites, not lower faculties like cautiousness, but higher ones like benevolence, hope, and veneration.[24] He became a firm friend of the American Unitarian William Henry Channing (1814–84), and like Channing he rebelled against the prevailing anthropomorphic conception of God the Father. Roger Cooter plausibly suggests that in all this Combe was rebelling against the memory of his own unloving father, and it may be significant that he first took up phrenology in 1815, the year of his father's death.

And yet, as we have noticed before, there was an ambivalence in these theological positions, and much resemblance beneath the surface between worshipping a God of love and worshipping a God of fear. Cooter has perceptively pointed out that, for all his antagonism to the Calvinists, Combe ended up by preaching virtues and values almost identical to theirs. Outside Edinburgh, where Calvinism was so strong, evangelical beliefs proved less of a barrier to the adoption of phrenology, so that Combe felt his influence to be stronger in Manchester than in Edinburgh, where 'the orthodox and metaphysicians rule . . . with undisputed sway'.[25] Though the terminology differed, the idea of one's better self conquering baser instincts was common to both evangelicalism and phrenology.

[22] [George Combe], 'Archbishop Whately—scripture and science', *Phrenological Journal*, 7 (1831–2), 321–34.
[23] G. Combe to Whately, ?1831, Gibbon, *Life of George Combe*, i. 264–6.
[24] Ibid., i. 205, 223–5, 236–43.
[25] G. Combe to William Ellis, 20 Apr. 1848, ibid., ii. 246.

'Elevating their minds above their passionate flesh', was how Chalmers put it. Indeed, Combe was to complain that Chalmers's Bridgewater Treatise *On the Moral and Intellectual Constitution of Man* had lifted many ideas from his own *Constitution of Man* without acknowledgement.[26] He was adamant that a Christian life requires right conduct as well as right worship, but then only extreme evangelicals like Irving or some of the wilder Edinburgh Calvinists would have disagreed. He could not see it, but Chalmers's 'expulsive power of a new affection' was not so very different from his own religion of hope and veneration.

This point emerges clearly from a correspondence between Combe and his lifelong friend and ally Richard Cobden, in which the latter attempted to defend evangelicals from Combe's disparagement.

With reference to your remarks as to the evangelical dissenters and religionists generally, and their views of your philosophy of morals, I will confess to you that *I* am not so inclined to quarrel with that class of my countrymen. I see the full force of what you urge, but am inclined to hope more from them, *in time*, than any other party in the state. Gradually, and *imperceptibly to themselves*, they are catching the spirit of the age, so far as to recognise the moral laws as a part of our natural organisation. . . . John Calvin and George Combe act upon different theories, and rely upon different motives, and start from very different premises, but they recognise the self-same ends, secularly speaking, and I cannot quarrel with either.

Combe's response to this rebuke is revealing. He acknowledged that evangelicals appreciated the supremacy of moral law, but thought that it was an 'enormous waste of religious, moral, and intellectual power' to seek its basis, as they did, 'in the supernatural', where no consensus is possible, 'instead of in the *natural*, . . . concerning which general agreement *is* possible'. He conceded, however, that 'the English mind is much more practical than logical', and that English evangelicals, if not their Scottish counterparts, 'do much practical good in spite of their erroneous belief'. Then he concluded, without realizing how close he was to proclaiming a moderate evangelical state of grace:

After I saw clearly the system of divine administration of the world through natural laws, instead of clashing and discordant sentiments, I attained to harmony and peace of mind. Instead of looking only to heaven to find God, I saw him

---

[26] Ibid., i. 296–7. Combe was indignant that phrenology was not considered sufficiently scientific to be allotted a Bridgewater Treatise of its own. On one occasion Combe commended a sermon of Chalmers, 'in which he demonstrated that the very act of obeying the laws of God is its own recompense. He boldly said that heaven is just holiness of mind, and not a place where enjoyment of other kinds is to be paid as the wages of holiness.' Ibid., i. 252.

in every institution of nature. . . . I felt myself living every moment in the presence of God; and this state of mind is my constant experience and delight.[27]

Even in his response to natural calamities Combe differed from his antagonists less than he supposed. When the cholera came in 1831, the *Phrenological Journal* carried an article which Combe said would gratify philosophers and horrify evangelicals. Predictably, its aim was to challenge 'the connexion between cholera and sin', and to deny the efficacy of repentance and supplication as a cure for physical malfunction.

Sins ought to be repented of, because they are sins, and all sins carry their own punishment; but reason can see no connexion between issuing a forged bill, or demanding sevenpence for a yard of cloth which ought to be sold at sixpence, or telling a lie on the Stock Exchange, and the irregular action of the blood-vessels, nerves, and muscles of the body. If God should at times send diseases like the cholera, which are purely organic, as a punishment of sins which are purely mental; and if He removes these diseases on our supplication independently of physiological causes, then He has given us reason in vain; for we cannot discover the connexion between the sin and the disease.

So far so good—cholera could not be a punishment for general spiritual depravity. But when the author (who was almost certainly Combe) turns to what it might be a punishment for, we find once again that the gap between the phrenologists and the evangelicals is not so very great. When working-men succumb to cholera it is probably because they are intemperate and debilitated, which fits the phrenological position, but when members of the higher classes are afflicted it is probably a retribution for having neglected the moral and physical condition of the people. Their covetous Mammonism has caused them to herd the poor together in grossly overcrowded cities, in which cholera thrives and infects themselves in turn. The writer believed that this was different from evangelical notions of retribution because it was not a case of providence 'punishing, in an arbitrary manner, sin in general', but a specific cause-and-effect chastisement which could only awaken the victim's sense of God's true power and goodness.[28] Though he did not see it, his quarrel here was only with the extreme pre-millenarians and not with the moderate evangelicals. Nor was there anything specifically un-evangelical in the *Phrenological Journal*'s cheerful view that cholera was killing off weaker strains in the human race. A difference can perhaps be discerned with respect to the *Journal*'s argument that cholera would rouse the rich to do something permanent about the condition of the towns. Preventive

---

[27] Cobden to G. Combe, 1 Aug. 1846, and G. Combe to Cobden, 13 Aug. 1846, ibid., ii. 217–22.

[28] [Anon.], 'Cholera morbus—effects of ignorance and knowledge', *Phrenological Journal*, 7 (1831–2), 463–76, esp. 473–4; Gibbon, *Life of George Combe*, i. 253.

checks were a central theme of phrenology — Combe's brother Andrew placed quite as much emphasis on the *prevention* as on the cure of disease, making every effort to befriend his patients and to show them that, God's laws being invariable, cold feet will eventually lead to a chill and must in Christian duty be avoided.[29] Nothing in this would have offended Chalmers, who had distinguished between 'a charity for indigence' and 'a charity for disease', and yet it *is* noteworthy that he and other moderate evangelicals took little heed of prevention with respect to the physical 'health of towns'.

The explanation may be that Chalmerian values were rural rather than urban, and this in turn would point up an important difference between evangelical and phrenological modes, which was their appeal to rival sections of the community. The phrenological approach to Free Trade was optimistic in tone and attracted radical and Utopian reformers, anxious to promote social mobility and to sweep away the privileges which fed on mercantilism. A 'true reformer' and a Whig, with many friends who called themselves Radicals, Combe imbued Cobden with his sense of a universal moral law and his belief that *laissez-faire* and self-help were the means to uncover it.[30] Cobden in turn greatly approved of phrenology, and Manchester — thanks perhaps 'to the enlightening chemical and mechanical studies with which our industry is allied, and to the mind-invigorating effects of our energetic devotion to commerce' — provided Combe with some of his largest and most appreciative audiences, making his stay there one 'constant Jubilee'.[31] This Whiggish or radical approach to *laissez-faire* contrasted with the more pessimistic Chalmerian mode, which mainly appealed to the comfortably well-off *nouveaux riches* who, opposing privilege, nevertheless defended the existing social order: notably the salaried, professional, and *rentier* classes most susceptible to the ideas of the evangelical intelligentsia.

Ostensibly, therefore, phrenology was part of an optimistic, radical critique, but it could easily slip into bourgeois rationalization of emerging industrial society, an attempt to hegemonize and discipline the potentially dangerous workforce by instilling desires for self-improvement through hard work.[32] Whereas the values of evangelicalism were those of progressive agrarian society and finance capital, phrenology flattered the

---

[29] G. Combe, *Life of Andrew Combe*, pp. 238–9.

[30] W. H. Greenleaf, *The British Political Tradition. Vol. 2: The Ideological Heritage* (1983), 35. See below, pp. 246–7.

[31] Cobden to Combe, ?1836, Gibbon, *Life of George Combe*, i. 314–15. 'How I pity you in Scotland', added Cobden, 'the only country in the world in which a wealthy and intelligent middling-class submits to the domination of a spiritual tyranny.' Ibid., ii. 10–11.

[32] In this paragraph I have relied extensively on the stimulating discussion in Cooter, 'The cultural meaning of popular science', pp. 76–121.

industrial bourgeoisie by its emphasis on Smilesian respectability, while *The Constitution of Man* propagated what might be called a Calvinist work ethic. This volume reached an enormous popular audience after about 1835, 100,000 copies having been sold in Britain by 1860 and another 200,000 in America, most of them being in popular editions, and indeed it was possibly the most widely read book after the Bible, *Pilgrim's Progress*, and *Robinson Crusoe* during the second quarter of the nineteenth century. Its aim was to inculcate values and to encourage conduct in keeping with the needs of work discipline—thrift, time-keeping, cleanliness, order, and self-help—while deprecating such debased habits as the eating of spicy foods and early marriage. Its message, in Cooter's formulation, was that 'to achieve happiness—or at least stave off suffering—it was imperative to come into harmony with the social, political and legal external relations laid down by the new secular priesthood, to find your social niche and make the best of it'. Cooter sees the preoccupation with *heads* as asserting the importance of intelligence and meritocratic values, not only as against aristocratic privilege (inheritance of grey cells replacing inheritance of property) but also in opposition to the labouring classes, whose symbolic strength lay in their hands and sinew. Moreover, the very simplicity of phrenological science was a challenge to the arcane mysteries propagated by metaphysical lackeys of the old intelligentsia. Anyone could feel and understand bumps, just as anyone could classify rocks, without having to be initiated into the élitist lore of churches and universities. Again, phrenologists asserted the orderliness of nature, perhaps as a way of coming to terms with the bewildering pace of change. Thus Combe explained the hierarchy of brain functions, just as the Hutchinsonians revealed order in the structure of the earth's crust, and Andrew Ure demonstrated the virtuous symmetry to be found in mechanized factories.[33] To back up such notions of natural order, Combe and his associates naturally employed organismic and uniformitarian metaphors, quite unlike the atomistic, corpuscular, and catastrophic language popular with evangelical moralists. The point remains, however, that though the imagery, self-perception, and class appeal were so different, phrenology's 'secular Methodism', as Cooter calls it,[34] propagated values which were not so very unlike those of evangelicalism.

[33] Andrew Ure, *The Philosophy of Manufactures: Or, an Exposition of the Scientific, Moral, and Commercial Economy of the Factory System of Great Britain* (1835), esp. 55–66. Ure identified three 'principles of action' or 'organic systems' in manufacturing—the mechanical, the moral, and the commercial. They were fed respectively by labour, science, and capital, and were comparable to 'the muscular, the nervous, and the sanguiferous systems of an animal'.

[34] Cooter, 'The cultural meaning of popular science', pp. 118–20.

It is only to be expected that Combe should have played an important part in the popular dissemination of political economy. He had read Malthus in 1805, and seems to have derived from him and Ricardo some of his 'fondness for system' and belief in the workings of universal laws. The *Phrenological Journal* defended political economy against 'practical men', who invariably possessed enormous organs of mere *knowing* (induction) in the lower regions of the forehead, but who had far too tiny organs of *reflection* (comparison, causality, and wit) to enable them to appreciate an abstract subject like political economy.[35] Combe was fascinated by the idea of 'division of labour'—in a sense it was the principle that he had applied to the head—but he naturally had no patience with the evangelicalization of population theory by Sumner and Chalmers. He refused to consider 'the grounds cursed, and the human mind in its elementary dispositions desperately wicked',[36] while philoprogenitiveness (like benevolence) was in his view unfortunate only if it got out of control. Turning to currency and banking problems after the 1825–6 commercial crisis, Combe was particularly concerned to analyse the psychological causes of over-speculation, which like Chalmers he thought might best be extirpated by sound religious advice. He attributed the troubles to his equivalents of original sin: acquisitiveness and self-esteem, lower propensities which were bound to cause 'continually-recurring misery', but he also saw that such failings were exacerbated by the morally dangerous system of paper currency, a point reiterated in his *Moral Philosophy*, written after his experiences in America during 1839, a year notorious for its bankruptcies. Paper interfered with natural justice, he argued, since the real culprits could often throw their losses on to innocents. The commercial crises of 1847 and 1855 led to further articles in the *Scotsman* in praise of the 1844 Bank Charter Act, and naturally they were commended by the intellectual leader of the Currency School, Lord Overstone. According to Combe, the laws which regulate the production and distribution of wealth 'are based in nature and are universal in their operation'; money and banking exist merely to facilitate that operation, and are 'as thoroughly subject to the same laws as the motions of a satellite are to those of the principal planet'. But for the whole system to work *naturally*, notes must be equal in value to specie, and issues would have to be contracted periodically in order to maintain convertibility.[37] Only then will actions committed in a spirit of 'pure, generous, and

---

[35] [Anon.], 'The press and political economy', *Phrenological Journal*, 3 (1825–6), 47–51.

[36] G. Combe to Whately, 24 Feb. 1847, loc. cit.

[37] [Anon.], 'Commercial distress', *Phrenological Journal*, 3 (1825–6), 313–22; the *Scotsman*, 29 Dec. 1847; Gibbon, *Life of George Combe*, i. 204–5, ii. 202, 272–4, 340–1.

disinterested' love lead to results which are gratifying to covetousness, self-esteem, and love of approbation.

William Ellis (1800–81), who founded the Birkbeck Colleges, was the friend of both Combe and J. S. Mill, but it was Combe whom he 'revered'. He had abandoned political economy in despair during the 1820s, but took it up again twenty years later as a result of Combe's demonstration that such evils as hunger could be conquered if man would but adapt, and 'place himself in harmony with the laws of Nature'.[38] Like Ellis, Combe had a passion for education. To those who argued that *secular* education was immoral, he countered that 'a knowledge of God's order of creation and providence, is *highly moral*'—and here, of course, his quarrel was not with moderate evangelicals but with Tractarians like Denison who could not accept the value of any truth outside revelation.[39] Education was part and parcel of his individualism, a feature which marks him out as a creature of the earlier, not the middle or later, nineteenth century. When he visited New Lanark in 1820 he saw at once, just as Chalmers did, that Owen's communitarian paternalism could not work because it did not allow for the development of individual character, developments which would inevitably create contending interests and destroy the community. He concluded that *sentiment* over-predominated in Owen's skull.[40] Thirty years later he wrote to Ellis:

It appears to me that all attempts, such as are now making in Paris, and such as are proposed here, to organise labour in the form of Socialism, Fourierism, Owenism, or any other 'ism' which shall aim at communicating to brute labour—by which I mean the labour of the muscles—the reward which Providence has allotted only to intelligent labour, or labour enlightened, directed and controlled by a cultivated intellect and trained moral sentiments—labour, in short, which shall be capable of exerting its powers in accordance with the order of God's natural laws—will end in disappointment. . . . Before labour in general can reach a higher reward than it now receives, workmen in general must come more nearly into the mental condition of those in the middle ranks who combine capital and labour.

Intelligence and moral restraint, in other words, were indispensable to the production and accumulation of wealth, 'and without its accumulation in *their own hands*, the labouring classes never can improve their condition,

[38] Ellis to W. B. Hodgson, 19 Aug. 1847, *Life of William Ellis*, by Edmund Kell Blyth (1889), 58–9; *Memoir of William Ellis and an Account of His Conduct-Teaching*, by Ethel E. Ellis (1888), 53–7. Ellis regarded every merchant as a speculator, and as such 'neither a good nor a bad man'. Ellis to Hodgson, 1 Sept. 1847, Ellis, *Memoir of Ellis*, p. 58.

[39] G. Combe to James Clark, 14 Apr. 1847, Gibbon, *Life of George Combe*, ii. 237–9.

[40] Ibid., i. 133. Compare Torrens's view that 'a copulation between vanity and benevolence' had 'engendered madness' in Owen's brain. Torrens to Place, 11 Sept. 1817, Place Papers, BL Add. MS 37949, fos. 50–2.

or attain a reasonable independence'.[41] So much for the labour theory of value—here Combe's bourgeois ethos parts company with that of the Ricardian Socialist, Thomas Hodgkin, with so many of whose other views he seems to agree. So much also for the ideas of Christian Socialists and other paternalists, which were to flourish in mid-century. Despite his 'softness' on fundamental theological issues, Combe was, as we have seen, a child of the earlier nineteenth century: he saw God's moral law as retributive and corrective, and he saw Free Trade as necessary to realize its operations. Free Trade would prove that social inequalities were natural in the sense of being divinely ordained, and it would also give maximum effect to that division of labour which God had clearly intended when he endowed us all with different faculties. Meanwhile it would be dangerous, as he told another phrenologist, Charles Bray, to give working-men allotments or votes before they had learned 'to comply with the natural laws which govern the production and distribution of wealth'— that is, to be moral, restrained, and hard-working.[42] In this way, as Cooter points out, Combe actually reinforced Manchester economics. No wonder that he was friendly with McCulloch, and greatly admired John Stuart Mill's *Principles of Political Economy* (1848). Bray, as we shall see, belonged to a later and more radical generation of phrenologists, one which saw the science as disproving laws of political economy in relation to the distribution of wealth. For him there was no free will, 'no virtue in the ordinary sense of that term', and no sin. Virtue was 'not that which is free, or spontaneous, or uncaused, but that which does good', and society should be so organized as to force men to do as much good as possible.[43]

Mentor of Cobden, approved by Overstone—evidence of Combe's influence turns up in all sorts of unlikely places, even though there was no 'school' as such. One of his greatest admirers, and the man who mediated Combean ethics most fully with political economy, was Whately, who became 'infatuated' with phrenology. Essentially Whately was a 'common sense', anti-Lockean philosopher, viewing the mind as an active agent, capable of sensation, perception, and conception. Like Reid, Stewart, and Butler, he referred to man's intellectual powers by the term 'understanding', and to his active powers by the term 'will'. Like them also he believed that men possess innate moral sense: 'the inculcation of virtue and reprobation of vice in Scripture are in such a tone as seems

---

[41] G. Combe to William Ellis, 10 Apr. 1848, ibid., ii. 265–6. For Ellis on bankruptcy see above, p. 161.
[42] G. Combe to Charles Bray, 20 Apr. 1848, National Library of Scotland, Combe MS 7391/425–7, quoted in Cooter, 'The cultural meaning of popular science', p. 269.
[43] *Phases of Opinion and Experience during a Long Life: An Autobiography*, by Charles Bray (1885), 17–18. See below, pp. 324–5.

to presuppose a natural power, or a capacity for acquiring the power, to distinguish them.[44] But, as Ray McKerrow points out, Whately rejected the 'common sense' assumption as to the uniformity of human nature, possibly as a result of Combe's influence, and accepted instead that different men possess different powers. The role of reason is to help a man recognize his own particular attributes, to direct them, and to moderate his illicit passions.[45] With his usual desire to demonstrate that natural society was in a state of harmony, Whately used the fact that there are these innate differences among men to justify the existence of social inequality. The latter is conducive to the division of labour and the efficient organization of human communities, and is therefore proof of God's benevolent intervention in human affairs.[46] By emphasizing the need for self-education and development, Whately and Combe were able to retain a dualistic conception of man's nature, but it is undoubtedly the case that in pointing toward the mid-century emphasis on fixity of character and personality, they helped to undermine the sway of evangelical and Butlerian ethics. Before we consider this development, however, we must look briefly at the world of politics to see how the philosophy of atonement affected public life in the earlier half of the century.

[44] Whately, *Lectures on Political Economy*, p. 34.

[45] See Ray E. McKerrow, 'Richard Whately on the nature of human knowledge in relation to ideas of his contemporaries', *Journal of the History of Ideas*, 42 (1981), 439–55, for a full account. McKerrow points out that though he has been ignored by leading philosophers and historians of philosophy, Whately's 'common sense' psychology was in fact the 'staple fare' of the readers of such journals as *Leisure Hour*, *Good Words*, *Catholic Layman*, and *Saturday Magazine*.

[46] Whately, *Lectures on Political Economy*, p. 153. See Corsi, 'Natural theology, the methodology of science, and the question of species' University of Oxford D.Phil. (1980), 127.

6

The Politics of Atonement

An ethic transmuted into a cult, this ideal of economical and therefore virtuous government passed from the hands of prigs like Pitt into those of high priests like Gladstone. It became a religion of financial orthodoxy whose Trinity was Free Trade, Balanced Budgets, and the Gold Standard, whose Original Sin was the National Debt.

Henry Roseveare, *The Treasury* (1969), 118

I have often told Wilberforce that I rank politics high among Christian Virtues; because I find no men so ready to forget, and forgive offences, to overlook injuries, and to act in the true spirit of conciliation, and charity as those who are initiated in this noble science, so useful to mankind.

Henry Bankes to George Canning, 31 July 1812, Leeds Archives, Harewood MSS, Canning 34a

Saints in Parliament

It is time to consider the impact of the evangelical ideology on politics and legislation. There is a problem in that public life cannot be explained in terms of ideology alone, and anyway there were competing ideologies which need to be taken into account. The picture that emerges here is inevitably distorted and partial, but it is an important picture nevertheless, since evangelicalism was as much a public ethic as it was a personal credo.

Anglican evangelicalism first obtruded into national life during 1779–82. Economic depression, Lord George Gordon, riots in London and the north, and humiliation at the hands of the American colonists provoked what John Torrance, in a stimulating essay,[1] has described as 'outbursts of anxious patriotic moralism among the middle classes, . . . an epidemic of moral indignation, amounting to a recrudescence of the Protestant ethic'. Torrance's Weberian analysis relates this mentality to the emergence of an upper middle-class consciousness, to values which had long existed in metropolitan circles but which spread to the provincial élites and laid claim to national recognition during the 1780s. If there was an economic

---

[1] John Torrance, 'Social class and bureaucratic innovation: the Commissioners for Examining the Public Accounts 1780–1787', *Past and Present*, 78 (1978), 56–81.

basis to this so-called 'class' it was financial: progressive and improving (as distinct from backwoods) landlords—property agents—engineers—attorneys—architects—government officials—military officers—bankers—financiers—the larger merchants—anyone in fact who managed to plug into the *rentier* economy that was growing commensurately with the National Debt.[2] The dominant ethos was that of professionalism, 'improvement' being as much a psychological necessity as an economic calculation, and one that affected the new evangelical clergymen with their 'professional' interest in the saving of souls. Its moral tone was that of genteel respectability, as is clear from the numerous philanthropic associations campaigning 'for the restoration of public and private manners', the 'suppression of vice', and the regeneration of the classes above and below themselves—the effete aristocracy and the licentious rabble. Hannah More's *Thoughts on the Importance of the Manners of the Great to General Society* (1788), Gisborne's *Enquiry into the Duties of Men in the Higher and Middle Classes* (1794), and Wilberforce's *Practical View* (1797) were powerful but conventional expressions of the new 'moral majoritarianism'.

Between 1779 and 1783, according to Torrance, this *haute bourgeoisie* participated in the County Associations for Economical Reform alongside the older and vastly different country opposition, but the decision of the Yorkshire Association under Wilberforce and Thornton to forsake radical reform in favour of Pittism in 1784 indicates the establishmentarian, as well as nationalist and patriotic, aspects of the new ideology. That Pitt should have been the first politician to benefit from it is ironic, for there was little of either the evangelical or the Butlerian in his personality. But publicly his assumption of 'virtue', and the contrast between his image and that of the debauched gambler Charles James Fox, brought him enormous esteem. It is hard to believe that he was entirely unaware of this, and certainly his policies, unlike Fox's, pandered to the new 'mystique of oeconomy'. Retrenchment, anti-corruption, and what was termed 'justice to the public creditor'—that is, the priority given to repaying a portion of National Debt, even at the cost of extra burthens on the taxpayer—won Pitt a reputation for supreme economic righteousness at the same time as it pleased the fundholders. He also fostered his credentials with those who supported Wilberforce's campaign to abolish the Slave Trade, which succeeded in 1807, just after his death.

If political evangelicalism was born in an atmosphere of guilt, alarm, and perplexity during the early 1780s, events in the middle and later

---

[2] The nominal amount of unredeemed capital of the National Debt was £126.6 m. in 1762, £127.3 m. in 1775, £231.8 m. in 1783, and £844.3 m. in 1819. See B. R. Mitchell and Phyllis Deane, *Abstract of British Historical Statistics* (Cambridge, 1962), 402.

nineties—the reign of terror in France, fears of domestic insurrection, war, the threat of invasion, scarcity, and Malthus's *Essay*—all greatly intensified such feelings. There ensued a temporary sense of relief following the Peace of Amiens, during which Paley's reassuring *Natural Theology* (1802) appeared, but then 'just as the delay of the invasion was lulling the Country into a false peace, it . . . pleased God to afflict us with an awful visitation—the sudden and desperate illness of the king'.[3] The years 1807–11 were characterized by further apocalyptic fears concerning revolution, invasion, blockade, food shortage, national debt, a mad king, and a general apprehension that England was about to be singled out for divine punishment. As Ian Bradley shows in his important study of 'The politics of Godliness', this sense of impending doom led to a considerable jump in evangelical membership of Parliament between 1807 and 1811.[4] Bradley identifies 112 Evangelical MPs in the period 1784–1832, a conservative estimate in that it includes very few whose evangelicalism was informal, in the sense of being a medley of attitudes and feelings imbibed from associates. Of these 112 about thirty are classified as Saints, meaning that they were adherents of the Clapham Sect. According to Bradley, they were mostly optimists and activists, supporters of the reformist Tories after 1820. The others were either Recordites, who tended to be activist and reactionary, or else of no particular groupings but pessimistic, passive, and conservative, like the bulk of evangelical clergy in the parishes.[5] Socially and constitutionally, all evangelicals were conservative at bottom, not only from their sense of man's sinfulness but also, as a perceptive historian has written, from 'a fundamental fear of the loneliness of liberty, a craving for authority and obedience'.[6] They felt a need to flirt with liberty, yet, not daring to follow the breeze wherever it listed, many found an appropriate haven in Liberal Toryism.

As liberal social theorists the Clapham evangelicals were very firmly in favour of Free Trade and little government, and hostile to all forms of economic paternalism. They helped, indeed, to give such potentially selfish policies an aura of economic righteousness. The main hero of the movement for economical reform between 1807 and 1822 was

---

[3] Hannah More's diary, 19 Feb. 1804, in Roberts, *Life and Correspondence of Hannah More*, p. iii.

[4] Ian Bradley, 'The politics of Godliness: Evangelicals in Parliament, 1784–1832', University of Oxford D.Phil. (1974), 15–17. I am much indebted to Dr Bradley's thesis on these points. See also J. Jerram, *Memoirs of Charles Jerram*, p. 274, on the great tide of evangelical enthusiasm which flowed in Surrey during 1810 and which transformed his reputation from being that of a pariah to that of a fashionable pundit. Chalmers's conversion dates from the same period.

[5] Bradley, 'The politics of Godliness', p. ii.

[6] Henriques, *Religious Toleration in England*, pp. 226–7.

Henry Bankes, a close associate of Wilberforce. As chairman of the Finance Committee set up by Perceval in 1807 to inquire into salaries and sinecures, he worked closely with Henry Thornton and Thomas Baring.[7] During the twenties he deserted the Saints to take up an extreme anti-Catholic stance, and left the leadership of the campaign for retrenchment to the Radical Joseph Hume, whose humourless pedantry and lack of moral fervour lessened its impact considerably in the political world.

Along with cheap government went dear money. Wilberforce, Bankes, and the *Christian Observer* campaigned vigorously in favour of Bullionism, and regarded the resumption of Cash Payments as a 'triumph of truth and justice over clamour, and prejudice, and sordid interest'.[8] They were anxious to see the Usury Laws repealed, and were opposed to governments dispensing financial aid to bail out business firms which found themselves in difficulties. Saints were also devoted to Free Trade, 'that truly Christian system of intercourse',[9] though this fact has been to some extent obscured by Wilberforce's speech and vote for the third reading of the notoriously protective Corn Law of 1815. In fact more Saints opposed than supported the Corn Law, despite their attachment to Liverpool's government, and Wilberforce's vote was given reluctantly and in return for government support on the slavery issue.[10] By the 1820s, most of those evangelicals who were not also ultra-Tories were in favour of Corn Law repeal, and from 1822 the *Christian Observer* maintained an assertive campaign.[11] Indeed, the most vociferous parliamentary advocate of repeal between Ricardo's death in 1823 and the beginning of C. P. Villiers's campaign in 1838 was William Wolryche Whitmore, a fervent evangelical from Shropshire and a Saint. As chairman of the local Board of Guardians, Whitmore was notorious for his harsh, less-eligibilist treatment of his poor,[12] and his approach to repeal was equally moralistic and retributive. In 1841 he explained to the future Lord Overstone that he was anxious to set up Exeter Hall as the focus of a London-based agitation on the lines of the anti-slavery campaign, with the hope of countering the political radicalism, economic ignorance, and ethical optimism of the Anti-Corn

[7] Michael Roberts, *The Whig Party 1807–1812* (1939), 186–90. Perceval and G. H. Rose, both extreme in their evangelicalism, opposed the Committee's more sweeping recommendations.

[8] *Christian Observer*, 18 (1819), 342; Bradley, 'The politics of Godliness', pp. 139–41.

[9] Bradley, 'The politics of Godliness', p. 158. See *Christian Observer*, 22 (1823), 131, welcoming Robinson's first budget.

[10] Wilberforce in House of Commons, 10 Mar. 1815, *Parliamentary Debates*, 1st series, xxx. 116–18. For Wilberforce's complex motivation see Robin Furneaux, *William Wilberforce* (1974), 342–4.

[11] See, for example, *Christian Observer*, 25 (1826), 319; 26 (1827), 191, 383–4; Bradley, 'The politics of Godliness', pp. 215–18.

[12] *Shropshire Conservative*, 5 June 1841.

Law League.[13] Villiers himself had entered politics as a disciple of Canning and Huskisson. His connections were mainly Whiggish and his approach to repeal probably owed more to utilitarianism than to religion, but he did not entirely ignore the moral lobby, referring to Chalmers in public as 'one of the most philosophical divines of Scotland, one of the most intellectual men that I can name, and a Conservative too', who had 'come to the conclusion that the Corn Laws literally foul the air of British society'. He also quoted *The Times* on how Protection was 'a sort of rebellion against Providence for which the people at large may be in daily expectation of some visitation'.[14] On such occasions he even sounded like the evangelical bishop John Bird Sumner, a strenuous extra-parliamentary advocate of Corn Law repeal.[15]

On the other hand, moderate or Clapham evangelicals in Parliament joined their colleagues of the SBCP in distrusting all forms of sentimental paternalism.[16] It is true that the elder Peel's Factory Act of 1802 has some claims to be considered an evangelical initiative, but, as Bradley has shown, there is no clear evidence that the Staffordshire philanthropist was in fact an evangelical. Wilberforce and his colleagues seem to have opposed the attempts by Whitbread and Sheridan in 1795 to secure a minimum wage, and by George Rose in 1808 to maintain the earnings of cotton weavers artificially.[17] Thomas Babington, who came from an important family of Saints and was afterwards a friend of Chalmers, denounced the Speenhamland system of wage supplements,[18] and overall there was a clear party line that poverty was the fault of those who suffered it. Wilberforce frequently animadverted to this effect, and so did Gisborne in his would-be *Friendly Observations to the Manufacturing Population*.[19] Hannah More argued that poverty was 'ordained' by providence and that the poor were especially favoured in God's sight. Wilberforce, who was apparently whole-hearted in his support for 'all' Chalmers's views on pauperism,[20] countered the 'greatest happiness' principle by claiming that social inequality 'combines the greatest measure of temporal comforts and spiritual privileges'. Then again, it was an evangelical (from Sheffield)

[13] Whitmore to Loyd, 1 Sept. 1841, Dudmarton MSS.
[14] Villiers, 'Speech in Manchester', 3 Jan. 1843, *The Free Trade Speeches of Charles Pelham Villiers, with a Political Memoir* (1883), i. 346.
[15] See Soloway, *Prelates and People*, pp. 219–22.
[16] See above, pp. 98–100.
[17] Bradley, 'The politics of Godliness', pp. 218–19.
[18] Babington in House of Commons, 1 Mar. 1816, *Parliamentary Debates*, 1st series, xxxii. 1054.
[19] T. Gisborne, *Friendly Observations Addressed to the Manufacturing Population of Great Britain* (3rd edn, 1827), 15.
[20] Chalmers to Wilberforce, 9 Feb. 1818, *A Selection from the Correspondence of the Late Thomas Chalmers*, ed. William Hanna (Edinburgh, 1853), 96.

who argued that combinations 'insult the Majesty of heaven' by indicating discontent with the working-man's divinely appointed lot, 'and bring down the curse of God upon themselves'.[21] In short, as we saw in Chapter 3, moderate evangelicals were anxious to be privately charitable but uninterested in fundamental social and economic reforms, or in organic paternalism of the Tory Radical type. In 1812 Wilberforce, Henry Thornton, and Charles Grant all fell asleep while Robert Owen was outlining his scheme for New Lanark to them.[22] Only when there were obvious *villains* did these saintly evangelicals get excited about social reform, as Bradley points out.[23] Thus they were prepared to campaign on behalf of climbing boys and negro slaves, though even here one cannot be sure that their most urgent desire was not to save the souls of the chimney sweeps and planters. They were anxious to curb royal extravagance and impeach corrupt ministers, prohibit bear-baiting and duelling, end abuse of the Sabbath, improve the efficacy of judicial punishment, and generally 'suppress vice'. And of course they wanted to see new churches built in the industrial cities, for like Chalmers they believed that economic *laissez-faire* could only work its social purpose if it was backed up with moral suasion. But also like Chalmers they considered soul-saving to be more important than eliminating pauperism. As one of the most outspoken of late eighteenth-century evangelicals in Parliament apostrophized, 'How much more to be dreaded is a famine of the word of truth, than a dearth of earthly food!'[24]

Perhaps the distinction is misleading, since spiritual and economic considerations were always intertwined, as in the case of sabbatarianism. Christopher Hill has suggested that in the seventeenth century sabbatarian fervour was fuelled by capitalist businessmen, keen to endorse the virtues of competition but anxious also to blunt the edge of rivalry by institutionalizing at least one day of rest in seven.[25] In the earlier nineteenth century also, moralists welcomed any practices that might stay the pace of what was perceived to be hectic economic growth. The leading parliamentary champion of sabbatarianism was Sir Andrew Agnew, a Scotsman and devotee of Chalmers. Agnew underwent an evangelical 'great change' in 1821 as a result of the agricultural depression, which forced him to cut down on servants, foreign travel, and entertaining.

[21] William Ibbotson, *Address to the Workmen in the File Trade* (1836), quoted in E. R. Wickham, *Church and People in an Industrial City* (1957), 106.

[22] R. I. and S. Wilberforce, *Life of Wilberforce*, iv. 91.

[23] Bradley, 'The politics of Godliness', pp. 192–3.

[24] Richard Hill to a clergyman, 10 Nov. 1800, *The Life of Sir Richard Hill*, by the Revd Edwin Sidney (1839), 472.

[25] Christopher Hill, *Society and Puritanism in Pre-Revolutionary England* (1964), 151–3.

According to his biographer, retrenchment and economy made him very happy. His 'providential seclusion from the gaieties and follies of the world' was his 'Kilmany'—a reference to Chalmers's own conversion experience.[26] Agnew's new evangelical passion latched on to Lord's Day Observance, a cause about which Chalmers himself remained fairly cool, but on which his advice was characteristic. In God's well-regulated universe virtue is rewarded, and so it is 'a well-known economic law, that . . . every addition to the quantity of work is attended by a corresponding reduction in the rate of wages'. Sunday working will invariably 'overstock the labour market', and Sunday Observance must be in the workers' 'best and highest interests, even in this world as well as in that which is to come'.[27] Agnew was eventually, and at his own wish, buried alongside Chalmers in Edinburgh's Grange Cemetery.

Religious and financial motives are particularly hard to disentangle with respect to anti-slavery, which was the supreme example of the politics of atonement, and provided public evangelicalism with its most potent *raison d'être*; so much so, that the passing of the Abolition Act in 1833 had as enfeebling an effect as repeal of the Corn Laws was to have on Manchester politics ten years later. There has been much argument among historians as to whether the evangelical campaign against slavery and the Slave Trade was a cause of economic self-interest masquerading as moral righteousness, or whether it was a supreme instance of capitalist self-sacrifice.[28] The debate is too well known to need rehearsal here, but it seems clear that Duncan Rice's view as to the supremacy of spiritual considerations among Scottish abolitionists also applies to the Clapham Sect. The reformers were no doubt sincerely revolted by the material horrors of West Indian slavery, but they derived their zeal and urgency, in Rice's opinion, from the fact that slavery was 'the symbolic opposite of free agency under God'. Emancipation would be 'an act of atonement for national sins, as well as a first victory in the wider battle against enslavement to sin. The eschatological importance of emancipation was that of an act of redemption—redemption of the abolitionists as well as redemption of the slaves.'[29] Not that Wilberforce had made any secret of this, for he wrote to Bathurst, Secretary for War and the Colonies, in 1816:

I consider it my duty to endeavour to deliver these poor creatures from their present darkness and degradation, not merely out of a direct regard for their well being . . . but also from a firm persuasion that both the colonists and we

[26] *Memoirs of Sir Andrew Agnew*, by Thomas McCrie (1850), 63–7.
[27] Chalmers to Agnew, ?1838–9, *Memoirs of Agnew*, 345–7.
[28] See, for example, Eric Williams, *Capitalism and Slavery* (1964), 178–96; Seymour Drescher, *Econocide: British Slavery in the Era of Abolition* (Pittsburgh, 1977), 162–86.
[29] Rice, *The Scots Abolitionists*, p. 26. See Anstey, *The Atlantic Slave Trade and British Abolition*, pp. 184–99.

ourselves shall be otherwise the sufferers. The judicial and penal visitations of Providence occur commonly in the way of natural consequence and it is in that way I should expect the evils to occur.[30]

The elder James Stephen, on the other hand, believed that *un*natural or 'special' punishments were also likely to result from Britain's West Indian possessions, since 'independently of all such second causes' as war and economic depression, 'I look to that almighty hand which holds the fate of nations, which weaves out of their crimes in general a scourge for their chastisement'.[31] But then Stephen, unlike Wilberforce and unlike his own son, held strongly to a belief in a 'universally particular' providence— particular, that is, not only occasionally and in matters of great moment but in *all* the daily occurrences of life.[32]

If abolition of the Slave Trade seemed the only way to stave off the danger of a French invasion, then the cessation of slavery in the British colonies in 1834, at a cost to the nation of twenty million pounds, was undertaken at a time of equally apocalyptic anxiety. The penitential elements in British abolitionism have been thoroughly and subtly explored in the important work of David Brion Davis. The problem with slavery was that it was so obviously unfair that it challenged the liberal evangelical belief in a just distribution of rewards and punishments in the natural world. Davis sees 1807 and 1833 as 'genuine rituals', evoking fantasies of death and rebirth, and 'designed to revitalize Christianity and atone for national guilt'[33]—rituals so potent, moreover, that even the slave owners, whose ruin they entailed, succumbed to the moral philosophy underlying them.

The Scottish evangelical Congregationalist (and devotee of Chalmers) Ralph Wardlaw described emancipation day as a 'Jubilee', which was a reference to Leviticus and the day of emancipation and Atonement in the seventh month following seven sabbatical years. But, as Davis points out, this exultation did not stop him from welcoming the almost simultaneous introduction of Poor Law slavery at home. Yet really there was no contradiction—for, as Davis puts it, the emancipated slaves were rendered *free* to 'be judged by the standards of the mother country' and made 'individually responsible for their own fate'. It has already been shown that Wardlaw's Utopian vision of universal love and mercy, gradually

---

[30] Wilberforce to Bathurst, 4 July 1816, *Historical Manuscripts Commission Report on the Manuscripts of Earl Bathurst*, p. 418.

[31] James Stephen to Robert Peel, 17 Aug. 1822, Peel Papers, BL Add. MS 40350, fo. 3. Peel's reply was polite but non-committal. Ibid., 40350 fo. 5.

[32] *The Memoirs of James Stephen, Written by Himself for the Use of his Children*, ed. Merle M. Bevington (1954), 26–8.

[33] David Brion Davis, *Slavery and Human Progress* (New York and Oxford, 1984), 118–28.

achieved, was quite compatible with—was even predicated on—a belief in the need for free market individualism. Davis explains this in terms of tension between 'a basically secular belief in the possibility of continuous, gradual improvement in accordance with the natural laws of cause and effect' on the one hand, and on the other belief 'in what Paul Tillich has called *kairos*, "a decisive moment" of qualitative change that must be distinguished from *chronos*, that is, chronological or "watch time"'. Such victories are not predictable fulfilments but represent 'victory over a particular power of destruction, a victory over a demonic power'. Evangelical reform, for Davis, attempted to 'fuse the two conceptions of change, channelling sacred inspiration into the controllable world of secular power'.[34] To this analysis it is only necessary to add that the tension alluded to is not so much between the sacred and the secular as between the post-millennial and pre-millennial visions, between the two competing views of providence which have been a major focus of this study.

After the Saints: Pre-millennialists in Parliament

This discussion leads us back to the split within evangelicalism. We have already noticed the differences in social thought between the moderate and extreme wings of the movement.[35] Irving and Drummond opposed the Abolitionists' attempts to interfere with the negroes' divinely-appointed lot. 'The mystery of Divine Providence' was the 'guide and the comfort of those souls which in such inequality are stationed; teaching one who is a master that there is no iniquity in having many servants, or even slaves, under him'.[36] From about 1825 there was an increase in the number of pre-millenarian and Recordite MPs, and these, for reasons explained above, were both more conservative and more inclined to be paternalistic. They were activated by dislike of the liberal shift in politics in the 1820s, and especially by hostility to Catholic Emancipation, that act of 'national apostasy' which was perpetrated in 1829. Whereas Saints were divided in their attitude to Emancipation, the Recordites and their associates were quick to see in Popery a harbinger of anti-Christ. They joined in certain of the moderate evangelical campaigns, such as sabbatarianism, though their point was not that Sunday working would lead 'by way of natural consequence' to economic hardship, as Chalmers thought, but rather that it would attract the 'special' wrath of God. Pre-millennarian sabbatarians, accordingly, gave great prominence to railway accidents that occurred

---

[34] Ibid., p. 129.   [35] See above, pp. 10–22, 91–100.
[36] Edward Irving, *The Last Days: A Discourse on the Evil Character of These Our Times* (1828), 531, quoted in Steven E. Swartzman, 'Crisis of Principle: the English Evangelicals', Harvard University BA thesis (1986), 37.

on the sabbath.[37] But, unlike their moderate counterparts, such evangelicals did not stop at moral reform. With Recordites and crypto-Recordites in Parliament it becomes possible for the first time to identify a bloc of evangelicals with movements for social reform as well. Sadler, who tried eight times to secure poor laws for Ireland between 1830 and 1832, was not himself a Recordite, but he supported the Recordite campaign in Parliament, and was in turn backed firmly by the Scottish Recordite leader, John Briscoe. His Select Committee of 1832, which marked the effective starting-point of the Ten Hours campaign, included the 'prophetic' Recordites, Spencer Perceval junior, Bucknall Estcourt, and Robert Inglis, as well as less outspoken followers like John Weyland and G. H. Rose.[38] Seeley, who wrote for the *Record*, and the apocalypticians G. S. Bull and Edward Bickersteth, all supported the Ten Hours Movement, and Ashley, who took over the leadership of the movement after Sadler's removal from Parliament in 1832, was a devotee of Irving and Haldane and has been called a crypto-Recordite, though he sometimes found the *Record*'s language a little too strident. The place of evangelicalism in Ashley's politics has been admirably elucidated by G. B. A. M. Finlayson. His starting-points were the 'great doctrine of Man's corruption and infirmity', and 'the prodigy of . . . the great, necessary and most comfortable doctrine of the Atonement'. He illustrates the so much less joyous aspects of evangelicalism which took over from Clapham in the 1830s, its 'stiff-necked, unconquerable pride', its philistinism and morose, intolerant barrenness.[39] And he was, of course, a pre-millenarian, believing that the judicial and penal visitations of providence occurred not in a constant or 'direct' way of 'natural consequence' but immediately and by special fiat. Moreover, the Second Coming, which was imminent, would secure the release of 'deceitful . . . and desperately wicked' man as well as the conversion of the Jews. Like his pre-millenarian friends Seeley, Inglis, and Bickersteth, Ashley was for a long time a protectionist, though he was persuaded late in the day of the need for Corn Law repeal on moral grounds.[40]

The Ten Hours Movement, more than anything else, exposed the division in evangelical ranks. We saw above[41] how Chalmers (who agreed that 'if Free Trade be right, the Ten Hours' Bill is wrong') clashed

[37] Harrison, 'Victorian philanthropy', *Victorian Studies*, 9 (1965–6), 356.

[38] The Saint and moderate evangelical T. F. Buxton was also on the committee.

[39] Charles Whibley, *Lord John Manners and His Friends* (1925), i. 164.

[40] Ashley was abroad when the New Poor Law was enacted and his attitude to it is unclear, but he did not subsequently join the Anti-Poor Law Movement, thereby prompting Oastler's reproach: 'You slumbered and slept.' Finlayson, *The Seventh Earl of Shaftesbury*, pp. 126, 134–5 n. 92. However, despite its paternalist leanings, the *Record*, 11 Aug. 1834, approved of the 'thoroughly good' Poor Law Amendment Act.

[41] See above, p. 92.

brutally with Oastler on this issue, and their disagreement was reflected in Parliament. For while Ashley, Sadler, and Oastler were prominent campaigners, it is evident that evangelicals as a body, and the more Saintly especially, opposed the movement for factory reform. Rennie has shown how they disliked its paternalist implications, and how they preferred to salve their consciences with fresh appeals to 'No Popery', which they affected to believe was a greater evil than the industrial system.[42] The *Christian Observer* gave some grudging support to Sadler on moral grounds, while insisting that protection of women and children must not be seen as a precedent for overthrowing the 'sacred rule' of non-interference in such matters where adults were concerned. It is well known that Ashley complained over and over again in the 1840s that he could win very little help from most of the evangelicals in Parliament.[43] In so far as moderate evangelicals did participate, moreover, one cannot be sure that concern for the souls of exploiting factory owners was not a more potent argument in favour of reform than the plight of the employees.

It is in a sense paradoxical that the extreme or apocalyptic evangelicals should have been paternalistic in their social outlook. Why did those who believed in the world's imminent destruction bother about bettering the lot of the poor? The answer, as we have seen above,[44] is that such paternalists did not think of their social interventions as somehow *improving* the world. (Indeed, it was the post-millennial Claphamites who wanted to improve the world, though they saw this as a matter of morality and self-reliance rather than economic comfort and material well-being.) The paternalists, far from seeking to *improve* their inferiors, sought merely to protect them from the stormy blasts, and were wont to cite the reproach of Jesus to Jerusalem: 'How often would I have gathered thy children together, even as a hen gathereth her chickens under her wings, and ye would not' (Matthew, 23: 37 and Luke, 13: 34).

At all events, it was these extremists who, so far as fashionable society was concerned, began to give providence a bad name. The chronological connection between appeasement of Roman Catholics and national disasters could hardly be overlooked, since Emancipation in 1829 led directly to cholera in 1831–2 and the Maynooth Grant of 1845 led to the Irish potato famine. Carlyle memorably described the frenzied phantasms that seized so many imaginations in the wake of Emancipation, the widespread feeling that society 'is fast falling in pieces; and a time of

---

[42] Ian S. Rennie, 'Evangelicalism and English public life 1823–1850', University of Toronto Ph.D. (1962), 390–4 (typescript in Cambridge University Library).

[43] *The Life and Work of the Seventh Earl of Shaftesbury*, by Edwin Hodder (1886), i. 325, 346; ii. 76, 209.

[44] See above, pp. 16–17.

unmixed evil is come'.[45] Successive shocks—another revolution in France, the Last Labourers' Revolt or 'Swing' riots, the cholera, and the Reform crisis, during which the Church of England and her bishops were widely attacked as tools of Anti-Christ—merely intensified this sense of crisis. As a united political and moral force, evangelicalism was broken by the bitter divisions of these years. While hundreds of sermons heralded 'the special interposition of divine providence' in recognition of national sins, there were many others which savaged the notion that God would 'invade the regularity' of his own general laws merely because he did not like a particular Act of Parliament.[46] Ervine has described the 'vulgarity and vitriol' with which the *Record* and its parliamentary hero, J. E. Gordon, attacked all liberals, but especially the moderate wing of the evangelical party during the second half of 1830.[47] Against a barrage of radical opposition, the Recordites in Parliament managed to secure the institution of a National Fast Day (21 March 1832) in acknowledgement of what was to them a clear case of special providence. 'Cant, humbug, and hypocrisy! Ostentatious sanctity!' fulminated Joseph Hume and the radical reformers, who demanded a National *Feast* Day instead. Briscoe and Inglis then tried to persuade the Commons to declare solemnly that 'it hath pleased Almighty God to visit the United Kingdom with the disease called the Cholera', but were eventually induced to withdraw their motion by the more moderately evangelical leader of the House, Lord Althorp.[48] Soon after, on 20 March, came an amazing speech on cholera and the Second Coming by Spencer Perceval junior. Drooling, shaking, resisting attempts by friend and foe to sit him down, Perceval denounced the House's unwillingness to make this formal recognition of God's hand in the affliction.

Will ye not listen for a few moments to one who speaketh in the name of the Lord? I stand here to warn you of the righteous judgment of God, which is coming on you, and which is now near at hand. . . . Ye have in the midst of you a scourge of pestilence, which has crossed the world to reach ye. Ye brought a bill into the House to retard its approaches, and ye refused in that bill to insert a recognition of your God. . . . I told Ministers it was not God they worshipped. The people is the god before whom they bow down in absurd and degraded worship. . . . This mockery of religion God will not away with, he will bring

[45] Thomas Carlyle, 'Signs of the times', *Edinburgh Review*, 49 (1829), 441 [*Centenary Edition of the Works of Thomas Carlyle*, xxvii. 58].

[46] See, for example, the 'old Whig' Bishop of Chichester, Edward Maltby, *A Sermon Preached in the Abbey Church of Westminster on 21 March 1832* (1832), 7–9.

[47] W. J. C. Ervine, 'Doctrine and diplomacy: some aspects of the life and thought of the Anglican evangelical clergy, 1797 to 1837', University of Cambridge Ph.D. (1979), 251–307.

[48] Debate in House of Commons, 15 and 16 Feb. 1832, *Parliamentary Debates*, 3rd series, x. 392–3, 438–41.

on [ye] fasting and humiliation, woe and sorrow, weeping and lamentation, flame and confusion. . . . I tell ye that this land will soon be desolate: a little time and ye shall howl one and all in your streets, . . .[49]

According to Hansard, 'indescribable confusion prevailed', a raucous and ribald cacophany of derision and indignation. Yet Perceval merely spelled out in an exaggerated form what many of his high Tory contemporaries believed—that God punished mankind in a paternalist or discretionary way, and that he delegated similar powers, 'sacred, as well as secular, . . . functions',[50] to judges and magistrates, his representatives on earth. It was a doctrine deeply offensive to the growing number of liberal statesmen.

Punishment—Human and Divine

Even while we are rebelling against his dispensations, we are taking our hints in the economy of public and private life, from the economy of Providence in the administration of the world. We govern our country by laws emulative of those by which he governs his creatures:—we train our children by probationary discipline, as he trains his servants. Penal laws in states, like those of the Divine Legislator, indicate no hatred to those to whom they are proclaimed, for every man is at liberty not to break them; they are enacted in the first instance for admonition rather than chastisement, and serve as much for prevention as punishment. . . . The intelligent child perceives his father's motive for restraining him, till the act of obedience having induced the habit, and both having broken in his rebellious will, he loves the parent the more for the restraint.[51]

Nineteenth-century disputes over penal theory bring out particularly well two of the central themes of this study: the similarity between moderate evangelicalism and natural law utilitarianism,[52] and the marked contrast between both of these and the thought of extreme evangelicals. Many of the latter supported the death penalty for murder, and took a severe line on punishment generally. 'Whoso sheddeth man's blood, by man shall his blood be shed' (Genesis 9: 6) and 'He that spareth his rod hateth his son' (Proverbs 13: 24) were quoted with relish by the extremists S. R. Bosanquet and R. B. Seeley.[53] On the other hand, moderates like Hannah More, quoted above, did not like the idea of executing

---

[49] Perceval in House of Commons, 20 Mar. 1832, ibid., xi. 577–81.

[50] Vaughan Thomas, *The Scriptural Character of Civil Punishment Vindicated in a Sermon* (Oxford, 1830), 32.

[51] Hannah More, *Christian Morals* (1813), i. 69–70.

[52] For the relationship between evangelicals and utilitarians on the question of lunacy reform see Andrew T. Scull, *Museums of Madness: The Social Organization of Insanity in Nineteenth-Century England* (1979), 55–9.

[53] Bosanquet, *Principia*, p. 60; Seeley, *Remedies for 'The Perils of the Nation'*, pp. 58–9.

unregenerates, and they regarded most forms of physical correction as too demeaning to be reformative. Psychological intimidation was preferred, particularly in the form of solitary confinement, during which the lonely sinner could be brought to reflect and repent. Michael Ignatieff has explained how the evangelical reformer John Howard, for instance, developed a 'technology of salvation' for use on criminals, and how he was 'one of those rare men whose private compulsions seem to capture the imagination of their class'. He also points out that, as we have seen in other spheres, this evangelical ethos meshed with the utilitarian:

Thus Howard and Bentham both denied criminal incorrigibility, but from diametrically opposed positions—one accepting the idea of original sin, the other denying it. One insisted on the universality of guilt, the other on the universality of reason. Materialists like Bentham and Priestley asserted that men could be improved by correctly socializing their instincts for pleasure. Howard believed men could be changed by awakening their consciousness of sin.

Though Howard's concern was primarily spiritual, deriving from Wesleyan vernacular rather than from natural law mechanicism, it derived sustenance from the latter, as Ignatieff further explains:

During the 1770s the Hartleian climate of belief in reformist circles did provide the context necessary for the acceptance of Howard's disciplinary ideas. Materialist psychology, by collapsing the mind–body distinction, seemed to offer a scientific explanation for Howard's claim that men's moral behavior could be altered by disciplining their bodies. Materialist psychology implied that a regimen applied to the body by the external force of authority would first become a habit and then gradually be transformed into a moral preference. Through routinization and repetition, the regimens of discipline would be internalized as moral duties.[54]

Somewhere in the middle, straddling the utilitarian and evangelical approaches, was Benjamin Rush. He was in the difficult position of believing that individuals must undergo a 'great awakening' while not believing in original sin, and out of the dilemma came a firm advocacy of solitary confinement.

Too much cannot be said in favor of SOLITUDE as a means of reformation, which should be the *only* end of *all* punishment. Men are wicked only from not *thinking*. 'O! that they would *consider*,' is the language of inspiration [Deut 32: 29]. A wheelbarrow, a whipping post, nay even a gibbet, are all light punishments compared with letting a man's conscience loose upon him in solitude. Company, conversation, and even business are the opiates of the spirit of God in the human

[54] Michael Ignatieff, *A Just Measure of Pain: The Penitentiary in the Industrial Revolution 1750–1850* (1978), 57, 66–7.

heart. For this reason, a bad man should be left for some time without anything to employ his hands in his confinement. Every *thought* should recoil wholly upon *himself*.[55]

At least this was not a doctrine of salvation through labour. Rush persistently refused to beat his unfortunate children, despite their entreaties. Chalmers also opposed corporal punishment, preferring Captain Alexander Maconochie's 'mark system' of prison discipline as a means to universal moral regeneration. The earth (that is, liberty) might be a 'school of suffering', but prison should provide a regimen of 'properly stimulated exertion and self-restraint'. Maconochie's point was that sentences should be expressed in terms of a certain number of tasks to be performed rather than of time to be served, an idea which had much in common with Whately's views on penal reform. Chalmers congratulated Maconochie on a system 'beautifully simple while original and true to human nature. . . . It strikes me as being not less practically sound, than profoundly philosophical to make the discipline of the prison graduate as you have done with the discipline of nature in society and in the world.[56]

This observation indicates ways in which evangelical and Benthamite thinking diverges, since utilitarians did not believe in the discipline of nature. Senior, echoing Paley and Bentham, argued that 'human justice is solely expedient and preventive; it has no relation to moral guilt' — hence he could believe that 'the same cause which diminishes the guilt, the force of the temptation, may often justly increase the punishment'.[57] Moderate evangelicals, on the other hand, regarded the 'discipline in nature' as a guide to penologists. Thus the younger Bicheno, propagandist of population theory,[58] believed that human law should correspond as far as possible to divine law, which, unlike his extreme evangelical father, he regarded as a constant. Political economy helped men to formulate criminal law because it offered insights into God's intentions.

We must endeavour to discover the general laws by which the affairs of mankind are naturally regulated without any interference on the part of human legislatures; and must make ourselves acquainted with the orderly succession of events, to which all things, both in the physical and moral world, have a tendency, and

---

[55] Rush to Enos Hitchcock, 24 Apr. 1789, Butterfield, *Letters of Rush*, i. 512. On Rush see above, pp. 157–61.

[56] Chalmers to Maconochie, 20 Jan. 1846, copy in Brougham Papers, University College London, 36251; A. Maconochie, *Secondary Punishment: The Mark System* (1848), 3. See Maconochie, *Crime and Punishment: The Mark System, Framed to Mix Persuasion with Punishment, and Make their Effect Improving, yet their Operation Severe* (1846), p. viii: 'surround with motives, as well as walls'.

[57] Levy, *Nassau W. Senior*, p. 215.   [58] See above, p. 78.

the means which nature has adopted to rectify the discrepancies which are incidental to this constitution of things.[59]

It may possibly be more appropriate to trace the spiritual origins of nineteenth-century liberalism to these debates about justice and repression, as Ignatieff and David Brion Davis do among others, than to debates about the economy. Yet the two were closely connected, the economy being generally regarded as a huge arena of natural justice. The more pressing problem now is to consider the extent to which those who formulated government policy were moved by 'spiritual liberalism' at all.

Liberal Toryism and the Evangelical Ethos

The first point to make is that many politicians were utterly untouched by vital religion. Wholly lacking in vitality was John Charles Herries, a career politician of markedly high Tory leanings, and hostile to the fashion for liberal economic policies. His diaries contain many rudimentary and conventional pieties, but markedly lack religious *feeling* of the type that was becoming so fashionable. Tormented by the death of his wife in childbirth, he derived consolation in behaving well—bearing up— rather than in thoughts on providence and the afterlife, and his fatherly advice to his son mainly concerned the figure he should cut in the eyes of the world.[60] A private memorandum on his own late father displays similarly unevangelical attitudes to the world of commerce. Herries senior had been a 'guiltless and guileless soul' whose high animal spirits and sanguine temperament did not 'allow him to secure with prudence and to spend with providence what he had gained by ability'. The failure of the firm in 1798 had proved a 'happy circumstance', for by terminating his mercantile career it had enabled him to live out twenty-one years in 'calm and gentle sunshine' on a pension engineered by George III.[61] None of Lord Overstone's 'storms and tempests' for Herries, but rather their antithesis—a life of anodyne contentment.

One politician about whose religiosity there will be no disputing is Spencer Perceval, dubbed the 'Evangelical Prime Minister'. As it happens, his was not the type of faith which fuelled liberalism, for he was on the extreme wing of the movement. Ultra-Protestant and reactionary, he was instinctively opposed to the new liberal trend in social and economic policy. Thus he showed some sympathy towards proposals for minimum wage legislation, and wished to extend the elder Peel's 1802 bill for the protection

---

[59] J. E. Bicheno, *Observations on the Philosophy of Criminal Jurisprudence, being an Investigation of the Principles Necessary to be Kept in View during the Revision of the Penal Code, with Remarks on Penitentiary Prisons* (1819), pp. v–viii.

[60] Herries's MS diary, 1819, Herries Papers, BL Add. MS 57445, fos. 14–20, 46–76.

[61] Herries's MS notes on the death of his father, 1819, ibid., 57447, fos. 1–3.

of cotton apprentices. His financial plan of 1810, though never executed, suggested a most unrighteous 'raid' on the Sinking Fund in order to provide for the military needs of the year, and presaged an end to Pitt's policy of debt redemption. He opposed the Bullion Report on the grounds that resumption of cash payments would choke the war effort, while he also supported protectionist restraints on commerce.[62] Opposing slavery, he nevertheless distanced himself firmly from the Saints.[63] It is therefore not surprising to find that theologically Perceval, like his more florid son and namesake, leant towards pre-millennialism. 'Like many of the "weaker vessels among the evangelicals"', writes his biographer, 'he was a keen student of biblical prophecy.' He calculated that the world would end in 1926—a consummation date which (while it showed some foresight) was less imminently apocalyptic than most extremists would have chosen—and identified Napoleon as the woman in Revelation 17: 3–6, 'who rides upon the beast, who is drunk with the blood of the saints, the mother of harlots'. That he conceived of providence as operating in a discretionary and not a mechanical manner is clear from this comment on the French Revolution, which he regarded as a divine instrument to destroy Roman Catholicism.

If you will take up your map, and look at the countries where the French power and opinions have made their greatest impression, I think you will be of opinion that they have been raised up by Providence for the overthrow of the popish superstitions; for except with some few exceptions, *which may have been permitted to prevent this object of God's Providence from being too strikingly apparent*, you will find their progress most destructive where the popish super-stitions most prevailed.[64]

Clearly, Perceval's evangelicalism was not of the liberal type we have in mind when we talk about its influence over the 'official mind' and 'public doctrines' of the period.

For the way in which evangelicals made an impact out of all proportion to their numbers was by establishing a moral hegemony over public life. In order to establish this claim it will be necessary to investigate the attitudes of Liberal Tories such as Liverpool, Canning, and Peel, since it was they and their like who were responsible for most of the important economic legislation of the period, for Free Trade, sound money, retrenchment, and deflation. They were not a coherent party, Canning and Peel being divided on the Catholic Question, for example,

---

[62] Denis Gray, *Spencer Perceval: The Evangelical Prime Minister 1762–1812* (Manchester, 1963), 56–7, 174–5, 368–89, 467.

[63] Ibid., pp. 25–7, 99–100, 260. Wilberforce referred to his 'differing so much' from Perceval in a diary entry of 1810. R. I. and S. Wilberforce, *Life of William Wilberforce*, iii. 458.

[64] Gray, *Spencer Perceval*, pp. 18–19, 45–6 (italics added).

and although they agreed about social and economic policy it would be wrong to imply that they were primarily inspired by moral, religious, or any sort of ideological considerations. Liberal Tories tended to be reticent in such matters—nevertheless, they held to a fairly coherent set of attitudes and beliefs.

All Tories, according to Brock, had 'a sense of the harmony of society',[65] but it is obvious that Liberal Tories and High Tories conceived of social harmony in different ways. The latter's was an organic conception of nature as a complex web of phenomena which had grown, developed, been woven, fostered, and survived. To mortal eyes life was not logical or constant, least of all was it fair, but it *was* the outcome of divine intention, and to meddle, as reformers wished to do, with any part of the patchwork—or 'fabric', as it was called—would be both impious and socially destructive. God had placed certain groups at the head of society, to manage affairs and to be protective and paternal toward the lowly. Most paternalism would be exercised locally—by magistrates (as at Speenhamland), by factory owners, Sunday School teachers, and the like—but there were also certain inescapable functions of central government, such as maintaining law and order and public solvency, securing food supplies, and attending to defence and diplomacy, and these too should, they thought, be performed in a managerial fashion. It was a philosophy which Coleridge had articulated in his discussion of the 'spirit of state', but it derived from eighteenth-century tradition, in part from the Country Party under Anne and Walpole.

The so-called Liberal Tories were younger than the Highs, being born after 1770 for the most part and so 'formed' in the wake of the French Revolution, which profoundly affected them, and amid the darkening gloom of Malthusianism. This made them far more susceptible to the evangelical sway and to the reaction in favour of a systematic or 'muscular-corpuscular' philosophy. For if 'love of *system*' prevailed 'over the love of *truth*', as Whately complained, and men were prone to what Keats called an 'irritable reaching after fact and reason', then Carlyle was also correct to discern that 'Nowhere is the deep, almost exclusive faith, we have in Mechanism, more visible than in the Politics of this time.'[66] Certainly, the sense of harmony which infused the Liberal Tories was of this mechanical sort, a confidence that, if only one could rid the natural machine of friction—by stripping away anomalous powers, monopolies,

---

[65] W. R. Brock, *Lord Liverpool and Liberal Toryism 1820 to 1827* (Cambridge, 1941), 35.

[66] Richard Whately, *Detached Thoughts and Apophthegms* (1st series, 1854), 43; Keats to his brothers George and Thomas, 21 Dec. 1817, *The Letters of John Keats*, ed. M. B. Forman (3rd revised edn, 1947), 72; Carlyle, 'Signs of the times', *Edinburgh Review*, 49 (1829), 447 [*Works*, xxvii 66].

preferences, special favours, and backstairs influences—then society would run itself so as to create, if not a Paleyan context of beauty and happiness, at least a Butlerian framework of moral harmony, truth, and justice. The point can be illustrated with respect to foreign policy. Canning's understanding of strategy did not differ greatly from Castlereagh's; but whereas the latter liked to work through congresses and diplomatic negotiations, Canning denounced all such 'cabal and intrigue' and tried instead to systematize diplomacy,[67] to lay down permanent principles and trust to the force of national righteousness: 'The Age of Areopagus and the like is gone by. Each nation for itself and God for us all.' Canning's diplomatic rhetoric was always constructed around the notions of harmony, balance, and equilibrium: 'England should hold the balance', he once said, 'not only between contending nations, but between conflicting principles'; 'I called the New World into existence to redress the balance of the Old'; 'foreign policy should be a scheme of policy regulated by fixed principles of action, and, operating to produce, definite, and foreseen results'; or, varying the mechanical metaphor, 'the true policy of England was to move steadily in her own orbit, without looking too nicely to the conduct of the Powers in alliance with her'. In exactly the same way, Peel as Home Secretary detested Sidmouth's methods of maintaining law and order through the use of secret contacts, spies, and *agents provocateurs*; nor did he approve of the eighteenth-century judicial system which, as Douglas Hay has memorably shown,[68] deliberately gave judges and justices a considerable latitude over sentencing. By reducing such paternalistic discretion, discouraging reprievals, and putting the law officers of the Crown into visible uniform, Peel was systematizing—that is, encouraging individual citizens to weigh up, with some degree of certainty, the probable consequences of different courses of action. Similarly, in economic affairs, Huskisson hated Vansittart's hand-to-mouth financing, his perpetual juggling with accounts, and the way he exploited his contacts with City magnates such as Rothschild and Baring to keep the government's head just above the financial waterline. Huskisson referred to such methods in terms of the 'encroachments of powers and the errors of empiricism', and quite sincerely believed that, as the perpetrator of such evils, Vansittart was 'the real *blot* and *sin* of the Government'.[69]

[67] Harold Temperley, *The Foreign Policy of Canning 1822–1827: England, the Neo-Holy Alliance, and the New World* (1925), 470–1.

[68] Hay, 'Property, authority and the criminal law', in *Albion's Fatal Tree: Crime and Society in Eighteenth-Century England*, ed. Douglas Hay and others (1975), 17–63.

[69] As reported by Croker to Peel, 16 Aug. 1822, in *The Croker Papers: The Correspondence and Diaries of John Wilson Croker*, ed. Louis J. Jennings (1884), i. 229; Huskisson in House of Commons, 18 Mar. 1830, *Parliamentary Debates*, 2nd series, xxiii. 584.

Of course, one must not exaggerate these theoretical differences between Liberal and High Tories. Many of the former were self-conscious meritocrats, who simply did not possess any contact with those powers whose encroachments into public affairs they found so baneful. Canning lacked Castlereagh's social and diplomatic connections, Huskisson possibly envied Vansittart and Herries their influence with City magnates, and there was certainly a hint of personal pride and paranoia mixed up with his love of 'system'. Then again, if we are to rely on language as a guide to mentality, it is important to stress that while Liberal Tories frequently slipped into mechanistic metaphor when talking about social, economic, and diplomatic relations, at other times they often indulged in the language of organicism. Thus they endlessly defended the 'fabric of the constitution', a usage which may reflect the fact that Liberal and High Tories concurred in opposing parliamentary reform. It is also the case that the two modes of thought, though incompatible if pushed to extremes, could cohabit. Notably Burke, whom most Tories of whichever type acknowledged as their philosophical mentor, oscillated between a natural law systematic on economic matters and a romantic organicism where, for example, the *ancien régime* in France was concerned. One might even say that Burke, with his views on 'cogent expediency', made a theory of pragmatism or sense out of sensibility. For these and other reasons, modern scholars have tended to play down the gap between Liberal and High Toryism. Yet, as William Brock wrote in his wise and perceptive study, there was for all that a 'deep antagonism between the spirit of Canning and the spirit of Eldon',[70] an antagonism which helps to explain why Liberal and High Tories clashed so bitterly on social and economic policy.

We have already presented Chalmers as a guru whose preaching Canning, Huskisson, Peel, and company adored, and we have seen how Chalmers himself 'hailed with delight' the 'great and glorious advance' in economic policy which (he supposed) only public opinion was preventing Huskisson and Robinson from carrying still further.[71] In fact, Free Trade was not a particularly important source of conflict between Liberal and High Tories before the 1840s, commercial policies being governed more by pragmatic and political considerations than by ideological ones. Huskisson was adamant in claiming that a free trade in corn, without any restrictions or protecting duty, would secure high prices for the agriculturalists, and that this in turn would benefit the manufacturing and labouring classes.[72] Much more divisive was the 1819 decision to

[70] Brock, *Lord Liverpool and Liberal Toryism*, p. 34.
[71] See above, pp. 57–62; Hanna, *Life of Chalmers*, iii. 117.
[72] Huskisson in House of Commons, 14 June 1827, *Parliamentary Debates*, 2nd series, xvii. 1293.

implement the Bullion Report by resuming cash payments at the old par value. There is no space here for a detailed discussion, but certain points can confidently be made. First, it was very clearly a Liberal Tory policy, being pushed with moralistic fervour by Huskisson, Canning, and eventually Peel. High Tories, on the other hand, opposed the measure, some of them—Vansittart, Castlereagh, Eldon, Sidmouth, and Herries—with considerable energy. It was also one of those rare instances in which it is possible to ascribe a tangible and decisive influence over the decision-making process to a clerical economist. Of all the hundreds of pamphlets that appeared on either side of the topic in 1819, it was Copleston's two public *Letters to Peel*, chairman of the Commons' Secret Committee of Inquiry, which caught the most notice and which Peel himself singled out, publicly and privately, as having had a decisive effect on his thinking.[73] It is also clear that one of the attractions of specie payments for Liberal Tories was that, in theory at least, they instituted an automatic, self-regulating mechanism for fixing the money supply, and removed much of its discretionary power from the Bank of England. Huskisson promised that

The Bank would be the great steam engine of the state to keep the channel of the circulation always pressing full, and the power of converting its notes at any time into gold bullion at 78s the ounce the regulator and index of the engine, by which the extent of its operations and the sufficiency of the supply would be determined and ascertained.[74]

Significantly, a back-bench High Tory who opposed resumption—Peel's father, the philanthropist—employed organicist metaphor to defend the bank restriction, describing it as a 'mighty fabric erected by the immortal Pitt':[75] 'mighty' because it had enabled the nation to subsidize the defeat of Napoleon, 'fabric' because the subsidy system had constituted a network of financial contacts and connections. Bullionists, on the other hand, responded to popular demonology by castigating the Treasury's contacts and connections as wicked and improvident speculators. In their judgment, convertibility would kill off the 'noxious weeds' of unsound and fictitious business, while leaving stolid but solid commerce unaffected. In this sense, far from being a policy for growth, resumption was essentially deflationary, a policy to favour the professional and official classes living on fees and fixed incomes, the fundholders and investing groups, rather than the industrial wealth-creators whose lot was periodically to borrow money.

---

[73] On Copleston's views see above, pp. 107–8, 130 and on his influence see below, pp. 234–5.
[74] W. Huskisson, 'Rough draft on coin and currency', 1818, Huskisson Papers, BL Add. MS 38741, fos. 242–52.
[75] House of Commons, 24 May 1819, *Parliamentary Debates*, 1st series, xl. 673.

Having taken the decisive step in 1819, ministers had then to struggle to sustain the Gold Standard against pressure from the many influential groups damaged by it. During parliamentary debates of 1821–2, several Liberal Tories managed to imply that much of the nation's wartime wealth had been speculative and fictitious, that convertibility would justly squeeze out the many economic gangsters who had won fortunes in those years. Convertibility also appealed because it relieved the government of the need for a money supply policy. This was not just a case of laziness or political convenience: individual citizens must fend for themselves and take the economic consequences of their own actions, and in order that they should not be able to blame central government for any economic misfortunes, the policies of that government, particularly in the monetary sphere, should be strictly neutral. Such views were expressed most clearly in the quarrel which erupted in cabinet in the aftermath of the financial crash of December 1825. On that occasion High Tories wished to bail out certain distressed firms by lending exchequer bills to tide them over the crisis; the Liberals, however, with further moralistic severity, insisted that there must be no 'asylum in the government' if capitalists were to be brought through retribution to a Christian liberality. The most striking remark was Peel's, as he argued as forcefully as anyone against relief measures: 'Ultimate good, after some severe suffering, will result.'[76] All Peel's subsequent policies were cast in the same vein, and defence of the Gold Standard, threatened by a further monetary crisis in 1839, became perhaps the main keynote of his career. He regarded his Bank Charter Act of 1844 as 'the complement and defence of the Act of 1819',[77] a further curtailment of the Bank's powers of independent control over the money supply, convertibility alone having proved insufficient to force responsibility on that institution.

There is another relevant point to be made about Peel's intentions in 1844, which is that they were severely deflationary. If the Act had operated as it was intended to do, the limitation on Bank issues (to the amount of bullion in the vaults plus a fiduciary leeway) would have been so restrictive that it is hard to see how the famous mid-Victorian boom could have occurred. In fact the Act probably facilitated expansion by forcing the use of alternative sources of money, which like Overstone and other members of the Currency School Peel did not recognize as money—that is, cheques and deposits. Moreover, the mid-century gold finds eventually increased the amount of specie holdings in London so that the limitation on Bank paper was to be less stringent than anticipated. What matters

---

[76] Peel to E. J. Littleton, 23 Dec. 1825, in C. S. Parker, *Sir Robert Peel from His Private Papers* (1891–9), i. 383; Hilton, *Corn, Cash, Commerce*, p. 209.
[77] Peel to Brougham, 17 May 1844, Peel Papers, BL Add. MS 40482, fo. 42.

here, however, is not the effect of the legislation but Peel's intentions; there can be no doubt that he shared the essentially static vision of Chalmers and Overstone, rather than the better-known, growth-oriented political economy of Ricardo, Senior, and Cobden.

The same consideration applies to Liberal Tory support for Combination Law repeal in 1824–5. It may seem odd that Huskisson and Place should have worked so well together in the matter, but the minister's sympathy towards trades unions derived, not from any populist streak, but from a theory that economic distress was the child of over-production, of an economy that had been building too fast. Strikes might precipitate recovery, not by redistributing profits and wages, but by removing workers from active production until the 'market could come round'. As the *Phrenological Journal* put it in supporting the brave but controversial decision of 'our present excellent ministers' to repeal the Combination Laws, strikes were a 'natural check' to over-production. Masters whose men had stood out longest were now in the best position, since they had sold their stocks while prices were high — a clear indication of 'the laws of the Creator and the wisdom of ministers'.[78] Further indications of an anti-growth philosophy are to be found in the ministerial attitude to public works as a means of alleviating distress. Generally speaking, Liberal Tories opposed such expedients as contradicting their policy of *laissez-faire*, and on the rare occasions that they resorted to them the intention clearly was that public works, by being so much less efficient economically than private enterprise, would slow the economy down until the demand for over-stocked products could revive.[79]

The sharpest policy disagreement between High and Liberal Tories was over the treatment of the poor. For Liberals *paternalism* stopped short at moral exhortation and education: they laid great store by the provision of 'Commissioner' or 'Waterloo' churches in urban areas, and in 1837 Peel made great play with Chalmers's point, as expressed in the *Lectures on National Establishments*, that the laws of supply and demand could not be applied to religion, there being no natural craving for spiritual refreshment: 'The demand for religious instruction may not only not be in the direct ratio, but absolutely in the inverse ratio of its necessity (loud cheers).'[80] So far as material relief went, however, Liberals were negatively doctrinaire, Peel, Graham, and other front-bench Tories in the 1830s and 1840s being fully supportive of the Whigs' Poor Law Amendment Act of 1834. High Tories, meanwhile, from the 'Young

---

[78] [Anon.], 'Commercial distress', *Phrenological Journal*, 3 (1825–6), 321.
[79] Hilton, *Corn, Cash, Commerce*, pp. 82–7.
[80] *A Correct Report of the Speeches delivered by Sir Robert Peel at Glasgow* (7th edn, 1837), 61–2.

England' gang to such Tory-Radicals as Oastler and Bull, were appalled by the inhumanity of the 1834 legislation.[81] Their attitude was summed up by Eldon, whose piety was of that 'high and dry' kind which found Bible Society enthusiasm so rebarbative, and who had long abhorred the trend towards liberal individualism within his party. He denounced the New Poor Law on both constitutional and social grounds: 'Heaven grant that this new mode of treating the poor and needy may not bring forth those fruits, which I for one anticipate.'[82] There was a similar conflict over the question of the working-man's day, since Peel and Graham would have no truck with Ashley's campaign for Ten Hours. Education of factory children was one thing, but restraints on labour would merely diminish profits, which in turn would diminish the wages fund. Again, despite his genuine hatred of commercial speculation, Peel refused to sanction moves by Dalhousie, his minister, to regulate and control the mid-1840s rash of railway promotions.[83] Commercial probity could only be achieved, in Peel's opinion, 'after some severe suffering' at the hands of market forces.

It has been easy enough to show that Liberal Tory social and economic policies fitted the evangelical ideology; a more difficult question is, were they inspired by it? Brock commented that most of Liverpool's ministers had fallen under evangelical influence,[84] but he did not elaborate the point and subsequent historians have not taken up his suggestion. Unfortunately, the Liverpool and Peel ministries were ideologically reticent, and had to be, since the events of 1789 had made *all* political theory suspect among the governing classes. Even so, there is some evidence for thinking that the government had a dogmatic cast of mind. At least four of Lord Liverpool's ministers—Grant, Goulburn, Harrowby, and Vansittart—can be called Evangelical in a formal sense. Charles Grant, later Baron Glenelg, the son of a Clapham philanthropist of the same name, was from boyhood a very close friend of John William Cunningham, John Venn's curate and later Vicar of Harrow, an honorary life-governor of the Church Missionary Society, and editor of the *Christian Observer* (1850–8). (According to Simeon, Cunningham was an early and fervent advocate of Chalmers and all his works.) Grant was an extreme free trader, and resigned from the new Wellington Ministry in 1828 because it would not reduce the Corn Law further. Henry Goulburn was a cautiously liberal Chancellor of the Exchequer 1828–30 and 1841–6, very close to his

[81] On whom see Nichols C. Edsall, *The Anti-Poor Law Movement 1833–44* (Manchester, 1971), 77–8, 175–86.

[82] Eldon to his daughter, 23 July 1834, *The Public and Private Life of Lord Chancellor Eldon, with Selections from His Correspondence*, by Horace Twiss (1844), iii. 233.

[83] H. Parris, 'Railway policy in Peel's administration, 1841–1846', *Bulletin of the Institute of Historical Research*, 33 (1960), 194.

[84] Brock, *Lord Liverpool and Liberal Toryism*, p. 115.

mentor Peel, by whom he was somewhat overshadowed. Dudley Ryder, 1st Earl Harrowby, was a brother of the evangelical Bishop of Gloucester.[85] He was hardly a Liberal Tory, being opposed to the resumption of cash payments, and not at all close to Wilberforce and Clapham. Nicholas Vansittart (created Baron Bexley in 1823) was the most holy of all. 'Liverpool is pious enough', spat Bentham, 'but Vansittart is still more conspicuously pious!'[86] He succeeded Teignmouth as President of the British and Foreign Bible Society in 1834, and was a warm supporter of the CMS, the Prayer Book Society, and the Homily Society. It must be said at once that Vansittart does not fit the thesis presented here. His evangelicalism *appears* to have been moderate enough, and he associated often with the Saints in Parliament—yet he was a High Tory and an opponent of liberal economic policies. It was he who erected Anti-Bullionism into an aggressive principle in 1811, and who actually carried out Perceval's policy of successive raids on the Sinking Fund. As we saw, his hand-to-mouth financial strategy, as well as his secretive and complicated accounting methods, made him seem like a '*blot* and *sin*' to Liberal Tories such as Huskisson. It would therefore be reassuring if we could show that theologically he was sympathetic to the Recordites, since this would fit in with his anti-individualistic economic philosophy, but evidence of such leanings is sadly meagre: merely that in 1831 he felt moved to congratulate a Hulsean prize essayist, Frederick Myers, who had written on *The Futility of Attempts to Represent the Miracles Recorded in Scripture as Effects Produced in the Ordinary Course of Nature*. Myers's was 'an inquiry at all times interesting, but of peculiar importance at the present, when so many attempts are made to evade the force and invalidate the evidence of the Christian miracles'.[87] It is a slender point—probably we should just accept that Vansittart was a maverick, and be comforted by Bradley's remark that he divorced his political life from his religion, something which the Saints conspicuously did not do.[88]

That Lord Liverpool himself was deeply religious is beyond doubt. It is true that he had an abhorrence of what he called 'Calvinism', and that he sometimes crudely equated evangelicals with Calvinists. It is true also that Wilberforce was moved to complain that Low Churchmen were often

[85] William J. Baker, 'Henry Ryder of Gloucester, 1815–1824: England's first Evangelical Bishop', *Transactions of the Bristol and Gloucestershire Archaeological Society*, 89 (1970), 130–44.

[86] University College London MSS, Bentham Papers, Box 7, quoted in Bradley, 'The politics of Godliness', p. 287.

[87] Lord Bexley to Dr Myers, 21 Mar. 1831, Trinity College Cambridge MS, Myers 17[8].

[88] Bradley, 'The politics of Godliness', pp. 62–3. Wilberforce thought Vansittart good but dull and narrow.

overlooked in matters of preferment. On the other hand, Liverpool seems to have done his best to accommodate Wilberforce's desires, and he certainly gave a warm support to the BFBS.[89] Indeed, when Irving first burst on the London scene at the Hatton Gardens chapel—this was in 1822, four years before his 'Second Coming-out'—Liverpool seems to have led the throng of titled and notable personages who rushed to hear him. 'Lord Liverpool . . . is said to have made his way through one of the windows, and from thence let himself down into the interior of the chapel', wrote an outraged and probably mendacious observer. 'We think it quite natural that Mr. Canning and Mr. Brougham, for instance, should feel some curiosity to ascertain the pretensions of a rival orator. . . . [But] they should make it a rule to go in at the door.' Another disgusted scribbler complained at the way in which Vansittart, Canning, Peel, Huskisson, and Lansdowne, as well as Liverpool, showed such an abnormal fascination with the phoney Caledonian phenomenon.[90] The point for now is that doctrinally, though not ecclesiastically, the Prime Minister's instincts were low.

Perhaps because he was also witty and brilliant, Canning is not usually thought of as devout, yet according to Greville, who had it from Charles Grant, who had it from James Scarlett, Wilberforce offered Canning the leadership of the Saints in Parliament when he 'retired' in 1823. It is certain that the two men were very close, and that the Saints bothered themselves constantly over the condition of Canning's soul, which they feared must be corroded by worldly ambition and intrigue, as well as by his many associates from Liverpool who had West India connections.[91] Several of Canning's intimate friends were notably evangelical, such as Granville Leveson-Gower, 1st Viscount and Ambassador in Paris, and Lord William Bentinck. The latter, appointed Governor General of Bengal in 1827 and of all India in 1833, had become a Canningite shortly after his evangelical marriage and conversion (c.1808–11). According to his biographer, becoming a Liberal 'went together with the gradual deepening of his religious feeling', which in his case was a more important ingredient than

[89] Brock, *Lord Liverpool and Liberal Toryism*, pp. 92–4, 199–200; *Life of Charles Richard Sumner*, by G. H. Sumner (1876), 56–63; A. B. Webster, *Joshua Watson: The Story of a Layman 1771–1855* (1954), 25; Wilberforce to Liverpool, 16 and 30 Sept. 1820, Liverpool Papers, BL Add. MS 38191, fos. 274–8, 280–3. For Liverpool to Wilberforce, 26 Sept. 1820, see Best, 'The Evangelicals and the Established Church in the early nineteenth century', *Journal of Theological Studies*, NS 10 (1959), 74–5; H. W. C. Davis, *The Age of Grey and Peel* (Oxford, 1929), 150.

[90] James Fleming, *The Life and Writings of the Rev. Edward Irving* (1823), 29; [Anon.], *Trial of the Rev. Edward Irving, M.A.: A Cento of Criticism* (8th edn, 1823), 1.

[91] *The Greville Memoirs: A Journal of the Reigns of King George IV and King William IV by the late Charles C. F. Greville*, ed. Henry Reeve (1874), ii. 125 [7 Mar. 1831]; Bradley, 'The politics of Godliness', p. 67.

utilitarianism, though that was also present.[92] It is in no way incongruous that such men should have respected Canning, whose domestic life was notably pure, and whose trust in 'Christ's atoning blood', expressed in some conventional but affecting verses on the death of his eldest son,[93] was unselfconscious and sincere. Impulsive and warm-hearted, simple and sentimental, Canning's feelings were easily roused by devotional fervour. We have already seen him following Chalmers from pulpit to pulpit with tears in his eyes. In fact it was common for him to be 'struck by' a sermon and to request a copy—he did this, for instance, with one of William Vernon Harcourt's.[94] Once, in the Commons, James Mackintosh borrowed a commonplace phrase he had heard on the lips of Irving—something about orphans being 'thrown upon the fatherhood of God'. An orphan of sorts himself, Canning 'started' deeply moved, and then determined to hear the northerner at first hand, becoming one of the several celebrities to 'fly' at Irving 'in all directions', as Creevey put it sardonically soon afterwards.[95]

Peel's religious propensities were paraded with much less perfervour, yet there is evidence of deep faith and a basically evangelical temper. Just as in secular affairs a distinction needs to be drawn between his doctrinaire, theoretical approach to legislation and his highly cautious, pragmatic approach to administration and politics, so in spiritual matters Peel combined an empirical approach to ecclesiastical issues with a fairly dogmatic approach to theology. His was, as Gash points out, 'a simple, rational, pious Protestantism',[96] but it was none the less powerful for being uncomplicated. Admittedly the dry and somewhat academic correspondence with his former tutor at Christ Church, Charles Lloyd, on doctrinal topics such as absolution, does not betray much emotional involvement.[97] This is found rather in his occasional public statements of belief. Though Newman protested against the allegedly shallow and syncretic rationalism of Peel's *Address at the Opening of the Tamworth Reading Room* (1841), its message was that scientific knowledge would 'make men not merely believe in the cold doctrines of natural religion,

---

[92] John Rosselli, *Lord William Bentinck: The Making of a Liberal Imperialist 1774–1839* (1974), 56–68, 82–7, 321–5.

[93] Quoted in H. W. V. Temperley, *Life of Canning* (1905), 242.

[94] Harcourt, *The Harcourt Papers*, xiii. 168.

[95] Creevey to Miss Ord, 18 Jan. 1825, *The Creevey Papers: A Selection from the Correspondence and Diaries of the late Thomas Creevey*, ed. Sir Herbert Maxwell (1903), ii. 85; Oliphant, *Life of Irving*, i. 158–9; *Memoirs of the Life of Sir James Mackintosh*, by R. J. Mackintosh (1835), ii. 477.

[96] Norman Gash, *Sir Robert Peel: The Life of Sir Robert Peel after 1830* (1972), 185. But it is not the case that Peel had 'little dogmatic content to his . . . mind'. Ibid., pp. 186–7. See Boyd Hilton, 'Peel: a reappraisal', *Historical Journal*, 22 (1979), 585–614.

[97] See, for example, Peel to Lloyd, 11 Feb. 1826, Peel Papers, BL Add. MS 40342, fos. 320–1.

but that it will so prepare and temper the spirit and understanding, that they will be better qualified to comprehend the great scheme of human redemption'.[98] Later he was entranced by the 'doctrinal portion' of one of J. B. Sumner's *Charges*, a solemn statement of the need for atonement and of justification by faith, and it seemed to Gladstone that he regarded the evangelical bishop 'as a type' or exemplar of true Christianity.[99] His religious sentiments may have been suppressed for much of the time, but they were fervently held nevertheless.

Peel also exemplifies what Keats meant by lack of negative capability. A clever but impressionable young man, he was undoubtedly affected by the 'syllogistic reasoning dominant in Oxford'. His schematic mind was attracted to theories which were coherent or at least holistic, being unable to cope with incongruities and anomalies. This facet is brought out particularly well in his conversion to bullionist theory in 1819. Thus he wrote to Lloyd that the authors of the 1810 Bullion Report had provided therein 'complete' proof of the doctrines they propounded:

Still, there are facts apparently at variance with their theory. If the demonstration is complete, this can only be so apparently. They are like the triangles that I used to bring to Bridge [The Revd R. Bridge, who had coached him in mathematics], and declare that the angles of those particular triangles amounted to more than two right angles. The answer in each case is the same. There is some error in the fact, and in the triangle, not in the proof, which was as applicable to that fact, and to that triangle, as to any other.[1]

'Stanley swallows "a fact" too easily', he complained in 1846, when the two men were bitterly at loggerheads over Repeal; 'There seem to me very few facts, at least ascertainable facts, in politics. He is not wise in intermeddling with the doctrines of political economy.'[2] No wonder Peel found the theory of *laissez-faire* seductive, and though his inclination in this direction was tempered throughout by caution and political instinct, it derived from his Butlerian vision of society as an efficient moral mechanism. He told an audience invited to celebrate his inauguration as Lord Rector of Glasgow University in 1837 that government was a 'great machine':

---

[98] 'Sir Robert Peel's address on the establishment of a library and reading-room at Tamworth', as reported in *The Times*, 26 Jan. 1841, p. 3b–e.

[99] Gladstone's note of 3 Aug. 1843, *The Prime Minister's Papers: W. E. Gladstone*, ed. for the Royal Commission on Historical Manuscripts by John Brooke and Mary Sorensen (1971–81), ii. 218. J. B. Sumner, *A Charge delivered to the Clergy of the Diocese of Chester* (1841), 20–6.

[1] Peel to Lloyd, 1819, Peel Papers, BL Add. MS 40342, fos. 26–7, quoted in Parker, *Peel*, i. 293–4, and Hilton, 'Peel', op. cit., pp. 589–90. The phrase 'facts apparently at variance with their theory' closely echoes a remark in Copleston, *Letter to Peel on a Variable Standard of Value* (1819), 2–3.

[2] Peel to Brougham, 13 June 1846, in Parker, *Peel*, iii. 357, and Hilton, 'Peel', op. cit., p. 606.

I wish to see that great machine in the discharge of its proper functions, beating with a healthful and regular motion—animating industry, encouraging production, rewarding toil, correcting what is irregular, purifying what is stagnant or corrupt; but let me tell you that in the social, as in the material machine, . . . the movements cannot be regular unless the foundations of the edifice are stable and secure, and the main springs and organs of action are free from perpetual disturbance.

God, he consoled a working-men's audience, had instituted a wonderful 'system of social retribution'. Society fluctuates like a

great ocean, whereof one part seems depressed and another elevated, if it be regarded hastily and only for an instant of time; but presenting, if viewed attentively for a longer period, constant vicissitude—that which is at one time the lowest, assuming, in its turn, the station of the highest. The fluctuations of the waves are caused by physical and fortuitous influences; but they are moral influences which affect the fluctuations of society. Industry, sobriety, honesty, and intelligence will as assuredly elevate the low, as idleness, profligacy, and vice will depress, and justly depress, those who are in high stations.[3]

Canning and Peel were mainstays of Liverpool's ministry but not obviously philosophical in their approach to politics. A more vivid insight into the administration's ideological complexion is provided by its relations with Lord Grenville and his adherent Edward Copleston. Grenville was a Pittite Whig who had helped Fox to abolish the Slave Trade in 1807, but by 1820 he had adopted a more or less neutral, elder statesmanlike role. In December 1821 his party adhered formally to the government, but long before that Grenville had liaised closely with the Prime Minister on matters of public policy, economic issues especially. The Grenvill*ites* are usually dismissed as a time-serving band of toadies; Grenville himself was scholarly, devout in an evangelical way, a frigid moralist 'who condemned moderate as well as excessive vices',[4] an ardent Bullionist, and a notably doctrinaire exponent of the ideas of Adam Smith. He could be utterly uncompromising in his espousal of *laissez-faire* policies, as on the occasion of the grain shortage of 1800,[5] and he led the assault of a minority of Peers against the 1815 Corn Law.[6] Only the 'rapid accumulation, and profitable application of capital in the employment of labour' could ensure the improvement of the mass of mankind, while

---

[3] *A Correct Report of the Speeches delivered by Sir Robert Peel at Glasgow*, pp. 42–3, 59–60.

[4] Peter Jupp, 'The aims and achievements of Lord Grenville', *Essays Presented to Michael Roberts*, ed. John Bossy and Peter Jupp (Belfast, 1976), 93.

[5] Piers Mackesy, *War without Victory: The Downfall of Pitt 1799–1802* (Oxford, 1984), 177–9.

[6] Grenville in House of Lords, 15 Mar. 1815, *Parliamentary Debates*, 1st series, xxx. 187–202.

government's role should be limited to providing moral and religious instruction and to protecting property, 'not only against lawless invasion, but against the invasion of the laws themselves, in the too common form of commercial regulations'.[7] However, the inspiration behind his economic philosophy seems to have been Butlerian rather than Benthamite. Among the Dropmore manuscripts are fragments of his projected essay on political economy, dated 1826–8. Its premiss is the 'entire coincidence of public and private morality', an anti-utilitarian presumption that seemed to him as basic as gravity and the revolution of the planets. Science develops by successive subdivisions—a commonplace thought and the intellectual equivalent of Adam Smith's pin factory. In the beginning was religion, then as a subsidiary came ethics or the science of human happiness, then politics or the science of social and institutional happiness, and lastly political economy, which treats of the ways in which wealth can make social and institutional man happy. The doctrines of political economy are deducible 'from the consciousness of what passes within our own breasts, and from our observations of the qualities of other men'. They support Free Trade because of man's original instincts to truck and barter; they condemn debasements because money has a fixed value 'in the estimation of society'. 'Hence it follows that this, like every other branch of politics, must of necessity rest all its theorems, not on the evidence of sense or demonstration'—not, that is, on Whately's empiricism or Ricardo's deductivism—'but on that of moral probability, "the very guide of life". See the excellent introduction to Butler's Analogy, in which the subject of moral probability is fully and most satisfactorily explained. To that statement nothing can be added.'[8] Grenville's conclusion is more forcefully stated in a published tirade against the Sinking Fund:

The proper aim of legislation in these matters is not the multiplication of wealth, but the multiplication of that social happiness which is derived from wealth, and which consists essentially in its use: in its wise, and virtuous, but free use. And that this freedom, while it gives to wealth its highest value, has also been made, through the provident constitution of our nature, the most effective instrument of its increase, is the beautiful discovery of modern science.[9]

The moment of final identification with the Tories came with Grenville's attack on Lansdowne in the Lords on 30 November 1819 over the conduct

[7] Grenville to Sir John Newport, 25 Oct. 1818, Newport Papers, Duke University, William R. Perkins Library, North Carolina, MS XVIII-F.

[8] Lord Grenville, 'Draft of essay on political economy ?1826–8', Additional Dropmore Papers, BL Add. MS 59434, fos. 1–24. It may be relevant that Grenville defended John Locke's 'expulsion' from Oxford University in 1684 against Dugald Stewart's strictures in the Edinburgh Review. Lord Grenville, Oxford and Locke (1829), 65–6 and passim.

[9] Grenville, Essay on the Supposed Advantages of a Sinking Fund (2nd corrected edn, 1828), 82.

of the Peterloo magistrates. With ministers embarrassed, Grenville conducted the defence on that occasion, and never was 'doom and gloom' propagated with such statesmanlike grandeur. They were living, he opined, in the shadow of the French Revolution, 'that terrible convulsion of the world' and disruption of God's natural order. 'Naturally' capital, and therefore employment, increase faster than population, but war and paper money had, by the unnatural tendencies, arrested the increase of capital, while at the same time a generous system of poor relief had led to improvidence and over-population. The remedy lay, not with legislatures, but 'there only, where it is placed by Providence, in the admirable disposition of moral as well as of natural causes'. All that the government could do in the meantime was resolutely suppress the 'inflammatory and poisonous publications' which were fomenting such mischief.[10]

Grenville's most notable contribution to the economic ideology of the day was his assault on the Sinking Fund, that curious contrivance which, from having been a symbol of purity under Pitt—that is, of the nation's resolve to pay off its debts—became in the 1820s almost a byword for iniquity. It had been suggested to Pitt by the Socinian and post-millennialist Richard Price, who claimed that by investing money at compound interest the nation might pay off portions of its debt without taxing itself unduly. It thus reflected the glorious optimism still to be found in the 1780s, compound interest being regarded by many as a magical device, like the division of labour, to secure ever more happiness and wealth. It was of course a delusion, and the man who more than any other played 'Malthus' to Price's 'Smith', by demonstrating that the national debt could not be liquidated without pain—that is, by levying new taxes or borrowing also at compound interest—was Robert Hamilton (1743–1829), Professor of Mathematics at Aberdeen University. Hamilton wrote extensively on topics of political economy, especially on pauperism, being 'on strong grounds, always hostile' to poor rates.[11] Despite this he was highly philanthropic—'in his charities, which were as extensive as his circumstances permitted, he was solicitous that "his left hand should not know what his right hand did" '.[12] His piety was described as 'rational, fervent, and unostentatious', which is an excellent description of the moderate evangelical temper we have been describing. He was a member of the Anti-Slavery Society and of the Aberdeen branch of the BFBS, and hostile to those who stirred trouble over the Apocrypha. His *Inquiry concerning the National Debt* (1813) boldly proclaimed that the only true

[10] Grenville in the House of Lords, 30 Nov. 1819, *Parliamentary Debates*, 1st series, xli. 450–4, 460.

[11] Robert Hamilton, *The Progress of Society* (1830), p. xiii.

[12] Ibid., p. xviii.

Sinking Fund was one which consisted in an excess of revenue over expenditure.[13] Hamilton's work was widely quoted and imitated, so that by 1828, when Grenville weighed in with his philippic, the 'sort of hocus-pocus' (as Overstone called it) had come to seem as ridiculous as the rest of Vansittart's policies, and it was in fact formally abandoned that same year.

As Chancellor of the University of Oxford (1810–34) Grenville was much engaged in lobbying the government on intellectual matters. He became warmly attached to Copleston, who visited Dropmore at least as early as 1813 and was later described by an acute observer as clever but 'dogmatic' and 'too much of the Grenville school'.[14] Copleston can be said to have exercised a direct influence on events, not only in 1819, but in policy interviews arranged for him by T. P. Courtenay with Peel (May 1821), Huskisson (April 1822), and Canning (June 1825), the main purpose of which was to strengthen the ministers in their resolve not to tamper with the newly restored Gold Standard.[15] A warm admirer of Malthus on population and of Huskisson's *Essay on the Depreciation of Our Currency* (1810), Copleston was anxious to protect monied proprietors and annuitants from depreciationists like Lord Lauderdale,[16] and adamant that any blame for the fall in prices should be laid at the door of the Bank restriction, not of its termination. He figures prominently in one or two squabbles over patronage, incidents which give us some insight into the intellectual currents which charged Liberal Toryism.

There was, for example, a series of tussles between Copleston and Charles Lloyd, a High Churchman, High Tory, and the Professor of Divinity at Oxford (1822–9). They intensified with the growing importance of the Liberal Tories after 1822 and climaxed in 1826. In that year Copleston canvassed on Canning's behalf when a vacancy occurred in the representation of Oxford University, but the more conservative colleges were implacably hostile. Lloyd admitted to Peel, who remained studiously neutral, that he himself was 'responsible' for Canning's 'not being proposed', and that if Canning 'knew all he would not love me the more'. It was therefore slightly disingenuous of him to grow indignant when Canning did apparently show some bitterness. Yes, he had been 'responsible' for Canning's rejection, but 'How, in the name of Heaven, should [Canning]

[13] Robert Hamilton, *An Inquiry concerning the Rise and Progress, the Redemption and Present State, and the Management of the National Debt of Great Britain* (Edinburgh, 1813; 2nd enlarged edn, 1814), 10 and *passim*.

[14] MS diary of John Louis Mallet, 15 Dec. 1824, v. 144, in the possession of Mr P. L. V. Mallet.

[15] Salim Rashid, 'Edward Copleston, Robert Peel, and cash payments', *History of Political Economy*, 15 (1983), 249–59.

[16] Copleston to Peel, 13 May 1821, Copleston to his father, 13 Jan. 1811 and 29 Jan. 1814, *Memoir of Copleston*, pp. 41, 47–9.

know this? I have attended no public board, and only spoken to Copleston in the most friendly manner.'[17] Lloyd scored again shortly afterwards when he beat Copleston—pushed by Canning—for the See of Oxford. On this occasion Lloyd represented to Peel that he ought to be found preferment within Oxford, as 'I hope to be a great Divine and to found a School of Theology',[18] an appeal which is pathetic in retrospect. Lloyd hated—and frequently baited—the evangelicals, especially young John Newman whom he bullied mercilessly,[19] and if he founded a school it was only in the negative sense that his crusty pedantry drove many of Oxford's more virile minds into Tractarianism. Copleston, meanwhile, had been dished, but Liverpool consoled him with the deanery of Chester in 1826, and in 1827 Frederick Robinson, now Lord Goderich, made him Bishop of Llandaff and Dean of St Paul's.

Patronage had not always gone Lloyd's way, however, as is clear from the career of William Buckland, Professor of Mineralogy at Oxford since 1813 and Reader in Geology since 1819. His work as a Scriptural Geologist of sorts has already been touched on.[20] Here it is important to note the esteem in which he was held by certain sections of the government. Among his backers were prominent evangelicals like J. B. Sumner, and it was one of them, Shute Barrington, Bishop of Durham 1791–1826 and the dedicatee of *Reliquiae Diluvianae*, who first pressed him for preferment, unsuccessfully, in 1823. Barrington urged on Liverpool the 'great public importance' of keeping Buckland at Oxford. Geology was 'capable of abuse and mischief', but Buckland had 'applied himself to clearing it from all its most dangerous doubts and difficulties; and making it a very useful auxiliary to the cause of revealed Religion'.[21] Buckland's claims were taken up enthusiastically by Copleston and Grenville, and Liverpool himself acknowledged his desire to find 'some suitable provision and reward' for Buckland's high services.[22] He finally offered a canonry at Christ Church in 1825, much to the chagrin of Lloyd, who was anxious to push Gaisford and irritated by Liverpool's 'mania for the modern sciences' in preference to Greek and Latin. 'Buckland has filled all their heads'—meaning Grenville, Liverpool, and Barrington—'with the idea

---

[17] Lloyd to Peel, 10 and 28 Feb. 1826, Peel Papers, BL Add. MS 40342, fos. 318–19, 328–9.

[18] Lloyd to Peel, 28 Feb. 1826, loc. cit.

[19] William J. Baker, *Beyond Port and Prejudice: Charles Lloyd of Oxford, 1784–1829* (Oxford, 1981), 56, 79, 106.

[20] See above, pp. 150–2

[21] Barrington to Liverpool, 10 Feb. 1823, Additional Liverpool Papers, BL Add. MS 61818, fos. 103–4 (provisional). See Rupke, *The Great Chain of History*, pp. 14, 64.

[22] Liverpool to Buckland, 19 Feb. 1824, draft in Liverpool Papers, ibid., 38298, fos. 204–5. Copleston to Grenville, 1 Sept. 1823, Additional Dropmore Papers, ibid., 59416, fos. 92–3.

that, if it had not been for his exertions, Geology would have become in this Country, the tool of Atheism: and that nothing has prevented this, but the discoveries which he has made in favor of a deluge.—All this is sheer nonesense.' Somewhat surprisingly, Lloyd considered that Buckland's 'loose desultory habits' would not fit in at Christ Church, but he also realized that Liverpool was utterly committed to 'the Grenvilles' and they to Buckland.[23] Peel said little to Lloyd, but he too must have been impressed by *Reliquiae Diluvianae*. As Prime Minister he was later to appoint Buckland to the deanery of Westminster in 1845, and to claim that he 'never advised an appointment of which I was more proud';[24] while Buckland was also said to be very close to Peel and 'hardly ever absent' from the parties held for distinguished men of arts and science at Drayton Manor.[25]

Although political historians have been reluctant to adduce ideological overtones to Peelism, historians of science have recently been less reticent. Desmond has suggested that Richard Owen's anti-transformism and repudiation of 'Lamarckian-radical thought' acted as an intellectual buttress of Peelite conservatism; Neve has depicted science in Bristol in the same way; and McLeod has linked Peel to the 1830–48 reform movement within the Royal Society.[26] These delineations have yet to be conclusively demonstrated, but it seems evident that the mid-century identification of Peelism with Prince Albert, the Great Exhibition, and 'professional' government had a prelude in the middle-class craze for science during the 1830s.

As the tenuous nature of some of the above evidence suggests, Liberal Toryism as an ideology has to be searched out, and one is in danger of distorting it by doing so. The search is worth while nevertheless, since, transmuted into Peelism and then, with further changes, into Gladstonian liberalism, it turns out to have been the germ of something that would have a profound impact on the 'English mind'. However, Gladstonian liberalism clearly had roots in the Whig tradition as well as in that of the Tories. Though they were in power for a relatively short time during the Age of Atonement, it will be necessary to consider briefly how the Whigs fit into the picture.

[23] Lloyd to Peel, 4 Jan. 1825, Peel Papers, ibid., 40342, fos. 187–9; Liverpool to Buckland, 2 July 1825, Liverpool Papers, ibid., 38300, fo. 126.
[24] *The Life and Correspondence of William Buckland*, by Mrs Gordon (1894), 219.
[25] Ibid., p. 165.
[26] Adrian Desmond, 'Richard Owen's reaction to transmutation in the 1830s', *The British Journal for the History of Science*, 18 (1985), 46–50; Michael Neve, 'Science in a commercial city: Bristol 1820–60', *Metropolis and Province: Science in British Culture, 1780–1850*, ed. Ian Inkster and Jack Morrell (1983), 181; Roy MacLeod, 'Whigs and savants: reflections on the reform movement in the Royal Society, 1830–48', ibid., pp. 58, 62–74, 87–8.

Piety and Poverty in the 1830s

Since the Whig interpretation of history went out of fashion, it has been usual to regard the Whig governments of the 1830s as devoid of intellectual content and motivated mainly by political calculation. However, recent studies by Peter Dunkley on the Poor Law and Paul Richards on the handloom weavers, and unpublished work by Peter Mandler on social and economic policy and Richard Brent on religion, seem likely to rescue the Whigs from such disparagement. As a group they too were touched by the evangelical wave, though much less so than their opponents, and the balance between evangelical and utilitarian elements tended to tilt more toward the latter.

There were, of course, some outspoken anti-evangelicals, none more virulently so than Alexander Baring, a junior minister. But then Baring was also at the anti-liberal end of the spectrum and opposed to the 'politics of atonement' at most points. Although he had had something to do with putting Free Trade on to the parliamentary agenda in 1820, by the 1830s he had become one of the most influential defenders of Protection. He also opposed the resumption of cash payments in 1821 and the Bank Charter Act of 1844, while he supported the introduction of limited liability in evidence before a commission of inquiry in 1837.[27] It is entirely characteristic that a man with such views on economic policy should have been so virulently hostile to vital religion. It was said of him that 'there are two things he hates — an abolitionist and a saint'; he also 'hated' Romans 5: 12, 'Wherefore, as by one man sin entered into the world, and death by sin; and so death passed upon all men, for that all have sinned.'[28]

On the other hand, there were notable Whig evangelicals, such as Alexander's nephew Francis Thornhill Baring, Chancellor of the Exchequer 1839–41 and active in most of the important missionary and charitable societies. Thomas Spring Rice, Lord Monteagle, who preceded Baring as Chancellor, was also devout in a lowish sort of way, as befitted a friend of Pryme, and it was not only on the Poor Laws that his opinions were 'in all respects those of Dr. Chalmers'.[29] There was Henry Labouchere and also Edward Stanley, who had written a highly evangelical book on the Parables and served on the committee of the Hibernian School Society. He was now on the way to becoming a High Churchman as well a 'high'

---

[27] On this question see below, pp. 255–67; on Baring's views see Hilton, *Corn, Cash, Commerce*, pp. 92–5, 174.

[28] Marianne Thornton to Hannah More, 29 Dec. 1825, Forster, *Marianne Thornton*, p. 117.

[29] Spring Rice to Napier, 15 Nov. 1830, Macvey Napier Papers, BL Add. MS 34614, fo. 431.

Conservative, though as late as 1839 the evangelical publishers Seeley and Burnside published an anonymous volume in which he sought to demonstrate to children how the 'active exercise of His Almighty Power, in overruling the course of nature' in the miracles of Christ, was testimony to his divine affection and protection.[30] Most of all, perhaps, there was Sir George Grey, aptly described by Brent as 'the Evangelical equivalent of Gladstone'.[31] He was the son of a friend of Chalmers and unquestionably devout like his wife, a Ryder. Grey worked under Grant at the Colonial Office (1834–9), and was later many times Home Secretary (1846–52, 1855–8, 1861–6). His religion is described by his biographer in the following terms:

He had laid a firm grasp on the vital principles of the Christian faith, and held to them with unswerving tenacity. His religious belief was firmly incorporated into his inmost being, and formed part of himself. . . . The central point of his own religious feeling was the Atonement, which he did not undertake to explain, but which he felt to be absolutely necessary. The sense of sin was ever present with him, and he found in the Cross of Christ the sense of forgiveness and reconciliation with God. But on all other points concerning theology he was exceedingly tolerant of diversities of opinion.[32]

During the Chartist disturbances, for handling which he was of course responsible, Grey became very 'providence-conscious', and to the dismay of the thoroughly secular *Economist* newspaper he acceded to calls by Howley and Sumner—the evangelical primate and arch-evangelical prelate—for a National Fast Day of Humiliation in reference to the Irish Famine.[33] At least this must have pleased Peel, who, as Gladstone had noted earlier, was 'very loth to believe that Grey would not be in unison with' so great a clergyman as the Bishop of Chester.[34]

The most important nucleus of evangelical piety, however, centred on Althorp, Chancellor of the Exchequer before Spring Rice. Ellis Wasson has identified a 'Young Whig' party, entering politics round about 1809 and led by three noble sprigs, Tavistock, Althorp, and Milton. Their group included Lord Ebrington, whose sepulchral religiosity made him

[30] [Edward G. G. S. Stanley], *The Miracles of Our Lord Explained in a Correspondence between a Mother and Daughter* (1839), pp. vi–viii. See Grant, *Memoirs of Sir George Sinclair*, pp. 331–2.

[31] Richard Brent, 'The emergence of Liberal Anglican politics: the Whigs and the church 1830–1841', University of Oxford D.Phil. (1985), 141.

[32] *Memoir of Sir George Grey*, by Mandell Creighton (privately printed, Newcastle upon Tyne, 1884), 119–20.

[33] *The Economist*, 3 Apr. 1847, p. 382. It may also be significant that like his predecessor as Home Secretary, Graham, Grey was 'puritanically' reluctant to use spies and informers, as distinct from policemen, in tracking down agitators. F. C. Mather, *Public Order in the Age of the Chartists* (Manchester, 1959), 200, 202.

[34] Gladstone's note of 3 Aug. 1843, loc. cit.

(in Wasson's words) a 'young Whig stereotype', and W. H. Lyttelton, whose particular obsession was with the demoralizing effect of national lotteries.[35] Then there was the evangelical Henry Parnell, who along with Poulett Thomson was to advise Althorp closely during the latter's term at the Exchequer (1830–4). And there was Lord Radnor, whose views on charity were typical of his generation. 'Assuredly', he once pontificated, 'no man can suppose that a just God . . . will punish any rich man for the mere fact of his being rich, but the punishment is inflicted for not having made a good use of his riches.'[36] All these men were active in Bible Societies and suchlike organizations for bringing spiritual succour to the poor.

Althorp and Milton were to all intents and purposes evangelicals, though they did not use the term, and were often lampooned as 'Presbyterians' or 'Puritans'. Wasson aptly describes Milton as the 'scourge of the Corn Laws and the Thersites of the ruling class'; he had, in Sydney Smith's opinion, a 'hard anabaptist nature', while to Lady Spencer he looked 'exactly like Praise God bare bones raised from the grave'.[37] They were both high-minded, introspective, pure, and (as Wasson puts it) 'enthusiastic about God' in a way that was as incomprehensible as it was reprehensible to the older generation of Foxite Whigs. Though neither went to such extremes of spirituality as their brothers the Revd Wriothesley Russell and George Spencer, both read the Bible conscientiously, as they also (and in the same frame of mind) imbibed the new sciences—political economy, geology, biology, zoology, chemistry, physics, and agronomy. They were active in Bible Societies, punctilious in their family orisons as well as in their charities, and simple in their pleasures. After the early death of his wife in childbirth, Althorp completely abandoned fox-hunting, partly because he loved it so much that deprivation was a genuine penance, what Wasson calls 'a hair shirt'. Further, he 'closed up houses and sold property', not only because he was in debt but because 'it was a great relief for him to do so. He hated the life of a grandee.'[38] What did make him happy was his simple faith, 'first in an active reliance on the Goodness of God, and in a perfect resignation to his Will, secondly in Charity toward men in the spiritual sense of the word Charity, and thirdly in an humbleness of mind which estimates one's self only through

[35] Betty Askwith, *The Lytteltons: A Family Chronicle of the Nineteenth Century* (1975), 14–15.

[36] Radnor, sermon of 1844, quoted in Brent, 'The emergence of Liberal Anglican politics', pp. 136–7.

[37] Smith to Lady Holland, 4 Nov. 1825, *The Letters of Sydney Smith*, ed. Nowell C. Smith (Oxford, 1953), i. 419–20; E. A. Wasson, 'The Young Whigs: Lords Althorp, Milton, and Tavistock and the Whig party 1809–1830', University of Cambridge Ph.D. (1976), 212. I have relied extensively on Wasson's unpublished work in this section.

[38] Wasson, 'The Young Whigs', pp. 20–3, 27, 172.

the merits of the Atonement'.[39] In public life, the Young Whigs were severe on any forms of immorality. In fact it was the Duke of York scandal in 1809 which first made them politically aware, and which severed Althorp's hitherto warm relations with his mentors, William and Thomas Grenville. Their sense of duty also made them resolute, as Wasson puts it, 'to do what was right even against their economic interest'. Admittedly, their urgent desire to abandon the Sinking Fund and reduce taxation could be said to have been self-regarding. But they were also the most ardent Bullionists, and sternly resisted attempts by the agricultural interests to devalue the currency during the 1820s. Free Trade, meanwhile, took on what Wasson calls 'an almost religious character', and they certainly believed that the Corn Laws showed the aristocracy as selfish and unfit to rule. Thus 'scientific economics was given a back seat to moral passion and political principle'. Milton, it seems, felt driven to atone for his 'sin' in having voted for the Corn Law of 1815, while religion was almost certainly a stronger influence on Althorp than utilitarianism, Zachary Macaulay a closer associate than James Mill or Francis Place.[40]

Still, both strands of thought were in evidence. 'My two lines of reading', wrote Althorp as early as 1818, 'are divinity and political economy: the first to do myself good: the other, to enable me to do good to others.'[41] Five years later he was elected a member of the Political Economy Club. Milton was a keen attendant at McCulloch's London lectures and genuinely anxious to improve the working-man's lot, supporting railways and industrial expansion as stoutly as his father opposed them. Indeed, a deep Whiggish faith in progress via breeding, agronomy, and chemistry suffused all the Young Whigs. Althorp and Milton both believed that dense industrial populations could be sober and orderly, and so did not fear political economy. As for Malthus, they accepted his view of population increase but refused to regard it as an evil, since more people meant more wealth and a larger stock of national capital.[42] Parnell was confident that 'the removal of obstacles is all that is required of the legislature for the success of trade', which unlike Chalmers he believed was 'still very far from having arrived at a limit', and he was confident that happiness would accrue from the expansion of industry and wealth.[43] Radnor, it is written, 'genuinely

[39] Althorp to the Bishop of Bristol, 25 Nov. 1834, *Journals and Correspondence of Sir Francis Baring from 1808 to 1852*, ed. the Earl of Northbrook (privately printed, Winchester, 1905), i. 113.

[40] Wasson, 'The Young Whigs', pp. 212–15, 224–5.

[41] Althorp to Bishop Allen, 9 Sept. 1818, *Memoir of John Charles Viscount Althorp Third Earl Spencer*, by Denis Le Marchant (1876), 169.

[42] Milton in House of Commons, 24 May 1821, *Parliamentary Debates*, 2nd series, v. 997; Wasson, 'The Young Whigs', pp. 24–5, 188–91, 202.

[43] Henry Parnell, *On Financial Reform* (1830), 21–2, 310.

believed that Scripture endorsed Adam Smith and that free-trade meant prosperity for all'.[44]

It was this optimistic faith in growth and progress which separated even susceptible Whigs and Whig–Liberals like Milton and Althorp off from the ideology of the Age of Atonement. Peel and Chalmers, for example, espoused *laissez-faire* policies as the means to a juster society, one in which reward would square with virtue, but they did not suppose that economic expansion would so increase national wealth that material happiness could be dispensed to all. In this respect the Whig-Liberal cosmology was a more anodyne affair, high on rectitude but low on retribution. A characteristic exponent was Lord Morpeth, and also Robert Slaney, whose career has been perceptively analysed by Paul Richards. Slaney was a country gentleman MP, and a pioneer of social reform, especially in his work for the Health of Towns Association. As a young politician he hero-worshipped Althorp, Brougham, and McCulloch, whose London lectures he attended. Having very much a 'this' rather than 'other-worldly' approach to matters, he was a convinced environmentalist, and inherited some of his father's eighteenth-century paternalism. He felt that it could 'be shown clearly that there is a quality of the human mind named Benevolence, Kindness of Heart, a good nature according to its degree of perfection which more than any other endowment contributes to our happiness and that of those around us'.[45] Slaney had all the usual sort of evangelical sobriety, seeing misfortune as an admonition to do his duty of stewardship, and by 1836 he had decided to set aside a 'Christian portion' of his annual income for charity. But political economy — Malthus, Smith, Ricardo, and later Chadwick — was probably the more important ingredient, which helps to account for the Utopian elements in his thought. Thus his *Essay on the Beneficial Direction of Rural Expenditure* (1824) was, as Paul Richards says, 'a major defence of an expanding industrial capitalism based on free trade'. He ignored the Ten Hours Movement and the pleas of the handloom weavers, and supported wholeheartedly the New Poor Law of 1834.[46] His vision was of a model town — with parks, loan societies, and schools, whereby workers would be integrated peacefully into the economic system and imbued with thrift and self-help. Clearly the vision is not very far from that which Chalmers held, but the ethos is crucially different, if only because the end of eliminating pauperism seemed to take priority over the saving of souls.

[44] Ronald K. Huch, *The Radical Lord Radnor: The Public Life of Viscount Folkestone, Third Earl of Radnor (1779–1869)* (Minneapolis, 1977), 136–7, 168.

[45] Slaney's notebook for 1854 quoted in Paul Richards, 'R. A. Slaney, the industrial town, and early Victorian social policy', *Social History*, 4 (1979), 87.

[46] Ibid., pp. 88–9.

The tension between an optimistic and a retributive application of political economy pertains particularly to the New Poor Law of 1834, which was not only the most important single piece of social legislation in the first half of the nineteenth century, but one in which much overt evangelical influence may be traced. If nothing else, the part played by Althorp, who introduced the bill to the Commons, by Radnor—the bill's 'patron and protector' in the Lords—and by Harriet Martineau, who, along with Edwin Chadwick and Sturges Bourne, advised the ministers, certainly suggests that class moralism played some part in deciding the issue. Without going into detail, therefore, something should be said, first about the balance between theory and pragmatism in the making of the Act, and then about the balance between the evangelical and utilitarian— retributive and optimistic—static and expansionist—elements which were mingled in that theory.

We have already seen that the Old Poor Law was a focus of considerable abuse among moderate evangelical social theorists. Very few, it is true, contemplated the total abolition of all legal relief, even Chalmers being more equivocal in practice than he was in theory. The fact remains that, in theory at least, the New Poor Law of 1834 marked a significant step towards a harsh and brutal treatment of the English poor, especially in those (mainly southern) rural areas where previously the generous Speenhamland system of outdoor relief had operated. Consequently its sponsors looked confidently for Chalmers's support, and had indeed made use of his expertise. Scotland, with its mixture of assessed and unassessed parishes,[47] provided a convenient unit for testing the effects of compulsory poor relief. Senior, the government's main economic adviser, made it clear that he was not able 'to believe, with McCulloch and Black, that assessment and prosperity go hand in hand',[48] and he sent an assistant commissioner (Tufnell) up to Edinburgh to be briefed by Chalmers. Tufnell's report lauded Chalmers's approach to poor relief as against 'McCulloch's doctrine',[49] and so it came as something of a shock when Chalmers criticized the 1834 legislation. 'The best which can be said . . . is that in some of its sterner, though in none of its kindlier features, it does somewhat approximate to the right and wholesome charity of principle.' However, it deterred not only the undeserving poor, which was excellent, but also the deserving poor, while its workhouses would undermine the

---

[47] In 1818 about 17% of the population lived in parishes with a legal assessment, and relied for relief on a voluntary system run by the church; by 1839 the proportion had increased to 45%. *Report by a Committee of the General Assembly on the Management of the Poor in Scotland*, 1839, 163–341; Brown, *Chalmers and the Godly Commonwealth*, p. 289.

[48] Senior to Chalmers, 28 July 1832, Chalmers Papers, New College Edinburgh MS CHA.4.189.57–8.

[49] Tufnell's report in Chalmers, *Works*, xvi. 437–44.

family, the parish, and other units of private and communitarian philanthropy.[50] Chalmers was to be even angrier when the Whigs extended a similar system of relief to Ireland in 1838 and when Peel's government, following the recommendations of a commission of inquiry, did the same for Scotland in 1845. Whereas the English measure had at least reduced the amount of monies compulsorily raised for the poor, the same system in Scotland and Ireland entailed a fatal increase in the amount of support.[51]

This is not the place to consider in detail the making of the New Poor Law. It seems clear that the Whigs had formulated their opinions before taking office in 1830, and that their approach was mainly doctrinaire, despite Brundage's claim that political motives predominated. Almost the first thing they did was to set up a committee under Spring Rice to investigate the state of poverty in Ireland. Chalmers's evidence to that committee made, as his biographer says,[52] a 'profound impression' on Senior, who—even more than Edwin Chadwick—master-minded the new act. As for England, Althorp claimed later that he had looked for a sweeping change in the 'whole existing framework of society' since at least 1830,[53] and Peter Dunkley argues that he, Grey, and Senior were all determined from the moment they gained power to kill the allowance system, on the grounds that making up wages from rates could only lead to over-population, low wages, 'idleness and improvidence'. What was needed to restore harmony to the countryside was a deterrent system of poor relief, together with tough, exemplary punishment of rioters by the Home Office.[54] To this end the government immediately put matters into the hands of Brougham, whose 'views had been forged in the immediate post-war . . . heyday of Malthusian, abolitionist sentiment', and who still agreed 'heartily' with all Chalmers's views on the question.[55]

---

[50] T. Chalmers, *The Sufficiency of a Parochial System, Without a Poor Rate, for the Right Management of the Poor* (1841) in *Works*, xxi. 139, 152–3.

[51] The Scottish legislation was not, however, designed so as to be over-generous toward the poor. 'It is part of the supreme law of nature which no system of human law can disregard with impunity, that as a man sows he must expect to reap. A comfortable subsistence ought to be looked for, only as the fruit of industry and economy.' *Report from Her Majesty's Commissioners for Inquiring into the Administration and Practical Operation of the Poor Laws in Scotland*, p. liv [PP 1844, xx. 60]. Accordingly, it was held that official relief should be kept to a bare minimum, and that private charity should 'restrain its hand'.

[52] Brown, *Chalmers and the Godly Commonwealth*, p. 192.

[53] Spencer to Chadwick, 8 May 1841, Chadwick Papers, University College London MSS.

[54] Peter Dunkley, 'Whigs and paupers: the reform of the English Poor Laws, 1830–1834', *Journal of British Studies* 20 (1981), 124–49. There is a more detailed exposition in Peter Dunkley, *The Crisis of the Old Poor Law in England 1795–1834: An Interpretive Essay* (New York and London, 1982), 113–43.

[55] Dunkley, 'Whigs and paupers', loc. cit., p. 130; Brougham to Sinclair, 22 July 1847, Grant, *Memoirs of Sir George Sinclair*, pp. 352–3; Chalmers to Brougham, 13 Sept. 1841, Brougham Papers, University College London MSS, 470.

Eventually, in February 1832, ministers decided to set up a commission of inquiry. Brundage argues that this was merely a cosmetic prelude to introducing a preconceived measure; Dunkley, on the other hand, suggests that the 1831 riots in rural England had made ministers more cautious, and that they hoped by appointing a commission to forestall Brougham's tactless enthusiasm, and get away with something less than full-scale reform.[56] There is certainly much evidence to support the former view. Most striking is the letter which seems to have initiated behind-the-scenes discussion, from Thomas Hyde Villiers, Vice-Secretary of the Board of Control, to Howick on 19 January 1832. Villiers clearly knew what had to be done, knew that it would be politically unpopular, and advocated the commission as a ploy whereby 'Government might at once relieve themselves from difficulty and responsibility . . . , do their duty to the country—and earn for themselves a just praise and popularity'.[57] Once in action the commissioners clearly knew what conclusions they would reach. Thus in June 1833 Senior told Le Marchant that the commissioners could perfectly well report at once (since 'Chadwick has the bill in his head')[58] but that it would be prudent to wait for evidence and 'make our report in the way in which I should wish, that is constantly referring to the evidence and defending ourselves not on general principles, but by facts, and opinions of magistrates and clergymen and practical people, and figures'.[59] Such evidence was bound to be corroboratory, since Chadwick 'has an admirable faculty of endowing the purposes of his examinees with words, [like] a French cook who can make an excellent ragout out of a pair of shoes'.[60] From all this it seems clear that the legislation was mainly based on theory: the theory that 'no relief shall be given to the able bodied, or to their families, except in return for work, and that work as hard as it can be made, or in the workhouse, and that workhouse as disagreeable as it can be made'.[61]

In so far as the New Poor Law was master-minded by certain ministers, it owed something to the retributive philosophy of evangelicalism. Villiers, for example, described by the Webbs as 'one of the channels through which much Benthamism reached the minds of Ministers',[62] was also susceptible

---

[56] Dunkley, 'Whigs and paupers', loc. cit., pp. 132–4; Anthony Brundage, *The Making of the New Poor Law. The Politics of Inquiry, Enactment and Implementation, 1832–39* (1978), 16–18.

[57] T. H. Villiers to Howick, 19 Jan. 1832, copy in Senior Papers, National Library of Wales MS, C855.

[58] Senior to Le Marchant, 28 June 1833, Brougham Papers, 10857.

[59] Senior to Brougham, 9 Mar. 1833, ibid., 44843.

[60] Senior to Brougham, 4 Jan. 1833, ibid., 44437.

[61] Senior to Brougham, 9 Mar. 1833, loc. cit.

[62] Sidney and Beatrice Webb, *English Poor Law History: Part II: The Last Hundred Years* (1929), i. 48 n.

to the moralistic approach, and considered that the principle of population must be 'the very foundation of any useful reform'. In recommending commissioners, and trying to avoid men 'who cannot rise to a general view of any question', he first suggested J. B. Sumner on account of his *very great* performance' on population in the *Records of Creation*, and his accurate views as to poor relief in the *Encyclopaedia Britannica*.[63] If, on the other hand, Dunkley is correct to say that Brougham was excluded from the policy discussions, and that the commissioners were 'pivotal' in deciding for reform, then the motivating philosophy was not evangelicalism, or even the fatalistic pessimism of the Whigs as to the divinely ordained ineradicability of poverty, but the optimistic, growth-oriented capitalism espoused by Senior and Chadwick. They were confident that there was no real surplus of population in the rural districts of the south, and that population pressure, famines, and pestilence were avoidable. What was needed was to remove restrictions on the contractual relations between master and labourer, and an enforced sobriety, hard work, and self-preservation on the part of the latter would then lead to high wages and increased comforts. Competition, in other words, could reveal the harmonies of the universe.[64]

David Brion Davis has noted that anti-slavery gave rise to 'extraordinary conjunction of two seemingly antithetical realms of language, thought, and rhetoric: the evangelical appeals to sin, guilt, retribution, and deliverance . . . and a highly utilitarian analysis of punishment, nutrition, land use, labor incentives, productivity, and revenue, accompanied by the premise that such a rational calculus would enable the government to maximize the benefits at minimal cost to slaves, planters, merchants, taxpayers, and consumers'.[65] Clearly, the same conjunction can be found in the campaign for poor law reform, the same blend of evangelical retribution and utilitarian optimism. It is, in fact, one of the main arguments of this book that an evangelical, backward-looking pessimism could lead men to the same competitive policy conclusions as growth-oriented optimism, and since many thinkers oscillated ambivalently between the two modes, it would be futile to make the distinction too rigorously. Whichever dominated, it is clear that 'less eligibility' and the workhouse test constituted a mechanical and impersonal system of relief which disrupted power-paternalism,[66] but it also contradicted the central plank of Chalmerian views of philanthropy—that it should be voluntary. Dunkley sees this as a dramatic moment in the transition to capitalism: 'a

---

[63] Villiers to Howick, loc. cit. He also suggested Senior, James Mill, and possibly Henry Warburton, with Henry Taylor's father an executive secretary.

[64] Dunkley, 'Whigs and paupers', op. cit., pp. 134–9.

[65] Davis, *Slavery and Human Progress*, p. 211.

[66] Dunkley, 'Whigs and paupers', op. cit., p. 148.

"rational" system of precise, consistent, and universally applied guidelines
. . . imperiled the entire mental structure of paternalism and obligation.
In 1834, the Whigs made clear where their sympathies lay.'[67]

Whig sympathies may also have lain increasingly with Free Trade,
but they did little to forward it until the end of their decade in office.
The free trade movement began to swell at that time, especially in the
provinces, and it undoubtedly had religious overtones, but religion was
not its core as it was in the case of the Tory free traders, nor was it of
an evangelical type. Cobden emphasized his standing as a Churchman,
knowing that many supporters of the Anti-Corn Law League were
prepared to sacrifice social status in what was to them a spiritual cause.[68]
The League's envelopes were decorated with biblical texts, and much
publicity was derived from the famous conference of nearly seven hundred
ministers at Manchester in August 1841, organized and orchestrated by
George Thompson to proclaim 'the politics which flow from pity, the
politics of the gospel'.[69] However, the religion of the League was hardly
retributive; in part it looked back to the eighteenth-century, Paleyan
version of natural theology, in part forward to the 'Good Samaritan'
humanism of the 1850s and 1860s. Whereas Chalmers rejected cosmopolitan ideals of 'universal citizenship', on the grounds that only small
communities could provide a field for redeeming sinful individuals,[70]
Cobden's premiss was that providence had designed commerce to unify
and 'moralize' mankind, and that Free Trade was the international law
of God, to 'spread *Christianity through commerce*, over the world'.[71]
Moreover,

If we can keep the world from actual war—and I trust railroads, steam-boats,
cheap-postage, and our own example in Free Trade will do that—a great impulse
will, from this time, be given to social reforms. The public mind is in a practical

---

[67] Dunkley, 'Whigs and paupers', op. cit., p. 144. See also Peter Dunkley,
'Paternalism, the magistracy and poor relief in England, 1795–1834', *International Review
of Social History* 24 (1979), 371–97.

[68] Cobden to Combe, 1 Aug. 1846, Gibbon, *Life of Combe*, ii. 218–19.

[69] *Report of the Conference of Ministers of All Denominations on the Corn Laws,
Held in Manchester* (1841); Asa Briggs, *The Age of Improvement* (1959), 317; Norman
McCord, *The Anti-Corn Law League 1838–1846* (1958), 103–7. For the 1842 Conference
of Ministers at Edinburgh see *The Life and Work of Duncan McLaren*, by J. B. Mackie
(1888), i. 232–7.

[70] Chalmers, *On the Power Wisdom and Goodness of God*, i. 225–6 [*Works*, ii. 64].

[71] Cobden to Combe, 1 Aug. 1846, loc. cit. Viner, *Providence in the Social Order*,
p. 50, is surely wrong to say that such arguments were rarely used in the nineteenth century.
For just one of very many examples see the Congregationalist J. Baldwin Brown, *Buying
and Selling and Getting Gain: A Pastoral for the Times* (1871), 7: 'Commerce is in the
lower sphere what religion . . . is in the higher sphere, man's ministry to man.' But for
some cogent doubts as to the influence of the idea on practical missionary work see Andrew
Porter, ' "Commerce and Christianity": the rise and fall of a nineteenth-century missionary
slogan', *Historical Journal*, 28 (1985), 597–621.

mood, and it will now precipitate itself upon education, temperance, reform of criminals, care of physical health, &c., &c., with greater zeal than ever.[72]

Combe, Cobden's intellectual mentor, congratulated him on having 'reached the *moral and intellectual* faculties of the poeple', before which all purely selfish feelings died away,[73] but it could hardly be said that the League touched specifically spiritual chords. Cobden himself could display intense piety—as for example when his son died—but instinctively he rejected evangelical attitudes, both in his work for the League and in his later crusade for pacifism. '*If* there be a God ruling the world on principles of retributive justice we ought to tremble for the punishment which awaits this nation', he sceptically remarked of Britain's 'deeds of blood and violence in the East'.[74] He acknowledged the role of the Saints in abolishing slavery, but was otherwise cool about the 'religious revival', and also considered that Palmerston's generation had 'so dragged our protestantism through blood, and flames, and *poison* in India and China, that the nations are all laughing at our pretensions to any scruples about the slave trade'.[75]

Of all the League's prominent supporters, Baptist Noel was probably the most overtly evangelical, but he had strong dissenting contacts (becoming a Baptist in 1848—hence the sobriquet) and shrank from the retributive philosophy common among Anglican evangelicals. Like Cobden he had a Utopian confidence in future progress, and expected Free Trade to remove the fetters on industry and bring 'unbounded prosperity to the whole nation'.[76] He agreed entirely with George Thompson that 'the chastisements we are enduring are self-inflicted; our national distresses are the result of a departure, by human legislation, from the spirit and mandates of the divine law'.[77] Orthodox believers were often scandalized by this way of blaming economic distress on Corn Laws rather than on original sin.

What! the miseries and distress of our land no proof of sin—no token of God's displeasure—due to no fault in those who suffer—but merely the result of 'restraints on man's natural rights and liberty!' The cause of our calamities

---

[72] Cobden to Combe, 14 July 1846, Cobden Papers, BL Add. MS 43660, fos. 46–51. For the post-millennial aspects of Cobdenism see Alexander Tyrrell, 'Making the millennium: the mid-nineteenth century peace movement', *Historical Journal*, 21 (1978), 75–95.

[73] Combe to Cobden, 14 Feb. 1845, Cobden Papers, BL Add. MS 43660, fo. 19.

[74] Cobden to Sturge, 28 Apr. 1857, Sturge Papers, BL Add. MS 43722, fos. 236–7 (italics added).

[75] Cobden to Sturge, 15 Oct. 1858, ibid., fos. 312–13.

[76] Hon. and Revd Baptist W. Noel, *A Plea for the Poor, Showing How the Proposed Repeal of the Existing Corn Laws will Affect the Interests of the Working Classes* (1841), 35.

[77] *Report of the Conference of Ministers on the Corn Laws*, p. 129.

is not, it seems, disobedience to the laws of God, but the existence of certain laws of man![78]

Ultimately, Whigs, Radicals, and Leaguers owed less to Christian morality than to the secular culture of the day, to political economy, science and pseudo-science, and the passion for improvement. It was only the Liberal Tories, largely (though not entirely) insulated from that culture, whose instincts for Free Trade developed in a context of piety and pessimism.

Famine and the Corn Laws

The Whiggish-Radical-Cobdenite statement of the case for Free Trade was officially paraded in the 1840 report of the Select Committee on Import Duties, of which Joseph Hume was chairman. Peel claimed not to have read it. Whether or not this was strictly true, Peel was certainly justified in implying that his route to Free Trade was not that of the Committee. It can be argued that Peel's commitment to Free Trade had its origin in the 1820s, and that his apparent support of Protection in the election of 1841 was to some extent disingenuous.[79] The point here is not merely a question of whether Peel was being dishonest in 1841. It is rather that if Peel was converted to Free Trade after 1841, then in so far as there was an ideological dimension to that conversion, we might plausibly locate it in the radical and cosmopolitan optimism of Cobden and Combe, instead of in the Malthusian, underconsumptionist climate of the 1820s. To a degree such an ascription would be justified. Peel claimed afterwards that he had turned against Protection partly because of the market theory of wages—Cobden's demonstration that Free Trade would raise wages by increasing the demand for labour.[80] A sense that it could benefit everyone, working-men and agriculturalists as well as manufacturers and exporters, was a central plank in Cobden's argument for repeal. Even so, it seems clear that Peel shared the earlier, Liberal Tory view that benefits should be proportioned to desert, that a just economy was more to be sought after than an expanding one. He certainly shared his colleague Graham's underconsumptionist alarms and desire to cool the economy down. Graham, who was as close as anyone to Peel by 1840, put it as follows: 'Advances of capital made by banking speculations, and rivalry aided by improved machinery perpetually displacing adult manual labour, have so stimulated and increased

[78] [Anon.], 'Christianity and the Corn Laws', the *Church of England Quarterly Review*, 10 (1841), 444.
[79] Boyd Hilton, 'Peel: a reappraisal', *Historical Journal*, 22 (1979), 585–614.
[80] Ibid., pp. 599–600.

production that the civilised world cannot consume our articles with sufficient rapidity.'[81]

Graham is normally portrayed as a cold administrator, but there was also a whiff of the Recordite about him. His mother was an ardent evangelical and he himself was always susceptible to apocalyptic alarms. Thus he prophesied in 1839 that a week-long suspension of either credit or food would create 'such a scene of havoc, of bloodshed and of horrors as the civilized world has not yet witnessed'.[82] It is therefore not surprising that he should have seen the hand of a special providence behind the Irish potato blight. That the Famine provided an occasion and an excuse for repeal, rather than converting Peel and Graham to the policy, is now clear. Nevertheless, their response to it shows up their very different eschatologies. In October 1845 Graham concluded a note to Peel on the rotten potatoes in Ireland with the following observations on the way that special providence can smite:

It is awful to observe how the Almighty humbles the pride of nations. The Sword, the Pestilence, and Famine are the instruments of his displeasure; the Canker-worm and the Locust are his Armies; he gives the word; a single Crop is blighted, and we see a nation prostrate, and stretching out its Hands for Bread. These are solemn warnings, and they fill me with reverence; they proclaim with a voice not to be mistaken, that 'doubtless there is a God, who judgeth the earth'.[83]

We saw above that Chalmers was prepared to ditch *laissez-faire* in 1846 because he could see that the Famine was a 'rare' instance of special providence. Just so, Graham told the Lord Lieutenant of Ireland that, while normally the Relief Commissioners should only give food to those who had earned wages from public works projects, 'Yet in the last extremity of want, *especially where it arises from a dispensation of Providence* these rules must necessarily be relaxed.'[84]

Almost certainly Peel saw the 'solemn warnings' of Graham's 'Almighty' in an entirely different light. He would have agreed that sword, pestilence, and famine were 'instruments'—but of God's mercy rather than of his 'displeasure'. Peel's evangelical instincts were of that rational sort which held God to act—even in matters concerning redemption—more often by the known laws of science. Typical of him was the way he once put down J. E. Gordon, one of the fiercest of the extreme evangelicals, who had described the Dissenters' Chapel Bill of 1844 as suffused with moral

---

[81] Graham to Peel, 17 Oct. 1841, Peel Papers, BL Add. MS 40446, fos. 60–1, in *Life and Letters of Sir James Graham 1792–1861*, by C. S. Parker (1907), i. 328.
[82] Graham to Peel, 20 Jan. 1839, copy in Graham Papers, General series, Bundle 37A.
[83] Graham to Peel, 18 Oct. 1845, Peel Papers, BL Add. MS 40451, fos. 400–1.
[84] Graham to Heytesbury, 26 Nov. 1845, copy in Graham Papers, General series, Bundle 95B (italics added). On Chalmers see above, pp. 108–12.

guilt: 'Mr. Gordon would act more in conformity with the spirit of the religion he professes if he were less peremptory in imputing moral guilt to those who may conscientiously differ in opinion from himself, and less presumptuous in undertaking to determine who are the proper objects of divine vengeance.'[85] So it is not likely that he saw the Famine in terms of obedient locusts and canker-worms. Suffering had its purpose ('ultimate good, after some severe suffering, will result') but this purpose could only be realized in a society where God's natural laws reigned uninterruptedly. If we wish to see to the heart of Liberal Toryism, we should look to the peroration to Peel's great speech of 16 February 1846 on the Corn Laws. He could not, he told the House, be *certain* that the Corn Laws were the cause of distress; but it was obvious that they might be, and therefore they should be repealed, so that,

When you are again exhorting a suffering people to fortitude under their privations, when you are telling them, 'These are the chastenings of an all-wise and merciful Providence, sent for some inscrutable but just and beneficent purpose—it may be, to humble our pride, or to punish our unfaithfulness, or to impress us with the sense of our own nothingness and dependence on His mercy'; when you are thus addressing your suffering fellow subjects, and encouraging them to bear without repining the dispensations of Providence, may God grant that by your decision of this night you may have laid in store for yourselves the consolation of reflecting that such calamities are, in truth, the dispensations of Providence—that they have not been caused, they have not been aggravated by laws of man restricting, in the hour of scarcity, the supply of food![86]

This surely encapsulates both the mechanicism and providentialist fatalism of Liberal Tory social philosophy.

Certainly the Famine helped to discredit providence theory, and by the 1850s it had dropped out of the public agenda. Prime Minister Palmerston's contempt for such modes of address is well known, and Aberdeen was equally dismissive. On several occasions Archbishop Sumner advocated special prayers, for the preservation of the armed forces or for protection against cholera, and was refused. Aberdeen would have preferred, for the sake of morale, to order prayers of gratitude for 'our glorious victories' in the Crimea, 'but unfortunately they have been accompanied by a cruel loss of life, and as they have led to no final result,

---

[85] Peel to Gordon, 5 June 1844, Peel Papers, BL Add. MS 40546, fo. 127.
[86] Peel in House of Commons, 16 Feb. 1846, *Parliamentary Debates*, 3rd series, lxxxiii. 1043. Of course, there was an element of cliché in these remarks. See Graham to Peel, 15 Aug. 1845, Peel Papers, BL Add. MS 40451, fos. 182–3: 'The question always returns what is the legislation which most aggravates or mitigates this dispensation of Providence?'

we had better be silent'.[87] By the 1850s, clearly, evangelical attitudes were waning, and a sign of this was the triumph of limited liability legislation in 1856.

[87] Aberdeen to Sumner, 28 Aug. and 28 Nov. 1854, Sumner to Aberdeen, 25 Sept., 24 and 29 Nov. 1854, Aberdeen Papers, BL Add. MS 43195, fos. 128–30, 142–7.

PART THREE

After the Age of Atonement

7

'Incarnate and Incorporate': the Lord of Limit

It is impossible to deny that this question [Limited Liability] is one almost purely economic. It goes directly to the sources of wealth — to the flow of it — to the distribution of it — to the employment of it — and to the increase of it. Yet it is equally undeniable that it cannot be probed to the bottom without taking into account a thousand facts and considerations which concern metaphysics, jurisprudence, politics, morals, and even religion.

> Duke of Argyll, *The Unseen Foundations of Society* (1893), 557

All the world seems to be divided into Political Economists, Poor Law Commissioners, Guardians, Policemen, and Philanthropists, Enthusiasts, and Christian Socialists. Is there not a large intermediate ground which anyone who can write might occupy, and who could combine a real knowledge of the problems to be solved with the enthusiasm which impels a person to devote their life to solving them? The way would be to hide the philanthropy altogether as a weakness of the flesh; and sensible people would then be willing to listen.

> B. Jowett to F. P. Cobbe, 24 Sept. ?1860, *Life of Frances Power Cobbe* (1894), i. 316.17

The Triumph of Limited Liability

By the eighteen-fifties the evangelical or retributive version of free trade ideology, with its essentially agrarian or physiocratic, *rentier*, nationalist, and static or cyclical view of the economy, was rapidly losing ground to the more optimistic and expansionist, industrializing, and cosmopolitan vision of Cobden. Parliament endorsed this development symbolically in 1855, and again more fully in 1856, when it made provision for general limited liability.[1] As Peter Cotterell has written, 'it is extremely difficult to account for this sharp and dramatic change':

---

[1] For details of this legislation see John Saville, 'Sleeping partnerships and limited liability, 1850–1856', *Economic History Review*, 2nd series, 8 (1955–6), 418–33; H. A. Shannon, 'The coming of general limited liability', *Economic History (Economic Journal Supplement)* 2 (1930–3), 267–91; B. C. Hunt, *The Development of the Business*

The total reform of English company law during the years between 1855 and 1862 marks a sudden and sharp break; change both before and subsequently was a long drawn out, gradual process. Not only was the pace suddenly quickened, but the law itself was turned upside down, with all the barriers in the way of company formation being removed. This extreme degree of permissiveness was to become the hallmark of English law.[2]

A brief history of company legislation in the nineteenth century will show that limited liability was essentially a Whig and Radical policy, and was opposed by most Tories, whether High or Liberal.

The Bubble Act of 1720 was a belated and vain attempt to douse 'South Sea' speculation by forbidding the incorporation of new joint stock companies without the grant of a special and expensive charter from Crown or Parliament. Joint stock activity dwindled and played little part in eighteenth-century industrialization, though incorporations were frequently made for public utilities like gas and water companies. Atavistic prejudice against joint stock companies was reinforced by Adam Smith's argument that, since most of their shareholders were sleeping partners, and day to day control devolved on boards of directors, affairs were likely to be conducted with less vigilance and prudence than in an ordinary partnership, where each member was bound to take a personal concern in the management.[3]

Attitudes gradually changed after 1800 as more and more capital-intensive schemes were floated, and joint stock came to seem a convenient method of organizing investment. In June 1825 the Bubble Act was repealed by Liverpool, Huskisson, and Peel, all of whom wished to encourage domestic investment in 'just and laudable objects', rather than see capital scurrying abroad into baseless South American projects. They may also have wished to extend the privilege of incorporation beyond the circle of those who were rich enough to cajole MPs into granting them a charter, or able to curry favour with royalty. However, these Liberal

---

Corporation in England, 1800–1867 (Harvard, 1936), 116–44; James B. Jefferys, *Business Organisation in Great Britain 1856–1914* (New York, 1977), pp. 19–53. I shall not enter into technicalities of the debate concerning *en commandite* partnerships, in which only those partners who took an active part in management would be fully liable, the rest being liable only to the extent of their subscriptions. Saville, 'Sleeping partnerships', p. 422, points out that until 1854 most reformers argued in favour of such partnerships rather than for the *société anonyme* or general limited liability. The most extensive account of how bankruptcy law worked is in Ian P. H. Duffy, 'Bankruptcy and insolvency in London in the late eighteenth and early nineteenth centuries', Oxford University D.Phil. (1973).

[2] P. L. Cottrell, *Industrial Finance 1830–1914. The Finance and Organization of English Manufacturing Industry* (1980), 45, 54.

[3] Adam Smith, *Additions and Corrections to the First and Second Editions of An Inquiry into the Nature and Causes of the Wealth of Nations* (1784), 59–60 [ed. R. H. Campbell, A. S. Skinner, and W. B. Todd for *The Glasgow Edition of the Works and Correspondence of Adam Smith* (Oxford, 1976), ii. 740–1].

Tories decidedly did *not* want to accompany Bubble Act repeal with access to limited liability, the most significant of the privileges usually associated with joint stock status. Here they agreed with the High Tory Lord Eldon that each man who invested in a scheme from which massive dividends were expected must also expect to have to pay the debts of the company in the event of its failure 'to his last shilling and acre'. They fully subscribed to the vulgar view, enshrined in the famous judgment of 1793 in *Waugh* v. *Carver*, that 'he who feels the benefit should also feel the burden'.

Support for limited liability came mainly from utilitarian economists such as Bentham, Senior, and J. S. Mill, and later from Cobden and Bright.[4] 'Were it lawful for every one to engage in commercial undertakings for a limited amount, how many facilities would be afforded to men of genius! All classes of society would furnish assistance to inventive industry. . . . The spirit of gaming, diverted from its pernicious direction, might serve to increase the productive energy of commerce and art.'[5] Such views carried weight with the Whig governments of the 1830s, and following a sudden burst of joint stock formation in 1835–6 they were aired officially in Bellenden Ker's *Parliamentary Report on the Law of Partnership* in 1837. The return of Peel in 1841 set the cause back, however. Gladstone's Joint Stock Company Registration and Regulation Act (1844) drew a firm legislative distinction between a joint stock company and an ordinary partnership, granting the former certain privileges in return for certain conditions as to publicity, but it did *not* grant the right of limited liability, which remained a prerogative of the rich, and also of certain types of company, mainly railways. So while the United States and all Continental countries (except Sweden) enjoyed limited liability, Britain moralistically resisted it.

Limited liability was discussed at great length and with great excitement in the early 1850s, but in 1854 a Royal Commission on Mercantile Law recommended by five votes to four that no change should be made.[6] Nevertheless, the House of Commons carried a motion in favour of 'diminished responsibility' (as it was often called by its opponents) in

[4] C. E. Amsler, R. L. Bartlett, C. J. Bolton, 'Thoughts of some British economists on early limited liability and corporate legislation', *History of Political Economy*, 13 (1981), 774–93. Senior's evidence in H. Bellenden Ker, *Report on the Law of Partnership*, pp. 63–4 [PP 1837, xliv. 461–2].

[5] J. Bentham, 'A Manual of Political Economy', *The Works of Jeremy Bentham*, ed. John Bowring (1843), iii. 48. See J. S. Mill, *Principles of Political Economy with Some of their Applications to Social Philosophy* (1848), ii. 461–2 [ed. V. W. Bladen for *The Collected Works of John Stuart Mill*, general editor J. M. Robson (1963–   ), iii. 898].

[6] *Report from the Select Committee on Investments for the Savings of the Middle and Working Classes*, 1850 [PP 1850, xix. 169–294]; *Report from the Select Committee on the Law of Partnership*, 1851 [PP 1851, xviii. 1–231]; *First Report of the Commissioners appointed to inquire into the Mercantile Laws and the Law of Partnership*, 1854 [PP 1854, xxvii. 445–750].

June 1854, against the pleadings of the Coalition government. The latter
fell in January 1855, however, giving way to Palmerston's Whig/Liberal
administration. Of the Peelites, Aberdeen and Newcastle were excluded,
while Graham, Gladstone, and Herbert soon went into opposition. As
they were all opposed to limited liability, their departure cleared the way
for its passage, to which Palmerston personally was very committed.[7]
Acts of 1855 and 1856 allowed such status to any association of seven
or more persons who wanted it in most fields of enterprise, so long as
they complied with certain stipulations as to promotion, publicity, and
winding up. Banks were included within the scope of the legislation in
1858 and insurance companies in 1862, when the whole was codified
in a statute which was to remain the basis of company law until 1948.
Effectively, the legislation removed the power to sue individual investors,
and also removed the power of individual creditors to sue at all.

The parliamentary doyen of limited liability was Palmerston's Vice-
President of the Board of Trade, Robert Lowe, who regarded the Act of
1856 as the most important contribution of his long career. A large section
of public opinion supported him, and in particular *The Times*, run by
his friend John Delane. In debate the Peelites Cardwell and Goulburn
were antipathetic, while Gladstone, who voted against the bill in crucial
divisions, later described the legislation as ill-conceived. But the really
hysterical opposition came from the Lords, where, as the Liberal leader
Granville admitted, the three best political economists—Monteagle, Grey,
and Overstone—were all hostile.[8] Monteagle, as we have seen, was very
devout and had been a friend and admirer of Chalmers. Grey was a great
admirer of Huskisson's economic policies and of Overstone's writings,
and held to an extreme version of the evangelical dogma on currency and
finance. The only step that Parliament could take to stem the rising tide
of over-trading and speculation was to 'make the laws of bankruptcy more
stringent, and the responsibility of all traders more severe'. He criticized
the 1844 Act only for being too mild in its attack on the 'little-shilling
men' from Birmingham. Peel should not have temporized, and given
businessmen an impression that the Bank would be permitted to rescue
them *in extremis*.[9] Overstone called the 1856 legislation a fraud upon

[7] For the hostility of the Peelites, Cardwell and Goulburn, see Cardwell to Aberdeen,
4 Feb. 1853, Aberdeen Papers, BL Add. MS 43197 fos. 258–9; Goulburn to Cardwell,
11 Feb. 1853, ibid., fo. 260; *The Times*, 7 Aug. 1855, p. 8*f*.

[8] Granville himself favoured limited liability—but then he had never read Bishop
Butler. Granville to Lord Canning, 18 Mar. 1856, Fitzmaurice, *Life of Lord Granville*,
i. 170–2. Russell was 'disposed' to condemn limited liability, 'though the current, at present,
runs all the other way'. Russell to McCulloch, 5 May 1856, O'Brien, *Correspondence
of Overstone*, ii. 646.

[9] Earl Grey to Sir Charles Wood, 14 and 24 Nov. 1857, Hickleton Papers, A4.55.4
(microfilm in Cambridge University Library).

creditors, and a harbinger of 'reckless speculation'. 'A great disease . . . was likely to settle upon this country—the indiscriminate desire for limited liability', which was a ruse to enable speculators to trade with the capital of unknown shareholders.[10] 'Lord Overstone would cheerfully march to the stake', mocked *The Times*, 'or send anyone else there in the unholy cause of Unlimited Liability.' In this he perpetuated the traditional British attitude toward investment, which was: ' "Drink deep, or taste not" . . . a cry inspired, as it was thought, by eternal justice.'[11]

Eternal justice was important, but even more important was the question: *would* limited liability encourage 'fraud, collusion, and robbery',[12] damage the interest of creditors, and ruin Britain's reputation for commercial probity? On this question there was frank disagreement. One party considered that merchants could only achieve a state of commercial grace by being redeemed, and that sudden disasters encouraged such redemption; the other believed that a gradual process of education would take place, as businessmen realized that in order to raise capital they must first have a reputation for honesty. The former feared that limitation would make partners more careless, the latter retorted that it would make creditors more vigilant. Whatever the truth, the decision to allow limit of liability to the extent of each shareholder's own investment clearly marks a retreat from retributive or evangelical economics. Bishop Butler had elaborated a theory of society in which men are governed by rewards and punishments, and Chalmers and Overstone had adapted that insight to the workings of a capitalist economy, business failure being an essential part of a process whereby original economic sin might be atoned. In the 1850s, when the limited liability idea 'was laying rapid hold of the public',[13] such attitudes gave way to the more optimistic liberalism of J. S. Mill, with its confidence in mercantile virtue and common sense. Thus, in introducing the measure, Lowe denounced the evangelical emphasis on natural depravity: 'Unless we deal with each other upon some presumption of confidence . . . the disruption of human society must necessarily follow.

---

[10] Overstone in House of Lords, 22 May 1855, *Parliamentary Debates*, 3rd series, cxxxviii. 869.

[11] *The Times*, 2 Feb. 1856, p. 8 d.

[12] G. F. Muntz in House of Commons, 4 July 1856, *Parliamentary Debates*, 3rd series, cxliii. 338. Muntz, a Birmingham banker, thought that the 1856 bill was 'one of the worst measures that had ever been introduced'. T. Baring remarked on 8 February 1856 that it would place a premium on fraud. Ibid., cxl. 477–9. It is worth pointing out that despite Spooner and Muntz the Birmingham Chamber of Commerce supported limited liability, whereas the Manchester Chamber was hostile. Saville, 'Sleeping partnerships', loc. cit., pp. 431–2. In previous debates also, Birmingham had tended to side with debtor interests and Manchester with creditors.

[13] *The Life of George Joachim First Viscount Goschen 1831–1907*, by A. D. Elliot (1911), i. 60. Overstone claimed, however, that *The Times* gave a false impression of public opinion.

Fraud and wickedness are not to be presumed in individuals.'[14] The opposite view was most memorably expressed by McCulloch, who, though not himself an evangelical, was old enough to have imbibed the ethos of the Clapham generation, with its emphasis on man's need for forgiveness:

In the scheme laid down by Providence for the government of the world, there is no shifting or narrowing of responsibilities, every man being personally answerable to the utmost extent for all his actions. But the advocates of limited liability proclaim in their superior wisdom that the scheme of Providence may be advantageously modified, and that debts and contracts may be contracted which the debtors though they have the means, shall not be bound to discharge.[15]

To the reformers it seemed 'unnatural' to hold the total sequestration of all his property over the trembling businessman, but McCulloch belonged to a generation that thought such hammer-blows entirely natural, like volcanoes. As Professor O'Brien has reminded us, McCulloch is not to be seen as a mere popularizer of Ricardo, for he held independent views derived from the Scottish context, and agreed wholeheartedly with his close friend and former pupil, Lord Overstone, that 'hope of unlimited profit' should continue to be 'associated with and corrected by the sense of unlimited responsibility'.[16]

Now there is an interesting semantic problem arising from the debates on commercial law, which is that both sides claimed—passionately—to be acting in favour of Free Trade. Of course they *had* to, given the mystique which that doctrine was rapidly acquiring, but still the claims are paradoxical. 'It is a question of Free Trade against Monopoly', declared Palmerston, and Lowe echoed him:

The principle is the freedom of contract, and the right of unlimited association. . . . I am arguing in favour of human liberty. . . . We should do well to profit

---

[14] Lowe in House of Commons, 1 Feb. 1856, *Parliamentary Debates*, 3rd series, cxl.124. Lowe also, unevangelically, wished to remove temptation from company directors, on the grounds that temptation was a bad thing. Ibid., p. 126.

[15] J. R. McCulloch, *Considerations on Partnerships with Limited Liability* (1856), 10–11. See [J. R. McCulloch], 'Partnership, limited and unlimited liability', *Encyclopaedia Britannica* (8th edition, 1853–60), xvii. 321. Long before, in the wake of the 1825–6 crash, McCulloch had recommended withholding 'all relief, except in cases of extreme necessity, from those who have had the misfortune to be involved'. [J. R. McCulloch], 'Commercial revulsions', *Edinburgh Review* 44 (1826), 77. McCulloch would have agreed with Combe that 'Freedom of the *will* would be inconsistent with responsibility. If will is not determined by the strongest motive, law would have no basis to rest on.' Combe to Spencer Perceval jun., 10 Jan. 1827, Perceval Papers, BL Add. MS 49191 fos. 123–4.

[16] Overstone's evidence in *First Report on the Mercantile Laws and the Law of Partnership*, p. 93 [PP 1854, xxvii. 537].

by the lesson which that science [political economy] has taught. That lesson is this—[not] to interfere with and abridge men's liberty.[17]

Meanwhile, Overstone complained that Palmerston and Lowe were merely 'fanning a popular cry for the purpose of putting [us] down', when they 'endeavoured through the most flimsy sophistry to associate [limited liability] with the principle of Free Trade; matters which have the same relation to each other which Darkness has to Light'.[18] And McCulloch considered that limited liability had as much to do with Free Trade as it had to do with 'the theory of the tides'.[19]

The explanation is, of course, that the two sides meant different things by 'Free Trade'. In one sense the miscomprehension can be seen in terms of the difference, already noted,[20] between Liberal Tory notions of Free Trade—cyclical, nationalist, physiocratic, retributive—and Whig or Liberal notions—expansionist, urban, cosmopolitan. Then again we can see it as a conflict between *political* and *economic* modes; between a *rights* way of thinking about Free Trade and a *market* way of thinking about it. Market free traders favoured unlimited liability because it seemed to them to chime with their market views of nature: man should be left both to win and to lose. If a man limits his risks, he should also limit his profits by (say) lending money at fixed interest instead of buying shares.[21] Rights theorists, on the other hand, argued that capitalists should be 'permitted to deal how and with whom they choose, without the officious interference of the state', and 'to associate in whatever form they think best', so long as they are honest about it. Limited companies are harmless since no man is obliged to trade with one, and none will do so unless the company enjoys a good reputation. (The same disagreements obtained in the contemporary debate on trade unions, rights theorists defending them on the grounds of men's right to associate with whomever they chose, market theorists condemning them because their monopoly power threatened the autonomy of individual, free market competition.) Finally, while both sides rested on assumptions derived from natural theology, the market free traders—as one would expect—interpreted these in a more anthropomorphic light than the political rights theorists. Thus Lowe,

---

[17] Palmerston in House of Commons, 26 July 1855, *Parliamentary Debates*, 3rd series, cxxxix. 1389–90; Lowe in House of Commons, 1 Feb. 1856, ibid., cxl. 129–31, 138.
[18] Overstone to Granville, 21 Mar. 1856, O'Brien, *Correspondence of Overstone*, ii. 643. Overstone also believed that the Cobden/Chevalier Treaty of 1860 was a retreat from 'pure' Free Trade back to reciprocity. Overstone to Reeve, 16 Feb. 1860, ibid., ii. 909–10.
[19] McCulloch, *Considerations on Partnerships with Limited Liability*, p. 27.
[20] See above, pp. 64–70.
[21] [Anon.], *How to Mismanage a Bank: a Review of the Western Bank of Scotland* (Edinburgh, 1859), 42.

whose conception of *laissez-faire* was 'political', trusted to 'laws planned by Infinite sagacity', which, without human direction, without even the need for human co-operation, did the work 'of correcting and of compensating errors—one extreme invariably producing another—dearness producing cheapness, and cheapness dearness; and thus the great machine of society is constantly kept oscillating to its centre'.[22] On the other hand, McCulloch, as we saw, made it clear that the 'scheme laid down by Providence' was founded on the need for 'personal responsibility' to the fullest extent.

The salient question is: *why* in the mid-nineteenth century did one model of Free Trade give way to another, both legislatively and in popular estimation? Cutting through the legalistic and moralistic debates of the day, Jefferys has recently made a convincing case for seeing limited liability as the child of an investors' lobby which was well represented in Parliament, mainly domiciled in the home counties, not interested in the management of companies, but very concerned by the recent fall in dividends and the narrowing of investment opportunities with the reduction of the national debt and the expected decline in gas and railway activity. Industrialists, it is claimed, were not too bothered, since they could invest in their own partnerships, but the *rentier* class, not content with consols at three per cent, wanted to grab thirty or forty, yet were chary of risking their whole fortunes in the failure of a single company.[23] A more traditional explanation is that the large number of railway companies, where limited liability effectively operated, was undermining the older system by stealth.

All this is plausible, but understandably it did not figure much in the public debate, which is where we must go to elicit underlying attitudes and assumptions. What caused one party to become so hysterical about this turning of the law 'upside down' overnight? Why, on the other hand, were so many MPs ready to swallow Lowe's somewhat spurious liberal optimism?[24]

In the first place, we can see that limited liability reflected new and less ambivalent attitudes to economic growth. Whereas during the first half of the century growth had seemed to be putting Britain out of step with the rest of the world, so making her susceptible to a dreadful recoil

---

[22] Lowe in House of Commons, 1 Feb. 1856, *Parliamentary Debates*, 3rd series, cxl. 138.

[23] Jefferys, *Business Organisation in Great Britain*, pp. 44–53; for some criticisms of the thesis see Cottrell, *Industrial Finance*, pp. 45–7.

[24] For Lowe's approach to limited liability see T. D. L. Morgan, 'All for a wise despotism? Robert Lowe and the politics of meritocracy 1852–1873', Cambridge University Ph.D. (1984), 88–106. I am grateful to Dr Morgan for much fruitful discussion of this subject.

and retribution, by 1856 it was assumed that the other nations would follow the same road to felicity. By this time, fear of the Malthusian peril had also subsided, which removed the greatest barrier to Utopian dreams of growth. In 1863 the Registrar-General proclaimed *ex cathedra* that capital could be made to multiply even more rapidly than population, and that capital was always convertible into manufacturing industry, 'which in the present state of commerce is *always convertible into "the means of subsistence"*'.[25] And so, whereas Liberal Tories had moved toward Free Trade as a way of stabilizing and containing the economy, expansion now seemed to be both normative and desirable, and limited liability—'the natural corollary and complement of the repeal of the Usury Laws'[26]—was intended to encourage greater investment in a society whose commercial fabric was based on credit. New attitudes to growth, investment, and business enterprise generally, are evident from the way in which the word 'speculation' began to be used in its non-pejorative sense, as in Bagehot's 'philanthropists or speculators'.[27] The fashionable complaint now was that capitalists were not investing enough, or were seeking safe unadventurous outlets and even foreign ones. Growth-oriented economists like Mill pointed to America as a land where limited liability had encouraged its citizens to invest in industrial ventures, confident that even if they failed they would not lose everything. Opponents retorted, of course, that America was notorious for its bankruptcies and chicanery. As it happened, limited liability was not to lead to the desired and dreaded surge in productive investment, but both sides certainly expected it to.

Accompanying this shift of attitudes was an adjustment in popular socio-economic demonology. Consciously or otherwise, Liberal Tory or Peelite economists had regarded debt as sinful, and their dear money policies had been designed to make things difficult for those who sinned. They were unimpressed by the argument that men who risked getting into debt in order to invest in productive business were economic heroes, while public creditors, lending their money safely at fixed rates of interest, were merely 'drones'. The late eighteenth century had seen 'a stern pro-creditor reaction' in English law.[28] Then in the 1830s Brougham, as we saw, attempted to move the law back towards the debtor. His Royal

---

[25] 'Census 1861 Report', PP 1863, liii. 26.

[26] Moffatt in House of Commons, 8 Feb. 1856, *Parliamentary Debates*, 3rd series, cxl. 476.

[27] See, for example, W. Bagehot, 'The character of Sir Robert Peel, *Biographical Studies*, ed. R. H. Hutton (1881), 6, 36 [St John-Stevas, *Collected Works of Bagehot*, iii. 245, 269]; William Morton, 'Some of the moral aspects of political economy', *Fraser's Magazine*, NS 16 (1877), 509.

[28] Joanna Innes, 'The King's Bench prison in the later eighteenth century: law, authority and order in a London debtors' prison', *An Ungovernable People: The English and their Law in the Seventeenth and Eighteenth Centuries* (1980), p. 260.

Commission reported in 1840, and in 1844 he sponsored an Act which made it practically impossible to recover small debts under twenty pounds. To its detractors this measure was a product of 'false and effeminate humanity',[29] and one which seemed to condone pillage and to subvert national morality, and so Graham—much to Brougham's annoyance—made adjustments back in favour of creditors in 1845 and 1846.[30] But in the 1850s attitudes switched sharply, so that the Deputy Governor of the Bank of England could advertise limited liability as 'a fair and just precaution against dishonest creditors'. 'There are such things as dishonest creditors as well as dishonest debtors', confirmed E. W. Field, a reforming solicitor, as if to unbelieving traditionalists.[31] Much to McCulloch's disgust, bankruptcy legislation of 1857 made it very much harder for creditors to regain what they were owed, even from companies whose liability remained unlimited. Hitherto they had been able to hound an individual party, and it had been up to the defendant to try and force his partners to make their contributions. After 1857 the only resource of a creditor against a company that said it could not pay him from general funds was to petition the Court of Chancery for winding up and recovery—a long and complicated process. 'Creditors might be left to take care of themselves' was the only comfort Lowe could offer.[32]

Clearly, then, limited liability reflected new attitudes to growth and speculation. Another reason for its adoption was a realization that the *unlimited* system was not working, partly because Whig reformers had drawn its teeth. As a result of Lord Brougham's legislation in the 1830s, abolishing arrest on *mesne process*, it had become possible for debtors to anticipate their victims, declare themselves bankrupt with no assets to distribute, and so avoid imprisonment. As a result bankruptcy became less of a deterrent and less effective in protecting creditors. The mania of 1847, fed by the railways but not confined to them, the notorious careers of John Sadleir ('Irish politician and swindler', as the *DNB* succinctly describes him) and George Hudson, all made it obvious that the

[29] [Anon.], 'Bankruptcy and insolvency', *The Westminster and Foreign Quarterly Review*, 46 (1847), 501.

[30] Graham to Brougham, 14 Aug. 1845, University College London MSS, Brougham Papers, 14234; Lyndhurst to Graham, 15 Aug. 1845, Graham Papers, Bundle 92. See *Report of the Commissioners for Inquiring into Bankruptcy and Insolvency* [PP 1840, xvi. 1–600] for the reformers' case.

[31] E. W. Field's evidence in *Report from the Select Committee on the Law of Partnership*, p. 145 (Q.939) [PP, 1851, xviii. 167]. Field [1804–71] was a Unitarian and a typical mid-Victorian (post-Romantic) sentimentalist, who wrote poems full of soppy conceits like that of the 'sunbeam's parting kiss of earth', &c. *Edwin Wilkins Field: A Memorial Sketch*, by Thomas Sadler (1872), 111. See E. W. Field, *Observations of a Solicitor on the Right of the Public to form Limited Liability Partnerships* (1854).

[32] Lowe's evidence in *First Report of the Commissioners on the Mercantile Laws and the Law of Partnership*, p. 84 [PP 1854, xxvii. 528].

problem of 'speculation' was not even being contained. It became fashionable to agree with J. S. Mill's sneer at Chalmers—that it was simply not possible to 'inculcate on capitalists the practice of a moral restraint in reference to the pursuit of gain'.[33] More and more pundits abandoned the elusive goal of economic conscience, and sought instead a market mechanism that would maximize the public benefits to be derived from profit-seeking.

Worse even than the fact that many villains survived the system was the realization that many of those who smashed were themselves innocent parties. It had been a central assumption of evangelical economics that no one who failed could be wholly guiltless, that commercial crashes somehow *found out* commercial guilt,[34] but this view began to change in the 1840s with the rise of the small shareholder. The *Report on Joint Stock Companies* (1844) insisted on the innocence of the widows, orphans, and other familiar archetypes of early Victorian literature, who found themselves caught up in business crashes. 'Victims . . . are usually persons of very limited means, who invest their savings in order to obtain the tempting returns which are offered. Old people, governesses, servants and persons of that description', are tempted to invest their little all'—presumably for security, not speculation— 'and when the concern stops, they are ruined.'[35] Dickens recognized that traffic in shares was '*bred*'— note the Malthusian terms—'*at first*, as many physical diseases are, in the wickedness of men, but then *disseminated* in their ignorance . . . and communicated to many sufferers who are neither ignorant nor wicked'.[36] Gladstone had hoped that provisions enacted in 1844 to ensure regular audit and full publicity would dispel the ignorance of shareholders and identify speculation with guilt once more. Nevertheless, the innocence of the average investor was a compelling argument in the Whig–Liberal case for reform during the 1850s.

In this context it is significant that the supporters of limited liability professed positive attitudes to social mobility. Initial moves came indeed from the Christian Socialists, anxious to encourage the formation of working-class co-operatives. F. D. Maurice, E. V. Neale, Thomas Hughes, and J. M. Ludlow first moved, through their parliamentary representatives R. A. Slaney and Viscount Goderich, for legal adjustments (including

---

[33] J. S. Mill, *Principles of Political Economy*, ii. 90 [*Collected Works*, iii. 571].

[34] See above, pp. 134–8.

[35] *First Report of the Select Committee on Joint Stock Companies*, 1844, p. xi [PP 1844, vii. 11]. Though it was pointed out that widows and children who invested their entire wealth in a suspended bank would lose as much under limited liability as they did already. William Romaine Callender, *The Commercial Crisis of 1857: its Causes and Results* (1858), 35–6 and n.

[36] Charles Dickens, *Little Dorrit*, Bk. II, ch. 13.

limited liability) that would enable working people to provide against 'the contingencies constantly occurring to them', and to 'give them the means of preserving their small savings'.[37] Goderich hoped that limited liability would open up opportunities for working-class investment, and further that a system of *en commandite* partnerships 'would enable the Manufacturer to give any of his workmen a more direct interest in his business, than he now can, without at the same time giving them some authority as to its management, and would thus remove one obstacle to that real union and association of all concerned in the work of production on the existence of which we can alone wisely depend for safety'.[38] As it happened, the Industrial and Provident Societies Act of 1852 having given this pressure group many of the securities it was looking for, the Christian Socialists largely detached themselves from the campaign for limited liability, which came to seem more and more a middle-class concern. Still, Lowe and Goderich urged in 1856 that the privilege should not be confined to the rich, and Henry Labouchere, a Radical-Liberal, later opined 'that the whole system of limited liability companies [was] really created in order to enable small men to act together and hold their own against the very rich men'.[39] It was only the latter, taunted Lowe, who clung to non-limitation.

Opponents of the change were naturally more outspoken on the social question. In Liberal Tory hands Free Trade had been an essentially retrogressive policy, competition a way of keeping down small men. Lord Liverpool had pointed out complacently in 1826 that 'where perfect liberty prevailed, each person having an equal right to invest his capital, the wealthier must in time drive out the weaker and less solvent'. He disliked a system in which 'any petty tradesman, any grocer or cheese-monger, however destitute of property, might set up a bank in any place'.[40] Crashes were periodically necessary to shake off too much productive investment, and to maintain the beneficial consumption of aristocrats and *rentiers*. Thirty years later Overstone opposed limited liability publicly on the grounds that it would encourage 'speculation, trickery and fraud',

---

[37] Slaney in House of Commons, 22 May 1849, *Parliamentary Debates*, 3rd series, cv. 874; Goderich in House of Commons, 27 June 1854, ibid., cxxxiv. 763; Saville, 'Sleeping partnership', op. cit., pp. 419–23; G. D. H. Cole, *A Century of Co-operation* (Manchester 1944), 114–26. Morgan, 'All for a wise despotism', pp. 91–106, points out that Lowe did not expect working-men to succeed in building up their capitals, but thought that they must be allowed to 'try the experiment, or they will never be satisfied'.

[38] Goderich to Bruce, 3 Dec. 1853, Ripon Papers, BL Add. MS, 43534 fo. 11.

[39] *The Life of Henry Labouchere*, by A. L. Thorold (1913), 421. On the wish to help small shareholders see Lowe in House of Commons, 1 Feb. 1856, *Parliamentary Debates*, 3rd series, cxl. 126–35; Harrowby in House of Lords, 14 Mar. 1856, ibid., cxli. 148–9.

[40] Liverpool in House of Lords, 17 Feb. 1826, *Parliamentary Debates*, 2nd series, xiv. 461–2.

but in a private letter of 1863 another motive emerged: 'Joint Stock Banks and Limited Liability Companies—are the order of the day—and the boldest man seems the most likely to be prosperous. . . . The world is going up and down stairs, *without laying hold of the bannister*.'[41]

But if limited liability can be seen in one way as a pointer to social mobility, it can also be seen as the moment when the middle classes suddenly opted out of the capitalist system *at the point where it stood to damage themselves*. Hitherto they had been able to justify its inequalities with the thought that they were not only more diligent and resourceful, but also more daring than the workers, and consequently more vulnerable. Risk of sudden loss had been inseparable in their minds from the enjoyment of rapid gains, and if they were harsh to the poor they were also, through their refusal to enact securities for investors, stern with themselves.[42] But *now*, complained Monteagle and Overstone, they were prepared to allow profit-making *without* commensurate risk. More people would be admitted to the share-holding élite, but the élite itself would be cushioned against danger. To this extent limited liability can be stigmatized as a gross example of middle-class selfishness. Yet this in itself forced many of the more conscience-stricken to seek another mode of justifying, or at least rationalizing, their social advantages, and this in turn impelled some of them to take a more positive attitude to working-class conditions.[43]

'Hide the Philanthropy': a New Approach to Social Reform

It is of course impossible to be more than tentative in considering the motives behind an entire generation of middle-class attitudes, but at least some people seem to have reasoned that, if they were no longer disciplining themselves, they could not go on disciplining the lower orders in the old way. Mill is just one thinker who moved from support of *laissez-faire* in industrial relations in 1848 to support for trade unions by the 1860s, for there was a growing consensus in favour of 'social reform'. In 1851 James Martineau, who was able as a Unitarian to survey society from a psychological distance, longed for the day when employers would put

---

[41] Overstone to Norman, 24 Oct. 1863, O'Brien, *Correspondence of Overstone*, iii. 1017. Overstone elsewhere called the existing distribution of capital 'natural, and therefore the legitimate and most beneficial distribution'. Humble shareholders would not be able to understand the risks of an undertaking, and real management would therefore pass to selfish parties with other interests. *First Report on the Mercantile Laws and the Law of Partnership*, pp. 94–6 [PP 1854, xxvii. 538–40].

[42] See above, pp. 115–20.

[43] Dicey claimed that limited liability 'has given room, and supplied arguments for State intervention' in many other areas of life. A. V. Dicey, *Lectures on the Relation between Law and Public Opinion in England during the Nineteenth Century* (1905; reprint of 2nd, 1914 edition, 1962), 246.

up 'a moral resistance to the full swing of economical laws'; yet by 1886 he was complaining that too many people (and nearly the 'whole body' of Anglican clergy) had, 'in their humanitarian enthusiasm, [been] betrayed . . . into vain and disastrous struggles against social and economic laws, which will be found as unyielding as the law of gravitation'.[44]

Now of course there were many, and sometimes conflicting, reasons for this new approach, such as a feeling that reform was necessary to placate the subversive masses and also, perhaps, a sense that those masses were now more peaceable and deserving. In terms of policy it should not be regarded as a dramatic ideological adjustment, merely the replacement of one conception of Free Trade by another. The reformers did not contemplate massive state intervention or increased public spending, and so had little in common with the 'New Liberalism', Fabianism, or even Socialism of forty years on. Their aim was rather directed towards improvements in the machinery of the state, and to ameliorations in the fields of law, sanitation, housing, industrial relations, conditions of work, psychiatry, penology, and so forth. What it undoubtedly did reflect was a mid-century change of mood. Kitson Clark noted that 'the tone of England became gentler' at about this time, while contemporary historians like Spencer Walpole and Harriet Martineau had marked 'the prevalence of kindly feelings', 'the spread of a spirit of peace—of a disinclination, that is, for brute violence'.[45] The establishment of an Anti-Duelling Association in 1843, leading to abolition in 1852, reflected the fact that it was now more chic to apologize than to fight—though it must be said that this was a view which many evangelicals (notably Wilberforce, More, and Rowland Ingram) had pressed for many years.[46] Then there was the adoption of surgical anaesthesia from 1847, the restriction of army floggings to only fifty lashes in 1846, the foundation of the Board of health (1848), the kinder treatment meted out to animals, children, lunatics, and paupers—all these, no less than limited liability, marked a new and more indulgent approach to human foibles. Sewell lamented in 1844 that an insidious Benthamism was undermining the older and more wholesome view of punishment as an 'exhibition of the moral law of retribution'. Instead of inflicting exemplary pain, reformers were anxious to achieve the 'inferior and hopeless objects of deterring by example, and of correcting

---

[44] Martineau to F. W. Newman, 29 Sept. 1851, Drummond and Upton, *Life and Letters of Martineau*, ii. 294–6; Martineau to the Revd Priestley Prime, 26 Dec. 1886, ibid., ii. 230. For Martineau see below, pp. 301–3.

[45] S. Walpole, *A History of England from the Conclusion of the Great War in 1815* (1878–86), v. 529; H. Martineau, *A History of England during the Thirty Years' Peace, 1816–1846* (1849–50), ii. 714.

[46] Donna T. Andrew, 'The code of honour and its critics: the opposition to duelling in England, 1700–1850', *Social History*, 5 (1980), 409–34, stresses the abolitionists' belief in 'the equal subordination of individuals to law and to the market place'.

the offender'.[47] Similarly, the *National Review* of October 1856 complained, with reference to an 'environmentalist' speech of Lord Stanley, that it was 'a growing habit to look upon the convict, not as a culpable person at all, but simply as an unfortunate one, who so far from having any atonement to make for his past career, is rather in a position to require that atonement to be made'.[48] Admittedly, this tendency towards a softer line on penal policy is obscured from view because the gradual cessation of the transportation system, under which incorrigible offenders had simply been eliminated from society, meant that British prisons had to deal with more hardened criminals than formerly. Superficially, therefore, the deterrent nature of the Penal Servitude Act of 1864 might seem to suggest a hardening of upper-class attitudes. But in fact the real development of the 1860s, as Jennifer Davis has shown, was the creation of a clear line demarcating deviants and habitual criminals from the remainder of the poor.[49] In the earlier years of the Industrial Revolution, criminality had been regarded in much the same way as fever, or speculation, or pauperism—a disease which might spread by moral zymosis and subvert the entire nation. Now, however, crime was becoming 'socialized', and although the treatment of individual offenders was still harsh at times, at least society felt able to contain and tolerate a criminal class.

It is not possible to examine the new approaches to social problems in any detail. A familiar example concerns the changing treatment of children. For all his liberal rhetoric, Thomas Arnold was as obsessed as any evangelical could have been by sin, and by the 'unimaginable wickedness of boys'. Corporal punishment was entirely proper for such 'inferior' creatures, incapable of any further degradation beyond that of boyhood itself.[50] The mid-century saw much softer attitudes, however, and even a feeling that childhood was a state of pre-corrupted innocence. The provision of reformatories for juvenile offenders, following on legislation of 1854, was one consequence of this new outlook.[51] Another

---

[47] W. Sewell, *Christian Politics* (1844), 354–5. For Sewell see above, p. 172.

[48] Cited in W. L. Burn, *The Age of Equipoise. A Study of the Mid-Victorian Generation* (1964), 20–1. Burn observes that Stanley's was still a minority view in 1856, but the point is that it was a rapidly growing one.

[49] Jennifer Davis, 'The London garrotting panic of 1862: a moral panic and the creation of a criminal class in mid-Victorian England', *Crime and the Law. The Social History of Crime in Western Europe since 1500*, ed. V. A. C. Gatrell, Bruce Lenman, and Geoffrey Parker (1980), 190–213.

[50] John Chandos, *Boys Together. English Public Schools 1800–1864* (1984), 118, 242, 256–8.

[51] *The Recorder of Birmingham. A Memoir of Matthew Davenport Hill; with Selections from his Correspondence*, by R. and F. Davenport-Hill (1878), 151–75. See ibid., p. 300, for Hill's 'Birmingham' views on currency. For information about the reformatory movement, and about social reform in general in this period, I am indebted

telling example of changing methods is provided by the Temperance Movement. Traditionally, reformers had insisted that there should be an absolutely free trade in alcohol, and that the only way to deter drinkers was by holding revivalist meetings, perhaps with a slobbering sot prominent on the platform as an earthly foretaste of the retribution that awaits all sinners. 'Graphic accounts of *delirium tremens* thrilled Exeter Hall', especially when given by the reformed drunkard J. B. Gough. Between 1848 and 1854, however, reformers turned against the idea of inducing terror, partly because it was not working and partly through moral revulsion. Now the only cure seemed to be to cut off alcoholic supplies at source, through licensing and urging the *pledge*. As Brian Harrison puts it, this shift from the 'moral suasion' approach of the evangelicals—redemption through suffering—to reliance on prevention and prohibition accompanied a realization that moral reform might have to precede religious conversion.[52] In the same way, Maurice hoped that co-operative associations of workmen would *prevent* 'extravagant and ruinous speculations', whereas Chalmers had thought a cure was only possible through the suffering which such evils bring in their wake.

This desire to *prevent* social evils clearly went with Owenite ideas of environmentalism and biological determinism, both of which militated against the Christian doctrines of original sin and free will. The consolation which Peel had derived from a crisis—'ultimate good, after some severe suffering, will result'—was no longer readily available. Quite suddenly almost everyone was saying the sort of things Southwood Smith had been saying, more or less to himself, for several decades, not only with respect to social reform but on the whole nature of Christianity.

The Afterlife: from Retribution to Restitution

In 1856 Sir Robert Peel's executors, Philip Stanhope and Edward Cardwell, set about preparing a volume of his correspondence on the Irish Famine and Corn Law crisis. When Stanhope came to Graham's diagnosis of 18 October 1845,[53] in which he ascribed the disaster to divine vengeance, he decided to omit the passage as irrelevant to 'the political bearing' of the letter. He conceded the propriety of Graham's 'reverent humbling . . . before

to Lawrence Goldman, who is writing on the activities of the Social Science Association. On the decline of evangelical penal practice in favour of a Nonconformist-inspired emphasis on the gospel of work and self-help, see U. R. Q. Henriques, 'The rise and decline of the separate system of prison discipline', *Past and Present*, 54 (1972), 61–93.

[52] Brian Harrison, *Drink and the Victorians: The Temperance Question in England 1815-1872* (1971), 179–218. Louis Billington, 'Popular religion and social reform: a study of revivalism and teetotalism, 1830–50', *Journal of Religious History*, 10 (1978–9), 266–93.

[53] See above, p. 249.

Almighty God at the apprehension of so dreadful a calamity', but insisted that such sentiments would be generally misunderstood.[54] Maybe he was being squeamish, but the incident does reflect the change that had taken place within a decade in the accepted idea of God's fatherhood. Geoffrey Rowell has charted the gradual but steady decline of realistic belief in Hell, and the rise of more cheerful notions such as 'universal restitution'. In 1854 Maurice was dismissed from his Chair at King's College, London, for claiming that Hell was a metaphorical concept, a state of heavenlessness, and that the word 'eternal' as applied to punishment meant, not for ever and ever, but a qualitative state: infinity rather than 'all sequential time'. In 1862 H. B. Wilson could still be prosecuted for an article on this subject in *Essays and Reviews*.[55] Yet by 1870 most Anglican clergymen, if not yet all their congregation, had accepted the dread neology. Acceptance took many different forms, of course. There were the Conditionalists, who argued for a sort of survival of the morally fittest unto eternal life, while the residuum merely passed away into nothingness. There were Universalists who believed in the eventual salvation of everybody. And there were those, perhaps the majority, who came to see Hell as a reformatory where sinners could submit to short sharp spiritual shock and finally purge themselves in preparation for Heaven. A few even regarded this purgatorial existence as specific to the Christian era, and supposed that in centuries to come Hell's fossil remains would be matter to excite the geologist.[56] But for all these nuances the central fact is that so many came to sympathize with William Rathbone Greg in rejecting as blasphemous the orthodox picture of a 'cruel, short-sighted, capricious, and unjust [God], punishing with infinite and endless torture men whom He had created weak, finite, and ephemeral,—nay, whom he had fore-ordained to sin'.[57] Greg's *Creed of Christendom* (1851) was identified by Morley as an especially significant example of the 'dissolvent literature' (the metaphor has commercial as well as chemical connotations) of the 1850s.[58]

[54] Stanhope to Graham, 13 July and 17 Sept. 1856, Netherby MSS, Graham Papers, General series, Bundle 130.

[55] Ieuan Ellis, *Seven Against Christ: A Study of 'Essays and Reviews'* (Leiden, 1980), 185.

[56] Geoffrey Rowell, *Hell and the Victorians: A Study of the Nineteenth-Century Theological Controversies concerning Eternal Punishment and the Future Life* (Oxford, 1974), *passim*. On the 'confessional revolution' in the Scottish church see A. C. Cheyne, *The Transforming of the Kirk: Victorian Scotland's Religious Revolution* (Edinburgh, 1983), 60–87.

[57] W. R. Greg, *The Creed of Christendom: Its Foundations and Superstructure* (1851), p. xiii.

[58] John Morley, *Critical Miscellanies* (1886), iii. 242–3.

Like Greg, Maurice was to some extent prepared for these developments by his Unitarian background, but why did they have such a widespread impact? It would be amusing to think that men ceased to have any need for Hell once they discovered that there were abundant signs of hell on earth. The evidence does not support such an interpretation, however. It seems clear that the eschatological revolution preceded late nineteenth-century awareness of the bitter cry of outcast Londoners. Probably a more important factor was the growing awareness that the harshness of orthodox doctrines was turning men away from Christianity altogether, and that it was therefore necessary to surrender the shadow of the valley in order to preserve the substance of the faith. But this does not of itself explain why so many believers were unable to go on stomaching harsh doctrines.

In 1955 Howard Murphy examined the problem of loss of faith as it was experienced by F. W. Newman, J. A. Froude, and George Eliot. He used these examples to illustrate his general point, which was that those persons in whom the higher criticism or geology and biology aroused religious doubt were already likely to have felt a moral repugnance against such doctrines as those of election, reprobation, future punishment, and especially vicarious sacrifice. For example, Newman had turned away from fierce Protestantism in the 1820s, but it was only in the 1840s that he came to regard the usual view of the Atonement as 'the product of ages of cruelty and credulity', and thereafter that he slipped into Unitarianism. Murphy believes that evolutionism and biblical criticism had been available to Newman in the 1820s and 1830s, but that they were only seized on when they fulfilled an ethical and emotional need.[59] Darwin, Sidgwick, and Leslie Stephen are just three other eminent Victorians who apparently lost their faith for similar reasons, but more telling still in favour of Murphy's thesis is the evidence of Susan Budd's recent study of the less eminent. Her analysis of the deconversion experiences of nearly three hundred and fifty free thinkers c.1840–1900 supports his contention that the crucial factor in loss of belief was a 'sense of moral outrage' in realizing that Christianity 'was *wrong*—i.e. morally wrong'.[60]

It is of course hard to be confident about the order in which such intangible changes occurred. Possibly moral repugnance only loomed so large because historical and scientific criticism of the Bible, dimly perceived if not openly embraced, had already forced believers to rely increasingly on the moral worth of Christianity. Thus Isaac Taylor had claimed that

[59] Howard R. Murphy, 'The ethical revolt against Christian orthodoxy in early Victorian England', *American Historical Review*, 60 (1955), 800–17.

[60] Susan Budd, *Varieties of Unbelief: Atheists and Agnostics in English Society 1850–1960* (1977), 106, 113–19. See Noel Annan, *Leslie Stephen: The Godless Victorian* (1984), 234–66.

certain events related in the New Testament *had* to be true because they were so beautiful and pure that our 'moral antennae' confirmed them for us. This was a commonplace, but more surprising was the claim that his intuitive method of investigation and proof was as 'rigorous' and as accurate as 'mathematical' and 'physical' methods, and was sufficient to establish Christianity as a 'religion of facts', historically proven.[61] Baring-Gould made a related point in the 1860s, when he argued that the best evidence for Christianity was that God had implanted spiritual instincts and tendencies in man.[62] At all events, early nineteenth-century religion was based on ethical more than on intellectual postulates, so it is not surprising that the retreat from religion should have taken an ethical form, even if there were other root causes. It is entirely plausible that an unconscious rejection of the scientific basis of the faith had led to a conscious emphasis on its ethical aspects, so that it was the latter of which the newly faithless were most aware when they came to tell their tales.

At all events, it is clear that moral revulsion did play an important role in the softening of evangelical Christianity. A conviction that the moral sense has an 'absolute right to reject as untrue any doctrine appearing to it immoral, whatever amount of (apparent) Scriptural evidence may be adduced in its favour', had, as one commentator put it, become 'present to the minds of men with a more than ordinary force'.[63] It is just one of many paradoxes surrounding this subject that Maurice had jettisoned his early Unitarian faith because of the very opposite distaste: 'I had a certain revolting, partly of intellect and partly of conscience, against what struck me as a feeble notion of the Divine perfections, one which represented *good nature* as the highest of them. . . . I despised the Universalist and Unitarian as weak.'[64] Maurice's bedrock—'Christ on the Cross . . . reconciling the world to Himself . . . consubstantial with the Father'—was thus for him a robustly realistic alternative to the sort of sentimental twaddle (as he now considered it) in which he had been nursed, whereas for Anglicans, steeped in decades of vulgar evangelical piety, the same resource offered an escape from holy terror.

There was then a decline in mid-century of the sort of evangelicalism which has been discussed in this book, though numerically the party suffered no declension. It even began to dominate appointments to high office in the Church of England, thanks to Shaftesbury's influence and

---

[61] Isaac Taylor, *Four Lectures on Spiritual Christianity* (1841), 9–37.

[62] S. Baring-Gould, *The Origin and Development of Religious Belief* (1878), pp. xv–xvi (the book was mainly written in the later 1860s).

[63] John H. Jellett, 'Future punishment', *Contemporary Review*, 32 (April–July 1878), 153–6.

[64] Maurice to Hort, 23 Nov. 1849, *The Life of Frederick Denison Maurice chiefly told in his own Letters*, ed. F. Maurice (1884), ii. 15.

Palmerston's complaisance,[65] so that Maurice could ruminate gloomily that they were now 'the most influential of all parties' in the Establishment.[66] What did decline was the old eschatology based on sin, trial, and judgment, and also the old revivalist fervour, so that even the Moody and Sankey pageants of the 1870s were sedately organized and soberly optimistic rather than urgently fervent (let alone chiliastic) in their appeal.[67] As the Cambridge theologian Fenton Hort put it, perhaps prematurely, 'disbelief in the existence of retributive justice . . . is now so widely spread through nearly all classes of people'.[68]

An interesting figure through which to trace this shift in religious sensibility is Frederic William Farrar, author of one of the two notable schoolboy novels of the Victorian era. *Eric; or, Little by Little* (1858)—the title reflects evolutionary gradualness and rejection of apocalyptic change— was a deliberate counter to 'the "Tom Brown" school of theology', and its juvenile version of 'the Sermon on the Mount—"if a boy smite thee on the one cheek, hit him on the other also" '.[69] Brought up in a narrow evangelical vein, Farrar's liberation began with the teaching of Maurice and Plumptre at King's College London (1847–50), the former reproving him sternly for his youthful fascination with the *Horae Apocalypticae* of Elliott. From London he went to Trinity College, Cambridge, where he became an Apostle, and it was as a Fellow there in 1857 that he won the Norrisian Prize essay with *The Christian Doctrine of the Atonement Not Inconsistent with the Justice and Goodness of God*. This showed Farrar to be very aware of the moral objections to orthodoxy, but also anxious to cling to it. Drawing heavily on Butler, he argued that it was presumptuous of man to expect to understand the inscrutable, and criticized those who tried to systematize the faith by devising 'philosophies of the plan of salvation' and other 'petty schemes of Aristotelian theology'.[70]

Both at school and university Farrar had won the reputation of being a nice swot, oozing 'purity and unselfish gentleness' of the sort that he paraded in *Eric*. A contemporary wrote that he appealed to 'a pure and

[65] On continuing evangelical vitality see Michael Hennell, *Sons of the Prophets: Evangelical Leaders of the Victorian Church* (1979), *passim*; Toon, *Evangelical Theology, 1833–1856*, pp. 78–109; J. Edwin Orr, *The Second Evangelical Awakening in Britain* (1949).

[66] Maurice to Revd D. J. Vaughan, 18 Jan. 1854, *Life of Maurice*, ii. 234.

[67] On 'the failure of English revivalism' in 1859 see John Kent, *Holding the Fort: Studies in Victorian Revivalism* (1978), 71–131, and on Moody and Sankey see ibid., pp. 132–235; also Billington, 'Popular religion and social reform', loc. cit., p. 293.

[68] Hort to Maurice, 16 Nov. 1849, *Life and Letters of Fenton John Anthony Hort*, ed. A. F. Hort (1896), i. 116–23.

[69] B. Gregory, *The Thorough Business Man*, pp. 16–17.

[70] F. W. Farrar, *The Christian Doctrine of the Atonement Not Inconsistent with the Justice and Goodness of God* (Cambridge, 1858), 18–19, 24–5.

exalted personal morality for all, not of the mere negative kind, but a very active one, and the imaginative literature illustrating such aspirations,— the *literae humaniores* in short. He delighted in "the cloud of witnesses".'[71] As an assistant master at Marlborough and Harrow (1854–71), Farrar stunned his rough and idle lower-fifth forms by his disinclination for the rule of law as 'the only incentive and the sole civiliser'. He introduced 'a new idea of life, and the conviction that we were made for something better and higher than to be caned and cuffed'. Corporal punishment, he would have agreed with C. J. Vaughan, 'is inconsistent with modern notions of personal dignity and modern habits of precocious manliness',[72] which reminds us that liberal 'manliness' was sharply opposed to the animality that had previously been supposed to lie at the root of human nature. Jam and cake, a little pathos, and much genial chaff were his weapons, a manly lachrymosity which some claimed touched, via *Eric* and *St Winifred's*, the 'deeper emotions' and 'inner chord . . . of boy life' in a way that 'no other writer has ever equalled'. It is entirely typical that he should have regarded the Parable of the Prodigal Son as 'the Epitome of the Gospel',[73] for in mid-century that and the Good Samaritan began to replace the Talents and the Unjust Steward in popularity. Needless to say, Farrar was not a games man, and in that sense not a forerunner of the coarsification of the public schools in the last two decades of the century. He represents a distinctly 'liberal' phase between Arnold and the Edwardian imperialists, a Headmaster who at Marlborough (1871–6) 'made up for want of firmness by excess of kindness'.

Farrar's *The Life of Christ* (1874) turned out to be the most successful of a very successful popular genre. It went through more than thirty editions and sold over one hundred thousand copies before 1914, and undoubtedly it helped to make its author a Canon of Westminster in 1876. But two years later his published sermons on *Eternal Hope* (1878), though reaching an equally wide audience—it sold through the first edition in three weeks, while the eighteenth appeared in 1901— aroused a storm of controversy among more conservative Churchmen. Its central theme was a Mauricean one, 'that the expressions which have been interpreted to mean physical and material agonies by worm and flame are metaphors for a state of remorse and alienation from God'. Eternal punishment may occur, not because God wills it, but as a logical

---

[71] *The Life of Frederic William Farrar, Sometime Dean of Canterbury*, by Reginald Farrar (1904; new and revised edn, 1905), 23–6, 46–51.

[72] C. J. Vaughan, *A Letter to Viscount Palmerston on the Monitorial System of Harrow School* (1853), 5–12, cited in Chandos, *Boys Together*, pp. 241–2.

[73] *The Atonement: a Clerical Symposium*, ed. F. Hastings (1883), p. 67. On Farrar as schoolmaster see *Life of Farrar*, esp. pp. 56–9, 81–2, 178, and, less indulgently, Chandos, *Boys Together*, p. 300.

consequence of vice. Even so, it is *never* too late to repent, since God's mercy can even extend to the soul after death, in the intermediate state (Purgatory) before final judgment. Farrar, in other words, went beyond annihilationism or conditional immortality, whereby the wicked would simply be destroyed, in favour of universalism, the view that all men would *eventually* be saved.[74] His son believed that these opinions probably cost the Canon of Westminster proper preferment, but consoled himself by reflecting that, in taking liberal theology down to the populace, Farrar had released thousands 'from the gloom and terrors of a fetich worship'.[75]

Eschatology and Social Reform

We must now consider whether there is a connection between this new eschatology and the call for a more humane treatment of social underdogs. In a very important sense, the emasculation of Godly terrors can be seen as a failure of middle-class nerve. For whereas the poor had a sporting chance of being whisked to Paradise, the well-to-do faced the prospect of a fiery workhouse beneath the earth, an afterlife of perpetual less eligibility.[76] In abolishing Hell, the middle and upper classes were making their futures more secure, but at the same time they were also removing a justification for their own material advantages. Hitherto they could have defended privilege by referring to their own spiritual vulnerability: God had intended them to have wealth and power, but was marking well what they did with it—not only *what*, but, more elusively, *how* and in what state of heart they did it. Now, quite simply, the rich and powerful were unable to bear this suspense any longer. For example, the story was told in 1858 of a society lady susceptible, like so many of her class (and especially, perhaps, her sex) to bouts of acute clinical depression.

What religious teaching she had in her youth was of a so called evangelical nature. No sooner did affliction come upon her, than these teachers came about her, wrote, and in short, kept her in a state of high nervous excitement. This will not do for everyday 'wear and tear', and for the last three years she has been in a constant alternation of feeling, obliged from position and circumstances to be always in society, and all the time fearing that she is falling from God because

---

[74] F. W. Farrar, *Eternal Hope: Five Sermons* (1878), pp. xi–lvi, 49–89. For opposition to Farrar see E. B. Pusey, *What is of Faith as to Everlasting Punishment?* (Oxford, 1880) and E. M. Goulburn, *Everlasting Punishment* (1880). Goulburn was a former moderate evangelical turned moderately High Churchman. See F. W. Farrar, *Mercy and Judgment: a Few Last Words on Christian Eschatology with reference to Dr. Pusey's 'What is of Faith?'* (1881), 483–5.

[75] Farrar, *Life of Farrar*, pp. 274–8.

[76] See above, p. 115–16.

she can no longer find in herself the highly wrought emotions which existed when she was in stronger health. Loved by all who come near her . . . , devoted to her poor . . . , she is thoroughly unhappy from the constant fear of the wrath of this inexorable Judge.

Apparently this lady was able to take enormous and immediate relief in Maurice's assurance 'that God is a God of love, and that He does not punish in anger'.[77]

We can now see more clearly what the Duke of Argyll, a member of the Cabinet that introduced limited liability, meant when he observed that the question could not be fully understood without reference to morals, metaphysics, and religion; what Muntz meant when he said that the company legislation was 'philosophic' rather than 'commercial'; and what Lowe meant when he 'repudiated the pretensions of unlimited liability to rest on the ground of natural justice'.[78] Limitation was, as we saw, a case of the well-off investing classes softening the rigours of capitalism *at the very point* where it threatened themselves. In the same way, the repeal of hell-fire can be regarded as unbuttoning a system of spiritual capitalism *at just the point* where the upper classes felt vulnerable. Maurice, one might say, was limiting the liability of sin. It was suggested above that the legislation of 1856 made it necessary to find a new way of rationalizing privilege, and the concomitant softening of spiritual sanctions added to the necessity. No doubt the vast majority of the well-to-do, carefree by disposition, were unmoved, but there were also many earnest souls—those who commit their thoughts to print and so reach the historian—who seem often to have felt that if one of the main justifications for social exploitation were removed, then the thing itself should be obliterated. It should be pointed out, however, that in adjusting to the more serene philosophy of the Age of Equipoise, fashionable thought was merely catching up with what formal political economy had long adumbrated. For though Adam Smith had insisted that religion should retain 'a place . . . for the punishment of the wicked, as well as one for the reward of the just',[79] Ricardo, Senior, Torrens, and J. S. Mill—the latter with splendidly rollicking defiance: 'to Hell I will go'—were all contemptuous of spiritual terrorism.[80]

---

[77] Charlotte Williams-Wynn to Maurice, Apr. 1858, *Memorials of Charlotte Williams-Wynn,* edited by her sister (1877), 246–7.

[78] Muntz in House of Commons, 6 Feb. 1856, *Parliamentary Debates,* 3rd series, cxl. 260–1; Lowe's evidence in *First Report on Mercantile Laws and the Law of Partnership,* p. 84 [PP, 1854, xxvii. 528]. Morgan, 'All for a Wise Despotism', pp. 281–2 n. 13.

[79] Adam Smith, *The Theory of Moral Sentiments* (enlarged 6th edn, 1790), i. 229 [*Works and Correspondence of Smith,* i. 91]. On Smith's eschatology and views about the Atonement see D. D. Raphael, 'Adam Smith and "the infection of David Hume's society"', *Journal of the History of Ideas,* 30 (1969), 225–48.

[80] See above, p. 189.

However, it is still far from clear whether religious changes preceded social ones or whether men with changed social visions searched for new eschatologies. Hort considered that disbelief in retribution was felt

especially in regard to social and political questions, [and] causes even men, whose theology teaches them to look upon God as a vindictive, lawless autocrat, to stigmatise as cruel and heathenish the belief that criminal law is bound to contemplate in punishment other ends beside the improvement of the offender himself and the deterring of others.[81]

In other words, Hort seems to have thought that social conscience preceded spiritual awakening, whereas Charles Gore, a Christian Socialist writing many years later, saw things the other way round. Discussing the mid-century breakdown in orthodox Christianity with reference to the effects of Darwin, textual criticism, and comparative religion, Gore commented:

Hardly less important among the causes of religious unsettlement was the revolt of the moral conscience — which in the middle of the last century, if it was singularly insensitive on some points, as for instance on the cruelties and injustices still involved in our industrial system, was acutely sensitive and insistent on others — against certain current doctrines of Christianity which are commonly, if not quite accurately, described as Calvinistic. The idea of absolute divine decrees condemning to eternal misery masses of men even before their birth — the teaching about the Atonement which represented God as content to punish the innocent in place of the guilty — the doctrine of an endless hell which was to be the lot of all who had not accepted a message which some of them had not even heard — such doctrines, which had no doubt been commonly preached from Christian pulpits for a long period, more or less suddenly began to produce a violent reaction. . . . [There was] a very widespread rebellion of conscience against everything in the current religious tradition which described the action of God as tyrannical, arbitrary and cruel.[82]

So, in Gore's view, moral revulsion preceded a compassionate concern for social justice. F. W. Newman illustrates the point, as his espousal of social reform came *after* he had abandoned a salvationist theology. 'Undoubtedly, if we are to expect our Master at cockcrowing, we shall not study the permanent improvement of this transitory scene.'[83] Earlier nineteenth-century almsgiving, as we saw, so often went unorganized because it was felt that individual effort was needed to redeem the sinful philanthropist, but now that efficiency and success mattered more than the

---

[81] Hort to Maurice, 16 Nov. 1849, loc. cit.
[82] Charles Gore, *Belief in God* (1921), 19–20.
[83] F. W. Newman, *Phases of Faith: Or, Passages from the History of My Creed* (1850), 204.

redemption of the rich, charity organization became the watchword.[84] Farrar welcomed this 'systematic and proportional charity', but James Martineau denounced the 'kind of systematic and semi-official and wholly officious philanthropy, which perverts the moral taste of the present day'.[85] Officious, maybe, but also unselfish. It has been pointed out that Dickens's heroes, in many ways exemplars of the new equipoise, are good-*natured*, in that they act benevolently by instinct rather than from fear or a sense of duty. Pickwick and Boffin 'act as they do because they cannot act otherwise. . . . They seem to have no temptations, difficulties, or struggles: they are uniform, unruffled, and unreflecting.'[86] 'That Dickens could identify this Romantic benevolence with Christian benevolence marks the decline of the older and sterner faith on which the latter had been placed', comments Houghton, who goes on to cite Fitzjames Stephen's condemnation of the period's 'vapid philanthropic sentiment'—'a creed of maudlin benevolence from which all the deeper and sterner elements of religious belief have been carefully purged away'.[87]

Three brief examples must suffice for the moment to illustrate these new attitudes. The first comes from changing interpretations of the Parable of the Talents, in which Jesus consigned the unprofitable servant to darkness. For A. B. Bruce, Professor of Apologetics at the Free Church College in Glasgow from 1875 to 1899, darkness could hardly signify flames, but must mean that he would be forever excluded from the festive inn of Heaven, left to wail and gnash his teeth outside. And for what sin was he thus punished? Not for having squandered his talent in riotous living, which had been the usual interpretation, but merely because he was timid, over-cautious, nervously afraid of responsibility when it came to investing his assets. Such was the urgency of the demand for work and profit, the need for growth in other words, that God would punish men for neglecting their economic duties. Furthermore, 'in teaching a morality of love Jesus virtually teaches a theology of grace', meaning that God loves kindness, and that being kind to the poor (by works) actually

---

[84] See Owen, *English Philanthropy*, pp. 215–46. Owen was quite correct to regard the Charity Organisation Society (founded in 1869) as taking over from Chalmers the belief that charity must foster individualism and self-dependence in the recipient, but possibly he did not appreciate the extent to which the COS's emphasis on systematization undermined those sacred ties between giver and taker which were so important to Chalmers. Ibid., pp. 225–8, and see above, pp. 88–9, 101–6.

[85] F. W. Farrar, *Social and Present-Day Questions* (1891), 95; Martineau to Revd T. E. Poynting, 24 Jan. 1848, Drummond and Upton, *Life and Letters of Martineau*, ii. 297–9. Martineau thought that philanthropists were now worrying too much about 'the *pecuniary* element of benevolence' and not enough about '*personal labour and intercourse*'.

[86] Humphry House, *The Dickens World* (1941), 39.

[87] Houghton, *Victorian Frame of Mind*, p. 275; *The Life of Sir James Fitzjames Stephen*, by Leslie Stephen (1895), 157.

entails grace, as the Parable of the Unjust Steward shows.[88] Nothing could be further from the theology of the earlier part of the century.

The second example concerns an evangelical Rector of St George the Martyr in Southwark, William Cadman (1815–91). Preaching in 1856, he was anxious to reassure his comfortably well-off congregation that, notwithstanding old-fashioned beliefs, the poor possessed no special advantages over them spiritually. Admittedly, there was the text, 'Hath not God chosen the poor of this world rich in faith, and heirs of the Kingdom which He hath promised to them that love Him' (James 2: 5), but this meant merely that *some* of the poor would be saved, that they were not *all* marked out for Hell. The inference he drew from this was that, since God had not entirely overlooked the claims of the poor with respect to the next world, rich men should not do so either with respect to this one. But while they should show personal benevolence, sympathy, and friendship to the poor, it was also necessary to make 'well organized plans' if they were to do the job properly. Most rich people would be too busy to do the work themselves, so they should support agencies for the purpose—district visitors, scripture readers, missionaries, and clergy. Clearly Cadman did not belong to the school which thought that one should become personally involved because personal salvation depended on the performance.[89]

Finally, there was the elderly clergyman who wrote—also in 1856—to congratulate the author of a new book, saying that nothing for a long time had moved him so much. It illustrated beyond cavil 'the greatest and most absorbing of all the principles of all religion—that *love* is the fulfilling of the law. . . . I most truly think that this book would be a better preparation for Orders for most persons than they commonly get.' The remarkable thing here is that the book, a treatise on criminology by Matthew Davenport Hill, the Birmingham reformer, while inveighing passionately against the place of retribution in penal theory, had nothing explicit to say about religion at all.[90] It is a vivid illustration of the way in which religious faith itself was becoming secularized and socialized.

A Scottish Challenge to the Cross

The clergyman in question was John Penrose (1778–1859), a High Churchman and a believer in God's miraculous powers. His tract *Of God;*

[88] A. B. Bruce, *The Parabolic Teaching of Christ: A Systematic and Critical Study of the Parables of Our Lord* (1882), 207–11, 375.

[89] W. Cadman, 'The sin of neglecting the poor', *The Pulpit*, 69 (1856), 516–22. On Cadman's evangelicalism see *A Memorial of the Rev. William Cadman*, ed. Leonard E. Shelford (for private circulation, 1899), *passim*.

[90] J. Penrose to M. D. Hill, 26 Aug. 1857, Davenport-Hill, *The Recorder of Birmingham*, pp. 315–16; Matthew Davenport Hill, *Suggestions for the Repression of Crime, contained in Charges delivered to Grand Juries of Birmingham: Supported by Additional Facts and Arguments* (1857), 182 and *passim*.

or of the Divine Mind (1849) expounded on the personalization of God in the divine *logos*, Christ, 'that human character in which is incorporated the full perfection of every human virtue and power'.[91] It appeared six years after a more dissolvent tract on *The Moral Principle of the Atonement*, which depicted the crucifixion as merely a moral example to mankind, entailing nothing forensic. He could not accept that Christ was 'a secondary Deity, perhaps a benignant God, in opposition to a Severe God, which is what he certainly is not'. On the contrary, the Atonement only works because its moral influence subdues sin and implants holiness, and so renders man meet for salvation — it does nothing more than that, and has no direct effect on God's will.[92]

It is time to look more closely at the doctrine of the Atonement. Along with hell-fire, liberal theologians of the 1850s and 1860s surrendered the idea that a loving God would inflict excruciating suffering on his son as a vicarious sacrifice for other men's sins. Such an action now seemed both unjust and, in a Benthamite sense, inefficacious.

That sinners can *only* be redeemed through the atoning sacrifice of Christ is at the centre of Christian theology and was given particular emphasis by nineteenth-century evangelicals.[93] 'It is an eternal and absolute law that sin deserves punishment.'[94] God has been wronged and must exact a recompense, for his law 'knows nothing of compromise, nothing of compassion, nothing of concession', and a blind eye to our sins on his part would 'shake the whole moral government of the universe'.[95] Some, of course, limited the efficacy of the Atonement to the Elect, calculating that the awfulness of Christ's suffering was an exact equivalent in amount to the sins of the chosen number and no more. But the more usual evangelical position had been that Christ's death opened the way to forgiveness for everyone who chose to embrace the opportunity. Christ was but one man, yet he was also infinite and therefore capable of taking on himself the task of paying for the sins of the entire world. Only by faith in the Atonement, and not by any other merits, could a man save his soul.

---

[91] [J. Penrose], *Of God: Or of the Divine Mind: And of the Doctrine of the Trinity, also of Pantheism: In a Series of Letters to an Undergraduate* (Oxford, 1849), 38–41.

[92] J. Penrose, *Of the Moral Principle of the Atonement: Also, of Faith: And of its Two Sorts, Conviction and Confidence, and of the Connexion between Them* (1843), 12–19 and *passim*.

[93] For the orthodox view see William Magee, *Discourses and Dissertations on the Scriptural Doctrines of Atonement and Sacrifice* (1809). Of many 'classic' statements a particularly comprehensive one is Revd R. P. Buddicom, 'The Atonement indispensable to the necessities of guilty man: and shown to stand and fall with the deity of our Lord Jesus Christ', *Unitarianism Confuted: a Series of Lectures by Thirteen Clergymen of the Church of England* (Liverpool, 1839), 437–520.

[94] R. W. Dale, 'The expiatory theory of the Atonement', *British Quarterly Review*, 46 (1867), 502.

[95] H. Stowell, 'The Atonement: A sermon', *The Pulpit*, 69 (1856), 222.

In order that a man may receive the atonement, he must be brought to despair of every alternative refuge, every succour, every substitute, but the One offering once for all offered upon the cross. The first great preparation for the reception of the atonement is for a man to come to an utter bankruptcy of all hope beside. The next thing to hope in the Christian's experience is despair.[96]

This forensic doctrine of the Atonement had helped moralists to explain away the fact that God's temporal dispensations were not always so just. The greatest sin of all in that period was conceived to be avarice, and bankrupts—to use the word literally now—could usually be presumed to have been cheats and speculators. But even when they were not, as in the case of a thousand widows and orphans, Chalmers and Overstone could console themselves that such sacrificial lambs atoned for the commercial spirit of the age. Such confidence only makes sense in the light of eschatological views concerning vicarious sacrifice and substitutionary punishment, and it is not coincidental that those who insisted most strongly on the 'fever of speculation' as a preliminary to redemption— Chalmers himself or Thomas Nolan[97]—also clung to a 'hard' interpretation of the Atonement.

Like Hell, this 'whipping-boy' theology came under widespread attack in mid-century. It began to be protested that, although one could substitute suffering, one can never substitute punishment, since only a guilty party is susceptible of punishment. Anyway, none but a cruel and vindictive God would make an innocent suffer. J. P. Hopps, a Unitarian, considered one of the signs of the times to be 'a disinclination to hold dogmas that shock the moral sense and cast a cloud over the perfections of God. . . . The vast majority have quietly drifted from the belief in an angry God who punished His Son as a victim.'[98] There was widespread acceptance of Bentham's view that the sole end of punishment was tutelage, and that mere retribution was barbaric. Then again the Atonement was, of all doctrines, the most vulnerable to anthropological attacks on orthodox Christianity. Discovery by anthropologists of the widespread practice of sacrificial offerings among countless tribes of Africa not only destroyed the uniqueness of the Christian message but was an acute embarrassment to apologists. It was hard to refute Baring-Gould's point that sacrifice was central to the religious sensibilities of savages as well as of Christians, having originated first in men's dealings with one another, and only becoming attached to notions of sin and responsibility to God later, 'when the idea of a moral Governor of the universe dawned on men's minds'. Thus the Greeks had regarded sacrifices not as expiations but as gifts

[96] H. Stowell, 'The Atonement: A second sermon', ibid., p. 228.
[97] See above, p. 125, and below, pp. 293–4.
[98] John Page Hopps, Sermons for the Times (1864), 54–5.

to their gods, and it was only with the Jews, ever conscious of their own 'shortcomings', that the idea of atonement had been introduced.[99] Biblical criticism was also especially harmful to the doctrine of the Atonement, since at this time it centred on disproving the Mosaic authorship of the Pentateuch. Such doubts called into question the theory of successive revelations, which depicted Moses as a prototype of Christ, performing a similarly mediatorial role between man and God.[1] Anything which contradicted such notions was bound eventually to reflect doubt on the Atonement itself.

The ideology of Atonement was, as we have seen, particularly strong in Scotland and in Oxford, while the challenge to orthodoxy came largely from Scotland and Cambridge. North of the border the force of the Westminster Confession was such as to provoke the first rebels against orthodox Atonement theology. John McLeod Campbell (1800–72), hitherto a warm admirer of Butler's *Analogy*, became minister at Row in September 1825. A great change of heart on doctrinal matters followed in the latter part of 1826 and early 1827. By his own account it began with a revulsion against the orthodox view of repentance, which now seemed to be nothing but a prudential and selfish calculation. One could only achieve 'singleness of heart and eye in the service of God' if one had assurance of faith. This thought led to a re-evaluation of the Atonement, since 'unless Christ had died *for all* . . . , there was no foundation in the record of God for the Assurance which I demanded, and which I saw to be essential to true holiness'. Campbell now turned away from the system of 'evidences', on which he had hitherto relied, as virtually contradicting 'the inherent power of a true apprehension of the grace of God to give peace with God'. The latter he called true *'evangelical repentance*, as distinct from repentance produced by the fear of wrath'.[2] By preaching universal pardon Campbell aroused local opposition, which eventually led to his deposition by the General Assembly in May 1831. Later, in the 1850s, he came to be regarded as a seer and martyr, but during the heyday of Chalmers he was a counter-cultural figure. It is a mark of Chalmers's greatness, in fact, that his death in 1847 hit even the

---

[99] Baring-Gould, *Origin and Development of Religious Belief*, i. 368–89, ii. 293–312.

[1] J. D. Yule, 'The impact of science on religious thought', Cambridge University Ph.D. (1976), 371–2.

[2] J. McLeod Campbell, *Reminiscences and Reflections, referring to his Early Ministry in the Parish of Row, 1825–31*, ed. Donald Campbell (1873), 24, 152–7; *Memorials of John McLeod Campbell: Being Selections from his Correspondence*, ed. Donald Campbell (1877), i. 50–1. For his subsequent doubts as to Butler's adequacy for nineteenth-century dilemmas see Campbell, *Memorials*, ii. 80, 169. On Scottish 'doctrinal-disciplinary' cases in this period see D. Chambers, 'Doctrinal attitudes in the Church of Scotland in the pre-Disruption era: the age of John McLeod Campbell and Edward Irving', *Journal of Religious History*, 8 (1974–5), 159–82.

unsympathetic Campbell with a sense of the 'emptying of the earth': 'a void that I did not anticipate, . . . greater than any consciousness of his existence that I previously had'.[3] Campbell had loved and admired Chalmers, but regretted that he had 'never . . . got out of the forms of the Scotch systematic theology'. In particular Chalmers had had a limited understanding of the Atonement. 'He came to *seek holiness* in the strength of the faith that he *was* freely pardoned and accepted in Christ, not in the hope that he *would be* conditionally.'

Inasmuch, however, as he did not see the relation between the ground of the forgiveness proclaimed in Christ, and the state of mind proposed to be produced by the knowledge of that forgiveness, he is continually left to be saved by the tenderness of his conscience alone from the error of being made less sensitive as to the evil of sin, or its danger, through his trust in the Atonement.[4]

Campbell also differed from Chalmers politically in that he was not unsympathetic to protectionism, while he steadfastly refused to accept that the victims of business failure were any more 'sinners above all men' than were the fortuitous victims of shipwrecks and earthquakes.[5] His conception of providence in ordinary life, that is, was not a mechanical one.

Another hero of the Scottish resistance was a layman, Thomas Erskine of Linlathen. *The Unconditional Freeness of the Gospel* (1828) argued that all men could accept God's pardon irrespective of faith *or* works. They should believe, not in order to be justified, but because they are justified. Campbell was greatly moved by it and the two men later became ardent friends. Chalmers also liked it, but fretted lest 'the train of his thoughts might ultimately lead Mr. Erskine to doubt the eternity of future punishment'.[6] Another martyr at the hands of the Scottish Establishment was A. J. Scott, who later became a Christian Socialist in London,[7] but the linkman most relevant to our purposes is Edward Irving.

---

[3] Campbell to T. Erskine, 18 June 1847, Campbell, *Memorials*, i. 207–8.

[4] Campbell to Miss Macnabb, 21 Feb. 1850, ibid., i. 218–20.

[5] Campbell to his brother, 5 July 1850 and 23 Feb. 1852, ibid., i. 220–1, 236–7. See Campbell to his son, 5 Nov. 1867, ibid., ii. 186–8, where he praises Chalmers for having seen that moral factors are mightier in economic affairs than physical ones, and regrets the tendency of recent social scientists to overrate the latter. Still, he believed that *laissez-faire* should go so far and no further, and accepted Factory Acts while deploring the selfishness of trade unions.

[6] John B. Logan, 'Thomas Erskine of Linlathen, lay theologian of the "Inner Light" ', *Scottish Journal of Theology*, 37 (1984), 23–40; Hanna, *Life of Chalmers*, iii. 247. Erskine was a lifelong friend of Chalmers, despite these serious disagreements, and greatly influenced Maurice. On Erskine's theology in respect to eternal punishment see Rowell, *Hell and the Victorians*, pp. 70–5.

[7] J. P. Newell, 'The other Christian Socialist: Alexander John Scott', *The Heythrop Journal*, 24 (1983), 278–89.

Irving has been presented as an extreme evangelical, his apocalyptic fantasies and speech in tongues being utterly opposed to the natural law philosophy of Wilberforce, Chalmers, and their kind.[8] But, as antithesis leads on to synthesis, Irving was also a forerunner of the Broad Church movement away from evangelicalism. Certainly he and Campbell seem to have played important roles in each other's development. They met in May 1828 when Irving visited Edinburgh to preach on the Apocalypse, and Campbell records the following conversation:

IRVING: I do not know how it is, but I see that the Reformers had a far deeper sense of sin than we have.
CAMPBELL: This is because they had a deeper sense of the love of God as embracing the sinner, and as what the Atonement reveals.
IRVING: [after pacing back and forward for a good while]: I believe you are right, and that you were sent to show me this.

'From that time', Campbell reflected, Irving 'preached the Atonement as for all, and the faith of the love manifested in it as the great power to awaken the deep sense of sin, as well as to quicken love to Him who first loved us.'[9] Partly as a result, Irving too was deposed from the Church of Scotland by the Presbytery of Annan in March 1833, and died disconsolate and demoralized in 1834. His mature message, which can be found in the *Morning Watch* (1829–33), surrounded by wild stuff on prophecy and the apocalypse, was that man must hold to the humanity, the personality, the incarnation of Christ, who bore our 'common human nature'. It was a deliberate challenge to 'the stock-jobbing theology of the religious world,—that God wanted punishment, and an infinite amount of it; which Christ gave for so many'.[10]

Campbell and Irving remained close friends to the end, but except on the questions of assurance and Atonement they remained far apart doctrinally. The real 'discoverer' of Irving was the Cambridge Apostle F. D. Maurice, who shared his fascination with the Apocalypse. Maurice loved and revered Irving as 'the man who felt most deeply and inwardly the truth of the old Puritan theocracy', though too little appreciated by his fellow sufferers, Scott, Erskine, and Campbell:[11]

He was utterly and purely a theologian; God was all in all to him. From God he must begin. And how to establish a relation between God and mankind on the Calvinistic hypothesis, which he nobly determined not to abandon for any Arminian or Semi-Arminian compromises; this was the problem in trying to solve

---

[8] See above, pp. 10–12, 131–2.
[9] Oliphant, *Life of Irving*, ii. 25–7; Campbell, *Memorials*, i. 50–4.
[10] [E. Irving], 'On the humanity of Christ', *The Morning Watch*, 1 (1829), 421–45.
[11] F. D. Maurice to J. M. Ludlow, 28 May 1862, Ludlow Papers, Cambridge University Library MSS, ADD. 7348/8/135, quoted in Maurice, *Life of Maurice*, ii. 403–4.

which he gave up his fame and his life, . . . the most vigorous Protestant against the religion of the newspapers and Exeter Hall that has appeared in our generation.[12]

Irving, according to Maurice, in the period of his greatest influence (1830–4) had insisted that evil had tempted Christ in just the same way that it tempted all the sons of Adam—which was a form of Manichaeanism, as distinct from the moderate evangelical belief in God's superintendence of both good and evil. The Westminster Confession, that cornerstone of the Scotch theology against which Irving had reacted, implied that

the race stood in Adam, and had fallen in Adam; then a scheme of salvation, of which the Incarnation formed a step, was necessary to rescue certain persons from the consequences of the fall. Mr. Irving had begun to regard the Incarnation not merely as a means to a certain end, in which some men were interested, but as the very manifestation of God to men—as the link between the creature and the Creator. But what could the Incarnation on his previous hypothesis be but the descent into a radically *evil* nature? Some of Mr. Irving's Scotch opponents perceived the difficulty, and resorted to the hypothesis of our Lord's taking the unfallen nature of Adam. He regarded the suggestion as a miserable subterfuge, which made the relation between Christ and actual men an utterly unreal one.

Adam, argued Maurice, fell because he tried to be 'something in himself', something other than God. Since he never possessed a nature independent of God, it cannot really be said that the race ever *stood* in Adam, as it clearly *does stand* in Christ. The latter *had* truly felt the temptations of evil on our behalf, and had redeemed us all because he, unlike Adam, never lost trust in God or tried to stand alone. The essence of Maurice's Christology (like Irving's) was that the Son possessed 'perfect humanity' and was not a mere puppet of the Father's 'scheme'.[13]

We see here a sort of dialectical progression at work. The Arminian bias of moderate evangelical orthodoxy, in which God *controls* both good and evil, led to an Irvingite reaction in which evil was seen as an independent force—a force so powerful, indeed, that one could not conceive of permanent natural laws controlling the universe. In turn Maurice seized on this idea to argue that, in defeating evil, Christ was uniting his will with the Father's: 'The entire union of the Father with the Son is what we have to assert if we would overcome the notion of a Son who changes the Father's will.'[14] In this sense Maurice's feet were firmly in the early nineteenth century, however much he heralded the mid-century movement away from it.

---

[12] Maurice to Ludlow, 30 May 1862, Ludlow Papers, ADD. 7348/8/136, quoted in Maurice, *Life of Maurice*, ii. 404–5.

[13] F. D. Maurice's letter appended to R. H. Hutton, 'The Incarnation and principles of evidence', *Tracts for Priests and People* (1861–2), ii. 65–6; Maurice, *Life of Maurice*, ii. 406–9.

[14] Maurice to D. J. Vaughan, 18 Sept. 1860, in Maurice, *Life of Maurice*, ii. 379.

Another interesting, but less important, link between Scotland and Cambridge was formed by the Vaughans, father and son. Edward Thomas Vaughan became a Fellow of Trinity College, Cambridge, in 1798, and was successively Vicar of All Saints and St Martin's in Leicester (1802–29). He and his large family—he had thirteen children—became close friends of Irving. According to the official biography, Irving's friends always credited Vaughan with an important role in Irving's theological development during the 1820s.[15] Drummond described him in 1826 as 'a great theologian' (though 'a horribly bad Political Economist').[16] He was certainly a fierce polemicist, an outspoken Calvinist, and an inveterate anti-Papist. His approach to charity—which no doubt offended Drummond—was that it should be unlimited but not indiscriminate (in other words, that it should squeeze the rich without releasing the most impoverished from the grip of penury), and he relished the prospect of the everlasting fiery punishment which awaited those who failed to clothe the naked and feed the hungry.[17] He had an overpowering sense of man's depravity ('your whole nature is corrupt: your body sensual, as that of the brutes'), and was assured that Christ died 'for' us, meaning 'as a substitute . . . in our room and stead', not merely 'for' our benefit.[18] Then in the mid-twenties, and with acknowledge-ments to Irving, he began to attack the complacency of the moderate evangelicals. His letter to the secretary of the Church Missionary Society complained that the establishment was full of 'faulty and filthy' Christians who failed to preach 'the message of a kingdom in which are damned ones as well as saved ones'. He seems to have moved in much the same spiritual direction as Drummond during the early to middle 1820s, and like him could not accept the CMS's vision of *man co-operating, as in a joint free partnership, with God, to do good; God working, and not working*. What was needful was a sense of most men's 'blindness', and of the invincibility of those chosen ones whom God had energized to rise in Christ.[19]

It is not clear how far Vaughan, who died in 1829, influenced his sons, David and Charles. The former was a Fellow of Trinity College Cambridge (1850–8) at the same time as his friends Westcott and Llewellyn Davies,

[15] Oliphant, *Life of Irving*, i. 218, ii. 60–1. Mrs Oliphant refers to a Mr W. Vaughan, but this is clearly a misprint. For identification see Campbell to his wife, 8 July 1860, Campbell, *Memorials*, i. 335; A. Temple Patterson, *Radical Leicester: A History of Leicester 1780–1850* (Leicester, 1954), 161–3.

[16] Drummond to Zachary Macaulay, 15 Nov. 1826, California, Huntington Library MSS, MY 218. Drummond may have been the obituarist in *The Morning Watch*, 1 (1829), 691, who described Vaughan as a theologian 'of the first order' and 'absolutely without a rival' in the Church of England.

[17] E. T. Vaughan, *Christian Benevolence Enforced: in a Sermon* (1802), 12–13, 28.

[18] E. T. Vaughan, *Blood Not Required: Or the Clergyman's Private Appeal to the Understanding and Conscience of his Hearers* (1819), 27, 41–7.

[19] E. T. Vaughan, *A Letter to the Rev. Edward Bickersteth, on the Lawfulness, Expediency, Conduct and Expectation of Missions* (Leicester, 1825), 14–21.

the latter became Headmaster of Harrow in 1844. David Vaughan's work on the Atonement (1859), much appreciated by Maurice, argued for 'the truth of an intercession that is still proceeding', as the only means of resisting 'the superstition of an ever-recurring sacrifice'.[20] Shortly after, he pointed out that the Pauline word most often used in describing Christ's work *for* man is not ἀντι but ὑπερ, which means *for our sake* or *on our behalf* and in no way implies *substitution*. Christ therefore is 'our natural and rightful Representative', undergoing hardships on our behalf, but in no sense our substitute.[21] By this time the *locus classicus* on these matters, Campbell's *The Nature of the Atonement, and its relation to Remission of Sins and Eternal Life* (Cambridge, 1856), had appeared, a book which went through five editions and had considerable influence, especially in Cambridge and in Scotland. One can indeed judge the success of the new ideas from the hysterical nature of the opposition. Thomas Archer, for example, was a Scotch United Presbyterian, very evangelical and utterly devoted to his friend, model, and former teacher Chalmers. For him the Atonement was part of God's plan, not merely a voluntary change of mind by man. What alarmed him most about the 'moral chloroform' prescribed by such as Campbell and Erskine was its appealing—even lovely—representation of Christ, which was all too likely to attract the minds of the young, yet contained 'not one word of sacrifice—not a word of atonement—not a word of bloodshed—of sacrificial martyrdom'.[22]

English Debates on the Atonement

Meanwhile, in England generally there had been little fuss about the Atonement before the 1850s. It had not figured prominently in the Tractarian controversy, unlike transubstantiation and baptismal regeneration, and Charles Edward Kennaway, Vicar of Campden, could write in 1849 that 'the faith of Christ crucified', besides being 'vehemently insisted on', was a subject of 'universal accord and tranquil acceptance'.[23] Kennaway did not attack the doctrine himself, but he did suggest, following

[20] D. J. Vaughan, *Three Sermons on the Atonement: With a Preface* (Cambridge, 1859), p. xvii; Maurice to Vaughan, 18 Sept. 1860, *Life of Maurice*, ii. 379.

[21] D. J. Vaughan, *Sermons on the Resurrection: With a Preface* (Cambridge, 1860), pp. xiii–xx. See also D. J. Vaughan, *Sermons on Sacrifice and Propitiation* (Cambridge, 1861), esp. 99–131.

[22] Thomas Archer, 'Philosophy of the Atonement: A lecture', *Lectures Delivered before the Young Men's Christian Association, in Exeter Hall, from November 1854, to February 1855* (1855), 147; *Memoir of Thomas Archer*, by John Macfarlane (1867), 7–9, 41.

[23] C. E. Kennaway, *Christ Crucified: or, the Incarnation and Atonement: An Ordination Sermon* (1849), 6–7. Unitarians, of course, protested against these evangelical views. See J. Martineau, *The Scheme of Vicarious Redemption Inconsistent with Itself, and with the Christian Idea of Salvation: A Lecture* (1839); W. Turner jun., *Remarks on the Commonly received Doctrine of Atonement and Sacrifice* (Newcastle upon Tyne, 1830).

Robert Wilberforce, that it had to be much more than an 'artifice of deliverance' and that its efficacy — 'nay, very existence' — was 'based on' and depended on the reality of the Incarnation. 'The incarnation was the root of the atonement, . . . the incarnation, and not the atonement, is . . . [the] fountain-centre of the redemption of man.' Christ had become the new representative of man's nature as Adam was formerly, and Christ had entire control over the material world, including questions of sickness and health.[24] In 1853 a future Archbishop of York delivered the first Bampton Lectures devoted to the Atonement since Veysies's rebuttal of Priestley in 1795. They were thoroughly academic in approach, entirely lacking in the brimstone of current controversy.[25] Soon after this, however, Maurice's notorious *Theological Essays* (1853) claimed that orthodox (by which he meant evangelical and patristic) versions of the Atonement 'outrage the conscience'. To those who argued that carnal beings like ourselves should not expect to understand such spiritual things, 'We can only answer, We prefer our carnal notion of justice to your spiritual one. We can forgive a fellow-creature a wrong done to us, without exacting an equivalent for it; we blame ourselves if we do not; we think we are offending against Christ's command, who said, "Be ye merciful as your Father in Heaven is merciful," if we do not.' Satisfaction to offended sovereignty was not what Maurice called justice, but still he did not go so far as to deny the principle of vicariousness; all he wished to do was render it joyful. Maurice was not out to deny the need for punishment, but in his squeamish way he wished to render the punishment painless.[26] *The Doctrine of Sacrifice deduced from the Scriptures* (Cambridge, 1854), also by Maurice, roused further evangelical uneasiness.[27]

Stirrings of discontent came to a head with Jowett's notes to an edition of the *Epistles of St Paul* in 1855. This year has been held to begin 'a new epoch' for British theology.[28] 'Can He impute to us', quipped Jowett, 'what we never did? Would He have punished us for what was not our fault? It is not the pride of human reason which suggests these questions, but the moral sense which He himself has implanted in the breast of each one

[24] Kennaway, *Christ Crucified*, pp. 17–22, 29–31; C. E. Kennaway, *Some Tones of the Voice of Prophecy and of the Voice of Miracle* (Oxford and London, 1867), 1–44. See also [Henry Rogers], *Selections from the Correspondence of R. E. H. Greyson* (1857), i. 295–310. Kennaway wanted urgent state action (including an Irish Poor Law) to deal with the Famine, which he refused to regard as a judgment. C. E. Kennaway, *Two Sermons: I. The Duty of Charity, Independent of State Measures of State Relief: II. The Doctrine of God's Visitations* (Brighton, 1847), 10–16, 33–51.
[25] W. Thomson, *The Atoning Work of Christ, Viewed in relation to some Current Theories*, 1853 Bampton Lectures (Oxford, 1853).
[26] F. D. Maurice, *Theological Essays* (Cambridge, 1853), 137–41.
[27] See, e.g., *The Evangelical Magazine, and Missionary Chronicle*, NS, 33 (1855), 21–7; *British and Foreign Evangelical Review*, 12 (1863), 7–8.
[28] *The Life of Robert Flint*, by Donald Macmillan (1914), 345–6.

of us.'[29] Predictably this called forth a vigorous evangelical restatement. Melvill pointed out that the ancient religions of the Old Testament had enjoyed a solemn day of expiation, when an atonement was made for the sins of the children of Israel. It was clearly possible to infer

from the character of the legal sacrifice that of the Christian. If you can once show that the sacrifices of the law typify the sacrifice of Christ, and that the sacrifices of the law were strictly propitiatory, it follows as an irresistible deduction—notwithstanding the cavils, objections, and theories of philosophising sects—that the Lamb of God died truly as a sin-offering, making, by His death, atonement for the world.[30]

Stowell backed him up by pointing out that the temporal law would become a laughing-stock if it failed to punish simply because a culprit expressed remorse, and argued that the proof of God's loving wisdom emerged from the way in which he had found it possible to forgive *without* undermining his own law.[31] There was also much anguished hostility to Jowett from within Oxford, with pamphlets by Charles Baring, Frederick Meyrick, and Edward Goulburn among others. 'Almost all *temporal* blessings are purchased at the expense of sorrow somewhere', commented the last of these, so it was merely cavilling to squirm at the idea of a lamb of sorrows.[32] This evangelical reaction reached a sophisticated climax in Mansel's Bampton Lectures of 1858, which tried to counter moral objections to sacrifice, whether Christ's or Isaac's, on the Butlerian grounds that divine morals are different from and unknowable by humans. But this attempt 'to defend orthodoxy on Kantian principles', which was how a contemporary saw it, merely 'breaks up the whole basis of revelation', for it was essential to the scheme that man should comprehend God's justice.[33] As Mansel left the matter it seemed that to God could be ascribed all wisdom and power, but not goodness as it was understood in the mortal world.[34]

[29] B. Jowett, *The Epistles of St. Paul to the Thessalonians, Galatians, Romans: With Critical Notes and Dissertations* (1855), ii. 468: 'the Christian [is] as one with Christ, . . . not in His death merely, but in all the stages of His existence'. Ibid., ii. 480. For Jowett's volume as a stimulus to 'liberal' thought see Mozley to R. W. Church, Jan. 1858, *Letters of the Rev. J. B. Mozley*, ed. Anne Mozley (1885), 238.

[30] Henry Melvill, 'The Day of Atonement: A sermon', *The Pulpit*, 69 (1856), 345.

[31] Stowell, 'The Atonement', ibid., pp. 222–3. See also Joseph B. Owen, 'The scripture and the catechism: A second sermon', ibid., p. 122.

[32] E. M. Goulburn, *The Goodness and Severity of God as Manifested in the Atonement: A Sermon* (Oxford, 1856), 35; C. Baring, *Christ's Death a Propitiatory Sacrifice: A Sermon* (Oxford, 1856); F. Meyrick, *God's Revelation and Man's Moral Sense considered in reference to the Sacrifice of the Cross: A Sermon* (Oxford, 1856). For further opposition to Jowett within Oxford see J. M. Prest, *Robert Scott and Benjamin Jowett* (supplement to *Balliol College Record*, 1966), 10–14.

[33] Mozley to Church, 13 Dec. 1858, *Letters of Mozley*, p. 240.

[34] H. L. Mansel, *The Limits of Religious Thought examined in Eight Lectures*, 1858 Bampton Lectures (Oxford, 1858), 108–13, 211–16. See Don Cupitt, 'Mansel's theory of regulative truth', *Journal of Theological Studies*, NS, 18 (1967), 105–6.

Meanwhile others were preparing to bend before Jowett's onslaught, if only because it was becoming obvious that bald restatements of the forensic position by popular preachers were driving many of the faithful into Socinianism and other heresies. It was not coincidental, perhaps, that in the middle fifties blame should be placed on the commercial terminology which was so frequently used to explain the mystery of the Atonement. It derived from Luther and ultimately from Anselm, and had been understandably popular in that first capitalist age. Heaven is God's merchandise. Sinners are debtors of God and ransomed to the Devil. A third party may redeem that ransom as well as the debtor himself. Such attitudes were deeply ingrained, and only scrutinized at all closely when they came under attack in the 1850s. As explicit a statement as any of what was very widely assumed can be found in Chalmers:

By the death of Christ a full penalty was rendered for sin. . . . He undertook to be surety for all who should believe, . . . the matter was closed, and the creditor now ceased from putting in any further claim. . . . In the covenanting of ordinary trade, a deficiency from our engagements brings us into debt; but should an able cautioner liquidate the whole, we, in him, may be said to have sustained the prosecution, and borne the damage, and are now clear of the weight of conscious debt—because in him we have made full and satisfactory payment. In our covenant with the Lawgiver of heaven and earth, a deficiency from our engagements brings us into guilt; but should a competent mediator take upon his own person the whole burden of its imputation and its penalty, we, in him, may be said to have been pursued even unto death which was its sentence, and should now feel clear of the weight of conscious guilt—because in him we have rendered a full atonement.[35]

Here the active role of man was stressed, but, as Chalmers put it elsewhere, the Atonement had been graciously planned 'in the upper counsels of heaven', as a means of disciplining man's 'alienated heart' and at the same time giving him a 'relish' for God's own character.[36] Orthodox believers explicitly stressed the 'non-limitation' of the Atonement, and attacked 'liberals' who would 'limit', not only man's personal liability for sin, but the spiritual efficacy of Christ's love. Quoting Chalmers, the *Evangelical Magazine* for 1856 insisted that 'in the offer of the gospel we must make no limitation whatever'.[37] Gethsemane was quite different from a heathen sacrifice, because it was not an attempt to bribe God and was based on

---

[35] T. Chalmers, *Lectures on the Epistle of Paul the Apostle to the Romans* (1837–42), ii. 96–7 [*Works*, xxiii. 92–3].

[36] T. Chalmers, 'The power of the Gospel to dissolve the enmity of the human heart against God', *The Atonement: Being Four Discourses* (1857), 35–44.

[37] *Evangelical Magazine*, NS, 34 (1856), 245–9, 293–312. For evangelical attacks on *Essays and Reviews* (1861) see B. E. Hardman, 'The Evangelical Party in the Church of England 1855–1865', Cambridge University Ph.D. (1964), 84–122.

love, not fear. The gestures of a husband for his wife are born of love, exuberance, and joy, and so entail no suffering, and the same would be true of our sacrifices to God if only we were not fallen. Many evangelicals thus cling defiantly to commercial terminology in expatiating on the 'scheme of divine philanthropy':[38]

The 'scheme of redemption', beset at every step with moral and philosophical difficulties to other men, seems to [the evangelical] the perfection . . . of Divine ingenuity. Its resemblance to a human commercial transaction strikes him as the most natural instead of the most offensive thing in the world.[39]

Froude had complained of the debt analogy in 1849,[40] but it was only after Jowett that apologists urgently began to shift their ground. In 1859 a former headmaster of Harrow complained of those who would reduce God 'to a party in an action at law', by making him out to be 'merely our *Creditor*' and us 'simply *debtors*'.[41] In 1856, mindful no doubt that the commercial law no longer took an instinctively creditor approach to debt, John Cotter MacDonnell argued that the monetary analogy was wholly inappropriate. The only biblical examples of a monetary contract being used to illuminate the relations between God and man were the Parables of the Unmerciful Servant and the Two Debtors, in both of which there was no mention of, or indeed room for, the question of mediation. The equation of sin with debt was a legitimate use of figurative language to convey an obscure truth, but was not to be taken literally. The truth conveyed is that each man feels guilty about the sin he has committed, and his state of mind can fairly be compared with that of an insolvent debtor.

Tell such a one that Christ has paid his debt; that on certain conditions he will be freely forgiven all; and no knowledge can be more real or practical than that which you impart, though you may still leave the actions of the dreaded creditor shrouded in mystery, and fail to explain either the origin of the debt or the ground of its remission.[42]

---

[38] *Evangelical Magazine*, NS, 33 (1855), 511.

[39] F. P. Cobbe, *Broken Lights: An Inquiry into the Present Condition and Future Prospects of Religious Faith* (1864), 37.

[40] James Froude, *The Nemesis of Faith* (1849), 69–71. The Scottish evangelical Congregationalist Ralph Wardlaw (1779–1853), on whom see above, pp. 86, 210, had apologized for the analogy with commercial justice when defending the doctrine of the Atonement against Erskine's criticisms. Wardlaw, *Two Essays: I. On the Assurance of Faith: II. On the Extent of the Atonement, and Universal Pardon* (Glasgow, 1830), 196–200.

[41] C. Wordsworth, 'On the doctrine of the Atonement', *Occasional Sermons, preached in Westminster Abbey* (7th series, 1859), 111.

[42] J. C. MacDonnell, *The Doctrine of the Atonement cleared from Popular Errors* (Dublin, 1856), 9–18.

Macdonnell developed these thoughts further in his 1857 Donnellan Lectures to the University of Dublin. Sacrificial images were, he conceded, employed in the Epistle to the Hebrews, but only because this was a mode which contemporaries would recognize, and they had no relevance to nineteenth-century man. Christianity was not 'a theology of blood and wounds', since 'vicariousness'—as was clear from Butler's *Analogy*, Part Two, chapter five—implied no more than that there are many cases, 'so familiar in God's natural government of the world', where a man will lose his own life or livelihood by interposing to save a friend from the natural consequences of folly or wickedness. The commercial analogy failed because it confused the substitution of *things*—one man's ten pounds was as good as, or equivalent to, another's—with the substitution of *acts*, where one is as good as another only if it produces a like effect, and this can only be so where the actor in some way represents those on whose behalf he is acting. Thus, while Christ's suffering and obedience were clearly coextensive in their effects with man's sin and guilt, it was not to be supposed that he literally 'endured pang for pang, just as in paying a debt, we must pay pound for pound'. Finally MacDonnell cited Chalmers's argument that, while natural religion on its own 'emits audibly a note of terror', the Atonement meets the cravings of the human heart for signs of God's mercy and love.[43] The future Archbishop Magee claimed that MacDonnell's lectures cleared the doctrine of 'all the incrustations that have grown on it', and had refuted Maurice and Jowett, not directly, but by attacking those false evangelical views which had for so long given the Socinians much of their purchase.[44]

Controversy was maintained in 1860 by Llewellyn Davies, who would have nothing to do with satisfaction or recompense. The Cross was all about love, God's forgiving and Christ's redeeming love, and was designed to make men love in return. 'God in Christ forgives and adopts men, that they may be His children.' In this sense Christ should be regarded as the son of man as well as the son of God.[45] Like Jowett, Davies roused predictable fury in evangelical circles. Thomas Nolan protested that vicarious sacrifice was 'the very essence of Christianity'; Charles Hebert went to great lengths in demonstrating exegetically that the doctrine was biblical; and the Congregationalist Henry Allon cited the 'forgiving cross' as able to do what, by itself, Christ's 'incarnate condescension and toilsome life' could *not* do—give men 'new spiritual

[43] J. C. MacDonnell, *The Doctrine of the Atonement deduced from Scripture, and Vindicated from Misrepresentations and Objections* (1858), 54–9, 165–70, 202–14. Chalmers, 'The power of the Gospel to dissolve enmity', op. cit., pp. 33–52.
[44] Magee to MacDonnell, 14 Sept. 1858, *The Life and Correspondence of William Connor Magee*, by J. C. MacDonnell (1896), i. 62–3.
[45] J. Llewellyn Davies, *The Word of Reconciliation: Two Sermons* (1860), pp. iii–vi.

life'.[46] If God was made to appear somewhat vindictive, it should be remembered that 'a wise father on earth has to punish in some shape', while 'weak parents, who fulfil not their own right threatenings, are not successful with their children'.[47]

But as with Jowett's critics, the most interesting responses came from those who saw the need to accommodate, such as the Cambridge New Testament scholars Hort and Westcott. Fenton Hort (1828–92) came from an evangelical background but fell under his friend Maurice's influence in the 1850s, and considered Campbell's *Nature of the Atonement* closer to his own views 'than any book I ever saw'.[48] Westcott (1825–1901) was close to Davies, who sent him a copy of his sermons in refutation of Hebert's *Atonement by Propitiation*.[49] What is interesting about the ruminations of these men is the way in which debate was turning away from lurid fantasies concerning God's wrath, to more analytical considerations of the nature of justice. Thus Westcott objected to analogies with human justice, of the type drawn by Melvill, since it was more concerned with the needs of society than with an individual's moral character. Divine justice required an extra dimension, which was the penitent's union with Christ.

If, then, we may represent suffering as the necessary consequence of sin, so that the sinner is in bondage, given over to the Prince of Evil, till his debt is paid, may we not represent to ourselves our Lord as taking humanity upon Him, and as man paying this debt—not as the debt of the individual, but as the debt of the nature which He assumed? . . . To my mind there is nothing in this which is against our instinctive notions of justice.[50]

Hort countered that current notions of human justice were inadequate even for their temporal purposes, since they were based on jural rather than moral values, and should be amended in the light of what we can comprehend of divine justice. The Bible clearly suggests that it is not unjust for an innocent to suffer and for the guilty to benefit thereby, and human life frequently affirms that this can occur.

[46] T. Nolan, *The Vicarious Sacrifice of Christ, the Only Foundation for the Sinner's Hope, the Only Motive to the Christian's Holiness* (1860), pp. v–vi; C. Hebert, *The Atonement by Propitiation: A Fragment of the Argument* (1860), 12–46; H. Allon, *Christ's Consecration and Ours* (1860), 25–6.

[47] C. Hebert, *Neology Not True, and Truth Not New: Three Short Treatises* (1861), 122.

[48] Hort to Revd Gerald Blunt, 18 and 26 Nov. 1855, *Life and Letters of Hort*, i. 314–16.

[49] J. Ll. Davies, *The Work of Christ: Or the World reconciled to God: Sermons, with a Preface on the Atonement Controversy* (1860).

[50] Westcott to Davies, 19 July 1860, *Life and Letters of Brooke Foss Westcott*, by A. Westcott (1903), i. 238–9; see Westcott to Hort, 6 Aug. 1860, ibid., i. 239–40.

But this is a very different thing from taking a human *explanation* or *interpretation* of the facts (as the 'forensic' 'plan of salvation') as itself a criterion of justice. That suffering may be a necessary consequence of sin, 'quite apart from free forgiveness', I most fully believe, and so I think does Davies. But surely the essence of the Atonement must consist in the forgiveness itself, and not in the abolition of such suffering; whether it involves at all any such abolition, I cannot yet make up my mind. Perhaps we may be too hasty in assuming an absolute necessity of absolutely proportional suffering. I confess I have no repugnance to the primitive doctrine of a ransom paid to Satan, though neither am I prepared to give full assent to it. But I can see no other possible form in which the doctrine of a ransom is at all tenable; anything is better than the notion of a ransom paid to *the Father*.[51]

If the standard response to the existence of suffering was to deny *either* God's amiableness *or* his power, Westcott and Hort were moving towards the latter position.[52] It took a form of Manichaeanism which moderate evangelicalism had avoided: Satan as independent force, to whom ransom was made by sin. On Westcott's other point, Hort agreed that the Atonement signified man's union with Christ, and deplored the popular and immoral notion of Christ substituting materially for man, but he also saw that this did not adequately answer the question as to the nature of 'satisfaction'.[53] In the same context Erskine claimed that 'man was created not to be tried but to be educated'.

The idea that we are in a state of trial or probation necessarily forces us to look on God as a Judge, and forces us also to be more occupied with the forgiveness of sins than with a deliverance from sinfulness. It is this idea which has given its character of substitution to the life and death of Christ, representing it as the ground on which God is justified in forgiving men, rather than as the actings of the root of the human tree, by which the sap is prepared for and propelled into the branches. It seems to me also that it is this idea which has made eternal punishment to be received as a principle in God's government. If it were believed that God had created us for education, . . . it would generally

---

[51] Hort to Westcott, 14 and 16 Aug. 1860, *Life and Letters of Hort*, i. 426–9.

[52] Dale developed the idea that, in punishing man for sin, God was simply (and to his great 'glory') obeying an 'eternal law', which existed 'antecedently to the Divine commands'. Dale, 'Expiatory theory of Atonement', *British Quarterly Review*, 46 (1867), 485–9. However, Dale seems to have retreated from this God/Law dualism in his *The Atonement: The Congregational Union Lecture for 1875* (1875), 370–2, where he claimed that God is not distinct from, but identical to, the Law.

[53] Hort to Westcott, 15 Oct. 1860, *Life and Letters of Hort*, i. 430. Erskine also believed with Maurice that Christ's work on earth must have had more point than 'a mere manifestation of the loving purpose of the Father, but must have accomplished something, and that was . . . the redemption of humanity by its purgation in its root'. Erskine to Bishop Alexander Ewing, Feb. 1861, *Letters of Thomas Erskine of Linlathen*, ed. William Hanna (Edinburgh, 1877), ii. 220–1.

be accepted without hesitation that the education must necessarily proceed in the next world.[54]

From this a Broad Church reassessment emerged, which maintained the need for a 'true' Atonement as necessary, not only to the redemption of sin, but also to give meaning to the Resurrection. Sacrifice was indeed 'vicarious', since ideas of 'self-atonement' were heathenish and futile, but it was also 'the acting out and the manifestation of an eternal sacrifice'; not a substitute for all other sacrifices, but a means of 'giving them the power and meaning which of themselves they could not have'.[55] If this was a brazen attempt to abolish the Cross and to keep it, the ruse helped to transform what had once been regarded as 'a manifestation of holy righteousness'[56] into a vehicle for holy love.[57]

If Hort is to be believed, the Atonement ceased to be quite such a subject of controversy in the late 1860s. In 1873 the Congregationalist Dale reflected that ordinary people would never be able to understand it properly until they recovered 'a far deeper sense of sin as sin', and of guilt as guilt, than they had at present. For him a 'larger truth' was the Incarnation, which older evangelicals had seen as 'a kind of after-thought in the mind of God, . . . contingent on human sin', but which for the younger generation 'lies deeper than the Atonement': 'it was God's eternal thought and purpose that the race should be one with Christ', and sin merely gave him an extra opportunity to show how much he loves us.[58] By now the Atonement was very widely seen as a supremely noble but essentially symbolic gesture by the son of God[59] — a case of willing self-sacrifice, an embrace of pain and humiliation in order to demonstrate his love for us — but *not* a literal redemption in the sight of God for the sins of man, since these — it was increasingly believed — could only be expiated by man himself. In current usage the word 'atone' came more and more to signify 'making amends for one's own misdeeds', while the authorized reference to Christ as him 'by whom we have now received

[54] Erskine to Ewing, 17 Aug. 1864, ibid., ii. 221–3. For a contemporary look at the influence of the four Scotsmen Campbell, Erskine, Ewing, and Norman Macleod, see D. J. Vaughan 'Scottish influence upon English theological thought', *Contemporary Review*, 32 (April–July 1878), 457–73.
[55] Hort to Bishop Harold Browne, 12 Nov. 1871, *Life and Letters of Hort*, ii. 157–8.
[56] R. Wardlaw, *Two Essays*, p. 190.
[57] See the summary in [C. E. Prichard], 'Modern views of the Atonement', *North British Review*, 46 (1867), 343–80.
[58] Hort to Browne, 12 Nov. 1871, loc. cit. R. W. Dale to J. Wilson, 4 July 1873, *Life of R. W. Dale of Birmingham*, by A. W. W. Dale (1898), 327. R. W. Dale, *The Old Evangelicalism and the New* (1889), 37–58.
[59] See C. C. J. Webb, *Studies in History of Natural Theology* (Oxford, 1915), 121, on how the Atonement came to be seen as an example of what Spencer and Comte had called 'altruism'.

the atonement' (Romans 5: 11) became, in the Revised Version of 1881, him 'through whom we have now received the reconciliation'.

It is not the case that limited liability legislation caused a major political confrontation. Apart from anything else the public was largely preoccupied with foreign affairs in 1855–6. It *is* the case that many people on both sides of the question became extremely agitated on the matter, and many more sensed that something momentous was occurring although they did not quite know what. Links between economic and theological thought mostly took place below the surface of consciousness, and usually have to be adduced, with caution, from linguistic parallels (such as Chalmers's description of the earth as a 'theatre of . . . competition').[60] The fact remains that the dominant mode of economic thought in the first half of the nineteenth century looked to religion as a powerful sanction, while religion itself, coloured as it was by moderate evangelicalism, resembled nothing so much as a type of spiritual capitalism in which, as Miss Cobbe put it, sinners acquired 'a saving interest in the Blood of Jesus'.[61] This being so, it seems fair to conclude that the virulent phase of *laissez-faire* capitalism (since about 1780) came to an end in 1856 when it was enacted that in future the blood of bankrupts should be sprinkled only, and not spilt.

[60] T. Chalmers, *Discourses on the Christian Revelation, Viewed in Connection with the Modern Astronomy* (Glasgow, 1817), 200 [*Works*, vii. 140].
[61] Cobbe, *Broken Lights*, pp. 36–7.

Incarnational Social Thought
in its Intellectual Context

Excitement performs in the moral world an office analogous to the attraction of gravitation in the physical world.

> Thomas Doubleday, *On Mundane Moral Government demonstrating its Analogy with the System of Material Government* (Edinburgh and London, 1852), 27

The theory of evolution shows that moral evil is rather failure on man's part to rise higher in the scale of being, and to respond to the true dignity of his nature, than a fall from a state of perfection which was his when he started upon his history.

> E. H. Askwith, 'Sin, and the need of atonement', *Essays on Some Theological Questions of the Day by Members of the University of Cambridge*, ed. H. B. Swete (1905), 177.

'Time! Time! Time!': the Common Context of Mid-Victorian Thought

So far we have considered incarnational theology entirely from an internalist point of view, as though it were merely a rebound off an earlier eschatology. But it was also one aspect of a mid-century doctrine of positivist liberalism whose main ethos, so far from being religious, was by implication secular. It may be helpful to consider this wider intellectual context, however sketchily, approaching it from scientific, philosophical, and literary angles in turn. In so doing, it will be necessary to rely extensively on the researches of the many scholars who have recently tackled this multi-faceted, mid-century phenomenon.

Irving has been presented as an extreme evangelical whose ideas led into the incarnationalist thought of the mid-century. Nevertheless, he could not break away from the earlier period's soteriological obsession with the Fall. In his view, Christ has been a 'sinful substance', perfectly holy no doubt, but only because he was acted on by the Holy Ghost indwelling in him and not inherently so. If it were not so, the doctrines of atonement, regeneration, and redemption would have been void and meaningless.[1] Such a view would have been quite out of keeping sixty years later, when Farrar felt able to expostulate to those who still regarded the Atonement as the 'key' to salvation: 'His Incarnation, His life, His example, as well as His death — should be "the key of the Evangelical position".'[2] Gone is the earlier obsession with sinfulness, Christ being regarded now as noble exemplar rather than primarily as saviour. The influence here of American Unitarians like Ralph Waldo Emerson, who made a highly successful tour of England in 1847–8, and William Ellery Channing, and to a lesser extent of the American Congregationalist Horace Bushnell,[3] is clearly important.

In the first half of the century incarnationalism had not usually taken a Christocentric form. For Joshua Watson and the Hackney Phalanx, as for the Tractarians, the Word was filtered through a corporate church which was seen as the key to salvation. For some extreme evangelicals it came immediately in the guise of divine inspiration. But after 1850, when the Incarnation actually began to displace the Atonement as the centrepiece of Anglican theology, the Word was attached more and more to the life of Jesus on earth. Christian Socialism was based on a belief that God had become *man* — had 'emptied himself' in first-century man — in order to teach us a code of everyday ethics.[4] It is therefore not surprising that from 1860 onwards historical reconstructions of the life of Jesus became enormously popular for the first time, became in fact 'a sort of vogue'.[5]

Up to a point this involved a shift of ground from natural theology to Revelation. In another sense it meant switching from a static natural theology based on 'evidences' to a more dynamic view of the natural world, God's wisdom, goodness, and power being detected more and more in 'development'. In other words, fascination with Jesus *as a man* was bound up with the new conceptions of the passage of time that accompanied mid-century scientific developments, especially in geology and biology.[6]

---

[1] 'The doctrine of the Incarnation opened in six sermons', in Edward Irving, *Sermons, Lectures, and Occasional Discourses* (1828), i. vi–vii and *passim*. See C. Gordon Strachan, *The Pentecostal Theology of Edward Irving* (1973), 25–52.

[2] Farrar in Hastings, *The Atonement*, p. 71. See ibid., pp. 83–6, for Farrar's dislike of the debt/credit view of the Atonement.

[3] For a sensitive account of Bushnell's 'Christocentric liberalism' and social gospel see Conrad Cherry, *Nature and Religious Imagination: From Edwards to Bushnell* (Philadelphia, 1980), 158–9.

[4] G. Kitson Clark, *Churchmen and the Condition of England 1832–1885: A Study in the Development of Social Ideas and Practice from the Old Regime to the Modern State* (1973), 290–341; David Newsome, 'The assault on mammon: Charles Gore and John Neville Figgis', *The Journal of Ecclesiastical History*, 17 (1966), 227–41.

[5] Daniel L. Pals, *The Victorian "Lives" of Jesus* (San Antonio, Texas, 1982), 3 and *passim* for a survey of later nineteenth-century devotional biography.

[6] For discussion of ideas of 'time' see Jerome Hamilton Buckley, *The Triumph of Time: A Study of the Victorian Concepts of Time, History, Progress, and Decadence*

It is not coincidental that 'forensic' or 'automatic' theories of the Atonement should have flourished from 1790 to 1850, when chemistry and mechanics dominated scientific debate. Nor is it coincidental that Scrope, who opposed evangelical social thought at every point—predictably, he supported limited liability—should have been among the early proponents of uniformitarianism in geology. 'The leading idea which is present in all our researches, and which accompanies every fresh observation, the sound of which to the ear of the student of Nature seems continually echoed from every part of her works, is—Time!—Time!—Time!', he wrote as early as 1827![7]

It took another quarter-century for most students of nature, and almost all plain men, to hear Scrope's march of time. Before about 1850 the world appeared to be locked in stasis, subject merely to cyclical fluctuation, and a marked discontinuity was assumed between life and the afterlife. Nature and grace being so obviously distinct, no one expected earth to partake of the blissfulness that is Heaven. Hence the continued purchase of natural theology, though, as we have seen, its practitioners were placed on the defensive by the gloomy nature of the times, and forced to emphasize the paradoxes of faith more than its evidences.[8] Designed to be a place of moral trial, the earth could be regarded as a mirror-image of Heaven, and suffering as a mark of God's mysterious regard, from which man should derive a masochistic uplift. It was a 'Hard Church' with a 'flogging theology', but at least it helped mankind to survive psychologically the blights of war, famine, and pestilence. It also complemented the prevailing scientific thought, for it is clear that 'vital religion' was the counterpart to vitalism in physiology, to catastrophism in geology, and to mechanistic dualism in natural philosophy generally. Unfortunately it was a religion which relied on what Hutton called 'fixed-skeleton truths' and fossil evidences, on 'the *inorganic* laws of human thought and action', and ignored 'the more delicate laws of growth and change discoverable in social and individual character'.[9]

(Cambridge, Mass. 1967), 1–65; Stephen Toulmin and June Goodfield, *The Discovery of Time* (1965), 232–44; J. W. Burrow, *Evolution and Society: A Study in Victorian Social Theory* (Cambridge, 1968), 98–100, 115–17, and *passim*.

[7] G. Poulett Scrope, *Memoir on the Geology of Central France: Including the Volcanic Formations of Auvergne, the Velay, and the Vivarais* (1827), 165, quoted in Rudwick, 'Poulett Scrope on the volcanoes of the Auvergne', op. cit., p. 205; see above, p. 154. See also R. Hooykaas, 'The principle of uniformity in geology, biology and theology', *Journal of the Transactions of the Victoria Institute or Philosophical Society of Great Britain*, 88 (1956), 101–16, 185–93.

[8] See above, pp. 182–3.

[9] Richard Holt Hutton, *Essays: Theological and Literary* (1871), i. 337–40. By 'Hard Church' Hutton meant the Broad Churchmen of his own day, but his description of its 'religion of common sense', originating in Paley—the theology, not the ethics—and based on Whately's logic and Mansel's metaphysics, also fits the sort of moderate evangelicalism we have been depicting.

In contrast to this static mental outlook, the mid-century saw a rapid spread of the idea of continuity. It showed itself, not only in the new sedimentary geology, but also in the way that history began to be written, in philology, ethnology, and jurisprudence, and in the fashion for anti-quarian and anthropological studies. Comtism, Marxism, *Spencerismus*, Social Darwinism, Gladstonian Liberalism — all these powerful currents of thought were fed by a new concept of the stream of time, and by a more Platonic, linear view of the future. 'Surely', reflected Hort, 'the continuity of life (or existence . . .) of a *person* depends directly on the operation of the Word, unless with the Manichaeans we set up two grounds of being.'[10]

There was, of course, a dark side to this development. It is not necessary to expatiate on the challenge posed to religious belief by Darwinian implications of randomness in natural selection. In many hands Social Darwinism encouraged conservative and authoritarian strains of thought: racism, imperialism, or a fondness for eugenics and social stratification. Within the religious tradition such trends are perhaps particularly notice-able among Unitarians, ironically in view of the fact that it was they who had kept alive a flicker of radical optimism during the overwhelmingly dominant Tory pessimism of the period before 1850. W. R. Greg, for example, objected to social reform as likely to interfere with the processes of natural selection, and looked to eugenics as a means of racial improve-ment. Having noticed that an unusually high proportion of his collection of old Irish skulls contained sutures along the frontal bone, he felt able to assure Darwin 'that the Irish remained *always* children, or assimilated more than we do to the lower animals'.[11]

In one sense the mid-century's dismissal of Hell and its relegation of the Cross marked a victory for Unitarian perspectives. 'Forty, fifty, or sixty years ago', declared Martineau in 1858, 'Unitarians stood absolutely and hopelessly alone, objects of general abhorrence and antipathy. Now the difficulty appears to be to find any person who really differs with us.'[12] Perhaps because of a temperamental need to feel that they were

---

[10] Hort to Maurice, 16 Nov. 1849, *Life and Letters of Hort*, i. 121. Technically Social Darwinism owed little to the Darwinian theory of evolution. See James Allen Rogers, 'Darwinism and Social Darwinism', *Journal of the History of Ideas*, 33 (1972), 265–80.

[11] W. R. Greg to Charles Darwin, 14 Mar. [?1874], Cambridge University Library, Darwin Papers, 90 fo. 130. On Greg's reactionary pessimism and eugenic theory see Peter Morton, *The Vital Science: Biology and the Literary Imagination, 1860–1900* (1984), 123–6.

[12] James Martineau, report of address to Hope Street Church, 31 Dec. 1858, J. Estlin Carpenter, *James Martineau Theologian and Teacher: A Study of His Life and Thought* (1905), 403. Martineau was successively Professor of Mental and Moral Philosophy and Political Economy (1840–57) and Professor of Mental, Moral, and Religious Philosophy (1857–69) at Manchester New College.

distinct, Unitarians derived little comfort from this development. As first Anglicans and then Nonconformists took up the Incarnation of Christ as their central tenet, Unitarians found that their own doctrine seemed less poweful than it had done. For them the Incarnation was true, 'not of Christ exclusively, but of man universally and God everlastingly'. Humanity was a 'susceptible organ of the divine', and Christ but one example of this fact.[13] By 1892 it had occurred to Martineau that the victory had been pyrrhic and the Unitarians themselves outflanked. As he commented ruefully,

The mission which had been consigned to us by our history is likely to pass to the Congregationalists in England and the Presbyterians in Scotland. Their escape from the old orthodox scheme is by a better path than ours. With us, insistence upon the simple Humanity of Christ has come to mean the *limitation of all Divineness* to the Father, leaving Man a mere item of creaturely existence under laws of Natural Necessity. With them the transfer of emphasis from the Atonement to the Incarnation means the retention of a Divine essence in Christ, as the Head and Type of Humanity in its realised Idea; so that Man and Life are lifted into kinship with God, instead of *what had been God* being reduced to the scale of mere Nature.

Unitarianism remained reasonable and true but had lost—Martineau thought irrevocably—its spirituality, whereas the 'liberalised orthodox' of other denominations, by bringing God down into everyday life, had retained their power to awaken piety, reverence, faith, devotion, and hopes of immortality.[14] Martineau, an 'Old Whig', represents the more pessimistic and conservative side of organicist social philosophy, not dissimilar to that of his fellow sectarians W. R. Greg and F. W. Newman.[15] The paradox is that Unitarians had been monists while all around them had been dualists; now that the fashion was for monism, they were reintroducing a form of dualism, Hort's 'two grounds of being', by distinguishing matter from spirit. Thus Martineau has been called 'the most able defender of the concept of dynamic causality in the third quarter of the nineteenth century',[16] and certainly he regarded man's 'active mind'

---

[13] Hector Macpherson, *A Century of Intellectual Development* (Edinburgh and London, 1907), 271–7.

[14] Martineau to the Revd Priestley Prime, 3 Jan. 1892, Drummond and Upton, *Life and Letters of James Martineau*, ii. 231. For a Unitarian view of the Atonement see James Martineau, 'Inconsistency of the scheme of Vicarious Redemption' (1839), and 'Mediatorial religion' (1856), *Studies of Christianity: a Series of Original Papers, now first collected, or new* (1858), 83–176.

[15] On Newman and the retreat from Unitarian radicalism see Corsi, 'Natural theology, the methodology of science and the question of species', University of Oxford D.Phil. (1980), 290–1.

[16] Roger Smith, 'Physiological psychology and the philosophy of nature', University of Cambridge Ph.D. (1970), 214–16.

as altogether separate from the matter which often imbues it with sensations. He argued from this that governments derive their authority from the fact that they represent a transcendent divinity, whose 'Universal Will' controls the entire cosmos. Spirit controls matter, and God's representatives on earth—that is, authoritarian states supported by 'national churches'—have the task of inculcating this spirit of higher morality. As Jacyna has put it, 'the distinction between spirit, the motive power, and matter, the moved, corresponded' in Martineau's opinion 'to that between the ruler and the ruled in society. Just as matter required force to attain order; so men needed authority to achieve a society.'[17]

So the notions of immanence and continuity had their dark sides, but in the heyday of incarnational thought (*c.*1860–80) it is proper to stress the predominantly optimistic and liberating aspects. If God was still working his purpose out, man's task was to work with him in eradicating evil and suffering, and to help build Maurice's 'organic Christian society', characterized by co-operation and brotherly love. Southwood Smith had battled for decades to convince conventional opinion that social reform would display and not undo God's providential handiwork, and now at last his views were gaining ground. Such social optimism found its apotheosis, perhaps, in a bizarrely Darwinistic work of enormous contemporary appeal, *Natural Law in the Spiritual World* (1883) by a young Scottish evangelical, Henry Drummond (1851–97), no relation of the homonymous Angel of the Irvingites, but a colleague of Moody and Sankey. His message was that the scientific principle of continuity extended from the physical universe to the spiritual world. Another writer to build a co-operative vision of society on the idea of continuity was A. R. Wallace, whose optimistic Social Darwinism exploited Combean psychology, Owenite socialism, Spencerean metaphysics, and Chambers's theory of mental development in celebrating man's ability to adapt to a rational world.[18] 'There were no absolutely bad men or women' in Wallace's opinion,[19] and the purpose of suffering was not to punish the sufferer but to arouse the Good Samaritan faculties in others. Injustice and pain assisted the development of human personality, pushing it towards a higher degree of spirituality after death.[20] As J. H. Brooke has put it,

---

[17] L. S. Jacyna, 'The physiology of mind, the unity of nature, and the moral order in Victorian thought', *British Journal for the History of Science*, 14 (1981), 122–3.

[18] John R. Durant, 'Scientific naturalism and social reform in the thought of Alfred Russel Wallace', *British Journal for the History of Science*, 12 (1979), 37–8. On Wallace's dislike of Malthus and *laissez-faire* economics see Roger Smith, 'Alfred Russel Wallace: philosophy of nature and man', ibid., 6 (1972–3), 177–99.

[19] Alfred Russel Wallace, *My Life: A Record of Events and Opinions* (1905), ii. 382–3.

[20] On Wallace's spiritualism see Frank Miller Turner, *Between Science and Religion: The Reaction to Scientific Naturalism in Late Victorian England* (New Haven and London, 1974), 68–103.

During the 1860s [Wallace] shifted the struggle for existence in human evolution away from competition between individuals towards competition between groups. He could then underline the survival value of co-operation rather than individual might. Whereas Darwin had appealed to the division of labour as a metaphor for evolutionary divergence, Wallace appealed to the same as a means of contrasting the individualism of the animal world with the 'mutual assistance' beneficial in human society. In contrast with blatant forms of social Darwinism, Wallace sought to minimise competition *within* a society.[21]

'Survival of the fittest' was therefore a concept which, if interpreted in moral terms, suited the progressive developmentalism of incarnational thought better than the rigours of competitive capitalism.

Although increasing specialization and the mathematical method were by this time lifting scientific research above the comprehension of ordinary educated laymen, the latter still looked eagerly to science for guidance and support. Technical treatises could still be devoured like novels, while social and political commentators still hoped to square their ideas with the latest scientific findings. In tracing the way in which such advances helped to condition (and may in part have been conditioned by) changing attitudes to time, it is necessary to consider not only geology and biology but chemistry, physiology, and physics, and to note how the earlier nineteenth century's dualistic assumptions came to be displaced by scientific uniformitarianism.

Natural science and the science of society

The origins of the Age of Atonement have been located in the 1780s and 1790s, in political disillusion and apprehensions of social catastrophe. Intellectually there was the challenge of *The Wealth of Nations* in 1776, and a still greater one in 1777 from *Disquisitions relating to Matter and Spirit* by the radical Joseph Priestley. Because Priestley ended up as a Unitarian, it is sometimes overlooked that he had earlier been a pre-millenarian, believing in special providences and the apocalypse, an imminent time of woe and tribulation prior to the millennium, as predicted in Matthew, 24: 6–14.[22] When the French Revolution burst

---

[21] J. H. Brooke, 'Photo-finish', *London Review of Books*, 7, No. 9 (1985), 12. A similar point is made in Bernard Semmel, *Imperialism and Social Reform: English Social-Imperial Thought 1895–1914* (1960), 29–31, and in Durant, 'Scientific naturalism and social reform', op. cit., pp. 41–2.

[22] Jack Fruchtman jun., 'The apocalyptic politics of Richard Price and Joseph Priestley: a study in late eighteenth-century English republican millennialism', *Transactions of the American Philosophical Society*, 73/4 (1983), 35–45. Unlike Priestley, Price was a post-millennialist, believing that the earth undergoes a process of 'continuous creation'. Ibid., p. 43.

out he heralded it as the 'great earthquake' foretold in Revelation.[23] He rejected completely the doctrines of the atonement and of the immortality of the soul, yet he believed in the resurrection of the body since this represented merely the reanimation and recomposition of man's sleeping dust. In other words, Priestley was a materialist and a monist, asserting what he liked to call 'the homogeneity of man', much like the pre-millenarians of a later generation, and it was this which rendered his ideas so shocking to the evangelical conscience.

Arnold Thackray has outlined some of the ways in which eighteenth-century evangelicals (including many Methodists) strove to maintain an 'unbridgeable divide between matter and spirit'. Before Priestley's time it was common for them to defend such dualism by postulating from Genesis the existence of an ethereal medium composed of fire, light, and air, but by the 1780s such theories were less easy to sustain.[24] Unable to maintain that a vital principle of life somehow animated matter, the faithful had instead to defend dualism by claiming that matter was itself utterly lifeless. In Thackray's words, 'the need to emphasize the inertness, grossness, and passivity of brute matter became increasingly urgent as the century progressed. . . . [For] if matter, beside extension, divisibility, mobility, and the *vis inertiae*, might also be taken to possess . . . such forces as those of gravity, etc., why might not thought and life themselves be merely a function of the complex organization of this remarkable— and still largely unknown—thing called matter?' This is why Priestley's *Disquisitions*, claiming that there was no such thing as solid matter, was widely seen, not only as a rebuttal of the matter/spirit dichotomy, but also as an extension of the author's necessarian philosophy and disbelief in immortality. In response, orthodox theologians of the 1790s and 1800s like William Jones and Bishop George Horne, as well as Scottish 'common sense' chemists like Chalmers's teacher, John Robison, strove anxiously to demonstrate that matter was made up of solid atoms.[25] Their attempts thereby to maintain a dualistic system led straight to John Dalton's *A New System of Chemical Philosophy* (1808–27). Its visual and realistic view of solid atoms, combining in a mechanical way according to weight, both fitted the 'vogue for numerical calculation' and, by promising to

[23] Joseph Priestley, *The Present State of Europe compared with Antient Prophecies: a Fast Sermon* (1794), 25–6.

[24] With a few notable exceptions (such as Whewell), scientists did not advocate the existence of ethereal fluids in the period *c.*1810–75, preferring mathematical and mechanical models instead. Thereafter ethers were taken up by those scientists who resorted to spiritualism in an attempt to reconcile religion and science. See G. N. Cantor, 'The theological significance of ethers', *Conceptions of Ether: Studies in the History of Ether Theories 1740–1900*, ed. G. N. Cantor and M. J. S. Hodge (Cambridge, 1981), 135–55.

[25] Arnold Thackray, *Atoms and Powers: An Essay on Newtonian Matter-Theory and the Development of Chemistry* (Cambridge, Mass., 1970), 146, 189–92, 244–52.

'reduce' chemistry to general laws 'of great simplicity', flattered the earlier nineteenth century's penchant for natural theology.[26] Dalton's insistence that combination was a mechanical process, thereby denying that there were forces of chemical affinity as such, has a parallel in utilitarian social thought, with its stress on consequentialism and associationism, and its denial of sympathy. As utility was held to be a measure of felicity, and gold-based currency of value, so the principle of combination according to proportions and equivalents served as an axiom of chemical mechanics.

Toward the middle of the nineteenth century the methods of Dalton's atomic chemistry began to be applied with equal success to organic as well as inorganic bodies, a development which greatly alarmed the orthodox. For since about 1800 the main battles over matter theory had been fought within medicine over the question of whether vitality was an independent principle or a function of organized matter.[27] More radical doctors, such as Thomas Charles Morgan (1783–1843), William Lawrence (1783–1867), and John Elliotson (1791–1868), the latter a leading phrenologist and later mesmerist, tended to follow Priestley in believing that mind was inseparable from the matter of the nervous system, and that the natural world was an organic whole with no basic discontinuity between living and non-living matter. Against them were ranged devout pluralists like John Abernethy (1764–1831) and Richard Saumarez (1764–1835) arguing for 'a series of basic interruptions in the fabric of the universe', and a view of nature as containing several sets of entities, each with its own aptitudes. Wohler's synthesis of urea in 1828 was perhaps the crucial step in discrediting such vitalist theories and demonstrating the link between organic and inorganic substances. If so, the year 1828 saw not only the beginnings of the rupture of Church and State, with the repeal of the Test and Corporation Acts, but also the scientific origins of the materialist philosophy which was to replace the old Church/State dualism.

Now the ideological overtones of this controversy are fairly obvious. The concomitant of natural pluralism was theological dualism and belief in the immortality of the soul. Dualists clearly used the existence of an other-worldly deity as a sanction to enforce obedience and morality in

---

[26] Ibid., pp. 256–69; Trevor H. Levere, 'The rich economy of nature: chemistry in the nineteenth century', *Nature and the Victorian Imagination*, ed. U. C. Knoepflmacher and G. B. Tennyson (Berkeley, Calif., 1977), 189–200.

[27] L. S. Jacyna, 'Immanence or transcendence: theories of life and organization in Britain, 1790–1835', *Isis*, 74 (1983), 311–29. I have relied heavily on Jacyna in this paragraph, as on Thackray in the last. Jacyna partly works through themes raised earlier in William F. Bynum, 'Time's noblest offspring: the problem of man in the British natural historical sciences, 1800–1863', University of Cambridge Ph.D. (1974), 118–64. See also June Goodfield–Toulmin, 'Some aspects of English physiology: 1780–1840', *Journal of the History of Biology*, 2 (1969), 283–320.

this world, while the monists' doctrine that all ideas could be traced to sensation and sensibility led to a form of ethical naturalism, clearly expatiated in Morgan's treatises of 1819 and 1822. In his view, the connectedness between men and animals proved that ethics must derive from the former's organic properties. Existing moral and legal systems were deficient precisely because of a failure to recognize that both society and men's minds are subject to laws of nature just as the physical world is. 'In the order of nature, God has given a precedency to this world over the other. . . . The motives for good conduct he has placed implicitly in the laws of nature; and if to strengthen their obligation he has deigned to add the sanction of future rewards and punishments, that sanction is still supplementary and secondary.'[28] Jacyna points out that Morgan's extreme *laissez-faire* economic and social views should be seen not as a bid for freedom against the God-exploiting tyranny of the Tories but as an alternative strategy, bourgeois rather than aristocratic, of social control.[29] And it is indeed the case that it was mainly Unitarians, militant Radicals, and phrenologists who raged against 'vitalism' and the basically Judaeo-Christian anthropology purveyed by the 'establishment'.

As we have seen,[30] the dominant groups in society invariably believed that healthy minds produce healthy bodies and that they do so by subduing the latter's inherently baser elements. There were, of course, dissenting outsiders, like the physician Southwood Smith and the devotional writer E. W. Grinfield. The latter edited and popularized the works of Tatham, that philosophical relativist who had desired that money ('the life-blood of the body politic') should flow abundantly.[31] As early as 1820, Grinfield claimed 'that life consists in organization', and also that it depends on 'a certain state and relation of the body towards the mind'.[32] By labouring to show that natural religion harmonizes with the revealed doctrine of the Resurrection, Grinfield proclaimed the difference between his own thought and that of moderate evangelicals, with their emphasis on the Atonement. Smith too believed that 'the mind is dependent on the body', and not vice versa. He was anxious to relate the mental and moral aspects of life to underlying physiological and neurological conditions, with the hope of finding a means for the 'spiritual and physical amelioration' of pain. Such approaches became commonplace after about 1850, as mind

[28] T. C. Morgan, *Sketches of the Philosophy of Life* (1818), 5–6; Morgan, *Sketches of the Philosophy of Morals* (1822), pp. xiii–xiv, 4–5, 235, partly quoted in Jacyna, 'Immanence or transcendence', op. cit., p. 320.

[29] Morgan, *Sketches of the Philosophy of Morals*, pp. 198, 269–70. The same point has been made with reference to Combe. See above, pp. 197–8.

[30] See above, p. 155. [31] See above, p. 128.

[32] E. W. Grinfield, *The Researches of Physiology, Illustrative of the Christian Doctrine of the Resurrection: A Discourse* (1820), 17.

came to be seen as a manifestation of matter.[33] Thus the society physician Henry Holland could write confidently in 1852 of 'that great law of continuity, which equally governs all mental and material phenomena', and of 'those . . . continuous relations, . . . those gradations of change, which bring extreme cases within common laws'.[34]

During the 1840s and 1850s, scientific naturalism made ever-increasing advances in many areas besides medicine. We have already noted the impact of uniformitarianism in geology with reference to Lyell and Scrope. The spread of evolutionary thought in biology between Robert Chambers's *Vestiges of the Natural History of Creation* (1844) and Darwin's *The Origin of Species* (1859) is too well known to require further comment. If Don Ospovat's thesis is correct, Darwin's basic ideas were formulated during 1838–44 and fitted the static conceptions of that period, being founded on perfect adaptation and the self-adjusting harmony of nature. Their final shape emerged alongside the new awareness of growth (or change) and development (or decay). It had something to do with the widespread realization that Britain was now in a state of industrial capitalism and was no longer an agrarian and aristocratic society. 'The idea of development that characterizes much of mid-nineteenth-century thought, both scientific and other, became a part of the theory of natural selection around 1857.'[35]

It could be argued that contemporaneous developments in natural philosophy (or physics) were of even greater moment than biology so far as non-scientific thought was concerned. The subject had emerged from a new conception of mechanical philosophy developed by Robison at Edinburgh around the turn of the century, and also from the use of mixed maths analysis at Cambridge in the 1820s. Fusion of these two schools, according to Crosbie Smith, led in the following decade to the 'unified physics' of J. D. Forbes (1809–68) and Whewell, which encompassed all

---

[33] T. Southwood Smith, *The Philosophy of Health: or, an Exposition of the Physiological and Sanitary Conditions Conducive to Longevity and Happiness* (1835; 11th edn, 1865), p. xi. See Pelling, *Cholera, Fever, and English Medicine*, pp. 7–9; Bruce Haley, *The Healthy Body and Victorian Culture* (Cambridge, Mass., 1978), esp. 3–119.

[34] Henry Holland, *Chapters on Mental Physiology* (1852), pp. viii, 301. See also [Thomas Laycock], 'Body and Mind', *Edinburgh Review*, 103 (1856), 423–52.

[35] Don Ospovat, *The Development of Darwin's Theory: Natural History, Natural Theology, and Natural Selection, 1838–1859* (Cambridge, 1981), 83–6, 231–3. The transition might be better termed as one from finance to industrial capitalism, but the underlying point stands. See Michael Ruse, 'Darwin's debt to philosophy: an examination of the influence of the philosophical ideas of John F. W. Herschel and William Whewell on the development of Charles Darwin's theory of evolution', *Studies in History and Philosophy of Science*, 6 (1975), 159–81, for the view that Darwin's theory was modelled on the Newtonian physics (especially astronomy) taught by Whewell and Herschel. On the development of ideas of 'continuous progression' in the 1850s see Peter J. Bowler, *Fossils and Progress: Paleontology and the Idea of Progressive Evolution in the Nineteenth Century* (New York, 1976), 93–115.

the empirical sciences such as chemistry, geology, mineralogy, electricity, and heat.[36] The dramatic breakthrough, however, and the one which directly challenged dualistic views of nature, came in the 1840s with the discovery of the conservation of energy (or first law of thermodynamics). According to the materialist John Tyndall many years later, that principle was 'of still wider grasp and more radical significance' than natural selection, for it 'binds nature fast in fate, to an extent not hitherto recognised'.[37] 'Every meal we eat, and every cup we drink, illustrates the mysterious control of Mind by Matter.'[38]

Conservation of energy has been described as a particularly notable example of 'simultaneous discovery' in science, having been formulated independently by Mayer (1842), Joule (1843), Colding (1843), and Helmholtz (1847), as well as being more or less grasped by at least eight other researchers at around the same time. Presumably, therefore, the idea had been lying 'close to the surface of scientific consciousness'.[39] Its essential point is the monistic one that the world of phenomena manifests only one force (energy), which is one and the same in all its different manifestations, and can be transformed (as from work to heat) but not created or destroyed. Until then it had been assumed that bodies remained at rest until acted on by an outside (transcendental) force; also that heat was caused by the presence in bodies of a weightless fluid (calorific), much as fever was thought to be caused by excitement of the blood and volcanoes by overflowing of lava. The discovery that heat was simply the effect of energy transferred from work, and that 'the grand agents of nature are by the Creator's fiat indestructible', suggested that the universe resembled not so much a Great Chain as a closed circuit. (Belief in 'connectedness' was reinforced by the 'rise' of zymotic pathology, or the science of the 'circulation of matter'—that is, recycling sewage, transforming waste matter 'from one beautiful and useful occupation to the next', which was a prominent feature of sanitary science in the 1850s and 1860s, espoused even by Christian Socialists such as Charles Kingsley.)[40]

The view that, 'humanly speaking, neither matter nor force can be created, and that an essential cause is unattainable—Causation, is the will,

---

[36] Crosbie Smith, ' "Mechanical philosophy" and the emergence of physics in Britain: 1800-1850', *Annals of Science*, 33 (1976), 3-29; Olson, *Scottish Philosophy and British Physics*, esp. pp. 157-61, 225-36.

[37] John Tyndall, 'The Belfast Address' (1874), *Fragments of Science: a Series of Detached Essays, Addresses, and Reviews* (6th edn, 1879), ii. 182.

[38] Ibid., ii. 192.

[39] Thomas S. Kuhn, *The Essential Tension: Selected Studies in Scientific Tradition and Change* (Chicago and London, 1977), 66-104. See also Yehuda Elkana, *The Discovery of the Conservation of Energy* (1974), 175-97.

[40] Christopher Hamlin, 'Providence and putrefaction: Victorian sanitarians and the natural theology of health and disease', *Victorian Studies*, 28 (1984-5), 381-411.

Creation, the act, of God', was presented in lectures to the London Institution in 1843 by William Grove, and published in 1846 in a treatise which went through six English editions as well as being translated into French and German.[41] The next important step was made by William Thomson, the future Lord Kelvin, who sought to reconcile the principle with its apparent antithesis—the dissipation of energy, which had been discovered by Sadi Carnot in the 1820s and was to become known as the second law of thermodynamics. David Wilson and Crosbie Smith have shown that theological considerations played an important part in Thomson's reconciliation, and so had a significant effect on the development of energy physics. Thomson's religious views derived from his time at Glasgow (where he was particularly influenced by John Pringle Nichol, the Professor of Astronomy) and at Cambridge in the 1840s, where he infiltrated the 'Cambridge network' and grew close to Whewell and Herschel especially. Like Whewell, whose Bridgewater Treatise greatly impressed him, Thomson had always believed in particular providences, miracles, and the apocalypse. The universe did show evidence of design, but only for a limited period, since all things are of finite duration and even the world itself must have an end. God works both through intermediaries and through natural laws, but his active and 'continual presence' is needed to sustain both, and having created the world he has to expend energy in order to sustain it. In Whewell's pre-thermodynamical formulation, 'perpetual change, perpetual progression, increase and diminution, appear to be the rules of the material world, and to prevail without exception'.[42] It was with this basic cosmogony that Thomson reflected on Joule's discoveries after about 1848, and which he employed to reconcile the apparently contradictory ideas of the conservation and dissipation of energy. The first and second laws of thermodynamics, as developed by Clausius in 1850, reassured Thomson that only God could destroy energy, so that the universe must be conserved along with it *unless* God should decide otherwise. The world *was* likely to prove transitory as Whewell had claimed, but not because of any inexorable natural laws. 2 Peter 3: 10–13 had spoken of the dissolution of the earth, as 'elements shall melt away with a fervent heat', to be followed by a new creation. In 1851, therefore, Thomson made the important claim that though heat *not* converted to useful work was 'irrevocably lost to man, and therefore "wasted"', at least it was not annihilated. The world is made up of three elements—matter, life, and energy—and the latter is created, preserved,

[41] W. R. Grove, *On the Correlation of Physical Forces: Being the Substance of a Course of Lectures* (1846), 50. I am grateful to Pietro Corsi for this reference.

[42] William Whewell, *Astronomy and General Physics Considered with Reference to Natural Theology*, Bridgewater Treatise No. 3 (1834), 203.

or dissipated according to the will of God, who had so far, in his mercy, exempted the universe from the 'heat death' predicted by the second law of thermodynamics.[43] In this sense, it was the anti-naturalistic elements of dualist thought, the philosophy of special rather than general providences, which had more in common with the monistic theories of the mid-century, just as it was Irvingism rather than Butlerism which anticipated and led on to incarnational theology.

Thomson's hope that thermodynamics might sustain belief in a providence that operated specially rather than through general laws suggests a religious interpretation of how physics was 'made'. A philosophical approach is equally plausible. It has been claimed that Herder's essay 'On the knowing and feeling of the human soul' (1778) was 'a turning point in the history of ideas' in that it marked a shift towards 'biologism' and away from the elementarism of Cartesian and Newtonian mechanics.[44] Following on from this Kuhn sees a partial explanation for the simultaneous discoveries of energy conservation in the influence of *Natürphilosophie*, which was at its peak on the Continent from about 1800 to 1825, the thought of Kant, Herder, Goethe, Novalis, Fichte, Oersted, and Schelling with its notion of the organism, a unifying principle for all natural phenomena in 'one great association'.[45] *Natürphilosophie* began to have a significant impact on thought in this country only after about 1845, among such thinkers as Lewes and Spencer, and we must now briefly review the philosophical movements (sometimes subsumed under the vague heading of 'Social Darwinism') which accompanied these scientific developments.

That the idea of energy conservation gained enormous currency among philosophers and the 'philosophically interested public'[46] was largely due to the influence of Herbert Spencer, a key figure in the mid-Victorian slide into unbelief. As a youth he had lived with his clerical uncle Thomas, and thus come to know in an extreme form the type of evangelical *laissez-faire* social thought that has been the subject of this book (though as a Nonconformist Thomas Spencer combined it with political radicalism).[47] Herbert got to know Combe well and showed an early and eager interest in phrenology and 'phreno-mesmerism'. His first book, *Social Statics* (1851), an extreme *laissez-faire* tract based on the idea of society as a biological organism, propagated a faculty psychology similar to that of

[43] Crosbie Smith, 'Natural philosophy and thermodynamics: William Thomson and "the dynamical theory of heat" ', *British Journal for the History of Science*, 9 (1976), 293–319; David B. Wilson, 'Kelvin's scientific realism: the theological context', *Philosophical Journal*, 11 (1974), 41–60.

[44] M. H. Abrams, *The Mirror and the Lamp: Romantic Theory and the Critical Tradition* (1953), 204.

[45] Kuhn, *The Essential Tension*, pp. 96–104.

[46] St G. Mivart, 'Force, energy and will', *The Nineteenth Century*, 3 (1878), 933–48.

[47] Burrow, *Evolution and Society*, pp. 183–4.

Combe. He attacked the utilitarians' emphasis on artificial rewards and punishments by the state, believing it was better to rely on man's innate moral sense. Public and private interests are in unison, and once they realize this men will act for the good of others. Spencer's faith in progress derived largely from his understanding of demography. We have seen how, despite the Famine, the Malthusian spectre ceased to haunt opinion in mid-century, and by the early 1850s Spencer had developed the view— 'a Godwinian revenge on Malthus', J. D. Y. Peel calls it—that population pressure is the 'proximate cause of progress. . . . It compelled men to . . . take to agriculture. . . . It forced men into the social state; made social organization inevitable; and has developed the social sentiments', which culminate in 'altruism'.[48] Thereafter, as R. M. Young has shown, Lewes's influence led Spencer to drop faculty psychology for associationism, and to develop a theory of evolution around a scheme of biological adaptation. *The Principles of Psychology* (1855), by elaborating ways in which such adaptations could occur, marks a final break with the epistemological dualism of the Locke tradition. In R. M. Young's words, 'Previous association psychologists had been concerned with the connections among mental phenomena. Natural scientists had concentrated on the connections between external phenomena. . . . Spencer's psychology was neither . . . [but rather] *"the continuous adjustment of internal relations to external relations"'*—meaning the processes of growth by which an organism becomes fitted for the ordinary functional activities of life, and the 'after-processes of adaptation' which fit it to special activities. By taking up a Lamarckian view of inherited acquired characteristics, Spencer was able to jump from biological to socio-cultural evolution, seeing both as part of one cosmic and necessary progression. Mental phenomena in this context could be regarded as 'incidents of the correspondence between the organism and its environment'.[49]

Spencer's conception of evolution by adaptation was centred on the idea that increasing specialization of function in developing societies (division of labour) mirrors the process whereby animal organisms develop from simple creatures of all one tissue to more advanced ones with organs adapted to separate functions: in von Baer's phrase, 'the development of every organism is a change from homogeneity to heterogeneity'. Change

[48] H. Spencer, 'A theory of population, deduced from the general law of animal fertility' (1852), 35; J. D. Y. Peel, *Herbert Spencer: The Evolution of a Sociologist* (1971), 139.

[49] Robert M. Young, *Mind, Brain and Adaptation in the Nineteenth Century: Cerebral Localization and its Biological Context from Gall to Ferrier* (Oxford, 1970), 150–72. H. Spencer, *The Principles of Psychology* (1855), 374–5, 584. See also C. U. M. Smith, 'Herbert Spencer's epigenetic epistemology', *Studies in History and Philosophy of Science*, 14 (1983), 1–22; Adrian Desmond, *Archetypes and Ancestors, Palaeontology in Victorian London 1850–1875* (1980), 95–101.

means differentiation, specialization, complexity, variety, heterogeneity: '*Every active force produces more than one change—every cause produces more than one effect*', whether in societies, individuals, or organisms.[50] But quite *why* evolution means differentiation Spencer could not say until 'there came the perception that the condition of homogeneity is an unstable condition . . . [and] the theorem passed into the region of physical science'. Thanks to the law of energy conservation, in other words, evolution became 'a question of causes and effects reduced to their simple forms—a question of molar and molecular forces and energies—a question of the never-ending re-distribution of matter and motion'.[51]

All this came together in the *First Principles* (1862), an extravaganza on the theme of Persistence of Force (energy conservation) which contained a great deal of what one commentator has called 'philosophy run riot'. In it the Unknowable is presented as a surrogate deity, the cause of all phenomenal existence. Scientific concepts like force, space, and time are mere representations of a reality we cannot understand, and just as heat, light, and motion are inter-transferable according to the 'law of correlation and equivalents', so they can also interchange with mental forces (sensations, emotions, thoughts) and social ones. Force, in other words, is an actual multiform substance, the basic element of consciousness, a 'relative reality indicating to us an Absolute Reality by which it is immediately produced'.[52]

Leaving Spencer's idiosyncratic metaphysics to one side, a simple and obvious point may be made. In the first half of the nineteenth century, moderate evangelicals—and natural theologians generally—would have agreed with J. H. Newman that 'the whole framework of Nature' was 'a tissue of antecedents and consequents',[53] 'predictable consequence' being taken as a sign of successful moral government over an ordered and essentially static world; now, however, the mentality of 'cause and effect' was being written into the idea of development, and taking in organic transformations from one *form* of activity (force) to another. Thus Alexander Bain, like Spencer a keen phrenologist in his youth, declared that 'the Conservation, Persistence, Correlation, Convertibility, Equivalence, Indestructibility of *Force* [i.e. Energy] is the highest expression of Cause and Effect. . . . Transferred energy is . . . the final and sufficing

---

[50] 'Progress: its law and cause' (1857), in Herbert Spencer, *Essays: Scientific, Political, and Speculative* (1858-74), i. 29. Compare Mill's view that as men's characters progress they will develop variety and eccentricity.

[51] Herbert Spencer, *An Autobiography* (1904), ii. 12; Peel, *Herbert Spencer*, p. 140.

[52] Herbert Spencer, *First Principles* (1862), *passim*. See Erwin N. Hiebert, 'The uses and abuses of thermodynamics in religion', *Daedalus: Journal of the American Academy of Arts and Sciences*, 95 (1966), 1054-6. Peel, *Herbert Spencer*, p. 140.

[53] J. H. Newman, 'The Tamworth Reading Room' (1841), *Discussions and Arguments on Various Subjects* (1872), 299.

explanation of all change, and the only explanation.'[54] And Tyndall heralded the conservation of energy as 'exacting from every antecedent its equivalent consequent, from every consequent its equivalent antecedent, and bringing vital as well as physical phenomena under the dominion of that [natural] law of causal connection'.[55] In this sense it did more to break down the division between mind and matter than even evolution, which was conceived entirely within the organic realm. As a result, the will came to be regarded, no longer in terms of faculty psychology, but as a series of transient volitions, each one representing expenditure of acquired energy.[56]

Literary Approaches to Incarnational Religion

Turning from the scientific to the literary ramifications of incarnational religion, we find that there are some suggestive links with the scientific developments just described. These have been subtly explored in recent years, notably by Gillian Beer in her brilliant study of 'evolutionary narrative' in fiction, and by Peter Morton in an interesting work on biology and the literary imagination.

An incarnational tradition had been maintained throughout the Age of Atonement by Coleridge, Wordsworth, Blake, and Carlyle. Their romantic opposition to Judaeo-Christian orthodoxy included a strong sense of childhood as innocent and pre-lapsarian,[57] at a time when most juvenile fiction was in the Mrs Trimmer/Mrs Sherwood/*Fairchild Family* mould—morally didactic, evangelical, and redemptive. After 1850 the romantic tradition was increasingly seen as normative, albeit in a somewhat debased, nostalgic form. 1862 has been seen as a seminal date in this development so far as children's literature is concerned, for within a few months of each other the Revd Charles Kingsley started on *The Water Babies*, the Revd C. L. Dodgson on *Alice's Adventures in Wonderland*, and the Revd George MacDonald on his immensely popular series of faerie fantasies for children.[58] MacDonald (1824–1905) was the Scotsman who inspired the 'Kailyard School', and whose novels were credited with helping to dispel the sway of Calvinism north of the border. A close friend of Maurice, A. J. Scott, and Octavia Hill, MacDonald purveyed an Erskinian eschatology, and in particular a view of death,

---

[54] Alexander Bain, *Logic* (1870), ii. 20–30.

[55] Tyndall, 'Belfast Address', op. cit., p. 182.

[56] Haley, *The Healthy Body and Victorian Culture*, pp. 41–2.

[57] Peter Coveney, *The Image of Childhood: The Individual and Society: a Study of the Theme in English Literature* (revised edn, Harmondsworth, Middlesex, 1967), 32–4, 192–3.

[58] Stephen Prickett, *Victorian Fantasy* (Hassocks, Sussex, 1979), 150–97.

not as the culmination of some evil disease, but the beginning of new life, wholesome and desirable. Thus his many death-bed scenes have none of the morbid sentimentality of evangelical fiction. Like Maurice he enjoyed a passionate trust in eternal help and forgiveness: God would make naughty boys and girls good, not wait until they are.[59] Like Maurice he was said to have provided ' a refuge from the storm' for many Scotsmen distressed by Calvinistic terrors. In his fantasies for children MacDonald developed an alternative world of faerie, working up Scotland's fast-disappearing myths and folk lore. Like his Pre-Raphaelite friends, he found an escape from cold rationalism in lands of enchantment and days of yore. He once said that 'fatherhood must be at the core of the universe', and like his literary successors C. S. Lewis and J. R. R. Tolkien his make-believe purveys 'the sacramental sequel to the Incarnation, for the Incarnation lies in the heart and soul of their creative genius'.[60] Because of his huge and loving acquaintance—he lived much of his life in London—MacDonald occupies an important place in the metropolitan culture of the sixties and seventies. One of his friends was Robert Browning, whose own theology of optimism was based on the existence of Absolute Good and its revelation in all human events. It may be the case that his 'impassioned conviction of a God-intoxicated man' was an 'impossible phantom', nothing more than 'a love that is ignorant of its subject', a 'blind impulse', and 'a moral consciousness that does not know the law'. Nevertheless, Browning's view of Hell as merely 'the consciousness of opportunities neglected, arrested growth', undoubtedly inspired a great many among the intelligentsia including Llewellyn Davies.[61]

In considering the switch from evangelicalism to Broad Churchmanship, however, it may be more interesting to consider, not committed incarnationalists like MacDonald and Browning, but two writers who, because of their personal backgrounds, exemplify some of the ambiguities involved in the transition: Charles Dickens and George Eliot.

Dennis Walder has shown how Dickens's persistent assaults on evangelicalism, in the guise of a Pardiggle, Chadband, or Pecksniff, were directed at 'something with which he is intimately connected'. As was the case with the agnostic George Eliot, Dickens's attacks came emotionally

[59] See Wolff, *Gains and Losses*, pp. 299–307, for the portrait of Maurice in MacDonald's novel *David Elginbrod* (1863); Robert Lee Wolff, *The Golden Key: A Study of the Fiction of George MacDonald* (New Haven, 1961), 180–265; Thomas G. Selby, *The Theology of Modern Fiction* (1896), 148–54; Annie Matheson in *Dictionary of National Biography*.

[60] Marion Lochhead, *The Renaissance of Wonder in Children's Literature* (Edinburgh, 1977), 5.

[61] Henry Jones, *Browning as a Philosophical and Religious Teacher* (Glasgow, 1891), 103, 123, 341, and *passim*.

from inside rather than outside the tradition. Walder considers various aspects of his thought in the course of a shifting relationship with evangelicalism: the 'innocent fall' in *Pickwick Papers* (1836–7), charity in *Oliver Twist* (1837–9), consoling death in *The Old Curiosity Shop* (1840–1), anti-popery in *Barnaby Rudge* (1841), conversion in *Martin Chuzzlewit* (1843–4), *A Christmas Carol* (1843), and *Dombey and Son* (1846–8), and the 'social gospel' in *David Copperfield* (1849–50) and *Bleak House* (1852–3). Walder does full justice to the influence of Channing and Emerson in Dickens's advance 'from a sense of individual to a sense of social sin'.[62] The most 'profound' and 'original expression of the religious aspect of Dickens's imagination' is held to be *Little Dorrit*, however, written in 1855–7, and having for its pervasive backdrop the theme of imprisonment for debt in London's notorious Marshalsea prison. 'In *Little Dorrit* the obsessive centre would seem to lie in the contrasting views of Mrs Clennam's imprisoning Old Testament ethos and Little Dorrit's liberating New Testament spirit. . . . Dickens specified in his notes . . . his intention to set "darkness and vengeance against the New Testament".' The hero Arthur Clennan is said to change in the course of the novel, most climactically while in the Marshalsea, in a way that reflects Dickens's own spiritual peregrination at that time. It is a movement from gloomy evangelicalism towards an affirmation of New Testament values and a belief in 'progressive revelation', similar to that which would soon be put forward by Colenso and Jowett.

Yet it is not as simple as this, for in some respects *Little Dorrit* represents, as Walder also points out, a retreat from the social gospel which he had been developing in *Copperfield* and *Bleak House*, where wickedness had been attributed at least in part to circumstance and environment. While evangelicalism is distinctly repudiated in the shape of Mrs Clennam's repressiveness, the idea of original sin is as clearly embodied in the character of Rigaud. In other respects, too, the novel catches the ethos of Atonement very carefully. Thus the process of Arthur Clennam's redemption begins while he is in the Marshalsea, whither he is sent having 'caught' the fever of speculation from Pancks, who himself had caught it from Casby's tenants in Bleeding Heart Yard, who had themselves had direct contact with the financial malignant himself, Merdle. But it is also the case that Arthur goes to prison partly of his own free will, as an act of 'real atonement' (bk. II, ch. 26). 'In doing so', writes Walder, 'he becomes a scapegoat for the sins of society; but he is not Christ, his

[62] Dennis Walder, *Dickens and Religion* (1981), 18, 114–16, 144. On Dickens and evangelicalism see Norris Pope, *Dickens and Charity* (1978), 13–41. On Dickens and 'idle Mammonism' in the 'Scrip Age' see Barry V. Qualls, *The Secular Pilgrims of Victorian Fiction: The Novel as Book of Life* (Cambridge, 1982), 125–6.

experience reflects Dickens's continuing belief in the idea that a profound crisis may precipitate a change of heart, bringing a new, redeemed vision.'[63] *Little Dorrit* shows the redemptive powers of mercy and forgiveness, as personified in Amy Dorrit, but its metaphysical dialectic between imprisoning darkness and heavenly light actually returns Dickens to a more evangelical outlook, or at least to the moderate evangelical's joy in the expulsive power of a new affection. William Myers points out that while Dickens considers the forgiveness of debts to be a virtue in creditors, he is far from thinking that debtors have any human right to be forgiven.[64] Similarly, N. N. Feltes shows how in *Little Dorrit* Dickens 'contrasts the "blind" and "anonymous" ambiance of "one of England's world-famed capitalists and merchant-princes" [Merdle] to the bond of mutual personal responsibility which links Arthur Clennam and Daniel Doyce'. Clennam's determination to take unlimited responsibility, to his last shilling and acre—' "I must work out as much of my fault—or crime—as is susceptible of being worked out, in the rest of my days" ' (bk. II, ch. 26)—is presented as a case of supreme nobility, and a contrast to Amy's 'tainted' feeling that Mr Dorrit should not have to pay his debts 'in life and money both'. 'In the persons it portrays and in its plot,' concludes Feltes, '*Little Dorrit* explores the meanings and the limits of human liability.' Merdle's is thus an earlier form of capitalism than that represented by Melmotte in Trollope's *The Way We Live Now* (1874–5). The latter, according to Feltes, typifies the era of the limited company, when liability was no longer 'even "a term in a contract" ', and as a consequence the novel's central theme is 'the radical isolation or separateness of most of the characters'.[65]

So, for all his social anger and compassion, Dickens retained a talent for expressing what Myers terms 'the simplifications of energetic belief', which was itself 'essentially bourgeois'. A more successful and self-conscious attempt to develop an organic–idealist philosophy through literature came from George Eliot, of whom it has recently been said that 'Incarnation summarises all that is most difficult for her and rewarding to her as a novelist.'[66] Margot Waddell has shown how her close associates— Charles Bray, George Combe, Robert Chambers, Herbert Spencer, and G. H. Lewes—all helped to provide an alternative to the evangelicalism of her upbringing, and to implant the germ of scientific naturalism—'the

---

[63] Walder, *Dickens and Religion*, pp. 170–95.

[64] William Myers, 'The radicalism of "Little Dorritt" ', *Literature and Politics in the Nineteenth Century: Essays*, ed. John Lucas (1971), 77–104.

[65] N. N. Feltes, 'Community and the limits of liability in two mid-Victorian novels', *Victorian Studies* 17 (1973–4), 355–69. See also Tony Tanner, 'Trollope's *The Way We Live Now*: its modern significance', *Critical Quarterly*, 9 (1967), 264–5.

[66] Gillian Beer, *Darwin's Plots: Evolutionary Narrative in Darwin, George Eliot and Nineteenth-Century Fiction* (1983), 154.

idea of a uniformity of nature as applied to the organic, the psychological and the social world'.[67] Belief in undeviating law and invariability of sequence, in the moral as well as the material world, gradually supplanted her earlier dualistic loyalties, based on a mind/body distinction. As Waddell succinctly explains, phrenologists and 'associationists'—that is, those who subscribed to the principle of association on which utilitarian philosophy was based—were both attempting to incorporate the study of human nature into their conception of scientific naturalism. Associationists did this in a somewhat abstract way, basing their human analogies on physics and chemistry, and deducing the nature of particular men from laws of mind in general (and a rather disembodied mind at that). Phrenologists, however, based their analogies on physiology and biology, seeing man as an organism and mind as a function of it. To cut (and sell) Waddell's long and subtle story short, Combe and Bray began the phrenological inquiries which Chambers then linked to evolutionism, while Mill and Bain linked associationism to psychology but did not tie it in with biologic evolutionism. It was therefore left to Lewes and Spencer to synthesize all three elements into a philosophy which Eliot could express in her novels.[68] The most explicitly political of these is *Felix Holt* (1866), where the hero's vision of harmony, consensus, 'gradual moral development and social progress' is counterpointed to the 'moral emptiness' of the Transome family, who are incapable of making connections between their own narrow concerns and the wider processes of existence: 'Mrs. Transome does not significantly change or grow. Her consciousness remains, as we found it—"absorbed by memories and prospects" and unable to integrate that actual past and possible future with a meaningful present.' Waddell sees as central George Eliot's 'doctrine of consequences', by which is meant a fairly mechanical process, not unlike that envisaged by J. S. Mill. Results of actions, judged according to pleasure and pain, lead persons to adapt their behaviour, and habitual behaviour in time determines the evolving character. Her nobler characters (Esther in the same novel) grow morally because they have a vision of continuity and outcome, whereas Mrs Transome has only 'superficial connectedness' or, in Eliot's own words, an 'habitual fear of consequences'.[69] The whole approach

---

[67] Margot Waddell, 'The idea of nature: George Eliot and her intellectual milieu', University of Cambridge Ph.D. (1976), 5–16, 47–52, and *passim*. On the way in which Eliot came to terms with her former 'enthusiastic' evangelicalism see U. C. Knoepflmacher, *Religious Humanism and the Victorian Novel: George Eliot, Walter Pater, and Samuel Butler* (Princeton, NJ, 1965), 24–71.

[68] Waddell, 'The idea of nature', p. 69. For an attempt to marry the utilitarian/ associationist position with evolutionism see Leslie Stephen, *The Science of Ethics* (1882), esp. 239–46, where he argues that altruism can be reconciled with egoism, and that our happiness is associated with the happiness of others.

[69] Waddell, 'The idea of nature', pp. 67–8, 155–64, 227, 234–6.

contrasts sharply with the static consequentialism of Bentham or the evangelicals, where change of heart comes suddenly through conversion rather than conservation, through expulsion rather than through peaceful adaptation and energetic growth.

Waddell believes that Eliot embodies not only a particular theory of nature but a particular class position. Less optimistic than Comte and Spencer, she remains, for all her progressivism, 'deeply attached to the traditions and customs embodied in an order [i.e. the feudal order of the Transomes] where the "nature of things"—and a possible basis for morality—was more straightforward and readily comprehensible'. Against this, Sally Shuttleworth has suggested that Eliot's use of organic metaphor is more 'exploratory and ambivalent', less 'conservative and constricting in its functions', than this implies. Where Waddell and Bernard Paris tend to regard Eliot's understanding of science in a somewhat static light, Shuttleworth prefers to stress the way in which her interests developed in line with science itself, moving from natural history or 'static organicism', through metabolic organic growth, to the 'dynamic organicism' of *Daniel Deronda* (1876), concerned as it is with such evolutionary themes as line, descent, race, and inheritance.[70] This critical disagreement serves to remind us of the ambiguities inherent in the mid-Victorian idea of development, and of the symbolic relationship between the thrill of 'progress' and the fear of 'degeneration'.

A Political Economy for 'Better, Wiser, and More Beautiful Beings'[71]

As we have seen, in the Age of Atonement, character—like virtue, or identity itself—was seen to be a precarious commodity. Acts of individual charity and personal commitment were recommended as a means of keeping one's character continually on the boil. But when Fanny claims that people are 'driven by their lives and characters' (*Little Dorrit*, bk. II. ch. 14), she is expressing a new sense that one's internal energy, one's steady state, can be as forceful a power as providence. The question to consider now is whether formal economic thought was affected by these wider intellectual developments.

Marginalist price theory is frequently regarded as analogous to Newtonian mechanics, with its virtual velocities and levers in equilibrium, but it has also been linked recently to the contemporary science of energetics. 'Neoclassical economic theory', writes Mirowski, 'was appropriated

---

[70] Ibid., pp. 231, 239–40, 248, 288; Bernard J. Paris, *Experiments in Life: George Eliot's Quest for Values* (Detroit, 1965), 72–90, 242–50, and *passim*. Sally Shuttleworth, *George Eliot and Nineteenth Century Science: The Make-Believe of a Beginning* (Cambridge, 1984), 26–8 and *passim*.

[71] For the quotation see Morton, *The Vital Science*, p. 53.

wholesale from mid-nineteenth century physics; utility was redefined so as to be identical with energy', and economic transactions were compared with energy transfers. Economists could not directly observe the marginal utility of traded goods for different persons, but they could nevertheless treat it mathematically, just as scientists treated unobservable potential energy.[72] Jevons wrote a great deal about scientific method as embracing all branches of knowledge, and strove to create a universal theory of economic behaviour, based on differential calculus, which would hold good for all times and places. Attacking the classical notion of intrinsic worth, he held that actual prices were the only real phenomena of value, and that they were determined mainly by the mental states of individuals. Economic decisions (whether to buy at a certain price) resulted from an imbalance of pleasures and pains in the mind, feelings being the main forces in determining behaviour.[73] By making psychology the basis of individual decision-making in this way, Jevons felt free to remove it from his macroeconomics. This led to his notorious explanation of economic fluctuations with reference to sun-spots. Where Overstone had blamed speculators and others blamed trade unions and wage rigidities, Jevons argued that cyclical disasters were nobody's fault but were the natural, and therefore beneficial, consequences of energy fluctuations.[74] Jevons placed great stress on the need for 'naturalness', perhaps because it provided a defence of Free Trade against those who argued that that policy was beginning to damage the country's economic well-being.[75]

Jevons had been brought up in the Unitarian tradition and continued to regard it as 'the most simple & truth-like' of creeds. Despite bouts of scepticism he retained his 'faith in Humanity; in the fact that man was created for happiness'. God for him was a 'principle' of 'abstract good', Christ an example of 'Perfect man'. Humanity was a more enigmatic affair, but clearly no one could have been created for the purpose of being damned. 'There is no foundation for any religion but in the feelings of the human heart', he confided to his sister in 1857, a view which perhaps reflects his belief in the introspective determination of economic value.[76]

---

[72] Philip Mirowski, 'Physics and the "marginalist revolution"', *Cambridge Journal of Economics*, 8 (1984), 361–79.

[73] Margaret Schabas, 'The "worldly philosophy" of William Stanley Jevons', *Victorian Studies*, 28 (1984–5), 129–47.

[74] Mirowski, 'Macroeconomic instability and the "natural" processes in early neo-classical economics', *The Journal of Economic History*, 44 (1984), 345–54.

[75] Mirowski makes the fascinating suggestion that Englishmen may have clung to Free Trade long after Continentals because, unlike them, they saw economic relations as grounded in a physical (not physiological) analogy. Philip Mirowski, 'Macroeconomic instability and the "natural" processes', ibid., p. 348.

[76] Jevons to his sister Henrietta, 3 May 1856, 4 Jan. 1857, 21 Jan. 1858, Jevons to his sister Lucy, 16 June 1857, Collison Black, *Papers and Correspondence of Jevons*, ii. 225–6, 258, 288, 311–12.

In this respect it is interesting that he should have described himself as a 'dependent moralist', one who did not believe in an inherent moral sense.[77]

Most of the neoclassicals were fascinated by physics, but Mirowski's point is not so much that they consciously extrapolated from it as that, by taking energetics as a metaphor, they 'surreptitiously' assumed (without altogether understanding) certain of its basic concepts. The conservation principle in particular was tacitly assumed, yet if all goods are transformable into other goods by trading, just like energy, then money is inessential and we have what is virtually a barter economy. Again, if income and endowments within the system are conserved, then the new theory reads very like the old one based on Say's Law. One neoclassical who *did* understand thermodynamics was Alfred Marshall, and he of course refrained from reliance on the physical metaphor (though Mirowski believes that it affected his thought none the less).[78] Instead Marshall plumped for 'economic biology' and the organic metaphor in working out his theories of the 'noble life' of economics.[79] His optimistic belief in social altruism and 'economic chivalry' derived in part from Hegel, Mill, and Spencer, being based on the possibility of man's capacity for 'self-actualization' and potential for 'higher' conduct. His faith in economic efficiency, activity, 'energy', and a high-wage economy replaced the classical model with its Malthusian emphasis on the relationship between capital accumulation, income distribution, and economic growth.[80]

This book is less concerned with original economic thinkers like Marshall than with conventional morality. What did Scott Holland *mean* when he wrote that 'it was the Incarnation . . . with which they desired to see the laws of political economy brought into contact'?[81] Like 'evangelical economists', incarnationalists assumed the existence of divine social laws which were not to be interfered with, and like them they saw both scope and need for the exercise of individual conscience, but their understanding of the latter was different. 'Conscience is the organ in the individual personality of the impulse towards collective life in the region

---

[77] Ibid., i. 66.

[78] Mirowski, 'Physics and the marginalist revolution', op. cit., pp. 372–6.

[79] J. Hirshleifer, 'Economics from a biological viewpoint', *The Journal of Law and Economics*, 20 (1977), 1–52; A. L. Levine, 'Marshall's *Principles* and the "biological viewpoint": a reconsideration', *Manchester School*, 51 (1983), 276–93. For Marshall's use of chemistry see Reba N. Soffer, *Ethics and Society in England: The Revolution in the Social Sciences, 1870–1914* (Berkeley, Calif., 1978), 97.

[80] John Dennis Chasse, 'Marshall, the human agent and economic growth: wants and activities revisited', *History of Political Economy*, 16 (1984), 381–404. Chasse successfully challenges the earlier view that by 'higher faculties' Marshall meant 'Protestant' values such as thrift and hard work.

[81] H. S. Holland's preface to Wilfrid Richmond, *Economic Morals: Four Lectures* (1890), p. xi.

of action.'[82] Yet far from being collectivist or socialist, far from attacking *laissez-faire*, most of them merely sought to replace one concept of *laissez-faire* by another. They differed from their predecessors by virtue of their optimistic belief in worldly progress and development. Religion and morality loomed large in their normative economics, but it was a sentimental, one-sided religion, Godly rule by reward and not punishment. Such attitudes were particularly suited to the outgoing, self-confident society of 1850–80, buttressed by the mid-Victorian boom, social stability, and equipoise. Suddenly every other twopenny pamphleteer was boasting about the 'sanitary influence' of religion—a version of the Combean theory that disease is caused by breaking moral laws (e.g. gluttony) and can be avoided—or about the 'Sabbath as a sanitary agent'. 'Belief in the Church', it was proudly announced, 'is the true key to all social science', a priority which would have dismayed Wilberforce and Chalmers.[83] Incarnational economists assumed a natural harmony of society and the probability of a future reign of natural justice, even Herbert Spencer—often thought of as a crude exponent of *laissez-faire* theory—being well within this anti-Malthusian tradition.[84] It is significant that their writings made frequent use of organic metaphors which, as Greta Jones points out, had formerly been put to the service of Tory and hierarchical values (as in Coleridge) but were now being accommodated more frequently to liberal progressive thought.[85]

The best way to convey the flavour of incarnationalism is probably to treat a selection of its exponents individually. This will make for rather motley presentation, since it is not being suggested that the following writers formed anything like a 'school'. We may begin with three whose ideas, while pointing forward, were mainly formed before 1850, and represent an older, protectionist approach to organicism, though one in which 'radical' elements predominate over High Toryism.

In some senses a pioneer of this way of thought, though a boring, repetitive, and opaque one, was William Atkinson, who exploited his positions in the Statistical Society of London and the Central Agricultural Society to expose 'a latent error of the greatest magnitude' in the current political economy.[86] Since about 1833 he had been obsessed by what he

[82] Wilfrid Richmond, *An Essay on Personality as a Philosophical Principle* (1900), 24.

[83] William Ewart, *Sanitary Influence of Belief in the Church* (1860), 31 and *passim*; Horatio Goodday, *The Sabbath: the First Sanitary Agent, or Means of Life* (1860), 10–11 and *passim*.

[84] Mark Francis, 'Herbert Spencer and the myth of *laissez-faire*', *Journal of the History of Ideas*, 39 (1978), 317–28.

[85] Greta Jones, *Social Darwinism and English Thought. The Interaction between Biological and Social Theory* (Harvester, Sussex, 1980), 40–1. See Beer, *Darwin's Plots*, pp. 167–80, on the 'web of affinities' metaphor. Earlier the 'fabric' metaphor had been used by Burkean High Tories.

[86] William Atkinson, *The State of the Science of Political Economy Investigated: wherein is shewn the Defective Character of the Arguments which have hitherto*

regarded as the Ricardian error, the belief that foreign trade is more advantageous, and more conducive to capital formation, than home trade.[87] He abominated the New Poor Law[88] and was appalled by some of the attitudes expressed in the Handloom Weavers Commission, on which he served. His main point was that capital increases geometrically, population only arithmetically, so that although the present destitution was indeed caused by population outstripping capital, this was not because of God's immutable laws but because the competitive system was misdirecting human industry and inhibiting capital freedom. He defended the Corn Laws, and was willing to allow capitalists to limit their liabilities.[89] Above all he could not tolerate the prevailing abstentionist or 'moral' theory of political economy, in which 'misers' were lauded as heroically unfolding the Creator's intentions.[90] 'The free principle of commerce is false' because 'immoral', he wrote in 1840:

It has its origins in *self-will*. This passion is declared to be the right source or true principle of motion. . . . It follows, that the greater the impulse given by this power to the numerous divisions and subdivisions of labour, the more ample will be the development of the material things which have been ordained to conduce to the temporal well-being of mankind. Thus are connected, as cause and effect, the selfish and the social, or, good springing out of evil.[91]

The proper way to reveal the workings of an all-wise and beneficent Creator was not through competition but co-operation, or what he termed 'the great social law of the Christian faith'.[92]

Man is placed upon the earth by his Creator, without anything in possession, but with a capacity to procure an unlimited variety. His labour is the means,—the earth is the object upon which it is to be exerted. With the great and exalted power of providing or creating matter he has nothing to do. The sphere assigned for his exertion is that of acting upon, or modifying, the matter given. He is free within a wide circle; but the bounds of the circle he cannot pass.[93]

---

been advanced for Elucidating the Laws of the Formation of Wealth (1838), p. v.

[87] Atkinson to Charles Babbage, 30 May 1833, Babbage Papers, BL Add. MS 37187 fos. 550–1.

[88] William Atkinson, *The Spirit of Magna Charta: or Universal Representation the Genius of the British Constitution* (1841), 65–72.

[89] Atkinson to Thomas Phillipps, 23 May 1839, Bodleian Library MSS, Phillipps–Robinson Papers, c.466 fos. 17–18; Atkinson, *The State of the Science of Political Economy*, pp. 47–63.

[90] Atkinson, *The State of the Science of Political Economy*, pp. 64–9.

[91] William Atkinson, *Principles of Political Economy: or, the Laws of the Formation of National Wealth: developed by Means of the Christian Law of Government* (1840), 136–9.

[92] W. Atkinson to [?Whewell], 15 Sept. 1840, Trinity College Cambridge Add. MSS, c.75².

[93] Atkinson, *Principles of Political Economy*, p. 155.

It is not likely that anyone took much notice of Atkinson, though it is interesting to note his instinctive grasp of energy conservation as early as 1840. Another who turned to writing after abortive attempts at lobbying behind the scenes was Samuel Laing, a far more widely read and appreciated moralist. In an early attempt to synthesize moral and physical science with political economy, Laing depicted society, not as a 'dead machine', but as a *'living* mass, held together by inappreciable *atomic* forces'.

> The good deeds of individuals, every act of duty, every act of charity, nay, every kind look, and expression, however trifling, of goodwill and brotherhood between man and man, are the attractive forces. — Every harsh, unjust, cruel, selfish deed, again, is a repulsive force. The man who does his duty in his appointed station is the true Conservative; the man who fails to do that duty, the true Destructive.

Only moral goodness, not the prescriptions of political economists, could help society, and moral goodness can only be nurtured by an intervening government, not by *laissez-faire*.[94] As an active Railway Commissioner under Dalhousie (1842–6), Laing particularly wanted to regulate the speculative promotion of railway companies, but was thwarted by Peel.

Laing's analysis of 1844, for all its emphasis on morals, is still Newtonian in conception. Forty years later his *Modern Science and Modern Thought*, in attempting 'to show how much of religion can be saved from the shipwreck of theology', revealed an awareness of more recent scientific developments. Two discoveries struck him as being of pre-eminent importance. 'The law of polarity . . . seems to prevail universally throughout the material, as it does also throughout the moral world, [so] that you cannot have a North without a South Pole, a positive without a negative, a right without a wrong.' On this reckoning error consisted merely of going too far in one direction. Secondly, there was the doctrine of the conservation of energy and concomitant rejection of dualism. 'Matter is alike everywhere', and primitive energy is the same in all its different manifestations. It can be transformed but not created or destroyed.[95]

Even more influential was Charles Bray (1811–84), friend and younger colleague of George Combe, friend and in some senses mentor of Spencer and George Eliot. Bray used the insights of phrenology to advocate very different social and economic policies from Combe, partly by wedding them to a doctrine of philosophical necessity. Like Combe, he believed that sinfulness was not original but resulted from bad institutions and human ignorance; unlike him, he advocated co-operation and association, for 'until the present system of individual interests is altered, however

[94] Samuel Laing, *National Distress: Its Causes and Remedies* (1844), 56–64.
[95] Samuel Laing, *Modern Science and Modern Thought* (1885), pp. v, 62–3, 66.

much it may be on the lips, the law of love will never be in the heart'. Mental, moral, and social science was only possible because 'law reigned equally in Mind and in Matter'. Bray claimed 'that the mind of man is not an exception to nature's other works; that like everything else it has received a determinate character; that all our knowledge of it is precisely of the same kind as that of material things, and consists in the observation of *its order* of action, or of the relation of cause and effect'. In *On Force, Its Mental and Moral Correlates* (1866), Bray used Spencer's 'persistence of force' to argue the monistic position that 'physical force creates the mind and the mind creates the world', that forces are in fact more often mental than physical, and that a coming spirit world of beautiful things might evolve from the atmosphere as a result of present cerebration.[96] This lurch into physics and phreno-mesmerism has its counterpart in Spencer's abandonment of faculty psychology for associationism and adaptationism, and it explains how Bray could combine phrenology with support for Owenism, whose environmentalist approach to social problems seems on the surface to be incompatible.

Social evolution follows the law of organic modification. It is the exercise of the feelings we wish to predominate that alone will strengthen them and increase the size of the organs with which they are connected. The commercial age in which we live . . . is making all men better off. . . . When a man is well off and happy he desires to make others so, exercising his benevolence.[97]

Needless to say, as an Owenite Bray ridiculed all of political economy, from the Malthusian doctrine to the selfish cry for Free Trade which, though necessary in its day, would 'fill the country with towns such as Manchester and Glasgow!' Joint stock companies, with labourers and capitalists sharing the profits equally, would be a first step towards realizing the moral law of universal brotherhood and 'unperverted Christianity'.[98] We can see what he understood by perversion from his attacks on sacrificial versions of the Atonement and on the nightmare of future punishment, both of which struck him as 'blasphemous slanders upon the character of God'.[99]

---

[96] Charles Bray, *The Philosophy of Necessity: or, the Law of Consequences: as Applicable to Mental, Moral, and Social Science* (1841), i. 6, ii. 437; Bray, *Phases of Opinion*, pp. 92–3, 98; Charles Bray, *On Force, its Mental and Moral Correlates: And on that which is Supposed to Underlie all Phenomena: With Speculations on Spiritualism, and Other Abnormal Conditions of Mind* (1866), 35–49, 144–6. See above, p. 201.

[97] Charles Bray, *'The Reign of Law' in Mind as in Matter, and its Bearing upon Christian Dogma and Moral Responsibility* (1874), ii. 23.

[98] Bray, *Philosophy of Necessity*, ii. 347–66, 391–403, 428–37, 484–92, and *passim*.

[99] Charles Bray, *Christianity: Viewed in the Light of our Present Knowledge and Moral Sense* (1876), 38–41; Bray, *Phases of Opinion*, pp. 166–202.

As protectionists, paternalists, and in Bray's case a socialist, the above writers must be seen as forerunners rather than exponents of incarnational economics. An early example of the real thing was Alexander Alison, whose *Second Reformation* (1851) and *The Future* (1852) captured widespread attention.[1] Their purpose was to base moral philosophy squarely on physical science. 'God governs man by general and not by particular laws', all events are natural, and 'nature is perfect', so 'to legislate contrary to nature is to produce Evil'. Since protection was 'unnatural, . . . an arbitrary interference with the Laws of Nature', Alison believed ardently in 'universal Free Trade', as well as in direct taxation, while his thoughts on poor laws were similar to those of Chalmers.[2] He also agreed that 'want of soul' was the cause of 'over-trading' and financial panics, but despite all this he diverged from evangelical thought in his belief that creditors had the law still too much on their side in enforcing rights over debtors,[3] and this germ of a humane attitude strengthened during the fifties. *The Improvement of Society* (1862) drew on Emerson and McCosh to assert the power of the principle of goodness in the world. The Incarnation was now seen to be central, and Old Testament or sacrificial interpretations of the Atonement were rejected. Any suggestion in St Paul, moreover, that justification was possible without works could hardly be meant to apply to all countries and all times. 'The Atonement of the New Testament is not blood, but *a new creature*, . . . following the example and precepts of our Lord', and until this was widely realized no social reformation would be possible. Wilberforce and Chalmers, he now believed, had erred in only attacking evil 'at the outside'. Assuredly a reformation would take place, however, for though 'the events of History do not change, man's capacity to interpret these events does change, showing that History, like Theology, is a progressive science'.[4]

Patrick Dove (1815–73) was a country-house philosopher whose work was much praised by Sir William Hamilton and Thomas Carlyle. It looked forward post-millennially to a 'reign of justice' in attempting to adapt natural theology to an age which had passed beyond physics, metaphysics, and mathematics to the physico-psychological. For Dove as for Alison, 'progressive development' signified the expansion of man's knowledge, divine reality remaining always the same. Political economy's present

---

[1] See A. Alison, *To the Electors: Universal Free Trade* (1852; Eighth Thousand Edition, 1852), Appendix pp. 1–20.

[2] A. Alison, *The Second Reformation: or Christianity Developed* (2nd edn, 1851), 21, 112, 211–12; Alison, *To the Electors*, pp. 31–5; A. Alison, *The Future: Or, the Science of Politics* (1852), 109–10.

[3] Alison, *The Future*, pp. 95–6; A. Alison, *The Philosophy and History of Civilisation* (1860), 369–70.

[4] A. Alison, *The Improvement of Society and Public Opinion* (1862), 19, 33–4, 42, 87, 104–5, 135; Alison, *The Second Reformation*, pp. 60–4.

domination of intellectual culture represented merely a stage in man's development from barbarism, when combativeness and loose passions had reigned, to the *telos* of a Christian brotherhood, when benevolence would flourish. After the present stage there was just one more to pass through before that *telos* was reached—a reign of equity, when what would exercise mankind was not the means of creating wealth (relations with external nature) but the means of distributing it (relations with each other, or 'justice').[5] He saw his own task as helping to effect a transition to this next stage, since 'political economy, in fact, is the natural preparative for a science of equity. All its questions solved', which they nearly were beyond dispute, 'there yet remains the question, "Who is the *proprietor* of the created value?" And this question arises necessarily so soon as political-economy has discovered *who* creates the value.'[6]As this last comment suggests, Dove believed that it was time to give the labourer his due share. He could not accept with Whately and others that there was a presumption in favour of the existing state of society, since this would be to suggest that God was monstrously unfair. The existing state of affairs must therefore have been brought about by an *interference* with nature.[7] Poverty, like maldistribution, occurred because artificial legislation thwarted God's plans for plentiful provision.[8] 'We do not believe . . . that pauperism comes from God. It is man's doing, and man's doing alone'[9]—not the pauper's own doing, it should be added, but man's social arrangements, which are based on superstition rather than knowledge.

In Dove's view there had been two great triumphs of truth in the recent past: abolition of slavery and Corn Law repeal. God had played the catalyst on corn, by sending abundant harvests in 1835–6 and forcing farmers to sell at a natural price while paying taxes and rents at inflated prices, thereby showing them the impolicy of 'legislation which attempted to amend the order of Providence'. Also the low price of corn had 'let the manufacturer into a secret', had given him precious 'knowledge'. It had taught him the market theory of wages—that low prices do not depress wages, but leave working-men with more disposable income to buy his own products. The consequent 'great combination . . . of knowledge and reason' had doomed the Corn Laws.[10] And justly so, for land belongs to the entire nation, and rents should bear the entire burden

[5] [P. E. Dove], *The Theory of Human Progression, and Natural Probability of a Reign of Justice* (1850), 424–504.

[6] Ibid., p. 462.

[7] Patrick Edward Dove, *The Elements of Political Science: In Two Books* (Edinburgh, 1854), 331–401.

[8] Ibid., pp. 116–19.   [9] [Dove], *Theory of Human Progression*, pp. 311–15.

[10] Ibid., pp. 142–9.

of taxation. A system which gave one shilling a day to the labourer and one thousand pounds a day to the landlord was ripe for national disaster. 'The great requisite, then, is to return to the laws of Nature, of Providence, of God—to let the skilful and industrious man be rich, and not to accord wealth to those who produce nothing for the welfare of mankind.' Taxes on labour disunite society, make the nation 'only an aggregation of unassociated individuals', whereas taxes on rent unite society—'it makes the nation a community bound together by the ties of a common interest, and a common welfare. . . . He who will give the greatest rent for the soil becomes its cultivator, and pays the rent to the nation for the benefit of the whole community.' Labour will be rewarded justly, the welfare of one will be the welfare of all, and men will bond together in true citizenship and Christian brotherhood.[11] Not surprisingly, Dove's work was greatly praised by Henry George, yet it is essential to point out that he was emphatically not a socialist but an individualist. His work represents a distinct stage—an attempt to wed individualism and Free Trade to post-millennial theological optimism.

George Rickards was Drummond Professor of Political Economy at Oxford from 1851 to 1857 and an advocate of limited liability. Acknowledging Sumner and Chalmers among his forerunners, he quickly distanced himself from them by citing as his chief teachers Whately, Jones, and Bastiat, who had done more to justify political economy on moral and religious grounds by demonstrating the 'agreeableness' and 'harmony' of its doctrines. Thus Whately had shown how men possess an unconscious social instinct which governs their economic lives. Jones had shown that benefits enjoyed by one class over another are always short-lived, and that stable growth is possible only where all partake of its fruits. Bastiat's *Harmonies Economiques* too had demonstrated that self-interest works for everyone's benefit. There was also, perhaps, though unacknowledged, a debt to Combe, since Rickards found the 'primary source of all the conclusions of true Political Economy' in 'the fixed laws of Providence exemplified in the constitution of man's nature and in the fundamental arrangements of society'.[12] A term like 'social' rather than 'political' economy would, he thought, have better pointed the analogy with physiology, and emphasized its descriptive, as distinct from normative, role.

On the other hand Rickards could not, in the moral climate of the mid-century, fall back on the old utilitarian argument that private vices were public benefits. By implying that material growth was tantamount

---

[11] Dove, *Elements of Political Science*, pp. 328–30.
[12] George K. Rickards, *Three Lectures delivered before the University of Oxford* (Oxford and London, 1852), 13, 31–5.

to moral degeneration, such theories created 'utter moral confusion'. True political economy, on the other hand, would reveal divine wisdom *and* benevolence, showing up all suffering to be the consequence of meddling human laws in restraint of trade. Thanks to their removal, Malthusian population theory no longer implies social catastrophe; the principle of self-interest, which if unchecked would tend to infinity, is in practice beneficially curbed by the magic of competition; commerce 'divides the losses and multiplies the gains of the inter-trading countries'; and so on. All this was in refutation of the socialists, who merely saw discordance in the natural order and stigmatized one man's self-interest as another man's exploitation. Rickards, on the contrary, looked forward to the reign of *laissez-faire*;

We should see . . . jealousy give way to sympathy, exclusion to intercourse, rivalry to co-operation, restraint to freedom. We should see restrictions, barriers, penalties, monopolies, the war of classes, the antipathies of nations gradually diminished. We should see a great mitigation of those calamities which man is far more concerned than nature in producing, dearths, gluts, panics, fluctuation of prices, commercial crises and revulsions.[13]

However, to remind us that what is changing is more the tone than the content of Christian economics, Rickards denounces those who say

that it matters not, economically speaking, how wealth is expended so long as labour is employed, and that he who circulates his money fastest, the reckless spendthrift, does more good to society than the frugal and provident man who lays up capital for investment—what must we conclude but that if this doctrine be well founded, wealth and virtue are irreconcileably [*sic*] opposed.[14]

Unlike Malthus, Chalmers, and the underconsumptionists, Rickards accepted the Ricardian view that accumulation of capital is legitimate and virtuous, providing a man with credit and trust, whereas spending is not far from immorality.

There are many others whom one might consider at this stage: G. N. Boardman, who deified Say's Law as revealing how beneficent providence, successively improving man through the ages, can overcome gluts;[15] Richard Jennings, who devised a somewhat *dirigiste* political economy based on physiological and psychological principles;[16] F. W. Newman, who taught political economy at Manchester College;[17] C. J. Vaughan,

[13] Ibid., pp. 38–49, 63. [14] Ibid., pp. 23–4.
[15] G. N. Boardman, *Political Economy of the Christian Ministry* (1866), *passim*.
[16] '*Value* is not a *condition of matter*, but a *purely human* condition, . . . a natural phenomenon of the human mind'; however, 'the laws . . . of human action are, in the same sense in which other laws of Nature are so, fixed and invariable'. Richard Jennings, *Natural Elements of Political Economy* (1855), 140, 202–3, and *passim*.
[17] F. W. Newman, *Lectures on Political Economy* (1851), *passim*.

David's brother, who begged his readers not to dwell on the pain involved in the crucifixion, but to concentrate on 'the entireness of the Incarnation and the *Incorporation*. We must not suffer even the Divinity to overshadow or to eclipse the Humanity.'[18] Incorporation was in turn based on co-operation and association. 'The power of association' was, added Gilbart, the 'offspring of modern science'.[19] Then again, the moralism of Samuel Smiles fits the incarnational approach. Though many of his strictures on frugality and competitiveness resemble those of the evangelicals, he differs from them in his relish for social mobility, and more subtly in his view that 'thrift' cannot be a natural instinct, but must be developed through intelligence and education. Anti-evangelical also is Smiles's emphasis on a phrase from the Lord's Prayer which had been little mentioned during the Age of Atonement—'Lead us not into temptation'. As we saw, temptation—even deliberate self-titillation—was crucial to evangelical concepts of self-control, whereas Smiles thought that true manliness required one to develop habits of not being tempted.[20] 'God tempts no one', reassured the incarnationalist son of an extreme pre-millenarian evangelical, Edward Bickersteth.[21] But perhaps the most explicit statements of incarnational economics can be found in Llewellyn Davies's *Theology and Morality* (1873) and in Wilfrid Richmond's *Christian Economics* (1888) and *Economic Morals* (1890).

A confirmation sermon of 1856 gave Davies an opportunity to challenge those who urged that competition and selfish motives were the mainsprings of society. Such a view was contradicted in his opinion by Confirmation, which admitted churchmen to a single family whose member spirits are bound 'with the cords of love'. 'We must not venture to *limit* the Spirit of God.'[22] Christianity for him was based on 'thankfulness'—on 'joy, . . . gladness and delight'. Sacrifice implied not self-denial, but surrendering our own wills to that of the loving God.[23] The Sermon on the Mount speaks practically to our own times, and contains the economic precepts of Christianity. 'The most effectual way of checking improvidence is to awaken the sense of duty, the care for higher things, the feelings and habits

---

[18] C. J. Vaughan, *Words from the Cross, and Thoughts for These Times* (1875), 2.

[19] J. W. Gilbart, *Moral and Religious Duties of Public Companies*, p. 46.

[20] Samuel Smiles, *Thrift* (1875), 2, 242-3.

[21] Edward Bickersteth (the younger), *The Revised Version of the New Testament: A Lecture* (1885), 24-6. Consistently, Bickersteth also defended the Revised Version's 'Deliver us from the Evil One' in place of 'from Evil'.

[22] J. Llewellyn Davies, *Confirmation: Or, the Laying On of Hands: A Parochial Address* (1856), 20-3. See also J. Llewellyn Davies, *St. Paul and Modern Thought: Remarks on Some of the Views advanced in Professor Jowett's Commentary on St. Paul* (Cambridge, 1856), 29-38.

[23] J. Llewellyn Davies, *Morality According to the Sacrament of the Lord's Supper: Three Discourses on the Names Eucharist, Sacrifice, and Communion* (London and Cambridge, 1867), 16-17, 46-8.

of one who thinks of human beings as the redeemed of Christ and God's children.' '*Give to him that asketh thee and from him that would borrow of thee turn not thou away*' (Matthew 5: 42).[24] In fact, Davies was as hostile to indiscriminate alms-giving as Chalmers, but, partly because of this, he was all for modern charity organization.[25] He admitted that the existing distribution of wealth was 'painfully unlike the Christian ideal', while firmly repudiating any suggestion of an equation between pain and virtue.[26] His post-millennial vision of society's peaceful progress towards a perfect day of manly and egalitarian brotherhood was spelled out most fully in his Hulsean Lectures of 1890.[27]

Meanwhile we can discover what incarnational man would be like to deal with in the market from Richmond, a former Oxford don and a founding member of the Christian Social Union of 1889:[28]

He will be, to start with, a unit of co-operation, not a unit of competition. . . . As the steward of a life which is God's gift, and of resources for which he is bound to render an account, he will seek to satisfy his needs without waste. . . . He will be sensitive to the bearing of his action on the members of his family, his trade, of every social unity to which he belongs. . . . His profession or trade will be to him a form of public service, as his whole life is a service of God. . . . In his dealings with his fellows he will be guided by the spirit of justice, by the desire to give *quid pro quo*, service for service, life for life, and to find the fair return for what he receives, by finding common ground with the man with whom he has to agree. But, as in his dealings with men he will more and more be brought face to face with the inequalities and wrongs of his life, . . . so the dominant desire of his life will more and more become this—to do the greatest good he can in his generation, the most to lift men to a higher level of happiness. Personal sacrifices which this task demands will take their natural place in a life whose ruling spirit has become the spirit of self-devotion.[29]

If this seems Utopian, it needs to be remembered that Richmond believed—in sharp contrast to Copleston and earlier moralists—'that it was the function of the law to promote moral action'.[30] Still, it clearly has some affinity with cranks like the Scottish Drummond, whose *The Ascent of Man* (1894) argued that the struggle for life would gradually become

[24] J. Llewellyn Davies, *Social Questions from the Point of View of Christian Theology* (1885), 270–4.

[25] Ibid., pp. 273–90.

[26] J. Llewellyn Davies, *Competition and Self-Surrender: A Sermon* (Marlborough, 1874), 9; J. Llewellyn Davies, *Theology and Morality: Essays on Questions of Belief and Practice* (1873), 25–7.

[27] J. Llewellyn Davies, *Order and Growth as Involved in the Spiritual Constitution of Human Society* (1891), 110–41.

[28] Peter d'A. Jones, *The Christian Socialist Revival 1877–1914: Religion, Class, and Social Conscience in Late-Victorian England* (Princeton, NJ, 1968), 175–7.

[29] Wilfrid Richmond, *Economic Morals: Four Lectures* (1890), 111–12.

[30] Ibid., pp. 19, 114.

altruistic, a struggle for other men's lives, and that the object of evolution was love. Better to be an animal eaten by another, wrote Drummond fatuously, than never to have existed at all. But, more soberly, Richmond's vision also has an affinity with that of Alfred Marshall, whose economics celebrated 'the marvellous growth in recent times of a spirit of honesty and uprightness in commercial matters'.[31]

Richmond waxed even more rhapsodical in his *Christian Economics*, a medley of post-millennial energetics. Commercial and industrial life is a 'moral fabric' and man is made in a glorious image, right worthy of being multiplied. Competition is the 'law of life', and what is called division of labour should really be called 'combination', since it depicts men organizing and uniting their forces in industrial fellowship. Justice is the law of exchange and love the law of distribution, since both entail putting the interests of others before one's own, so manifesting sacrificially 'the energy of self-devotion, . . . the self-satisfying energy of life'. Labour is blessed because it involves the full 'employment of energy': 'How did the words ever come to sound other than a blessing, "In the sweat of thy brow thou shalt eat bread"?' The economic body is corporate and organic, and only healthy when all its parts co-operate with each other. Richmond had no patience with the classical economists' ascetic emphasis on production. 'Wealth should be consumed, and be consumed with joy. Life, laborious and self-denying life, should be graced with beauty and filled with many pleasures.' Economic freedom was of paramount importance, not Adam Smith's freedom *from* legal restraint for the sake of wealth, but 'freedom to do something—to enjoy'. 'The enjoyment of wealth means . . . the freedom of energy, a system of life in which all objects of desire fulfil their function in evoking energy, and in giving the pleasure which attends its exercise, in which the energies of all are called forth to their fullest extent.'[32]

An Enthusiasm of Humanity

It will be clear from all this that what we are dealing with is as much as anything a question of *mood* and *tone*, a sense of contentment and a determination to be like 'Gentle Jesus, meek and mild'. The Governor Eyre controversy in 1865 became a moral touchstone precisely because it centred on the place of gentleness and compassion in public life. Thus Carlyle, who was steeped in the old corpuscular, not the new muscular,

---

[31] Alfred Marshall, *Principles of Economics* (1890), 365. See also William Morton, 'Moral aspects of political economy', *Fraser's Magazine*, NS, 16 (1877), 505–15, on the need for self-culture and commercial honour.

[32] Wilfrid Richmond, *Christian Economics* (1888), 31–4, 49, 96–100, 164–79, 241, 267–9, and *passim*.

tradition of Christianity, could not understand why Mill and most other Liberals (but, interestingly, not Dickens) should have behaved so fastidiously about a little blood-spilling. 'Manliness' became divested of *machismo*, and men no longer felt the need to apologize for being unassertive. This again was in stark contrast to the retributive attitudes current before 1850, when gentleness had been regarded as moral and physical weakness, as exemplified by the defensive tones in which Mrs Samuel Greg defended her husband, a Unitarian born in 1804 and the philanthropic elder brother of William: 'There was much of the feminine element in his constitution. He rather lacked that harder, tougher fibre, both of mind and frame, which makes the battle of life so easy and so successful to many men. He had nothing *hard* about him, and was not made for conflict. . . . He would have come out best, shone brightest, and achieved most, in sunshine.'[33] Unfortunately, Samuel Greg had lived in times when, as Overstone put it, storms were felt to be necessary, in moral as in physical life,[34] but the following generation from 1850 to 1875 preferred sunshine, which is partly why it worshipped a Christ of 'almost feminine tenderness and humanity'.[35] A characteristic figure might be J. A. Froude, who hated political economy and *laissez-faire* individualism, and who greatly regretted the loss of the old agricultural England with its independent smallholders. Acutely sensitive to suffering, the Irish Famine seems to have played a part in the process of his conversion from Christianity. As Burrow has shown, he was *half* attracted by the apocalyptic vulcanism prevalent in his youth, yet really his mind had a much 'gentler tenor': 'It is part of my plague that I cannot be angry with anybody.' When writing he took his imagery from sedimentary rather than from violent geology, from botany, meteorology, and navigation. Thus in describing the spiritual dilemmas of his own generation he alludes, not to 'struggle and flight', but to the sea's desolate (but stormless) immensity: 'all round us, the intellectual lightships had broken from their moorings. . . . [We were out] in an open spiritual ocean, . . . the lights all drifting, the compasses all awry, and nothing left to steer by except the stars.'[36] Nothingness and existlessness have replaced hell-fire in the mythology of doubt.

[33] Samuel Greg, *A Layman's Legacy in Prose and Verse*, edited with a memoir by his wife (1877), 54.

[34] See above, p. 134.

[35] [J. R. Seeley], *Ecce Homo: A Survey of the Life and Work of Jesus Christ* (London and Cambridge, 1866), 177.

[36] James Anthony Froude, *Thomas Carlyle: A History of His Life in London 1834–1881* (1884), i. 290–1; J. W. Burrow, *A Liberal Descent: Victorian Historians and the English Past* (Cambridge, 1981), 238–40, 256; Collini, Winch, and Burrow, *That Noble Science*, p. 190; *James Anthony Froude: A Biography*, by Waldo Hilary Dunn (Oxford, 1961–3), i. 159.

Another historian, J. R. Seeley, provides further insight into the mores of the sunshine generation. While sons of moderate evangelicals often suffered from religious doubt during the 1850s and 1860s, the offspring of extreme evangelicals typically took the Irving/Maurice path to incarnationalism.[37] Seeley was the son of an apocalyptic evangelical, the paternalist R. B. Seeley, but he early rejected the supernatural religion of revelation in favour of what he called an 'enthusiasm of humanity'.[38] As Richard Shannon has shown, he had strong views about the need to *prevent* poverty instead of merely indulging in occasional philanthropy. He called for an economically literate clergy to inculcate national morality through education, and appealed to English history as a record of national moral development up to the present hour. In this way the nation might recover its former unsentimental and 'masculine grasp of reality'. His enormously popular *Ecce Homo*, with its emphasis on Christ's humanity, appeared in 1865, but when a friend asked him whether he intended to write a sequel on Christ's divinity, he unexpectedly answered that he had already done so with his *Life and Times of Stein*. From this extraordinary remark it seems that Seeley regarded Stein as embodying a divine principle, a prophet evangel who had providentially rescued Prussia from the abyss by instilling national morality. As Shannon points out, Seeley's 'morality' is a more optimistic version of Matthew Arnold's 'culture'.[39] 'Humanity'—his keyword—remains the clue to the Christian's moral reformation, but it 'changed', as a result of the mid-century shift in sensibility, 'from a restraint to a motive, . . . from being a feeble, restraining power to be an inspiring passion'.[40]

We can perhaps form some idea of what Seeley meant by this keyword from the following comment by Octavia Hill, a well-known philanthropist, who specialized in the area of housing reform. Octavia's father was a businessman in somewhat precarious circumstances, and she was probably influenced more by her guardian, Thomas Southwood Smith. Then in the 1850s she fell under the spell of Maurice. Here she is commenting to a friend on the difficulties involved in instilling a sense of duty into poor children.

I dare not hope that I shall have the power of creating it. I dare not disbelieve that I ought to be the agent in awakening it. It is a very wonderful work on which

---

[37] The Vaughan brothers are obvious examples. Less obvious might be Sir James Stephen, son of the *fairly* extreme evangelical, James Stephen. By 1850 the son had come to deny the eternity of future punishment, the divinity of Christ, and the literal efficacy of the Atonement.

[38] Deborah Wormell, *Sir John Seeley and the Uses of History* (Cambridge, 1980), 12–47.

[39] R. T. Shannon, 'John Robert Seeley and the idea of a national church', *Ideas and Institutions of Victorian Britain*, ed. Robert Robson (1967), 236–67.

[40] [Seeley], *Ecce Homo*, p. 186.

we are engaged. It is a very awful work, when you feel how easily you can reach their hearts, how hard it is to reach their consciences; they will do anything *for you*, they will do hardly anything because it is right. And tho' this is dangerous, because so false a ground to stand upon, yet this inclination testifies of a precious truth. It might teach us, if we would only learn, how much all human beings must crave for personality, how cold, how dead, how distant are all abstractions. . . . If evil is all vague, all mysterious, and yet most real, is there no Person stronger than it, mysterious through His divinity? Yes! then all history, all life will testify there is such a one . . . this Conqueror, this Knight, . . . God's warrior, [who] came not to crush but to raise. . . . I do hope we may be able to awaken in the hearts of these children a knowledge that they are called soldiers of Christ.[41]

Here we can see the affinities between Broad Church religion and the mid-Victorian fascination with medievalism, crusades, and Camelot. But above all, incarnationalist religion centred on an immanentist belief in divine will, which was working its purpose out in man's actions and thoughts.[42] Christ came, as Westcott put it, 'to effect the perfection no less than the redemption of finite being, . . . to bring a perfect unity of humanity without destroying the personality of any one man'.[43]

Such individualistic confidence was, of course, short-lived, undermined by *fin de siècle* pessimism on the one hand, and by the growth of socialist and collectivist philosophies on the other. It was confined to a single generation which enjoyed an interlude of calm — 'equipoise', it has been called — between the passing of the Chartist anxieties and worries about the Great Depression and renewed social discontent. It must not be confused with socialist ideology in any strict sense (though there is an obvious affinity with certain 'come to Jesus' elements in the Labour party of Hardie, Snowden, and MacDonald). Thus, incarnational economists still believed in providence, and in the operation of divine social laws which must not be interfered with. Also, they continued to believe in 'conscience' as the key to right behaviour. What happened was that conscience and providence became sentimentalized — as d'Arcy Jones has put it, God came to resemble Santa Claus. Hell departed into metaphor, while Heaven retained its felicitousness, as indeed it had to do if it was to attract mankind once Hell had shed its terrors, but at the same time it became domesticated. The strategy now was not to frighten sinners into Heaven but to beckon them there by promising more of the good

---

[41] Octavia Hill to Mary Harrison, 16 July 1855, *Life of Octavia Hill as Told in her Letters*, ed. C. E. Maurice (1913), 49–51. See Nancy Boyd, *Josephine Butler, Octavia Hill, Florence Nightingale: Three Victorian Women Who Changed Their World* (1982), 129–30 and *passim*, for the contrast between Butler's evangelical wrestling with the powers of darkness and Hill's Mauricean belief that evil is merely an absence of good.

[42] Bernard M. G. Reardon, *From Coleridge to Gore: A Century of Religious Thought in Britain* (1971), 436–55.

[43] B. F. Westcott, quoted in Newsome, *Two Classes of Men*, p. 82.

things they had enjoyed in life. So as Hell ceased to be a fiery furnace, Heaven became a cosy fireside where long-lost loved ones congregated. Alexander Welsh has spoken of 'the Victorian readiness to make a heaven of hearth and home',[44] and this was the other side of making a home out of Heaven. As Farrar put it, Heaven was not a 'pagoda of jewels . . . and hallelujah choruses', as had once been imagined, but 'a place of . . . growth and progress upward and onward, of endless and beneficent activity, of a love which knows no fear. . . . '[45]—in other words, Home Sweet Home. In such a climate all was serene—God and nature seemed to be on man's side, and no one needed a theology of the Cross. In David Newsome's words, this was a 'very favoured' generation, which 'felt no brooding sense of cosmic disaster', and 'had no experience or even memory of the ugliness of war', nor yet of revolution.[46]

The fact that evangelists could now portray Heaven as a continuation of the good life means that they and their audience must have thought that life was good. And it is probably the case that the naturalistic version of Heaven, like the craze for spiritualism (conversing with the departed) and for childhood fantasy in literature, was an outgrowth of post-millennial assurance. Against this it has been suggested[47] that the fashion for fantasy was due to escapist yearnings, a retreat from 'the weary and the fever and the fret' of industrial awfulness, but, as the source of the quotation indicates, this was surely an earlier mode. Incarnationalism seems rather to have represented a brief interlude of insouciant self-satisfaction before the Rowntrees and Booths moved in with their breadlines and 'bitter cries'. George Orwell marvelled that Dickens could be so sentimental about happy endings ('a huge, loving family of three or four generations, all crammed together in the same house and constantly multiplying, like a bed of oysters'), but he also appreciated that such scenes of idle and idyllic cosiness were 'genuinely happy' ones, that Dickens 'could combine such purposelessness with so much vitality'.[48] The point is not that Dickens was unique, but that the 'spirit of the age' as represented by Browning, Swinburne, and Meredith was one which luxuriated in an optimism that was energetic as well as sentimental. Houghton considered that Mill, Morley, Dickens, Browning, and Eliot were untypical Victorians in so far as they regarded 'enthusiasm' and 'aspiration' as more important qualities than 'earnestness'

---

[44] Alexander Welsh, *The City of Dickens* (Oxford, 1971), p. vi.

[45] Farrar, *Life of Farrar*, p. 282.

[46] Newsome, *Two Classes of Men*, p. 88.

[47] Humphrey Carpenter, *Secret Gardens: The Golden Age of Children's Literature* (1985), 13–19.

[48] *The Collected Essays, Journalism and Letters of George Orwell*, ed. Sonia Orwell and Ian Angus (1968), i. 447–8.

and 'performance of duty',[49] but in fact their preference reflected a particular mid-Victorian phase.

The Eclipse of Bishop Butler

Newsome sees the emergence of incarnationalism as a case of Cambridge Platonism overtaking Oxford's Aristotelian bias. Maurice had been nurtured by that 'gallant band of Platonico-Wordsworthian-Coleridgean anti-Utilitarians',[50] the Cambridge Apostles—Julius Hare and Connop Thirlwall—and he in turn inspired Hort and (less directly) Westcott. However, when in the 1860s and 1870s Oxford too turned to incarnationalism, thanks to Gore, Scott Holland, and the group that would later produce *Lux Mundi*, the catalyst was, as Newsome shows, not Cambridge influence, but the substitution of Plato for the Aristotelian Butler in the syllabus, and the platonist influence within the University of Matthew Arnold, Jowett, Pattison, and T. H. Green.[51]

Maurice deeply admired Butler, but found it necessary to reinterpret him. Where evangelicals had found the great Bishop insufficiently salvationist, Maurice thought him excessively so. This is to a friend in 1865:

I go great lengths with you in your bold saying that Butler's 'Analogy' should be written over again in our time . . . that it may be reconciled with his own doctrine on the conscience. If he was right . . . in the sermon on the Conscience, it could not be necessary that he should help out his argument on moral probability by an ignominious appeal to men's fears; by showing them how perilous it might be not to act even upon the hundredth chance of the evidence for the Gospel (!) being true.

If God governs the world, it is dangerous to depict that world as out of joint, and conscience as an authority in the mind, independent of God. Rather conscience should be regarded as the mental organ through which God reveals his law to men;[52] though one may wonder whether this really differs from Butler's observation that conscience is 'the voice of God within us'. Maurice is forced to conclude, therefore, that in some respects Butler's arguments are inferior to George Combe's, whom he evidently admired. Butler had believed that moral antecedents produce certain consequences, painful or pleasant, and Combe argued the same

---

[49] Houghton, *The Victorian Frame of Mind*, pp. 263–5.

[50] R. C. Trench, quoted in Newsome, *Two Classes of Men*, p. 78.

[51] For Green's influence see Melvin Richter, *The Politics of Conscience: T. H. Green and His Age* (1964), 118–29, 330–49, and *passim*. For reservations see D. M. Mackinnon, 'Some aspects of the treatment of Christianity by the British idealists', *Religious Studies*, 20 (1984), 133–44.

[52] Maurice to D. J. Vaughan, 22 Nov. 1865, *Life of Maurice*, ii. 510–11; Swanston, *Ideas of Order*, pp. 82–4.

for *physical* antecedents, but the latter were based on scientific observation (induction) whereas Butler's, Maurice regretted to say, had been mere guesses or presumptions.[53]

Swanston comments that by the later 1850s many commentators, concerned at the rising wave of scepticism, and feeling the need for a new apologetic, were happy to link Butler and Paley as twin spokesmen of an outmoded theology. It began to be pointed out that, while Butler's language made his theology *seem* orthodox, so that evangelicals like Mansel could claim him as their forerunner, in fact, and looked at more carefully, Butler's great principle—that God treats everyone according to their personal deserts—strikes 'at the very root of the whole doctrine concerning the Scheme of Redemption and Salvation so largely taught as orthodox'. His demonstrations that in the natural world the sins of A often hurt B, while the sufferings of X often help Y, had nothing whatever to do with the doctrine of vicarious or substitutionary punishment, since Butler had never supposed, for instance, that a murderer will be dealt with less severely in the next world merely because an innocent person has been hanged for his offence.[54] It also began to be argued that the celebrated doctrine of conscience was either tautological ('like saying that conscience decides by the rule of conscience'), or else it depended on psychological premises which looked shaky in the wake of Kant.[55] In an age attracted to agnosticism, positivism, and evolution, Butler's refutations of deism merely begged all the important questions. Leslie Stephen's *History of English Thought in the Eighteenth Century* (1876), and the disdainful comments of Goldwin Smith (1861) and Matthew Arnold (1877), typified a rather widespread 'exaggeration of dispraise' in relation to Butler, which was itself 'a re-action from the extravagance and absolutism of a previous homage'.[56] Anthropological studies popularized the view that religions develop as a means of explaining and justifying the various anomalies of life, an interpretation which removed much of the lustre from Butler's reasoning that the failure of revelation to contradict nature strengthens the case for Christianity. Also, Butler's argument from design (or final causes) made little impression on evolutionists and positivists. As Mackinnon

---

[53] Maurice, *Theological Essays*, pp. 213–21, 232–4. For Maurice's miscomprehension of Butler on this and other points see J. B. Mozley, *Essays Historical and Theological* (1878), ii. 257–72.

[54] M. P. W. Bolton, *Inquisitio Philosophica: An Examination of the Principles of Kant and Hamilton* (1866), 263–70.

[55] J. C. Shairp, 'The moral dynamic', *Studies in Poetry and Philosophy* (Edinburgh, 1868), 383–6. As Cupitt points out, Mansel's Bampton Lectures were an attempt to recast the *Analogy* for a post-Kantian world. Cupitt, 'Mansel's theory of regulative truth', *Journal of Theological Studies*, 18 (1967), 104.

[56] Revd John R. T. Eaton, *Bishop Butler and His Critics: Two Public Lectures* (Oxford and London, 1877), 5.

puts it, 'the importance of teleological considerations in Butler's scheme left him *prima facie* vulnerable to the first impact of Darwin'.[57]

And so in 1864, ten years after the Commission appointed by Parliament had reported on the condition of the University, the *Analogy* was removed from its central position in the Oxford Examination Statutes, mainly thanks to 'a liberal board of examiners' led by Mark Pattison.[58] It was reported in 1870 that Butler had been 'out of fashion for some time now' and taken up only 'very infrequently': 'It is not excluded, but being an optional subject it is one that has been discouraged. He is gone out of fashion: I do not know why.'[59]

[57] Ibid., pp. 34–41; Mackinnon, 'Some aspects of the treatment of Christianity', op. cit., p. 141.

[58] Swanston, *Ideas of Order*, p. 10; Mark Pattison, *Memoirs* (1885), 135.

[59] Evidence of D. P. Chase in *Report from the Select Committee of the House of Lords on University Tests*, pp. 17, 32 [PP 1871, ix. 109, 124].

Gladstonian Liberalism:
the Last Days of Atonement

Let us with a Gladstone mind
Praise the Lord for He is kind.

The Last Butlerian

No one was more distressed by the eclipse of Bishop Butler than William
Gladstone. He is alleged to have fulminated at the time of the Oxford
University Commission that dropping Butler from the syllabus would be
worse than the loss of four colleges, though he did not specify which
ones.[1] Gladstone had, of course, been reared an evangelical, but had
suffered a reaction at Oxford, where he was dismayed by the extremism
of the St Ebbes set under Bulteel. Like many other sons of evangelical
businessmen coming of age round about 1830, he detested the growing
influence of the pentecostalists and prophesiers, and he considered
evangelicalism's scope for 'private judgment' altogether too anarchical—
too 'individualising'—for a period of revolutionary alarms. He not only
ceased to be an evangelical, but became a lifelong and devoted member
of its antithesis, the High Church. Yet for all his attachment to the historic
and corporate Church as an institution, he clung fervently to the central
tenets of moderate evangelicals: providence, sin, conversion, conscience,
Atonement, salvation, and Judgment. Moreover, they were to inform his
entire approach to political action.[2]

But not straight away, for there was to be a curious interlude of medieval
fantasy. In a sense the fault lay with Chalmers. Gladstone had developed
an intense veneration for Chalmers, whom he had first come to know
well during a visit to Edinburgh in 1833. 'One of Nature's nobles' was
Chalmers, with 'his warrior-grandeur, his rich and glowing eloquence,

[1] Mozley to Church, 25 Dec. 1853, *Letters of Mozley*, pp. 222–3.
[2] This section is based on Hilton, 'Gladstone's theological politics', in Bentley and
Stevenson, *High and Low Politics*, pp. 28–57. See also Perry Butler, *Gladstone: Church,
State, and Tractarianism: A Study of his Religious Ideas and Attitudes 1809–59* (Oxford,
1982), *passim*; H. C. G. Matthew in Foot and Matthew, *The Gladstone Diaries*, iii. xxiii–
lvi; Deryck Schreuder, 'Gladstone and the conscience of the state', in Marsh, *Conscience
of the Victorian State*, pp. 73–143.

his absorbed and absorbing earnestness', his 'zealous and truly noble propagandism'.[3] Yet he was bitterly disappointed by Chalmers's London lectures in 1838,[4] by their lukewarm, even utilitarian, defence of the Establishment, and by their inadequate conception of the Visible Church and the Apostolic Succession. Gladstone was moved to a riposte which probably went further than he really intended, and which very soon made him uneasy. *The State in its Relations with the Church* (1838) was a Coleridgean extravaganza which pitched the case for establishment in the very highest organicist terms. There was no such thing as an individual conscience, and the 'system of individual morality' was a 'degraded', 'injurious legacy' of Locke. Citizens should be regarded, 'not as individuals, but only as constituents of the active power of . . . the life of the state', which was 'the self-governing energy of the nation made objective'. In order to achieve moral awareness, men must plug into this organic national conscience, by submitting to the dictation of the state over their lives and thoughts.[5]

Gladstone's gradual rediscovery of 'individual conscience' went *pari passu* with his emergence as a Peelite. Not many years after his 1838 manifesto, he found himself engaged on a 'process of lowering the religious tone of the State, letting it down, demoralizing it—i.e., stripping it of its ethical character, and assisting its transition into one which is mechanical'.[6] The Maynooth crisis of 1845 left him reflecting that 'the State cannot be said now to have a conscience . . . inasmuch as I think it acts . . . as no conscience—that is, no personal conscience (*which is the only real form of one*)—can endure'.[7] The tribulations of the Oxford Movement and the Gorham Judgment completed Gladstone's disillusion, and in 1853 he put forward a budget in which the people's role was not to *be* moralized but to impose its own morality on potentially corrupt governments by taking control of the purse strings.[8] The year 1853 turned Gladstone's earlier theocracy on its head, and foreshadowed his future career as a Liberal.

---

[3] Quoted in W. Forbes Gray, 'Chalmers and Gladstone: an unrecorded episode', *Records of the Scottish Church History Society*, 10 (1950), 10. For Gladstone's respectful, but occasionally critical, notes of September 1835 on Chalmers's Bridgewater Treatise see Gladstone Papers, BL Add. MS, 44724 fos. 176–80.

[4] See above, p. 61.

[5] W. E. Gladstone, *The State in its Relations with the Church* (1838; 4th revised edn, 1841), i. 73–8, 88, 124, 149, and 296–7. See Foot and Matthew, *The Gladstone Diaries*, iii. xxv–xxviii; Alec R. Vidler, *The Orb and the Cross: A Normative Study in the Relations of Church and State with reference to Gladstone's Early Writings* (1945), 26–47.

[6] Gladstone to Manning, 19 Apr. 1846, *Correspondence on Church and Religion of William Ewart Gladstone*, ed. D. C. Lathbury (1910), ii. 272.

[7] Gladstone to Newman, 19 Apr. 1845, ibid., i. 72 (italics added).

[8] H. C. G. Matthew, 'Disraeli, Gladstone, and the politics of mid-Victorian budgets', *Historical Journal*, 22 (1979), 626–30.

Maynooth was an important moment in Gladstone's rediscovery of 'conscience',[9] but there was also an intellectual component in the writings of Bishop Butler. Gladstone had read Butler at Oxford in 1830–1 and had been revolted by the ethical psychology of the *Rolls Sermons*. He recalled later that the 'teaching in the sermons on our moral nature was not integrated so to speak until several years later by large perusal of the works of St. Augustine'.[10] In 1884 he was still contending that Augustine's 'doctrine of human nature is substantially that of Bishop Butler; and he converted me about forty-five years ago to Bishop Butler's doctrine'.[11] Systematic investigation of Butler followed during the aftermath of Maynooth, in June and July 1845, and quickly became an obsession. That Butler was 'a guide of life' became a great Gladstonian refrain, a guide moreover 'as much in *practical* as in speculative things'. 'I never take a step in life without thinking how Butler would have advised me.'[12] He was still saying the same, in an embarrassingly outmoded way, when in 1896 he published an edition of Butler's *Works* along with his own *Subsidiary Studies*. There is no doubt that Butler's assault on the sensationalist psychology of Locke, and his concept of a 'superintending faculty' called 'conscience', which *knew* certain things to be right even though they gave pain (and vice versa), were important ingredients in Gladstone's development as a 'liberal-individualist'.

In this sense Butler enabled Gladstone to return to some of his evangelical roots, based as they too were on the centrality of conscience. Yet more than once Gladstone credited Butler with having 'helped to emancipate me from the narrow evangelicalism of my boyhood'.[13] The comment has two possible explanations. In the first place, whereas evangelicals had a dismally 'negative' attitude to sacraments and liturgy, Butler's emphasis on the importance of such external forms led him, not less than Gladstone, to be accused of crypto-Romanism by nineteenth-century critics. More relevant here is the way in which Butler—together with Hooker and Palmer—helped Gladstone overcome certain other evangelical 'negatives'. The 'narrowest' aspect of the old creed was its insistence that, since faith was requisite for salvation, God must have condemned to eternal perdition millions of souls who had never even heard of him. Like his heroes Canning

---

[9] M. D. Stephen, 'Liberty, church and state: Gladstone's relations with Manning and Acton, 1832–70', *Journal of Religious History*, 1 (1960–1), 223–6.

[10] Gladstone's memorandum, 1894, Brooke and Sorensen, *The Prime Ministers' Papers*, i. 140–1, 150.

[11] Gladstone to Revd Charles Beard, 23 Aug. 1884, Lathbury, *Correspondence on Church and Religion*, ii. 325.

[12] Gladstone to his son Willy, 1 Aug. 1860, ibid., ii. 164.

[13] Gladstone's 'Autobiographical retrospect', 1894, Brooke and Sorensen, *The Prime Ministers' Papers*, i. 38.

and Peel,[14] and like the philosopher of mid-Victorian Liberalism, J. S. Mill, Gladstone was appalled by the 'damnatory clauses' of the Athanasian Creed. He was to write much later about his retreat from evangelicalism:

At this moment I am as closely an adherent to the doctrines of grace generally and to the general sense of St. Augustine [as in 1828]. I hope that my mind has dropped nothing affirmative. But I hope also that there has been dropped from it all the damnatory part of the opinions taught by the Evangelical school; not only as respects the Roman Catholic religion, but also as to heretics and heathens; Nonconformists and Presbyterians I think that I always let off pretty easily.[15]

It is clear that the 'affirmatives' not dropped were those more salvationist elements of the evangelical (and Augustinian) gospel scheme, such as providence, sin, and redemption.

Another way in which Gladstone ditched his evangelical past was by his sensitivity to the mid-century reformulation of theories about the passage of time. Thus when in later life the Grand Old Man of 'movement' had to explain why he had opposed parliamentary reform in 1832, he blamed evangelicalism for having blinded him to that 'greatest of historical facts', the fact that society is divine.[16] He meant, presumably, that as an evangelical he had looked on the world merely as a place of moral trial and a prelude to eternity. Certainly, 'becoming a Liberal' meant that God was to be seen as directing the progress of society and not merely receiving saved souls. From the fifties onwards his rhetoric is studded with metaphors appealing to a linear sense of destiny: to 'the great social forces which move onwards in their might and majesty', 'silent changes in the earth's crust', 'the great subterranean movements of society', 'silent changes in the very bed and basis of modern society'. Or, as he chided opponents of parliamentary reform, 'you cannot fight against the future. Time is on our side.'[17] Britain was passing, he more soberly said, 'from a stationary into a progressive period',[18] and in accepting this the natural theologian in Gladstone stopped looking for evidence of God's omnipotence in the workings of the machine, and found it instead in the moral improvement of society: 'When we contemplate many of the political societies, such as the Roman, the British, the American, their movement

---

[14] Canning to Phillpotts, 11 May 1825, *Some Official Correspondence of George Canning*, ed. Edward J. Stapleton (1887), i. 363.

[15] Brooke and Sorensen, *The Prime Ministers' Papers*, i. 152.

[16] Gladstone's 'Autobiographical retrospect', ibid., i. 38.

[17] Gladstone in House of Commons, 27 Apr. 1866, *Parliamentary Debates*, 3rd series, clxxxiii. 152.

[18] W. E. Gladstone, *A Chapter of Autobiography* (10th edn, 1868), 11, reprinted in Gladstone, *Gleanings of Past Years*, vii. 101–2.

through successive stages is astonishing. But each of these stages is a new presentation of the argument of design.'[19]

For this reason Gladstone was one of those Christians who, despite an attachment to certain fundamentalist doctrines, did not balk at Darwinism. He wrote to Jevons in 1874: 'Indeed, I must say that the doctrine of Evolution, if it be true, enhances in my judgment the proper idea of the greatness of God, for it makes every stage of creation a legible prophecy of all those which are to follow it.'[20] The significant word here is 'legible'. In 1845 he had called the Irish Famine a 'calamity legibly divine' because of the 'total absence of such second causes as might tempt us to explain it away'. In other words, it had been an example of special providence, just as Chalmers averred.[21] The trouble with such dispensations is, of course, that they can be interpreted in any number of ways, each of which will appear arbitrary to many people. Darwinism therefore appealed to some providentialists because it introduced some scientific stiffening into the religious interpretation of natural 'history'. As Gladstone quipped in *Studies Subsidiary to Butler*, 'evolution' might be better termed 'devolution', since it proved how God, rather than making a 'sudden or special creation', had 'still more admirably' devolved the task on secondary or scientific laws.

The more we have of system and fixity in nature, the better. For, in the method of natural second causes, God as it were takes the map of His own counsels out of the recesses of His own idea, and graciously lays it near our view; condescending, as it were, to make us partakers of His thought.[22]

Reflecting on Butler's view as to the evolution of conscience, and on his speculations as to the possible immortality of brutes, Gladstone was able to reassure himself that 'the idea of evolution is without doubt deeply ingrained in Butler'.[23]

But for all this Gladstone did not ditch the basic tenets of evangelical eschatology and evangelical moral philosophy; indeed it was his success in reconciling them with the mid-Victorian period's worldly optimism which gave Gladstonian Liberalism its purchase. No reader of Gladstone's private diaries can doubt, for example, his conviction of personal depravity, his belief 'in a degeneracy of man, in the Fall — in *sin* in the intensity and

---

[19] Gladstone, *Studies Subsidiary to Butler*, p. 305.
[20] Gladstone to Stanley Jevons, 10 May 1874, Lathbury, *Correspondence on Church and Religion*, ii. 101.
[21] See below, p. 351, and on Chalmers's views above, pp. 110–11.
[22] Gladstone, *Studies Subsidiary to Butler*, pp. 306–9.
[23] Gladstone to Argyll, 9 Dec. 1895, John Morley, *The Life of William Ewart Gladstone* (1903), iii. 521. See Gladstone to Müller, 24 Dec. 1872, Max Müller Papers, Bodleian Library MSS, d.170.

virulence of sin'.[24] Like Daniel Wilson and other apologists, Gladstone had to explain away the lack of 'evangelical flavour, or unction' in Butler by pointing out that his philosophical purpose had not led in that direction. Nevertheless, looked at carefully, Butler's works left the reader in no doubt as to his fundamentally lapsarian and soteriological approach. The only subject on which Butler's works might be regarded as boring and repetitious was the 'sad and solemn topic of the misery, debasement, and corruption which virulent and inveterate sin has brought about in the world'.[25] To the end Gladstone maintained that sin, righteousness, and Judgment made up a 'code of moral regeneration for mankind',[26] and that the key to that code was the Atonement. He was therefore dismayed by the mid-century softening of interpretation as to the meaning of the Crucifixion. He blamed it on the increasing 'tenderness' of the times, something which in other areas (such as social reform) he applauded. People objected to the orthodox conception of Christ as a whipping-boy, but only because they presupposed 'that *pain is essentially or at least universally an evil* . . . But this, it seems to me, ought to be denied. Pain is not in its nature an evil in the proper sense, nor is it universally attended with evil as a consequence.' Its most common effect, indeed, was to 'energise'—the verb is significant—'feelings of self-mortification and self-sacrifice',[27] which both evangelicals and Tractarians regarded as the surest harbingers of virtue, in nations as well as in individuals. Moreover, the doctrine of the Cross had to be seen in the context of the Incarnation, which had

brought righteousness out of the region of cold abstractions, clothed it in flesh and blood, . . . gave it the firmest command over the springs of human action, . . . by incorporating it in a person, and making it liable to love. Included in this great scheme, the doctrine of free pardon is not a passport for sin, nor a derogation from the moral order which carefully adapts reward and retribution to desert, but stands in the closest harmony with the component laws of our moral nature.[28]

A 'moral order which carefully adapts reward and retribution to desert': this phrase, an epicentre of Gladstonian Liberalism, introduces us to its

[24] Gladstone as reported by Mrs Humphry Ward, 8 Apr. 1888, *The Life of Mrs. Humphry Ward*, by Janet Penrose Trevelyan (1923), 59.

[25] Gladstone, *Studies Subsidiary to Butler*, pp. 112–13. See above, pp. 180–1.

[26] Gladstone to B. M. Malabari, 20 July 1889, Lathbury, *Correspondence on Church and Religion*, ii. 118.

[27] W. E. Gladstone, 'On the mediation of Christ', written in 1830 and printed as an appendix to *Studies Subsidiary to Butler*, pp. 328–9. See Gladstone to Manning, 16 Nov. 1869, *Life of Cardinal Manning*, by Edmund Sheridan Purcell (1895), ii. 407.

[28] W. E. Gladstone, 'True and false conceptions of the Atonement', *The Nineteenth Century*, 36 (1894), 328, reprinted in W. E. Gladstone, *Later Gleanings: Theological and Ecclesiastical* (1897), 331.

author's powerful sense of providence. God was no 'mere abstract idea dwelling in the air, and in the clouds', but a 'Divine Governing Power, which will some day call all of us to account for every thought we conceive, and for every word we utter'.[29] He retained throughout his life—and long after it had ceased to be fashionable—this transcendental view of God

> as standing in certain relations to us; as carrying on a moral government of the world. He is held to prescribe and favour what is right; to forbid and regard with displeasure what is wrong; and to dispose the courses of events in such a way that, in general and upon the whole, there is a tendency of virtue to bring satisfaction and happiness, and of vice to entail the reverse of these, even when appearances, and external advantages, might not convey such an indication.[30]

We saw above how Wilberforce preferred Butler to Paley because the latter had neglected God's holiness and justice.[31] Gladstone made exactly the same point about the incompleteness of Paley's natural theology: 'Although the argument of design took its rise within the precincts of the physical order, it did not end there. And Butler has here laid down for us the cardinal principle on which is founded its extension to the moral universe.'[32] Gladstone was naturally susceptible to the evangelical consolation that, since vice must be punished *either* here *or* in the next world, terrestrial misfortunes are really marks of divine favour, encouraging reformation and eternal safety. His response to family bankruptcy and to his daughter's dangerous illness was, typically, not self-pity, but a reflection that he had 'never seen the working of the prudential and moral laws of God's providence more signally exhibited'.[33]

It was essential, in Gladstone's view, that men should respond appropriately to the dispensations of providence. He attached enormous significance to the word 'action'.

> Our Almighty Father is continually, aye every day and hour, calling upon us, almost compelling us, to act. Now acting is not the mere discharge of an outward function. It is a continuing process, in which we are responsible throughout. What is meant by being responsible? It is meant that we expose ourselves to consequences flowing from our actions. These are (say) of two kinds. First, there is alteration of environment; which implies that in the future actings, which cannot be escaped, we shall have to cast our account anew with circumstances. The second cuts deeper still. It is that our action modifies, that is to say progressively

---

[29] Gladstone in House of Commons, 26 Apr. 1883, *Parliamentary Debates*, 3rd series, cclxxviii. 1193.

[30] W. E. Gladstone, 'On the influence of authority in matters of opinion', *The Nineteenth Century*, 1 (1877), 10.

[31] See above, p. 178.

[32] Gladstone, *Studies Subsidiary to Butler*, p. 293.

[33] Gladstone to Manning, 12 Mar. 1848, Lathbury, *Correspondence on Church and Religion*, ii. 279.

but silently alters, from time to time, and eventually shapes, our own mind and character.[34]

Gladstone explained such imperceptible character development with reference to Butler's doctrine of habit. By acting virtuously men acquire a habitude for virtue, and so improve themselves at the same time as their environment. It was thus that in those 'little tutored but yet reflective minds' of the Lancashire operatives, lauded by Gladstone for stoically supporting the cause of the Northern States against their own supposed economic interest, 'by a process of quiet instillation, opinions and sentiments gradually form themselves of which we for a long time remain unaware, but which, when at last they make their appearance, are found to be deep-rooted, mature, and ineradicable'.[35] And if action was the key to the good life, politics—an activity which Gladstone had formerly regarded as irredeemably sordid[36]—now came to be regarded as an arena for the grandest actions. 'The vital principle of the Liberal party,' Gladstone told Granville, 'like that of Greek art, is *action*.'[37] Providence would surreptitiously raise and moralize society, and the statesman's function was to see that laws were periodically adjusted so as to match society's rising awareness. Hence Gladstone's legislative restlessness and tilts at privilege. In the words of a recent authority, Gladstonian politics became 'practical experiments in truth . . . a series of evolving strategies, policies, postures, enthusiasms, missions, and tactical forays', endless attempts to evoke the sort of visceral 'response which his nature craved'.[38]

All very well, but *how* is one meant to act? Here Gladstone, who was no metaphysician, whose 'intellect would not bite' on philosophy,[39] remained unpardonably obscure, and grandiloquent appeals to the *Analogy of Religion* (Butler's 'sound principles applicable to the mode of Providential government'[40]) are not very helpful. But there is his celebrated analysis of his own political opportunism, which provides some clues. He claimed

---

[34] Gladstone, *Studies Subsidiary to Butler*, p. 9. See Butler, *Analogy of Religion*, p. 103 (Pt. I, ch. 5) [Butler, *Works*, ed. Halifax (1820), i. 144–5; ed. Gladstone (1896), i. 137]: 'There is a third thing, which may seem implied in the present world's being a state of probation; that it is a theatre of action, for the manifestation of persons' characters, with respect to a future one.'

[35] Gladstone in House of Commons, 27 Apr. 1866, *Parliamentary Debates*, 3rd series, clxxxiii, 148–9.

[36] Gladstone to Manning, 2 Apr. 1837, Lathbury, *Correspondence on Church and Religion*, i. 31–2.

[37] Gladstone to Granville, 19 May 1877, *The Political Correspondence of Mr. Gladstone and Lord Granville 1876–1886*, ed. Agatha Ramm (Oxford, 1962), i. 40.

[38] Schreuder, 'Gladstone and the conscience of the state', loc. cit., p. 85. See also Philip Magnus, *Gladstone: A Biography* (1954), 165.

[39] Henry Scott Holland, *Personal Studies* (1905), 41.

[40] Gladstone to Maud Stanley, 27 Jan. 1856, Lathbury, *Correspondence on Church and Religion*, ii. 30.

that providence had provided him with one 'striking gift', a gift of 'right-timing' or, 'at certain political junctures, . . . appreciation of the general situation and its result'. It was emphatically *not* a 'simple acceptance of public opinion', which was nearly always in arrears, but 'an insight into the facts of particular eras, and their relations one to another, which generates in the mind a conviction that the materials exist for forming a public opinion, and for directing it to a particular end'.[41] Butler was 'a guide of life' because, more than any other writer, he taught Gladstone how to set about achieving 'moral insight' into the facts of an era, and showed him where to look for evidence, or at least 'probable evidence'— Butler's dictum that 'probability is the guide of life' became another Gladstonian catch-phrase.[42] There was, perhaps unconsciously, a degree of wilful ambiguity in Gladstone's approach here. He had tried to knit himself a complete and 'systematic philosophy' in *The State in its Relations with the Church*, and the stitches had quickly come loose. He now made a virtue of incompleteness and uncertainty—hence his criticism of an avowed (but 'thoroughly unsound') Butlerian,[43] J. H. Newman.

I think there is nothing more characteristic of the unphilosophic mind than impatience of doubt and premature avidity for system. That seems to me . . . to have been Newman's snare all along. No man can grasp truth entire. Butler took it in fragments, but his wise instinct enabled him so to lay each stone that it would fit in with every other stone which might be well and truly laid in the double light of thought and experience. . . . Newman also laid his stones; but at every period of his life he seems to have been driven by a fatal necessity to piece them all together, to make a building of them, and he has made half a dozen; and when the winds blew and the floods beat they gave way.[44]

---

[41] Gladstone's 'General retrospect', Brooke and Sorensen, *The Prime Minsters' Papers*, i. 136. There are several analyses of this famous passage, of which perhaps the most interesting is in Magnus, *Gladstone*, pp. 190–1, 440–2.

[42] Gladstone, 'The law of probable evidence, and its application to conduct', written in 1845 and published (with a different title) in *The Nineteenth Century*, 5 (1879), 908–34, and reprinted in Gladstone, *Gleanings*, vii. 153–99, and also in Gladstone, *Studies Subsidiary to Butler*, pp. 334–70. See Gladstone to the Earl of Pembroke, 29 Sept. 1873, Lathbury, *Correspondence on Church and Religion*, ii. 94: 'Probable knowledge, or, to speak more accurately, probable evidence, may entail the obligation of action, the obligation of belief, as truly as knowledge which is demonstrative, and this probable knowledge is the "guide of life".'

[43] Gladstone to R. H. Hutton, 6 Oct. 1890, Lathbury, *Correspondence on Church and Religion*, i. 407.

[44] Gladstone to Sir F. Rogers, 25 Feb. 1866, ibid., ii. 301. For Newman's defence against such charges, see his criticisms of Peel and Brougham in J. H. Newman, *An Essay in Aid of a Grammar of Assent* (1870), p. 92, and Newman, 'The Tamworth reading room', *Discussions*, p. 295: 'Life is not long enough for a religion of inferences; we shall never have done beginning, if we determine to begin with proof. We shall ever be laying our foundations; we shall turn theology into evidences, and divines into textuaries. . . . I would rather be bound to defend the reasonableness of *assuming* that Christianity is true, than to *prove* [demonstrate] a moral governance from the physical world.'

Butler provided another clue to the 'facts of particular eras'—which was that providence operated in a dialectical manner, that there were 'laws of action and reaction in human thought'.[45] God 'takes sides in that conflict between virtue and vice, which incessantly prevails in the world'.[46] 'In the battle of good and evil, providence, though it may seem to be fighting in disguise, chooses its side and makes known its choice.'[47] It is a fascinating thought that Gladstone may have first derived such notions from an important review of *The State in its Relations with the Church* by yet another Butlerian, John Keble. The latter had applauded Gladstone's intentions, but had felt that the only hope for a church locked in mortal combat with the state was to break away from its enemy, if necessary by violence. Gladstone's vision of a revitalized church dominating the state from within struck Keble as hopelessly Utopian. It might work for a fortnight, but the long-term consequence would be the secularization of the clergy, not the spiritualization of the state. 'This is the sort of anticipation which most alarms us; and the more, because it seems to exclude persecution; whereas the violent separation of Church and State almost appears to involve it. There is no blood of martyrs in the former prospect, no seed of future diffusion and victory.'[48] Significantly, Gladstone considered Keble's review 'elevated and most interesting'; Keble must have 'the gift of prophecy in its larger sense, so accurately does he interpret many hidden meanings that are in my mind rather than my book'.[49]

Gladstone may also have been influenced by an idiosyncratic book which he read several times, Lord Lindsay's *Progression by Antagonism*. This Butlerian (and also Combean) tome was intended as a theoretical key to Lindsay's *magnum opus* on the historical development of Christian art, as well as a response to 'the cry that rises up on all sides, the yearning, agonising cry, from the youthful, ingenuous, truth-seeking hearts of England for a key to the enigma of our times'. Because of the Fall man was in a condition of 'internal anarchy', his senses and his intellect both at war with his potential spirituality, and only the supernatural influence of the Trinity (the will of God, the Incarnation, obedience, the Atonement, the Resurrection, and the Holy Ghost) could restore a harmonious subordination of the spirit. However, it was a general law of the moral government of God that progression could only occur through an antagonism of

---

[45] Gladstone, 'The evangelical movement: its parentage, progress, and issue', *The British Quarterly Review*, 70 (1879), 14, reprinted in *Gleanings*, vii. 221.

[46] Gladstone, *Studies Subsidiary to Butler*, p. 15.   [47] Ibid., p. 303.

[48] [J. Keble], 'Gladstone: *The State in its Relations with the Church*', *The British Critic and Quarterly Theological Review*, 26 (1839), 396.

[49] Foot and Matthew, *The Gladstone Diaries*, 8 Oct. 1839, ii. 631; Gladstone to J. R. Hope, 6 Nov. 1839, Lathbury, *Correspondence on Church and Religion*, i. 18, 46.

forces.[50] With respect to artistic endeavour the three life-forces were sense, mind, and spirit, respectively associated with Egyptian, Greek, and Christian cultures. Progress in Christian art had occurred dialectically, through an antagonism of half-truths, towards true spiritual awareness, but it had required a great artist in each era to inspire his contemporaries with the necessary vision, and to direct aesthetic opinion towards the desired end.[51] In Gladstone's view the politician's role was not at all dissimilar, which is why in a famous phrase he could refer to politics as 'at once a game and a high art'.[52] The statesman's function was to interpret providence to his contemporaries, and to make them 'feel the issue of the moment as part of the eternal duel between good and evil'.

Gladstone's first clear-cut espousal of dialectical moral politics came with the Corn Law crisis of 1845–6, an episode which had a profound effect on his mental development. If, as Colin Matthew has remarked in a seminal piece of interpretation, having abandoned theocracy Gladstone knitted 'an alternative if less elevated synthesis' out of 'colonial affairs, the morality of free trade and finance, and the morality of international affairs',[53] it remains a question: how could he have regarded the old and the new as in some sense equivalents? One explanation may be that whereas *The State in its Relations with the Church* presumed that truth would come to man through revelation, Gladstone's new passion for *laissez-faire*—in terms of international political relations as well as commercial ones—can be seen as an appeal to another main source of religious experience, which was natural theology; in other words, that he switched from a faith based on revelation to one based on nature. It was Gladstone the natural theologian who learned to praise God's providential 'counterpoises, both physical and social, for the advantage of His creatures', such as 'the wonderful monetary system of civilized

---

[50] Lord Lindsay, *Progression by Antagonism: A Theory, Involving Considerations touching the Present Position, Duties, and Destiny of Great Britain* (1846), pp. v–vi.

[51] Ibid., pp. 2–3. See also Lord Lindsay, *Sketches of the History of Christian Art* (1847), i. xii–xiv: 'Man is, in the strictest sense of the word, a progressive being, and with many periods of inaction and retrogression, has still held, upon the whole, a steady course towards the great end of his existence, the re-union and re-harmonizing of the three elements of his being, dislocated by the Fall, in the service of his God.' In 1877 Gladstone commented that Conservatism represented 'repose' like Egyptian art, whereas Liberalism contained 'the Greek idea of life and motion'. D. A. Hamer, *Liberal Politics in the Age of Gladstone and Rosebery: A Study in Leadership and Policy* (Oxford, 1972), 57.

[52] Gladstone to Max Müller, 25 Nov. 1872, Müller Papers, Bodleian Library MSS. d.170 fo. 183, quoted in J. P. Parry, 'Religion and the collapse of Gladstone's first government, 1870–1874', *Historical Journal*, 25 (1982), 72. Lindsay and Gladstone later conducted parallel researches into Olympian mythology and the theology of the Homeric Age. See Gladstone to Lindsay (Earl Crawford), 14 and 16 Feb. 1874, and Lindsay to Gladstone, 15 and 27 Feb. 1874, Gladstone Papers, BL Add. MS. 44442 fos. 230, 252–3, 264, and 272–3.

[53] Matthew in Foot and Matthew, *The Gladstone Diaries*, iii. xxxiv.

countries, which exhibits the balance of forces in a manner more curious and striking than any mere physical [i.e. human] ponderation can do it'.[54] For him, as for Peelites generally, Free Trade and sound (non-interventionist) finance were less matters of *enrichissez-vous* and social progress (though there were elements of these) than of leaving providence to its own devices, the better to display God's handiwork, his wise and moral economy of the world. But though theoretically Gladstone had moved to Free Trade some time before 1845, it was not until then that it became a burning moral issue. Before then, he told his father, he had been accustomed to speak of Protection, 'not as a thing good in principle but to be dealt with as tenderly and cautiously as might be according to circumstances, always running in the direction of Free Trade'. 1845 changed this: like others he was devastated by the Irish Famine, which ruled out his hitherto cautious approach to the tariff question, and commanded an immediate and firm commitment to principle, on one side or the other.

It was no longer open to me to pursue that cautious course: a great struggle was imminent in which it was plain that two parties only could really find place, on the one side for repeal, on the other side for the *permanent* maintenance of a corn law and a protective system generally and on principle.[55]

Now this is a remarkable admission. There is no sublunary reason why the Famine should have ruled out a cautiously pragmatic approach in favour of a war of principles; but then the Famine was not, in Gladstone's eyes, a sublunary phenomenon:

Here is a calamity legibly Divine; there is a total absence of such second causes as might tempt us to explain it away; it is the greatest horror of modern times, that in the richest age of the world, and in the richest country of that age, the people should be dying of famine by hundreds, and we, the English community, have scarcely as yet got even the feeblest notion of this horror in its aspect to us. No mere giving of money will do, it can only be met by national and personal humiliation.[56]

Where many politicians followed Trevelyan in seeing the hand of God as directed against the Irish themselves for their philogenitiveness and sloth, Gladstone saw only 'its aspect to us', its judgment on 'our usual tone of thoughtless joyous or ambitious life'. Ireland was not the object but 'the *minister* of God's retribution upon cruel and inveterate and but

---

[54] Gladstone, *Studies Subsidiary to Butler*, pp. 14–15.
[55] Gladstone to his father, 30 June 1849, Foot and Matthew, *The Gladstone Diaries*, iii. xxxviii–xxxix.
[56] Gladstone to Manning, 9 Mar. 1847, Lathbury, *Correspondence on Church and Religion*, ii. 275–6.

half-atoned injustice', and it forced the English ruling class to face up to those 'great social and great religious questions' which could not any longer be disregarded.[57]

There is no doubt that for Gladstone at least the repeal of the Corn Laws has to be regarded as an act of atonement. Unfortunately Peel's defeat in the Commons on another Irish issue (which Gladstone and Graham both regarded as a perfect example of 'Butler's doctrine of retribution in this world')[58] made the free traders' victory much less clear-cut, and so less morally purgative. Gladstone was frustrated by Peel's refusal during the next few years to reactivate the issue, which he could have done by withdrawing support from Russell's ministry and letting in a Tory government still committed to Protection. But Peel was not prepared to risk his achievement for the sake of a symbolic thrill, and when the Tories did take office once more, in 1852, the worst happened from Gladstone's point of view, in that Disraeli pronounced Protection to be 'dead and damned'. Gladstone's effective but immoderate, indeed almost manic, assault on the Tory budget marked his political resurrection after a spell of disillusionment and uncertainty. Shannon points out that from this time Gladstone hated Disraeli with a quite uncharacteristic venom, and ingeniously suggests that this may be because he projected on to the most obvious available candidate the self-loathing he felt with respect to his own disturbing ambition.[59] Whether or not this was the case, there is no doubt that he suffered a severe recrudescence of guilt and self-loathing at this time,[60] nor that he felt the force of his own ambitiousness. He may even have been aware that his 'total freedom from doubts' on the question of whether to accompany Hope-Scott and Manning to Rome in the wake of the Gorham Judgment was convenient from the point of view of someone who cherished a future in politics. Gladstone had previously wondered whether it had been 'sufficiently considered, how far pain may become the ground of enjoyment. How far satisfaction and even an action delighting in pain may be a true experimental phenomenon of the human mind. May not such virtue often exist, as shall find when the lower faculty is punished or straightened, a joy in the justice and in the beneficial effects of that chastisement.'[61] Now he began to put such reflections to the test in bouts of self-scourging, associated with his night-time rescue work, atoning by his own stripes

[57] Gladstone to his wife, 12 Oct. 1845, ibid., ii. 266 (italics added).

[58] Apparently because of Peel's equivocations on the subject of the sugar duties in 1841. See Gladstone's memorandum, 10 July 1846, Foot and Matthew, *The Gladstone Diaries*, iii. 557.

[59] Richard Shannon, *Gladstone: I. 1809–1865* (1982), 244, 256–63.

[60] See below, p. 356.

[61] Foot and Matthew, *The Gladstone Diaries*, 4 Jan. 1843, iii. 250–1.

for the sins of fallen women. It was an emotional and highly charged Gladstone that pounced on Disraeli's budget in 1852. But it is not the case, as is often supposed, that Disraeli offended because his espousal of Free Trade in 1852 was only half-hearted. His crime was rather to have abandoned Protection at all, and so destroyed the meaning which the tariff question had given politics for so long. Gladstone craved *meaning*, *legibility*, and clear-cut conflict, but Disraeli had disobligingly muddied the waters.

With corn off the agenda Gladstone looked round for some other great issue on which 'the blood of martyrs' might spill. But the Age of Equipoise was sadly lacking in polarization as even the agricultural lamb nestled up comfortably to the manufacturing lion. A clue to Gladstone's philosophy in this situation is to be found in his *Quarterly Review* diagnosis of the political malaise in 1856. The fundamental need, as he saw it, was to create an organic national union while allowing scope for individual conscience and freedom of action and the way to do this was through politics. Parliament's function was first to encourage, and then to legislate in response to, public initiatives, such 'responsible dialogue' between Parliament and public providing some degree of vertical cohesion in the nation. But in the 1850s Parliament was clearly failing in its task, and for reasons which went deeper than Palmerston's personal lack of political will. Parliament could not function because the public itself was no longer stirred into passionate advocacies. The heyday of moral politics had been 1832–46, when, according to Gladstone, two rigidly organized parties had held the legislature in a tight grip. There had been intense hatreds, but also — and more importantly — 'strong attachments', 'unwavering confidence', and 'warm devotion'. Though politics then 'were not profound, they were intelligible'. And all this had been possible because the country itself had been polarized socially and ideologically:

Town and country, upon the whole, represent the respective preponderances in Great Britain of Church and Dissent, of Authority and Will, of Antiquity and Novelty, of Conservation and Reform; and Town and Country had received from the Reform Act each its separate organization, acutely distinct and angular, while all the intermediate, nondescript, miscellaneous influences, that under the old system had darkened the dividing lines and softened the shock of the adverse powers, had been but too ruthlessly swept away.[62]

Needless to say this was nonsense, but it is central to any understanding of Gladstone's political demon. It is as though, frustrated by the mid-Victorian consensus, he was driven to creating conflict artificially — or so

---

[62] [W. E. Gladstone], 'The declining efficiency of parliament', *Quarterly Review*, 99 (1856), 527–8.

it seemed to his opponents—by pitting his vision of a morally enhanced future against the privileges of a fallen present. Thus did the most Burkean of statesmen become the most *un*-Burkean, ever interfering with society, and not even from sincere dictates of reason like Burke's despised *philosophes*, but gratuitously and from a conviction that societies which are not in political turmoil will stagnate. 'It is rapid growth in the body politic that renders stereotyped law intolerable.'[63] In place of the sacerdotal paternalism of 1838, Gladstone now proposed social self-flagellation, or the constant assault on privilege, as a way of securing vertical organic union within the nation. The body politic would divide, but laterally, one half of the upper ten thousand against the other half, and therefore without fundamental damage to social cohesion.

So began that series of what Schreuder calls 'practical experiments in truth'—those sudden convictions concerning Italy, slavery, Schleswig Holstein, Governor Eyre, Reform, Church Rates—where Gladstone seemed to be making bids in the hope of eliciting a popular political response. At length he hit an electoral jackpot when he hit on Irish Church Disestablishment in 1868. Magnus talks of Gladstone's 'seismic mind' and 'mental earthquakes',[64] but it may be more helpful to imagine his pilgrim progress through the sixties—not a decade when the Valley of Death cast its shadows before, but a relatively serene and self-confident time—as a series of energy transfers; not so much Lindsay's 'antagonism of forces' but 'persistence of force'. This is not the place to discuss the problem of Gladstone's sincerity. What *he* called discernment of those 'forces which will shape the future', his enemies called simple opportunism, or jumping in turn on to Italian, Yankee, Fenian, and (later) Bulgarian bandwagons. Where *they* saw tergiversation, he saw himself as participating in a moral dialectic, for if 'the idea of conversion requires and depends upon the idea of sin',[65] the fact that he had formerly been willing to accept the Confederacy made his championship of the Union all the more genuine. For after all, 'conversion' no longer signified a change from black to white so much as an energy transfer from one state of being to the next.

This point may be illuminated with reference to two intellectual commentators, Bagehot and Morley. Walter Bagehot was a lapsed Unitarian and an early devotee of Maurice, very aware of the importance of excitement (for good and ill) in Gladstonian Liberalism. His *Physics and Politics* (1872) purported, somewhat misleadingly, to apply biological evolutionary theory to the political world. Taking issue with H. T. Buckle's

---

[63] Ibid., p. 523.   [64] Magnus, *Gladstone*, pp. 49–50.
[65] Gladstone to Argyll, 14 July 1865, Lathbury, *Correspondence on Church and Religion*, ii. 87.

History of Civilisation in England (1857–61), Bagehot insisted that moral forces (or 'higher energy') were more important than material ones in securing progressive development, and that those forces did their work for the most part in little-tutored yet reflective minds.

It is the action of the will that causes the unconscious habit; it is the continual effort of the beginning that creates the hoarded energy of the end; it is the silent toil of the first generation that becomes the transmitted aptitude of the next. . . . The beginning is by the higher energy, the conservation and propagation only by the lower.[66]

Like Gladstone and Mill, Bagehot believed that citizens were nurtured best when public life was dominated by discussion and debate. More explicitly than Mill, he recommended intellectual discussion as a means to overcome residual Malthusian worries:

There is only a certain *quantum* of power in each of our race; if it goes in one way it is spent, and cannot go in another. The intellectual atmosphere abstracts strength to intellectual matters; it tends to divert that strength which the circumstances of early society directed to the multiplication of numbers.[67]

Borrowing from Lamarck and Huxley, Bagehot claimed that conscious effort produces habit, which then becomes 'fixed' by the nervous system, so that man's nervous organs or 'stores of will-made power' become 'charged with stored virtue and acquired faculty'. Fashion and imitation play a leading part in this physiology, and a leader such as Gladstone becomes in effect 'a great new causal factor whose influence radiates forth by the spontaneous working of the laws of imitation'.[68] It has been pointed out that Bagehot's theory of human nature, unlike Marx's, Spencer's, or Comte's, actually culminates in political life rather than in its supersession.[69]

John Morley's empathy with Gladstonian Liberalism was so strong that, were it not for Gladstone's own words on the subject, one might have suspected him of inventing it. He held a Comtist view of organic process whereby laws, institutions, and customs evolve step by step with men's

---

[66] Walter Bagehot, *Physics and Politics or Thoughts on the Application of the Principle of 'Natural Selection' and 'Inheritance' to Political Society* (1872), 11 [*The Collected Works of Walter Bagehot*, ed. Norman St John-Stevas (1965–86), vii. 22]. For Bagehot's view of Maurice see Richard Holt Hutton, *Essays on Some of the Modern Guides of English Thought in Matters of Faith* (1887), 306; for his misunderstanding of Darwinism see Gertrude Himmelfarb, *Darwin and the Darwinian Revolution* (1959), 351–5.

[67] Bagehot, *Physics and Politics*, pp. 199–200 [*Works*, vii. 130]. Contrast Bray, who thought it necessary to make most use of those organs one would wish to cultivate.

[68] C. H. Driver, 'Walter Bagehot and the social psychologists', in *The Social & Political Ideas of Some Representative Thinkers of the Victorian Age*, ed. F. J. C. Hearnshaw (1933), 203, 213.

[69] Collini, Winch, and Burrow, *That Noble Science*, pp. 180–1.

changing ideas about the world. 'Only "stages" mattered and it was idle to be in advance of one's time.'[70] He objected to Darwin's *The Descent of Man* (1870–1) for applying the principle of natural selection to civilized eras more subject to the operation of 'social evolution', by which he meant

the selection by a community, through its current opinion, laws, institutions, traditional usages, and so forth, of certain qualities, and ideals of character, for admiration. . . . The community is the organism, the unit. . . . The transmission is not physical, from father to son, but 'in the air' from generation to generation. That there are physical conditions cannot be doubted. But within the society itself, the characteristic habits of thought, rules of conduct, &c. are acquired through the non-physical medium of opinion, positive law &c. [71]

Morley's depiction of Gladstone's progression by 'stages' is excessively triumphal. It dwells little on the crushing tribulations that attended him from 1847 to 1852: the deaths of his daughter, and of his father, and then of his political 'father', Peel; the mortifying antics of his sister Helen; the shame and worry of his wife's family bankruptcy; thwarted political ambition; persistent 'temptations to impurity', causing agonies of remorse which could only be assuaged by what he uncoyly called 'the blessings of discipline'; and as a backdrop to all this, the gradual disintegration of the first Oxford Movement, beginning with Newman's apostasy and culminating in those of two friends 'in whom my trusts were carnal', Manning and Hope-Scott. Gladstone was devastated:

I have . . . a knowledge right in the very inmost parts of myself: that I am, even among guilty ones, the guiltiest. These two terrible years have really displaced and uprooted my heart from the Anglican Church, seen as a personal and *living* Church in the *body* of its Priests and members: and at the same time the two friends whom I might call the only supports for my intellect have been wrenched away from me, leaving me lacerated, and I may say barely conscious morally.[72]

Yet notwithstanding this fairly unequivocal gloom, sensitive critics have noted the heroic, redemptive aspects of these years. Morley wrote lyrically about 'the golden trumpet-notes of a new time', and G. M. Young, marvelling at the sudden relaxation of social tensions between 1848 and 1851, commented: 'It was in that Maytime of youth recaptured that Gladstonian Liberalism was conceived. It was the only atmosphere in which it could have been conceived, an atmosphere composed in equal

---

[70] Morley's words are reported in Austin Harrison, *Frederic Harrison: Thoughts and Memories* (1926), 177, and in D. A. Hamer, *John Morley: Liberal Intellectual in Politics* (Oxford, 1968), 382.

[71] Morley to Darwin, 30 Mar. 1871, Cambridge University Library, Darwin Papers, 87 fo. 170.

[72] Foot and Matthew, *The Gladstone Diaries*, 19 Aug. 1851, iv. 352–3.

measure of progress, confidence, and social union.'[73] It is important to juxtapose these two contrasting modes, 'gorgeous reckless optimism' and abject despair, because this is what Gladstonian Liberalism was all about. On the one hand, a rationalistic and tolerant confidence, the stuff of John Morley's *On Compromise*, and on the other an evangelical emphasis on sin and the need for salvation: it was the combination of the two which gave the movement its power to generate a 'visceral thrill' (in John Vincent's happy phrase),[74] its gift of redemptive expostulation. And it was of course a compound that at a spiritual level had characterized evangelicalism itself—a sense of depravity and danger on the one hand, and the joyous prospect of salvation on the other.

How the 'Nonconformist Conscience' Swallowed up Individual Conscience

This brings us back to Gladstone's relations with evangelicalism, a movement he reviewed critically but sympathetically in 1879. He complained that too many evangelicals—especially the extremists—had fallen into the Lutheran fallacy of regarding grace as something wholly external and 'unconditional', able to enter the frailest of human vessels, even without holy endeavour on their part. Certain others, mainly moderates, had by their careless terminology reduced the great doctrine of the atonement to the status of a 'forensic' process or, worse still, 'a sort of joint-stock transaction, . . . a bargain in a shop' affair. Yet on the whole Gladstone felt able to credit evangelicals with having nobly restored attention from the doctrine of justification to the person of Christ himself; by insisting that Justification requires constant and active faith, they had rightly presented the Atonement as a 'guarantee' of holiness, not a 'substitute' for it, and as 'serving the great end of sanctification'. He concluded that, although evangelicalism had had an inadequate appreciation of sacramental religion, 'all its other parts'—its 'juice and sap'—'have been appropriated by the Church of England at large, and have also been greatly and beneficially developed'.[75] In other words, it had played its part in forming the mid-Victorian religious consensus.

And yet, when another great moral challenge came to confront the nation in the form of Beaconsfieldism, Gladstone was dismayed to find that it was nonconformist churchmen, not Anglicans, who mainly responded to his prophetic admonitions. As Deryck Schreuder has pointed

---

[73] Morley, *Life of Gladstone*, i. 385; G. M. Young, *Today and Yesterday: Collected Essays and Addresses* (1948), 33.

[74] John Vincent, *Pollbooks: How Victorians Voted* (Cambridge, 1967), 47.

[75] Gladstone, 'The evangelical movement', *British Quarterly Review*, 70 (1879), 14–15 [*Gleanings*, vii. 221–2].

out, Midlothian was 'the radicalism of the Evangelical conscience, . . . not that of the Christian socialist or even the social gospeler',[76] and not surprisingly it made little impact on an established church[77] which was fast abandoning retributive doctrines in favour of Broad Church incarnationalism. Gladstone thought that the Church's failure to respond was the deadening result of her function as an establishment. 'He judged that her moral will had lost spontaneity, had grown timid and callous through a situation which impregnated her with the poison of a worldly Erastianism.'[78] The sympathy, ostensibly incongruous, which developed between Dissent and the archly High Church statesman was based on their common acceptance of a fundamentalist theology, now all but eclipsed in the Church of England. Vigour, moral energy, vital commitment all sprang from the Nonconformists' redemptive view of the world.

But from the 1880s even Nonconformists, running out of constitutional grievances and increasingly aware of their own social status, found it hard to keep redemptive angers fresh.[79] Gladstone was acutely conscious of the 'decline in the sense of sin, which, instead of being, as under the Christian system it ought to be, piercing and profound, is passing with very many into a shallow, feeble, and vague abstraction'.[80] As perturbing was the relegation of Hell 'to the far-off corners of the Christian mind, . . . there to sleep in deep shadow, as a thing needless in our enlightened and progressive age'.

A portion of Divine truth, which even if secondary is so needful, appears to be silently passing out of view, and . . . the danger of losing it ought at all costs to be averted. . . . It is not now sought to alarm men by magnifying the power of God and by exhibiting the strictures and severity of the law of righteousness. The anxiety now is to throw these subjects into the shade, lest the fastidiousness of human judgment and feeling should be so offended as to rise in rebellion against God for His harshness and austerity.[81]

In the same way, the new and softer interpretations of the Atonement were dulling our sensibility to 'corrective' or 'remedial' justice, and making it harder for us to feel that 'kind of actual joy in salutary pain'

---

[76] Schreuder, 'Gladstone and the conscience of the state', op. cit., p. 125. For Gladstone's evangelical and 'Butlerian' response to the Eastern Crisis see Matthew in Foot and Matthew, *The Gladstone Diaries*, ix. xxxiii–lxix.

[77] R. T. Shannon, *Gladstone and the Bulgarian Agitation 1876* (1963), 171.

[78] Holland, *Personal Studies*, p. 52.

[79] On the decline of Nonconformist fundamentalism see Richard J. Helmstadter 'The Nonconformist conscience', Marsh, *Conscience of the Victorian State*, pp. 140–4.

[80] Gladstone to Malabari, 20 July 1889, Lathbury, *Correspondence on Church and Religion*, ii. 118.

[81] Gladstone, *Studies Subsidiary to Butler*, pp. 199–201, 206.

that had so wonderfully galvanized Gladstone himself from time to time.[82]

Newcastle's death in 1864 had left Gladstone feeling isolated, a political dinosaur, relic of an earlier evangelical era. And for all his belief in progress, which he anyway conceived more in moral and spiritual than in material terms, Gladstone's social philosophy retained—like his theology—strong traces of earlier nineteenth-century individualism. He wished that money should fructify in the pockets of the people, but he also retained a strong sense of the moral imperatives of political economy. Extra-parliamentary speaking gave him opportunities for some full-blooded statements of the less eligibility principle, as in this address to the workmen of St Pancras in 1879:

It is necessary that the independent labourer of this country should not be solicited and tempted to forgo his duty to his wife, his children, and the community by thinking he could do better for himself by making himself a charge upon that community. There is no more subtle poison that could be infused into the nation at large than a system of that kind. We were in danger of it some fifty or sixty years ago, but the spirit and the courage of the Parliament of 1834 and of the Government of that day introduced a sounder and a wiser system. . . . It is very good for those who belong to the wealthier classes to be brought . . . into contact with you, . . . for we live in an age when most of us have forgotten that the Gospel of our Saviour Christ . . . was above all a Gospel of the poor . . . ; that from His own mouth proceeded the words which showed us in reference to temporal circumstances that a time will come when many of the first shall be last and many of the last first. Blessed, no doubt, are the rich men if they confront the many and subtle temptations of the life they have to live, but blessed, also, are the poor who accept with cheerfulness the limited circumstances and conditions in which they have to pass these few fleeting years.[83]

Even as late as 1897, and in spite of highland clearances and a Great Depression, Gladstone could still herald 'Lord Althorp of 'thirty-four as the saviour of the English peasantry'.[84]

But what most exercised Gladstone was 'the spirit of plutocracy'.

I think that in a political view the spirit of plutocracy requires to be vigilantly watched and checked. It is a bastard aristocracy and aristocracy shows too much disposition, in Parliament especially, to join hands with this bastard.

[82] Gladstone, 'True and false conceptions of the Atonement', *Nineteenth Century*, 36 (1894), 327 [*Later Gleanings*, p. 329].

[83] Report in *The Times*, 22 Aug. 1879, p. 8d., partly cited by Matthew in Foot and Matthew, *The Gladstone Diaries*, ix. lxviii.

[84] Brooke and Sorensen, *The Prime Ministers' Papers*, i. 55. Gladstone had always believed that Chalmers 'much overstated' the mischief done by legal assessments for poor relief. See notes of 1835 in Gladstone Papers, BL Add. MS, 44724 fos. 176–80.

In a religious point of view I believe the case to be yet worse, and I groan over the silence and impotence of the pulpit. I almost wish for a Savonarola or part of one. Manning has said some good things about it. . . .[85]

Plutocracy lay at the heart of the national moral disease which was 'Beaconsfieldism', denounced so savagely by the Savonarola of Midlothian. Disraeli's fiscal and financial irresponsibility, adventures such as the purchase of the Suez Canal shares, and the backstairs influence of Rothschild in the matter, no doubt reminded Gladstone of those 'blot and sin' manœuvres of Vansittart, from which Huskisson and Peel had emancipated the nation. The need to make responsible use of one's money, publicly and privately, was perhaps the most important article in Gladstone's creed, and affected policy in many disparate areas—his budgets, his Exchequer reforms, his approach to Church Rates and to Irish Home Rule. 'Religion and Christian virtue,' he observed in 1843 with reference to Wesley and the duty of frugality, 'like the faculty of taste and the perception of beauty,[86] have their place, aye and that the first place, in political economy, as the means of creating and preserving wealth.'[87] So it is not surprising that he should have entertained the gravest doubts about limited liability legislation, voting against the measure on 24 and 26 July 1855. In his 1879 address as Lord Rector of Glasgow University—shades of Peel on the 'great system of social retribution' forty years before!—Gladstone bemoaned a 'derangement' in the affairs of the country: a growth of luxury and capital outstripping even the rise in wages, and the emergence of a new and powerful 'class of hybrid or bastard men of business', drawn from many walks of life including the most comfortable.

The bond that unites them is the bond of gain; not the legitimate produce of toil by hand or brain—in most cases not fenced off from rashness, as in former times, by liability to ruinous loss in the event of failure, but to be had without the conditions which alone make pecuniary profit truly honourable.[88]

---

[85] Gladstone to Lord Houghton, 13 Sept. 1871, Trinity College Cambridge MSS, Houghton Papers, 9[186]; Henry Edward Manning, The Four Great Evils of the Day (2nd edn, 1871), 54–60.

[86] The question of whether there was such a thing as innate aesthetic taste was a major debating-point, and seen to be analogous with the debate on moral sense or conscience. Gladstone despaired of his own countrymen in this respect. Which other country would select its leading palazzo architect to design a perpendicular Palace of Westminster, and its leading architect in the pointed style for an Italianate Foreign Office? Gladstone, 'Ritualism and ritual', The Contemporary Review, 24 (1874), 668 [Gleanings, vi. 117–18].

[87] [Gladstone], 'Course of commercial policy at home and abroad', The Foreign and Colonial Quarterly Review, 1 (1843), 253, cited by Matthew in Foot and Matthew, The Gladstone Diaries, iii. xxxvii.

[88] W. E. Gladstone, Political Speeches in Scotland, November and December 1879 (Revised edn, Edinburgh, 1880), i. 237–8, cited by Matthew in Foot and Matthew, The Gladstone Diaries, ix. lxv.

The 'conditions' that Gladstone clearly had in mind here were *risk* and *indeterminacy*, such as had characterized the mental world of the earlier nineteenth century.

Three Types of Evangelical Survival

Gladstone's fizz resulted from a combination of progressive optimism and old evangelical fundamentalism, even though his *Butlerismus* and his flagellatory politics ('If this age has pride, and if its pride requires a whipping')[89] were looking fossilized by the nineties. Most evangelicals in the later nineteenth century turned their backs on the new science and retreated into literal fundamentalism. Still, there were some who struggled to adapt the older evangelical frame of mind to the new intellectual conditions: men such as McCosh, Argyll, and Birks. But in order to understand their very different responses, we must first return to Thomas Chalmers.

A serious problem for moderate evangelical theologians had always been: how to combine belief in predictable natural laws with the idea of a God who was capable of, and on occasions resorted to, intervention. Surely, if the great clock-maker was all-wise, he would have perfected his machinery at the outset and would not have to keep making adjustments to it. Moreover, how could the existence of permanent natural laws be squared with Revelation, in which was predicted the end of the earth? Chalmers's response to these difficulties, which has been acutely analysed by Crosbie Smith,[90] grew out of his early training in Scottish physics and was of particular significance. He conceded at once that the world was in 'utter derangement' and contained symptoms of decay—Paley had been quite mistaken to suppose that it manifested God's benevolence as well as his power[91]—but this was because only the visible realm was apparent to man and not the invisible. God may frequently answer the prayers of men in the invisible realm, but only occasionally will he do so by way of miracle, that is by tampering with the uniformity of visible nature.

It is thus that we reconcile all the experience which man has of nature's uniformity, with the effect and significancy of his prayers to the God of nature. It is thus

---

[89] W. E. Gladstone, 'The paths of honour and of shame', *The Nineteenth Century*, 3 (1878), 591.

[90] Crosbie Smith, 'From design to dissolution: Thomas Chalmers' debt to John Robison', *British Journal for the History of Science*, 12 (1979), 59–70, on which this paragraph is largely based.

[91] See above, p. 179.

that at one and the same time, do we live under the care of a presiding God; and among the regularities of a harmonious universe.[92]

His point was that the universe is in fact composed of a myriad of particles, which all obey the several laws of nature such as gravity, but which also possess different degrees of *vis viva* acting in any one of a number of directions. What makes the present world special, and what gives it its predictable orderliness, is the particular *arrangement* or 'collocation' of these various forces. Physics and chemistry may 'account for the evolution of things or substances collocated in a certain way'—hence the predictability of successive events, cause and effect—but 'they did not originate the collocations'. 'The laws of nature may keep up the working of the machinery—but they did not and could not set up the machine', nor keep it running contrary to the Creator's will.[93] 'The things which are seen are temporal; but the things which are not seen are eternal' (Corinthians 4: 18). It followed that the visible world was transitory and might be wound up at any time, but also that God, who was eternal, might then rearrange its various particles to make another world, one perchance that was not fallen but bathed in righteousness.[94]

Chalmers's distinction between *laws* and *collocations* of matter was taken extremely seriously by many who followed—by scientists such as William Thomson and James Clerk Maxwell, and by economists such as J. S. Mill and W. S. Jevons.[95] Indeed, it took on extra significance with the discovery of the first two laws of thermodynamics, and affected the way in which many evangelicals came to terms with the increasing evidence of uniformity in nature.

James McCosh (1811–94) was a Scottish Free Churchman and devotee of Chalmers, under whom he had studied theology as a student. His best-selling *Method of the Divine Government* (1850) so inspired the Lord Lieutenant of Ireland, Lord Clarendon, that McCosh was given the Chair of Logic and Metaphysics at Queen's College, Belfast, in 1851. He held strongly to Butler's and Chalmers's ideas on intuition and moral sense, but differed from them in his view that God was 'all-acting'. All the hairs of one's head being numbered, and not a sparrow falling to the ground without God's say-so, McCosh was adamant that the earth was ruled

[92] 'On the consistency between the efficacy of prayer—and the uniformity of nature', in Chalmers, *Works*, vii. 241. The date of this piece is unclear, but it was written during a cholera epidemic, and was a response to the contempt with which several MPs had flouted the idea of a National Fast.

[93] Chalmers, *On the Power Wisdom and Goodness of God*, i. 16–29 [*Works*, i. 206–26].

[94] 'On the new heavens and the new earth', in Chalmers, *Works*, vii. 280–99.

[95] W. Stanley Jevons, *The Principles of Science: A Treatise on Logic and Scientific Method* (1874), ii. 434.

more by particular than by general providence. Thus he went out of his way to castigate George Combe's *Constitution of Man* for having overlooked

that adjustment of natural laws to each other, whereby the results are often of the most complicated character, and such that they cannot be anticipated by human foresight. While all events are occurring according to the law of cause and effect, they are not happening in that orderly and regular manner which we call a general law. On the contrary, many events are falling out in an accidental unforeseen manner, which is fitted to make man feel his helplessness.

Because of his error Combe had denied the efficacy of prayer, as well as the need for faith, dependence, submission, meekness, patience, and consolation.[96] Faced nine years later with Darwin's demonstration that in nature the strong live and the weak die, McCosh was able to recoup his position by arguing that intellectual strength is 'stronger' than physical strength, just as moral strength outstrips intellectual strength. 'The Word becoming flesh and tabernacling on the earth' was the essential link in God's unfolding plan, and far from worshipping 'force' as Carlyle averred, we should rather parade our meekness in the wake of Jesus Christ. McCosh was an optimist, seeing abundant signs of progress in agriculture, arts, and science. There was a law in the divine mind before it appeared as a law of nature. Where Chalmers had drawn his argument of design from collocations (not laws) of matter, McCosh insisted that collocations, or mutual adaptations, were always implied in general laws.[97]

Among McCosh's friends was the Duke of Argyll, Gladstone's ally first as a Peelite and then until 1881 as a Liberal, who is quoted above on the religious implications of limited liability legislation, and who probably drew many of his ideas as to the working of 'Law in the Realm of Mind' from *The Method of Divine Government*.[98] Not formally an evangelical, he nevertheless perpetuated the Chalmerian ethic in difficult times. He began to read Butler carefully from 1852 onwards, and found in the *Analogy* confirmation of all he had instinctively apprehended from his

[96] James McCosh, *The Method of the Divine Government, Physical and Moral* (2nd edn, Edinburgh, 1850), 192–4. For Chalmers's influence on McCosh see J. David Hoeveler, *James McCosh and the Scottish Intellectual Tradition from Glasgow to Princeton* (Princeton, NJ, 1981), esp. 47–53. On McCosh's platonico-biological idealism see Philip F. Rehbock, *The Philosophical Naturalists: Themes in Early Nineteenth-Century British Biology* (Madison, Wis., 1983), 98–101. For Magee's concurrence with McCosh on the doctrine of conscience see Magee to MacDonnell, 31 Dec. 1864, MacDonnell, *Life of Magee*, i. 108.

[97] James McCosh, *Christianity and Positivism: a Series of Lectures to the Times on Natural Theology and Apologetics* (1871), 35, 53–62, 91–5.

[98] *The Life of James McCosh: A Record Chiefly Autobiographical*, ed. William Milligan Sloane (Edinburgh, 1896), 141–3.

youthful studies of animal mechanics.[99] As a scientist he was quaintly but unswervingly old-fashioned. He grew up in and clung to the cataclysmal school of geology, and denounced all the 'gutter theories' of the evolutionists. Whereas McCosh used a distorted version of Darwin, Argyll remained very hostile, and he also indulged in polemics against Spencer and T. H. Huxley, claiming that all *apparent* upward progress and evolution was not material but planned and directed by 'mind'. Ethnologically, he remained a 'degenerationist', arguing that barbarian tribes were the 'fallen' remains of once civilized races, which had been pushed in the struggle for existence out to remote and uncivilizable regions of the globe.[1] In mechanics Argyll remained firmly wedded to Newtonianism, telling Stokes privately as late as 1898 that he could not accept the modern theory that waves or vibrations of light were 'transverse to the line of propagation'. 'It is inconceivable to me that any form of energy can be "*propagated*" in a direction in which that energy does not itself exert *some* impulse.'[2]

In his social thought Argyll was very strongly in favour of Free Trade, and from *The Reign of Law* in 1867 to *The Unseen Foundations of Society* in 1893 he attempted to maintain a pure strain of individualism against the creeping tides of corporatism and collectivism. Attacking that 'master fallacy', the labour theory of value, he spoke up for Jevons's view that value was a function of effective demand, though unlike Jevons he ascribed most of the credit for channelling such demand to 'the possessory principle' (or private property) and the 'conceiving mind'.[3] We can see from his article on Christian Socialism in 1894 that his political economy was as much of a throwback to the first half of the century as were his scientific ideas. It contained great praise of Chalmers ('a splendid intellect') and of his views on poor laws. Christian Socialists erred because they thought that legislation (or direct action of the human will) could make life better, forgetting that all successful political institutions have been 'founded on natural laws which have been unconsciously and instinctively obeyed'. Man has a will, but it cannot, for example, alter his price-tag (wage), for this depends on thousands of other wills over which he has no control. Fortunately, we can learn to read economic laws, for like all natural laws they assign success to strength and virtue. Divine laws

---

[99] Argyll, *Autobiography and Memoirs*, i. 354–5.

[1] This was an attempt to resuscitate Whately's view that barbarians were the fallen descendants of once civilized men, a view which Lubbock, Tylor, and others had shown to be nonsense. Whately had been adamant, against the evolutionists, that man could not civilize himself without divine assistance. See Andrew D. White, *A History of the Warfare of Science with Theology in Christendom* (New York, 1896), i. 303–9.

[2] Argyll to G. G. Stokes, 10 Feb. 1898, Stokes Papers, Cambridge University Library MSS, Add. 7656, A801.

[3] John W. Mason, 'Political economy and the response to socialism in Britain, 1870–1914', *Historical Journal*, 23 (1980), 578–80.

act 'by way of natural consequence, in the direction of rebuke and of recovery. . . . It is only by way of natural and necessary consequence that anything can be accomplished.' It followed that such injunctions as 'Blessed are they who considereth the poor' mean precisely *that*—they who *think about* the causes of poverty, and do not take refuge in the easy but crude escape of indiscriminate alms-giving.[4]

Finally there was Thomas Rawson Birks (1810–83), who succeeded Maurice as Knightbridge Professor of Moral Philosophy at Cambridge in 1873. A founder and for twenty-one years secretary of the Evangelical Alliance, son-in-law and former curate of Edward Bickersteth, Birks believed strongly in prophecy, inspiration, pre-millennialism, and the eternal punishment of the wicked. He was originally a Baptist but moved towards the Church of England, partly as a result of reading Irving's *Babylon and Infidelity Foredoomed of God* (1826), a tract for 'these latter times' which greatly affected Birks and left him with a strong distaste for 'modern progress'. He was a fervent Conservative, despairing of Gladstone and of threats to the Establishment, and regarded the Election of 1880 as a moment of national catastrophe.[5] As an undergraduate he had shown brilliant mathematical promise, and it was a shock to many when he only came out Second Wrangler in 1834. However, he had already caught attention with a Trinity Prize Essay which Whewell, Chalmers, and William Wordsworth all thought philosophically profound, novel, and morally elevating, and which formed the basis of many of his later speculations. Its gist was that the laws of mind and of morals are as certain as those of mathematics and of matter.[6]

In saying this Birks was not subscribing to necessarianism. Rejecting physiological and instinctive theories of morals, he paraded the conscience, which was 'the conscious possession of a reasonable will, an inward power of choice'. 'Conscience discloses to us a law of union in the moral world, as wide and far reaching as the law of universal attraction, but of a nobler and higher kind'; for 'matter is subject to a law of physical compulsion, . . . but moral beings have a power of choice', and may look to the hills for help.[7]

Applying these insights to political economy, Birks deduced that commerce should be free from selfish and unnecessary restrictions which

[4] Argyll, 'Christian socialism', *The Nineteenth Century*, 36 (1894), 694–5, 704–6. For Argyll in his cultural context see Desmond, *Archetypes and Ancestors*, pp. 176–81.
[5] *The Record*, 27 July 1883, p. 741.
[6] T. R. Birks, 'Mathematical and moral certainty' (1833), reprinted in T. R. Birks, *First Principles of Moral Science, a Course of Lectures* (1873), 291–320. Whewell to J. C. Hare, 25 Dec. 1833, Whewell Papers, Trinity College Cambridge Add. MSS, a.215[29]; Whewell to his sister, 14 Jan. 1834, ibid., c.191[136]; Wordsworth to Whewell, 14 May ?1834, ibid., c.91[107]; Chalmers to Whewell, 4 Mar. 1834, ibid., a.202[25].
[7] Birks, *First Principles of Moral Science*, pp. 94–5, 128.

diminish wealth, but should remain subject to restrictions whose aim is to promote morals and happiness. Otherwise 'the cold, hard, iron selfishness of trade' would lead to distortion of the divine law. Yet trade can only succeed through personal prudence and morality, and confidence is vital to it. Political economists, who habitually ascribe its progress entirely to self-interest, separate the *body* of wealth (price) from its *soul*, without which it is worthless. The soul consists in the application of wealth to some beneficial end, otherwise it is waste and poison. Political economy was merely a form of 'natural chrematics', whereas what was needed was

Moral chrematics, or the laws of social duty, by which man is bound both to God and his fellow-men in the right use, social adaptation, and religious consecration, of all outward and visible things. It is not universal free trade, least of all its freedom from moral restraints, but universal uprightness, integrity, and brotherly kindness, in trade, labour, commerce, and all social relations, which is the true and effectual remedy for . . . threatening evils.

In this blithe mood he prophesied a day when businessmen would realize the great law of love, and when trade would revolve harmoniously in its own orbit, bathed in celestial light.[8]

Birks's confidence in this respect derived from an old-fashioned trust in God's moral government. Morality *had* to be based on consequences, since intuitionism was vague and unreal, but actions did not become right or wrong just because their consequences were good or bad. Fortunately 'an all-wise Providence secures that, soon or late, their moral tendency, from their own nature, shall prevail over every adverse and evil influence; "so that men shall say, Verily there is a reward for the righteous: doubtless there is a God that judgeth in the earth"'. 'In' the earth, note, and not the earth itself. This is earlier nineteenth-century evangelicalism, a static approach based on individual conversion, adapted to the sentimental optimism of a later age. 'Like sunlight reflected from the countless dewdrops of morning, the laws of righteousness, while they can gain no new force, shine with more conspicuous beauty, when they are seen in their combination with all the innumerable events of Providence, and human history in this lower world.'[9]

Birks's overriding aim was to combat attempts, by Positivists and others, to erect a comprehensive scientific philosophy which would effectively destroy religious faith. As one might expect, he refused to believe that the doctrine of evolution had been satisfactorily proved.[10] But it was modern physics which really appalled him, and in particular the theory

---

[8] Ibid., pp. 142–63.   [9] Ibid., p. 287.
[10] James R. Moore, *The Post-Darwinian Controversies: A Study of the Protestant Struggle to Come to Terms with Darwin in Great Britain and America 1870–1900* (Cambridge, 1979), 201–2.

of the conservation of energy, to which heresy he returned again and again. Matter was bidding to become a 'new divinity'—'Heat is identified with motion, and becomes a subtler branch of Mechanics.' Birks clung to Bacon's 'vast dual system of matter and ether' as against the monism of the materialists. He also invoked Newton when he claimed that the great divine law, 'love thy neighbour as thyself', was as simple and as absolute as gravitation.[11]

Birks was not alone in detesting the law of the conservation of energy as bestowing on matter certain 'vital' properties of mutation.[12] There were, even among scientists themselves, serious attempts at that time to refute the materialism which the social psychologists were deducing from thermodynamics. Most notably, perhaps, Balfour Stewart's and P. G. Tait's *Unseen Universe* (1875) employed the conservation and dissipation of energy, together with ethers and the vortex atom, as concepts to support belief in miracles. Immortality was 'strictly in accordance with the principle of Continuity (rightly viewed)', and with the principle of the uniformity of nature. For if mind and matter were linked, why not nature and the supernatural also? The Creation and the Resurrection were brought about 'by an intelligent Agent operating in the universe', though resident outside it in the invisible realm, whose operations were subject to the law of conservation of energy. Therefore miracles were not discontinuities or examples of special providence but subject to law. If the second law of thermodynamics (dissipation of energy) ensures that the universe must end, and the first law (conservation of energy) means that it must go somewhere, then clearly there must be a somewhere beyond the universe. Providence clearly operates by transferring energy from the invisible to the visible realm, in accordance with its own natural laws.[13] There was also the Cambridge physicist George Gabriel Stokes, a pious and rather 'literalist' evangelical who nevertheless believed in conditional immortality and placed the Incarnation at the centre of his faith. An

---

[11] Birks, *First Principles of Moral Science*, pp. 8, 67.

[12] If Birks's appointment as professor was theologically retrograde, it was paralleled less dramatically in Oxford by the elevation of J. R. T. Eaton, a Butlerian, to the Whyte's Professorship of Moral Philosophy in 1874. It is interesting to note that Eaton also adhered to an older physics, which he termed Aristotelian. Motion was *not* 'immanent in' inert matter, and bodies remain at rest until acted on by an outside force. J. R. T. Eaton, *The Permanence of Christianity*, 1872 Bampton Lectures (London, Oxford, and Cambridge, 1873), p. xvii.

[13] B. Stewart and P. G. Tait, *The Unseen Universe or Physical Speculations on a Future State* (1875; 4th revised edn, 1876), x, 89–90, 198–200, 241–56, and *passim*. P. M. Heimann, 'The *Unseen Universe*: physics and the philosophy of nature in Victorian Britain', *British Journal for the History of Science*, 6 (1972–3), 73–9. See also Brian Wynne, 'Physics and psychics: science, symbolic action, and social control in late Victorian England', in *Natural Order: Historical Studies of Scientific Culture*, ed. Barry Barnes and Steven Shapin (1979), 167–86.

exponent of dualistic idealism against the materialists, and a bitter opponent of evolutionism, Stokes's god was an interventionist god, though capable of ruling through natural laws if he wished. The second law of thermodynamics seemed to him to prove divine creation of the universe, but it was the conservation of energy which gave him most religious inspiration. He did not, like Stewart and Tait, deduce a belief in immortality from it, for he held that the Will lay outside the operation of energy transfers and conversions. Coining the word 'directionism', Stokes claimed that human beings possess a non-material aspect (Will) which stands outside the body's energy transactions and can—like the 'vital forces' of an earlier science—'direct' its physical activity. As the historian David Wilson has concluded:

Not long after Kelvin had wielded thermodynamics against the geological uniformitarianism which undergirded the naturalism of Darwinian natural selection, Stokes was pitting physics against biology and, thus, science against materialism. Of similar view to Stokes were the religious physicists Joule, Kelvin, Tait, Stewart, and Lodge. Broadly speaking, Stokes's physicists's alternative to materialism represented an older, clergy–gentry, Newtonian tradition in counterpoint to the newer (and growing), middle-class, professional, scientific naturalism epitomised by the biologist–philosopher T. H. Huxley.[14]

All this suggests that it was mainstream science, and especially classical physics, which attempted to maintain the theological assumptions of moderate evangelicals, while the latter's sons and daughters, if they had not drifted into secularism, were rapidly turning their backs on science and taking refuge in biblical fundamentalism.

At any rate many believers in the 1870s regarded thermodynamics as a greater threat than biology, especially as the doctrine of evolution was meeting with a good deal of scientific scepticism at that time. Birks particularly disliked the way that Spencer had used energy conservation (or Persistence of Force) to underpin his *First Principles*. But though this was his explicit target, equally vulnerable were Bray, Dove, and the gamut of 'mental evolutionary' writers of the 1860s and 1870s. The danger, in Birks's eyes, was that physics was setting itself up as the sole science, so that material phenomena were coming to be regarded as 'the only field of thought, in which knowledge is attainable'. In turn social, political, and moral philosophy, as well as psychology, were being seen as 'only branches of physics', applications of the theories of matter, motion, physical force, and atomic change. In this view the course of physical change had been 'one immense series of oscillations of alternate evolution

---

[14] David B. Wilson, 'A physicist's alternative to materialism: the religious thought of George Gabriel Stokes', *Victorian Studies*, 28 (1984–5), 69–96. G. G. Stokes, *Natural Theology* (1891–3), ii. 46–57.

and dissolution', leading from a state of nature in 'intellectual chaos' (where every possible subject of thought 'is pronounced unthinkable') to our present state of 'practical knowledge' and apparent reality. But the future held merely a return to hypothesis, to 'thoughts more or less continuous, which no real person thinks', where there is no reality but mere 'counterfeit', a reign of unknowability once more. In such a fatalistic view religion came nowhere — it was mere 'blind emotion, or vague yearning after the unknowable'. Against such views Birks argued at length that there was scope for choice and will in physical laws. The law of gravitation proved, as Newton had shown, that all second causes·lead up to 'the great First Cause, and that this First Cause is not mechanical, but a true, living, intelligent, and omnipresent Mind'. It was absurd to suppose that each atom could, of its own accord and without help from the Creator, discern intuitively its own distance at each moment from every other material particle in the entire universe, and perform its part in the Newtonian universe accordingly.[15] It was all very well Spencer opining that 'continuity or eternity of motion' was the foremost of all a priori truths, but other physicists were claiming that there was dissipation of energy. Birks found both notions futile, and offensive to his natural theology. 'We may be perfectly sure that there is no real waste-heap in God's glorious universe', and that what some saw as ceaseless dissipation into infinite space was really 'ceaseless circulation'.

> The true key to the problem will be found, I believe, in a strict application of dynamical reasoning to a vast dual system of matter and ether. It is confirmed by the double analogy of air and ocean currents on the surface of our globe. Radiant light and heat cannot be lost. If part travels out to other systems, the celestial exchanges cannot be all on one side. Our imports must surely balance, or nearly balance our exports.[16]

In developing his traditionalist belief in future punishment, Birks so far accommodated himself to the objectors that his eschatology even contains some resemblances to that of Maurice.[17] In particular he called for a recovery of a biblical perspective which would put Hell into the context of 'that historical plan of redemption, from Genesis onward, which centres in the death and resurrection of Christ, and in His future return,

---

[15] T. R. Birks, *Modern Physical Fatalism and the Doctrine of Evolution, including an Examination of Mr. H. Spencer's First Principles* (1876), 77, 107–27, 217–38, and *passim*.

[16] T. R. Birks, *The Uncertainties of Modern Physical Science* (1876), esp. 13, 23–6. See T. R. Birks, *On Matter and Ether or Secret Laws of Physical Change* (Cambridge and London, 1862), 12 and *passim*, for the existence of a luminous ethereal medium.

[17] But only *some*. For the contrast with Maurice see the chapter on 'The Kingdom of Christ' in T. R. Birks, *Outlines of Unfulfilled Propehcy, Being an Inquiry into the Scripture Testimony Respecting the 'Good Things to Come'* (1854), 184–212.

and the resurrection of His people'. Here he was of course reiterating a common complaint, especially among certain Nonconformists and more extreme evangelicals, that the moderate evangelicals had exaggerated the importance of personal immortality at the expense of the promise of a general resurrection of bodies, to be accomplished by miraculous means. 'Every created being . . . has a personal and individual, but also a relative and federal character', and salvation must be understood corporately as well as individually.[18]

In the same way Birks tried to retain a sacrificial version of the Atonement, which he regarded as 'the heart and life of Christianity', while meeting mid-century susceptibilities.

All sin has two different, almost opposite, characters. In one of these it can, in the other it cannot, be transferred. It is an act done once for all, which cannot be undone. Once committed, it stands engraven on the scheme of Providence, a transgression of God's law, a rebellion against the Supreme Lawgiver, which needs some public vindication of His outraged authority. But it is also the act of a conscious agent, the sign of his present state, which may be changed or even reversed, but which, while it lasts, must make him hateful in the sight of a holy God.

Sin is a debt, and also a disease. It is a transgression of the Divine Law, without and above the sinner. It is a transgression, also, against the health and life of the spirit within. . . . The debt needs a ransom, the disease a cure. If sin were only a disease, there would be much room for sympathy, none for substitution. Atonement and propitiation would be wholly out of place. Our only want would be the healing, soothing power of some attractive pattern of perfect love. If sin were only a debt, substitution would be a complete Gospel, and all for whom an atonement was made would be heirs of salvation, because of that substitition alone.

But in fact these two elements 'enter into the whole economy of redemption'.

The Law exhibits a perfect standard, and exacts a penalty for every failure. The Gospel assumes the moral bankruptcy of those to whom it is given, and provides a ransom for their guilt, and healing medicine for their moral and spiritual sickness. . . .

Sin is a debt, a moral bankruptcy, a just exposure to death and the curse, which no mere repentance can do away, and which it needs a sin-offering to remove.

But the Atonement was not merely a mechanical equivalent, in the same way that the mechanical equivalent of heat is 778 ft./lb. For, to be efficacious, a change of heart is necessary, a genuine faith in 'the magnetic, transforming power of the Cross of Christ'.

---

[18] Rowell, *Hell and the Victorians*, pp. 123–9; T. R. Birks, *The Victory of Divine Goodness* (London, Oxford, and Cambridge, 1867), 11, 42, 53.

The claim of God's holiness is ill explained by a law of mechanical compensation, as if the sufferings, for a few days and nights, of an Infinite Person, were exactly equal to those of the multitudes of mankind throughout a whole eternity of ruin and sorrow. Sin and its punishment are not such finite, measurable things.[19]

The Atonement, then, was not only a ransom but a 'moral magnet', and could operate only in conjunction with the Incarnation.

Birks's 'moral magnet' is not all that different from Chalmers's 'expulsive power', and yet the metaphorical difference is crucial. One stresses the attractiveness of the good, the other stresses victory over what is bad. The dominance of moderate evangelicalism, based on the Atonement, turns out to have been a relatively short-lived phenomenon, and it was the more extreme evangelicals who contributed most, though in different ways, to the more positivistic thought of the second half of the century. First, Irving influenced Campbell, who influenced Maurice and the incarnationalists; while among evangelicals it was Irvingism, with its emphasis on the miraculous survival of the body, rather than Clapham with its emphasis on the immortality of individual souls, which survived. In a sense, moderate evangelicalism had been predicated on a distinction between the mind/soul and the body, this dualism in nature being reconcilable only by spiritual at-one-ment. As the distinction collapsed under the weight of scientific naturalism and philosophic uniformitarianism, so believers abandoned a federal theology of sacrifice and turned instead either to an evangelical emphasis on bodily resurrection or else a religion which made mind and soul a function of the body, of the Word made Flesh.

The historian Albert Hirschman has demonstrated that in the eighteenth century moralists often thought of commerce as a virtuous activity because it engendered habits of civic and political behaviour more altruistic than natural instincts, such as martial pride and vainglory. In this sense, men's 'interests' could be called on to harness and so counteract their passions. This 'vision' then evaporated as Adam Smith inaugurated a defence of capitalism which, instead of postulating tension between vice and virtue, claimed that self-interest was justified because it disposed human relationships in such a way as to maximize happiness.[20] Among conservative thinkers, at any rate, such consolatory doctrines were short-lived. The pessimism of the Age of Atonement, itself fuelled by Malthus's discoveries, re-created a dualistic tension in social thought, but the key to understanding and to happiness was now thought to lie in another

---

[19] Birks, *Victory of Divine Goodness*, pp. 147–66.
[20] Albert O. Hirschman, *The Passions and the Interests: Political Arguments for Capitalism before its Triumph* (Princeton, NJ, 1977), *passim*.

world—in scientific vitalism and in 'vital religion'. And this gave way, in its turn as we have seen, to a mid-century monism which restored harmony to God's creation by stressing continuous development or spontaneous energetic growth.

This harmony was to be short-lived also. In particular, the second law of thermodynamics implied that after all nature was not compatible with durable happiness on earth. In the words of Toulmin and Goodfield,

Hutton and Lyell had been deceived: though Newton and his successors satisfied themselves that the planetary system was *dynamically* stable, they could not at the same time prove that it was *thermodynamically* changeless. The ambition to explain the structure of the Earth's crust by appealing to a permanent balance between constructive and destructive forces had been misconceived, and geologists could no longer make unlimited demands on antiquity. Thermodynamics placed limits on what was possible, and the History of Nature must adapt itself to these limits.[21]

The Age of the Incarnation ended in the eighteen-eighties, as calls for state intervention reflected an awakened sense of danger in the creation, as well as in society, and a belief that human wisdom was required to tame and remedy it.

[21] Toulmin and Goodfield, *The Discovery of Time*, p. 223.

EPILOGUE

Would I suffer for him that I love? So wouldst thou—
    So wilt thou!
So shall crown thee the topmost, ineffablest, utter-
    most crown—
And thy love fill infinitude wholly, nor leave up nor
    down,
One spot for the creature to stand in! It is by no
    breath,
Turn of eye, wave of hand, that salvation joins issue
    with death.

             Robert Browning, *Saul* (1855), § 18

Most of the arguments put forward in this book were formulated some years ago. It is important to emphasize this because they have since acquired a certain contemporary resonance. The nineteen-eighties has seen a revival of evangelical and charismatic worship, while it is no longer philosophically unrespectable to believe in God. Catastrophism is fashionable in many branches of science, and the deregulation of the stock market is envisaged as a 'big bang'. The spectre has arisen of a providential illness which wreaks retribution on the promiscuous, and it has led to cries for a return to abstinence and the so-called 'Victorian values'. On a similar Malthusian note, *The Times* tells us that penitential fasting, not 'Live Aid', is the European's proper response to famine in Africa.[1] In Britain the 'health of towns' is once more 'on the agenda', and the chairman of the Tory party reminds us that urban riots are the consequences of original sin, not unemployment or physical deprivation. When a Church of England report on *Faith in the City* (1985) suggests otherwise, it is castigated by the *Sunday Telegraph* for elevating false social gospels above the one true gospel: '"Repent so ye be saved". . . . From the Christian viewpoint, the most pressing need in the inner cities—far more pressing than the need for more houses, etc.—is for ordinary people to be shocked into . . . the paths of righteousness for fear of eternal damnation?' 'Thatcherites', we are informed, consider individual poverty

---

[1] Editorial in *The Times*, 26 Jan. 1985.

to be 'God's will—divine retribution for past sins'. 'The plight of the sub-class is a national scandal' no doubt, 'but it cannot be put right by paying them higher wages or even by organising better welfare services on their behalf. Nor is re-training the answer. For what many of them need is not so much to be re-trained as to be re-born.'[2] Or as Margaret Thatcher has put it, 'economics are the method' but 'the object is to change the heart and soul'.[3] Other prominent politicians call for our nation to produce more millionaires—even though that will mean more bankrupts as well.[4] We are to forgive our creditors and not blame our debts on hire purchase. Above all this din is heard the siren song of the shires in a thousand letters to right-wing editors: we must, as a nation, wake up to 'a greater awareness of danger—of life and death', and that cannot happen 'so long as failures are subsidised by the successful'.[5]

The likeness between all this and the earlier nineteenth century is tempting but misleading, for we are not really living in another Age of Atonement. In our century the principles of relativity and uncertainty have put paid to providentialism, which was at the core of earlier nineteenth-century thinking, if only because it was then so widely alleged that God had *not* provided for the sustenance of his creatures. In seeking to justify to man this neglect on God's part, moralists made virtues of suffering and restraint, qualities which have nothing in common with present-day hedonism or the ideal of an 'enterprise culture'. Indeed, when nineteenth-century evangelicals used the word 'enterprise', it was usually pejoratively so as to imply foolhardiness. 'We must restrain the enterprises of fancy', cautioned Chalmers, thus emphasizing the link between enterprise and fiction, while the link with 'speculation', that other object of abhorrence, is suggested by a sneering remark of Isaac Taylor: 'Theology offers no field to men fond of intellectual enterprise.'[6]

It is hardly paradoxical that the years which gave birth to economics as an intellectual discipline should also have seen the invention by Sumner, Chalmers, and others of a moral discipline which might be called 'anti-economics'. 'Anti-economists' regarded nature as representing stability and tradition in a world consumed by growth and flux. They blamed the boom years of the Napoleonic Wars on a bubble of fictitious paper, and they half-welcomed the periodic business crises which set in after

---

[2] P. Worsthorne, 'Hell, sin and the inner cities', *Sunday Telegraph*, 8 Dec. 1985; *idem*, 'When dogma meets dogma . . . ', ibid., 7 Oct. 1984; *idem*, 'Kinnock's castration of Christian socialism', ibid., 7 Sept. 1986.

[3] Margaret Thatcher in the *Sunday Times*, 3 May 1981.

[4] Paul Flather, 'High priest, mad monk or seeker after truth? Profile of Sir Keith Joseph', *The Times Higher Education Supplement*, 11 Jan. 1985.

[5] Correspondent from Oxfordshire to the *Daily Telegraph*, 3 Apr. 1981.

[6] T. Chalmers, *The evidence and authority of the Christian Revelation* (1814; 3rd edn, 1816), 194; I. Taylor, *Natural History of Enthusiasm* (1829), 79.

1815 as a necessary and purgative retribution on society, corresponding to the volcanoes and earthquakes, floods and fevers which distended and distorted the natural world. They thought that monopoly and Protection had spawned over-production, and that Free Trade would reduce the level of activity to that of the community's real needs. They also thought that the Speenhamland system and suchlike paternalist welfare policies had led to over-population, and they hoped that self-help and a free labour market would restore a balance between the supply of food and the need for it. If they supported the right of working men to combine, it was because they thought that strikes would usefully cut back on manufacturing production. For the same reason they were able to tolerate the diversion of capital into inefficient channels such as public works, and they positively applauded conspicuous and unuseful consumption by the idle rich. Savings banks were advocated, not as stepping-stones to a people's capitalism, but in order to provide funds which would keep working men in idleness until the market should 'come round'. These policies reflected pre-Victorian values, albeit ones which survived into the early decades of the Queen's reign, and they have nothing to do with creating an enterprise culture.

And this is understandable, for the ideology of Atonement was espoused, not by the rude thrusting industrialists of the north, but by those in the City, the service economy, and the professions, all of whom subscribed mainly to 'progressive gentry', *rentier*, and metropolitan values. In this respect it differed from the ideology of American capitalism, as interpreted by Gerhard Ditz in his recent reformulation of the ideas of Weber and Tawney.

Calvin designated rational, wealth-oriented work-effort as the principal sacrament for those who felt called and wanted to be chosen. . . . For the first time in history the two capital producing prescriptions, maximization of production and minimization of consumption became components of the same ethical matrix. . . . Calvinism . . . put saving ethically above spending, investing above saving. . . . Risk-taking came under the imperative of stewardship . . . [because it] was congruent with spiritual indeterminacy. . . . Financial risk-taking for the would-be-saints had been programmed into their earthly life. Trying to avoid it meant losing it all.[7]

Accordingly, Ditz attributes what he sees as a decline in the capitalist ethic in twentieth-century America to a retreat from Calvinism and a new assurance about universal salvation. The latter point is reminiscent of what happened in Britain during the 1850s and 1860s. The difference is that in Britain the fashionable theology had not been Calvinist, and

[7] Gerhard W. Ditz, 'The protestant ethic and the market economy', *Kyklos*, 33 (1980), 623–57.

had not emphasized the sacramental value of wealth in itself or of business success as a fulfilment of one's calling. In the terms used by Ditz, it had put spending ethically above saving and saving above investing. In so far as it had provided ideological support to a social élite, that élite was not composed of manufacturing entrepreneurs as in America, but of the gentrified, professional, cosmopolitan classes.

This raises a question as to the *function* of evangelical ideas, one which has only been addressed by implication in this study. For the most part, changes in social and economic thought have been related to changes in the prevailing eschatology, which in Chapter 7 was explained in mainly internalist terms. The justification for such an approach is the fact that there is a long history of oscillation between what might be called 'supply-side religion' based on the Creation and the Incarnation, and 'demand-side religion' based on external goals such as Heaven and Hell, first one being fashionable and then the other. For example, belief in Hell had declined among the privileged classes in late seventeenth and early eighteenth-century England, though at that time such disbelief could not be announced publicly since Hell remained the best sanction for securing good behaviour among the poor.[8] Chapter 8 attempted to broaden the scope of this internalist type of explanation by relating the eschatological shift of the 1850s and 1860s to what may have been a still more basic change in man's scientific understanding of the universe, in particular to an abandonment of the old dualistic conception of mind and matter as requiring metaphysical at-one-ment. What this book cannot claim to have fronted, however, is the question of how the evangelical system of belief functioned, and how it related to material reality and the interplay of social relationships.

If there is a 'peculiarity' about English capitalism—to use a term made famous by the 'New Left' debates of the 1960s—it is the subordination of industrial capital to the financial and landed-gentry capital of the metropolis. And if there is a cultural corollary of that peculiarity, then Corelli Barnett would locate it squarely in the enfeeblingly wet embrace of evangelicalism.[9] Almost certainly Barnett underestimates the 'robustness' of the Clapham Sect and other mainstream evangelicals, whose social and economic ideas were much less close to those of Lord Shaftesbury and correspondingly much closer to his own than he realizes. Nevertheless, it is no doubt the case that the ideology of moderate evangelicalism

---

[8] D. P. Walker, *The Decline of Hell: Seventeenth-Century Discussions of Eternal Torment* (1964), 262–3 and *passim*.

[9] Tom Nairn, 'The British political élite', *New Left Review*, 23 (1964); Perry Anderson, 'Origins of the present crisis', ibid.; E. P. Thompson, 'The peculiarities of the English', *The Socialist Register* (1965), and reprinted in *The Poverty of Theory* (1978), 35–91; Corelli Barnett, *The Collapse of British Power* (1972), *passim*.

rationalized and defended the existing social and economic structure of society. When Chalmers promised that 'the blood of a satisfying Atonement is offered to every human creature . . . who will venture to place his reliance upon it',[10] his characteristic use of a business term reminds us that he spoke for a bourgeois élite whose assets were movable and precarious, an élite which protected its ventures with a body of commercial law based on the sacred nature of contracts, in deliberate challenge to an older, land-based common law. If moderate evangelicalism was a contractual religion, its scheme of redemption a species of joint stock whereby one 'acquired a saving interest in the blood of Jesus', then that sacred blood was a type of movable property for sinful properties which were also movable. For just as conversion could be—and ought to be— instantaneous, so sins could be expiated by remorse and the slate wiped clean. All this mirrored a type of capitalism in which riches were often made overnight rather than by patient and laborious cumulation, and then lost just as quickly.

As we have seen, such contractual ideology went out of fashion in mid-century, when dissolvent writers like W. R. Greg professed to be appalled at the ease with which evangelicals thought that one could 'start afresh' spiritually. For Greg it was necessary to foster one's personality, like one's assets. Truth was no longer to be telegraphed providentially, but 'wrung from nature's close reserve'—Browning's final word reminding us, not only of Newman's epistemology, but of the nation's increasingly assured creditor status in the world economy.

> And having thus created me,
>   Thus rooted me, he bade me grow,
> Guiltless for ever, like a tree
>   That buds and blooms . . .
> Yes, yes, a tree which must ascend,
>   No poison-gourd foredoomed to stoop!

Browning's *Johannes Agricola in Meditation* signals a return to the days of Paley, who had argued against the evangelicals that many mortals do not need to undergo a conversion experience, having been brought up in God and never having deviated from him.[11] In this perspective, moral evil came to be seen rather as 'a failure on man's part to rise higher in the scale of being, and to respond to the true dignity of his nature, than

---

[10] Chalmers to Napier, 15 Jan. 1837, Macvey Napier Papers, BL Add. MS 34618 fo. 169.

[11] W. Paley, 'On the doctrine of conscience', *Sermons on Several Subjects* (7th edn, 1815), 112–35.

a fall from a state of perfection'.[12] But *why* did mid-Victorian man stop trying to get 'under the blood' of Jesus and begin to emulate his life and example, and *why* did doctors think that blood was spurting less forcefully from their patients' veins than in the 1820s, and *why* was it suddenly decided in 1856 that the blood of bankrupt capitalists should not be spilled? Whether the new paradigm was more than a paradigm—more, that is, than a way of interpreting the world—whether it reflected the changed nature of British capitalism, is the question that needs to be addressed next.

[12] E. H. Askwith, 'Sin and the need of atonement', *Essays on Some Theological Questions of the Day by Members of the University of Cambridge*, ed. H. B. Swete (1905), 177.

BIBLIOGRAPHICAL APPENDIX

This book is based on such a wide range of reference that it is not feasible to provide a conventional bibliography. I have tried to make as many specific acknowledgements as possible in the footnotes, though of course there are many important books which are not cited because I owe them a general rather than a specific debt. The following notes briefly review some of the relevant literature which has appeared since this book was written.

Chapter 1

It remains the case, as lamented on p. 7, that most of the best work on evangelicalism is unpublished. The most distinguished recent contribution is Doreen M. Rosman, *Evangelicals and Culture* (1984), briefly mentioned on p. 20, a compelling if slightly solemn corrective to the traditional view that evangelicals were irredeemably anti-intellectual and philistine, and there is a new appraisal of the earlier phases of the evangelical revival in Gordon Rupp, *Religion in England 1688–1791* (Oxford, 1986). A prosopographical appendix on 550 missionaries to India is included in Stuart Piggin's important *Making Evangelical Missionaries, 1789–1858: The Social Background, Motives, and Training of British Protestant Missionaries to India* (Abingdon, 1985). Piggin concludes that most evangelical missionaries were influenced by the enlightenment, hostile to enthusiasm, serenely confident in the power of human reason, and 'dedicated to the ethical value of efficiency and usefulness'.

Chapter 2

Richard B. Sher, *Church and University in the Scottish Enlightenment: The Moderate Literati of Edinburgh* (Edinburgh, 1985) mainly covers the period before 1780, but is nevertheless essential background reading on Scotland's intellectual contribution to public debate thereafter. The mechanisms by which 'Scotch knowledge' permeated England in the nineteenth century are examined in Anand C. Chitnis, *The Scottish Enlightenment and Early Victorian English Society* (1986), which contains a useful prosopography of Scotsmen working south of the border. Biancamaria Fontana's work, used here in thesis form, has been published as *Rethinking the Politics of Commercial Society: the* Edinburgh Review *1802–1832* (Cambridge, 1985). The role of Copleston and Whately in mediating between Stewart and Senior is noted in Salim Rashid, 'Dugald Stewart, "Baconian" methodology, and political economy', *Journal of the History of Ideas,*

46 (1985), 245–57, which points out that Canning had a hand in urging Copleston to review the first volume of Stewart's *Elements* for the *Quarterly* (which in the event did not publish it).

Chapter 3

The Malthus industry, especially that branch of it devoted to Malthusian theodicy, flourishes: see M. B. Harvey-Phillips, 'Malthus' theodicy: the intellectual background of his contribution to political economy', *History of Political Economy*, 16 (1984), 591–608 (qualifying the arguments of Le Mahieu and Pullen) and Salim Rashid, 'Malthus' theology: an overlooked letter and some comments', ibid., 135–8, which agrees with the view presented on pp. 89–91 that late in life Malthus became increasingly identified with evangelicals such as Chalmers and their assumption that life was a state of trial. There are also several useful essays in *Malthus and his Time*, edited by Michael Turner (1986). Samuel Hollander, 'On Malthus's population principle and social reform', *History of Political Economy*, 18 (1986), 187–235, bravely suggests that Malthus's message was less dismal, more reformist and egalitarian than is usually thought. An opposite viewpoint is presented in Gertrude Himmelfarb's account of changing social perceptions in *The Idea of Poverty: England in the Early Industrial Age* (London and Boston, 1984), mentioned briefly on p. 75 above. Himmelfarb rightly plays down the so-called 'forerunners' of Malthusian population theory and emphasizes the dramatic way in which the *Essay* shattered Smithian optimism and 'gripped the imagination of contemporaries for half a century, making even more fearful a period fraught with anxiety and insecurity' and a 'profound sense of moral and social disarray' (pp. 525–6). Himmelfarb is not concerned with the religious ingredients of social thought, and she underestimates (pp. 121–3) the impact made by Malthus's notion of 'moral restraint', especially as developed by later writers. An important contribution to Malthus studies will be made by A. M. C. Waterman, who kindly showed me some advance chapters of his forthcoming book, as well as commenting acutely on my own.

A stimulating contribution to our understanding of early nineteenth-century social thought is Catherine Gallagher, *The Industrial Reformation of English Fiction: Social Discourse and Narrative Form 1832–1867* (Chicago, 1985), which seeks to vindicate the industrial novel of the period by showing how features which have been perceived as faults (ambiguities of tone, contradictions 'between plot and character, narrator and character, or the beginning and the end of the story') are in fact appropriate reflections of the current 'Condition of England' debate and of the authors' own philosophical, social, and political views. This investigation is conducted with reference to three contemporary 'tensions'—between free will and social determinism (allegories on providence), between the family and the nation as social organisms, and between fact and value (the politics of representation yielding insights into the representation of values in literary texts). This is all enormously suggestive, but it should be pointed out that Gallagher's touch in religious matters is sometimes unsure. For example, it is not the case that Hannah More rejected the idea of a mechanical, watchmaker-type of providence, such as was espoused by deists and by the later novelist Harriet

Martineau, in favour of a 'chaotic and irrational' providence which 'intervened daily in people's affairs, overturning their plans, thwarting their desires' (pp. 37–41). Gallagher's contention to this effect is supported by reference to a single poem, 'Turn the Carpet', but in fact More's message here is not that providence is capricious, merely that its full purport cannot be grasped this side of Paradise. According to *Hannah More: A Biographical Study* by Annette M. B. Meakin (1911), p. 317, it was this very same poem of which Beilby Porteus, the evangelical (or evangelically inclined) Bishop of London, said: 'Here you have Bishop Butler's *Analogy*, all for a halfpenny!' As this suggests, More's actual conception of providence was that of the moderate evangelical. God's 'prescience' was an essential part of that providence, and the 'unbroken regularity, perpetual uniformity, and systematic beauty' of the creation is as much a proof of his superintendence as the occasional earthquake [*Christian Morals* (1813), i. 39–40]. 'Nothing happens but by divine appointment', and we should keep up 'a sense of God's agency in common as well as in extraordinary occurrences', but this does not imply that we are like flies to wanton boys, for most of life's calamities — sickness, shame, pain, often even death — originate with ourselves (ibid., i. 61–6). Accordingly, More attacked 'the fanciful, frivolous and bold familiarity with which [God's] supreme dictation and government are cited on the most trivial occasions, and adduced in a manner dishonourable to infinite wisdom. . . . It is not more foolish and presumptuous to deny it altogether, than to expect that God's Particular Providence will interpose' in such everyday occurrences (ibid., i. 71). If in fact More's fiction suggests a different conception of providence than this, Gallagher may need to acknowledge an unwelcome incongruity between it and More's other writings. In discussing Charlotte Elizabeth Tonna's novels (pp. 47–8, 61), Gallagher refers to her 'anti-providential territory', meaning that her imaginary town 'M' in *Helen Fleetwood* is a place which induces to spiritual suicide, unlike the habitats depicted by More and Martineau which induce to grace and redemption. This is a perceptive point, and is connected with the fact that Tonna's evangelicalism was of the pre- rather than post-millenarian variety, as is shown on p. 97 above.

Chapter 4

The intricacies of business behaviour as depicted in fiction are usefully surveyed by Norman Russell in *The Novelist and Mammon: Literary Responses to the World of Commerce in the Nineteenth Century* (Oxford, 1986). There are some tantalizing references to the anti-bullionist and anti-dualist philosopher Tatham in *The History of the University of Oxford: Volume V: The Eighteenth Century*, edited by L. S. Sutherland and L. G. Mitchell (Oxford, 1986). John V. Pickstone, 'Ferriar's fever to Kay's cholera: disease and social structure in cottonopolis', *History of Science*, 22 (1984), 401–19, discusses theories of psychological dualism, whereby the body was supposed to be kept in check by man's rational mind. It notes that the biological representation of social grades and class differences shifted from a hierarchical animal series (*c.*1800) to a hierarchy of properties within individuals, and then relates this shift to growing middle-class fears of the poor. This article has directed me to an essay which I had overlooked by Roger Cooter on 'Anticontagionism and history's medical record', in *The Problem of Medical Knowledge: Examining the Social Constitution of Medicine*, edited by Peter Wright and Andrew Treacher (Edinburgh, 1982), pp. 87–108. Cooter refines Ackerknecht's position and relates anticontagionism to socio-political developments by analysing the linguistic and metaphorical habits of the disputants. He shows that the earlier nineteenth century had a 'dirt fetish', that fear of filth went with fear of social disorder, that disease was assumed to be a punishment for the sin of filth, and that there was a 'vast cosmological difference between contagionists and anti-contagionists'. The anticontagionist position signified belief in rational and uniform social laws, it being significant in this context that Southwood Smith abandoned Calvinism for Unitarianism.

Chapter 5

The assumptions behind the nineteenth-century acceptance of Butler's probabilism are illuminated, though the question is not directly addressed, in Theodore M. Porter, *The Rise of Statistical Thinking 1820–1900* (Princeton, NJ, 1986), which includes a discussion of the breakdown of 'classical probability theory'. Roger Cooter's fine study of phrenology, used in thesis form for the section on Combe in Chapter 4 above, has been published as *The Cultural Meaning of Popular Science: Phrenology and the Organization of Consent in Nineteenth-Century Britain* (Cambridge, 1984). Combe also figures in Postlethwaite's *Making it Whole*, discussed below under Chapter 8, and in Michael Lynch, ' "Here is adhesiveness": from friendship to homosexuality', *Victorian Studies*, 29 (1985–6), 67–96, which analyses 'the contribution made by the science of phrenology, and particularly by men-loving men who were drawn to phrenology, to the emergence of the modern homosexual'.

Chapter 6

There have been few recent developments in political history. J. P. Jupp, *Lord Grenville 1759–1834* (Oxford, 1985), is a welcome and long overdue study, but it is not an intellectual biography. The moralistic assumptions behind penal reform are examined in Randall McGowen, 'A powerful sympathy: terror, the prison, and humanitarian reform in early nineteenth-century Britain', *Journal of British Studies*, 25 (1986), 312–34. Its theme is that evangelical (and other) reformers, alarmed by what seemed to be increasing social differentiation and distance, devised a moral vocabulary (based on 'sympathy') which enabled them to combine contradictory aspirations—for individual autonomy on the one hand, and for social harmony and connection on the other. Although they opposed the old cruelties of state power, such as capital punishment, their emphasis on prisons and reformatories betokened merely more subtle means of social coercion. There is a powerful discussion of the intellectual ingredients of Whiggism and Whig-Liberalism in J. P. Parry, *Democracy and Religion: Gladstone and the Liberal Party, 1867–1875* (Cambridge, 1986), especially pp. 57–149.

Chapter 7

F. D. Maurice is one of eight 'intellectuals' whose ideas are discussed in Edward Norman's *The Victorian Christian Socialists* (Cambridge, 1987). Janet Oppenheim, *The Other World: Spiritualism and Psychical Research in England, 1850–1914* (Cambridge, 1985) discusses the part played by phrenology and the growing abhorrence of retributive theology in the rise of spiritualism. Belief in a happy — but all too familiar — afterlife, where parted ones might be reunited, was a counterpart of the domestication of Heaven, discussed on pp. 335–6 above. The first fruits of Laurence Goldman's important research (referred to above on p. 270) may be tasted in 'The Social Science Association, 1856–1886: a context for mid-Victorian Liberalism', *English Historical Review*, 101 (1986), 95–134, and in 'A peculiarity of the English? The Social Science Association and the absence of sociology in nineteenth-century Britain', *Past & Present*, 114 (1987), 133–71. Peter Hinchliff, 'Ethics, evolution and biblical criticism in the thought of Benjamin Jowett and John William Colenso', *Journal of Ecclesiastical History*, 37 (1986), 91–110, points out that the two men took a moral approach to both biblical criticism and science, and claims that in attacking the authenticity of Old Testament narratives, Colenso sought to acquit God of the charge that he was 'a bloodthirsty pagan tyrant'. Colenso's *The Pentateuch and the Book of Joshua Critically Examined* (1862–5), with its attack on the penal/substitutionary theories of the Atonement, is described as a 'liberation of the most positive kind'. George M. Tuttle, *So Rich a Soil: John McLeod Campbell on Christian Atonement* (Edinburgh, 1986) is a close account of McLeod Campbell's rejection of the doctrine of 'limited atonement' and of his part in helping to liberate Scottish theology from its preoccupation with guilt.

Chapter 8

Several recent books have tackled aspects of middle and late Victorian humanism. Norman Vance, *The Sinews of the Spirit: The Ideal of Christian Manliness in Victorian Literature and Religious Thought* (Cambridge, 1985) is an utterly enjoyable account of 'the unmanning of [Carlylean, Arnoldian, Kingsleyan, and Hughesian] manliness'. In *Making it Whole: A Victorian Circle and the Shape of their World* (Columbus, Ohio, 1984), Diana Postlethwaite discusses the Combe–Chambers–Bray–Martineau–Lewes–Spencer circle and its contribution to 'positivism, necessitarianism, and evolutionary theory'. Their common aim was to find an epistemological and monistic unity 'between head and heart' (p. 249). Comte provides one of the focuses of this study, as he does more formally in T. R. Wright, *The Religion of Humanity: The Impact of Comtean Positivism on Victorian England* (Cambridge, 1986). Humanism is convincingly presented as a non-religious species of ethics, arising out of a mid-century 'vortex' of religious, philosophical, and social ideas, in I. D. MacKillop, *The British Ethical Societies* (Cambridge, 1986). Finally, in 'Political economy and Christian polity: the influence of Henry George in England reassessed', *Victorian Studies*, 30 (1986–7), 235–52, John Plowright demonstrates that George sought not only to 'humanize' but to 'theologize' political economy by showing that its laws 'control the mental and moral as well as the physical status of humanity'.

Plowright also claims that George 'can only be appreciated by placing his ethically inspired economic thought in the broader cultural context of the conflict between science and religion'. Studies of that broader context are appearing with startling frequency, though the theme of 'conflict' tends more and more to be played down. David Knight, *The Age of Science: The Scientific World-View in the Nineteenth Century* (Oxford, 1986) is a brief but useful attempt to integrate it with other aspects of contemporary thought. Isaac Kramnick, 'Eighteenth-Century science and radical social theory: the case of Joseph Priestley's scientific liberalism', *Journal of British Studies*, 25 (1986), 1–30, shows how Priestley's circle linked political argument to conceptions of the natural world, and explores its ambivalent commitment to 'liberalism', which signified freedom from political, spiritual, and economic restraint on the one hand, discipline, regimen, and authority on the other. W. H. Brock, *From Protyle to Proton: William Prout and the Nature of Matter, 1785–1985* (Bristol and Boston, 1985), surveys the chemical vitalism of a devout natural theologian and author of the Bridgewater Treatise on chemistry, meteorology, and digestion. Christopher Hamlin, 'Providence and putrefaction: Victorian sanitarians and the natural theology of health and disease', *Victorian Studies*, 28 (1984–5), 381–411, mentioned briefly in the context of scientific monism on p. 309, is a fascinating discussion of the role played by natural theology in the formulation of sanitary (and especially zymotic) science in the period between the heyday of anticontagionism and the new bacteriology of the 1870s. Particularly interesting are the idea of disease as a process of moral contagion, the emphasis placed on the Creation in Leibig's chemistry, the part which putrefaction was assumed to play in natural cycles, and the widespread belief in what Hamlin calls 'a sort of cosmic sanitary dualism'. A crucial question for contemporaries was: Had God intended cities to be filthy and subject to epidemics? There are the makings of a major investigation here. If conservation of energy was an idea that had long been lying 'close to the surface of scientific consciousness', waiting for several people to discover it simultaneously (above, p. 309), then the same seems to be true of the use made of the concept by intellectual historians. Noteworthy here is Greg Myers, 'Nineteenth century popularizations of thermodynamics and the rhetoric of social prophecy', *Victorian Studies*, 29 (1985–6), 35–66, which discusses Tyndall, Thomson, Maxwell, Stewart, and (with a different message) Huxley, concluding that 'Conservation . . . implies a world of exchange without production. Dissipation suggests a universe of two levels, one producing and the other inevitably wasting. Molecules assure us the basic order of the universe is that of perfect and uniform "manufactured articles". Apparently, the order of nature supports the hierarchy of capitalist society.' Among various contributions to the history of science by literary critics is a religious—specifically evangelical—reading of Emily Brontë in Barbara Munson Goff, 'Between natural theology and natural selection: breeding the human animal in *Wuthering Heights*', *Victorian Studies*, 26 (1983–4), 477–508. Brontë's fundamental question seems to have been: 'Was Heathcliffe "God" or "unredeemed evil"?' There is much new and interesting information on Spencer especially, and on the varieties of 'Victorian cultural ideology' generally, in

George W. Stocking, Jun., *Victorian Anthropology*, (New York, 1987). Finally, Michael J. Crowe, *The Extraterrestrial Life Debate 1750–1900: The Idea of a Plurality of Worlds from Kant to Lowell* (Cambridge, 1986), is a comprehensive survey of its subject and one which, among other things, takes seriously the scientific contributions of Thomas Chalmers and T. R. Birks.

Chapter 9

Gladstone's theological politics are tackled in Richard Helmstadter, 'Conscience and politics: Gladstone's first book', in *The Gladstonian Turn of Mind: Essays presented to J. B. Conacher*, edited by Bruce L. Kinzer (Toronto, 1985), pp. 3–42 (though probably this interesting essay predates the real influence of Butler on Gladstone's thinking). The important influence of Aristotle on Gladstone, and the interactions between Aristotelian and Butlerian modes in his thought, are stressed in the newly written sections of H. C. G. Matthew, *Gladstone 1809–1874* (Oxford, 1986), especially pp. 24–58. The remainder of this book brings together the superb introductions which Matthew wrote for volumes 3, 5, and 7 of *The Gladstone Diaries*, the main thrust of this portrait of Gladstone being to illuminate 'the gallimaufrous nature of his mind, taken as a whole' (p. 34).

INDEX

Aberdeen, George Hamilton Gordon, 4th Earl (1784–1860), PM (1852–5) 63, 250–1, 258

Abernethy, John (1764–1831), surgeon and physiologist 306

abolitionism, *see* Slave Trade

Acland, Sir Thomas Dyke (1809–98), High Church MP of evangelical background 10

Addington, Henry Unwin (1790–1870), diplomat 36

Agnew, Sir Andrew (1793–1849), Scottish politician and Sabbatarian 208–9

Airy, Sir George Biddell (1801–92), Cambridge astronomer 60

Albert, Prince Consort (1819–61) 236

Alison, Alexander (*fl.* 1850–70), social improving theorist 326

Alison, Sir Archibald (1792–1867), lawyer and historian 20, 39 n., 62–3

Alison, William Pulteney (1790–1859), Edinburgh physician and social theorist 62–3, 87, 108, 111, 162

Allen, John (1771–1843), Whig journalist and *Edinburgh* reviewer 164

Allon, Henry (1818–92), Congregational divine 293

Althorp (Visc.), John Charles, 3rd Earl Spencer (1782–1845), evangelical 'Young Whig' Chanc. Exchequer (1830–4) 238–43, 359

altruism 296 n., 312, 318 and n., 321, 332, 371

analogy 149, 170, 174–5, 363–4

Angus, Joseph (1816–1902), Baptist, editor of Butler and Wayland 174, 181

anticontagionism 156–7, 159–61, 382, 384

Anti-Corn Law League 69, 206, 246–8

apocalypticism, *see* pre-millenarianism

Archer, Thomas (1806–64), Scottish evangelical Presbyterian 288

Argyll, George Douglas Campbell, 8th Duke (1823–1900), Whig politician and amateur scientist 175, 255, 277, 361, 363–5

Aristotle, Aristotelianism 45, 96, 128, 168, 172–3, 274, 337, 367 n., 385

Armstrong, John (1784–1829), physician and bloodletter 156

Arnold, Matthew (1822–88), poet and school inspector 173, 334, 337–8

Arnold, Thomas (1795–1842), Headmaster of Rugby and Prof. History, Oxford 28, 106, 131, 141, 172, 176, 269, 275

Ashley, (Lord), Anthony Ashley Cooper (1801–85), *see* Shaftesbury, 7th Earl

Askwith, Edward Harrison (1864–1946), Cambridge theologian 298, 378

associationist psychology 312, 318 and n., 325, 350 n.

assurance 18, 96, 153, 174, 283, 285, 336

astronomy x, 308 n.

Atkinson, William, member of Statistical Soc., London 322–4

Atonement, doctrine of 3, 5, 8, 20, 27, 33, 45, 84, 153, 159, 179–83, 187, 212, 230, 238, 240, 274, 277 n., 307, 326, 340, 345, 357, 370–1, 377

changing interpretations of 272, 278, 281–300, 302, 305, 316, 325, 334 n., 338, 349, 358, 383

Attwood, Thomas (1788–1856), Birmingham MP and currency reformer 121–2, 126, 128, 148

Augustine St, Augustinism 9, 181, 342

Austen, Jane (1775–1817), novelist 20, 29, 123

Babbage, Charles (1792–1871), Prof. Mathematics, Cambridge 30, 60

Babington, Géorge Gisborne (1794–1856), physician 131

Babington, Thomas (1758–1837), evangelical MP Leicester (1800–18) 59, 207

Bacon, Francis (1561–1626), philosophic Lord Chancellor 367

Baer, Karl Ernst von (1792–1876), German embryologist 312–13

Bagehot, Walter (1826–77), economist and journalist 174, 177, 185, 263, 354–5

Bailey, Samuel (1791–1870), Sheffield philosopher and economist 129, 166–7

Bain, Alexander (1818–1903), Prof. Logic, Aberdeen (1860–80) 313, 318

Bank Charter Act (1844) 199, 224, 237, 258

Bankes, Henry (1757–1834), 'Saintly' and independent MP 203, 206

Banking School 137

bankruptcy 117–20, 123, 125–6, 130, 135–47, 161–2, 256 n., 258, 316
and 'atonement' 136–47, 282, 284, 292–7
law of 263–4, 292

Baptists 136 n., 365

Baring, Alexander, 1st B. Ashburton (1774–1848), financier and statesman of independent views 221, 237

Baring, Charles Thomas (1807–79), Bp. Durham (1861–79) 290

Baring, Francis Thornhill, B. Northbrook (1796–1866), Whig Chanc. Exchequer (1839–41) 237

Baring, Thomas (1799–1873), financier, Chanc. Exchequer (1852, 1858) 206, 259 n.

Baring-Gould, Sabine (1834–1924), prolific writer and High Churchman 273, 282–3

Barrington, Shute (1734–1826), evangelical Bp. Durham (1791–1826) 23, 98–9, 235

Barrow, John (1764–1848), civil servant and *Quarterly* reviewer 151

Bastiat, Frédéric (1801–50), French *laissez-faire* journalist 328

Bathurst, Henry (1744–1837), evangelically inclined Bp. Norwich (1805–37) 173

Bathurst, Henry, 3rd Earl (1762–1834), evangelical Colonial Sec. vii, 209

Baxter, Richard (1615–91), Presbyterian divine 18 n., 183

Beattie, James (1735–1803), Prof. Moral Philosophy, Aberdeen 183, 186

Beeke, Henry (1751–1837), Dean of Bristol (1814–37), financial expert 41–2

Begg, Revd James (1808–83), Scottish evangelical Free Churchman 61

Begin, Louis Jacques, French physician 160

Bell, Sir Charles (1774–1842), Prof. Surgery, Edinburgh, and neurological scientist 189

benevolence, *see* philanthropy

Bentham, Jeremy (1748–1822), social and political philosopher 31, 33, 40, 144, 169, 176, 182, 186 n., 216–17, 227, 257, 282, 319
Benthamism 31, 32, 39, 74, 127, 183, 232, 244, 268, 281; *see also* utilitarianism

Bentinck, Lord William Cavendish (1774–1839), Gov.-Gen. India (1833–5) 228–9

Berkeley, George (1685–1753), Bp. Cloyne, anti-materialist philosopher 129, 168

Bernard, Sir Thomas (1750–1818), evangelist founder of SBCP 19, 23 n., 98–9, 101–3

Bessborough (Countess), Henrietta Frances (1761–1821), society lady 29

biblical criticism 177, 272, 278, 282, 383

Bicheno, James (1750?–1831), Baptist premillenarian writer 217

Bicheno, James Ebenezer (1785–1851), Irish Poor Law Commissioner and scientaster 78, 80, 95 n., 102, 107 n., 143, 183 n., 217–18

Bickersteth, Revd Edward (1786–1850), evangelical, Sec. CMS, turned premillenarian (1833) 7, 59, 85–6, 96–7, 212, 365

Bickersteth, Revd Edward (1814–92), High Churchman and New Testament reviser 330 and n.

Binning (Lord), Thomas Hamilton, 6th Earl Haddington (1780–1858), Canningite 57

biology x, 34, 51, 239, 270, 272, 299, 304, 308, 312, 314, 318, 321, 363 n., 368, 381

Birks, Revd Thomas Rawson (1810–83), Prof. Moral Philosophy, Cambridge 361, 365–71, 385

Birmingham Chamber of Commerce 259 n.

Blackwood's Edinburgh Magazine 36, 121

Blaikie, Revd William Gardon (1820–99), Scottish Free Churchman 56

Blake, William (1757–1827), poet and painter 314

Blomfield, Charles James (1786–1857), Bp. London (1828–56) 61, 101

bloodletting 156–61, 378

Blunt, John James (1794–1855), Prof. Divinity, Cambridge (1839–55) 181

Boardman, Revd George Nye (1825–1915), American Congregationalist 85, 329

Boardman, Revd Henry Augustus (1808–80), American Presbyterian and devotee of Chalmers 14 n., 102, 122, 142–4, 148

Booth, Charles (1840–1916), shipowner and social investigator 336

Bosanquet, Samuel Richard (1800–82), social and prophetic writer 96–7, 215

bourgeois culture, class, ideology ix–x, 38, 40, 67, 155, 161, 194–8, 203–5, 223, 236, 262, 266–7, 269, 276–7, 307, 308 n., 317, 324, 368, 375–8, 381, 384

Bourne, William Sturges (1769–1845), Liberal Tory politician 59, 242

Bowdler, John (1783–1815), evangelical propagandist 100 n.

Braxfield (Lord), Robert Macqueen (1722–99), Scottish judge 38

Bray, Charles (1811–84), Coventry ribbon manufacturer, freethinker, phrenologist 201, 319, 324–6, 355 n., 368, 383

Brewster, Sir David (1781–1868), Scottish Free Churchman, physicist 60, 152–3

Brewster, Revd Patrick (1788–1859), Scottish 'moral force' Chartist 108

Bridgewater Treatises 51 n., 64, 82, 177 n., 185–6, 195 and n., 310, 341

Brierley, James, Boroughreeve Manchester (1820–2) 58

Bright, John (1811–89), Radical MP 257

Briscoe, John Ivatt (1791–1870), extreme evangelical MP 212, 214

British and Foreign Bible Society 227–8, 233

British Association for the Advancement of Science 30, 60, 62

Broad Church 28–30, 285, 296, 300 n., 315, 335, 358

Brock, Revd William (1807–75), London dissenting philanthropist 136 n., 142

Brontë, Emily (1818–48), novelist and poet 384

Brougham, Henry Peter, 1st B. (1778–1868), Whig Lord Chancellor and natural theologian 38, 59–60, 69, 188–9, 241, 243–5, 263–4, 348 n.

Brown, James Baldwin (1820–84), liberal Congregational theologian 106, 246 n.

Brown, Dr John (1810–82), Scottish physician and essayist 61

Brown, Thomas (1778–1820), Prof. Moral Philosophy, Edinburgh (1810–20) 24–5, 39, 45, 179, 186, 191, 192 n.

Browning, Robert (1812–89), poet 315, 333, 373, 377

Bruce, Alexander Balmain (1831–99), Free Church Prof. Apologetics, Glasgow 279–80

Bubble Act (1720) 256–7

Buckland, William (1784–1856), Prof. Geology, Oxford 23, 60, 78 n., 150–2, 177 n., 235–6

Buckle, Henry Thomas (1821–62), free thinking historian of civilization 354–5

Budd, Revd Henry (1774–1853), evangelical divine 132

Buddicom, Revd Robert Pedder (1781?–1846), Prinicipal St Bees 281 n.

Bull, Revd George Stringer (1799–1865), evangelical philanthropist 95, 212, 226

Bullionism, anti-Bullionism 40, 43, 95, 125–30, 153, 199, 206, 219, 223, 227, 230–1, 240, 258, 269 n., 381

Bulteel, Revd Henry Bellenden (1800–68), Oxford Irvingite 340

Bulwer, Edward George Earle, B. Lytton (1803–73), novelist 147

Burke, Edmund (1729–97), political philosopher 130, 136, 147, 222, 322 n., 354

Bushnell, Horace (1802–76), American Congregational theologian 143, 299 and n.

business cycles 119, 121, 125, 130–1, 326; *see also* commercial crises

Butcher, Edmund, Devonshire Unitarian 116 n.

Butler, Joseph (1692–1752), theologian and Bp. Durham 135, 168, 204, 258 n., 290, 347
  and Chalmers 173, 176, 180, 183–4
  and conscience 175–8, 181–2, 185, 191
  decline of his influence 337–40
  and deism 174, 176–7
  and economic philosophy 188–9
  and evangelicalism 173–4, 176, 180–1, 183
  Gladstone's admiration of 172, 181, 340, 342, 344–9, 352, 358 n., 361, 385
  his influence 170–6, 181–3, 232, 274, 282 and n., 311, 342, 362–3, 367 n.
  his moral philosophy 163, 176, 181–3, 185, 191, 201–2
  his natural theology 175–84, 192, 221, 230, 259, 345–6, 352, 381
  and probabilism 174–5, 232, 348–9, 382
  his style 174, 180–1
  and soteriology 293, 344–5

Butler, Josephine Elizabeth (1828–1906), evangelical social reformer 335 n.

Buxton, Sir Thomas Fowell (1786–1845), evangelical philanthropist and abolitionist 59–60, 212 n.

Byron, George Gordon Noel, 6th B. (1788–1824), poet and romantic hero 29

Cadman, Revd William (1815–91), London evangelical 280
Callender, William Romaine (1825–76), cotton merchant and author 124 n., 265 n.
Calthorpe, George Gough-Calthorpe, 3rd B. (1787–1851), evangelical 59–61
Calvinism 8–10, 29–30, 76, 79, 87, 190, 194–5, 198, 227, 278, 285, 314–315, 375, 382
Cambridge University 12, 30, 35, 48–9, 51–2, 60, 133, 163, 171, 173, 274, 283, 287–8, 294, 308, 310, 337, 367
Campbell, John McLeod (1800–72), Scottish theologian 20, 283–5, 288, 294, 296 n., 371, 383
Canning, George (1770–1827), PM (1827) vii, 39, 57, 61, 129, 207, 219, 221–3, 228–9, 231, 234–5, 342, 380
Cardwell (Visc.), Edward (1813–86), Peelite politician 258, 270
Carlyle, Thomas (1795–1881), historian and sage 36–7, 149, 213–14, 220, 314, 326, 332–3, 363
Carnot, Sadi (1796–1832), French physicist 310
Carter, Thomas Thellusson (1808?–1901), prolific Anglican writer 172
Castlereagh (Visc.), Robert Stewart, 2nd Marquis Londonderry (1769–1822), Foreign Sec. (1812–22) vii, 129, 221–3
catastrophism 147, 150–3, 198, 300, 364, 373
causality, causation 211, 309, 302–3, 313–14, 362–3
Cazenove, John (1788–1879), founder member Political Economy Club 49, 64
Cecil, Revd Richard (1748–1810), evangelical propagandist 13, 20
Chadwick, Sir Edwin (1800–90), Poor Law and sanitary reformer 60, 241–5
Chalmers, Revd Thomas (1780–1847), 'lad o' pairts' 7, 26, 30, 143, 162, 207, 297, 374
  and the Atonement 282, 291, 293, 377
  and Butler 173, 176, 180, 183–4
  his career 20, 39, 55–63, 81–2, 183, 365
  and charity 89, 101–2, 104, 197, 245, 331
  and Combe 191, 195
  and conscience 183–8

and Free Trade 66–70, 109–12, 121, 126, 161, 197, 207
  influence of 55–62, 85–9, 209–10, 226, 237–8, 258, 283–4, 288, 328, 362
  and Irish Famine 108–12, 114, 249, 344
  and Liberal Toryism 61–3, 222, 229
  and Malthus 59–60, 64–7, 70, 91, 118 and n., 380
  his metaphysics 165–7, 176
  his moral paternalism 88–9, 208, 225
  and pauperism, Poor Laws 57–60, 62–3, 81, 86, 93–4, 99, 118, 122, 167, 242–3, 326, 359 n., 364
  and political economy 49–50, 64–70, 87–9, 108–10, 116–22, 144, 153, 225, 240–1, 259, 329, 374
  and population theory 76–7, 90, 184, 199
  and profit motive 116–17, 120–2, 124, 147, 265, 270
  and science 23, 96, 150, 153, 385
  and social policy 92, 107, 200, 209, 212–13, 217, 246, 322
  his theology 12, 14, 19, 23, 25, 31, 79–80, 83–4, 110–11, 153, 173, 178–88, 284–5, 361–4, 371
Chambers, Robert (1802–71), publisher and author 303, 308, 318, 383
Champneys, William Weldon (1807–75), prolific evangelical writer 142
Channing, William Ellery (1780–1842), American Unitarian 178 n., 194, 299, 316
charity, *see* philanthropy
Charity Organisation Society 88–9, 104, 279 n.
Chase, Revd Drummond Percy (1820–1902), Oxford classicist 339 n.
chemistry 14, 24, 34–5, 38, 40, 65 n., 148, 175 n., 197, 239–40, 271, 300, 304–6, 309, 318, 321 n., 362, 384
cholera 10, 43, 85, 112, 131, 155, 161, 172, 196, 213–14, 250, 362, 381
Christian Guardian (1809–49) 8–9, 23, 87
Christian Observer (1802–74) 9–10, 14 n., 15–16, 23, 90, 91 n., 100 and n., 117 n., 132, 178, 181, 206, 213, 226
Christian Socialism 6, 93 n., 201, 255, 265–6, 278, 284, 299, 309, 358, 364
Christian Socialist Union (1889) 331
Church Missionary Society 96, 287
Clapham Sect 7, 10, 12, 14–18, 25, 28, 42, 45, 55, 59, 98, 133, 203–13, 219, 227–8, 237, 247, 260, 371, 376

Clarendon, George William Frederick Villiers, 4th Earl (1800–70), Foreign Sec. (1865–6, 1868–70) 362

Clark, Revd Samuel (1810–75), educationalist 173–4

Clarkson, Thomas (1760–1846), evangelical philanthropist 59, 127

'classical economics' viii–ix, 6, 31–3, 36–40, 49, 54, 65–70, 87, 163–6, 321

Clausius, Rudolf Julius Emanuel (1822–88), German physicist 310

Clutterbuck, Henry (1767–1856), physician and bloodletter 156–7

Cobbe, Frances Power (1822–1904), philanthropist and devotional writer 292, 297

Cobbett, William (1762–1835), radical journalist 43, 131, 158, 184

Cobden, Richard (1804–65), statesman 54, 69, 141, 143, 146, 188, 195–7, 201, 225, 246–8, 255, 257, 261 n.

Cockburn (Lord), Henry Thomas (1779–1854), Scottish judge 38, 49

Colding, Ludvig August (1815–88), Danish physicist 309

Colenso, Revd John William (1814–83), Bp. Natal and neologian 316, 383

Coleridge, Samuel Taylor (1772–1834), poet and sage 36, 50, 60, 68, 120–1, 128–30, 148, 176, 182, 220, 314, 321, 337, 341

Colquhoun, John Campbell (1803–70), Scottish evangelical politician 60, 62

Colquhoun, Patrick (1745–1820), merchant and social theorist 122

Combe, Andrew (1797–1847), Scottish physiologist and phrenologist 190–1, 197

Combe, George (1788–1858), Scottish phrenologist 189–91, 194, 200–1
and bourgeois culture 197–8, 200–1
and Chalmers 191
and Cobden 195–7, 201, 247–8
his influence 198–9, 201–2, 311–12, 317–18, 322, 324, 328, 349, 383
his metaphysics 191–8, 260 n., 303, 337–8
and natural theology 192–3, 196, 363
and political economy 135, 199–200

commercial crises 117–25, 130–6, 145, 148, 152, 161, 199, 259, 265–7, 320, 329, 374–5

common sense 25, 39, 51 n., 164–5, 168–70, 186–7, 201–2, 300 n., 305

Comte, Auguste (1798–1857), French sociologist, humanist 296 n., 301, 319, 355, 383

Congregationalism 210, 292 n., 302, 306, 337

conscience 8, 117, 120, 175–8, 181–8, 191, 312, 321, 334–5, 337–8, 340–2, 344, 353, 357–62, 363 n., 365–6
nonconformist 357–61

consequentialism 181–2, 318, 366

Constable, Archibald (1774–1827), Scottish publisher 145

consumption 138–9, 156

contagionism, *see* anticontagionism

conversion 8–9, 316, 319, 340, 354, 366, 377

Conybeare, Revd William John (1815– 57), devotional writer 123, 138

Copleston, Edward (1776–1849), Oxford moralist, Bp. Llandaff
and Butler 174, 180
and evangelicalism 29–30, 107–8
and Grenville 234
his influence 231, 234–5, 379–80
his moral philosophy 100, 107–8, 116, 151, 187, 331
and Paley 172
and political economy 41–2, 50, 77, 116, 126–7, 130, 223, 230 n.

Corn Laws 35 n., 37, 40, 44, 66, 68, 77, 206–7, 209, 212, 222, 226, 230–1, 239–40, 246–50, 270–1, 323, 327, 350–3

corporal punishment 215–16, 268–9, 275

Courtenay, Thomas Peregrine (1782–1841), Tory politician 234

Craik, Mrs Dinah Maria Mulock (1826–87), novelist 140

Creevey, Thomas (1768–1838), Whig MP and socialite 229

Croker, John Wilson (1780–1857), Tory politician, *Quarterly* reviewer 92–4, 221

Crombie, Revd Alexander (1762-1840), philologist, economist, theologian 189

Cropper, James (1773–1840), Liverpool merchant, philanthropist, abolitionist 58

Crucifixion 273, 281, 288, 301, 330, 336, 345, 370

Cunningham, Revd John William (1780–1861), evangelical editor of *Christian Observer* (1850–8) 226

currency, *see* Bullionism

Currency School, 'Currency Principle' 43, 133–4, 137, 199, 224

Currie, James (1756–1805), Liverpool physician 34–5, 73–4, 158, 164

Cuvier (B.), Georges (1769–1832), French naturalist and geologist 150 cycles, *see* commercial crises

Dale, Robert William (1829–95), Birmingham liberal Congregational divine 281, 295 n., 296
Dalhousie, Sir James Andrew Broun Ramsay, 1st M. (1812–60), Peelite politician, Gov.-Gen. India (1847–56) 226, 324
Dalton, John (1766–1844), Manchester chemist 24, 58, 305–6
Darwin, Charles Robert (1809–82), naturalist 90 n., 151, 272, 301, 304, 308 and n., 339, 356, 363–4
  Darwinism 30, 90 n., 298, 301, 303, 344, 355 n., 368, 384
Darwin, Erasmus (1731–1802), physician, early evolutionary theorist 192
Daubeny, Charles Giles Bridle (1795–1867), Prof. Chemistry, Oxford 150, 153
Davies, John Llewelyn (1826–1916), Broad Church theologian 6, 287, 293–4, 315, 330–1
Davy, Sir Humphry (1778–1829), chemist, Pres. Royal Soc. (1820) 23 n., 49
Dealtry, Revd William (1775–1847), evangelical vicar and mathematician 55 n.
debt, *see* bankruptcy
degenerationism 364 and n.
deism 174, 176–7, 187, 338
Delane, John Thadeus (1817–79), editor of *The Times* 258
Denison, George Anthony (1805–96), High Church Archdeacon Taunton 200
De Quincey, Thomas (1785–1859), writer and Ricardian economist 65
Descartes, René (1596–1650), French philosopher, Cartesianism 311
Dicey, Albert Venn (1835–1922), Liberal jurist 267 n.
Dickens, Charles (1812–70), novelist 108, 139–40, 265, 279, 319, 333, 336
  and evangelicalism 315–17
diminishing returns 66, 77–8, 82
Disraeli, Benjamin, 1st Earl Beaconsfield (1804–81), PM (1868, 1874–80) 62, 145, 352–3
  Beaconsfieldism 357, 360
division of labour 198–202, 304, 312, 323, 332
Doddridge, Philip (1702–51), nonconformist divine 18 n.
Dodgson, Revd Charles Lutwidge (1832–98), mathematician, children's writer 314
Doubleday, Thomas (1790–1870), radical political economist 156, 298

Dove, Patrick Edward (1815–73), popular philosopher 56, 326–8, 368
Doyle, Sir Francis Hastings Charles (1810–88), lawyer 56
Drummond, Henry (1786–1860), banker, Tory MP, Angel of the Irvingites and founder of Oxford Chair of Political Economy 12, 14–15, 17, 42–8, 93, 95, 130–1, 153, 211, 287
Drummond, Henry (1851–97), Scottish evangelical theologian 303, 331–2
dualism 160, 202, 216, 295 n., 300, 304–7, 309, 311–12, 314, 318, 324, 367–9, 371, 376, 381, 384
Dudley, John William Ward, 1st Earl (1781–1833), Liberal Tory politician vii
duelling 208, 268 and n.

Eaton, Revd John Richard Turner (1825? – 1911), Prof. Moral Philosophy, Oxford (1874–81) 338–9, 367 n.
Ebrington (Visc.), Hugh, 2nd Earl Fortescue (1783–1861), Whig MP (1804–39) 238–9
Eclectic Society 18, 20
economical reform, *see* retrenchment
Economist, The 54, 69
Eden, Sir Frederick Morton (1766–1809), writer on Poor Laws 102
Edinburgh Review 38–9, 47, 58, 64, 69, 152, 164, 188, 232 n.
Edinburgh University 24–5, 34–5, 38–40, 60, 158, 183, 308
education 82, 200, 202, 226, 232, 247, 334
Edwards, Jonathan (1703–58), American Congregational theologian 157, 167
Eldon, John Scott, 1st Earl (1751–1838), High Tory Lord Chancellor (1801–6, 1807–27) vii, 222–3, 226, 257
Elgin, Thomas Bruce, 7th Earl (1766–1841), evangelical writer on pauperism and rescuer of marbles 57, 59
Eliot, George (1819–80), novelist 139, 272, 315, 317–19, 324, 336
Ellenborough, Edward Law, 1st Earl (1790–1871), Tory politician, Gov.-Gen. India (1841–4) vii
Elliotson, John (1791–1868), Prof. Clinical Medicine, London, phrenologist 306
Elliott, Edward Bishop (1793–1875), evangelical propheticist 274
Elliott, Henry Venn (1792–1865), Cambridge evangelical divine 7
Ellis, William (1800–81), economist, founder of Birkbeck schools 149, 161–2, 200–1

Emerson, Ralph Waldo (1803–82), American idealist and social critic 299, 316, 326

energy:
  conservation of 309–11, 313–14, 319, 321, 324, 354–5, 366–9, 384
  dissipation of 310–11, 313–14, 367–9, 372
  energetics 319–321, 332, 345, 354–5, 372

environmentalism 162, 241, 270, 316, 325

Erskine, Henry (1746–1817), Scottish evangelical and Whig Lord Advocate 38

Erskine, Thomas (1788–1870), liberal theologian 284–5, 288, 292 n., 295–6, 314

Estcourt, Thomas Grimston Bucknall (1775–1853), extreme evangelical MP (1805–47) 212

eternal punishment 8, 76, 85, 90, 153, 169, 178, 184, 190, 194, 271–3, 275–6, 278, 284, 287, 325, 334 n., 342, 365, 369, 373

ethers 305, 367, 369 n.

Evangelical Alliance 104, 365

Evangelical Magazine (1793–1904) 10, 291–2

evangelical theology 7–35, 55, 90, 116, 174, 177–8, 195
  extreme evangelicalism 10–11, 13–19, 21, 85, 93–8, 195–6, 206 n., 211–15, 227, 285, 298–9, 311, 334, 340, 370–1
  mid-century softening of 273, 276–81, 289, 291, 340–3, 357
  moderate evangelicalism 10, 13–19, 21, 23, 68–9, 83, 93–8, 98–100, 113–14, 131, 133, 143–4, 149, 153, 196–7, 200, 208, 211–18, 233, 286–7, 295, 297, 300 n., 307, 313, 316, 334, 340, 357, 361–2, 368, 370–1, 376–7, 381

evolution, theories of 34, 54 n., 272, 298, 301, 303–4, 308–9, 312–14, 319, 332, 338, 344, 354, 356, 364, 366, 368, 383–4

Ewing, Alexander (1814–73), Bp. Argyll and the Isles 75, 296 n.

Exeter Hall 206, 270, 286

Eyre, Edward John (1815–1901), Gov. Jamaica (1864–6) 332, 354

Faber, Revd George Stanley (1773–1854), prophetic pre-millenarian evangelical 23, 141

Fabianism 268

faculty psychology 165, 168–9, 187–9, 191–3, 199, 201, 311–12, 314, 325

Fall (the), *see* sin

Farrar, Frederic William (1831–1903), neological Dean of Canterbury (1895–1903) 274–6, 299, 336

fever 155–7, 159, 161, 269, 309, 375, 381

Fichte, Johann Gottlieb (1762–1814), German philosopher 311

Field, Edwin Wilkins (1804–71), Unitarian law reformer 264 and n.

final perseverance, doctrine of 140 n.

financial crash (1825) vii, 41, 118–19, 125, 130–3, 224, 260 n.

Fisk, Revd George (*c*.1810–74), religious writer 122–5, 135, 145

Forbes, James David (1809–68), Prof. Natural Philosophy, Edinburgh 60, 308

force 187, 310–314, 325, 367 n; *see also* energy; will

Fourier, François Marie Charles (1772–1837), French utopianist 200

Fox, Charles James (1749–1806), Whig statesman, Foxites 170, 204, 239

Free Trade vii–viii, 6, 16, 40, 44, 45 n., 52, 79–80, 86–7, 92, 95, 97–8, 108–10, 112, 116, 121, 126, 149, 164, 170, 188–9, 197, 201–2, 205–6, 212, 219, 222, 232, 237, 240–1, 246–50, 268, 320 and n., 323, 325–6, 328, 350–3, 364, 366, 375
  rival models of 64–70, 188, 241, 245, 255, 260–2, 266

Frend, William (1757–1841), Unitarian tutor of Malthus, proponent of Sinking Fund, scientific writer 90

Froude, James Anthony (1818–94), historian, loser of faith 272, 292, 333

Froude, Richard Hurrell (1803–36), early Tractarian controversialist 28

Fry, Elizabeth (1780–1845), Quaker prison reformer 60

future punishment, *see* eternal punishment

Gaisford, Thomas (1799–1855), Oxford Prof. Greek 235

Gall, Franz Joseph (1757–1828), Paris physician and first phrenologist 190–1

Galt, John (1779–1839), novelist 115, 148

Garnier, Revd Thomas (1809–63), Dean of Lincoln 105, 111

Gaskell, Peter (1806?–41), surgeon and Liberal social investigator 115 n.

geology x, 22–3, 34, 51, 82–3, 148–54, 162, 166, 198, 235–6, 271–2, 299–301, 304, 308–9, 333, 364, 368, 372

George, Henry (1839–97), American Christian economist and tax reformer 328, 383–4

Gifford, William (1756–1826), editor of *Quarterly Review* 151

Gilbart, James William (1794–1863), Banking School theorist 103, 105, 137–8, 330

Gilbert, Thomas (1720–98), barrister and Poor Law reformer 99

Girdlestone, Revd Charles (1797–1881), biblical commentator 23–4

Gisborne, Revd Thomas (1758–1846), evangelical moralist, scientist 22, 152, 176, 178, 204, 206

Gladstone, Sir John (1764–1851), Liverpool merchant 58, 145, 356

Gladstone, William Ewart (1809–98), four times PM 105 n., 115, 124, 230, 238, 258, 265, 363, 365, 385
and belief in 'progress' 343–5, 347–50
and belief in providence 113, 133, 345–8
and Butler 172, 181, 340, 342, 344–9, 352, 358 n., 361, 385
and Chalmers 20, 55, 60–2, 89, 340–1, 359 and n.
and evangelicalism 27, 340–3, 357–61
'Gladstonian liberalism' 236, 301, 344–5, 347, 350–7
opposes limited liability 257–8, 359–61
his political style 203, 347–8, 350–4, 356–7
his religious views 10, 27, 341–50
and theocratic politics 121, 340–1, 350, 354

Glasgow University 62–3, 230–1, 310

Gleig, Revd George Robert (1796–1888), army chaplain and writer 57

gluts 52, 66, 89, 117–20, 153, 156, 248–9, 329

Goderich (Visc.), George Frederick Robinson, 1st M. Ripon (1827–1909), Christian Socialist MP, statesman, Gov.-Gen. India 265–6

Godwin, William (1756–1836), atheist and utopian 74–5, 312

Goethe, Johann Wolfgang von (1749–1832), German romantic 311

Gold Standard 6, 107, 115, 125–30, 158, 203, 223–4, 234, 240

Good Samaritan, parable of 246, 275, 303

Gordon, Lord George (1751–93), Protestant agitator MP 203

Gordon, James Edward (1789–1864), Scottish evangelical MP 116, 214, 249–50

Gore, Mrs Catherine (Grace) Frances (1799–1861), novelist 143

Gore, Revd Charles (1853–1932), *Lux Mundi*-ite, founder CSU, Bp. Oxford 278, 337

Gorham, Revd George Cornelius (1787–1857), evangelical, Gorham Judgment 341, 352

Gough, John Ballantine (1817–86), lapsed drunkard 270

Goulburn, Edward Meyrick (1818–97), Dean of Norwich, evangelical turned High Churchman 276 n., 290

Goulburn, Henry (1784–1856), evangelical and Liberal Tory, Chanc. Exchequer (1828–30, 1841–6) vii, 131 n., 226–7, 258

Graham, Sir James Robert George (1792–1861), Peelite, Home Sec. (1841–6) 258
and Chalmers 62–3, 225–6, 238 n., 264
on providence and the Corn Laws 248–50, 270–1, 352

Grant, Charles (1746–1823), Clapham Sect MP (1802–18) and philanthropist 208

Grant, Charles, Lord Glenelg (1778–1866), evangelical, Liberal Tory and later Whig politician vii, 226, 228, 238

Grant, James (1802–79), evangelical journalist 94

Grant, Sir Robert (1779–1838), MP and Gov. Bombay 59

Granville, George Granville Leveson-Gower, 2nd Earl (1815–91), Liberal statesman 258 and n., 347

Green, Thomas Hill (1836–82), Prof. Moral Philosophy, Oxford (1878–82) 337

Greenhough, George Bellas (1778–1855), geologist and geographer 151

Greg, Samuel (1804–76), Unitarian philanthropist 333

Greg, William Rathbone (1809–91), mill owner, government official, and essayist 271–2, 301 and n., 302, 333, 377

Grenville, Thomas (1755–1846), Foxite MP and bibliophile 240

Grenville, William Wyndham, 1st B. (1759–1834), PM (1806–7) 57, 59, 127, 231–6, 240, 382

Greville, Charles Cavendish Fulke (1794–1865), civil servant and diarist 36, 228

Grey, Charles, 2nd Earl (1764–1845), PM (1830–4) 38, 243

Grey, Sir George (1799–1882), Home Sec. (1846–52, 1855–8, 1861–6) 59, 238

Grey, Sir Henry George, Visc. Howick and 3rd Earl (1802–94), Whig statesman 258

Grinfield, Edward William (1785–1864), biblical scholar 307

Grote, George (1794–1871), banker and historian 168–70
Grove, Sir William Robert (1811–96), judge and physicist 310
Gurney, Joseph John (1788–1847), evangelical Quaker philanthropist 20, 59–60, 116 n., 122, 146, 178–9

habit, doctrine of 185–7, 192–3, 216, 318, 347, 356
Hackney Phalanx 299
Haldane, Alexander (1800?–82), evangelical editor of *The Record* 10, 212
Haldane, James Alexander (1768–1851), Scottish evangelical Congregationalist 83
Halifax (Hallifax), Samuel (1733–90), Bp. St Asaph, Prof. Arabic and Civil Law, Cambridge 170, 174
Hamilton, Richard Winter (1794–1848), Congregational minister 173 n.
Hamilton, Robert (1743–1829), Prof. Maths and Science, Aberdeen 103, 233–4
Hamilton, Sir William (1788–1856), Prof. Logic and Metaphysics, Edinburgh 172, 326
Hamilton, Sir William Rowan (1805–65), Irish mathematician 60
Hampden, Renn Dickson (1793–1868), Prof. Divinity, Oxford, Bp. Hereford 172, 173 n.
handloom weavers 237, 241, 323
Harcourt, Revd William Vernon (1789–1871), Sec. BAAS 30–1, 229
Hardie, James Keir (1856–1915), Independent Labour MP 335
Hare, Revd Augustus William (1792–1834), Oxford divine and country vicar 30
Hare, Revd Julius Charles (1795–1855), Cambridge classicist 28, 30, 171, 337
Harrowby, Dudley Ryder, 1st Earl (1762–1847), Ld. Pres. Council 57, 226–7
Hartley, David (1705–57), philosopher 192, 216
Hazlitt, William (1778–1830), essayist, *Edinburgh* reviewer 56, 176
Heaven 8, 100, 137, 185, 195, 271, 279, 291, 300, 376
    new mid-century notions of 335–6, 383
Hebert, Revd Charles (1807–90), religious writer 293–4
Hegel, Georg Wilhelm Friedrich (1770–1831), German philosopher 321
Hell, hell-fire 8, 13, 90, 115, 133, 184, 190, 280–1, 376

mid-century softening of belief about 271–2, 275–80, 282, 301, 315, 333, 335–6, 358
    Maurice on 271–2
Helmholtz, Hermann Ludwig Ferdinand von (1821–94), German scientist 309
Herbert, Sidney, 1st B. (1810–61), Peelite politician 258
Herder, Johann Gottfried von (1744–1803), German theologian, philosopher 311
Herries, John Charles (1778–1855), High Tory Chanc. Exchequer (1827–8) 218, 222–3
Herschel, Sir John Frederick William (1792–1871), Cambridge astronomer 30, 49, 60, 187, 308 n., 310
High Tories, High Toryism vii–viii, 36, 92, 215, 218, 220–7, 236, 256–7, 322
Hill, Revd George (1750–1819), leader of the Scottish Moderate Party 25
Hill, Matthew Davenport (1792–1872), Recorder of Birmingham, criminal law reformer 269 and n., 280
Hill, Octavia (1838–1912), philanthropist and housing reformer 314, 334–5
Hill, Sir Richard (1732–1808), controversialist and evangelical MP 208
Hill, Revd Rowland (1744–1833), evangelical preacher 59
Hoare, Samuel (1751–1825), evangelical banker of Quaker background 19 n., 60
Hobbes, Thomas (1588–1679), philosopher 189
Hodgkin, Thomas (1798–1866), physician 201
Hole, Revd Richard (1746–1803), poet and critic 144 n.
Holland, Sir Henry (1788–1873), society physician 308, 337
Holland, Henry Scott (1847–1918), *Lux Mundi*-ite, High Church liberal theologian, social and economic pundit 6, 321, 337, 347
Hook, Revd Walter Farquhar (1798–1875), Leeds High Churchman 30
Hooker, Richard (1554?–1600), theologian 342
Hope, Samuel, Liverpool philanthropist 58
Hope, Thomas Charles (1766–1844), Prof. Chemistry, Edinburgh (1799–1843) 34
Hope-Scott, James Robert (1812–73), barrister, turned to Rome (1851) 352, 356
Hopps, John Page, prolific Unitarian writer 282

Horne, George (1730–92), Bp. Norwich (1790–2) 305

Horner, Francis (1778–1817), Whig politician 38–40, 68, 127, 129, 164

Horner, Leonard (1785–1864), geologist, educationalist, factory inspector 60

Hort, Fenton John Anthony (1828–92), Cambridge theologian 274, 278, 294–6, 301–2, 337

Horton, Sir Robert Wilmot (1784–1841), Tory MP, emigrationalist 59

Howard, John (1726?–90), evangelical prison reformer 216

Howels, Revd William (1778–1832), Welsh evangelical sermonizer 11

Howley, William (1766–1848), Abp. Canterbury (1828–48) 238

Hudson, George (1800–71), railway speculator 123, 264

Hughes, Thomas (1822–96), author and Christian Socialist 265

Hume, David (1711–76), philosopher and historian 24–5, 164–5, 168, 176 n., 190–1

Hume, Joseph (1777–1855), Radical MP 206, 248

Huskisson, William (1770–1830), Liberal Tory Pres. Bd. of Trade (1823–7) vii, 39, 41, 129, 207, 221–3, 225, 227–8, 234, 256, 258, 360
and Chalmers 57, 61–2

Hutcheson, Francis (1694–1746), 'common sense' philosopher 39, 165, 175, 190

Hutchings, Revd William Henry (1835?–?1911), theological maverick, firm believer in eternal punishment, but an Incarnationalist who recommended 'systematic and proportional' almsgiving 142–3

Hutchinson, John (1674–1737), religious typologist, Hutchinsonianism 198

Hutton, James (1726–97), uniformitarian geologist 149, 151–2, 372

Hutton, Richard Holt (1826–97), theologian and journalist 300

Huxley, Thomas Henry (1825–95), scientist 355, 364, 368, 384

Incarnation, doctrine of 5–6, 285–6, 289, 293, 296, 298–9, 302–4, 326, 330, 334–5, 337, 345, 349, 358, 363, 367, 371, 376
incarnational social thought 311–15, 320–37

Industrial and Provident Societies Act (1852) 266

Inglis, Sir Robert Henry (1786–1855), High Tory MP 60, 212, 214

Ingram, Revd Rowland (1765–?1849), evangelical opponent of duelling 268

Irish Famine 108–14, 133, 213, 238, 248–50, 270–1, 289 n., 312, 333, 344, 351, 359

Irving, Revd Edward (1792–1834), founder of Catholic Apostolic Church 11–12, 14–15, 17, 21–2, 30, 42, 60, 96, 131–2, 145, 172 n., 195, 211–12, 228–9, 287, 298–9, 334, 365
and charity 103, 105–6
Irvingism 45, 94, 286, 303, 371
and mid-century theological developments 284–6, 311, 371

Jacob, William (1762?–1851), statistician and MP 49

James, Revd John Angell (1785–1859), Birmingham Congregational divine 105

Jeffrey (Lord), Francis (1773–1850), editor of *Edinburgh Review* 38

Jellett, John Hewitt (1817–88), Dublin mathematician and theologian 273

Jennings, Richard (1814–91), lawyer and social theorist 329 and n.

Jerram, Revd Charles (1770–1853), Surrey evangelical 86, 180–1, 205 n.

Jesus as man 5, 98–100, 104–5, 136, 213, 279, 286, 288–9, 297, 299, 320, 332, 344, 362, 364

Jevons, William Stanley (1835–82), economist and logician 320–1, 344, 362, 364

Jocelyn, (Visc.), Robert, 3rd Earl Roden (1788–1870), extreme evangelical MP 94

Johnson, Dr Samuel (1709–84), lexicographer and sage 129

joint stock companies 136–8, 256–7, 325, 377

Jones, Richard (1790–1855), Prof. Political Economy, London and Haileybury 34, 49, 51–5, 60, 144, 163–4, 167 n., 328

Jones, William (1726–1800) 'of Nayland', High Church divine 305

Joule, James Prescott (1818–89), Manchester physicist 309–10, 368

Jowett, Benjamin (1817–93), Prof. Greek, Oxford 173, 255, 316
and the Atonement 289–93, 337, 383

Judgment 340, 345

justice, theories of 179, 191–2, 274, 278, 303, 327, 332, 352–3, 358, 371, 373–5, 383 justification 18–19, 183, 230, 284, 326, 357

Kames, Henry Hume, Lord (1696–1782), Scottish philosopher 175
Kant, Immanuel (1724–1804), German philosopher, Kantian 168, 171, 183 n., 290, 311, 338 and n.
Keats, John (1795–1821), poet 177, 220, 230
Keble, Revd John (1792–1866), Tractarian 27, 49, 121, 175, 349
Kennaway, Revd Charles Edward (1800–75), religious writer 288–9
Kennedy, Thomas Francis (1788–1879), Scottish Whig MP and Poor Law reformer 59, 60 n.
Ker, Charles Henry Bellenden (1785?–1871), legal reformer 257
Keynes, John Maynard, 1st B. (1883–1946), Cambridge Economist, Keynesianism 65, 67
Kingsley, Charles (1819–75), Christian Socialist author 29, 115, 309, 314

Labouchere, Henry, 1st B. Taunton (1798–1869), Liberal politician 237
Labouchere, Henry du Pré (1831–1912), journalist and politician 266
Laing, Samuel (1812–97), railway director, MP, scientific popularizer 324
laissez-faire individualism vii–ix, 7, 15–17, 32–3, 45, 70, 79, 87–8, 92–5, 97–100, 110–11, 116, 122, 130, 148, 197, 200–1, 208, 210–11, 225, 230–1, 241, 249, 284 n., 297, 303 n., 307, 311, 322, 324, 328–9, 333, 342, 350, 364
Lalor, John (1814–56), Unitarian and journalist 56, 86
Lamarck, Jean Baptiste (1744–1829), French naturalist and evolutionist, Lamarckism 236, 312, 355
Lansdowne, Sir Henry Petty-Fitzmaurice, 3rd M. (1780–1863), 'very moderate' Whig politician 38, 40, 60, 228, 232
Lauderdale, James Maitland, 8th Earl (1759–1839), Whig turned Tory, heterodox political economist 37–8, 164 n., 234
Lavater, Johann Caspar (1741–1801), Swiss physiognomist 61
Lawrence, Sir William (1783–1867), London surgeon and anatomist 306
Le Bas, Charles Webb (1779–1861), Prof. Maths, Haileybury 60

Leibniz, Gottfried Wilhelm (1646–1716), German philosopher, mathematician 179
Le Marchant, Sir Denis (1795–1874), Liberal politican 244
Leslie, Sir John (1766–1832), Prof. Maths and Natural Philosophy, Edinburgh 24–5, 34
Lessing, Gotthold Ephraim (1729–81), German writer and philosopher 168
Lethbridge, Sir Thomas Buckler (1778–1849), country MP (1806–12, 1820–30) 126
Leveson-Gower (Visc.), Granville, 1st Earl Granville (1773–1846), diplomat 228
Lewes, George Henry (1817–78), positivist philosopher 311–12, 318, 383
Liberal Tories, Liberal Toryism vii–viii, 68–9, 205, 215, 219–36, 248
  Chalmers and 61–3, 222, 229, 256–7, 261, 263, 266
  and evangelicalism 218–20, 226–30
  and scientific culture 235–6, 250
Liebig, Justus von (1803–73), German chemist 384
limited liability legislation (1855–62) 237, 251, 255–68, 277, 297, 300, 317, 323, 328, 360–1, 363, 378
Lindsay, Alexander William Crawford, 25th Earl Crawford and 8th Earl Balcarres (1812–80), bibliophile and writer 349–50, 354
Liverpool, Robert Banks, 2nd Earl (1770–1828), PM (1812–27) vii, 7, 39, 42, 62, 67 n., 206, 219, 226–8, 235–6, 256, 266
Lloyd, Charles (1784–1829), Prof. Divinity, Oxford (1822–9) and Bp. Oxford (1827–9) 229–30, 234–6
Lloyd, William Forster (1794–1852), mathematician, political economist 47, 50
Loch, Sir Charles Stewart (1849–1943), Sec. Charity Organisation Soc. 88–9
Locke, John (1632–1704), philosopher 24, 45, 48, 164, 190–1, 201, 232 n., 312, 341–2
Lodge, Sir Oliver Joseph (1851–1940), Prof. Physics, Liverpool (1881–1900) 368
London University 41, 43, 48, 60, 274
loss of faith 272–3, 311, 368
Lowe, Robert, 1st Visc. Sherbrooke (1811–92), Whig/Radical Chanc. Exchequer (1868–73) 69
  proposes limited liability 258–62, 264, 266 and n., 277
Loyd, Samuel Jones, *see* Overstone

Lubbock, John, 1st B. Avebury (1834–1913), banker and scientist 364 n.

Lubbock, Sir John William (1803–65), astronomer and mathematician 60

Ludlow, John Malcolm Forbes (1821–1911), Christian Socialist 265

lunacy reform 141, 215 n., 268

Lushington, Dr Stephen (1782–1873), Admiralty Ct. judge, reforming Whig MP 60

Lux Mundi (1889) 5, 337

Lyell, Sir Charles (1797–1875), Prof. Geology, King's Coll., London 150–4, 308, 372

Lyttelton, William Henry, 3rd B. (1782–1827), Whig MP (1807–20) 239

Macaulay, Thomas Babington, 1st B. (1800–59), Whig historian 131

Macaulay, Zachary (1768–1838), evangelical and abolitionist 7, 59–60, 100 n., 146, 240

McCosh, James (1811–94), Prof. Logic and Metaphysics, Belfast (1851–68) 326, 361–4

McCulloch, John Ramsay (1789–1864), Prof. Political Economy, London (1828–32) 39–41, 43, 45, 66, 201
and Chalmers 64–5, 240–2
opposes limited liability 260–2, 264

MacDonald, Revd George (1824–1905), Scottish poet and novelist 314–15

MacDonald, Ramsay (1866–1937), PM (1924, 1929–35) 335

MacDonnell, John Cotter (1841–1902), Dean of Cashel 292–3

Mackintosh, Sir James (1765–1832), Whig philosopher and publicist 38, 41 n., 57, 60, 229

Maclean, Charles (1788–1824), liberal and anticontagionist medical writer 159

McLeod, Revd Norman (1812–72), Scottish Presbyterian, pupil of Chalmers 296 n.

McNeile, Revd Hugh (1795–1879), evangelical Dean of Ripon (1868–75) 110, 138 n.

Maconochie, Alexander (1787–1860), naval captain and penal reformer 217

Magee, William (1766–1831), Prof. Maths and Abp. Dublin 281 n.

Magee, William Connor (1821–91), Bp. Peterborough and Abp. York 293, 363 n.

Magendie, François (1783–1855), French anticontagionist physiologist 159

Malan, César Jean Salomon (1812–94), Genevan High Calvinist 18

Mallet, John Lewis (b. 1775?), gov. official and diarist 234

Maltby, Edward (1770–1859), Whig and evangelicalish Bp. Durham (1836–56) 214

Malthus, Revd Thomas Robert (1766–1834), political economist 37, 40, 49, 52, 70, 147, 149, 153, 162, 164, 168, 185, 188, 199, 205, 233, 241, 303 n., 312, 329, 371
and Chalmers 59–60, 64–7, 91, 118 and n., 184, 380
Malthusianism 13, 24, 32, 39, 64–7, 70, 77 n., 80–1, 89, 139, 154, 177, 182, 220, 243, 248, 263, 265, 312, 321–2, 325, 329, 355, 373
on population 4, 34–5, 66, 73–9, 82, 100, 108, 117, 234, 240, 380
his *Principles of Political Economy* 117–18
his theology 90–1, 179, 380

Manchester Chamber of Commerce 259 n.

Manchester economics, *see laissez-faire* individualism

Mandeville, Bernard (1670?–1733), social theorist 165

Mandeville, George, 6th Duke Manchester (1799–1855), extreme evangelical MP 94

Manichaeanism 286, 295, 301

Manning, Henry Edward (1808–92), turned to Rome (1851) 10, 352, 356, 360 and n.

Mansel, Revd Henry Longueville (1820–71), High Church metaphysician 173 n., 290, 300 n., 338 and n.

Marcet, Mrs Jane (1769–1858), popularizer of science 40, 70, 81

marginalism 319–21

Marsh, Revd William (1775–1864), evangelical publicist 95

Marshall, Alfred (1842–1924), Prof. Political Economy, Cambridge (1884–1908) 32, 321–2, 332

Martin, John (1789–1854), apocalyptic painter 147, 149

Martineau, Harriet (1802–76), scientific popularizer 81, 97, 126, 242, 268, 380–1

Martineau, James (1805–1900), Unitarian divine 5, 267–8, 279, 301–3, 383

Marx, Karl (1818–83), revolutionist, Marxism 64, 155, 301, 355

materialism, scientific materialism, matter theory 302–3, 305–9, 314, 323–4, 365, 367–9, 376

Maurice, Revd Frederick Denison (1805–72), Broad Church leader 5, 30, 47–8, 161, 171, 265, 284 n., 285–6, 294, 303, 314–15, 355 n., 371, 383
and the Atonement 288–9, 293
and Butler 173 n., 337–8
and Hell 270–5, 277, 369
influence of 314, 334–5, 337, 354
Maxwell, James Clerk (1831–79), Prof. Experimental Physics, Cambridge 362
Mayer, Julius Robert (1814–78), German physicist and physiologist 309
mechanical philosophy 14, 33, 36, 45, 50, 68–70, 97, 124–5, 148, 177, 216, 220–3, 230–1, 250, 284, 300, 305–6, 308
mechanics 34–5, 148, 197, 300, 311, 319, 364, 367
medicine 154–62, 175 n., 197, 306–8
Melvill, Revd Henry (1798–1871), Principal East India Coll., Haileybury, popular evangelical preacher 10, 103, 290, 294
Melville, Robert Saunders, 2nd Visc. (1771–1851), 1st Ld. Adm. (1812–27) 39
Meredith, George (1828–1909), novelist and poet 140, 336
Merivale, Herman (1806–74), civil servant and political economist 47–8, 50
mesmerism 306, 311, 325
Methodism 10, 18 n., 35 n., 40 n., 155 n., 198, 305
Meyrick, Revd Frederick (1827–1906), evangelical controversialist 290
Mill, James (1773–1836), utilitarian philosopher 6, 37, 40, 43, 65, 166, 169, 174, 189, 240, 245 n.
Mill, John Stuart (1806–73), philosopher 6, 54, 69–70, 88, 169, 182, 200–1, 257, 259, 263, 265, 267, 277, 313 n., 318, 321, 333, 336, 343, 355, 362
Miller, Hugh (1802–56), Scottish geologist and Free Church apologist 55, 56 n.
Milman, Henry Hart (1791–1868), Oxford Liberal Anglican church historian 28
Milner, Revd Isaac (1750–1820), Cambridge evangelical, mathematician 7, 9, 30
Milner, Revd Joseph (1744–97), evangelical divine 9, 18 n., 116 n.
Milton (Visc.), Charles William Wentworth, Earl Fitzwilliam (1786–1857), Whig MP (1806–33) 238–41
mind/body distinction, *see* dualism
miracles 31, 85, 151, 227, 238, 280, 310, 361, 367, 370–1
Moderate Party of the Church in Scotland 24–6, 183, 186

monism 302, 305, 307, 309, 311, 325, 367, 372, 383–4
Montgomery, Robert (1807–55), evangelical poetaster 103, 127 n.
Moody, Dwight Lyman (1837–99) and Sankey, Ira David (1840–1908), American evangelists 274, 303
moral government (God's), *see* natural theology
moral sense, *see* conscience
moral trial, earth a state of 8, 13, 177–8, 183, 215, 224, 260, 295, 300, 341–3, 380 and *passim*
More, Hannah (1745–1833), popular evangelical moralist 7, 18, 19 n., 146, 204–5, 207, 215–16, 268, 380–1
Morgan, Thomas Charles (1783–1843), physician and philosopher 306–7
Morley (Visc.), John (1838–1923), Liberal politician 271, 336, 354–7
Morley, Samuel (1809–86), Congregationalist, Liberal MP, philanthropist 106, 141
Morning Watch (1829–33) 10, 15, 42, 285, 287 n.
Morpeth (Visc.), George Howard, 6th Earl of Carlisle (1773–1848) 241,
Moses, Jewish leader and lawgiver 283
Muntz, George Frederick (1794–1857), Birmingham reforming MP 259 and n., 277
Myers, Revd Frederic (1811–51), author and divine 227

Napier, Macvey (1776–1847), *Edinburgh Review* editor 38
Napoleon I (1769–1821), Emperor of the French 219, 223
Nares, Edward (1762–1841), Prof. History, Oxford (1813–41) 42
National Debt 119, 128, 203–5, 233–4, 262
natural selection, *see* Darwin, Charles: Darwinism
natural theology 8, 19–25, 31, 49–55, 82–5, 90, 99–100, 124, 143, 149, 151–2, 154–5, 165, 176–89, 192–7, 246, 250, 261–2, 281–2, 285, 293, 299–300, 305–7, 313, 326, 343, 346, 348–51, 361–2, 364–6, 369, 384
Neale, Edward Vansittart (1810–92), Christian Socialist and co-operator 265
necessarianism 305, 324, 365, 383
Newcastle, Henry Pelham Fiennes Pelham, 5th Lord Lincoln (1811–64), Peelite politician 258, 359

New Liberalism 268

Newman, Francis William (1805–97), Anglican turned Unitarian 272, 278, 302

Newman, John Henry (1801–90), Anglican turned Roman Catholic (1846) 10, 27–8, 37, 115, 121, 172, 173 n., 175, 178 n., 229, 235, 313, 348 and n., 356, 377

Newton, Sir Isaac (1642–1727), mathematician and physicist, Newtonianism 9, 308 n., 311, 319, 324, 364, 367–9, 372

Nichol, John Pringle (1804–59), Prof. Astronomy, Glasgow 310

Noel, Baptist Wriothesley (1798–1873), Anglican evangelical turned Baptist 60, 247

Nolan, Revd Frederick (1784–1864), evangelical theologian 22

Nolan, Revd Thomas (1809?–82), Anglican theologian 125, 132, 282, 293–4

Nonconformity 5 n., 21, 26, 38, 155 n., 173, 195, 247, 249, 302, 311, 353, 357–8, 370

Novalis, Georg Friedrich Philipp, Freiherr von Hardenberg (1772–1801), poet 311

Oastler, Richard (1789–1861), evangelical philanthropist 91–2, 95, 97–8, 147, 212 n., 213, 226

Oersted, Hans Christian (1777–1851), Danish physicist and chemist 311

Orders in Council 37

original sin, *see* sin

Otter, William (1768–1840), Bp. Chichester, friend of Malthus 90–1

Overstone, Samuel Jones Loyd, 1st B. (1796–1883), financier, politician, leader of Currency School 41, 133–6, 148, 168, 173, 199, 201, 206, 218, 224–5, 234, 282, 320, 333
  opposes limited liability 258–61, 266–7 and n.

Owen, Revd Joseph Butterworth (1809–72), prophetic evangelical writer 117

Owen, Sir Richard (1804–92), anatomist and naturalist 236

Owen, Robert (1771–1858), utopian philanthropist 87, 200 and n., 208, 270, 303, 325

Oxford Movement 27–8, 36, 47, 113, 121, 144, 149, 172–3, 200, 235, 288, 299, 340, 345, 356

Oxford University x, 35, 41–8, 50–2, 128, 150, 163, 171–4, 179, 230, 232 n., 234–6, 283, 290, 328, 337, 339 and n., 340, 367 n.

Paget, Revd Francis Edward (1806–82), High Church divine and social reformer 103

Paley, William (1743–1805), Archdeacon Carlisle and moral philosopher 4–5, 32, 45, 51, 53, 69, 75, 77, 80, 84, 90 n., 100 n., 102–4, 144, 154, 170–9, 182–3, 185, 188–9, 191 n., 205, 217, 221, 246, 300 n., 338, 346, 361, 377

Palmer, William (1803–85), Tractarian theologian 342

Palmerston, Henry John Temple, 3rd Visc. (1784–1865), PM (1855–8, 1859–65) 247, 250, 258, 260–1, 274, 353

Parnell, Henry Brooke, 1st B. Congleton (1776–1842), Whig politician and financial reformer 239–40

Pasteur, Louis (1822–95), French microbiologist 156

paternalism viii, 17, 43–4, 87–9, 91–8, 93, 95–6, 98–9, 107, 110, 121, 133–4, 200–1, 205, 207–8, 211–13, 215, 220–1, 225, 241, 245–6, 326, 334, 354, 375

Pattison, Mark (1813–84), Oxford scholar 173, 180, 337, 339

Peacock, Revd George (1791–1858), Cambridge mathematician 30

Peel, Sir Robert, 1st Bt. (1750–1830), manufacturer and MP 207, 218, 223

Peel, Sir Robert, 2nd Bt. (1788–1850), PM (1834–5, 1841–6) vii, ix, 39, 42, 44, 133–4, 148, 219, 221–4, 226, 228–31, 234–6, 241, 256, 258, 270, 324, 348 n., 352, 356, 360
  and anti-growth economic policy 224–5, 241
  and Chalmers 60–3, 225
  and Corn Laws 230, 248–50
  opposes limited liability 257
  Peelites 258, 263, 341, 351, 363
  and Poor Laws 225, 243
  and providence 210, 230–1, 248–50
  and religion 229–30, 238, 243
  and resumption of cash payments 223–4
  and science 235–6
  his social philosophy 230–1

Penal Servitude Act (1864) 269

penal theory 166, 169, 192, 215–18, 247, 268–9, 270 n., 278, 280, 282, 303, 382

Penrose, Revd John (1778–1859), religious writer 280–1

Perceval, Spencer (1762–1812), evangelical PM (1809–12) 206 and n., 218–19, 227

Perceval, Spencer (1795–1859), extreme evangelical MP 212, 214–15, 219

Peterloo massacre 232–3

philanthropy 15, 100–10, 111–13, 136, 142, 154, 156, 162, 197, 208, 233, 239, 241, 245, 255, 263, 265–70, 278–80, 287, 316, 319, 324–5, 327, 331, 334, 364–5

Phillpotts, Henry (1778–1869), Tory and High Church Bp. Exeter (1830–69) 61, 113

Phipps, Edmund (1808–57), author and financial expert 187

Phrenological Journal 196, 199, 225

phrenology 189–201, 306–7, 311, 313, 382–3
  and bourgeois culture 197–8, 324–5
  and natural theology 192–3, 196, 318
  and political economy 199

physics x, 175 n., 239, 304, 308–14, 318, 320–1, 326, 361–2, 366, 367 n., 368

physiocracy 37–8, 65–8, 189

physiology 154–62, 300, 304, 318, 320 n., 328–9, 365

Pitt, William (1759–1806), PM (1798–1801, 1804–6), Pittite 7, 42, 99, 125, 147, 170, 203, 204, 219, 223, 231, 233

Place, Francis (1771–1854), Radical tailor of London 43, 225, 240

Plato, Platonism 172, 301, 337, 363 n.

Plumptre, Revd Edward Hayes (1821–91), Prof. Pastoral Theology, King's Coll., London (1853–81) 274

Political Economy Club 37, 65, 163, 240

Poor Laws, pauperism 16, 46, 59–60, 86, 88, 91, 93–4, 96–7, 100, 107, 116–17, 122, 183, 206–8, 225–6, 233, 237, 268–9, 326–7, 359–60, 364–5
  Chalmers and 57–60, 63, 66 n., 81–5, 167, 279 n.
  Irish Poor Law 95, 101, 110–11, 153, 210, 212 and n., 243, 289 n.
  New Poor Law (1834) 86, 93, 95, 97, 133, 135, 212 n., 225–6, 241–6, 323, 359
  Scottish Poor Law 63, 94, 243 and n.
  softer mid-century attitudes towards 268, 279 and n., 280, 334
  Speenhamland system 37, 99, 207, 220, 233, 242, 375

Pope, Alexander (1688–1744), poet and satirist 188

population theory 4, 15, 34–5, 39, 50–2, 66, 73–83, 89–91, 100 n., 116, 118–20, 154 n., 168, 188, 199, 217, 233, 240, 245, 263, 312, 323, 329, 380

Porteus, Beilby (1731–1809), evangelicalish Bp. London (1787–1808) 381

positivism 298, 338, 361, 371, 383

post-millenarianism, post-millennialism 10, 80, 211, 233, 247, 304 n., 326, 328, 331–2, 336, 381

Potter, Sir Thomas (1773–1845), Unitarian, reformer, 1st Mayor of Manchester 58

Powell, Walter (1822–68), devout merchant 20, 105–6, 123, 133, 141–2, 274

Pratt, Revd Josiah (1768–1844), evangelical, Sec. CMS, founder BFBS 9 n., 18 n., 20

predestination 8, 29

pre-millenarianism, pre-millennialism 10, 14–19, 43–4, 80, 94–7, 131–2, 211–15, 219, 228, 304–5, 310, 330, 340, 365, 381

Price, Richard (1723–91), socinian, philosopher and economist 233, 304 n.

Priestley, Joseph (1733–1804), socinian, chemist, materialist philosopher 65 n., 216, 289, 304 and n., 306

probabilism 174–5, 232, 337, 348 and n., 382

probation (state of), *see* moral trial

Prodigal Son, parable of 275

progressivism 319, 322, 350 n., 359, 361, 364–5, 367

Property Tax 37

prophecy, *see* pre-millenarianism

Protection 66, 68, 87, 110, 207, 212, 219, 237, 248, 284, 326, 351–3, 375

providence, providentialism x, 8–9, 11, 13–17, 44–5, 53, 69–70, 75, 78, 82, 93–4, 98, 120 n., 124–5, 136, 144, 151, 155, 165, 200, 207, 210–11, 213, 215, 218, 233, 246, 250, 260, 262, 270–1, 284, 286, 289 n., 303, 310, 319, 327–8, 335, 340, 343–4, 346–51, 366, 370, 373–4, 377, 380
  general providence 85, 94, 109–12, 133–4, 147, 152–3, 192, 211, 215, 238, 249–50, 310–11, 380–1
  special providence 55, 85, 94, 109–12, 114, 134, 151–3, 155 n., 196, 205, 210–11, 219, 249, 304, 311, 344, 351, 362–3, 367–8, 381

Pryme, George (1781–1868), Prof. Political Economy, Cambridge, and evangelical 48, 164, 237

public works 225, 375

punishment, retribution, *see* justice

Purgatory 276

Pusey, Edward Bouverie (1800–82), Prof. Hebrew, Oxford, and Tractarian 37, 105, 115 n., 121

Quakers 59, 116 n., 131, 141, 157, 178
quarantine 158-9
Quarterly Review 77 n., 92, 151, 153, 181, 353-4, 380
Quesnay, François (1694-1774), French physiocratic economist 40, 189

Radnor, William Pleydell-Bouverie, 3rd Earl (1779-1869), evangelical Whig 239-42
Raikes, Revd Richard (1743-1823), evangelically-inclined writer on economics 166
Reade, Charles (1814-84), evangelical and novelist 140-1
Record, Recordites 10-11, 22, 94-8, 205, 211-12, 214, 227, 249
reformatory movement 269-70 and n.
Reid, Thomas (1710-96), 'common sense' philosopher and Prof. Moral Philosophy, Glasgow (1764-96) 25, 39, 45, 48, 164, 169, 172, 175, 176 n., 186, 191, 201
rent, theories of 65, 82-3, 163, 167
resumption of cash payments vii, 153, 184, 206, 219, 223, 227, 237
resurrection of the body 305, 370-1
Resurrection of Christ 296, 307, 349, 367, 369
retrenchment vii, 203-6, 209, 219
retribution, retributive justice, *see* justice
Ricardo, David (1772-1823), 'bear' financier and MP viii, 6, 37-40, 43, 48, 51-2, 54, 65-6, 70, 77, 82, 88, 101, 118, 127, 129, 144, 168, 189, 199, 206, 225, 232, 241, 260, 277
Ricardianism 22, 49, 51, 65-70, 118, 135, 163, 167, 201, 323, 329
Richmond, Revd Wilfrid John (1848?-1939), Christian Social Unionist 6, 330-2
Rickards, George Kettilby (1812-89), political economist 51, 328-9
Robinson, David, *Blackwood's* journalist, economist paternalist 36, 121
Robinson, Frederick John, Visc. Goderich, 1st Earl of Ripon (1782-1859), Liberal Tory PM (1827-8) vii, 39, 206 n., 222, 235
Robison John (1739-1805), Prof. Natural Philosophy, Edinburgh 183, 305, 308
Rogers, Henry (1806?-77), Congregational apologist and *Edinburgh* reviewer 173 n.
Romilly, Sir Samuel (1757-1818), Whig politician and law reformer 57
Rooke, John (1780-1856), political economist and geologist 22

Rose, George (1744-1818), placeman and Pittite 99, 207
Rose, George Henry (1771-1855), diplomat, MP, evangelical writer 206 n., 212
Rose, Revd Hugh James (1795-1838), High Church theologian 47
Rothschild, Lionel Nathan (1808-79), financier and MP 360
Rothschild, Nathan Meyer (1777-1836), international financier 221
Rowntree, Benjamin Seebohm (1871-1954), sociologist 336
Rush, Benjamin (1745-1813), American physician 157-9, 161, 216-17
Russell, Lord John, 1st Earl (1792-1878), PM (1846-52, 1865-6) 258 n., 352
Russell, Revd Wriothesley (1804-86), evangelical royal chaplain 239
Ryder, Henry (1777-1836), evangelical Bp. Gloucester and Lichfield 7

Sabbatarianism 208-9, 211-12
Sadleir, John (1814-56), Irish politician and swindler 123, 264
Sadler, Michael Thomas (1780-1835), evangelical social reforming MP 15, 87, 91, 95-6, 98-9, 212-13
St Andrews University 39, 64, 67
Saints, *see* Clapham Sect
Sandon (Visc.), Dudley Ryder, 2nd Earl Harrowby (1798-1882), Liberal Tory MP and evangelical 63
Saumarez, Richard (1764-1835), surgeon and physiologist 306
savings banks 89, 375
Say, Jean Baptiste (1767-1832), French economist 40, 168, 189
Say's Law 52, 65, 118, 321, 329
Scarlett, James, 1st B. Abinger (1769-1844), Tory politician, Att.-Gen. 228
Schelling, Friedrich Wilhelm Joseph von (1775-1854), German philosopher 311
scheme of redemption, *see* Atonement
science ix-x, 22-6, 51, 147-62, 164, 229, 235, 239, 248, 272-3, 299-300, 304-14, 319, 330, 361, 368, 384-5
scientific naturalism 305-14, 318, 368, 371
Scott, Alexander John (1805-66), Scottish liberal theologian and Chartist 284-5, 314
Scott, Revd Thomas (1747-1821), evangelical publicist 8-9, 183
Scott, Sir Walter (1771-1832), novelist and glamorous bankrupt 55
scriptural geology, *see* geology

Scrope, George Julius Poulett (1797–1876), geologist and political economist 46 n., 64, 153–4, 162, 300, 308

Second Coming, *see* pre-millenarianism

secularism, *see* loss of faith

Sedgwick, Adam (1785–1873), Prof. Geology, Cambridge 48–51, 54, 60, 171, 173, 177 n., 191 n.

Seeley, Sir John Robert (1834–95), Prof. Modern History, Cambridge (1869–95) 334

Seeley, Robert Benton (1798–1886), extreme evangelical, publisher, and social critic 95–6, 212, 215, 334

Seeley and Burnside, evangelical publishers 97, 238

self help 87–9, 197–8, 200–1, 241, 270 n., 321 n., 375

Senior, Nassau William (1790–1864), Whig political economist viii, 6, 32, 45–6, 52, 54, 60, 64, 69, 83, 167, 189, 217, 225, 242–5, 257, 277, 379

Sermon on the Mount 194, 330

Sewell, Revd William (1804–74), Prof. Moral Philosophy, Oxford (1836–41) 27, 47, 144, 172, 268–9

Shaftesbury, Anthony Ashley Cooper, 3rd Earl (1671–1713), philosopher 188

Shaftesbury, Anthony Ashley Cooper, Lord Ashley, 7th Earl (1801–85), evangelical social reforming politician 15, 17–18, 22, 95–6, 131, 212–13, 226, 273, 376

Shairp, John Campbell (1819–85), Prof. Poetry, Oxford (1877–87) 338

Shelburne, Sir William Petty, 1st M. Lansdowne, 2nd Earl (1737–1805), Prime Minister (1782–3) 31

Shelley, Percy Bysshe (1792–1822), poet 177

Sheridan, Richard Brinsley (1751–1816), Whig and playwright 207

Sherwood, Mrs Mary Martha (1775–1851), evangelical authoress 314

Sidgwick, Henry (1838–1900), Prof. Philosophy, Cambridge (1883–1900) 272

Sidmouth, Henry Addington, 1st Visc. (1757–1844), PM (1801–4), High Tory Home Sec. (1812–21) vii, 41–2, 221, 223

Simeon, Revd Charles (1783–1836), Cambridge evangelical 7, 9, 12, 30–1, 48, 56, 60, 111, 133, 226

sin 8, 90, 115–16, 182, 185 n., 194, 199, 216, 247, 270, 286–7, 298, 316, 324, 340, 343–5, 349, 354, 357–8, 370–1, 373, 377–8 and *passim*

as debt 317, 370–1

Sinclair, Sir George (1790–1868), Scots MP, Free Church evangelical 91–5, 102

Sinking Fund 37, 219, 227, 232–4, 240

Slaney, Robert Aglionby (1792–1862), 'Health of Towns' reforming MP 241, 265–6

Slave Trade, anti-slavery, abolitionism 15, 26, 98–9, 132, 204, 206, 208–11, 219, 231, 233, 237, 245, 247, 327, 354

Smiles, Samuel (1812–1904), social reformer 87, 198, 330

Smith, Adam (1723–90), Prof. Moral Philosophy and Political Economy, Glasgow viii, 14, 31–2, 35, 37–8, 40, 45, 48, 67, 109, 116, 120, 128, 149, 156, 165–6, 168, 178 n., 190–1, 231–3, 241, 256, 277 and n., 304, 332, 371, 380

Smith, Goldwin (1823–1910), Prof. Modern History, Oxford (1858–66) 54, 173, 338

Smith, Horace (1779–1849), popular writer and novelist 146

Smith, Robert 'Bobus' (1770–1845), wit and Canningite MP 57

Smith, Revd Sydney (1771–1845), Whig wit 56, 239

Smith, Thomas Southwood (1788–1861), Unitarian minister, Edinburgh, and sanitary reformer 179, 270, 307–8

and population theory 76–7, 79–80, 183

his theology 81, 84, 177, 189, 303, 334, 382

Smith, William (1756–1835), Whig evangelical MP 59

Smyth, William (1765–1849), Prof. Modern History, Cambridge 48

Snowden (Visc.), Philip (1864–1937), Chanc. Exchequer (1924, 1929–31) 335

Social Darwinism 6, 301, 303–4, 311

Socialism 200–1, 268, 322, 326, 328–9, 335

social reform, social gospel 267–70, 276–80, 301, 303, 316, 345, 372

Social Science Association 270 n., 383

Society for Bettering the Condition of the Poor 98–9, 207

Socinianism, *see* Unitarianism

Southcott, Joanna (1750–1814), pre-millenarian fanatic and 'self-convinced imposter' (DNB) 21

Southey, Robert (1774–1843), poet and *Quarterly* reviewer 36

speculation 115–25, 131–6, 144–7, 158, 161, 199, 200 n., 223–4, 226, 248–9, 258–9, 263–6, 269, 282, 316, 320, 324, 359–61, 374

Spence, William (1783–1860), economist and entomologist 37, 65–6

Spencer, George (1799–1864), devotionalist, turned to Rome (1830) 239

Spencer, Herbert (1820–1903), philosopher 296 n., 301, 303, 311–13, 318–19, 321–2, 324–5, 355, 364, 368–9, 383–5

Spencer (Countess), Lavinia (1762–1831), society beauty and wit 239

spiritualism 305 n., 336, 383

Spooner, Richard (1783–1864), evangelical ultra Protestant MP and Birmingham banker, opponent of limited liability 59, 259 n.

Spring Rice, Thomas, 1st B. Monteagle (1790–1866), Whig Chanc. Exchequer (1835–9) 60, 237–8, 243, 258, 267

Spurzheim, Johann Gaspar (1776–1832), German physician and phrenologist 190–1

Stanhope, Philip Henry, 5th Earl (1805–75), historian 270–1

Stanley, Arthur Penrhyn (1815–81), Broad Church Dean of Westminster 28

Stanley, Edward George Geoffrey Smith, 14th Earl of Derby (1799–1869), PM (1852, 1858–9, 1866–8) 10, 230, 237–8

Stanley, Edward Henry, 15th Earl of Derby (1826–93), Foreign Sec. 269

Stein, Heinrich Friedrich Karl, Freiherr von (1757–1831), Prussian patriot 334

Stephen, James (1758–1832), lawyer, Clapham Sect MP, abolitionist 210, 334 n.

Stephen, Sir James (1789–1859), Colonial Under-Sec. 7, 60, 210, 334 n.

Stephen, Sir James Fitzjames (1829–94), judge and journalist 188

Stephen, Sir Leslie (1832–1904), philosophic writer 174, 190, 272, 318 n., 338

Stevens, Revd James (1809?–43) of Bucks., writer on the Poor Laws 86

Stewart, Balfour (1828–87), Prof. Natural Philosophy, Manchester (1870–87) 367–8, 384

Stewart, Dugald (1753–1828), Prof. Moral Philosophy, Edinburgh 25, 34, 38–40, 45, 48, 62, 68, 77 n., 127, 164, 169–70, 172, 175, 183, 186, 190–1, 201, 232 n., 379–90

Stokes, Sir George Gabriel (1819–1903), Prof. Maths, Cambridge (1849–1903) 364, 367–8

Stowell, Revd Hugh (1799–1865), Salford evangelical preacher 13, 140 n., 146, 281–2, 290

Sturge, Joseph (1793–1859), Quaker abolitionist and philanthropist 141

substitutionary punishment, *see* Atonement

Sumner, Charles Richard (1790–1874), Bp. Winchester (1827–69) 7

Sumner, John Bird (1780–1862), evangelical Bp. Chester (1828–48) and Abp. Canterbury (1848–62) 7, 90, 91 n., 328, 374
  and Butler 173–4
  and Chalmers 60, 81 n.
  and charity 98, 100–2, 105
  and Corn Laws 207
  and geology 23, 150, 235
  his theology 230, 238, 250
  and theory of population 77–80, 91, 119, 199, 245

suspension of cash payments 37, 223, 234

Sweet, Revd James Bradby (1818?–80), apostolical Churchman 103

Swinburne, Algernon Charles (1837–1909), poet 336

Tait, Peter Guthrie (1831–1901), Prof. Natural Philosophy, Edinburgh (1860–1901) 367–8

Talents, Parable of the 116, 275, 279–80

taste 360 and n.

Tatham, Edward (1749–1834), Oxford philosopher and controversialist 41, 128, 307, 381

Tavistock (M.), Francis Russell, 7th Duke of Bedford (1788–1861), Whig MP (1809–32) 238

Taylor, Sir Henry (1800–?86), civil servant in Colonial Office 245 n.

Taylor, Isaac (1787–1865), artist and lay theologian 272–3, 374

Teignmouth, John Shore, 1st B. (1751–1834), Gov.-Gen. India, evangelical Pres. BFBS 59–60, 227

temperance 247, 270

temptation 260 n., 286, 330

Temptation in the Wilderness 143–4

Ten Hours Movement 92, 97, 212–13, 226, 241, 284 n.

Tennyson, Alfred, 1st B. (1809–92), Poet Laureate 145

Thackeray, William Makepeace (1811–63), novelist 140

Thatcher, Margaret (1925-), PM (1979-), Thatcherism 373-4

thermodynamics 309-11, 313-14, 319-21, 362, 367-8, 372, 384

Thirlwall, Connop (1797-1875), historian and Bp. St David's 28, 171, 337

Thomspon, George (1804-78), abolitionist and Corn Law repealer 246-7

Thompson, Thomas Perronet (1783-1869), Philosophic Radical MP 33, 64, 120 n., 186 n.

Thomson, Charles Edward Poulett, B. Sydenham (1799-1841), Whig MP 239

Thomson, William (1819-90), Abp. York 289

Thomson, William, 1st B. Kelvin (1824-1907), evangelical and Prof. Natural Philosophy, Glasgow (1846-99) 310, 362, 368, 384

Thornton, Henry (1760-1815), Clapham Sect MP, philanthropist and economist 7, 101, 122, 127, 129, 204, 206, 208

Thornton, Henry Sykes (1800-81), partner in Down, Free, and Thornton 146-7

Thornton, John (1720-90), evangelical banker 106

Tierney, George (1761-1830), Whig politician 127

time, cyclical and linear understandings of 33-4, 66-7, 152, 154, 161, 163, 211, 271, 298-301, 303-4, 308 and n., 313, 343, 372

Tonna, Charlotte Elizabeth (1790-1846), evangelical novelist 97, 381

Tooke, John Horne (1736-1812), Radical politician and philologist 192

Torrens, Robert (1780-1864), political economist MP 4, 37, 65, 189, 277

Tractarianism, *see* Oxford Movement

Trench, Richard Chenevix (1807-86), Prof. Divinity, London, Abp. Dublin 337

Trevelyan, Sir Charles Edward (1807-86), evangelical Sec. Treasury (1840-59) 7, 109-10, 113, 162, 351

Trimmer, Mrs Sarah (1741-1810), evangelical authoress 314

Trollope, Anthony (1815-1882), novelist 140

Tuckerman, Revd Joseph (1778-1840), Boston Unitarian 85

Tufnell, Edward Carleton (1806-86), Ass. Poor Law Commissioner 242

Turgot, Anne Robert Jacques (1727-81), French economist and reformer 38, 168, 189

Twiss, Sir Travers (1809-97), lawyer and political economist 48

Two Debtors, Parable of the 292

Tylor, Sir Edward Burnett (1832-1917), Prof. Anthropology, Oxford (1896-1909) 364 n.

Tyndall, John (1820-93), physicist and scientific popularizer 309, 314, 384

underconsumptionism, *see* gluts

uniformitarianism 150-1, 153, 160, 198, 300, 304, 308, 367-8, 371

Unitarianism 5, 21, 76, 84-5, 90, 131, 179, 194, 233, 264 n., 267, 270 n., 272, 273, 282, 288, 291, 293, 299, 301-3, 307, 320, 333, 354, 382

universalism, universal pardon 271, 273, 276, 283, 375

Unjust Steward, Parable of the 275, 280

Unmerciful Servant, Parable of the 292

Ure, Andrew (1778-1857), chemical and social analyst 198 and n.

urea, synthesis of (1828) 306

Usury Laws 95, 144, 206, 263

utilitarianism viii-ix, 6, 31-3, 50, 53-4, 84, 88, 92, 100 n., 108, 164-70, 175-7, 179, 181-3, 186, 207, 215-18, 232, 237, 240-2, 244-6, 257, 306, 312, 318 and n., 328, 337; *see also* Benthamism

value, theories of 127-30, 141, 155, 166-8, 201, 306, 320, 329 n., 364

Vansittart, Charles (1820?-78), Berks. vicar 113

Vansittart, Nicholas, 1st B. Bexley (1766-1851), Chanc. Exchequer (1812-23) vii, 42, 59, 126, 221-3, 226-8, 234, 360

Vaughan, Revd Charles John (1816-97), Dean of Llandaff 275, 287-8, 329-30, 334 n.

Vaughan, David James (1825-1905), Mauricean theologian and social reformer 287-8, 330, 334 n.

Vaughan, Revd Edward Thomas (1772-1829), Leicester pre-millenarian evangelical 17, 287 and n.

Venn, Revd Henry (1725-97), evangelical divine 8

Venn, Revd John (1759-1839), Clapham evangelical, founder CMS 7, 9, 55 n., 99 n., 226

vicarious sacrifice, *see* Atonement

Villiers, Charles Pelham (1802-98), Free Trade MP 206-7

Villiers, Thomas Hyde (1801-32), utilitarian MP 244-5

Virchow, Rudolf (1821–1902), German anticontagionist biologist and Liberal statesman 159

vitalism 300, 306–7, 367–8, 372

vital religion, *see* evangelical theology

wages, theories of 65, 82–3, 118, 200, 226, 243, 245, 248, 320, 327–8, 364

Wakefield, Gilbert (1756–1801), Unitarian controversialist 90

Wallace, Alfred Russel (1823–1913), naturalist and evolutionist 303–4

Wallace, Thomas, 1st B. (1768–1844), Liberal Tory politician vii

Walpole, Sir Robert, 1st Earl of Orford (1676–1745), PM (1721–42) 220

Walpole, Sir Spencer (1839–1907), historian and civil servant 268

Warburton, Henry (1784?–1858), Philosophic Radical MP 245 n.

Ward, Robert Plumer (1765–1846), novelist and politician 187

Wardlaw, Revd Ralph (1779–1853), Scottish evangelical Congregationalist 86, 180, 210–11, 292 n., 296

Watson, Revd Joshua (1771–1855), Hackney High Churchman and philanthropist 299

Watson, Sir Thomas (1792–1882), physician and Prof. Medicine, London (1828–40) 154–5, 156 n., 160 n.

Watt, James (1736–1819), engineer 35

Wayland, Revd Francis (1796–1865), American Baptist, Pres. Brown Univ. 85, 171 n., 175 n.

Webster, Noah (1758–1843), American lexicographer and medical theorist 157–8

Wellington, Arthur Wellesley, 1st Duke (1769–1852), PM (1828–30) vii

Welsh, Benjamin, Edinburgh bloodletter 156

Welsh, Revd David (1793–1845), Scottish divine 194

Werner, Abraham Gottlob (1750–1817), German geologist, neptunist 150

Wesley, John (1703–91), Methodist leader 7–8, 28, 101, 216, 360

West, Sir Edward (1782–1828), lawyer and political economist 41, 77

Westcott, Brooke Foss (1825–1901), Cambridge theologian, B. Durham 287, 294–5, 337

Weyland, John (1744–1854), MP and Poor Law publicist 76 n., 100, 212

Whately, Miss Elizabeth Jane (1822–93), devotional writer 140 n.

Whately, Richard (1787–1863), Oxford philosopher and Whig Abp. Dublin (1831–63)
and Butler 172, 183
and degenerationism 364 n.
his metaphysics 165, 183, 201–2, 220, 300 n.
and penal theory 217
his philanthropy 101
and phrenology 191–2, 201–2
his political economy 46–7, 49–55, 75, 80, 83, 102, 117, 165, 167, 201–2, 232, 328, 379
his theology 28, 49–55, 85, 177, 327
and theory of population 79

Whewell, William (1794–1866), Prof. Moral Philosophy, Cambridge (1838–55) 30, 91, 365
and Butler 171, 176
and Chalmers 60, 187
his moral philosophy 163, 176
and Paley 171, 173
and political economy 48–9, 51–5, 68, 163–4
his scientific thought 305 n., 308 and n., 310
his theology 51–5, 187

Whiggism, Whig-Liberalism 34, 38–40, 52, 188–9, 197, 207, 236–48, 257, 261, 265, 382

Whitbread, Samuel (1764–1815), brewer and Whig politician 207

Whitefield, George (1714–70), leader of Calvinist Methodists 8

Whitmore, William Wolryche (1787–1858), evangelical Free Trade MP 59–61, 206

Whytehead, Revd Robert (1808?–63), York evangelical 86

Wilberforce, Revd Robert Isaac (1802–57), Tractarian, turned to Rome (1854) 5, 10, 289

Wilberforce, William (1759–1833), evangelical and 'philanthropist' 3–4, 7–9, 14, 18 n., 20, 30–1, 93, 98, 100 n., 101, 133, 173, 203–4, 206–10, 219 n., 227–8, 268, 285, 322, 326, 346
and Chalmers 57, 59–61, 89, 183, 207

Wildman, Richard (1802–81), lawyer and theological writer 182

Wilks, Revd Samuel Charles (1789–1872), evangelical, editor of *Christian Observer* (1816–50) 23

will, theories of the 187, 189, 201, 260 n., 270, 355, 364–5, 368, 380; *see also* energy; force

Williams, Isaac (1802–65), poet and Tractarian 27, 175

Williams-Wynn (Lady), Charlotte Grenville (1807–69), friend of Maurice 277

Wilson, Daniel (1778–1858), evangelical Bp. Calcutta 7, 17, 19–20, 127, 173–4, 180–1, 345

Wilson, Revd Henry Bristow (1803–88), essayist and reviewer 271

Wilson, James (1805–60), political economist, MP, and journalist 69

Wilson, John ('Christopher North') (1785–1854), Tory Prof. Moral Philosophy, Edinburgh 39

Wilton, Revd Richard (1827–1903), Canon of York 148

Wise Steward, Parable of the 116

Wöhler, Friedrich (1808–82), German chemist 306

Woodd, Revd Basil (1760–1831), evangelical hymn writer 13, 18

Wordsworth, Christopher (1774–1846), Cambridge liberal High Churchman 30

Wordsworth, Christopher (1807–85), Bp. Lincoln 292

Wordsworth, William (1770–1850), Poet Laureate 30, 175, 177, 314, 337, 365

Worsthorne, Peregrine (1923–), editor of *Sunday Telegraph* 373–4

Yates, Edmund (1831–94), journalist and novelist 123, 145

York and Albany (Duke), Frederick Augustus (1763–1827), soldier 240

Young, Arthur (1741–1820), evangelical agriculturalist and travel writer 100

'Young England' 225–6

'Young Whigs' 238–41

zymotic pathology 269, 309, 384